101 Great Illustrators
From the Golden Age
1890–1925

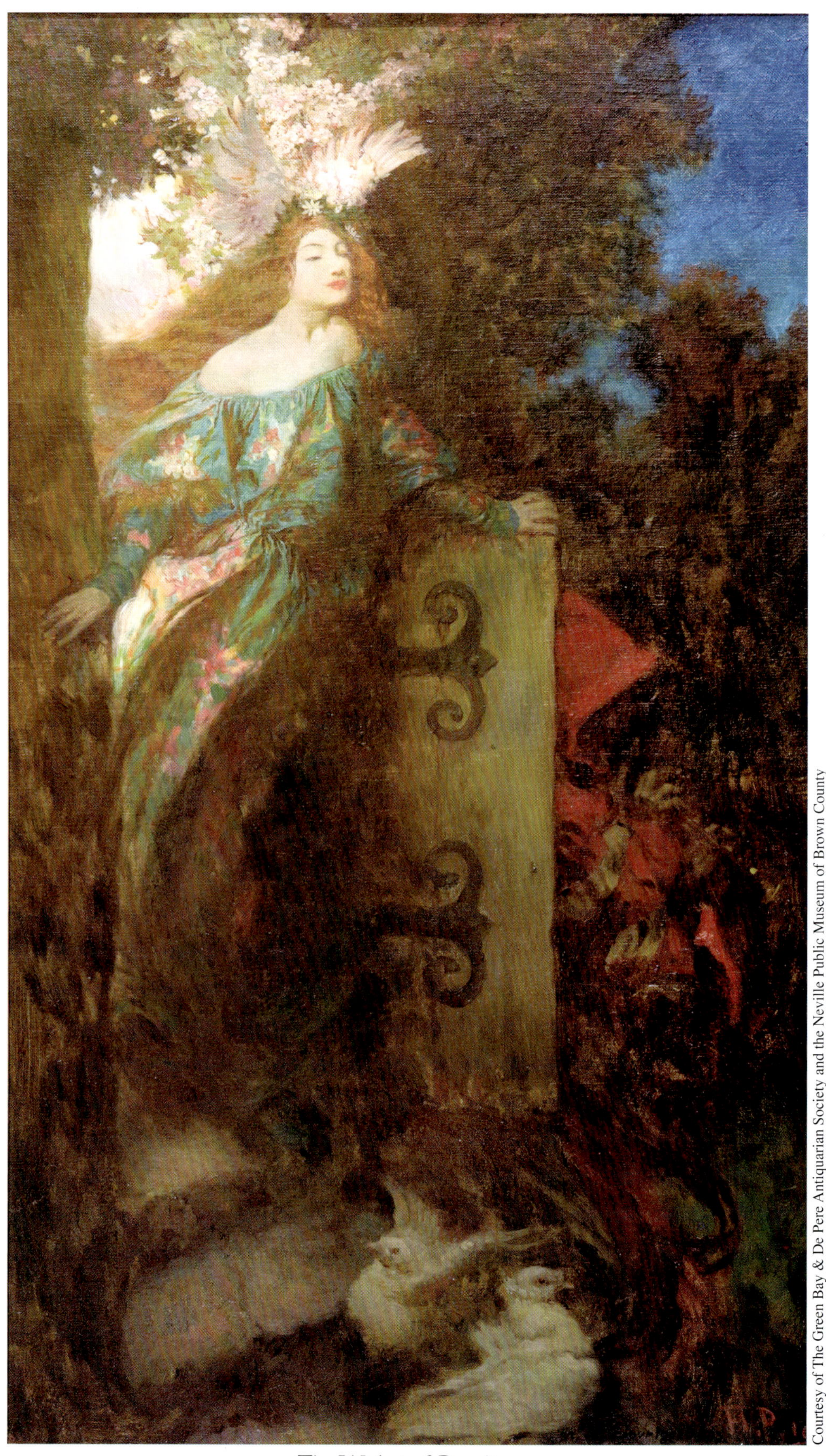

Courtesy of The Green Bay & De Pere Antiquarian Society and the Neville Public Museum of Brown County

The Wicket of Paradise

HOWARD PYLE, 1902

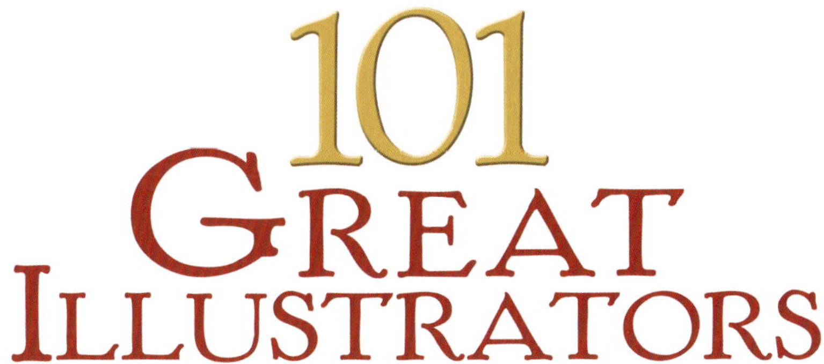

101 Great Illustrators from the Golden Age 1890–1925

Jeff A. Menges

Dover Publications
Garden City, New York

Bibliographical Note

101 Great Illustrators from the Golden Age, 1890–1925 is a new work,
first published by Dover Publications in 2016.

Library of Congress Cataloging-in-Publication Data

Names: Menges, Jeff A., author.
Title: 101 great illustrators from the golden age, 1890–1925 / Jeff A. Menges.
Other titles: One hundred and one great illustrators from the golden age, 1890–1925
Description: Garden City, New York : Dover Publications, 2016.
Identifiers: LCCN 2015040451| ISBN 9780486430812 (paperback) | ISBN 0486430812 ISBN 9780486816081 (hardback) | ISBN 0486816087
Subjects: LCSH: Illustration of books—19th century—Themes, motives. | Illustration of books—20th century—Themes, motives. | Magazine Illustration—19th century—Themes, motives. | Magazine illustration—20th Century—Themes, motives. | BISAC: ART / History / Modern (late 19th Century to 1945). | DESIGN / Graphic Arts / Illustration. | ART / Individual Artists / General. | ART / Reference.
Classification: LCC NC961.6 .M46 2016 | DDC 741.6092/2—dc23 LC record available at http://lccn.loc.gov/2015040451

Printed in China by Chang Jiang Printing Media Co., Ltd.
43081205 2023
www.doverpublications.com

Contents

Introduction

More information is gathered visually than by any other means. It is the first and fastest means by which we assess everything around us. It would not be unusual to think that the creation and reproduction of visual mages has become the most important aspect of communication in our modern age. Effective Illustration targets and shapes visual information, highlighting for viewers what the artist wants them to see, and removing what they don't.

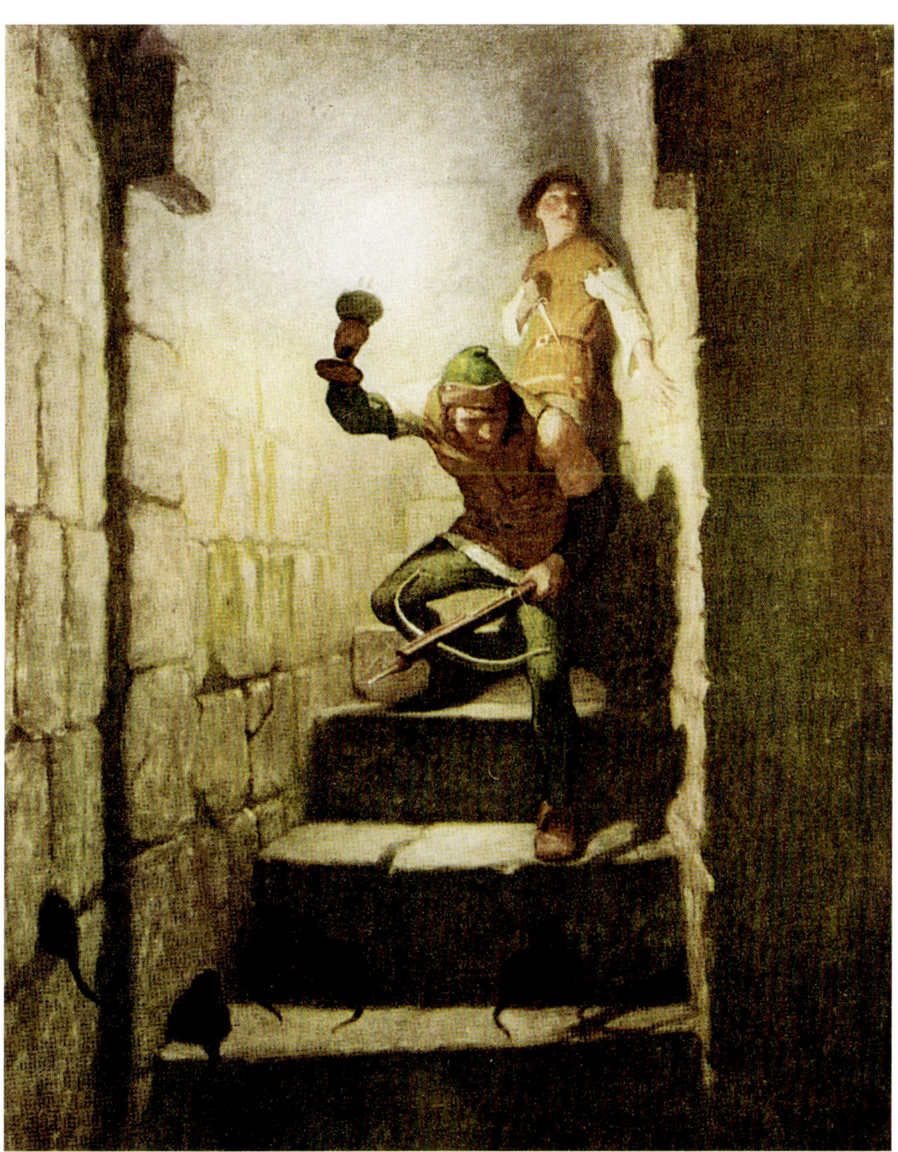

"We must be in the dungeons," Dick remarked.
From *The Black Arrow.* N. C. WYETH, 1916

Opportunity for advancement is greatest in times of transformation, and by the end of the nineteenth century, printing and publishing had blossomed into an industry that served all realms of public interest. With that development came the growth of Illustration as a profession. This collection is a tribute to some of the pioneers of Illustration, who were creating visuals at a time when every printed image seemed better than the previous one.

Some illustrators began as classically trained painters who later sought another avenue for income in an opportunistic field. Others grew up under the influence of even earlier illustrators. A few broke new ground aesthetically and stylistically. For those that could maintain quality under deadlines, professional assignments were plentiful, and the field grew. With printing technologies constantly moving forward, there were frequent opportunities to try something new, and the reproduction of artwork looked better with each new method the printers conceived. Some artists were innovative, insightful, or just plain lucky in their creative approaches. All of the illustrators in these pages made lasting impressions; some are like old friends whose work is still familiar to us today, others are people you may never have heard of but whose contributions to the field are worthy of notice.

This collection might inspire some debate. In selecting the material assembled here—in putting any label on it whatsoever—there have been judgments made, limitations established. These 101 Great Illustrators of the Golden Age may likely not be the same 101 illustrators another reader might pick. The definitions of the period vary, and it is possible to perceive involvement in it based upon a number of parameters. Inclusion here could be due to any of a number of reasons, including technical achievement, financial or artistic success, or lasting influence. Many of these artists have all of these critical qualities attached to their work.

What made it a "Golden Age"?

Before the period from 1890–1925, the potential of the printed image, its reach and effects, had not been fully realized. Nor did this medium seem to have the same impact after those years. Why? Printed matter was the primary source for news, entertainment, and all other social and business information at the time. Looking back to the American Civil War era, the need for accurate and timely news pushed a growing print industry to produce even more, and to make what was available more desirable to the reading public. One thing that encouraged publishing to grow at this point in history was better education. As more emphasis was placed upon access to proper education and succeeding generations became increasingly literate, print replaced word-of-mouth as the source for news—and with the printed word came the printed picture.

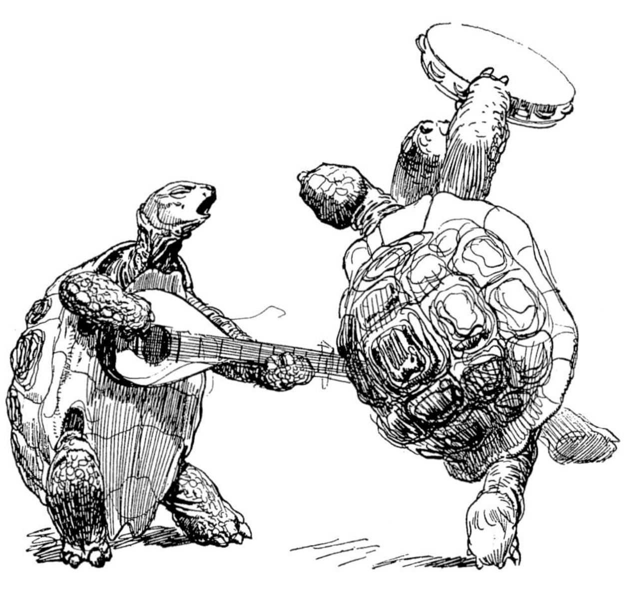

Heinrich Kley

The boom of technology during the Industrial Age also greatly aided the growth of publishing. Improved printing processes with more accurate forms of art reproduction and better color representation meant that artists were able to more directly bring their visions to a larger viewing audience. The very best of these illustrators became stars in their own right—adored by the public, sought after by the largest print houses, handsomely paid. Illustration became an occupation with more work than practitioners, and students flocked to established teachers to try to make a living in pursuit of their creative passion. Combined with the greatly improved networks of transportation, which provided books and magazines to the public with ever increasing frequency, print was king for those few decades.

Initially, this wave of printed progress was slowed by the advent of World War I, when paper use became restricted in many countries. Spending on lavishly produced books decreased considerably. While it was at the pinnacle of its popularity in the years leading up to World War I, print grew, and shaped itself to fit every need of a public clamoring for stories and images. Then in the 1920s, the age of radio began. This may have been the next factor in the diminution of the importance of print. People hearing their news, getting their weekly entertainment over the airwaves, spent less on getting it in print. Television would provide another, stronger alternative a generation later. Aside from isolated examples, the book industry never returned to the level of combined quantity and workmanship that had been achieved just prior to the war.

Why this 101?

There might be a consensus of forty to fifty illustrators of the period who can't be overlooked due to their success, longevity, and influence. Others that follow that group should be considered just as interesting. There are short but brilliant careers like Virginia Sterrett's. There are those who worked in specific aspects of Illustration, like Jules Guérin, or Oliver Kemp. Some are not as well known, but had some shining moments, like Stephen Reid. These artists dedicated their careers to their picture-making all the same, and put out relevant work worth bringing into discussion. But in some collections that review the "best" of the period, they might be overlooked. This was the impetus to select a field as deep as 101. There are many more than those included in this volume who are worthy of note, and as number 102 could qualify in the book. This is a solid selection of illustrators of the period, and I trust that you will find great enjoyment in their work, and perhaps discover some new names among them you may not have been familiar with.

How their work has influenced us for generations

Due to fortunately good timing and involvement in their profession during a period that can truly be labeled as Golden, these illustrators made large impressions, and their work became the foundation for the future century's illustrators. The generation that followed made some equally large impressions. Norman Rockwell, considered by many the most influential illustrator of the last century, idolized the top professionals in the field from this Golden Age, and brought a carefully curated selection of their best traits to his own work. Harvey Dunn and Stanley Arthurs—along with many of Howard Pyle's students—saw great value in the legacy their teacher had presented to them, and continued to make teaching a part of their own careers, creating a field that went back to their Golden Age roots.

The Legacy they have left us

Since artwork was first created for commercial application, that very usage has lessened its value in the view of most of the art world. Much of the original material was left to languish in dusty publishing storehouses, or was piled up in the studios of aging illustrators, with little opportunity to be seen again. In some cases illustrative artwork was discarded or destroyed, with hope abandoned that an audience might once again recognize and appreciate its significance.

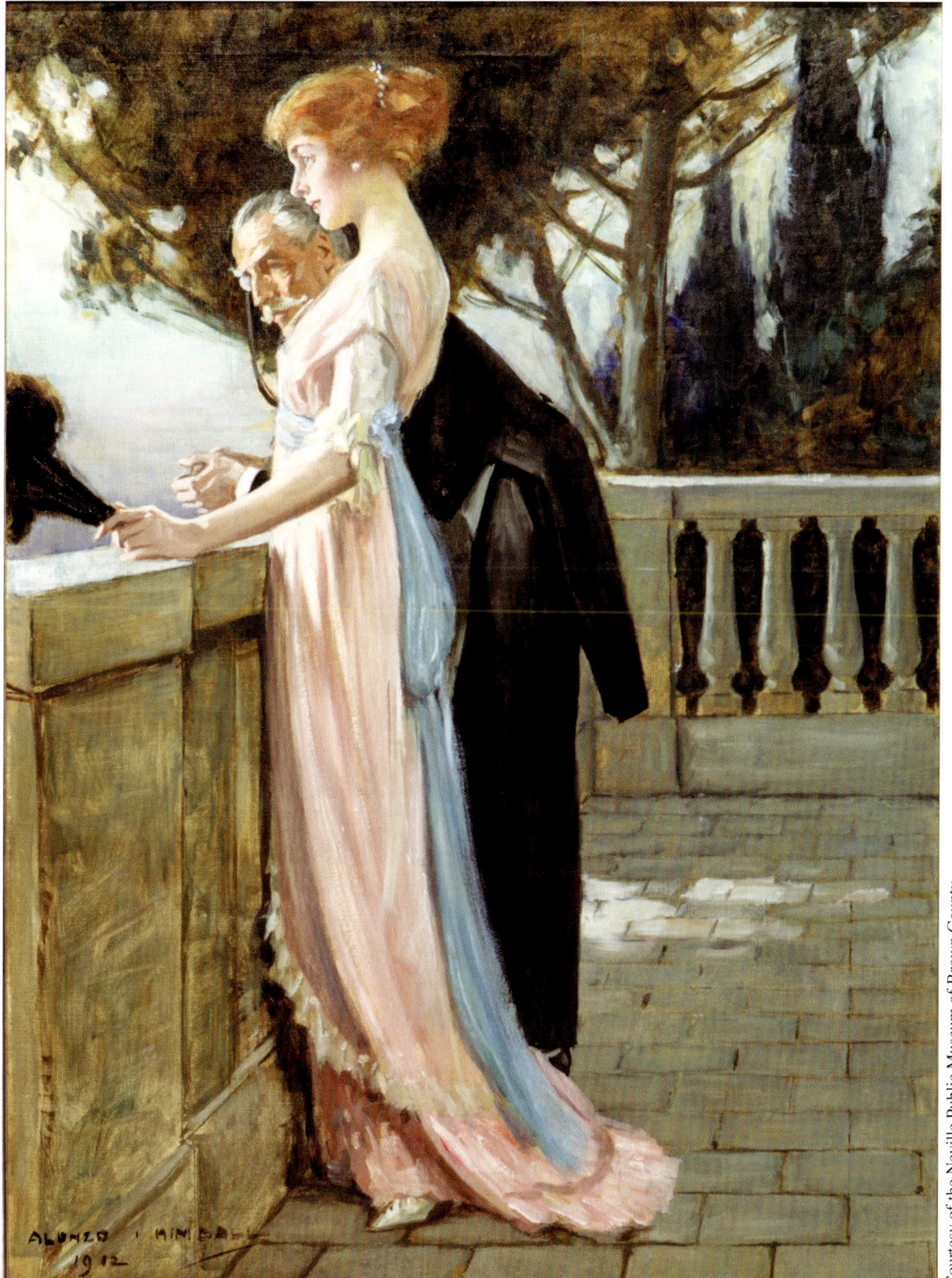

Courtesy of the Neville Public Museum of Brown County

The Conversation
Alonzo M. Kimball, 1912

However, the simple fact that it was published has let much of this imagery live for decades, and respect for the technical and creative mastery of the industry's best, has—over that time—let a wider audience see them for the artists that they truly are. A century after that Golden Age, museums that now show examples of work from this period are breaking attendance records for their events, auction houses are now actively pursuing illustration work for their auctions, and galleries that once shunned the commercial aspect of the work now welcome much of it onto their walls.

The illustrators who worked during this Golden Age informed and shaped generations. What still resonates in these works is the communication of ideas that—even a century later—continue to speak to every viewer who sees them.

Jeff A. Menges
April 2016

The Illustrators

EDWIN AUSTIN ABBEY
1852–1911, American

Edwin Austin Abbey was one of America's first great illustrators. From a very early age, his work was at a level worthy of publication, most notably for *Harper's Weekly*. *Harper's* hired him on as a staff illustrator when he was nineteen. His primary mediums of choice were pencil and ink, though the later parts of his career were spent on murals, with larger executions in oil. He was also an accomplished watercolor painter.

Abbey had a true penchant for depicting historical subjects in his work. That interest paid dividends when his publisher sent him to England in 1878, to gather inspiration for work on *Poetry of Robert Herrick*. This was the beginning of many trips to Europe for Abbey, and he would eventually settle in England in 1882. While there, he was thrilled to have the landscape, costumes, and props that populated his pictures in far greater quantity and availability than he had in the United States. In England, his success and recognition as an illustrator and painter continued to grow. Abbey was elected to be the president of The Royal Birmingham Society of Artists in 1901, and was selected to paint the coronation of Edward VII in 1902.

Abbey's preferred choice of subject matter was firmly rooted in English literature and history. The work he is best known for are the series of murals he painted for the Boston Library in 1890–1902, titled "The Quest for the Holy Grail." These works were created in England, and then shipped over for installation in America. Abbey's other major sources for imagery were Shakespearean subjects, and his deft skills with the pen landed him an assignment for *Harper's* in 1896: a four-volume set of *The Comedies of Shakespeare*. This series includes some of the most definitive imagery on Shakespeare done in the last 200 years.

The success of the murals at the Boston Library landed him a second major mural commission, one that would shape his last decade. He had finished extensive work on murals for the Pennsylvania State Capitol building, but succumbed to cancer in 1911, before the project was finished.

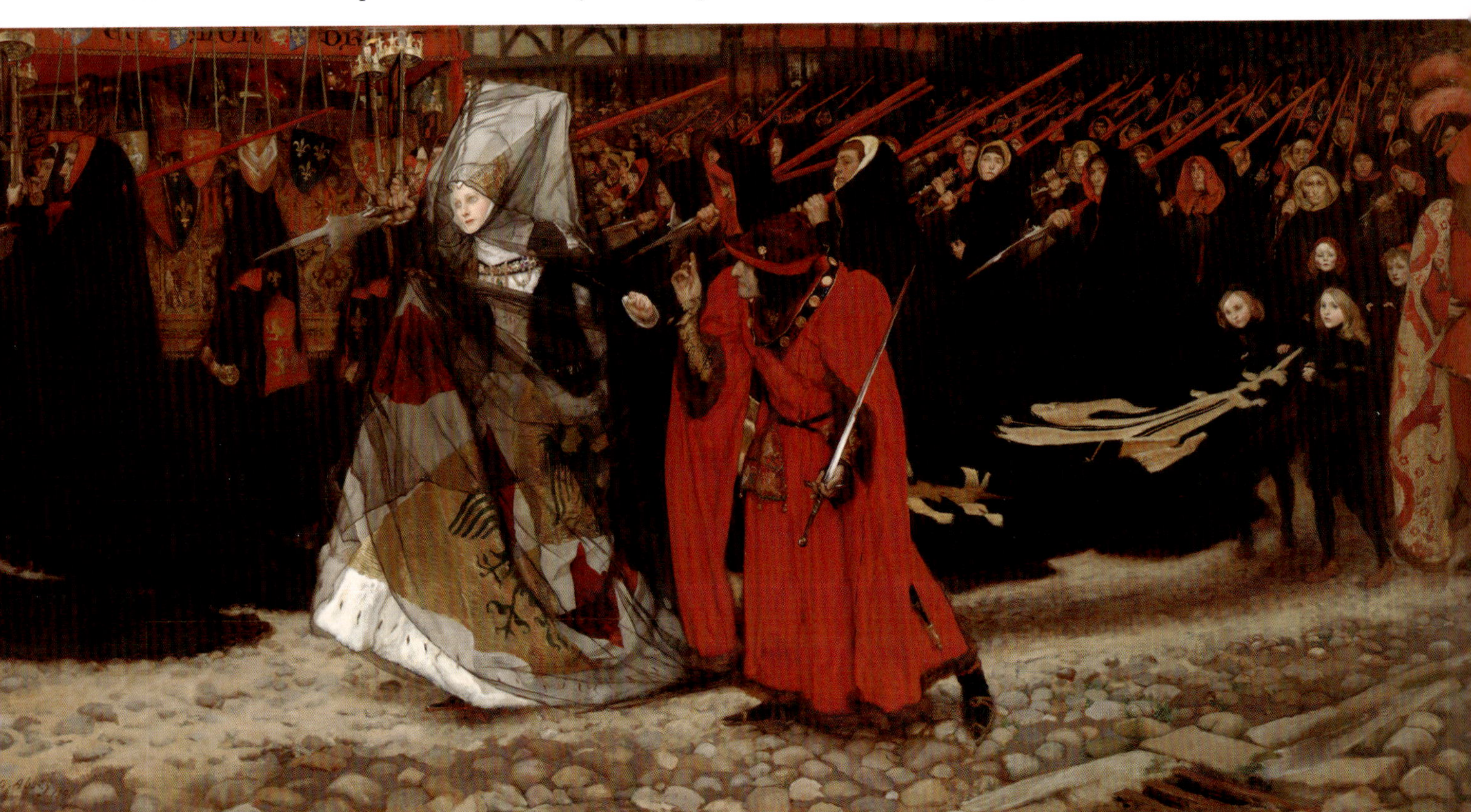

***Richard, Duke of Gloucester, and the Lady Anne.* 1896**

Courtesy of Yale University Art Gallery

An American Knight?

In 1907, Abbey declined a knighthood, because it would have meant renouncing his American citizenship.

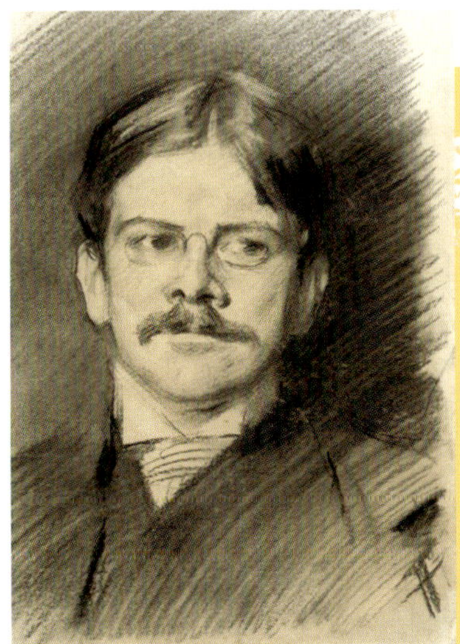

Abbey. By John Singer Sargent, c. 1889

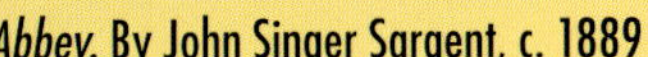

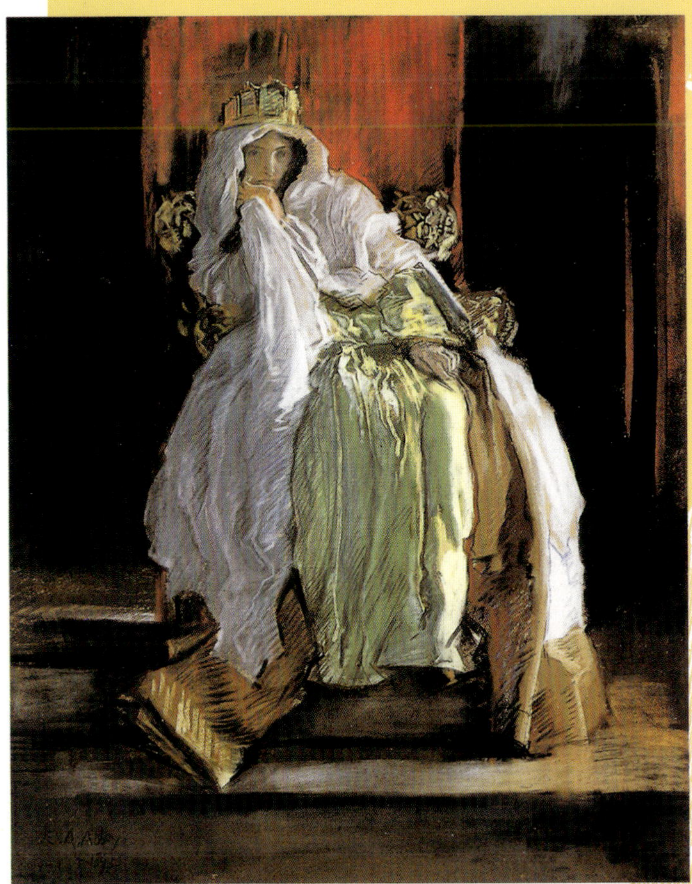

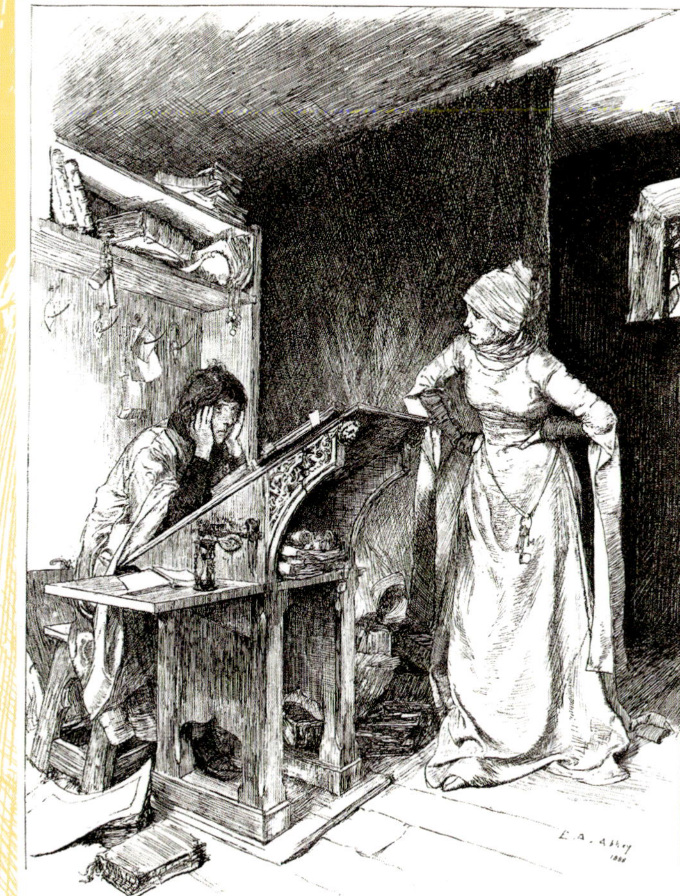

After Abbey's untimely death, the notable artist John Singer Sargent supervised the completion of the mural works that Abbey had started in Harrisburg, Pennsylvania. Violet Oakley, a student of the influential artist Howard Pyle, finished painting the areas he had not yet begun with her own designs.

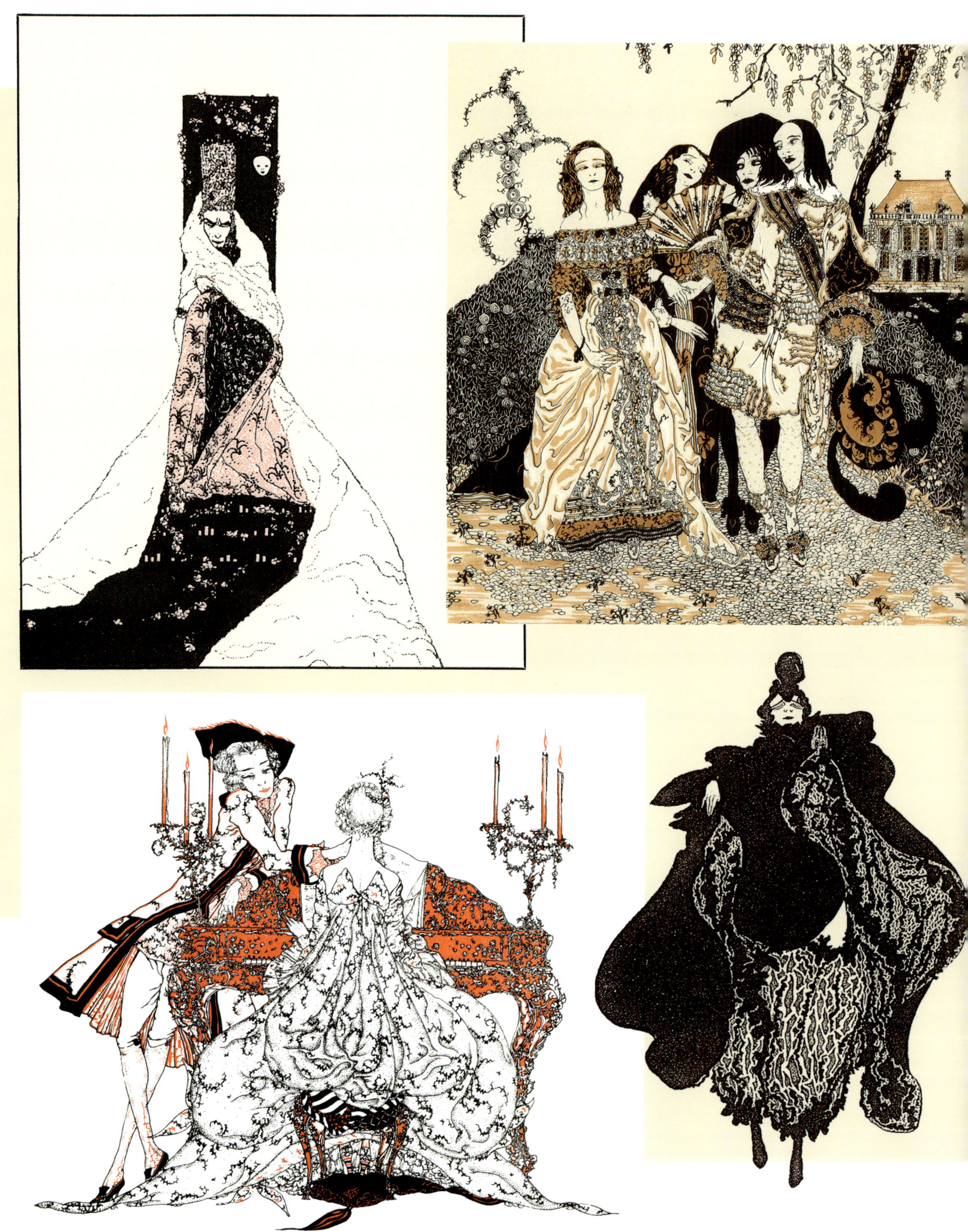

From *Forty-three Drawings*, 1914, and *Manon Lescoaux*, 1923

Alastair
1887–1969, German

An unusual artist who challenged the basic tenets of imagery on many levels, Alastair was a "nom de brush" of Baron Hans Henning Voight. The self-taught illustrator lived and breathed the Decadent art movement. His work was notably complicated, elegant, and often bawdy—he was known to push the limits of social acceptability in both his art and his lifestyle.

His earliest known published work is *Forty-three Drawings* (1914), which was his debut in the field of art and illustration. It made enough of an impact to secure Alastair some interest from potential publishers. Often compared to Aubrey Beardsley, Alastair followed a similar course in selection of material, and flourished with a highly graphic style, while also working with Aubrey Beardsley's original publisher, John Lane. Alastair's adventurous style was well-suited to the social climate of the 1920s, and it would remain the most prolific decade for his art. Among his works were publications with like-minded Oscar Wilde, for whom Alastair illustrated *The Sphinx,* in 1920, and two years later, *Salomé.* He would go on to illustrate *Les Liaisons dangereuses* and Poe's *The Fall of the House of Usher,* both in the late 1920s, along with a handful of other titles for *Éditions Narcisse.*

Throughout his life he had the ability to attract the interest of wealthy patrons and friends, who were able to provide him with needed security along the way. Waning interest in the Decadent style, and the difficulty Alastair had in navigating the hurdles of the publishing business both played a part in his departure from illustration in the early 1930s. For the next thirty-five years, he had little artistic output. Surprisingly, much of his time was filled with translating over 100 books into German. Before his death in 1969, he returned to display art publicly during the mid-1960s.

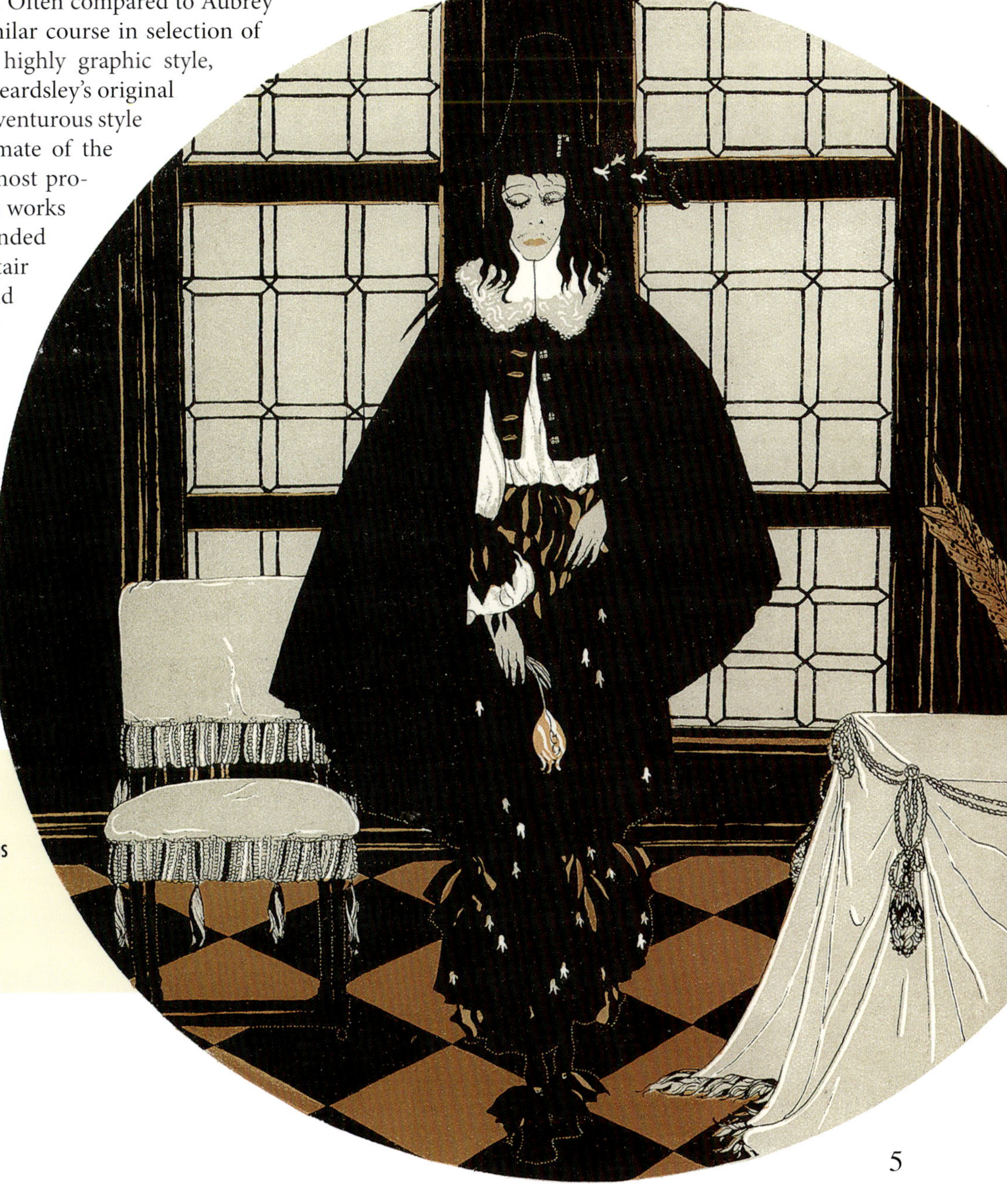

Finery and Pattern
With a delicate touch—and distinctive style—Alastair's work continues to find fans to this day.

Stanley Arthurs

1877–1950, American

A native of Delaware, Stanley Massey Arthurs did not have to travel far when the opportunity came for him to become one of Howard Pyle's students. Arthurs signed on early—first at Drexel in 1897—and later for the summer sessions at Chadds Ford, Pennsylvania, finally joining Pyle at the school in Wilmington.

Arthurs did not follow the crowd that Pyle had sent off to explore the world and paint from their experience. Arthurs resided in a small studio that had been part of the Pyle school; he bought it after Pyle's passing, and spent most of his career there, specializing in historical pieces. Arthurs took Pyle's teaching about historical accuracy to heart, and pursued it feverishly, focusing mostly on American subjects from the Revolution to the American Civil War. A book published in 1935 titled *The American Historical Scene* gathered many of his works from books, magazines, and commercial assignments into one volume.

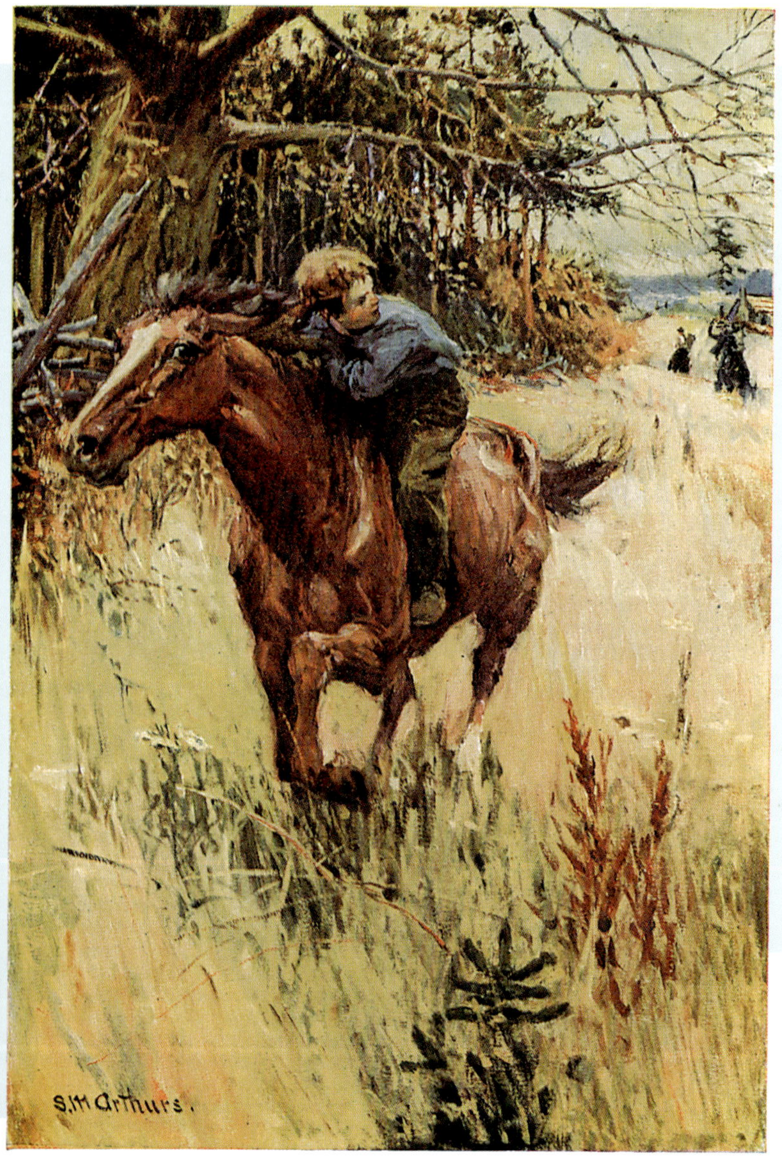

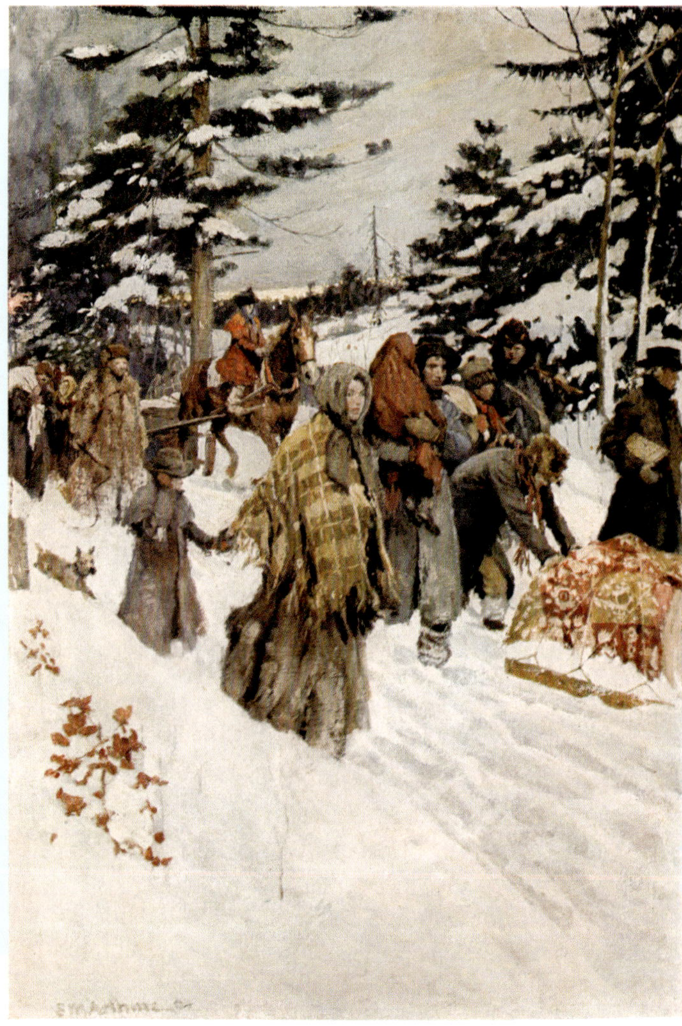

A Student of History
Like many of Pyle's students, Arthurs developed a deep appreciation for historical work. In 1935 University of Pennsylvania Press published *The American Historical Scene,* with many reprints of Arthurs' illustrated articles that had been previously printed in magazines.

Like his teacher, and some of his fellow Pyle school alumni, Arthurs included murals in his work as his experience matured. Arthurs' strength in historical painting made him a good choice for this type of art, and he did numerous works for his home state—as seen in the State Capitol and Delaware College.

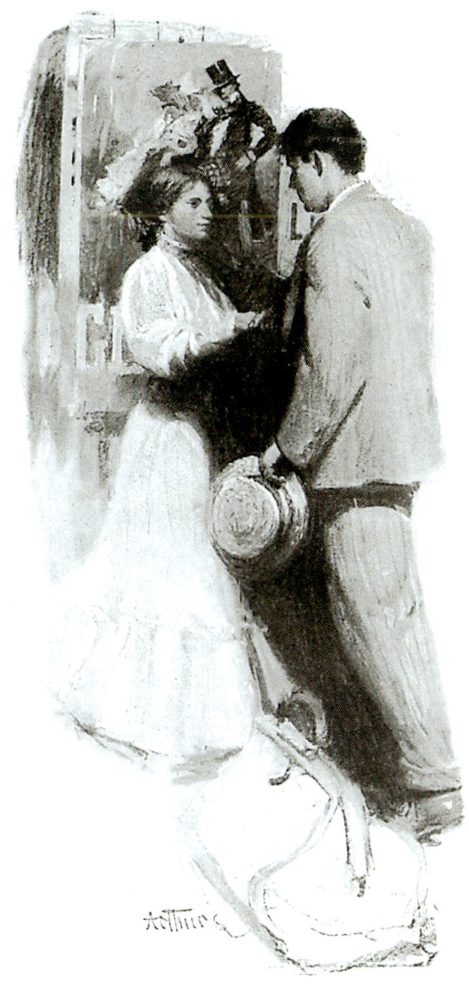

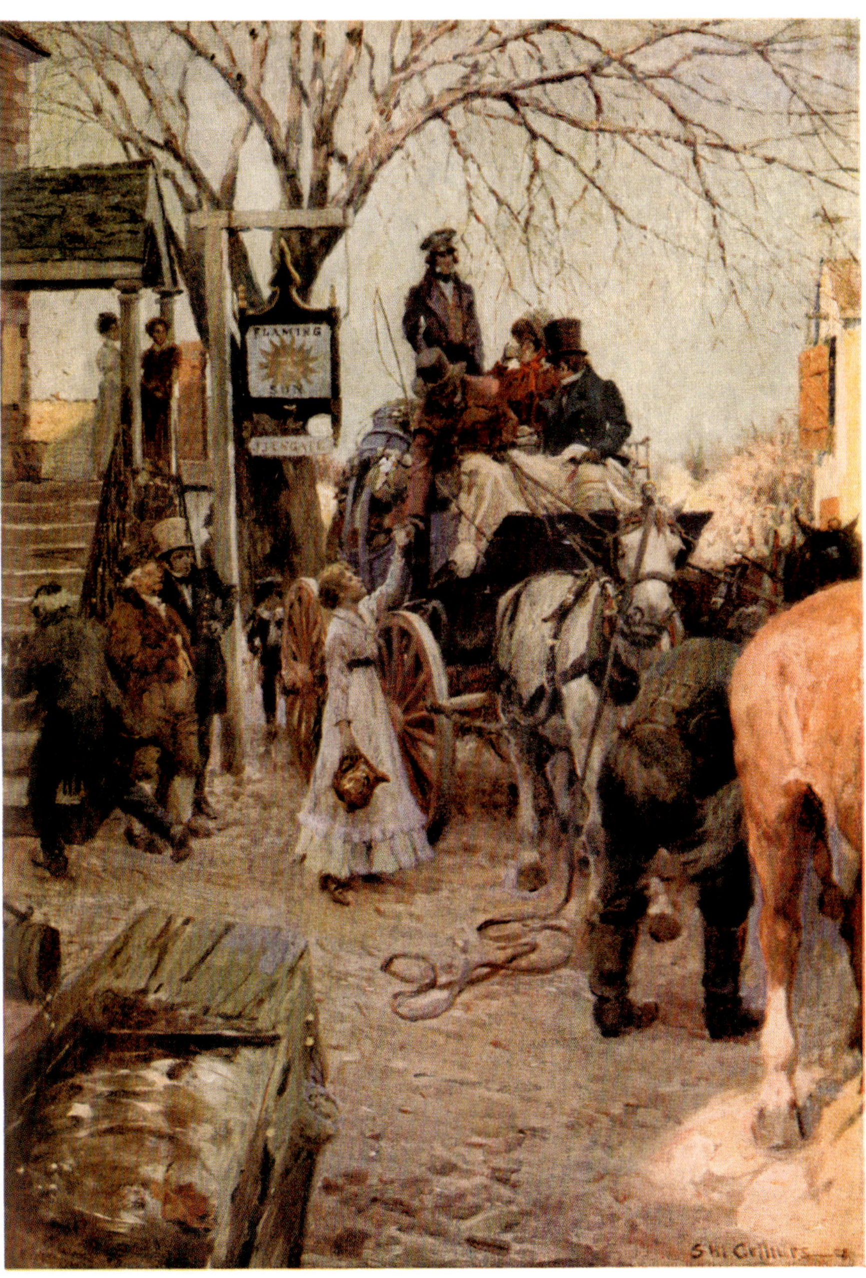

Clifford W. Ashley
1881–1947, American

Another product of the Howard Pyle school, Clifford Ashley was part of a group of promising students that came from the Boston area and met at the Eric Pape School there. The foursome included Ashley, Henry Peck (who was Ashley's cousin), Sidney Chase, and N. C. Wyeth. All of them would go on to have successful careers as illustrators, and all four went from Pape's school to join Howard Pyle in Delaware in 1901. Just a few years later, Ashley's work appeared regularly in magazines such as *Collier's*, *Delineator*, and *Success*.

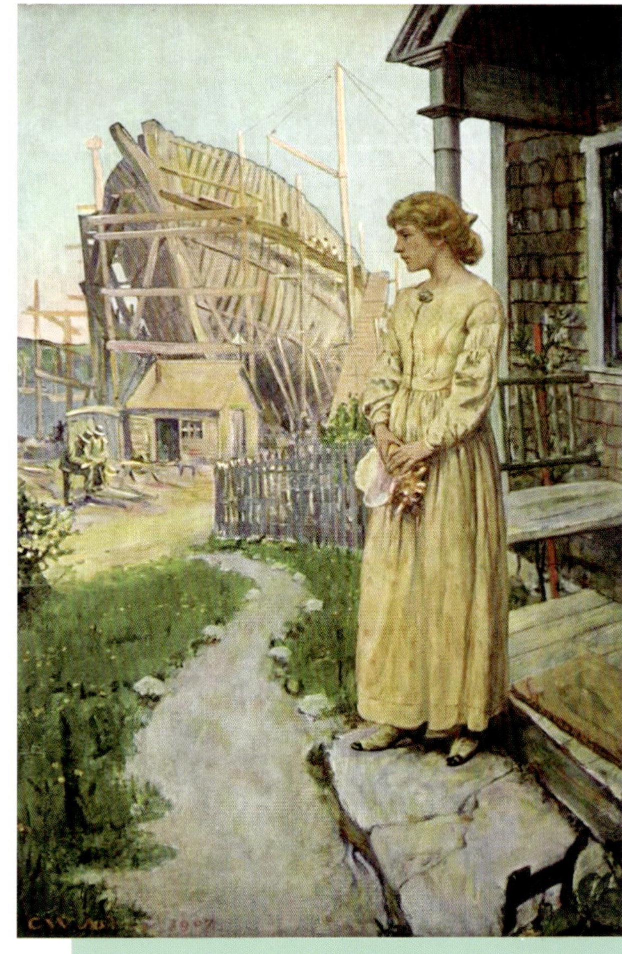

Ashley originally hailed from the whaling town of New Bedford, Massachusetts, and grew up during the end of the whaling era, which was so important to that area. The impact of that environment, and the influence of two uncles who were both ship captains, was significant. Ashley was one of several illustrators of the period who specialized in marine-themed work. The imagery was so ingrained in him that he was able to produce convincing scenes of ships, wharf areas, and other nautical subject matter with ease.

After Pyle's teachings, Ashley spent time sharing studio spaces with his cousin, Henry Peck, and Stanley Arthurs, before returning to Massachusetts and settling in the town of Fairhaven in 1916. Back on the New England coast, Ashley was motivated to continue working on marine subjects. During the next three decades, Ashley remained very active in the arts community; he was a member of such organizations as the Salmagundi Club, the Wilmington Society of the Fine Arts, and several historic and boating clubs as well. He married late in life in 1932, and had two daughters.

Three books came out of Ashley's combined interests in the sea and his illustration: *Yankee Whaler* in 1926, *Whaleships of New Bedford* in 1929, and *The Ashley Book of Knots* in 1944. The latter is the definitive book on nautical knots, and is still sought by sailors today.

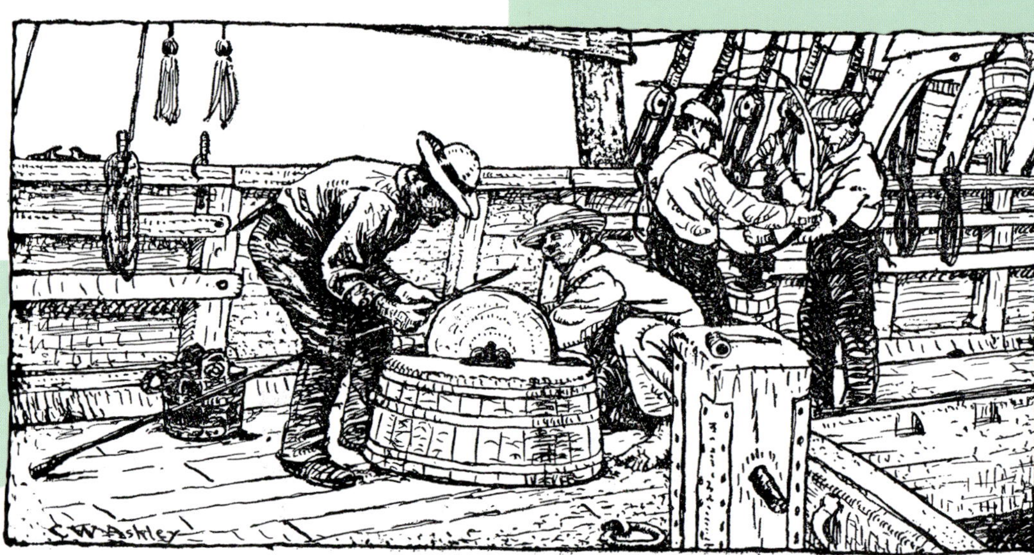

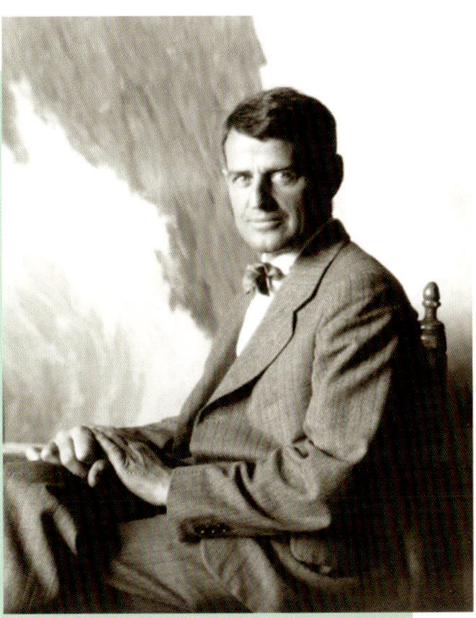

Strong ties to his youth

Growing up in New Bedford, Massachusetts, ships and whaling in particular were of great importance locally. The impression that it made deeply affected Ashley's work for most of his life.

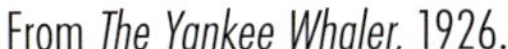

From *The Yankee Whaler*, 1926.

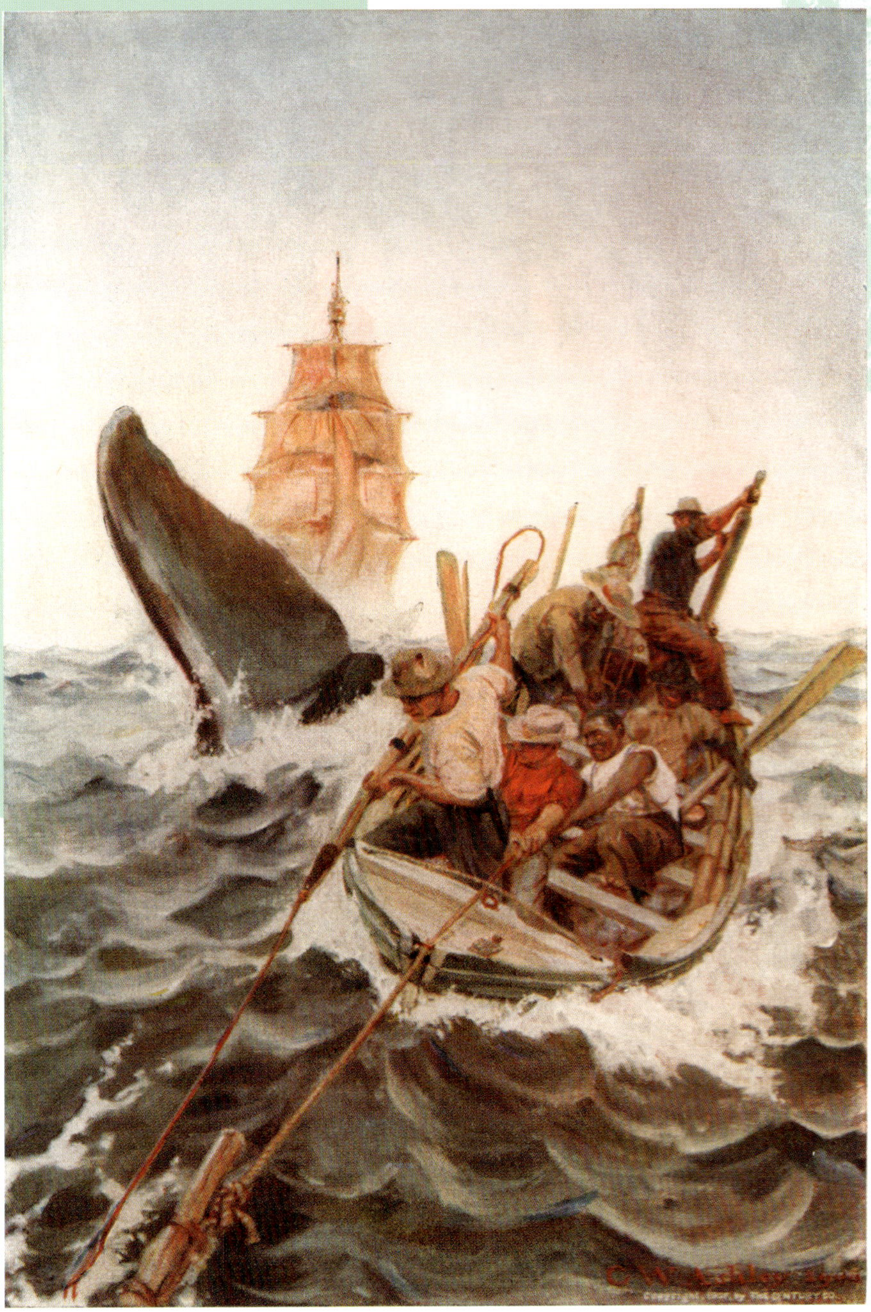

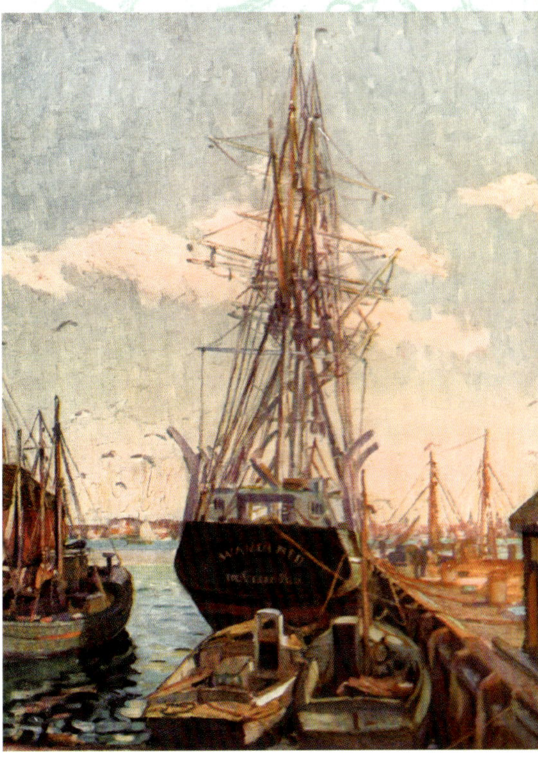

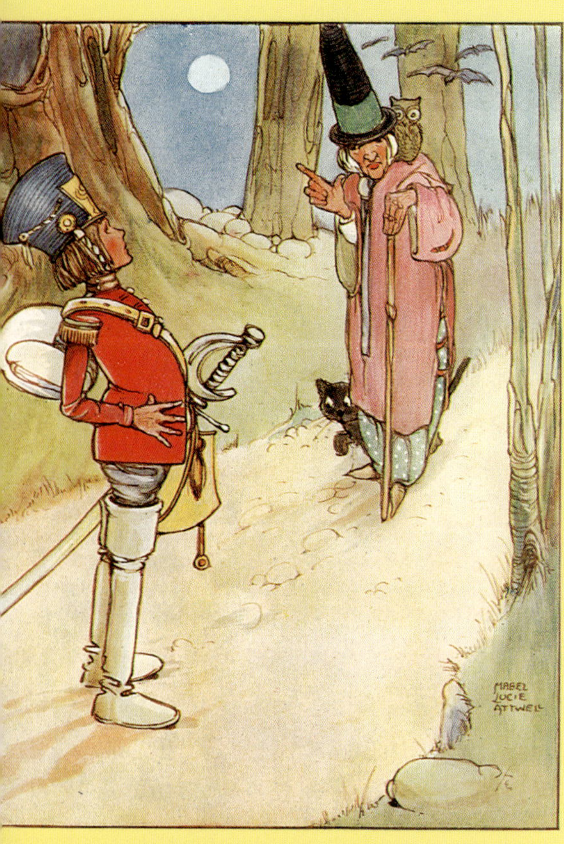

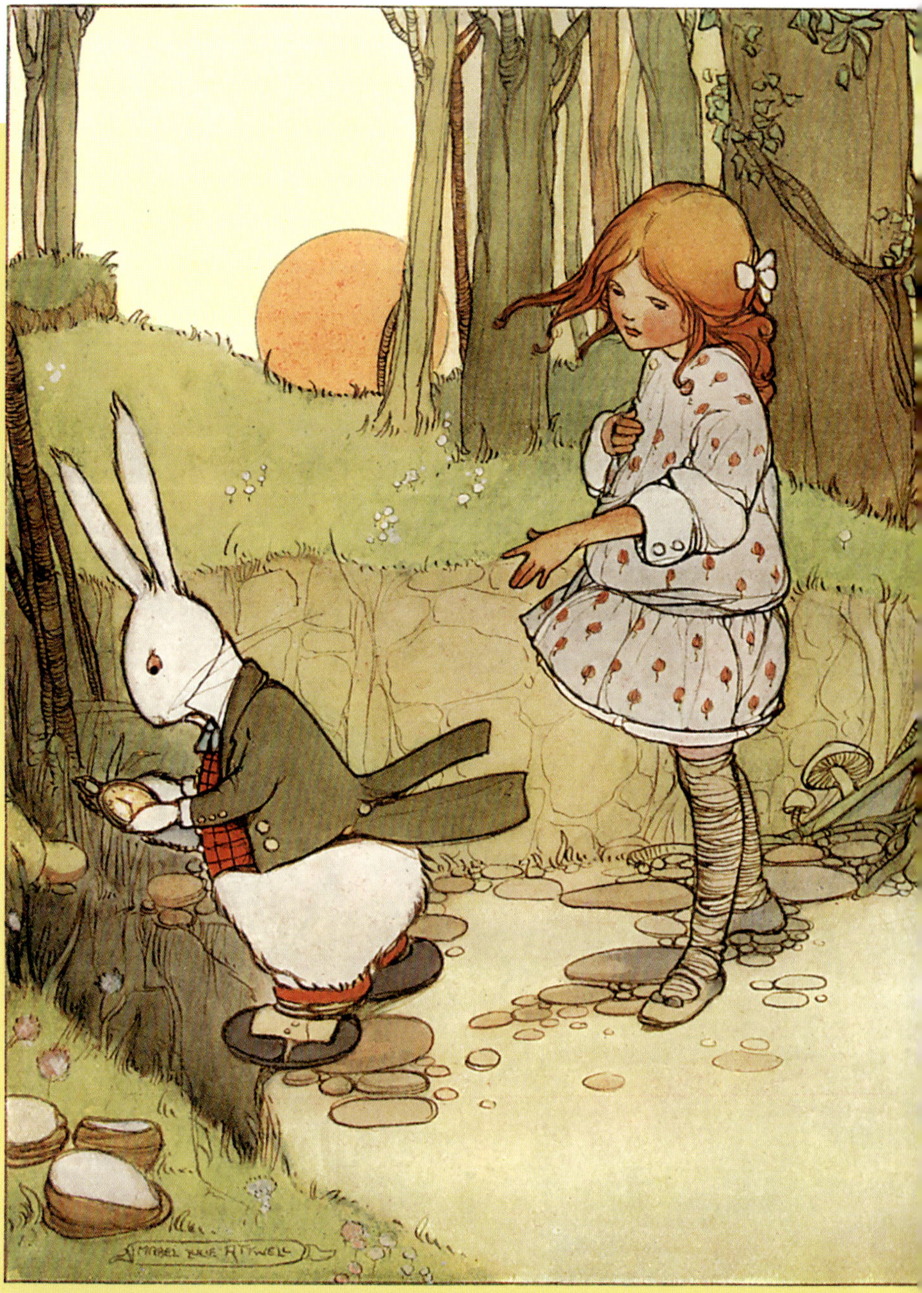

BY SPECIAL REQUEST

Attwell continued to receive numerous illustration commissions. In 1921, *Peter Pan* author J. M. Barrie asked her to illustrate a gift edition of *Peter Pan and Wendy* for British publisher Hodder and Stoughton.

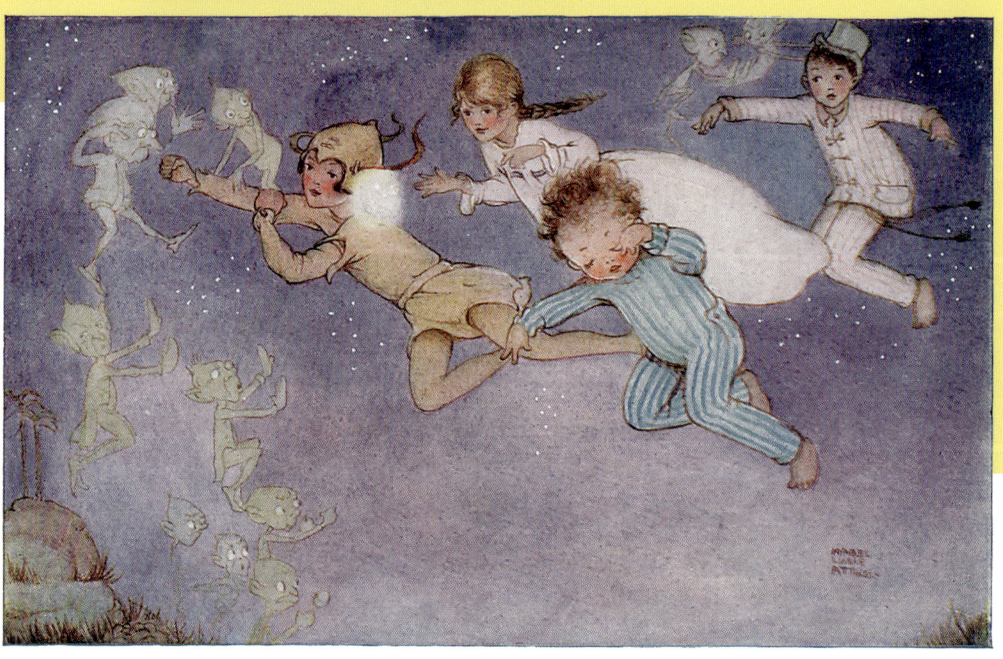

Mabel Lucie Attwell

1879–1964, British

Mabel Lucie Attwell did not find encouragement in art school. Attending at the end of the nineteenth century, her studies emphasized still-life drawing and a classical approach. Attwell had a vivid imagination, though, and wanted to develop it through her drawing. She left the confines of art school, and went out to seek her own path in illustration. By 1905, she was gaining steady commissions for work in children's stories. Within a few years her work caught the eye of some of Britain's major publishers—she worked for Cassell in 1910, and held a long-standing and productive relationship with Raphael Tuck, who printed her works from 1909 into the 1930s. Titles like *Grimm's Fairy Tales* (1910 and 1912), *Mother Goose* (1910), and *Alice in Wonderland* (1911) were all part of Attwell's rise in popularity. She also had a ten-book run with W. & R. Chambers, from 1905–1913.

Atwell married in 1908 and became a mother soon after. Inspiration from drawing her daughter Peggy brought a defining "feature" look to Attwell's illustrated children—one that the public took a strong liking to—and they became hungry for products that featured her elf-like children characters. The combination of Attwell's individual styling and the public's fondness for this look made her work market-worthy, and Attwell was able to capitalize on a few opportunities—her work became available on all sorts of children's materials, from nurseryware to figurines, to greeting cards and decorations of all types. Attwell's characters had an exceedingly strong presence in ceramics. As early as 1926, her designs were featured on children's chinaware for Shelley Potteries, and her work was still gracing their products some four decades later.

One of her greatest achievements came with the publication of the *Lucie Attwell Annual* in 1922. Publishing an Annual book was not uncommon during that era, but being driven by an individual entity was unusual, and it lived on for over 50 years. It kept her imagery fresh, in the forefront of the public eye, and remained solidly cherished by generations of children throughout the twentieth century.

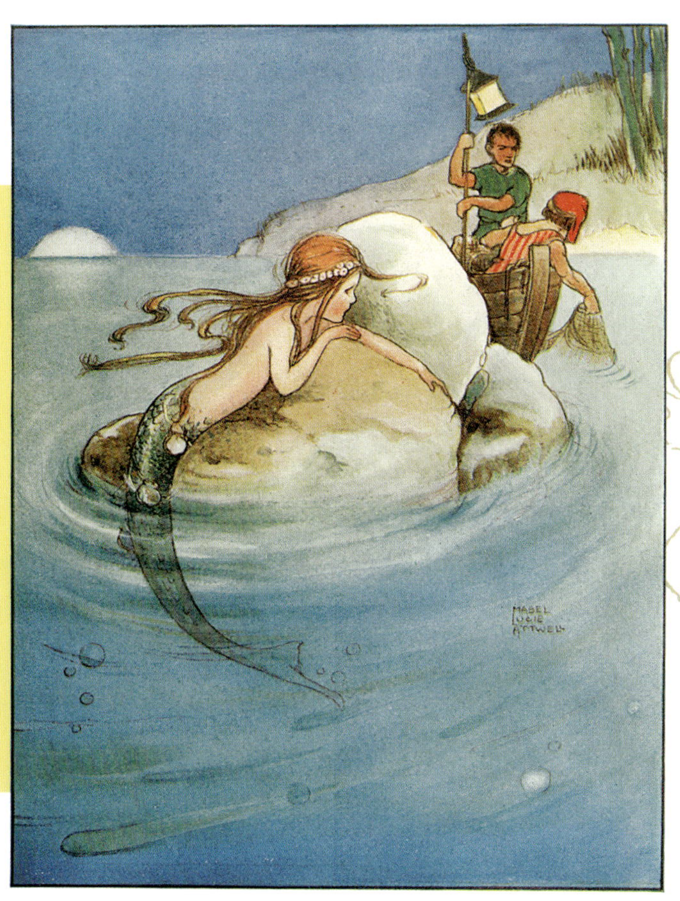

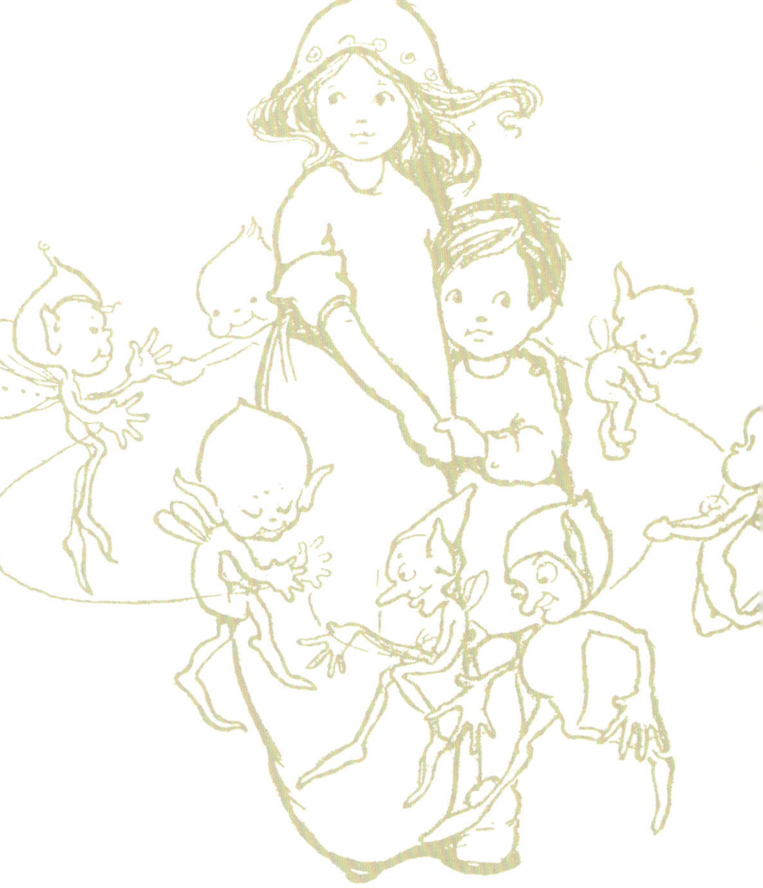

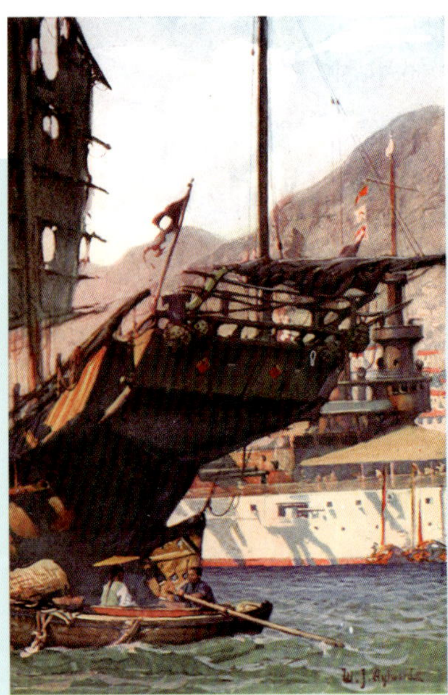

Masts, Rigging, and Whitecaps

Paint what you know. In Aylward's case, it was the sea and ships. He turned the knowledge he grew up with into his greatest ally when dealing with marine subjects, which made up the vast majority of his workload.

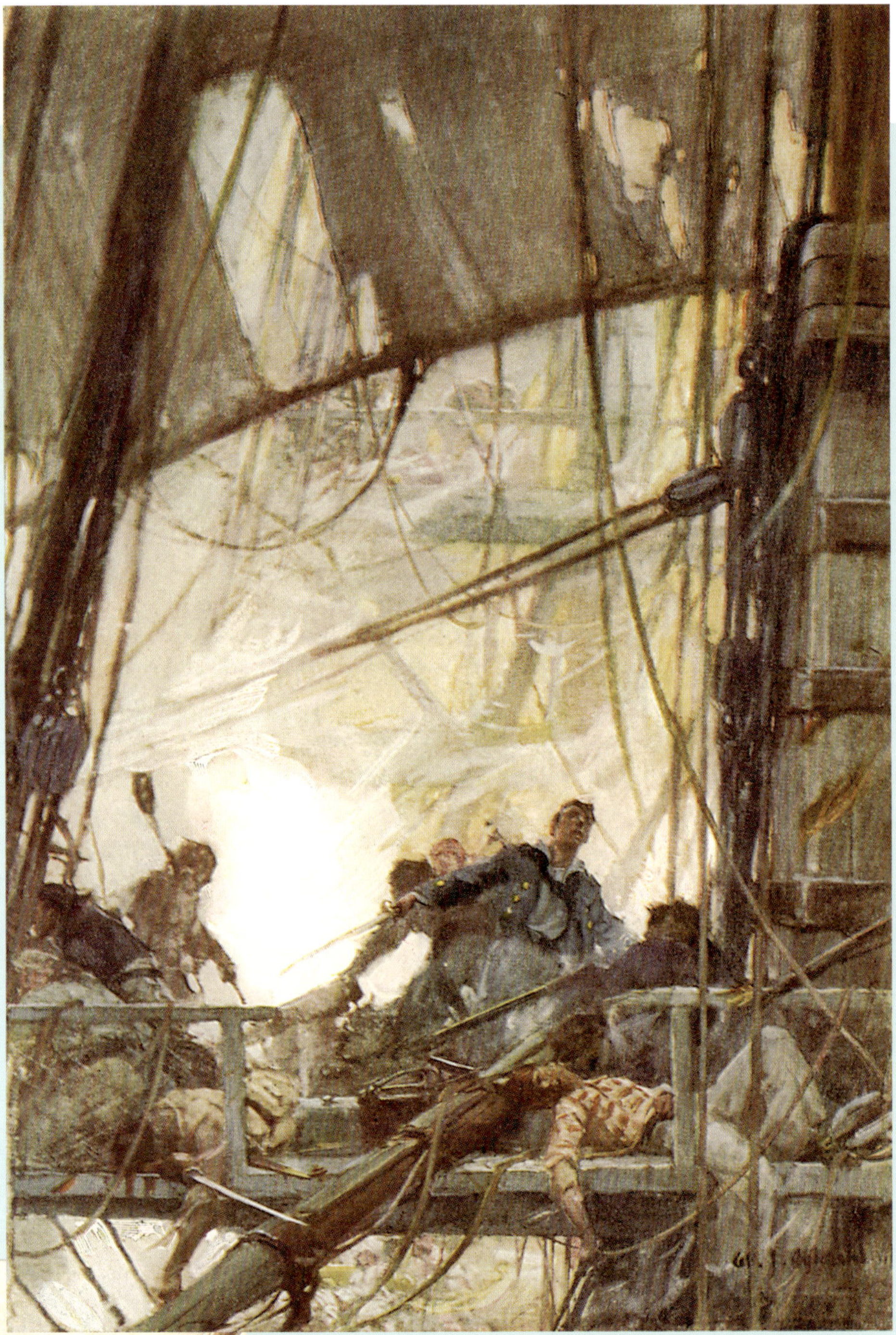

Aylward wrote and illustrated several articles for *Harper's* magazine, in which he explored local regions and their picturesque environments, including parts of New England, Long Island, and shipping on New Jersey's canals.

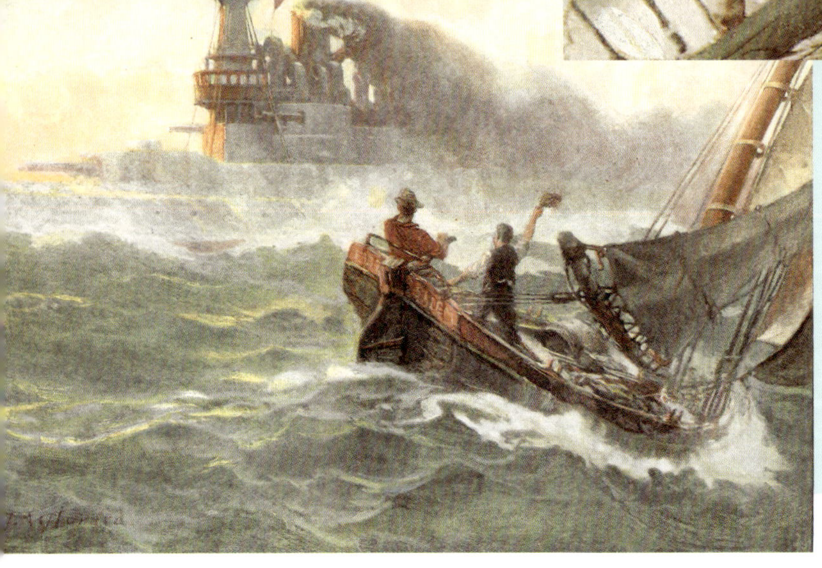

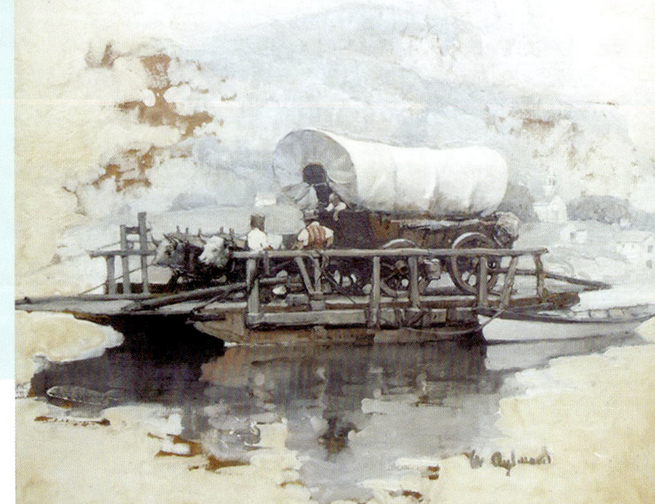

William J. Aylward
1875–1956, American

The son of a Great Lakes sea captain, it was no surprise that W. J. Aylward's career in illustration had marine painting at its core. The knowledge he acquired from growing up around ships gave him an understanding of their designs, and that experience came through in his nautical-themed work. A product of Howard Pyle's Brandywine school, Aylward, upon completion of his studies, was granted one of the work-associated trips that his mentor had arranged. He embarked on a trip halfway around the world by sea, on a ship escorting the floating dry dock "Dewey" from Brooklyn, N.Y., to the Philippines. During Aylward's trip he made numerous sketches and paintings, and upon his return they were published in an article on the experience for *Scribner's Magazine,* with no less than twenty illustrations by the author. The job established Aylward's expertise in marine work, while also providing a platform for him to display more figure-based illustrations as well. It also began a long-standing relationship with one of the largest employers of illustrators at the time—*Scribner's*—certainly a great start for what would be a lengthy career.

Aylward went on to do lots of magazine work, for the likes of *Youth's Companion, Scribner's,* and *Harper's* magazines, among others. In 1904, during the early part of his career, he caught a big break when he was assigned Jack London's *The Sea-Wolf.* That high-profile exposure made Aylward an illustrator of choice for marine work in books. He continued his marine illustration twenty years later, with the 1925 edition of Jules Verne's *20,000 Leagues Under the Sea.*

During World War I, Aylward put his expertise to good use when he was selected with seven other artists (including fellow Howard Pyle student Harvey Dunn) to be a member of the Engineer Reserve Corps, portraying war themes for records and for publication back in the United States. While in France, Aylward recorded Army troop movements while spending his spare time doing port studies in towns like Marseilles. After the war, his reputation for ship work made him the preferred artist for a ship's official portrait for many shipping lines. Aylward did many ship portraits for the United States line, the Norddeutscher Lloyd line, and the U.S. Navy.

Later in his career, Aylward taught at both Pratt Industrial Art School in Brooklyn and the Newark School of Fine and Industrial Art. In 1950, he published a small book through Pitman Publishing—*Ships and How to Draw Them.*

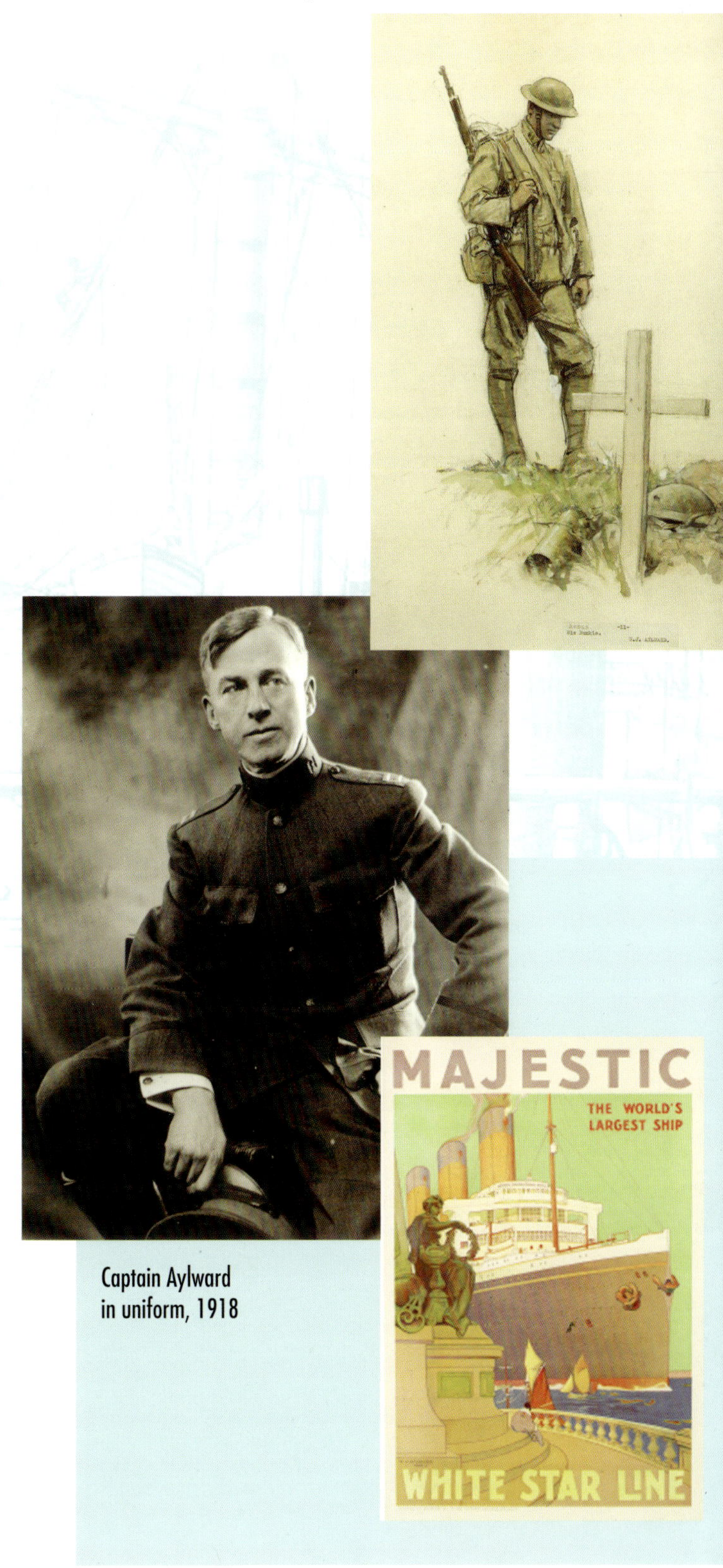

Captain Aylward in uniform, 1918

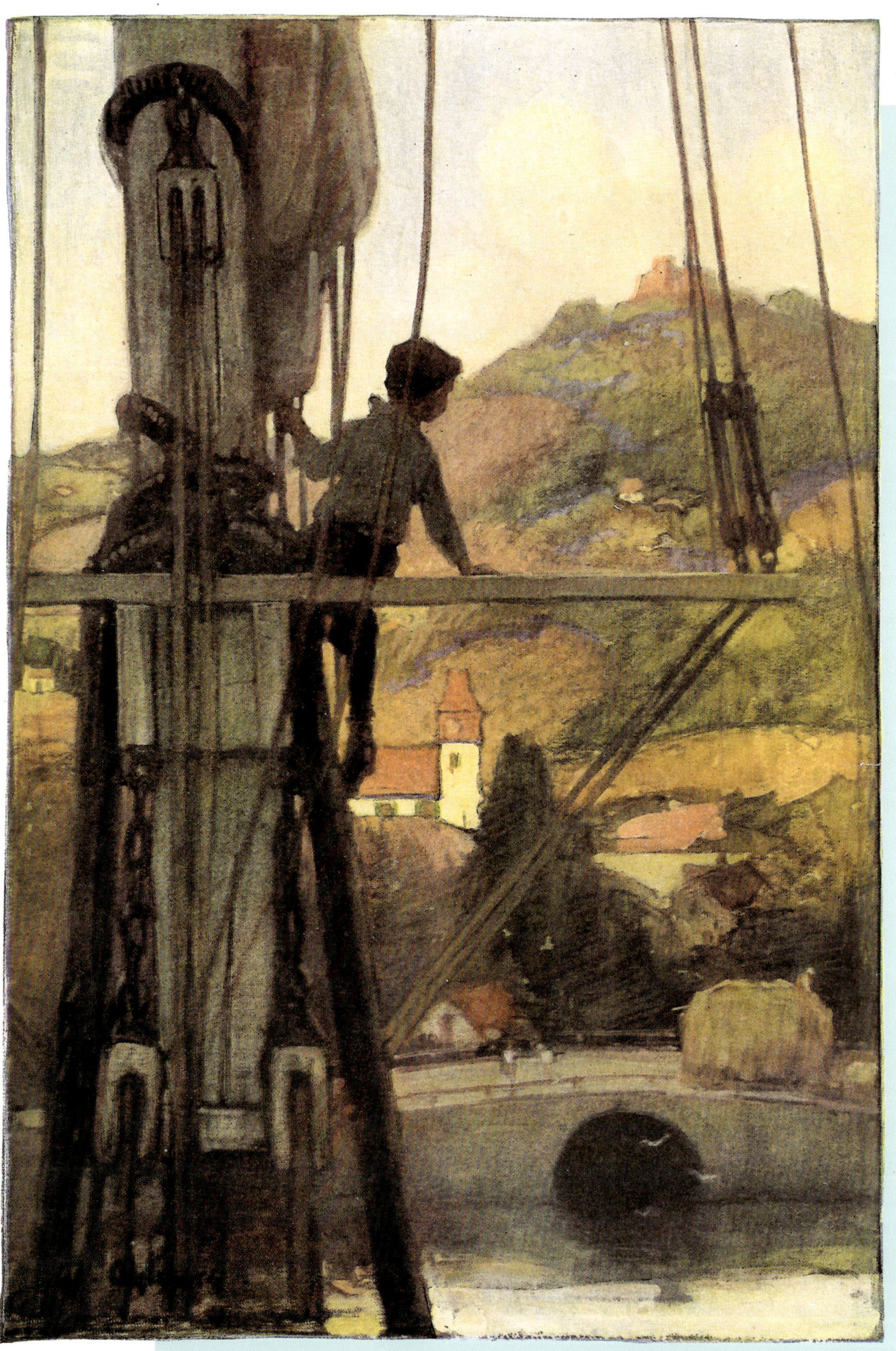

"This was my harbor, my ocean, my world." From *Harper's* magazine, February 1916.

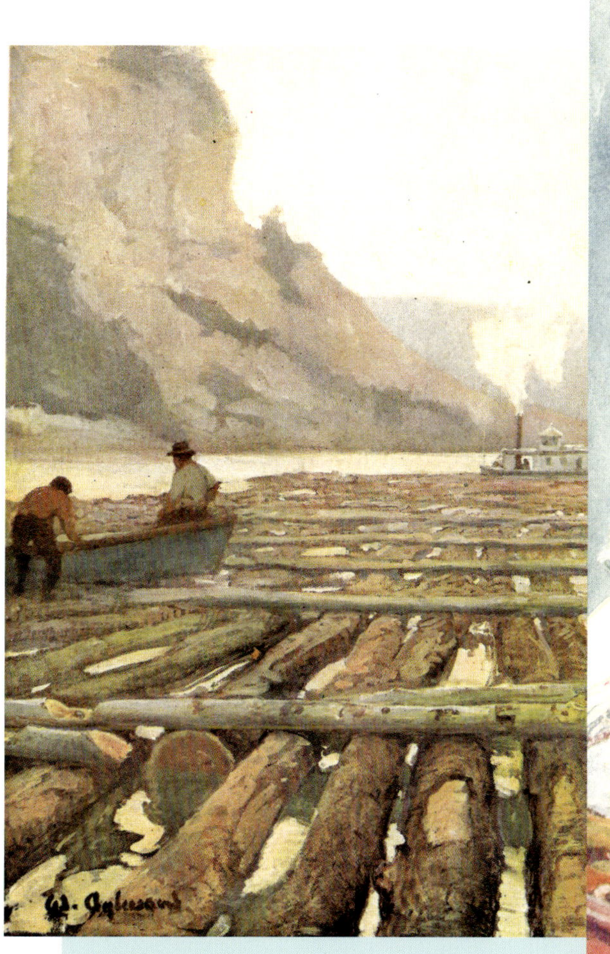

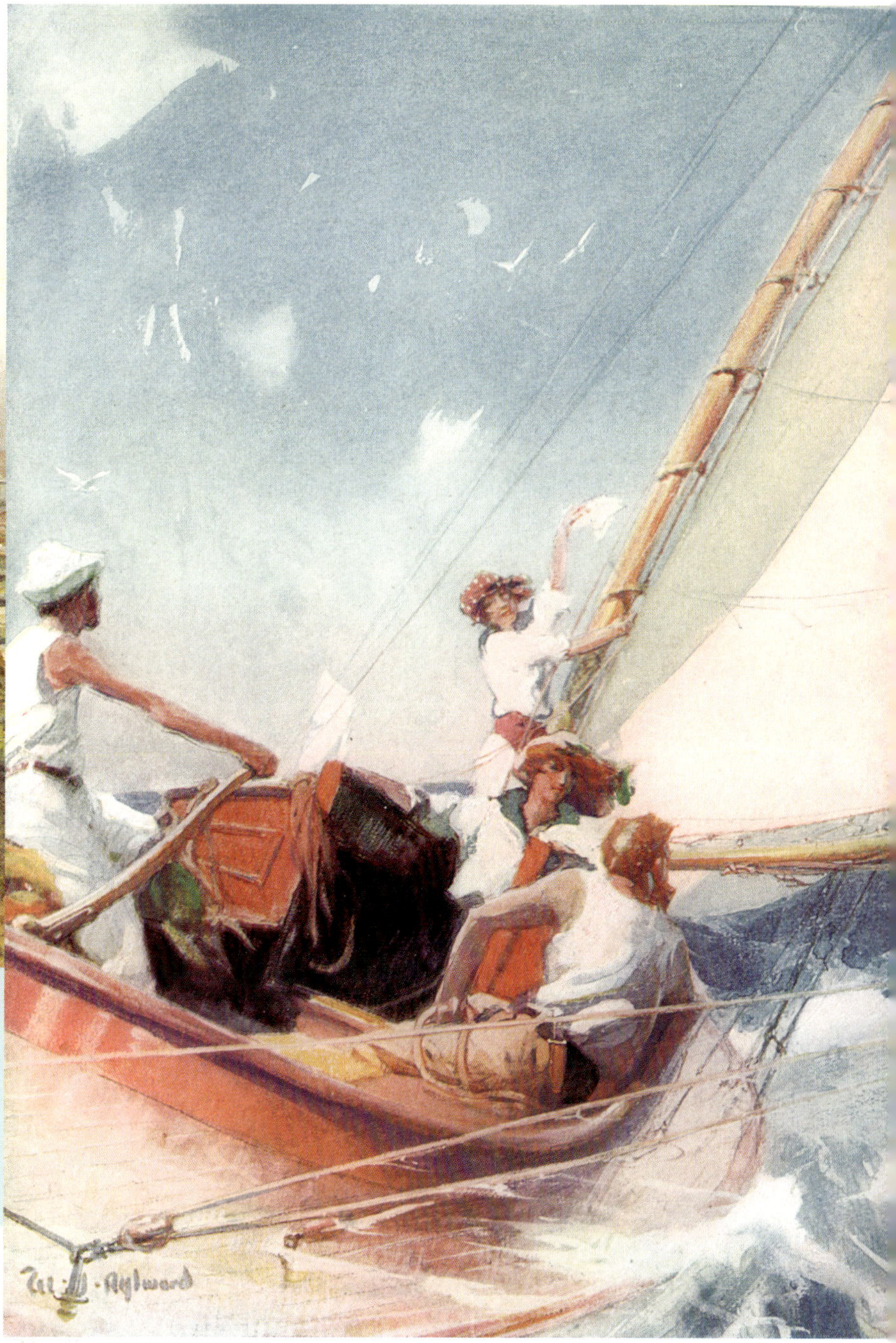

SELDOM FAR FROM WATER
River traffic, pleasure sailing, or the shallows of an inland creek—if boating was the assignment, Aylward was a solid candidate to depict it.

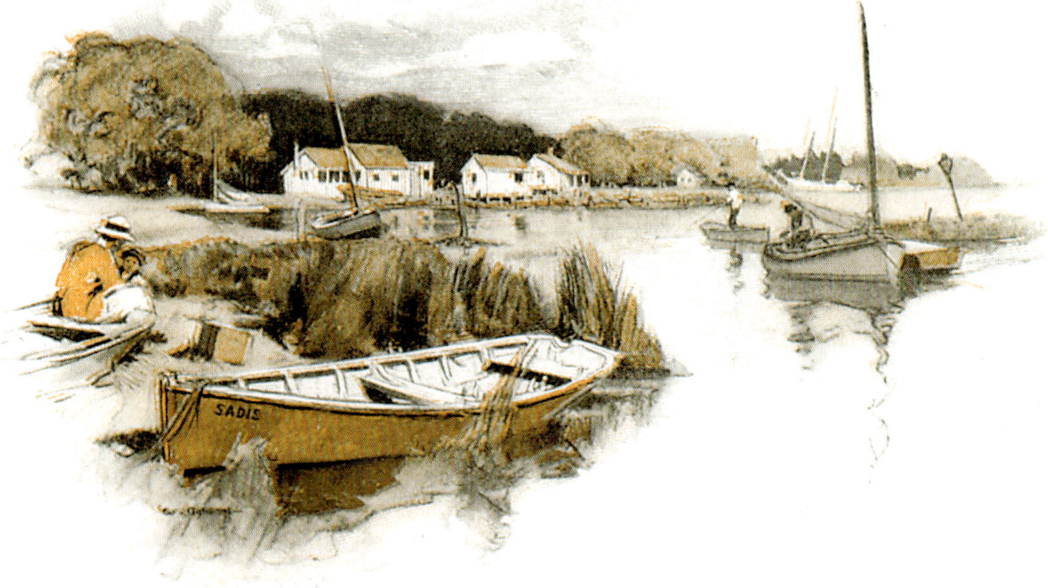

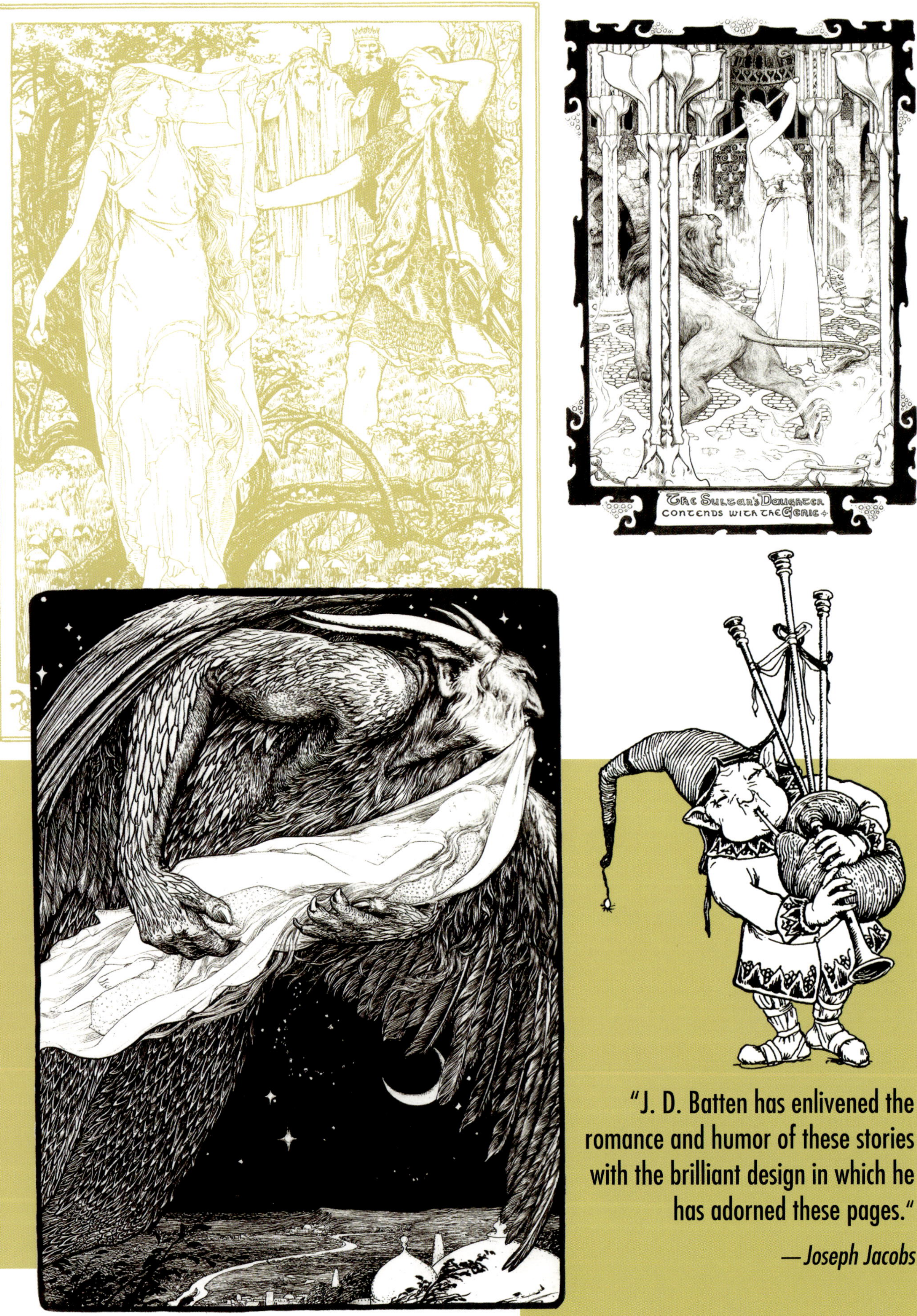

"J. D. Batten has enlivened the romance and humor of these stories with the brilliant design in which he has adorned these pages."

—Joseph Jacobs

John Batten

1860–1932, British

Though his output of illustration can be seen in just a few volumes of folk and fairy tales, the impact of John Dickson Batten's work on English children's literature was considerable. A friend and contemporary of illustrator H. J. Ford, Batten attended classes with Ford at the Slade School of Fine Art, and both studied under Alphonse Legros. Reflecting their parallel development, the two had remarkably similar paths to success, and both did outstanding line illustration.

In 1890 Batten was published in *English Fairy Tales,* with text from editor and historian Joseph Jacobs. Batten's work consisted of many smaller pieces, injecting the stories with humor and imagination. The partnership between Batten and Jacobs would prove a successful one that would continue for at least five more volumes over the next six years. Batten also contributed to a number of other projects during that time, most notably *Fairy Tales from the Arabian Nights* in 1893.

After 1896, Batten applied his creative efforts to more painterly pursuits—and left book illustration, for reasons that seem unclear. Perhaps his intention was to make what he thought would be more lasting statements with his work. He did, however, continue to produce imagery from fairy tales, and his beautiful color paintings would have been very fitting to the books he had worked on in the 1890s. Other painted works in his later years were done for various churches in England, such as Christchurch in Lichfield, and St. Martin's Church, Kensal Rise, London.

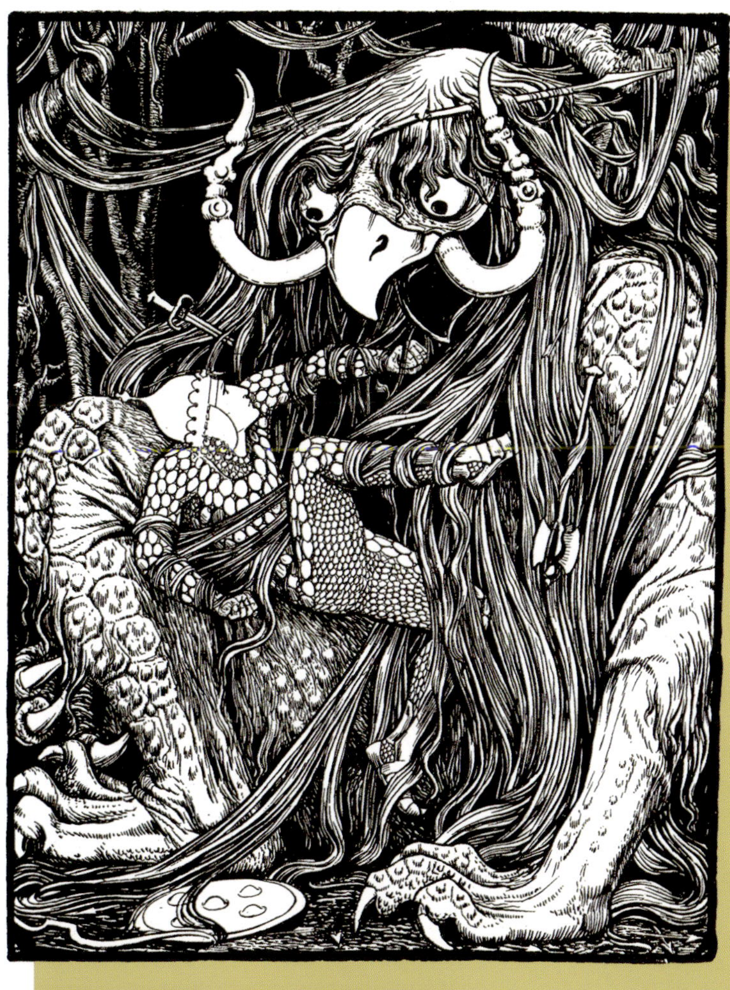

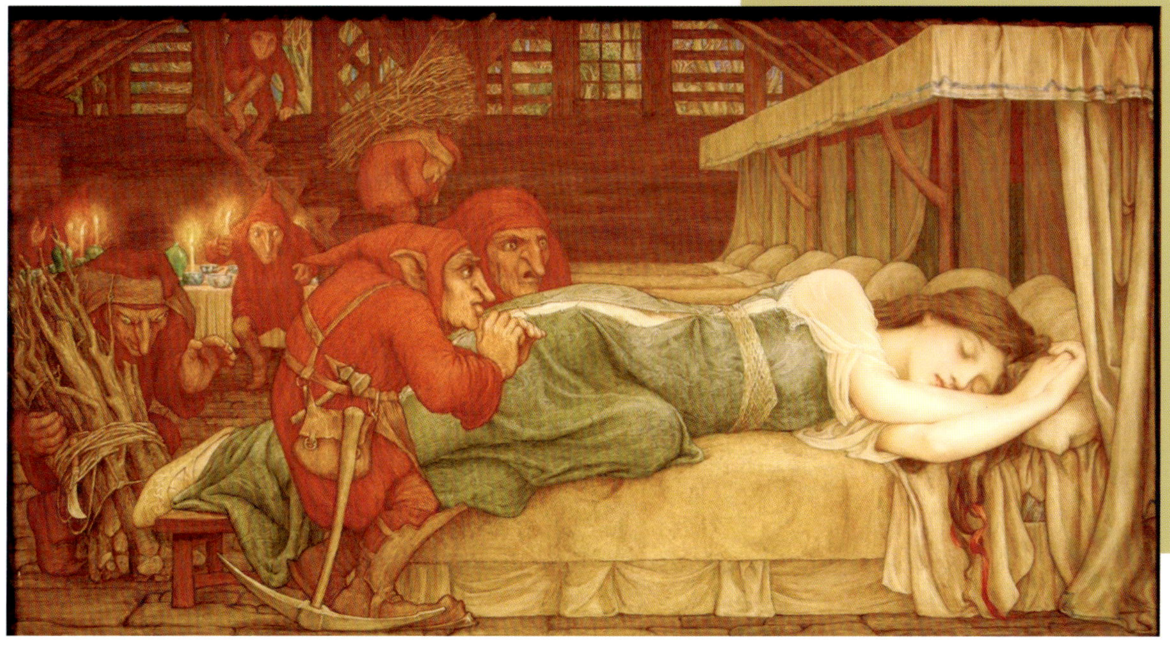

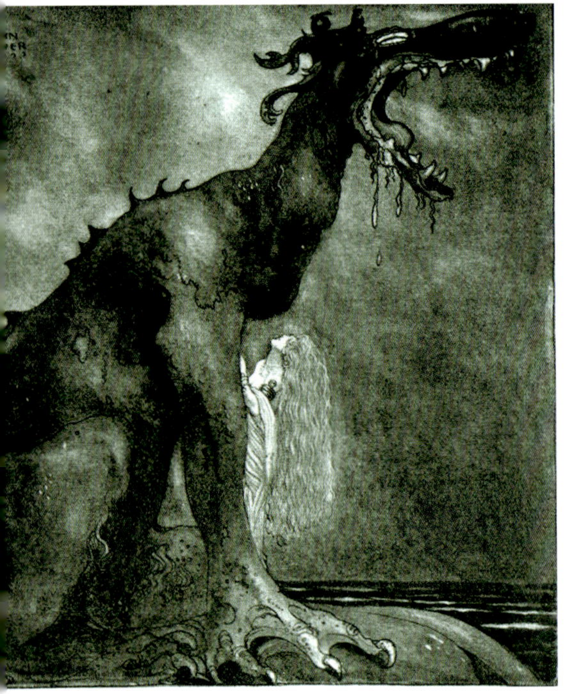

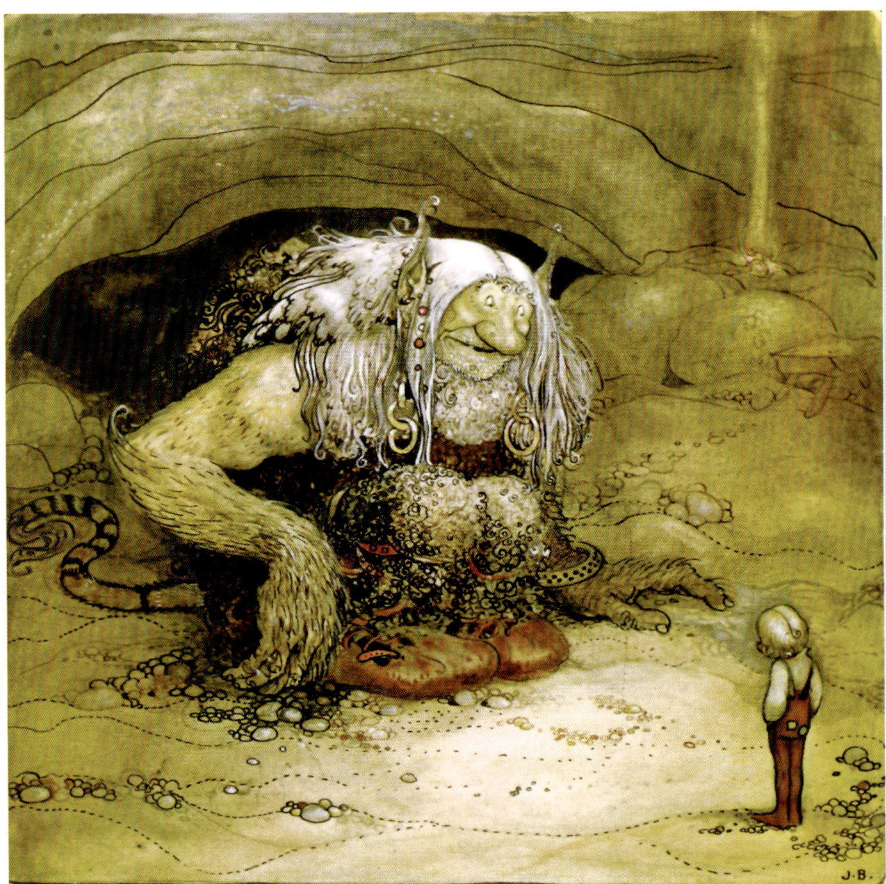

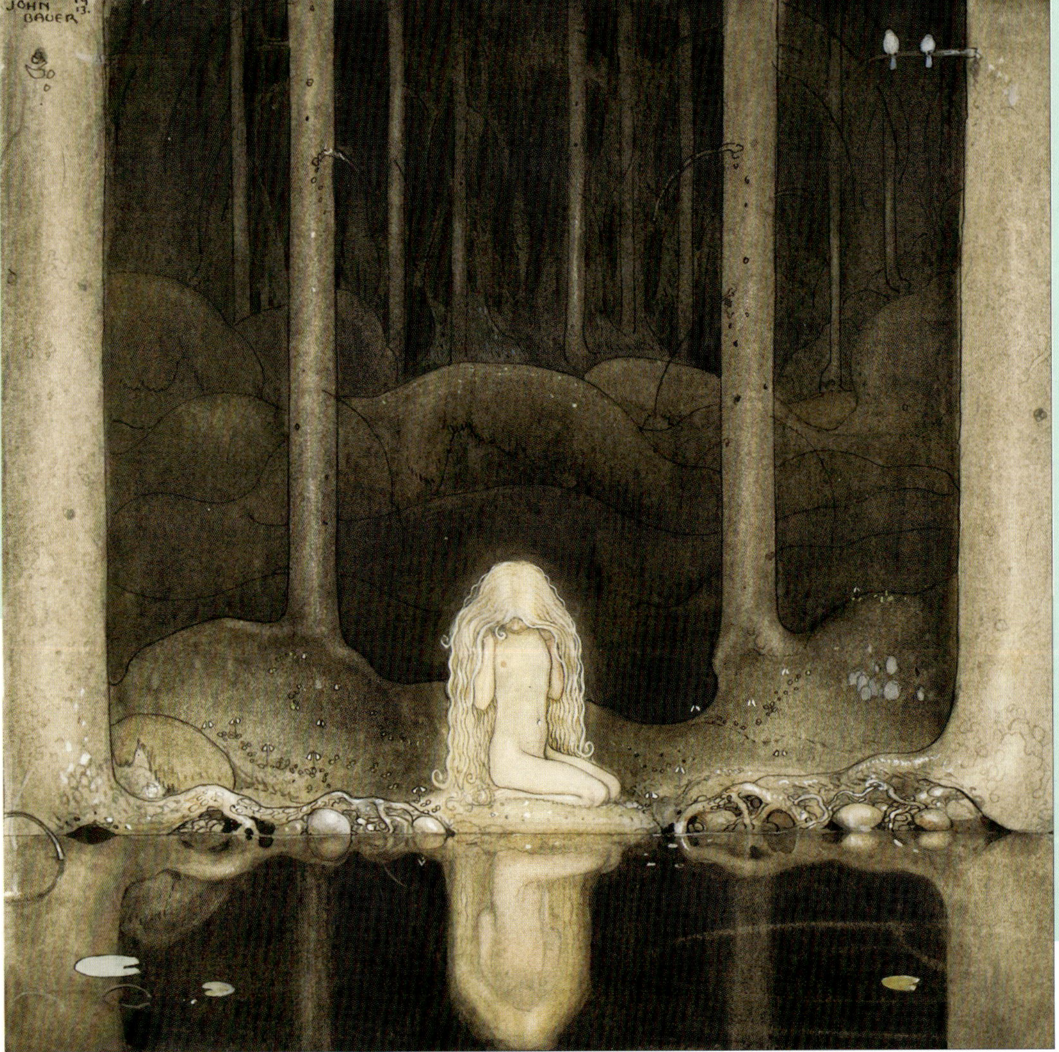

Almost a century after his death, Bauer's personal vision still reads as unique and fresh, and his work has influenced a great many creative illustrators that have followed him.

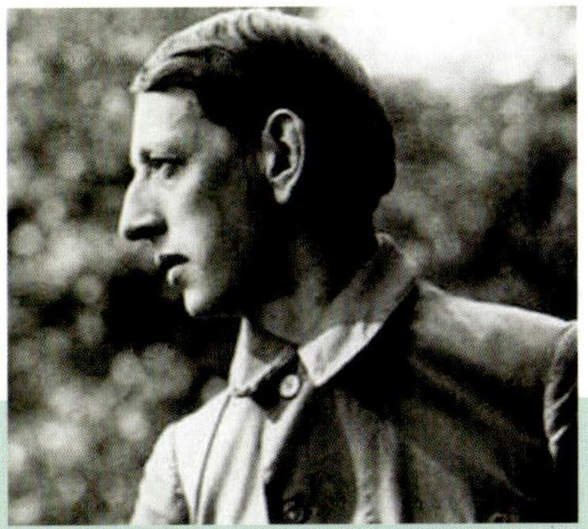

JOHN BAUER
1882~1918, SWEDISH

John Bauer came from modest surroundings and grew up in the countryside of Sweden, in Jönköping. His connection to the environment gave him great respect for the natural realm, something that would provide a spirit to his work for his entire career. His parents had more practical ideas, but allowed Bauer the opportunity to attend an art school in Stockholm. While Bauer watched the art world go through many changes and divisions at the turn of the twentieth century, he was passionate about the tales of his youth, and the characters that populated them.

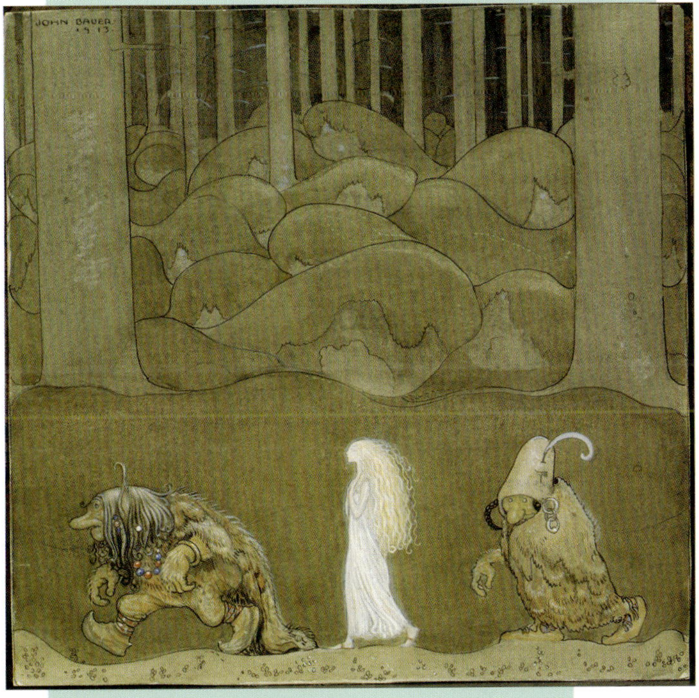

He had his first chance to share his view with a wider audience when his work was published in 1903, in *För Länge, Länge Sedan*. While his earliest illustrations show influences of the styles of other artists of the day, whispers of something different began to emerge. After some international traveling, Bauer found his place in 1907, with publication in *Among Gnomes and Trolls*. It was in this annual publication over the next few years that Bauer found his audience and his voice, through the characters in fairy tales. This was the subject matter that inspired him and the material for which he would be remembered. His love for the forests combined with the inspiration he found in both the native artists he grew up admiring and the Italian artists he discovered on recent journeys south. His characterizations of trolls, in particular, were embraced by his readership.

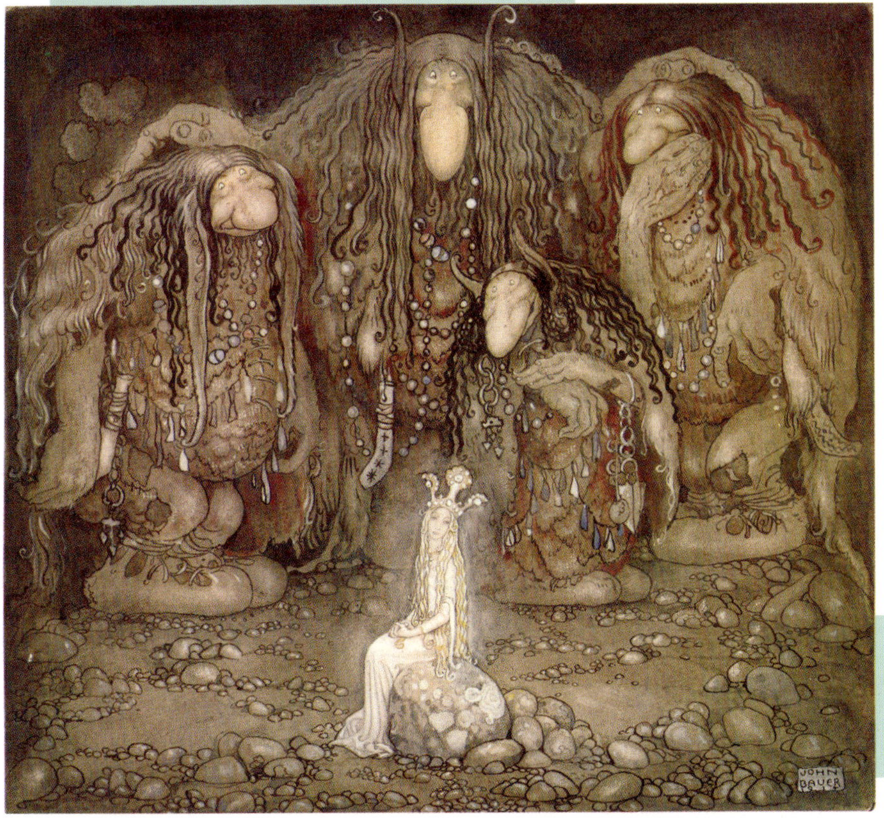

After finding recognition and success with his work in fairy tales, Bauer yearned for a more diverse means of expressing himself. His fame brought him those opportunities, with chances to do mural work or theater designs. But as World War I took a grip on Europe, some of those chances began to evaporate. In 1918, after some difficult personal years, things seemed to be looking up for Bauer and his young family—but tragedy struck when, during a ferry crossing on a stormy night, their boat capsized, and the family was lost. Today Bauer's work is a huge source of national identity and pride in Sweden.

Bauer's favorite character was a little troll called Humpe, whom Bauer used in numerous stories beginning in 1912.

"I have one aim—the grotesque. If I am not grotesque I am nothing."

—Aubrey Beardsley

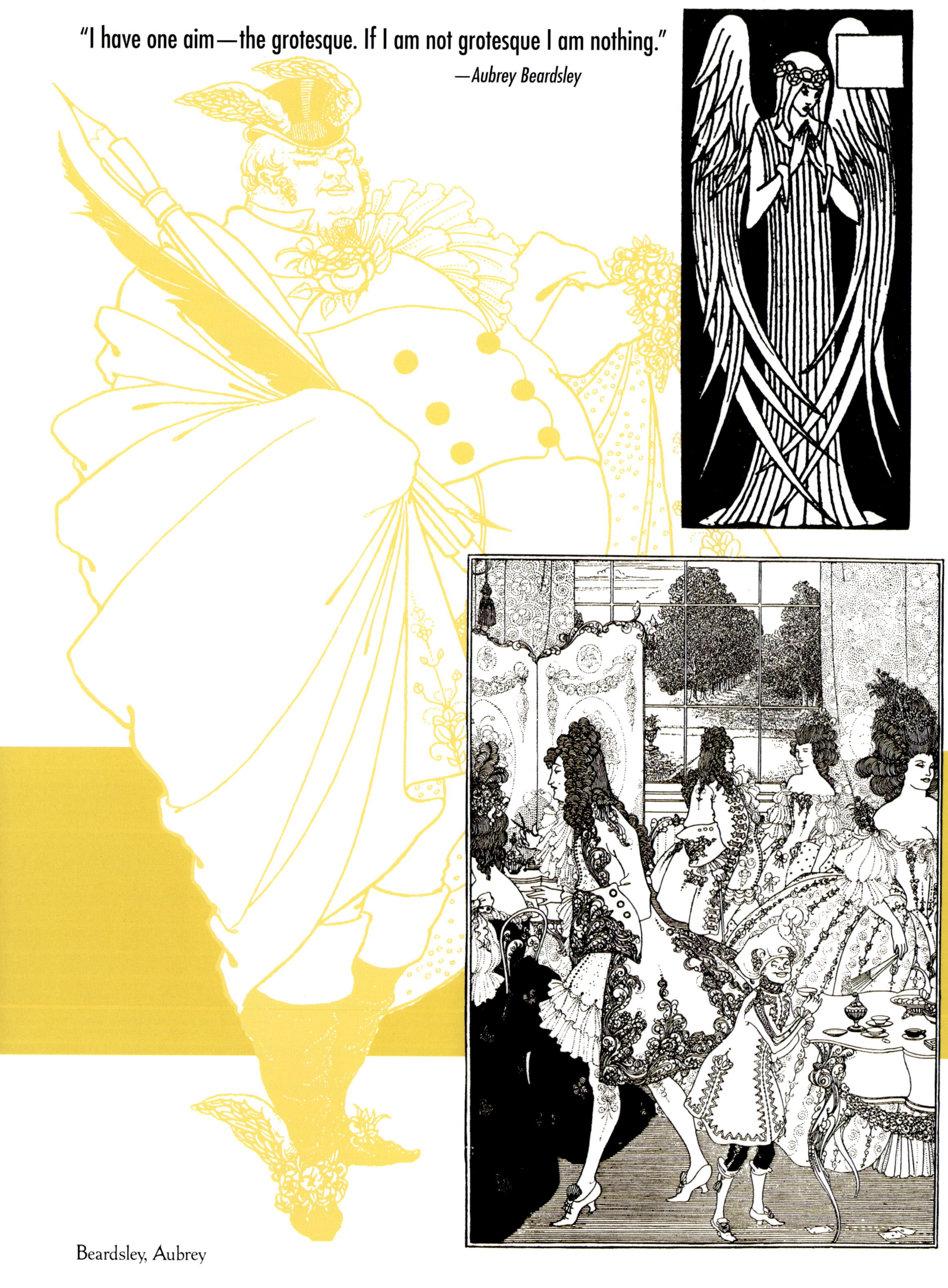

AUBREY BEARDSLEY
1872~1898, British

A brilliant designer and illustrator, Aubrey Beardsley's frail health cut his life and career very short, though the influence of his work has been long-lasting. Beardsley died of tuberculosis before the age of 26.

A prodigy of sorts from modest surroundings, Beardsley excelled in school, and at the age of 12 was performing in concerts with his sister, Mabel. In 1885 he wrote and performed a play with other students from Bristol Grammar School, and he began showing interest in drawing cartoons for the school paper at about the same time. After a start as a clerk in London-area offices, Beardsley got some encouragement from Pre-Raphaelite artist Edward Burne-Jones, who convinced Beardsley to pursue his art, and in 1892 he was off to study in Paris.

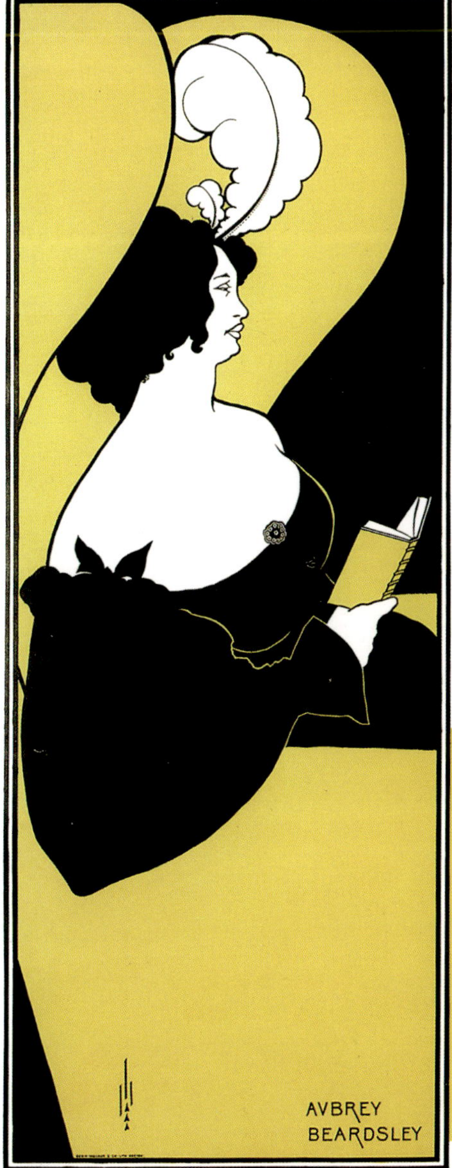

It was in Paris that Beardsley discovered two art forms that would be highly influential on his own work. The Art Nouveau work of Toulouse-Lautrec and Japanese print works both had considerable impact on the style that Beardsley would produce over the next few years. His return to England in 1893 also brought him his first major book commission, an edition of Malory's *Le Morte d'Arthur* for J. M. Dent. The volume had over 350 illustrations, and widely introduced Beardsley's decadent imagery to an English audience. His work, often erotic, and frequently shocking to his audience, was both praised for its innovation, and criticized for its lack of convention. Beardsley co-founded *The Yellow Book* with American Henry Harland in 1894, which allowed him to publish under his own direction. He had a similar arrangement in 1896 with *The Savoy,* and he was a regular contributor to *The Studio.*

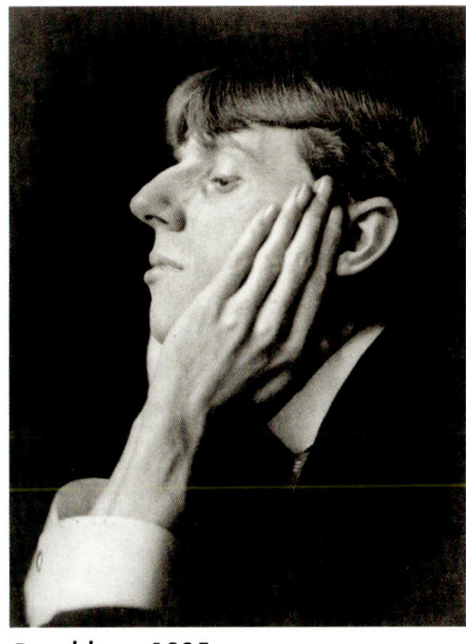
Beardsley, c.1895

He was known to be flamboyant and eccentric, and was associated with a crowd that included writer Oscar Wilde. The two worked together to produce an edition of *Salomé* in 1894. As Beardsley's health progressively worsened, he converted to Catholicism, and requested that copies of all his obscene drawings be destroyed. He died in Menton, France, in March of 1898.

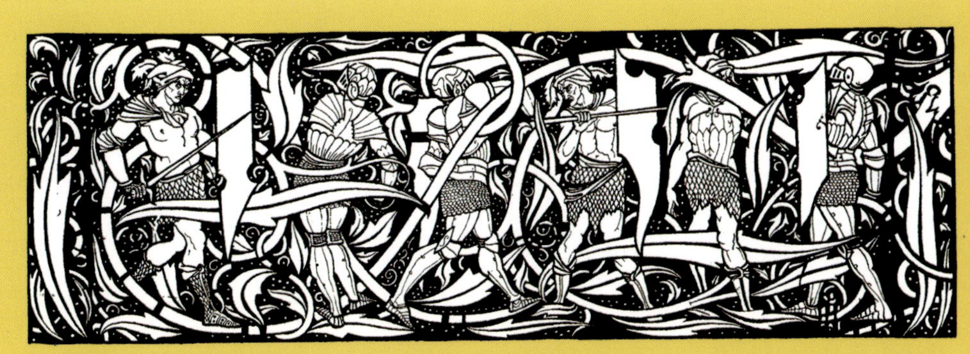

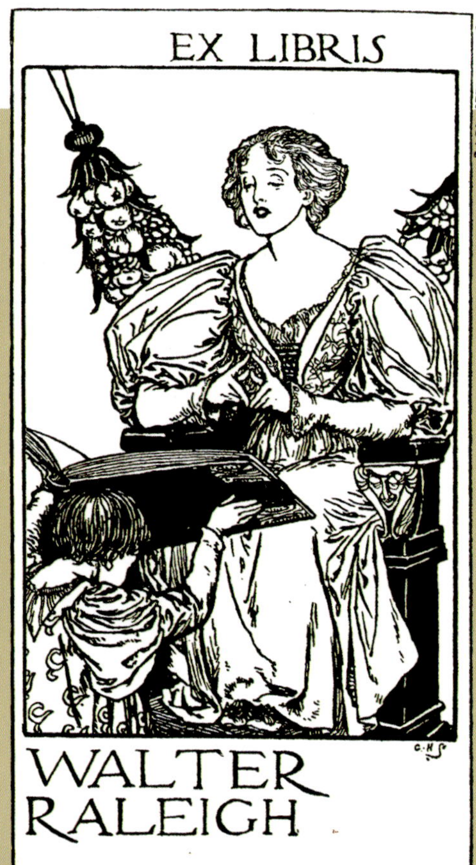

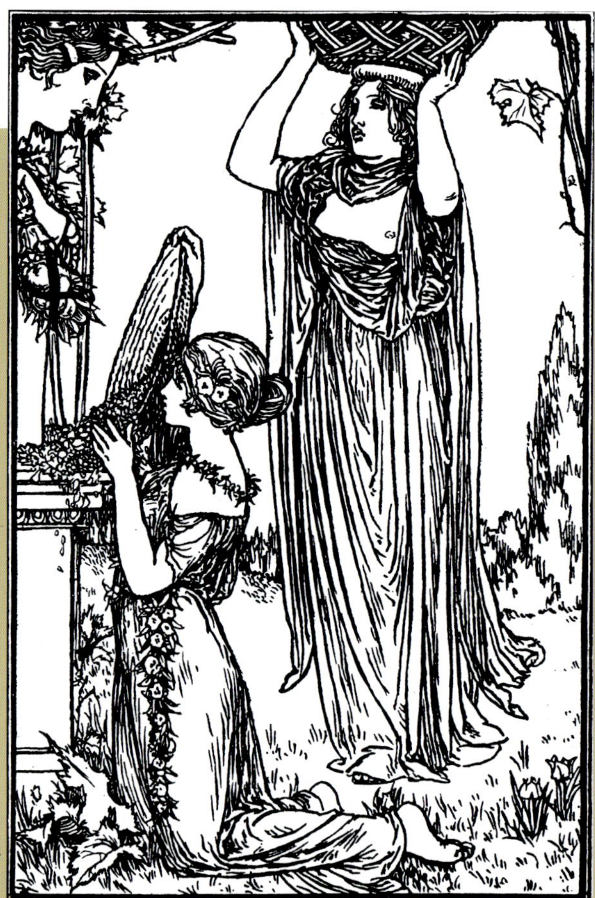

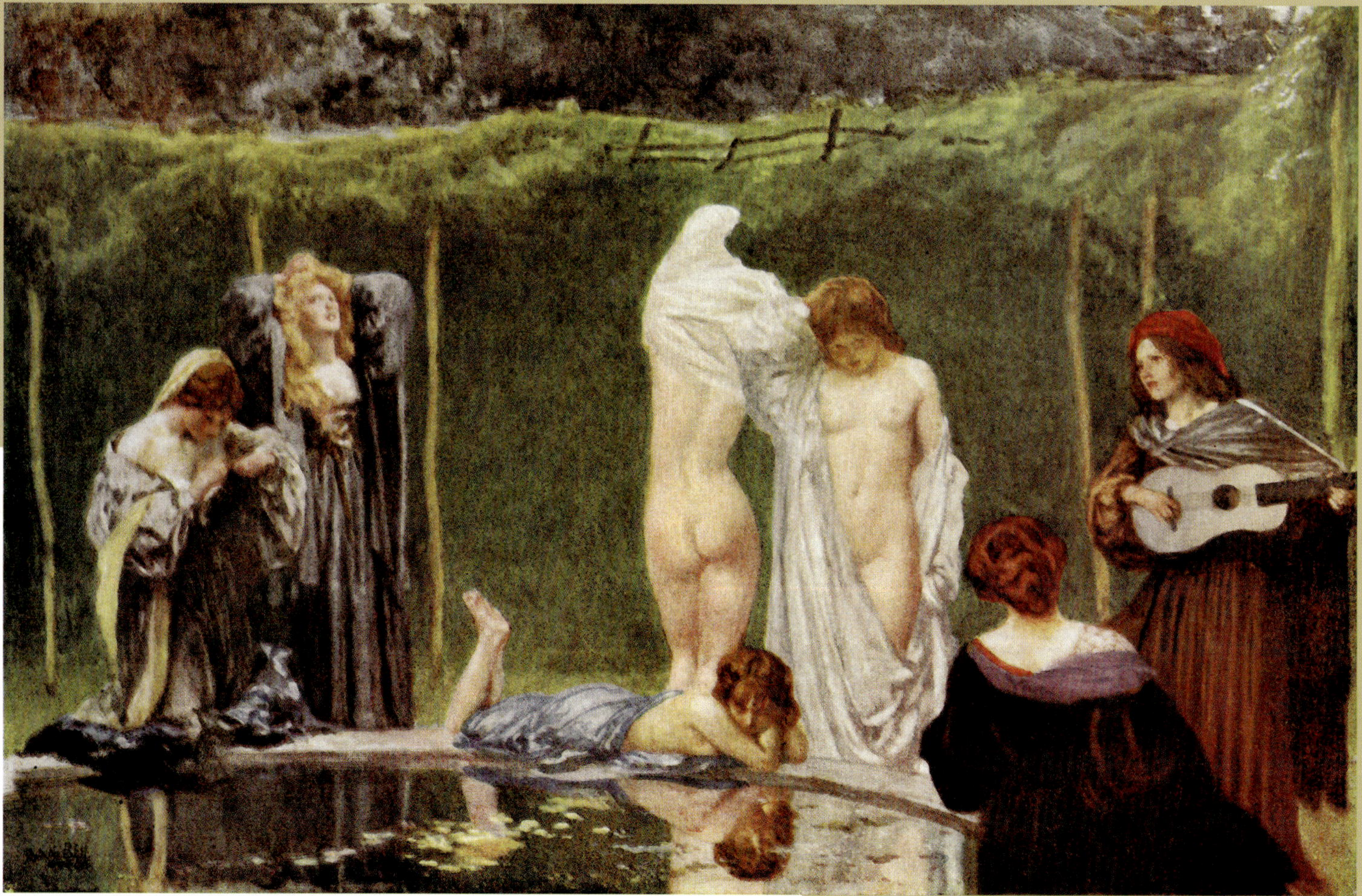

Bell, Robert Anning

Robert Anning Bell
1863–1933, British

An artist who had strengths in many disciplines, Robert Anning Bell began his studies at three different English schools before heading to Paris, where he studied under Aimé Morot. One of his first works was a series of designs for an altarpiece, which were eventually installed at the Church of St. Clare in Liverpool.

His earliest illustrations appeared in 1894, in fairy tales like *Jack the Giant Killer* and *Cinderella.* His style leaned toward more serious and complex material, rather than children's literature, and eventually he received more suitable assignments, such as Shakespeare's *Midsummer Night's Dream, The Tempest,* and works by Keats and Shelley.

Bell pursued teaching early in his career, becoming an instructor at Liverpool University in 1895. After four years there, his work in book design and illustration brought him some measure of success, and while he continued to paint throughout his career, he went on to teach again at the Glasgow School of Art in 1911, and later at the Royal College of Art from 1918 to 1924.

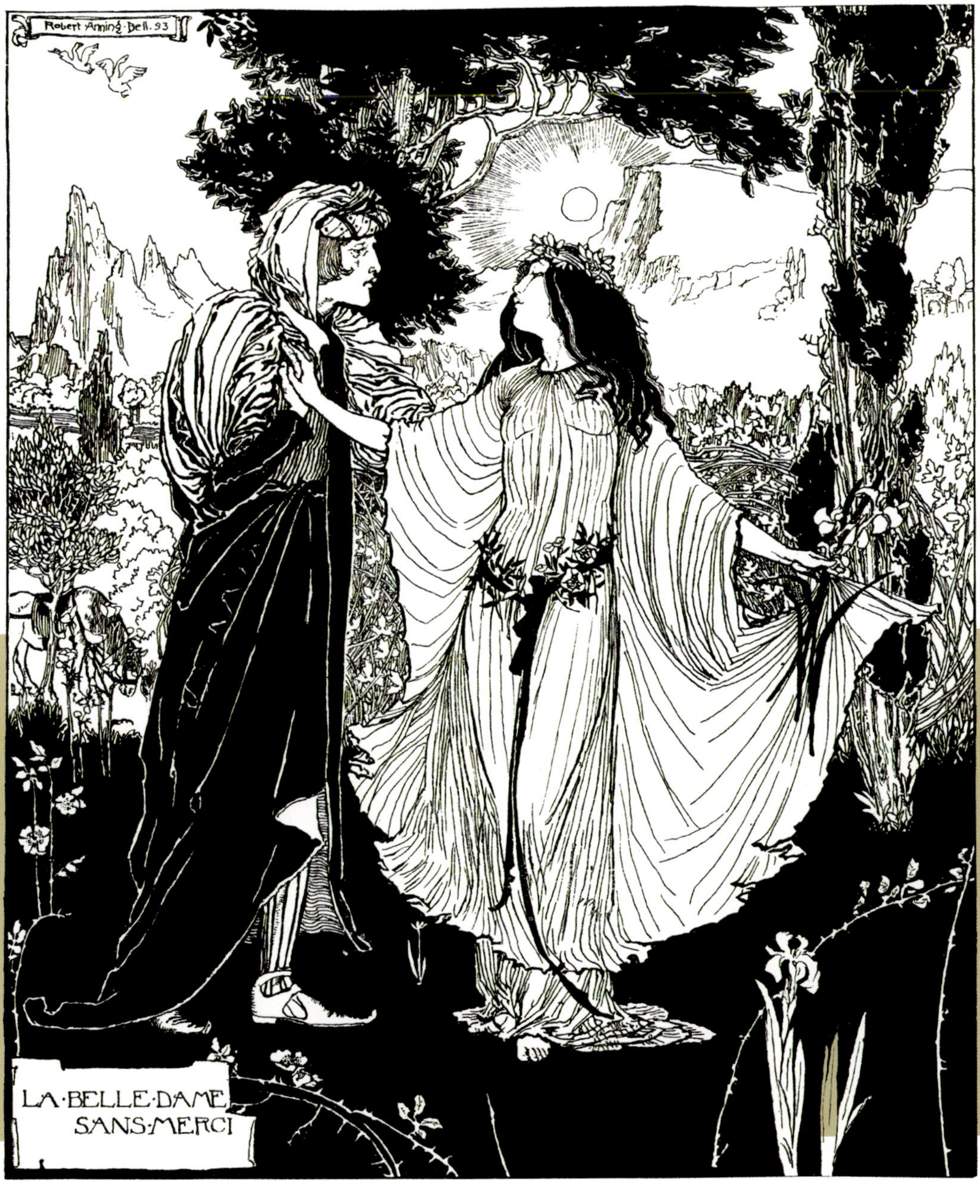

In his later years, mosaic work occupied a good deal of his time. Among the pieces he designed that are still visible today are the tympanum at Westminster Cathedral, and other mosaics for the Palace of Westminster.

While Bell explored new and different mediums, he continued to paint and to exhibit at the Royal Academy and the Royal Society of Painters in Water Colours, among others. He retained his love for myths and romantic subjects, revealing lasting influence from the Pre-Raphaelites.

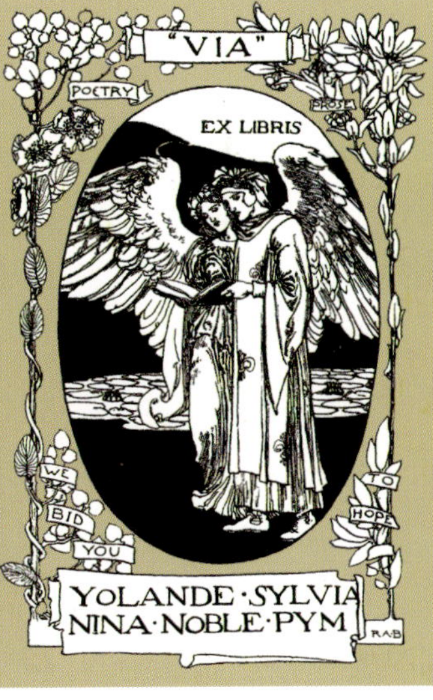

WLADYSLAW BENDA
1873–1948, POLISH

W. T. Benda began his art pursuits at Poland's Kraków College of Technology before attending the School of Fine Arts in Vienna. After visiting an aunt in California, Benda decided to stay in America, and moved to New York in 1902 to further his art. Among schools he attended in New York were the William Merritt Chase School and the Art Students League. He also studied with artist Robert Henri and American poster artist Edward Penfield.

Having previously done some illustration in Europe, his work had already developed a style before he came to America. Benda joined the Society of Illustrators in New York in 1907. His earliest work in America was for *Scribner's, McClure's,* and *St. Nicholas,* where he did magazine illustrations. His work had what can be called an "exotic" look, due to the different influences that Benda had compared to other American artists working at the time. That subtle difference gave his work a unique quality, which many publishers found desirable. The graphic and decorative qualities of his pieces complemented the Art Deco styling of the twenties.

Masks were an interest of Benda's, and they became a major part of his work in the latter part of his career. Not only did they appear in his paintings, but he created actual masks, which became sought after by the theater world. Benda lectured on the topic of modern masks, and was enough of an expert to write an article for *Encyclopedia Britannica* on the subject. In 1944 he wrote the book, *Masks,* for art publisher Watson-Guptill.

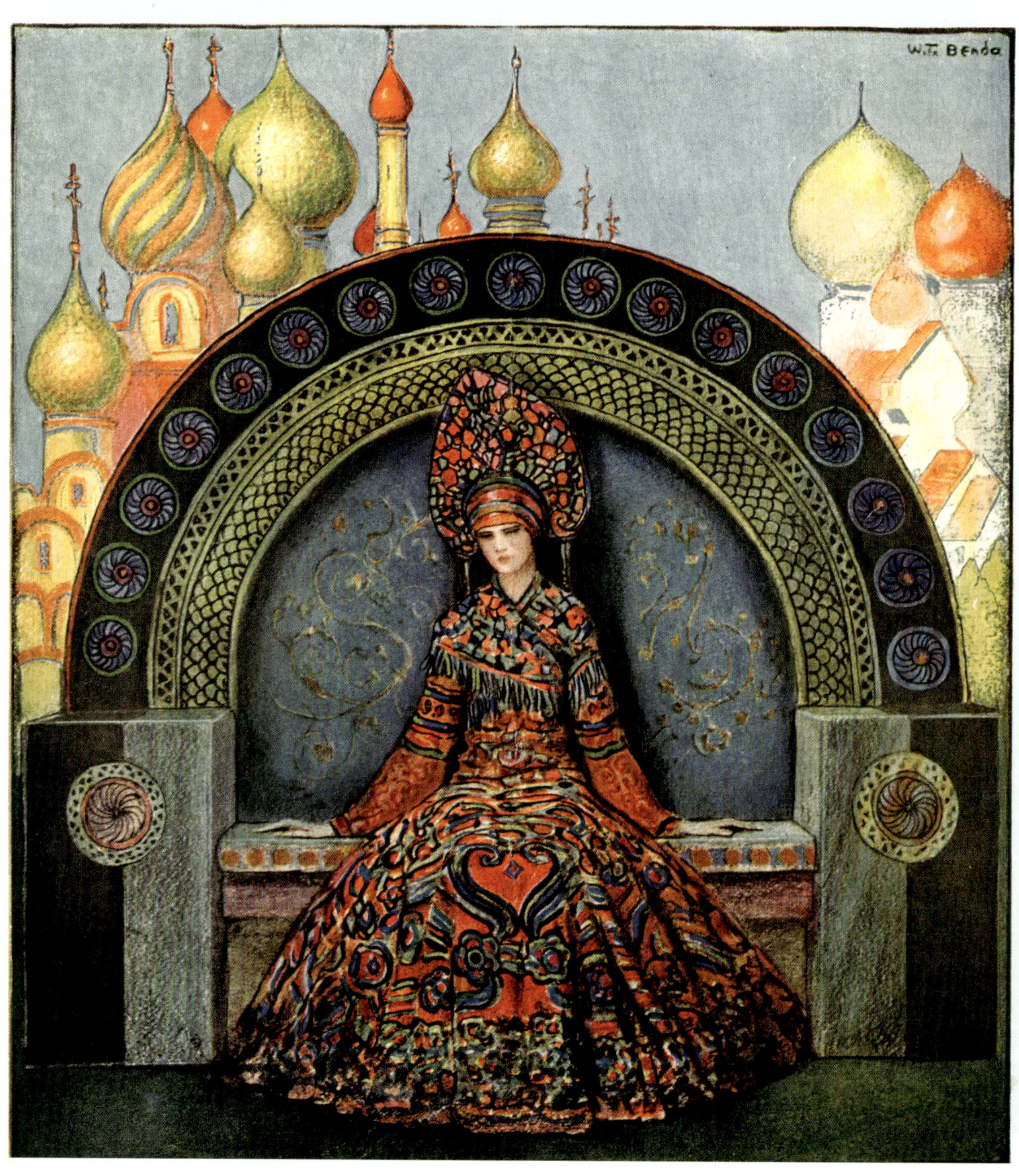

Benda, Wladyslaw

"...there are two kinds of people in the world, people that like W. T. Benda, and those that just aren't familiar with him."

—*Fred Taraba*

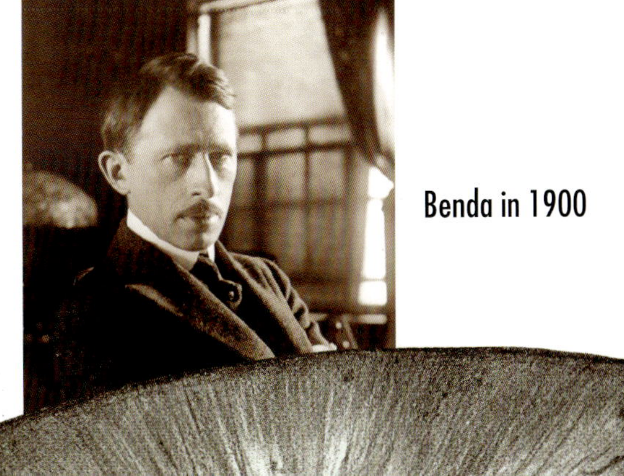

Benda in 1900

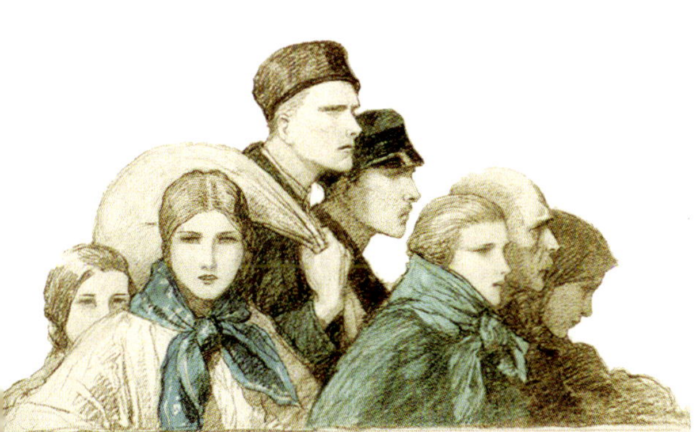

Benda continually received cover assignments from many high-profile magazine clients, such as *Life.*

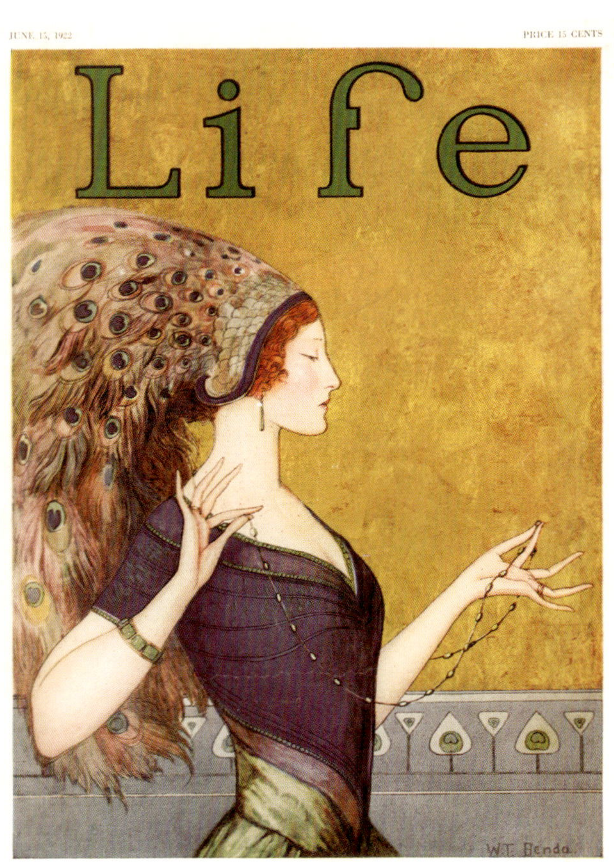

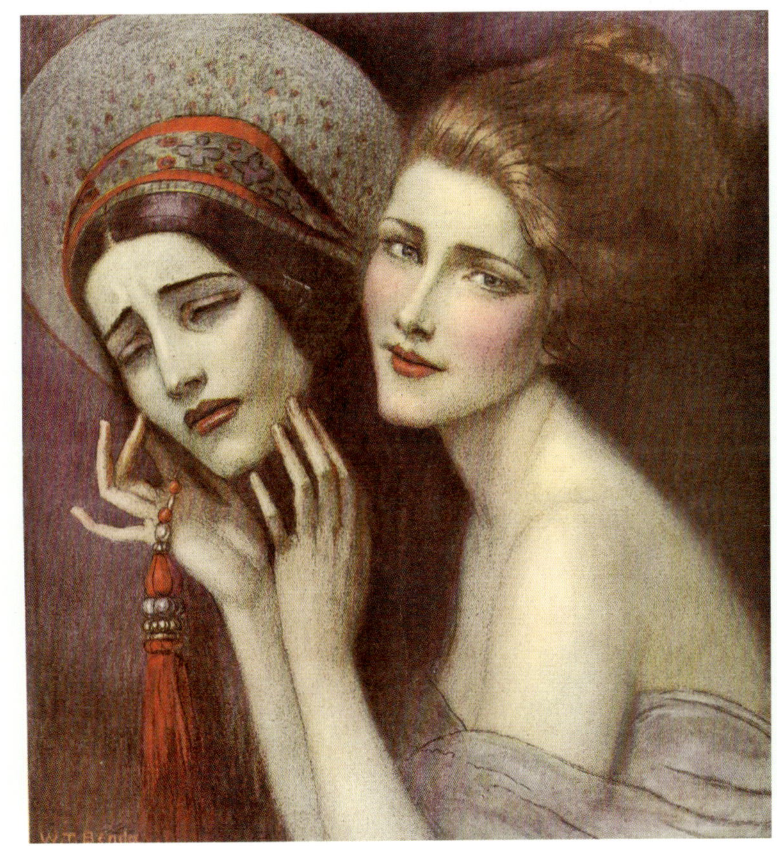

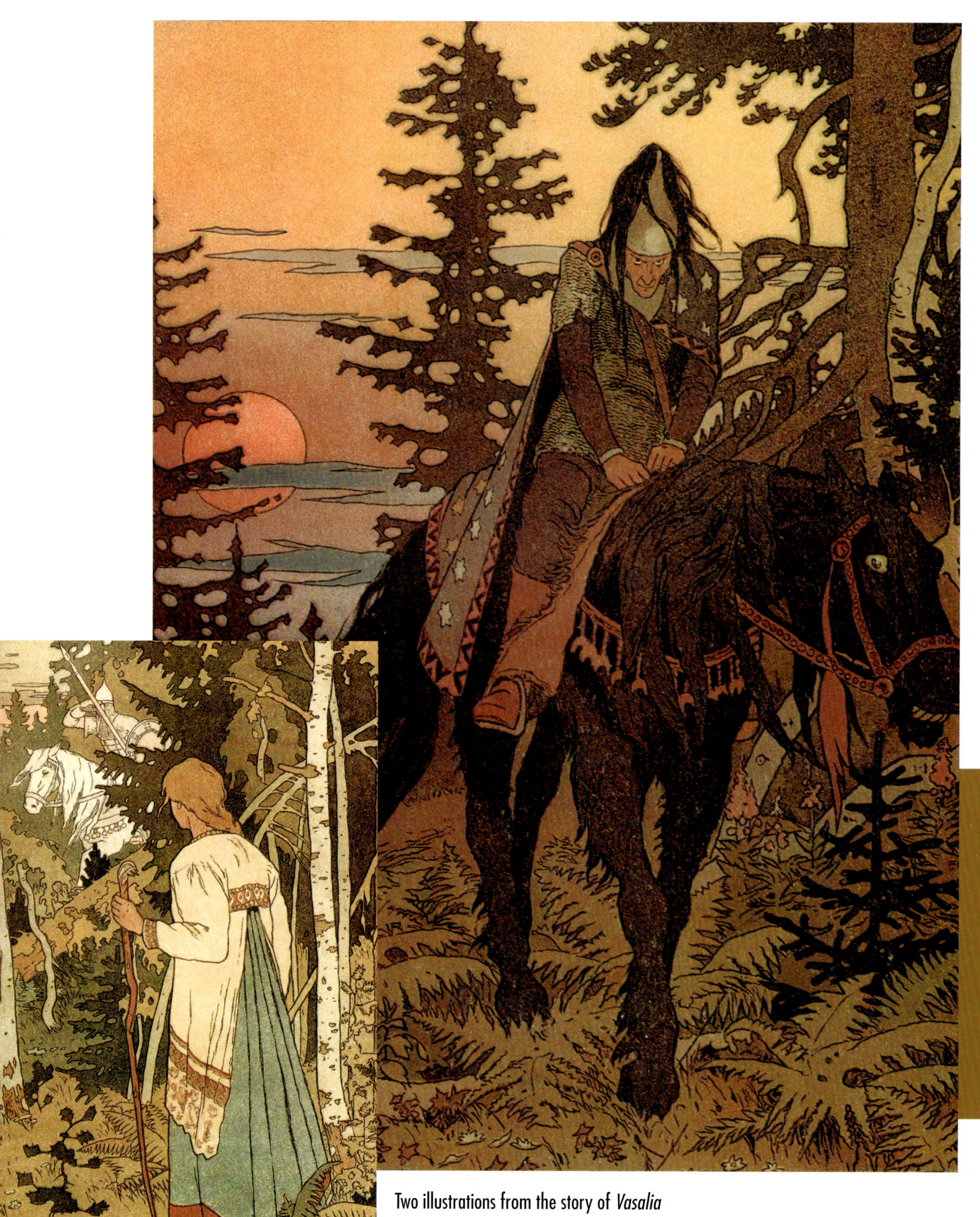

Two illustrations from the story of *Vasalia*

Ivan Bilibin
1876–1942, Russian

Ivan Bilibin is a name that has transcended the boundaries of his native Russia, with good reason. Not only did Bilibin become the premier illustrator of Russia's national tales and myths, but the unique style he developed, beautifully blended contemporary illustration with simple decorative graphics and native design. His art became a bridge linking the poster age, Russian cultural identity, and the oncoming Art Deco movement.

From 1896–1900, Bilibin studied law and art simultaneously; law at St. Petersburg University, and art at both the Drawing School of the Society for the Encouragement of the Arts and with the painter Ilya Repin. Perhaps it was this unlikely pairing of law and art that made him a good candidate to produce art for the Russian government. In 1902 Bilibin was commissioned by a department of the Russian Museum, and for two years he traveled through northern Russia, drawing and photographing the native people and their culture. This fueled his interest in their folk and fairy tales, and much of the work he would generate from 1900–1912 tied these influences together. Bilibin's watercolor style distinguished his work from earlier Russian painters, who had pursued a classical realistic approach. Bilibin's work demonstrated more of an influence of European poster art of the period. This work was better suited to print, and it made him an illustrator in high demand. He produced work for books, magazines, posters, and cards, and also discovered an interest in theater design. Much of the imagery he produced stemmed from his early successes with folk and fairy tales, and his strong background in the ethnic styles and designs of his native Russia.

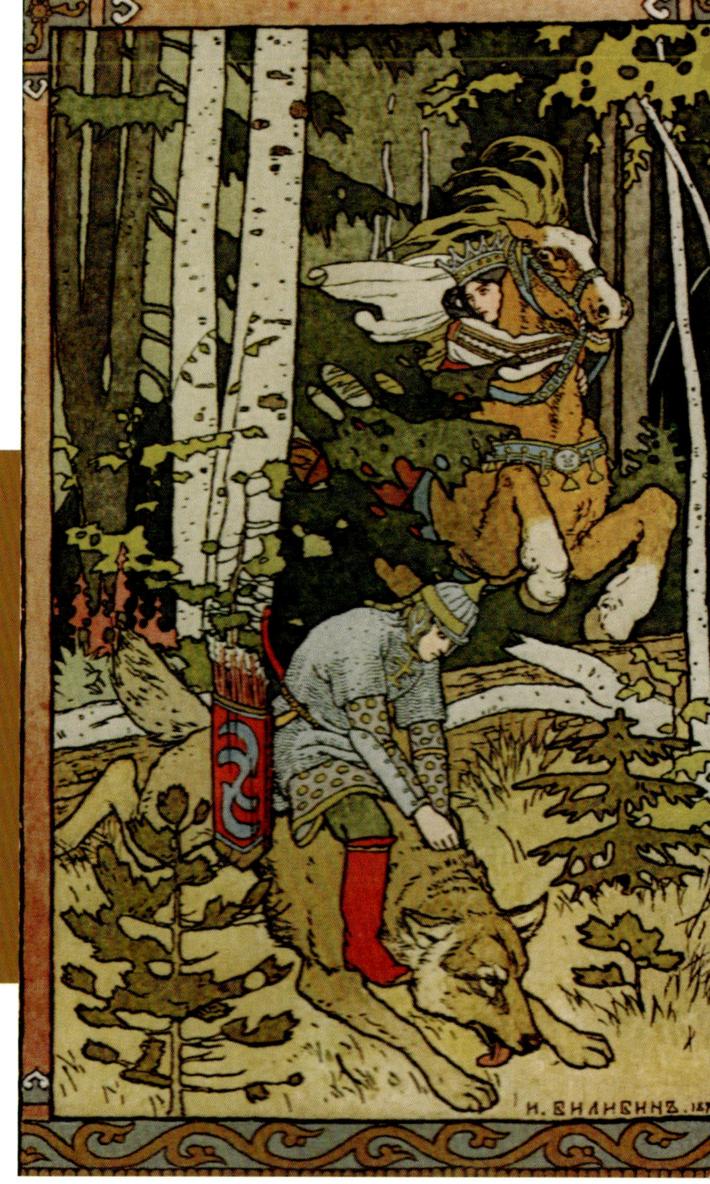

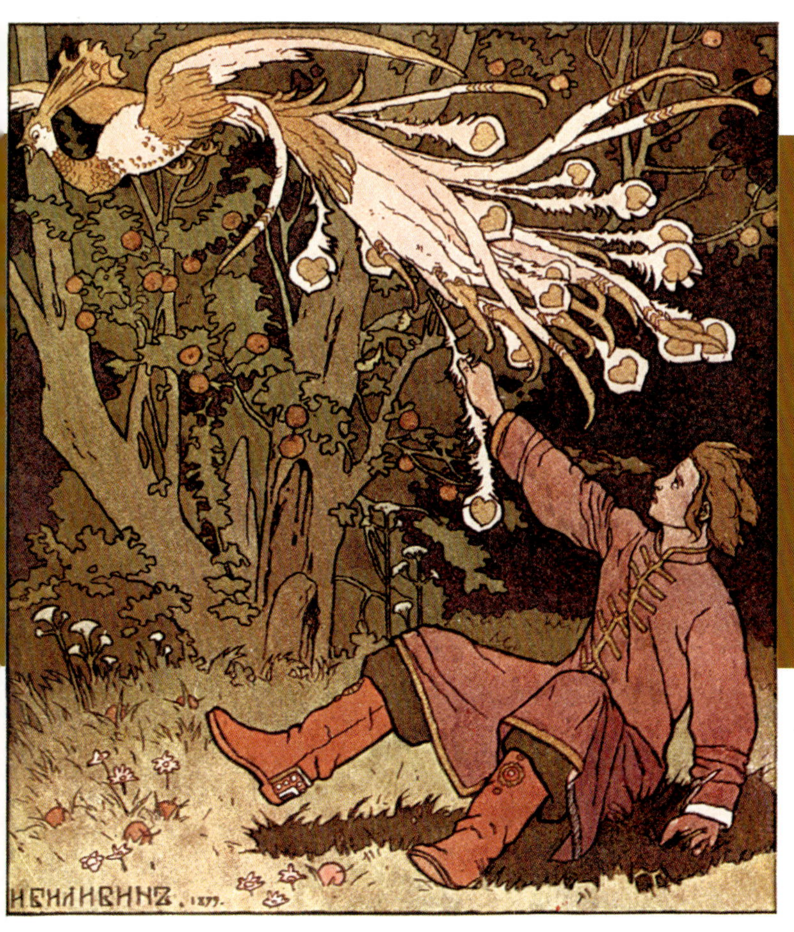

Franklin Booth
1874~1948, American

Among all great ink artists of the period, Booth is often regarded as having a unique style. As a child he had great admiration for the black and white works he saw reproduced in magazines like *Harper's* and *Scribner's*. Little did he know that the tones he saw that replicated values from paintings were not ink drawings but wood engravings. He developed his style trying to achieve those same effects with ink drawing, placing lines tightly together to create variations in perceived value. This gave his work a look that was far different from other ink artists of the period, and a unique painterly quality. Not only was his style distinct, but his draftsmanship was also exceptional. The two qualities together made him very much sought-after, and the appeal of his work is still strong today.

Booth was successful in advertising, with clients such as Bulova Watches, Whitman's Candy, and Rolls Royce. His ability to render sumptuous dream-like landscapes, expressing the kind of natural vastness that surrounded him in his Indiana youth, also made him an ideal selection for poetry. He illustrated many pages of poems in *Scribner's* magazine over the years.

Though he is renowned today for his ink work, he did venture into color work at times, choosing a watercolor method in one of his few book assignments with multiple plates—*The Flying Islands of the Night* by James Whitcomb Riley. It includes Booth's open compositions and his attention to classical forms, with skies filled with soft quiet washes of hues in place of fields of tone.

While Booth's style was reminiscent of a previous generation, it also put him at great risk for being out of fashion. When Art Deco became the dominant look of the period, and clean, smooth, continuous tones filled the pages of magazines, Booth's fully rendered and classically inspired works seemed like they belonged to yesterday. In later years, his pen-and-ink work was more often found in catalogs and commercial publications, but it never suffered for lack of quality.

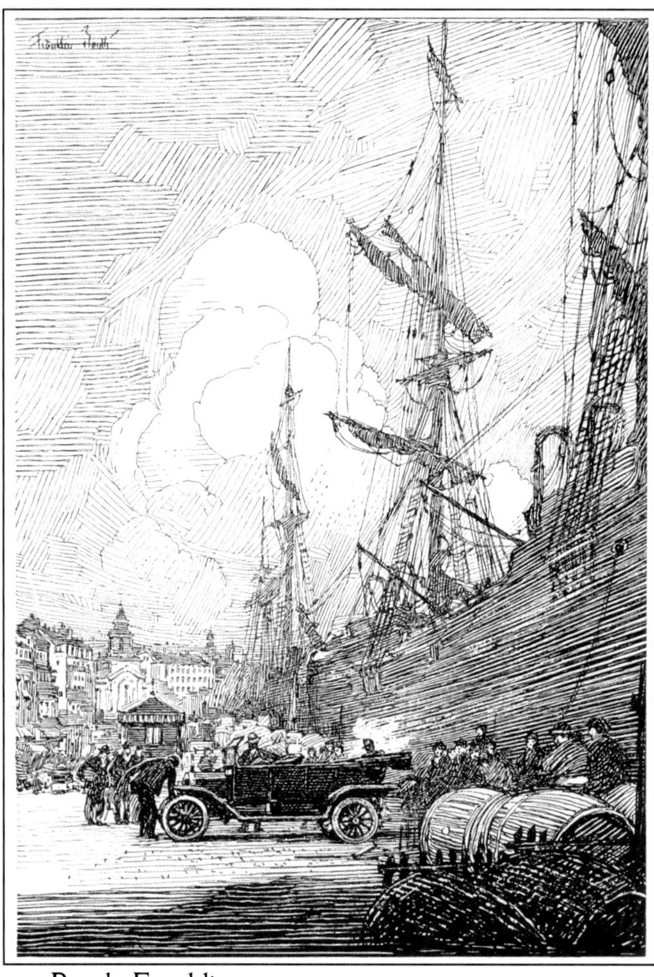

Booth, Franklin

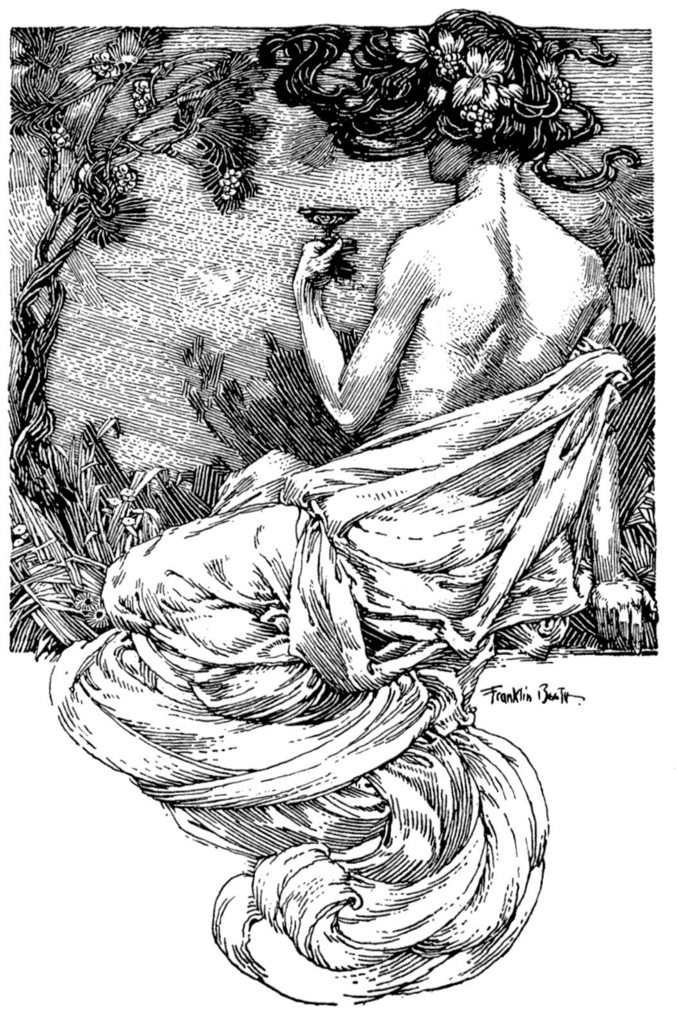

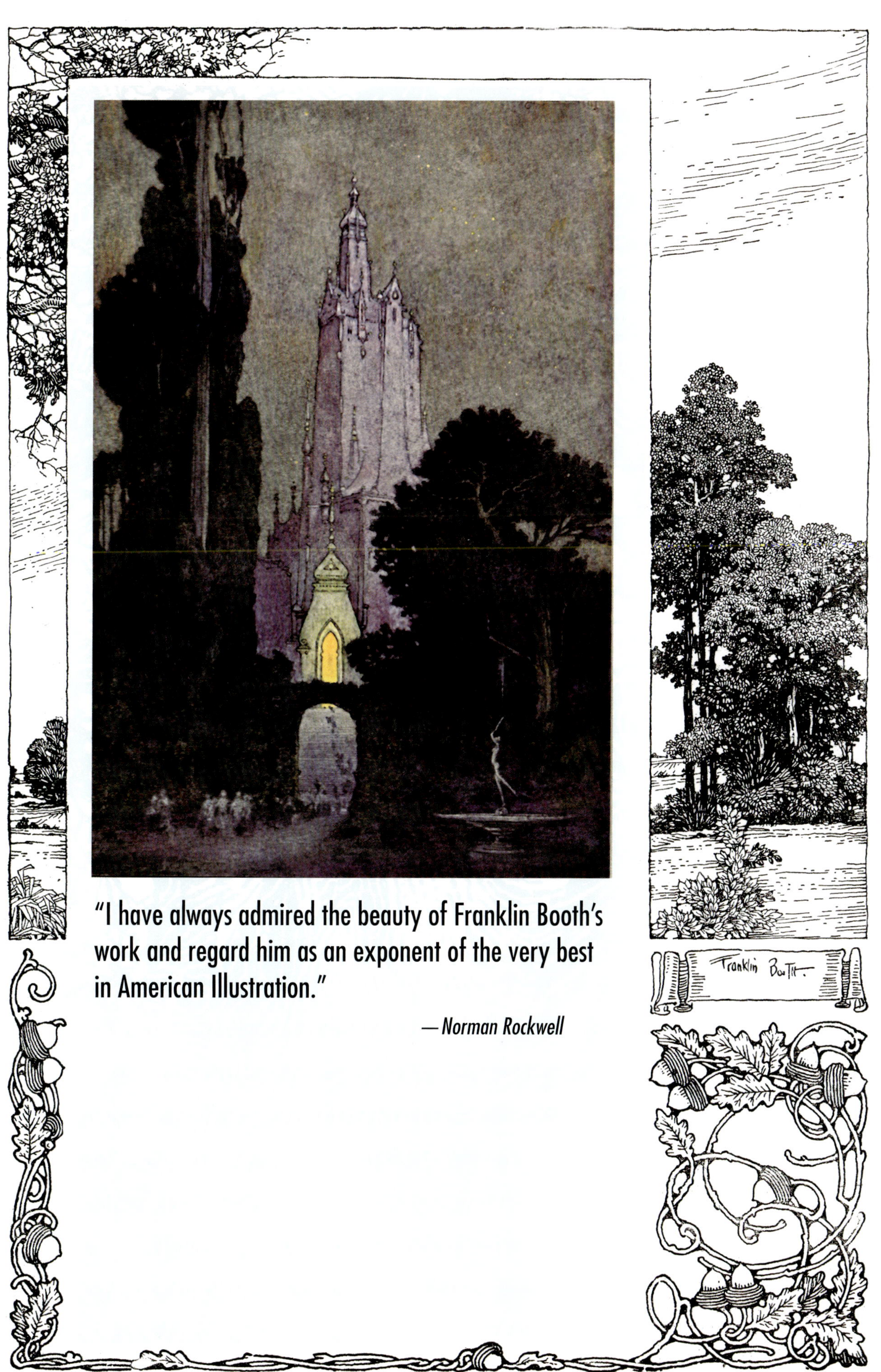

"I have always admired the beauty of Franklin Booth's work and regard him as an exponent of the very best in American Illustration."

—Norman Rockwell

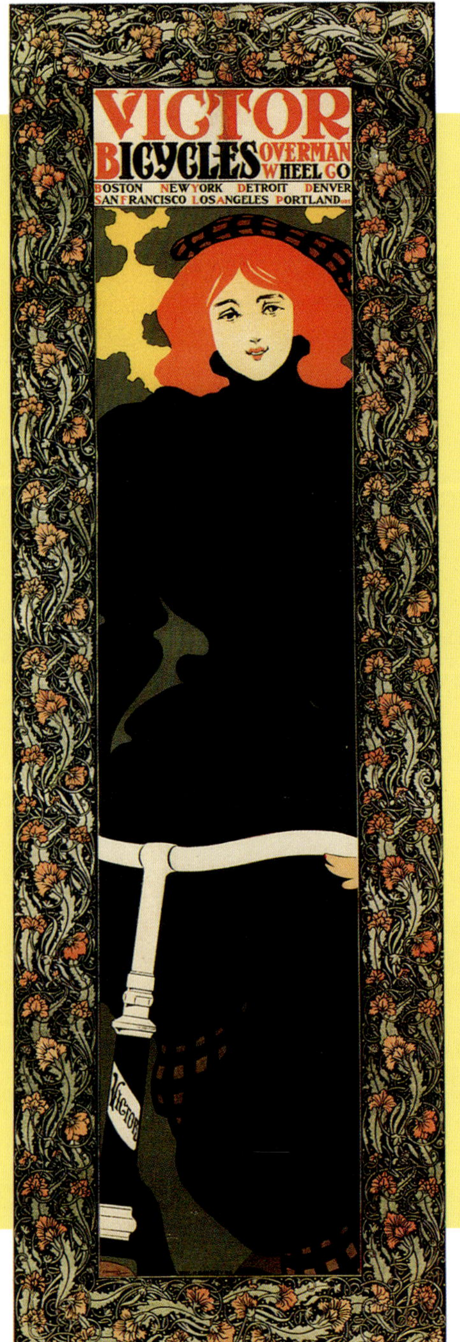

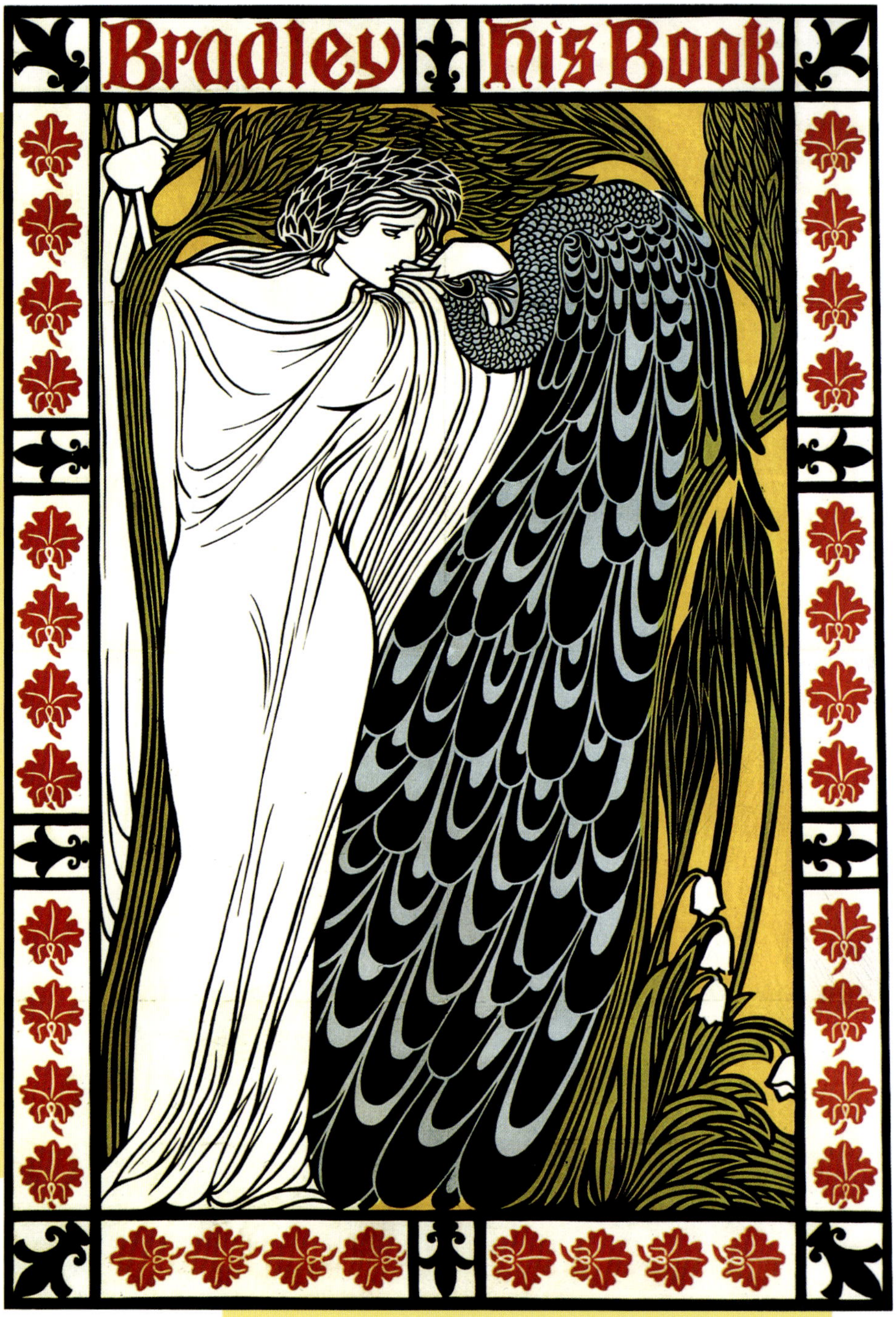

Bradley His Book

Will Bradley became known as the "Dean of American Designers"

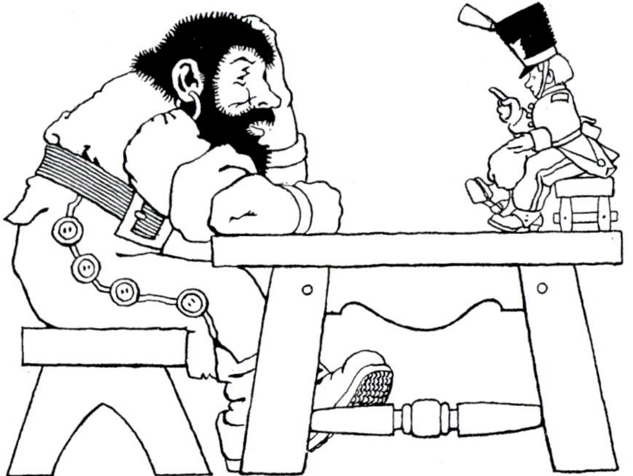

Bradley, Will H.

Will H. Bradley

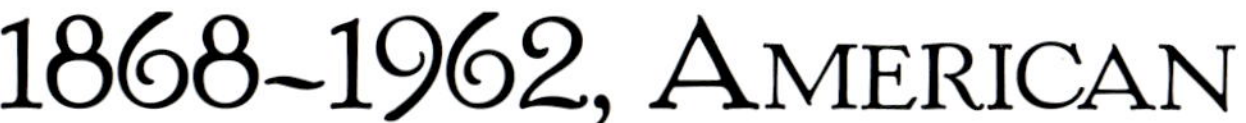

1868~1962, American

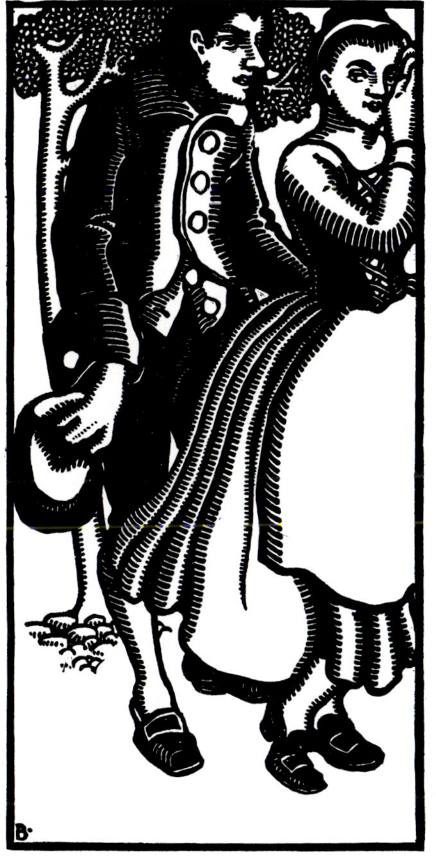

Designer, publisher, illustrator, typographer—all titles related to print media that require a separate type of mastery. Will Bradley mastered them all. Although he worked in various aspects of print production, his contributions as an illustrator should not be overlooked; he produced a large volume of images for book and magazine covers, advertisements, and poster art.

Bradley took to the print medium from a very young age in Northern Michigan. He was working for a printer at the age of 12; by age 15, he was a job foreman; and at 19, he was a designer in a Chicago print house. He spent time as a wood engraver and typographer, and then moved on to work as a freelance graphic designer. The 1890s were the height of the poster movement as an art form, and Will Bradley was in the forefront, with the influences of the Arts and Crafts movement and Art Nouveau permeating his designs. His work is often compared to that of Aubrey Beardsley, and his operations to those of British artist/publisher William Morris.

The same year that the World's Fair came to Chicago—1893—Will Bradley got his first book cover assignment, including a cover, title page, page decorations, and a poster. More cover work soon followed. It was The Inland Printer that really began to get Bradley's work seen. When asked to provide them with a new cover design to be used continually, month-to-month, Bradley made a proposal for the magazine to purchase a new design each month, which began his dominance on the early graphic design market. A trip to New York convinced Bradley that the design market was thriving, and he went back to the Boston area to start his own Wayside Press. Wayside was an artistic and commercial outlet for Bradley, who had built a small publishing industry before the age of thirty.

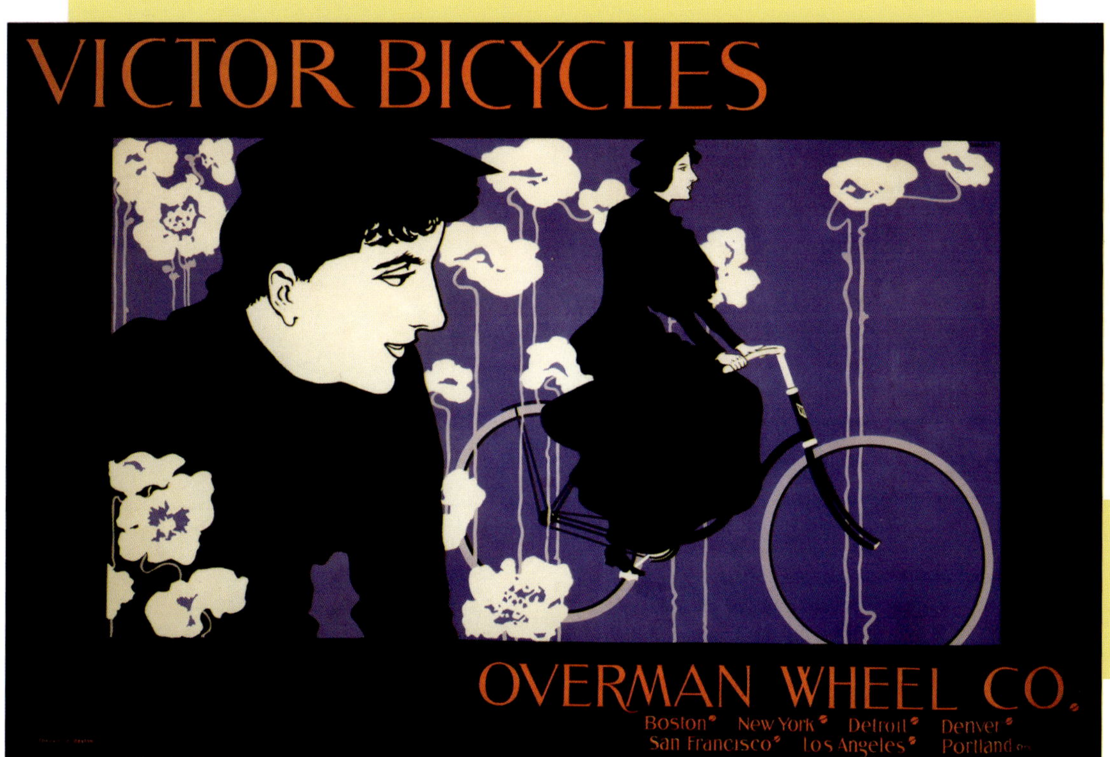

Bradley continued to learn and grow in publishing and design. As he developed new ideas, and reinvented old ones, the American printing industry seemed to follow his lead. He went on to work at *Collier's* magazines and shaped their look during the first decade of the twentieth century.

Sir Frank Brangwyn

1867~1956, Belgian-British

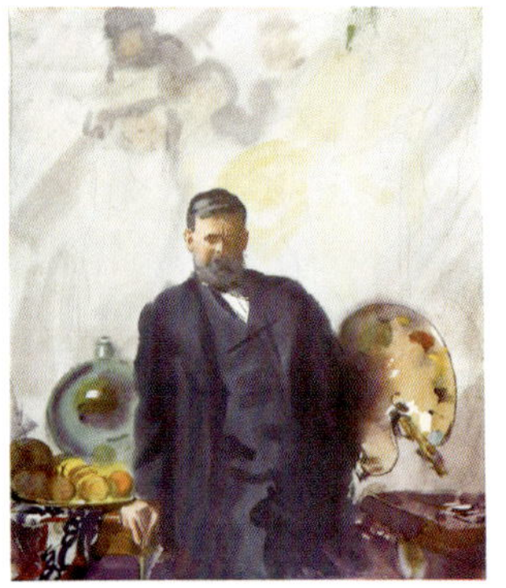

Brangwyn by Joseph Simpson, c. 1917

The contributions made by this artist are so varied and deep that it is hard at first to consider him merely an illustrator. With a bibliography of over 80 books that contain his images, it is impossible to consider him anything less.

Born in Bruges, Belgium, Brangwyn spent only part of his childhood there, before his English family returned to the United Kingdom. With only minimal instruction, Brangwyn managed to have his art accepted by the Royal Academy for a Summer Exhibition at the age of seventeen. The early success and recognition did much to launch his career along an artist's path.

Brangwyn would be remembered as one of the most prolific artists of the period, producing mountains of illustrations, posters, stained glass works, murals, and more. He was also a source of instruction for many of the painters of the next generation.

One of his most significant works were the British Empire Panels. These sixteen large pieces were commissioned to be placed in the Royal Gallery at the House of Lords. This group later refused to hang them there, fearing the images were too intense for the venue. Guildhall in Swansea altered its construction plan to allow for the works to be housed there, where they remain on display today. He also worked on murals in Canada and the United States.

Brangwyn illustrated scores of posters, both for wartime purposes and other promotions. He produced over 130 book plate designs for friends, and his book illustration dominated his career from 1891 up until his last few volumes, in 1948 and 1949. He was knighted in 1941.

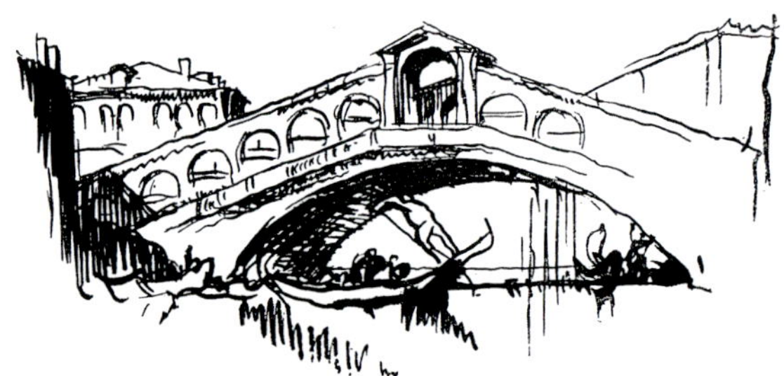

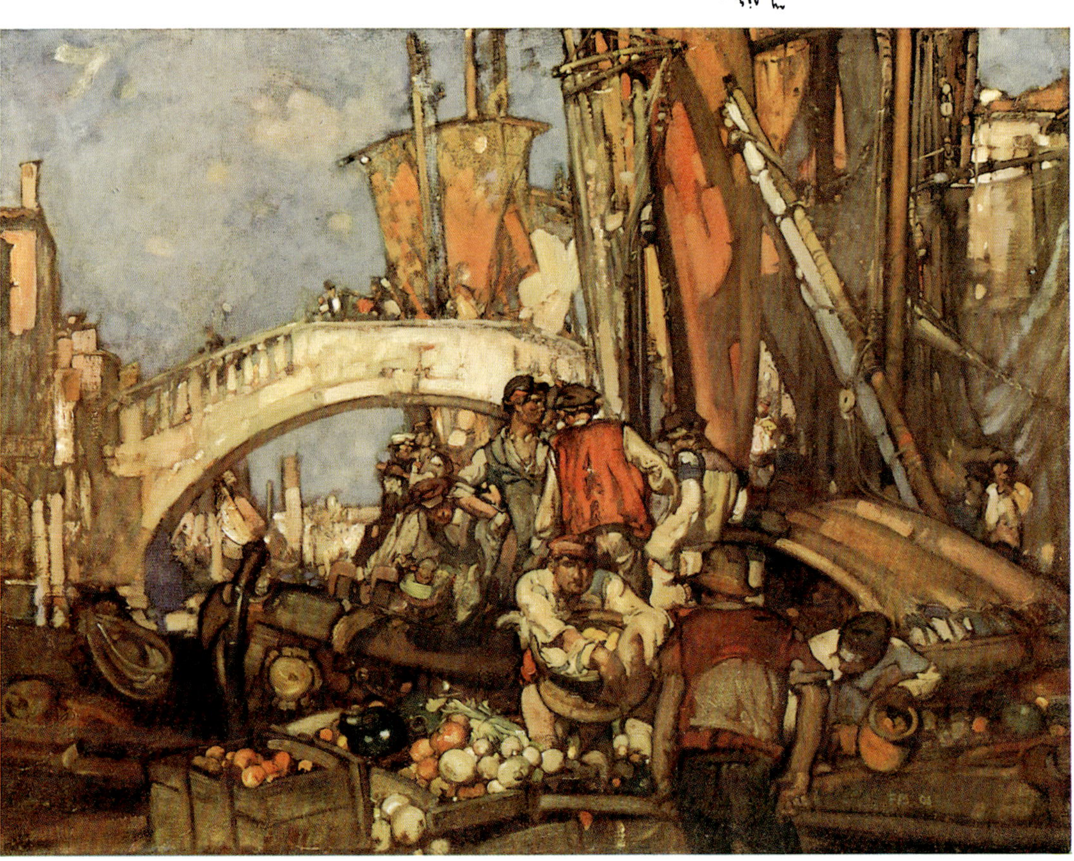

From *Pageant of Venice*, 1922

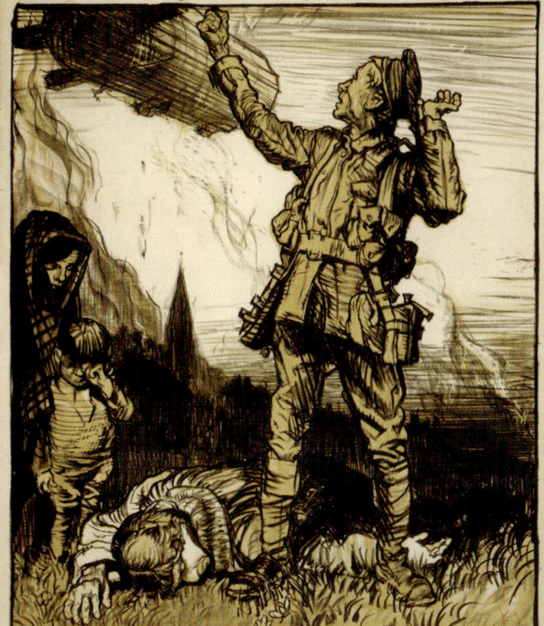

One of many British World War I posters that Brangwyn completed.

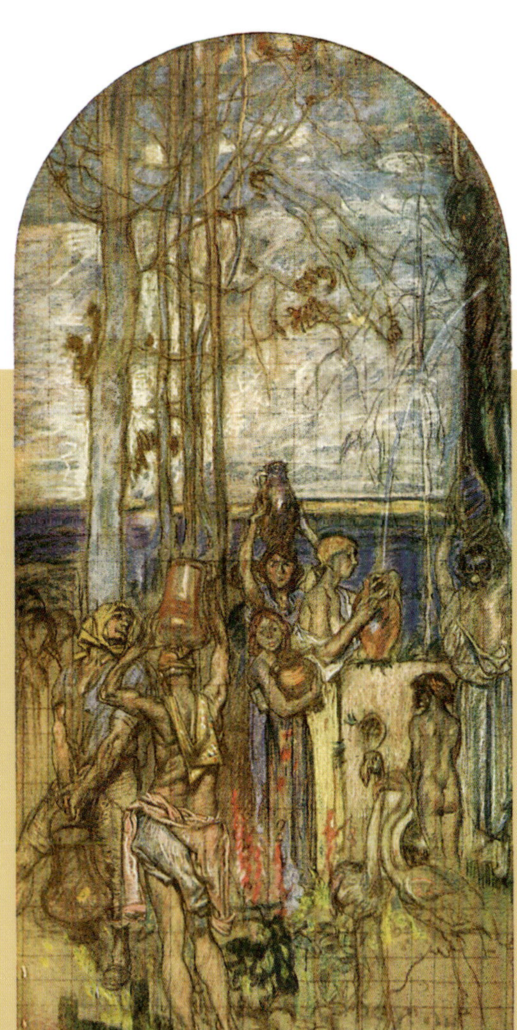

G. K. Chesterton termed Brangwyn:

"the most masculine of modern men of genius."

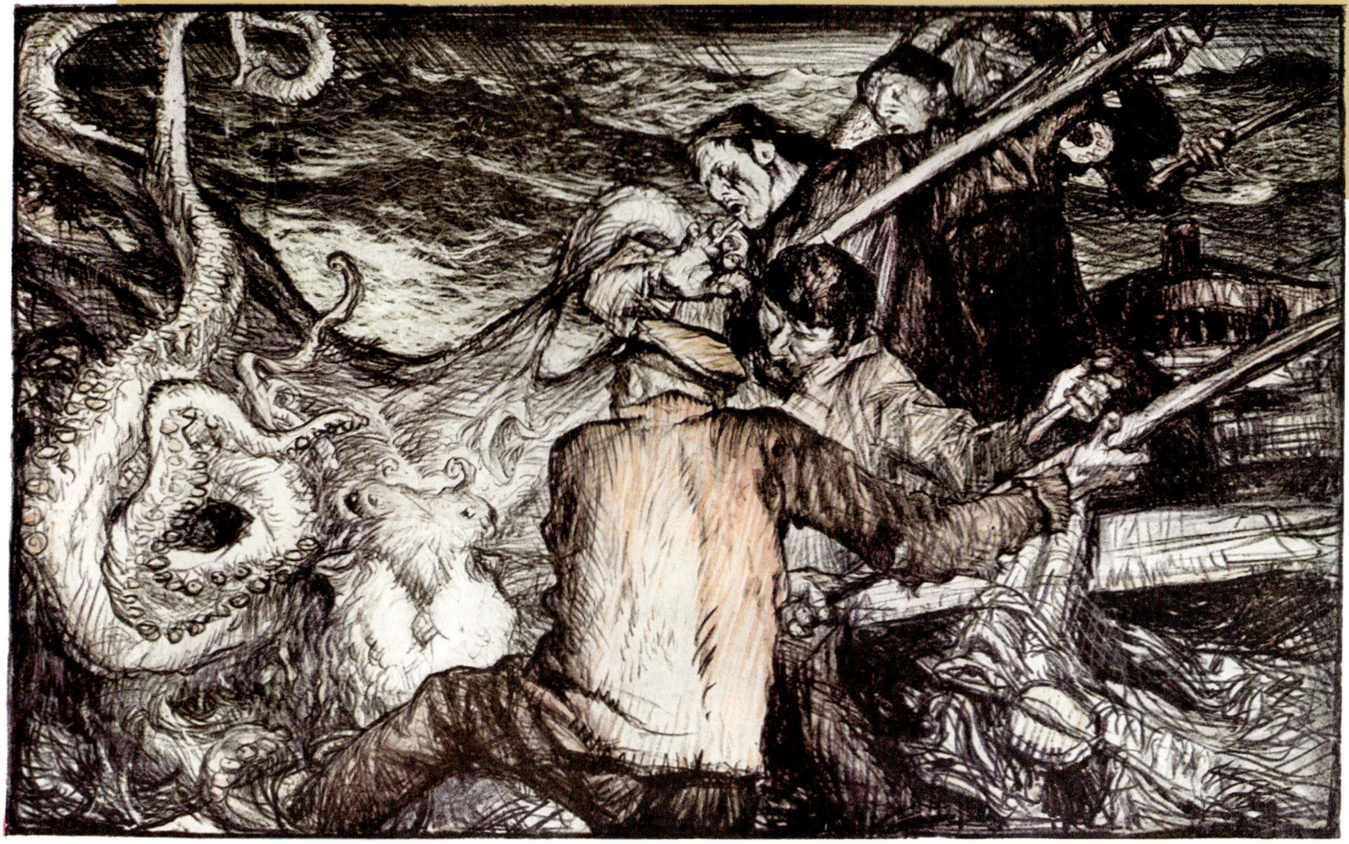

ELEANOR F. BRICKDALE

1871–1945, British

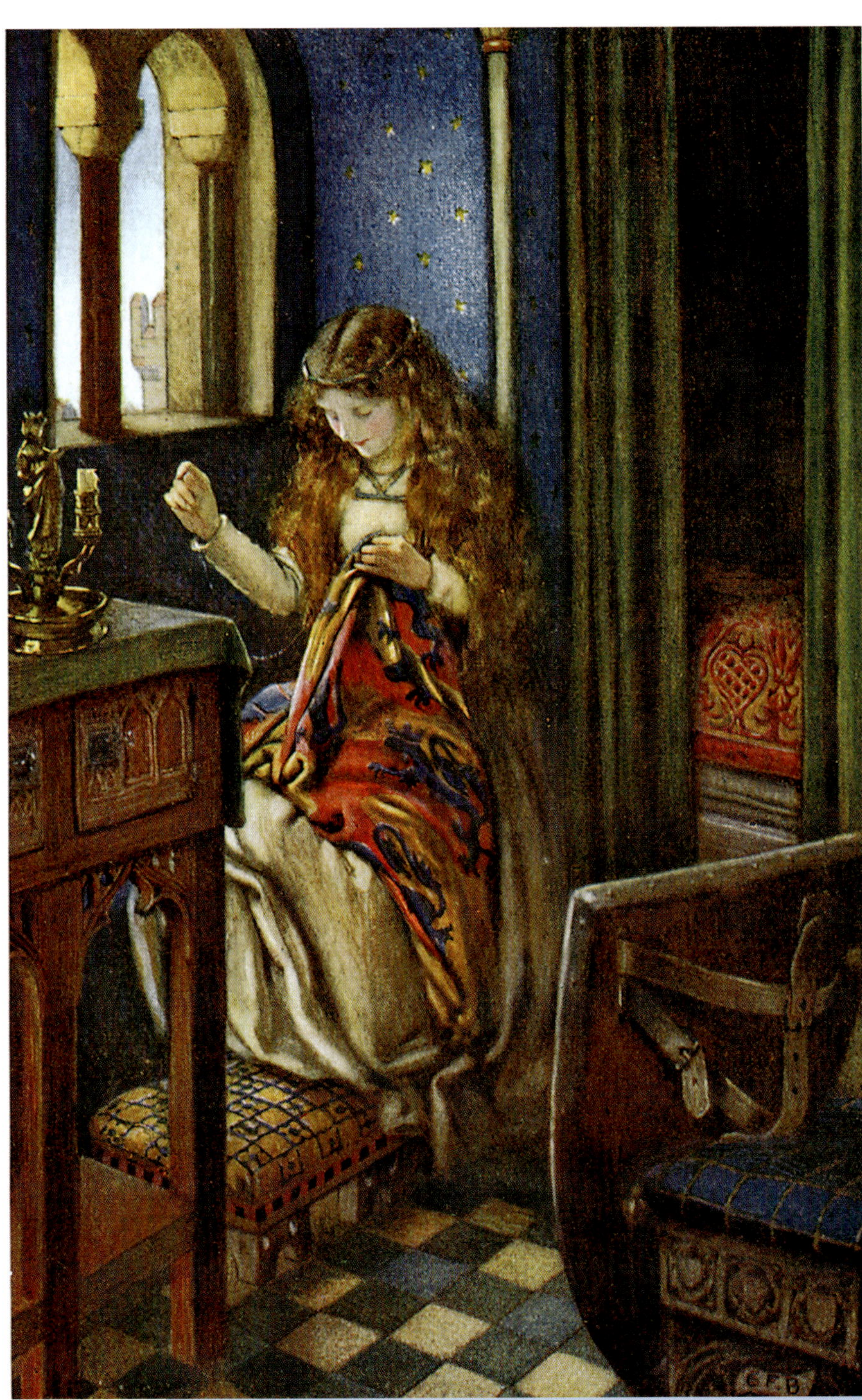

One artist in a group that maintained the ideals of the Pre-Raphaelite circle, Brickdale is sometimes referred to as "the last Pre-Raphaelite." Her subject matter of choice is often the idealized and romantic imagery that the movement was best known for.

Brickdale's earliest days at the Royal Academy led to exhibitions there, and she was greatly influenced by fellow artist John Liston Byam Shaw. Shaw opened a school in 1911, and enlisted Brickdale to become one of his teachers. Versatile in her work, comfortable with oil and watercolor, stained glass design, and book illustration, she was one of the first women to compete with male illustrators for the top jobs in the field, especially at the beginning of the century. Her illustration landed in some prime titles, including Tennyson's *Idylls of the King* for Hodder and Stoughton in 1911. Twenty-eight pieces were originally commissioned for the group by Leicester Galleries, and afterwards twenty-four were published with the text. Hodder and Stoughton went on to work with Brickdale for *The Book of Old English Songs and Ballads* in 1915. Her line work also appeared in British publications of the day, magazines, and annuals.

Later in her career, Brickdale was able to land the gallery attention sought after by other career illustrators. Her gallery painting often explored angelic and Christian themes—she was staunchly religious—and images of classical mythology and allegory, common themes favored by the Pre-Raphaelites. Flowing robes and atmosphere propelled her paintings to storytelling in the traditional style of painters from the past.

Another successful facet of her later work were her efforts as a stained-glass window designer. There are examples of her work that can still be seen today, both at Bristol Cathedral and also at Brixham. Brickdale designed more than twenty windows from 1914–1940.

Brickdale, Eleanor F.

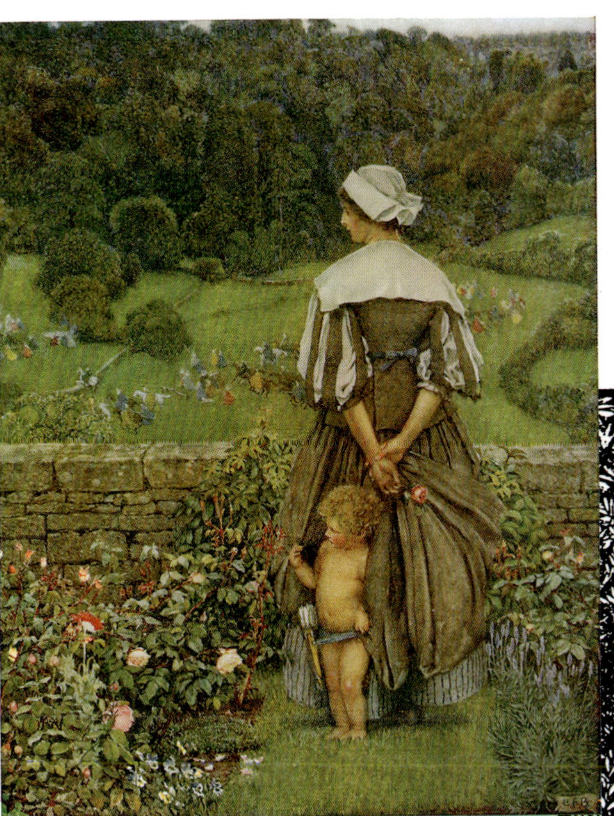

EQUALLY AT HOME WITH LINE OR COLOR
Brickdale mastered both styles of work, and her attention to detail and texture carried through in all her work.

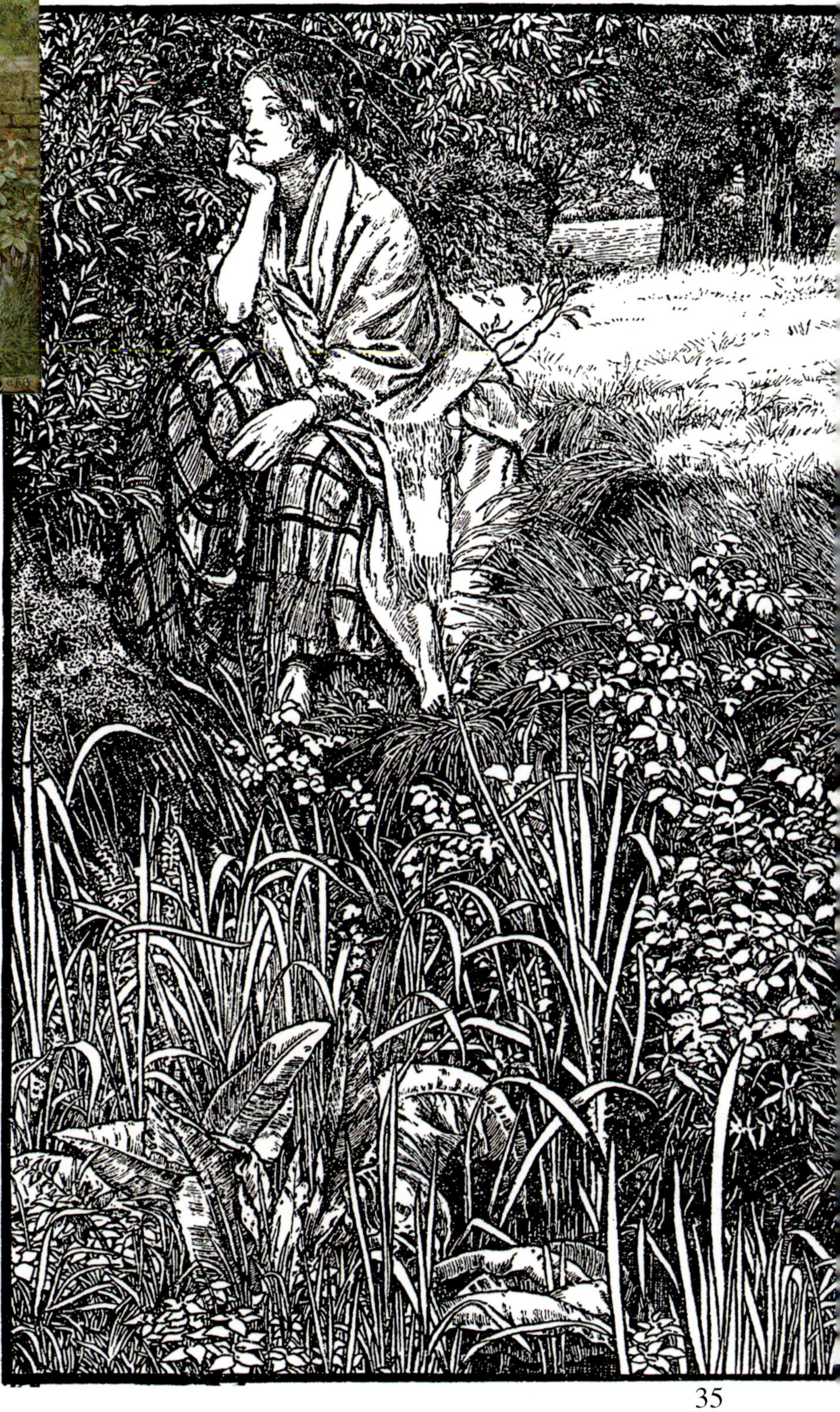

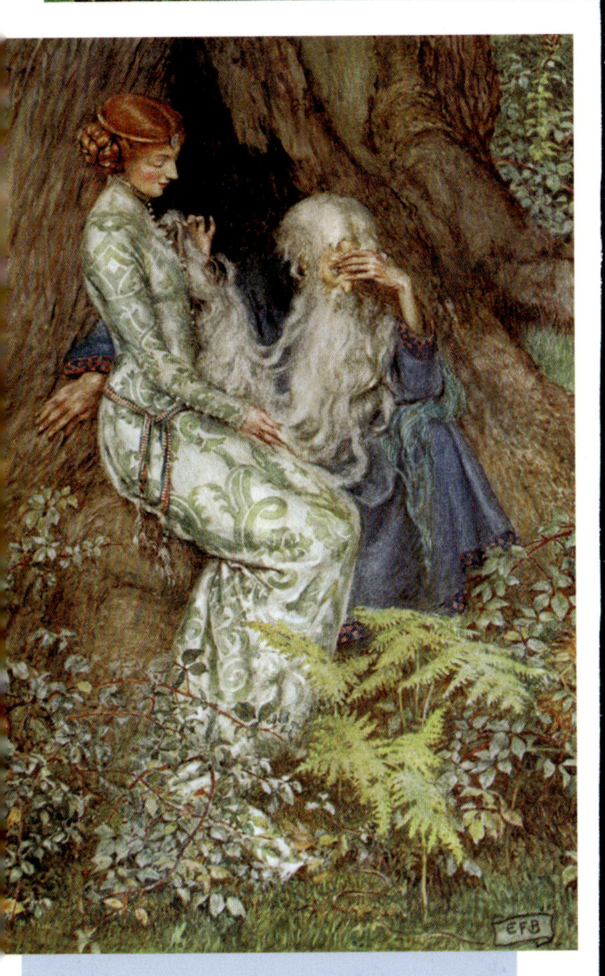

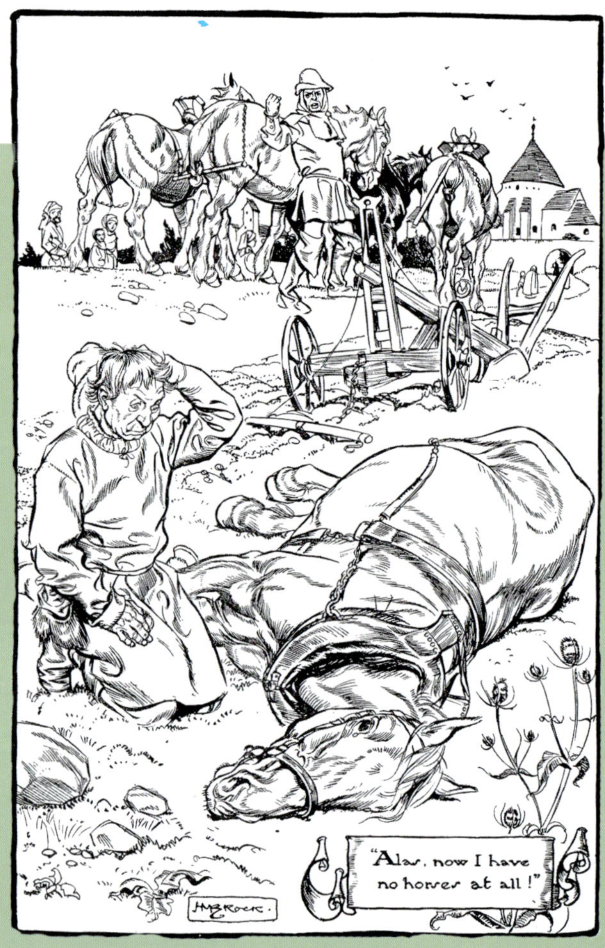

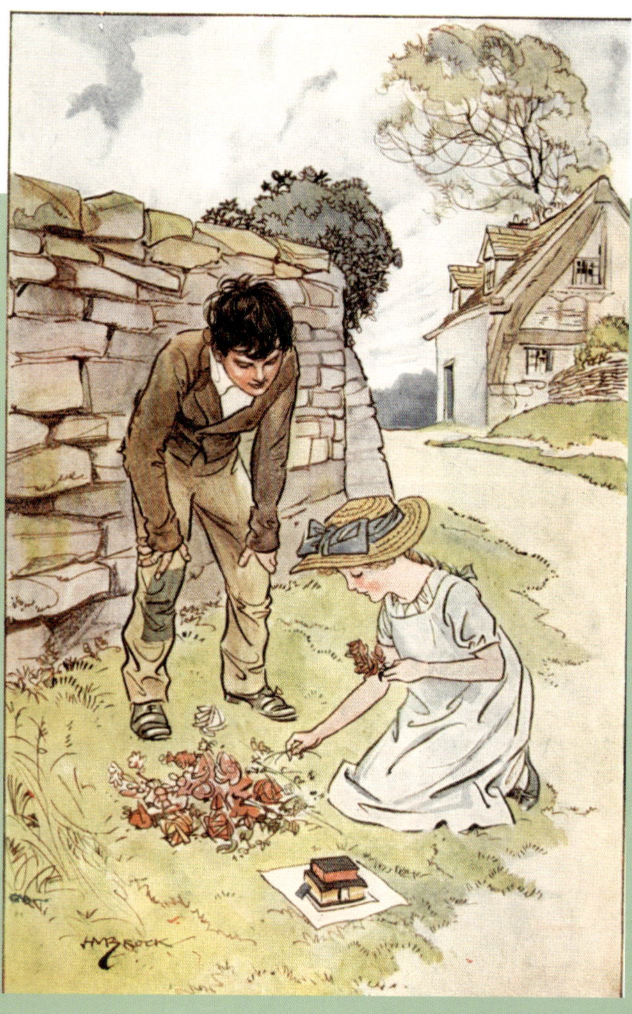

Above: from 1913's *Jackanapes*

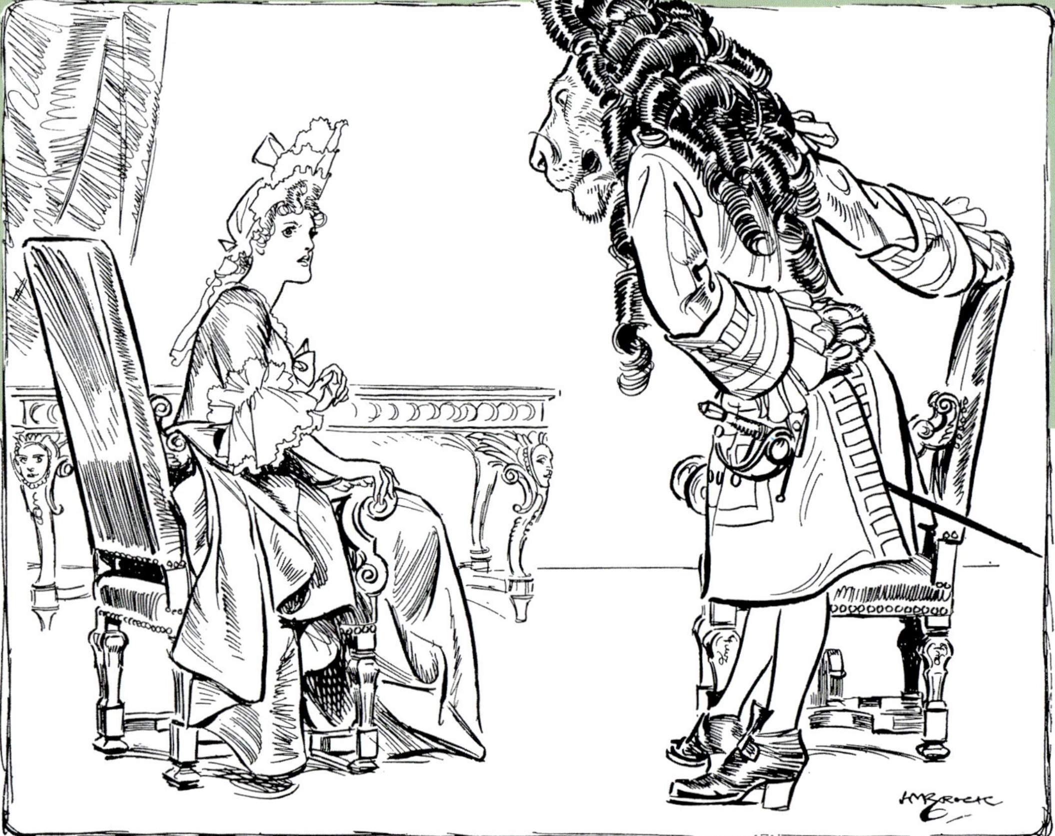

H. M. Brock
1875–1960, British

One of four brothers, H. M. Brock was not as well known as his older sibling Charles Edmund Brock. Charles pursued more gallery work and oil painting, and Henry Matthew was more active in advertising and book illustration. The two artistic brothers worked alongside each other, sharing a studio and a large collection of costumes and period furniture for reference, starting from 1894.

Henry's work was more focused on action stories and work in boys' magazines and annuals. However, like his brother, he was adept at the imagery of nineteenth-century England, and could illustrate the classic literature of that period as well. Austen, Dickens, Scott, and Stevenson were all part of H. M. Brock's portfolio. He also contributed to Sir Arthur Conan Doyle's Holmes story, *The Last Bow,* along with several other illustrators. H. M. Brock did poster work as well as illustration. The D'Oyly Carte Opera Company was a regular client for posters as well as ad material.

The distinction between the two brothers was largely evident in their choice of material. H.M. did a great deal more book work and he produced more for the juvenile market. C.E.'s illustration assignments were fewer, and those he did take included more literature. H.M.'s most notable children's books were a series of fairy stories that remained in print for many years. *The Fairy Library, The Old Fairy Tales, The Book of Fairy Tales,* and *The Book of Nursery Tales* were part of many children's libraries for generations in Britain.

Decreasing book sales changed the work available for H.M. in the 1930s and 1940s. He took on some assignments in comics in the late '30s, for *Sparkler* and later for *Knockout* and *Princess.*

Henry remained a painter as well. He exhibited regularly at the Royal Academy and the Walker Art Gallery in Liverpool, and continued to be a member of the Royal Institute of Painters in Watercolors. Henry remained an active illustrator for over 50 years, but failing eyesight kept him from working at the end of his life.

Below: The frontispiece from *Agothos, the Rocky Island, and Other Sunday Stories,* 1908

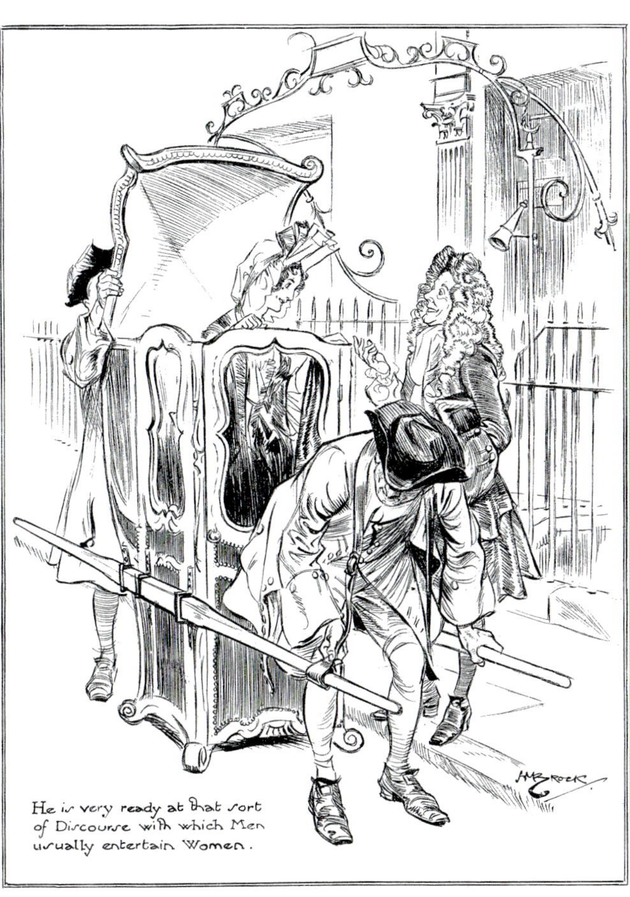

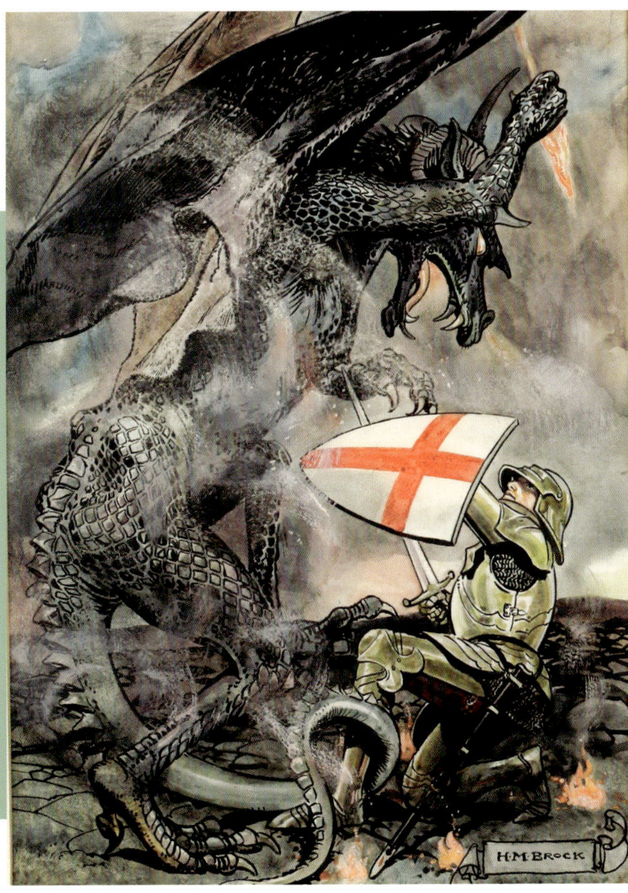

Charles Livingston Bull

1874–1932, American

A specialist in illustration, Charles Livingston Bull was an expert on wildlife. This resulted from Bull's early training as a taxidermist, specializing in birds. Though interested in art at an early age, Bull had a job working for Ward's Museum of Natural History in Rochester, N.Y. The strength of his work led to a later job at the National Museum in Washington D.C. Bull's training enabled him to understand the mechanics and construction of different species. He took that experience with him to the Philadelphia College of Art, and while there honed his skill to become one of the era's top wildlife illustrators.

Bull spent the latter part of his career living in the small town of Oradell, N.J., and he donated several of his works to the public library there.

His avid support of wildlife was instrumental in the campaign to save American eagles from extinction, and he was an active supporter of bird-banding. A member of the Salmagundi Club, the Society of Mural Painters, and the American Institute of Graphic Arts, he was elected to the Society of Illustrators' Hall of Fame in 2000.

Rather than join his fellow illustrators in the cities near their clients, Bull lived for some time in the Bronx, where he had his material to study close at hand. He also made many trips to further research varied species and environments, as far away as South America. Even the posters Bull created to raise support during World War I featured animals and birds as symbols of the countries at war.

Even in so specialized a market, Bull found work with many mainstream magazines. *The Saturday Evening Post, Life, Collier's, Outing,* and *Country Gentleman* were among his regular clients. He illustrated over 135 books in his career, including Jack London's *Call of the Wild,* and an edition of *Aesop's Fables,* in 1915. He worked on occasional ad campaigns as well; in 1920 he created a very successful "leaping tiger" poster for Ringling Brothers Barnum & Bailey Circus.

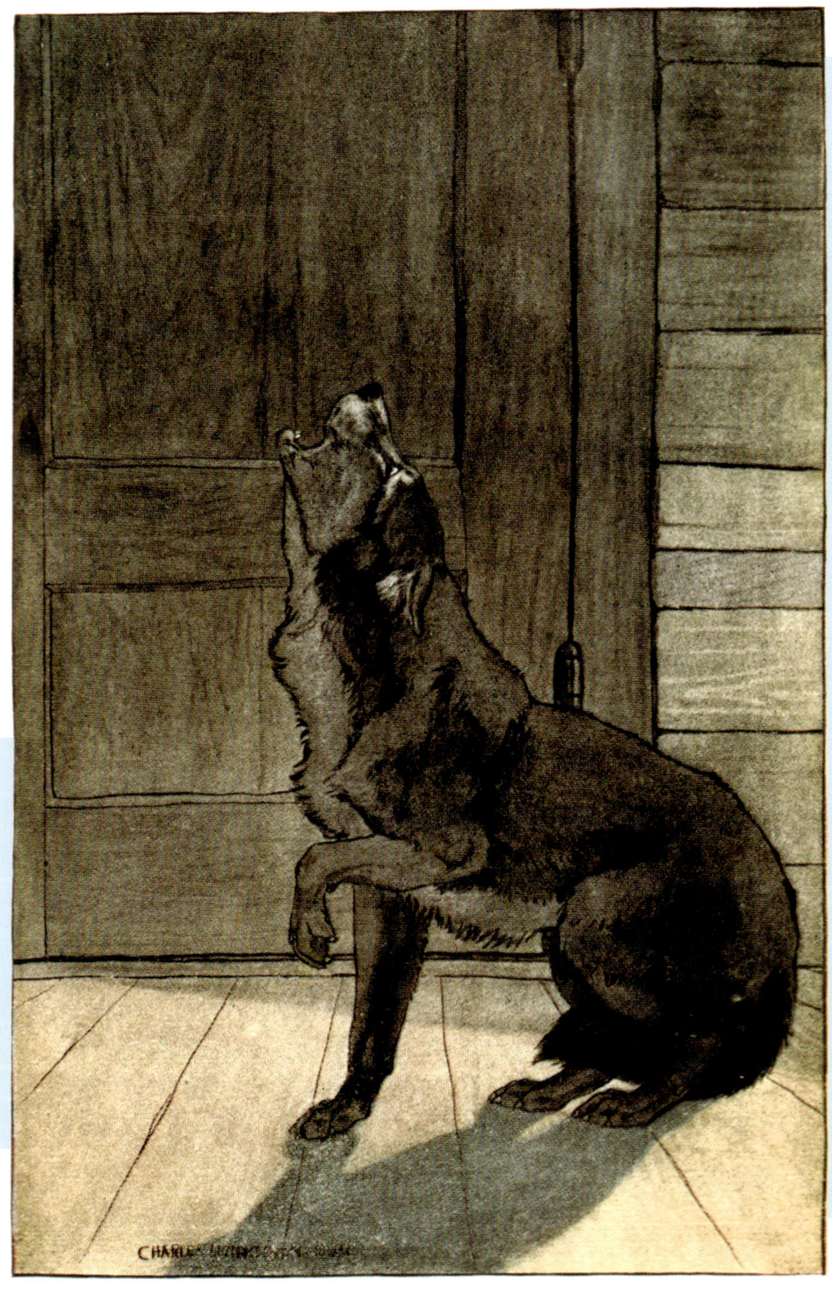

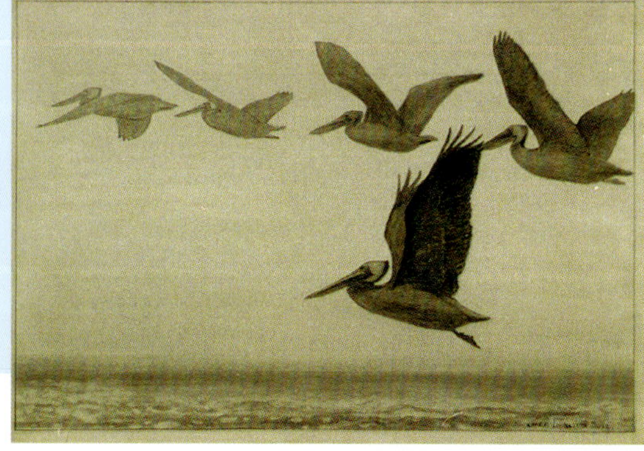

Bull, Charles Livingston

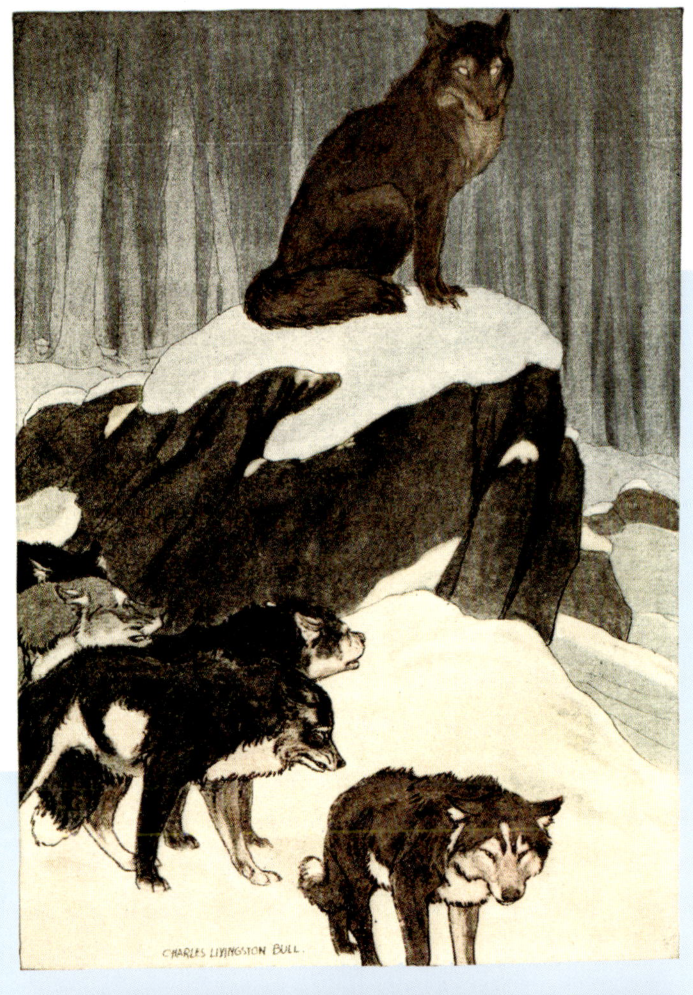
CHARLES LIVINGSTON BULL.

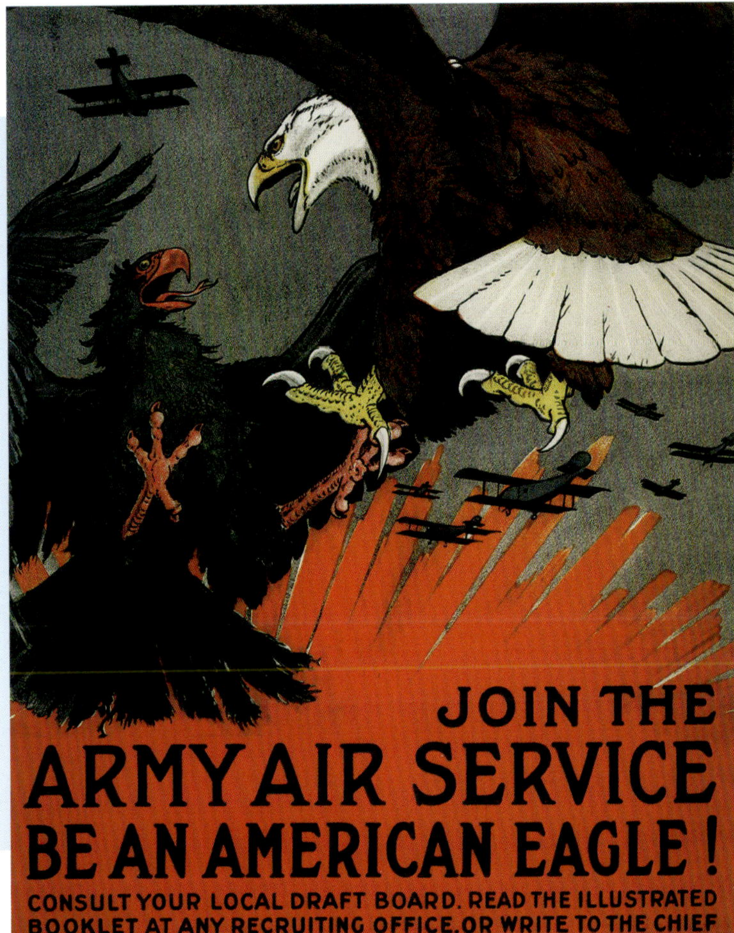
JOIN THE
ARMY AIR SERVICE
BE AN AMERICAN EAGLE!
CONSULT YOUR LOCAL DRAFT BOARD. READ THE ILLUSTRATED BOOKLET AT ANY RECRUITING OFFICE, OR WRITE TO THE CHIEF SIGNAL OFFICER OF THE ARMY, WASHINGTON, D.C.

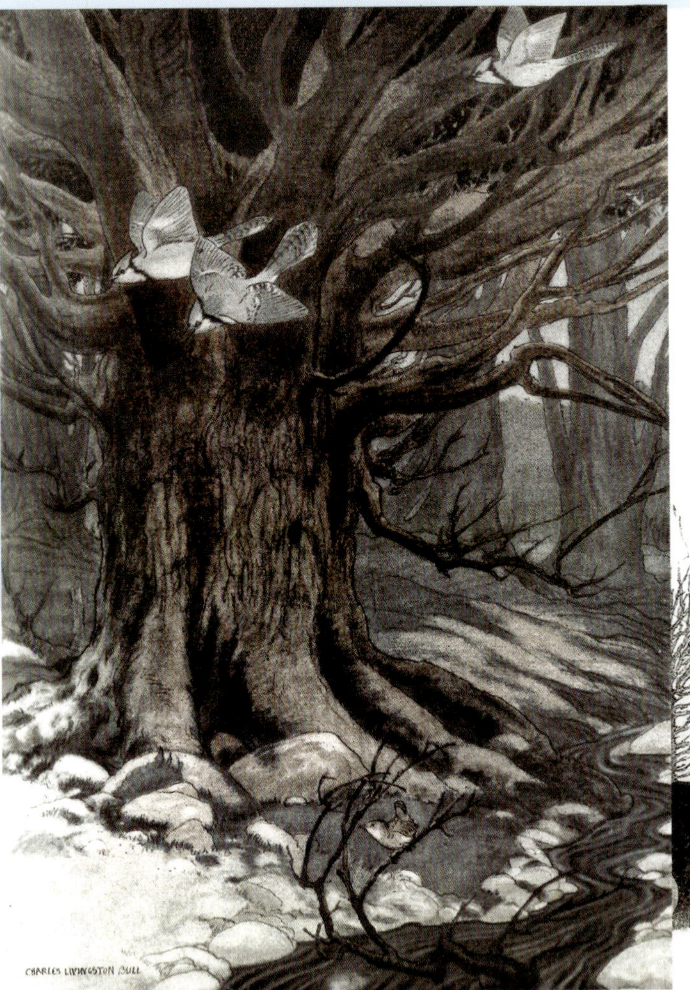
CHARLES LIVINGSTON BULL

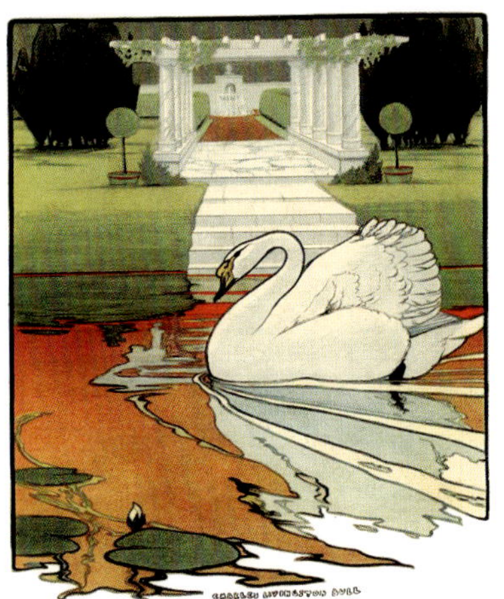

A Master Inker
Bull had a knack for a sinuous flowing line and great characterizations.

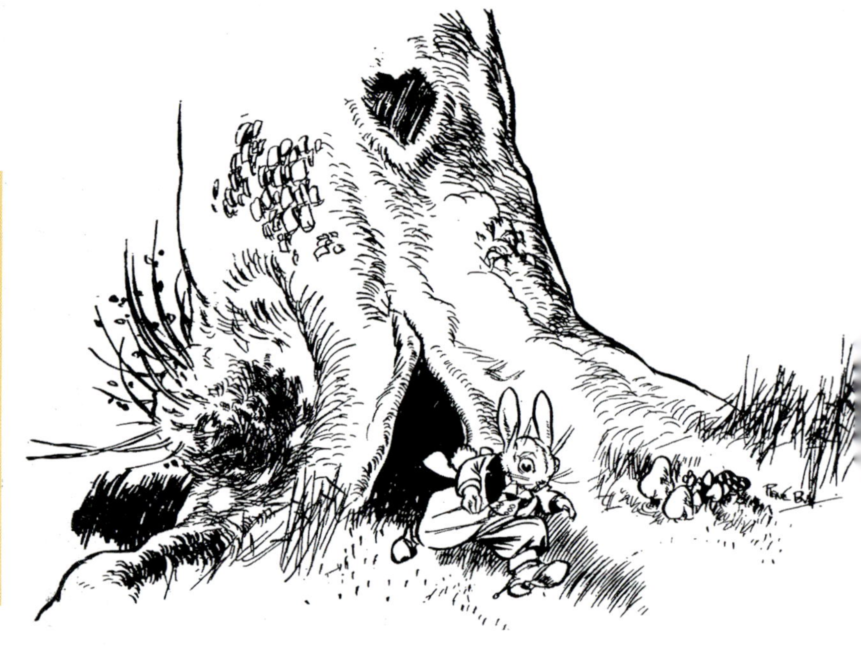

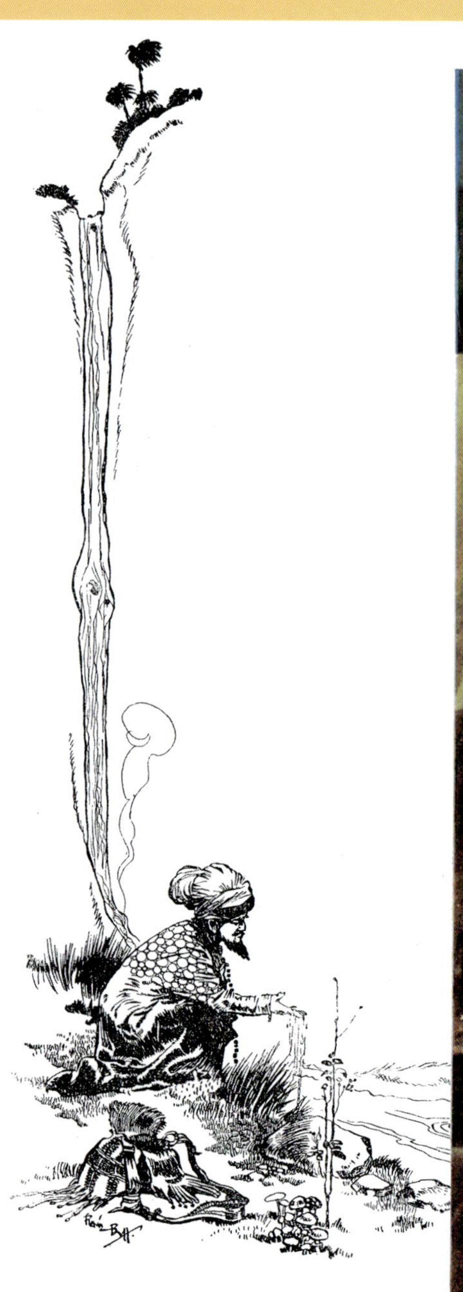

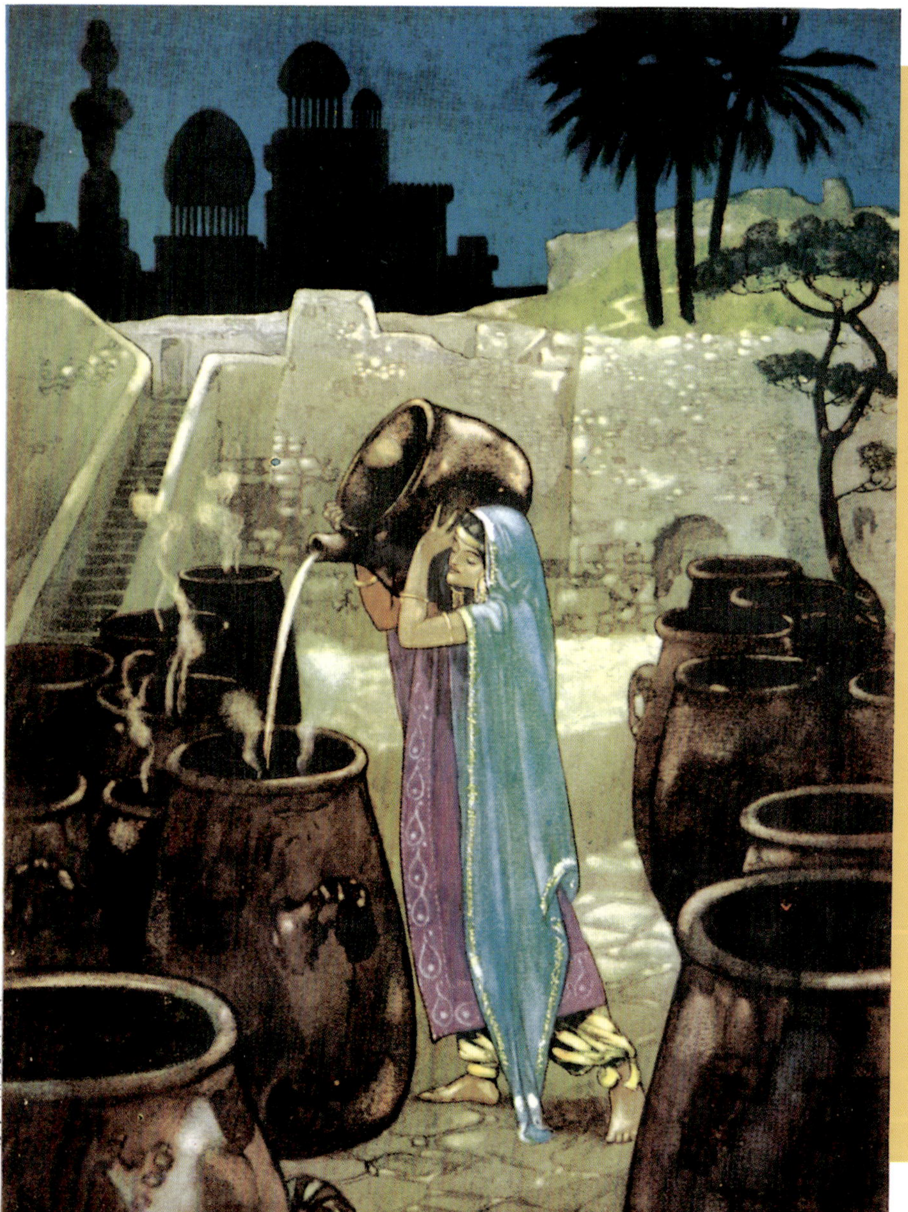

René Bull
1872–1942, Irish

While in Paris to study engineering, young René Bull met the artist and cartoonist Caran d'Ache, with whom he received drawing lessons. Bull soon began to pursue a career in illustration and found work in Ireland and England before signing with an illustrated newspaper in 1896. After joining the staff of the *Black and White* news magazine in 1896, he became a war correspondent, relaying his stories through his art. Well-suited for it, he stayed with the magazine to cover each war over the next decade, up to and including World War I. He began doing some book illustration while he was working for the paper, producing work for the book *Fables* in 1905 and *Uncle Remus* in 1906. Magazine work occupied him for a few years before he resumed book work in 1912.

Bull shared a love for imagery of the Far East with his friend and fellow illustrator Edmund Dulac. Bull had been to India and the Middle East as part of his work-related reporting. His memory for the architecture, costuming, and its colors lent an air of believability to his illustrations for *The Arabian Nights* (1912) and his *Rubáiyát of Omar Khayyám* (1913). A few other book projects followed after World War I, and then Bull's creative interests turned toward model-building. Though his illustrated works have endured as brilliant examples of artwork of the period, his limited output has prevented him from enjoying lasting fame.

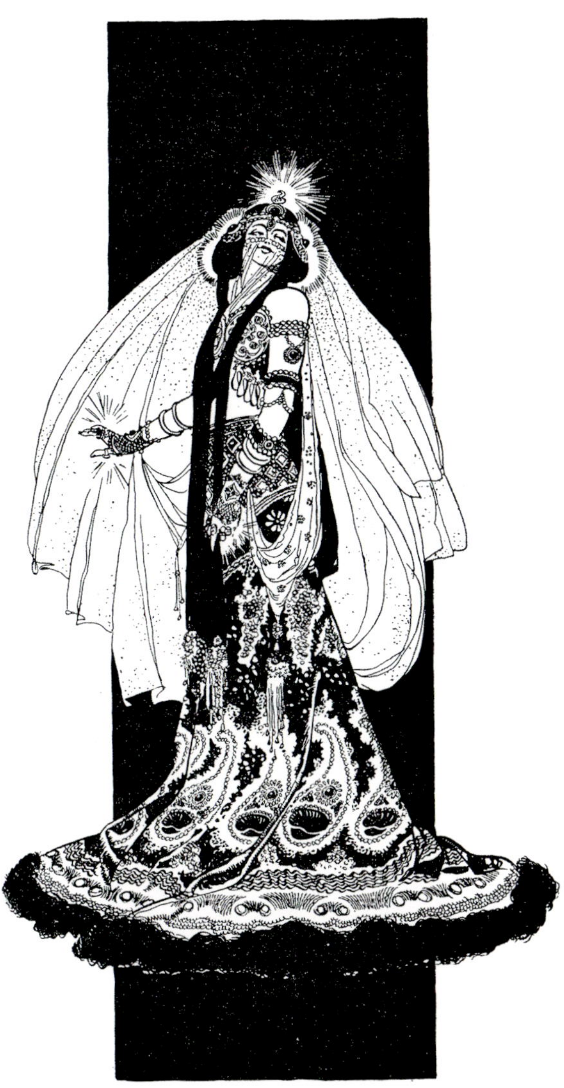

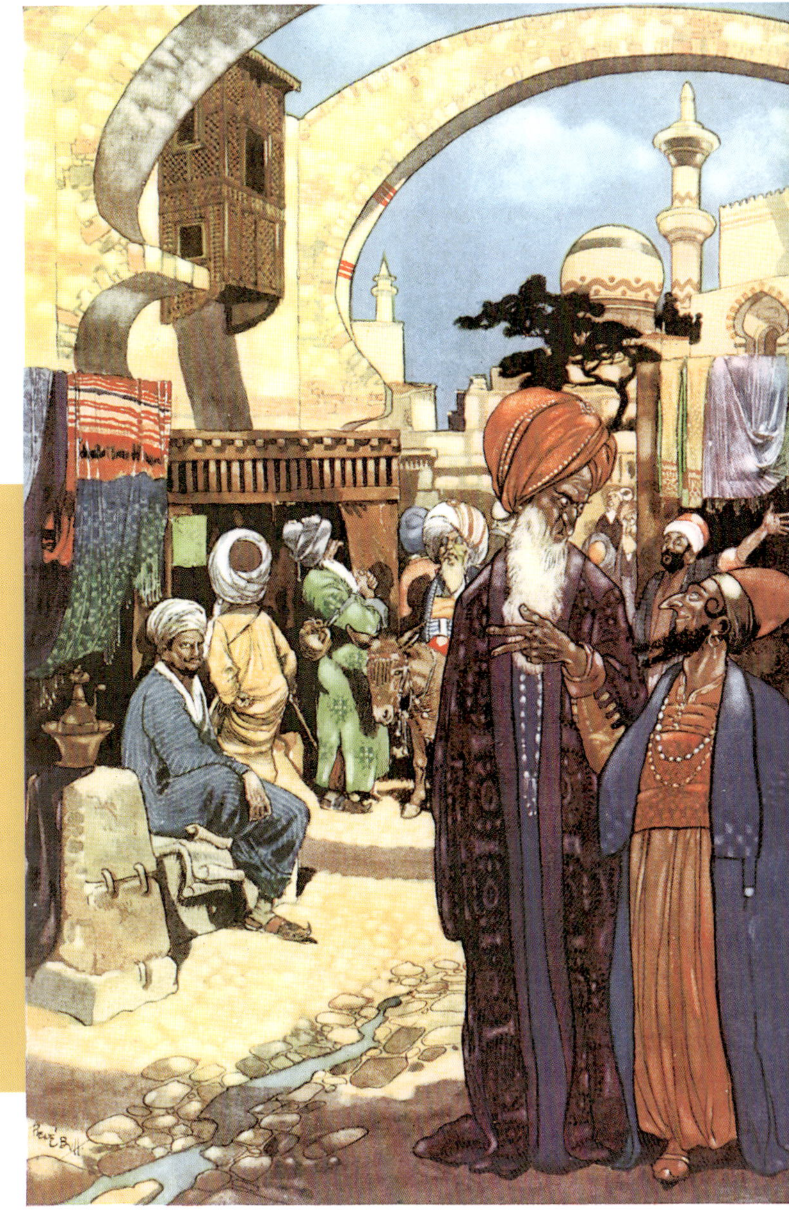

Charles E. Chambers

1883–1941, American

A steadfast non-genre illustrator, Charles Edward Chambers hailed from Ottumwa, Iowa. His earlier training was from the Chicago Art Institute, and later from the Art Students League in New York. One of his teachers was Fanny Munsell, a fellow illustrator, who later became his wife.

Chambers was comfortable with every type of assignment, and his name and work were held in high regard in his day. Assignments were well-balanced between advertising and editorial work. His ads were frequently mentioned for their strength and beauty. In the 1910s and 1920s, Chambers contributed to many recurring ad campaigns. Among them were Steinway & Sons (Chambers did a series of portraits of famous pianists of the day), Chesterfield Cigarettes, and Palmolive Soap. One of the Chesterfield pieces was cited as being "one of the most beautiful posters ever painted" (*Advertising Outdoors,* 1931).

Often noted are the transitions Chambers used in his paintings; shifts in value or color seemed smooth and flawless in Chambers's works. These soft edges seemed to help Chambers's work achieve the best possible reproduction. Chambers seemed to be in control of exactly how a painting was going to print, and sometimes followed his assignments all the way to the engraver who made the plates.

Chambers was recognized as a leader in the illustration field, working steadily for *Harper's* and *Redbook,* and eventually *Cosmopolitan,* who hired him on an exclusive contract for many years, and where he illustrated stories of literary figures such as Pearl S. Buck, Louis Bromfield, and W. Somerset Maugham.

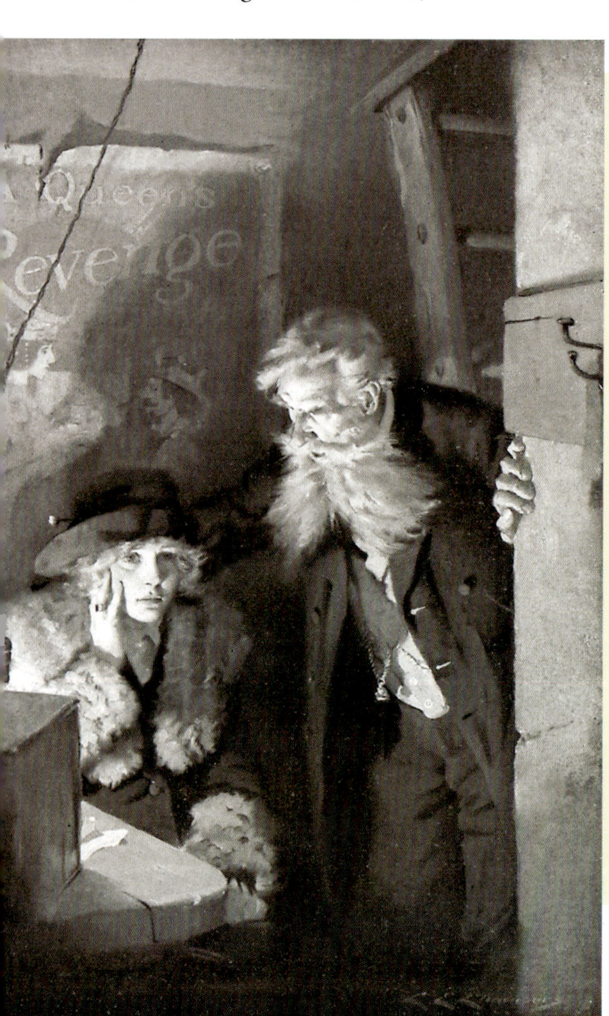

Chambers, Charles E.

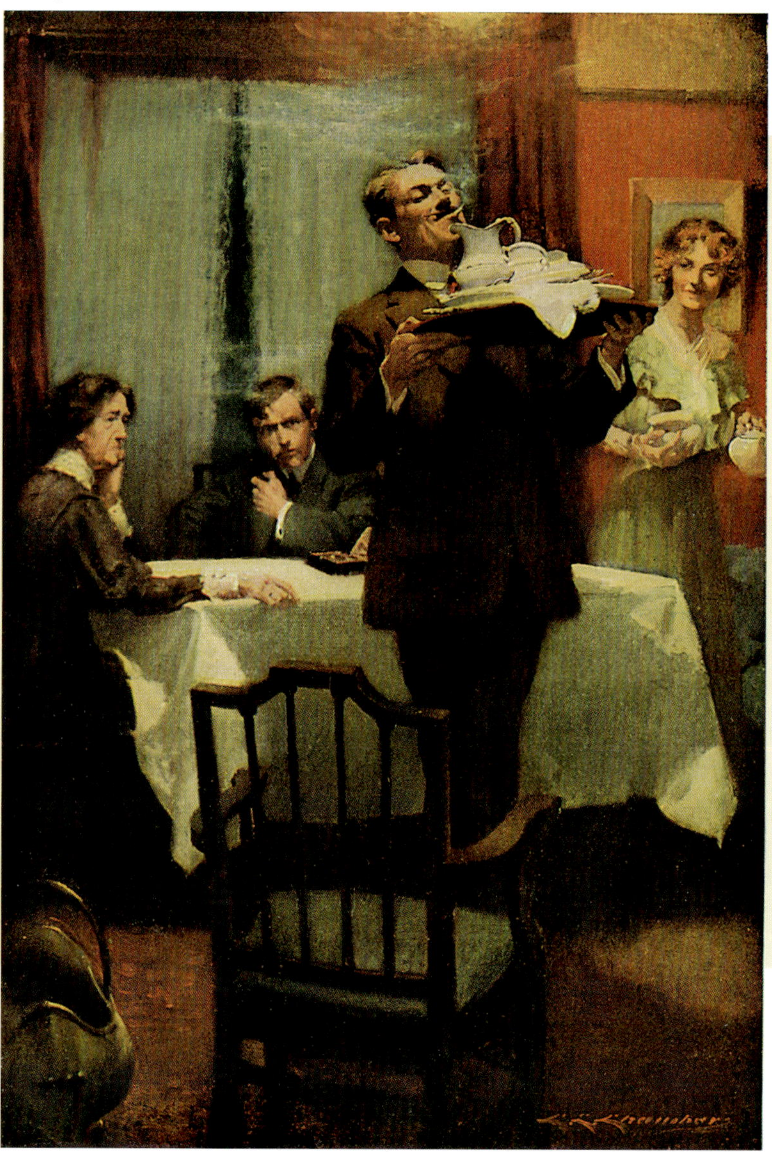

Probably no living American better typifies the successful illustrator than Charles E. Chambers."

—John D. Whiting, *author and art editor, 1920*

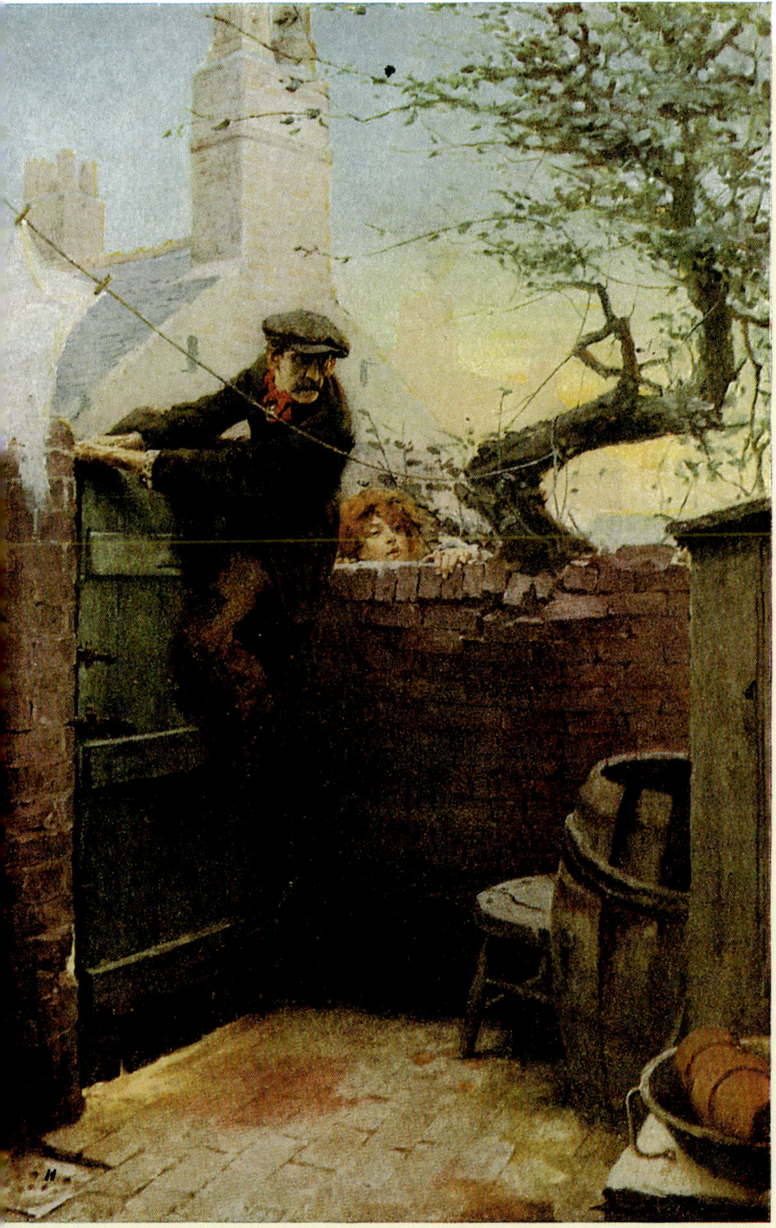

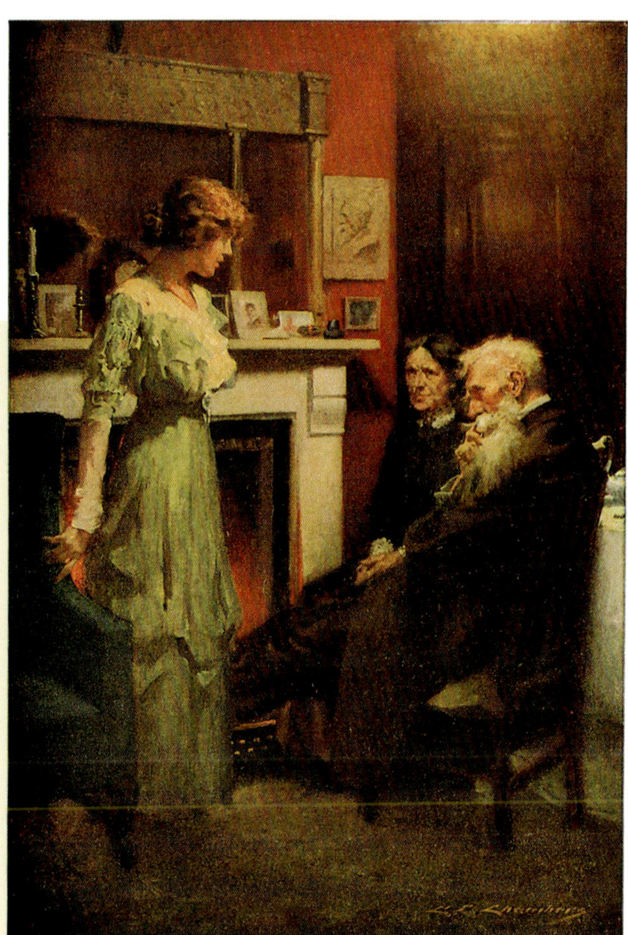

"Chambers' originals do stand the test of time and have much to be admired and to inspire the contemporary painter and illustrator."

—Walt Reed, *Illustration House*

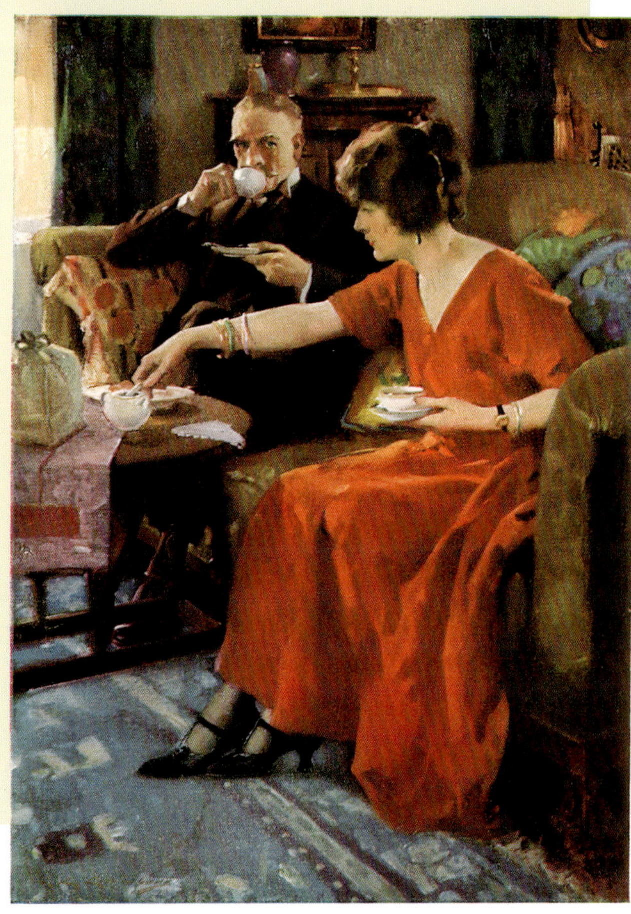

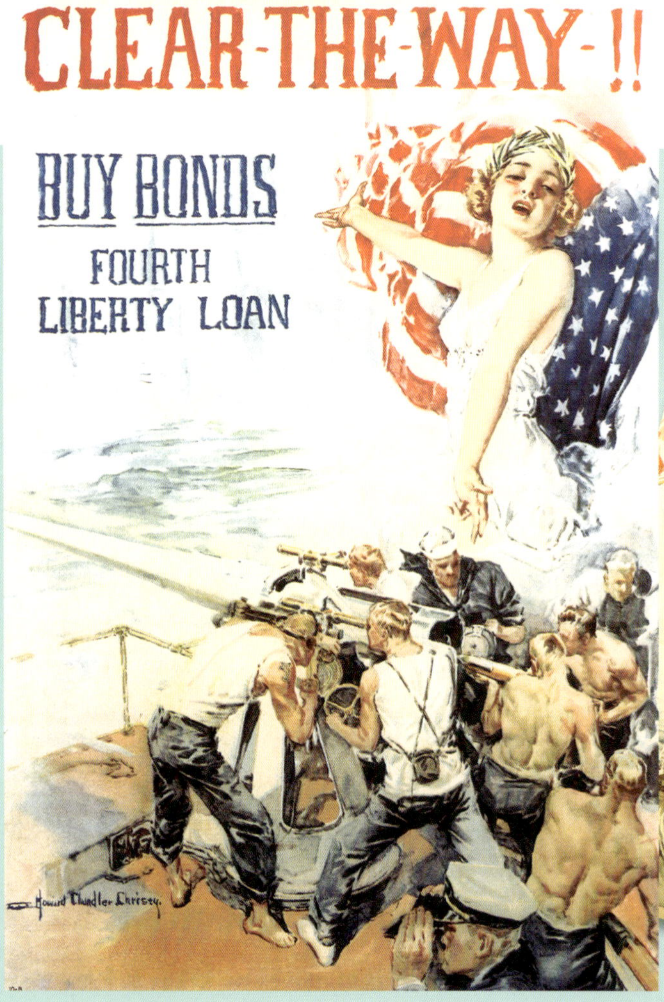

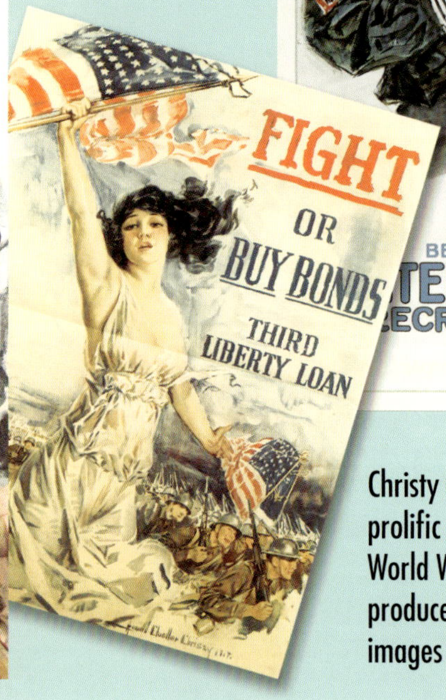

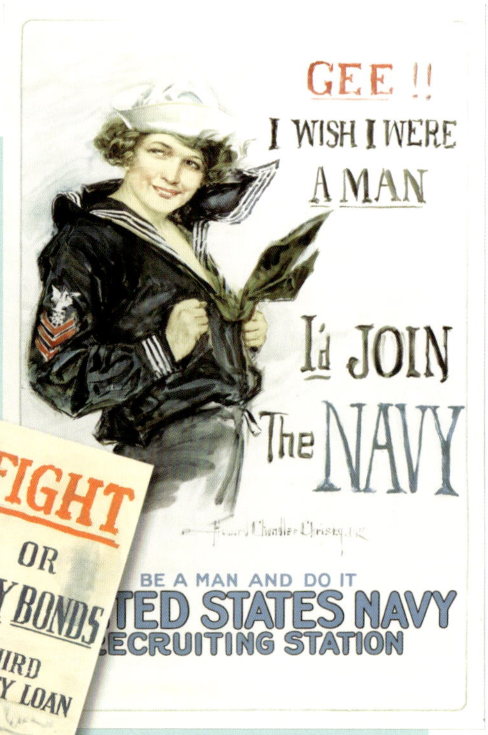

Christy was one of the most prolific artists for the World War I effort—he produced more than a dozen images for recruitment posters.

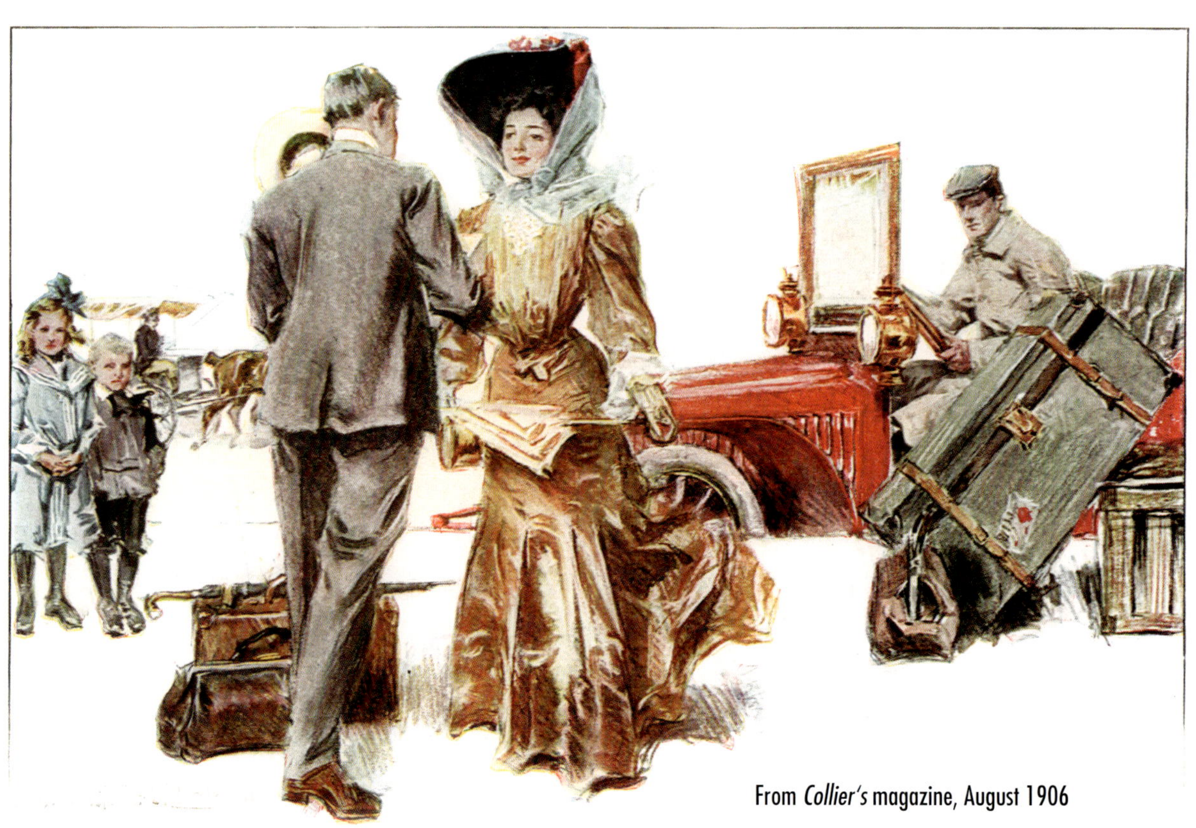

From *Collier's* magazine, August 1906

HOWARD C. CHRISTY
1873–1952, American

Originally from Ohio, Christy studied in New York at both the National Academy and the Art Students League. He was a society artist, who made a name for himself by giving the public a follow-up to the Gibson Girl. Christy's feminine images were a little more misty; his medium of choice was watercolor as opposed to Gibson's line—giving him an advantage when color began to dominate in publishing. The "Christy Girl"—as she was called—appeared regularly in magazines and in advertising, and Christy was tapped to do book works that featured heroines in his specific style. His feminine depictions were so popular, in fact, that he was able to author books featuring them in sketches and on color plates. Books like 1906's *The Christy Girl* started it all, and *Liberty Belles,* in 1912, solidified his place as the artist who presented idealized images of women.

Christy's unparalleled service to the effort during World War I gave us lasting memories of his work. During the Spanish-American War, Christy was a war reporter, doing sketches with a troop in Cuba for many of the magazines in the States. One of his pieces—which gained incredible popularity—was *Soldier's Dream,* and depicted a girl who was repeated in numerous publications for years to come. There were very few illustrators—certainly not one of Christy's commercial stature—who produced as much work for the World War I war effort. Christy produced posters for multiple branches of the service, war bonds, and other wartime promotions. Many of his war posters featured the feminine characters he had made so popular in his illustrations of the period.

Christy was also a popular teacher in the New York area, and a successful muralist. His subjects and venues ranged from larger-than-life nudes at the *Café des Artistes* in New York (which are still visible in a restored condition today) to "The Signing of the Constitution" at the Capitol rotunda in Washington, D.C.

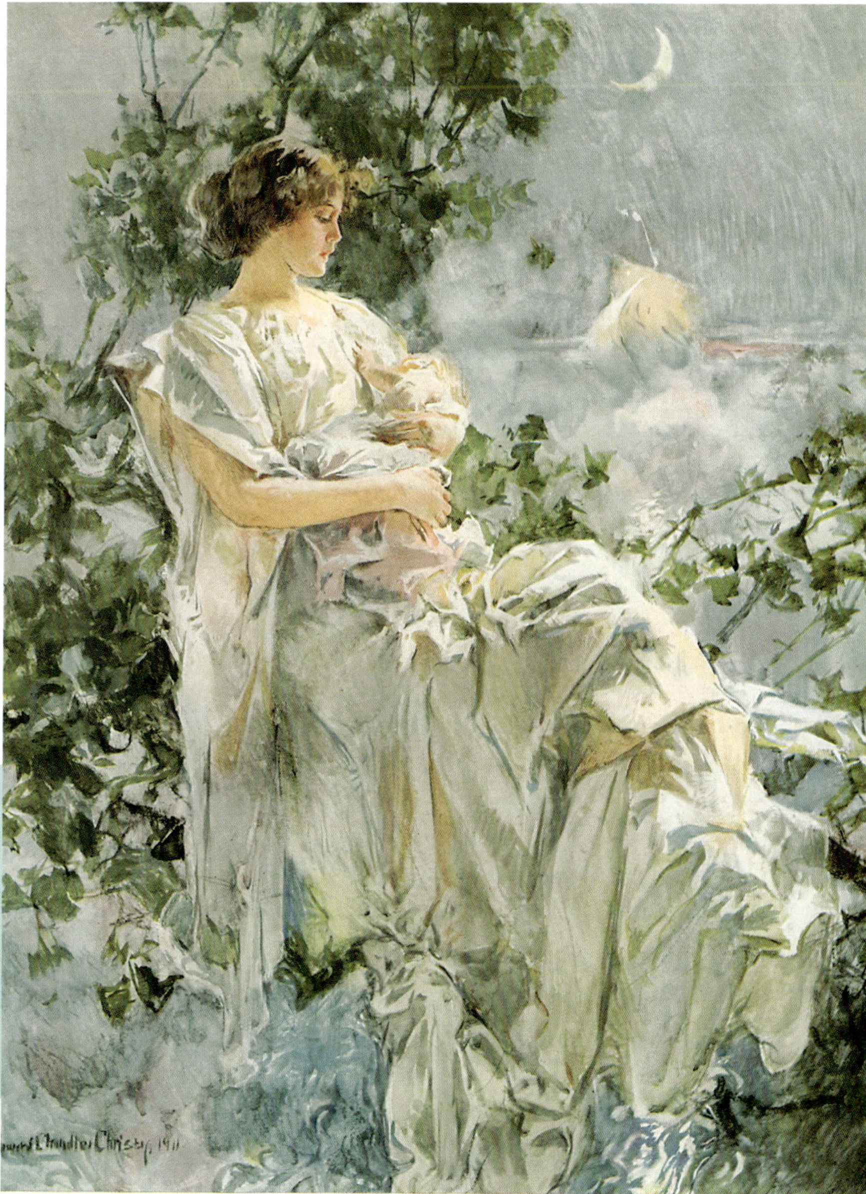

Christy in his studio, 1905

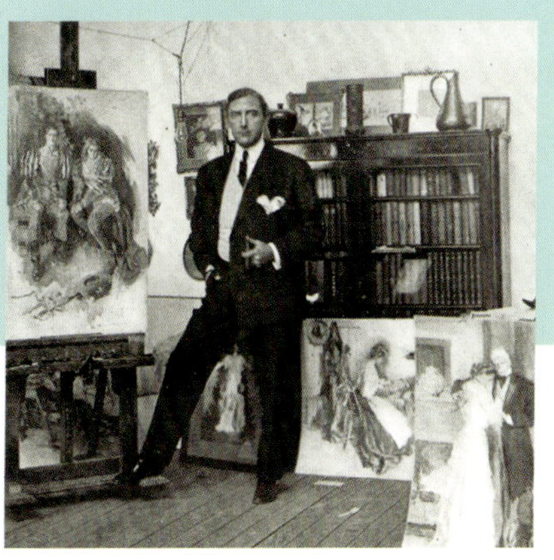

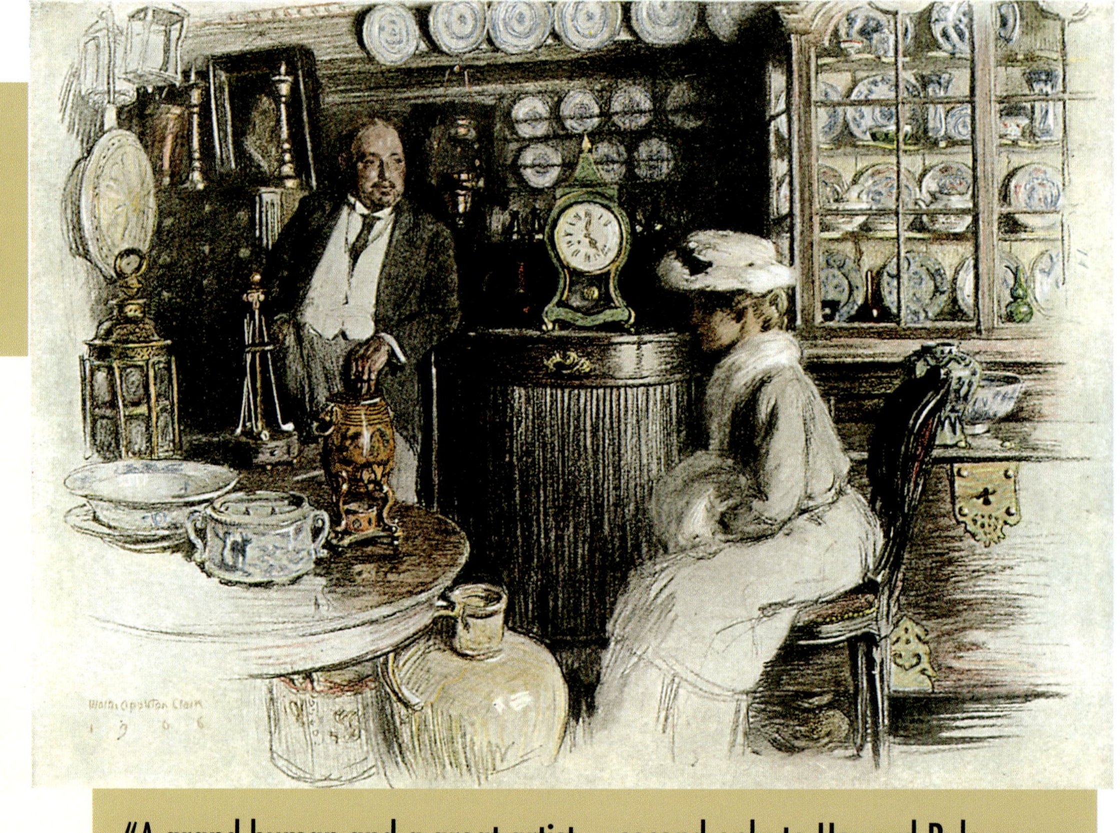

"A grand human and a great artist—second only to Howard Pyle as America's number one illustrator."

—James Montgomery Flagg

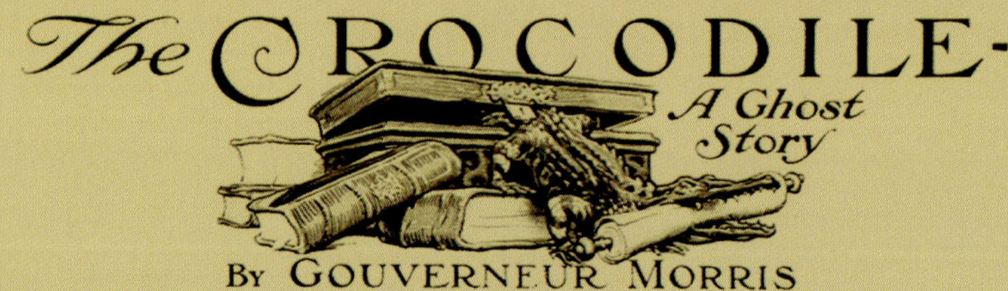

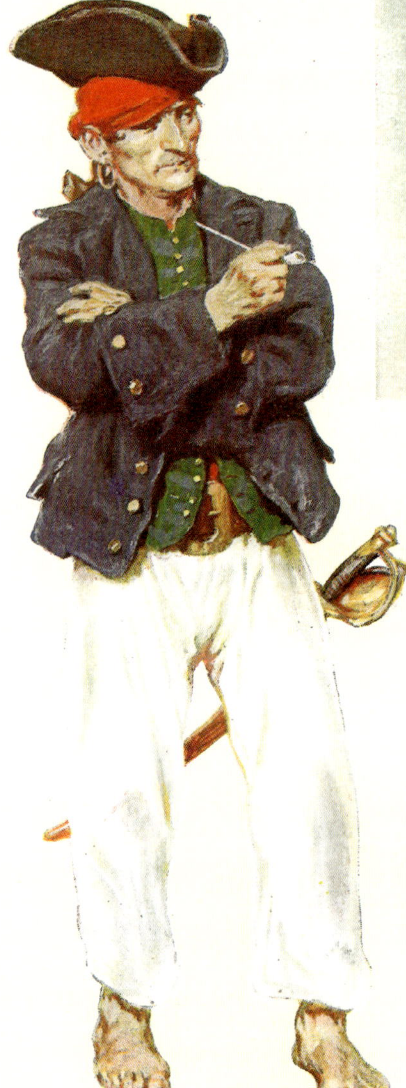

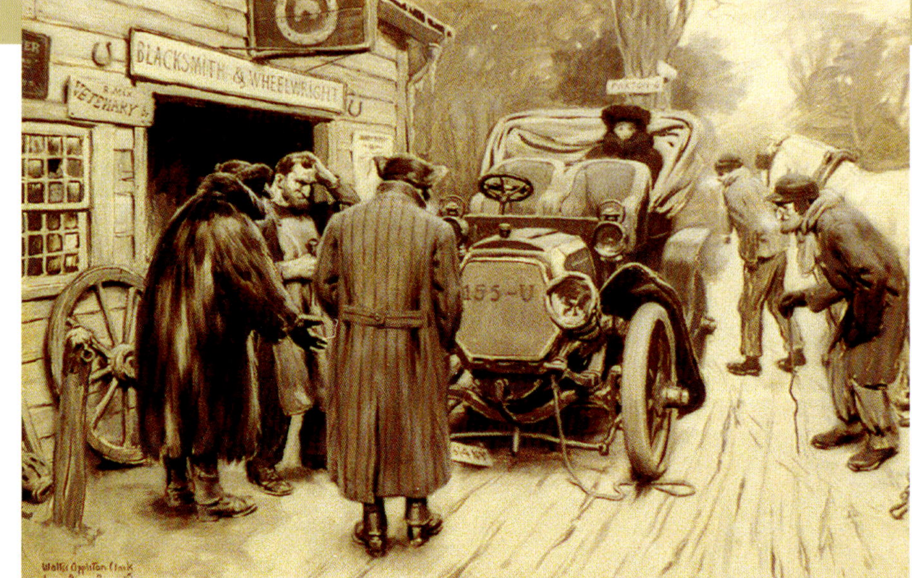

Clark, Walter A.

Walter A. Clark

1880–1906, American

With a career that spanned only a decade, Walter Appleton Clark still garners considerable respect when discussed alongside the great illustrators at the turn of the century. He was a close friend of James Montgomery Flagg, and the two were often together in New York and at the Art Students League. Spotted there by *Scribner's* art editor Joseph Chapin, Clark's career got off to a running start. His first assignment, in 1897, was a Rudyard Kipling story called ".007," which was the identification on a new locomotive. For the first four years of his creative output, he worked primarily with *Scribner's*—on their books and their monthly magazine.

One of the innovations that the young illustrator brought to the craft was the true vignette—where the shape of the subject was met by the white page, creating organic shapes for a magazine's type to wrap around. The look was attention-getting, and was soon being used by other illustrators. Clark was a perfectionist, even willing to scour the streets in search of the right model to suit his vision.

Despite his young age, he taught as well. Even though just a few years older than his students, he was sought after and shaped some high-quality artists, but he soon felt the need to return to full-time freelance work. For a change of atmosphere, he went to Paris in 1900, and again in late 1903 into 1904. He continued to work for his American clients while in Europe, but also explored new visuals and environments. He was among the leading illustrators of the day, often sharing pages with the likes of Howard Pyle and Charles Dana Gibson.

A few months after his return to New York, he signed a contract to work exclusively for *Collier's* magazine, which had some of the biggest names in the field of illustration under similar contracts. But his success there was brief; Clark developed typhoid fever in late 1906, and after fighting the disease for a few weeks, he passed away just before Christmas of that year.

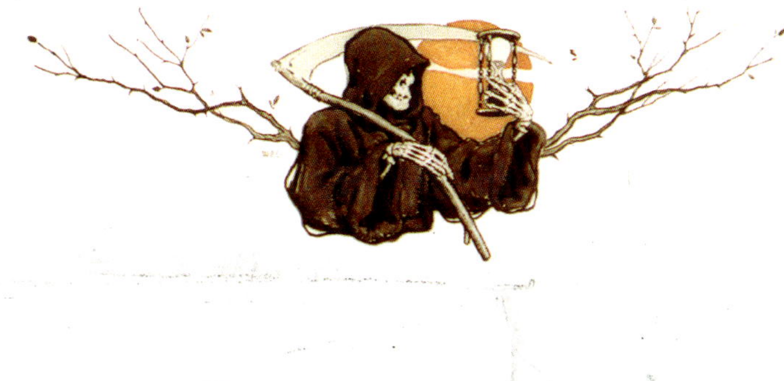

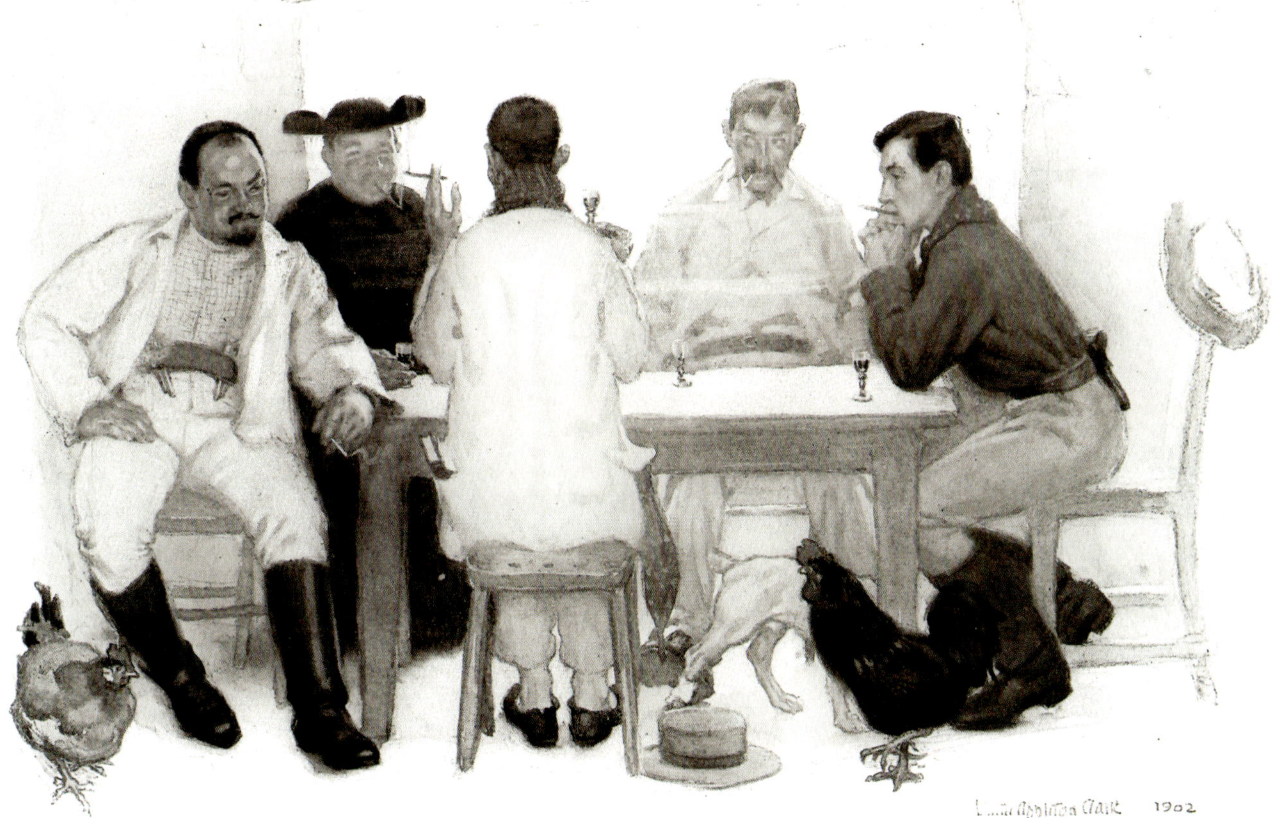

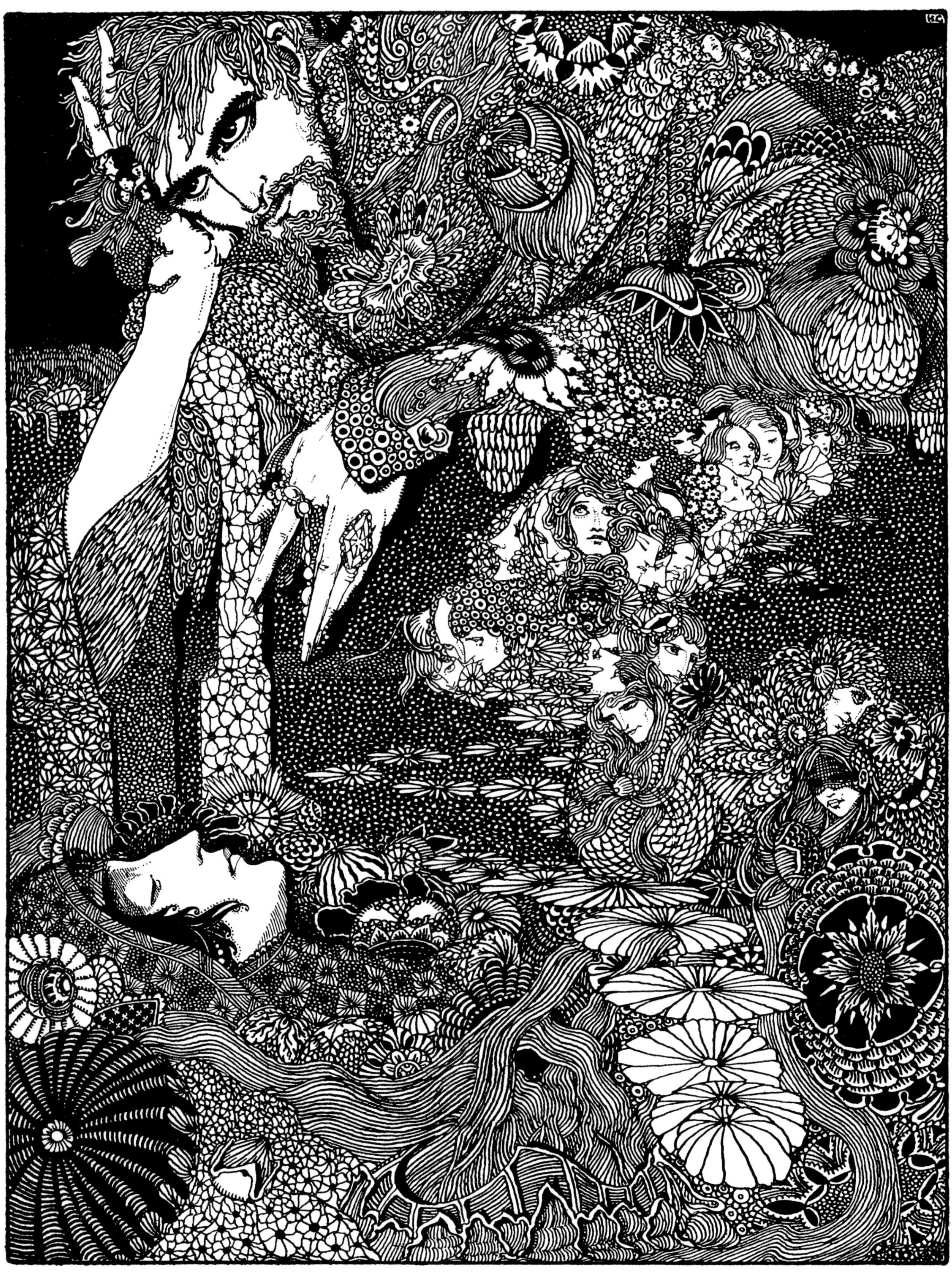

Clarke, Harry

Harry Clarke

1889–1931, Irish

Having apprenticed in stained glass design, Harry Clarke became adept at composing with flat shapes. That design sense carried over into his illustration work as well. Clarke became one of Ireland's leading figures of the Symbolist movement, applying his craftsmanship and design to the artistic ideals of the day. Throughout a good part of his career, he did both glass work—in a studio that would eventually bear his name—and some truly noteworthy book illustration.

Clarke became well known for the stylized appearance of his drawing, somewhat influenced by Aubrey Beardsley's "decadent" look. He used elongated stylized figures, solid flat areas, and large amounts of delicate and elaborate details. Clarke's work had its own distinct quality and its uniqueness brought him to the attention of one of the biggest publishers in London. His earliest published work in books occurred in 1916, with the Harrap edition of *Fairy Tales by Hans Christian Andersen.* Soon afterwards, Clarke followed with illustrations for *Tales of Mystery and Imagination* by Edgar Allan Poe. That book featured Clarke's intricate ink work and wild imagination, and was so successful that a second edition quickly followed the first, with an additional eight plates in color. His penchant for the bizarre imagery in Poe's tales would be encouraged again when he illustrated *Faust* in 1923.

Tales of Mystery and Imagination is to this day viewed as a definitive treatment of Poe illustration, and it established Clarke among the leading gift book illustrators working in London at that time.

Clarke's successes in both his illustration and his glass work pulled more from him than he had to give. In the late 1920s his health began to suffer. Following the death of both his father and then his brother (with whom he shared the work at the stained glass studio), he succumbed to tuberculosis before he was forty-two.

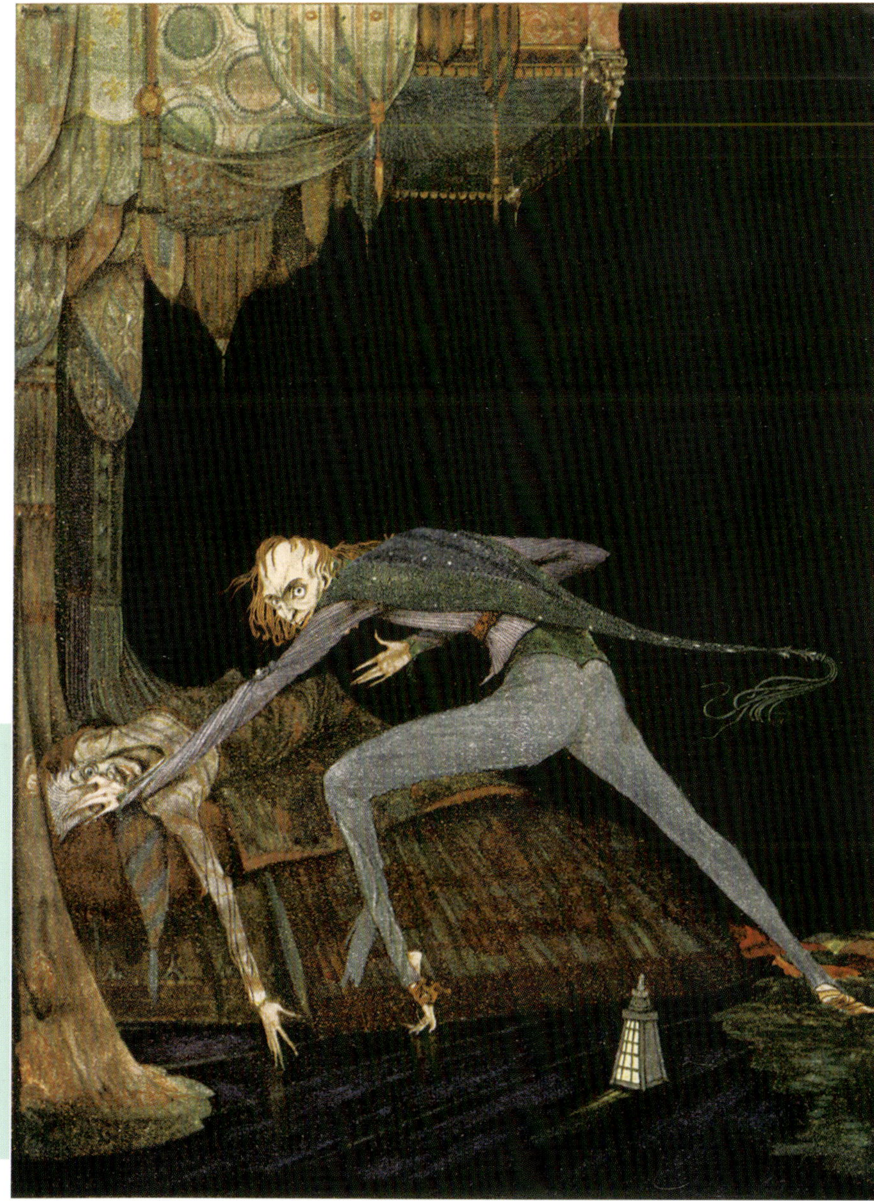

FOREVER LINKED WITH POE
After the initial release of Clarke's illustrations for *Tales of Mystery and Imagination* in 1919, the sales were so brisk that a larger edition with eight added color plates was put into production. This collection remains a definitive illustrated edition of Poe's work.

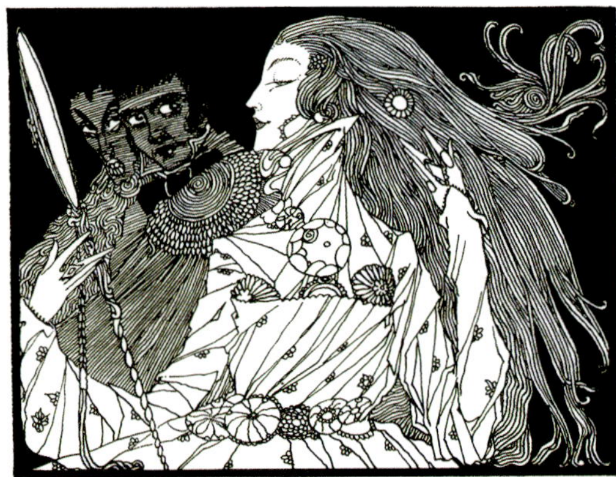

Successful in print, perhaps more so in stained glass

While we revere him here for the contributions he made in publishing, Clarke felt closest to the work he produced in his stained glass studio.

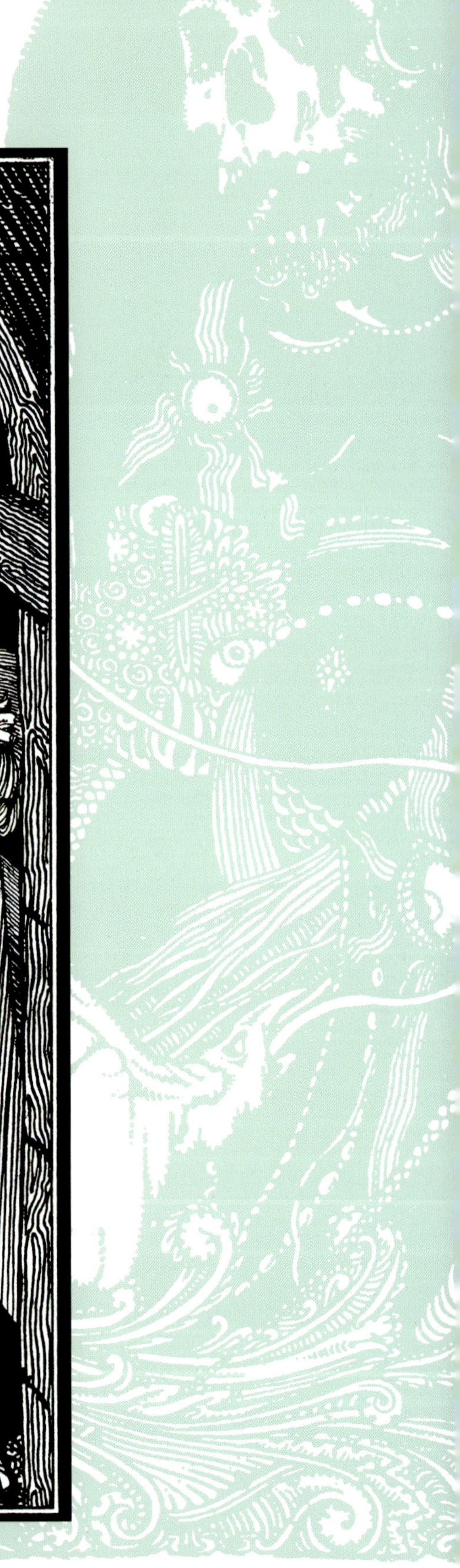

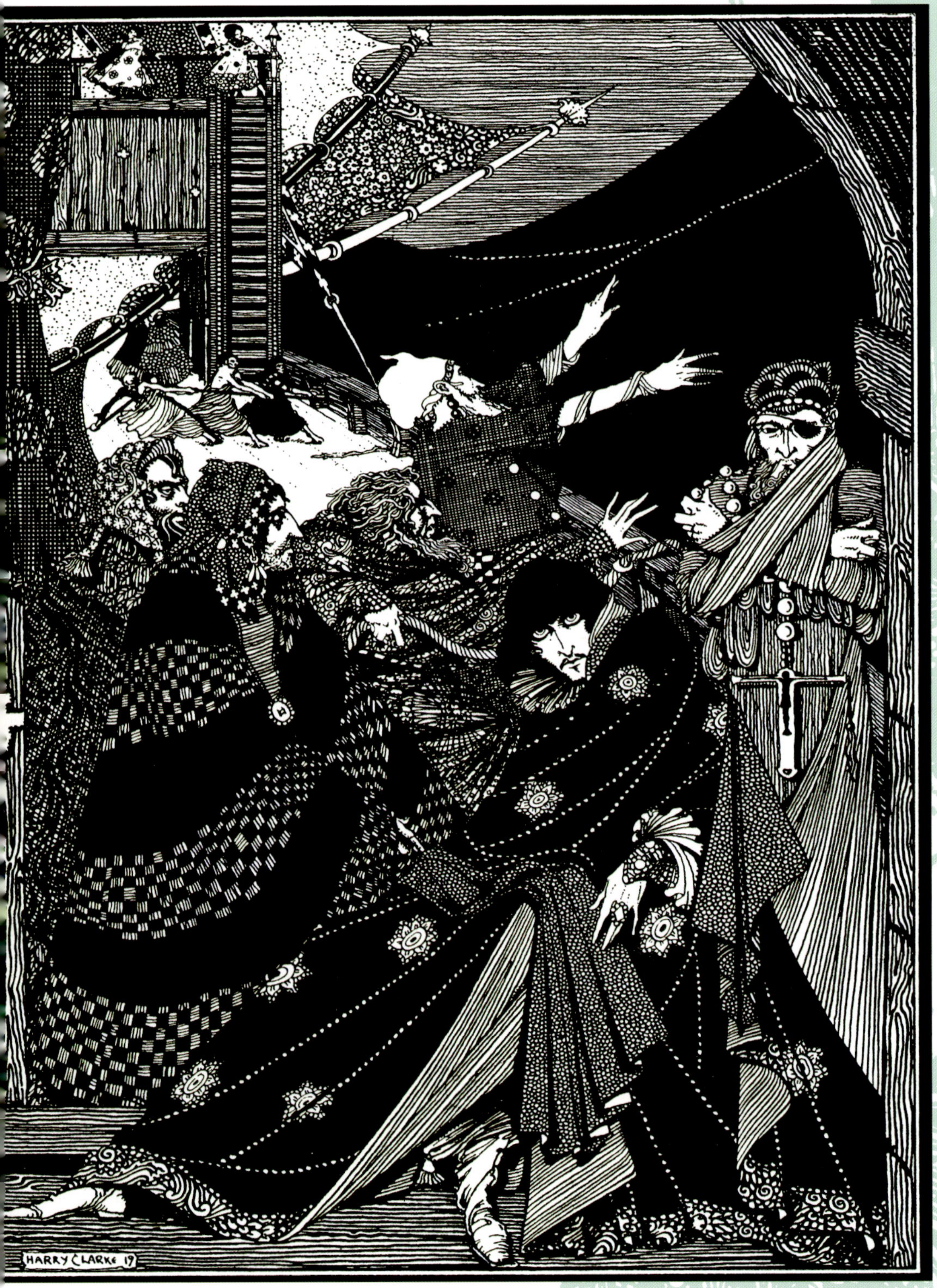

Clarke, Harry

The Destruction of the Rime

Clarke did a large number of drawings for an edition of Coleridge's *Rime of the Ancient Mariner,* predating his work on Andersen's—but most of the work was destroyed in the Easter Uprising of 1916, and it never saw print.

Clarke, c. 1925.

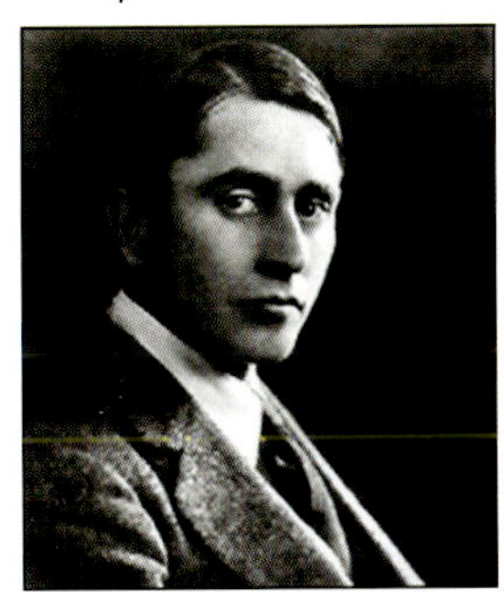

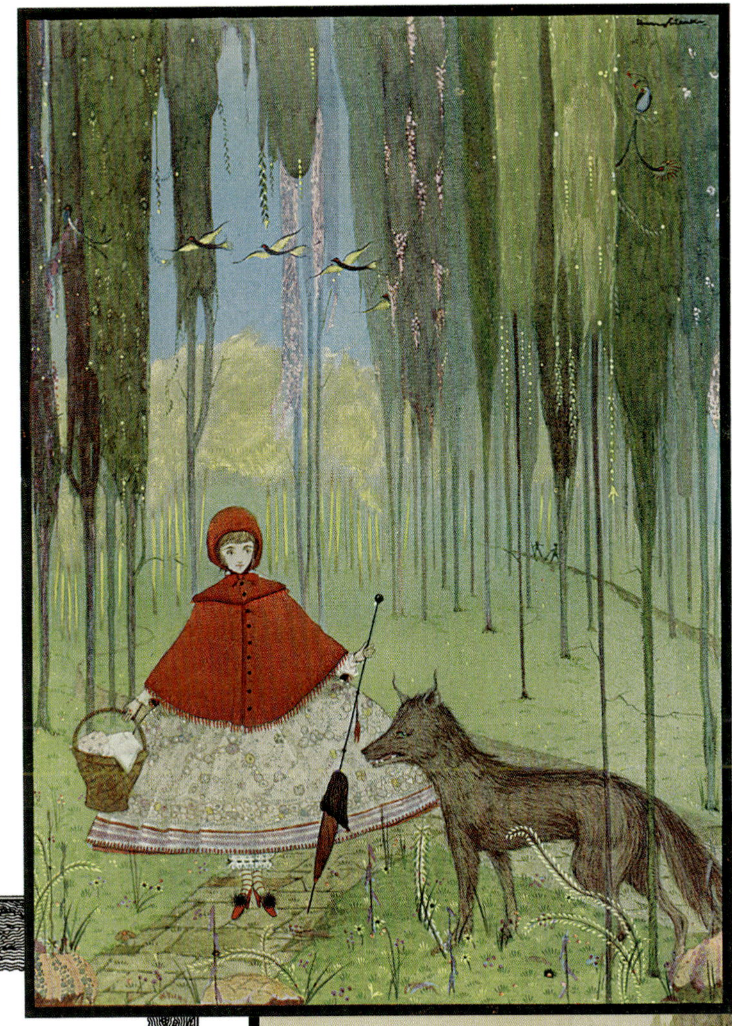

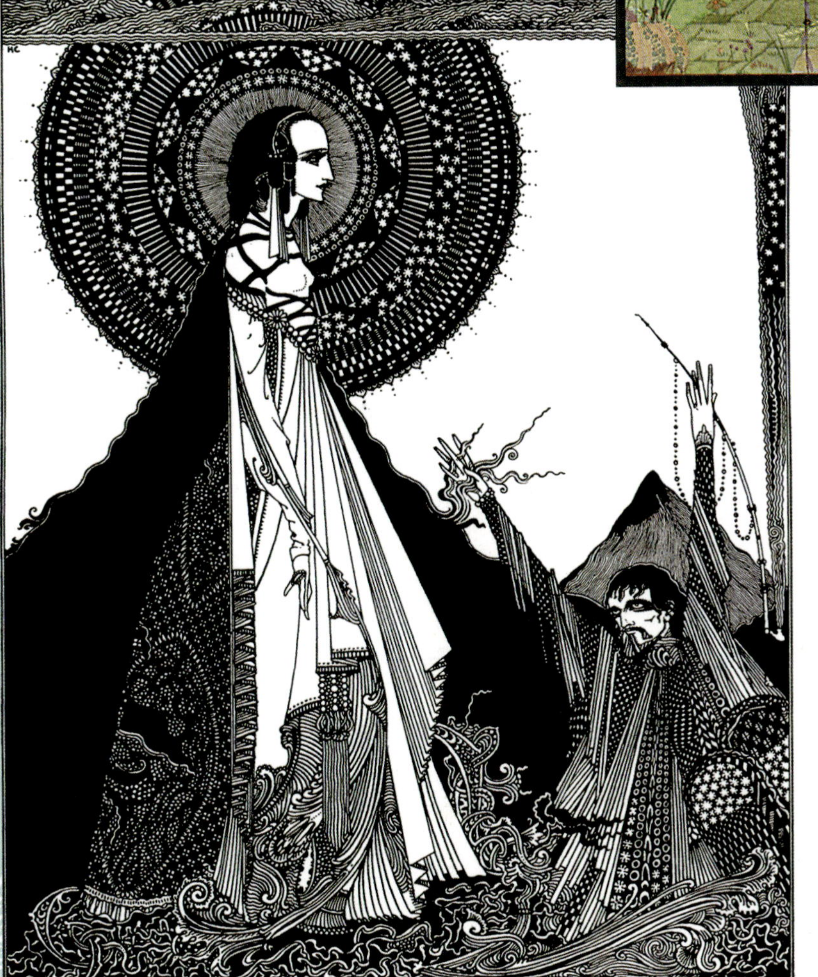

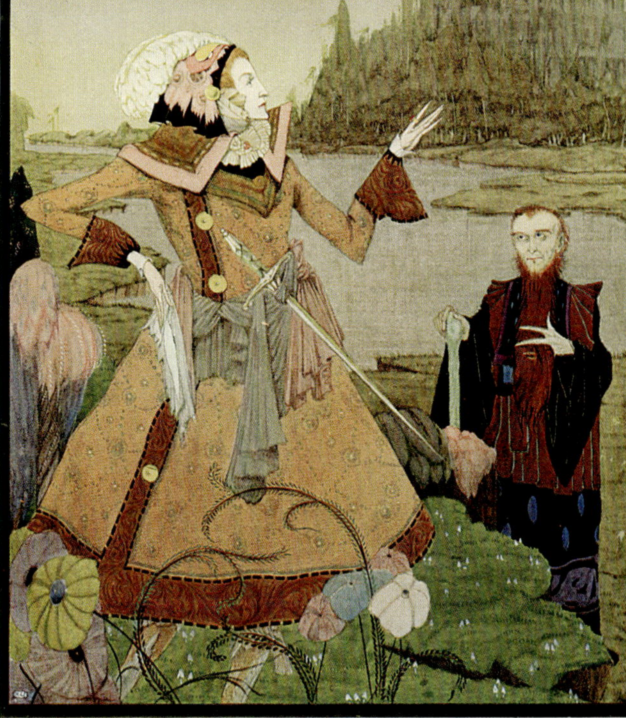

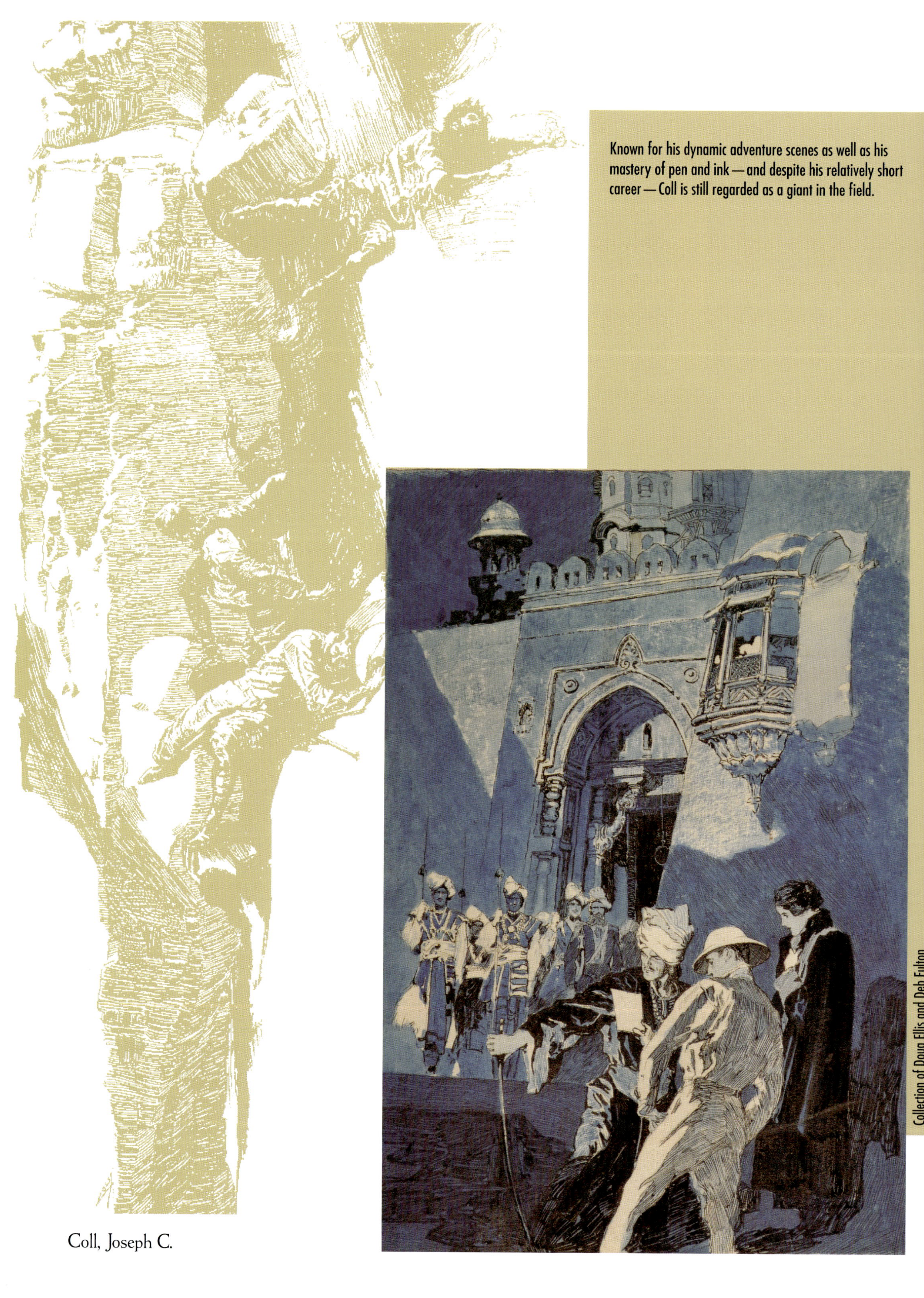

Known for his dynamic adventure scenes as well as his mastery of pen and ink — and despite his relatively short career — Coll is still regarded as a giant in the field.

Collection of Doug Ellis and Deb Fulton

Coll, Joseph C.

Joseph C. Coll

1881–1921, American

There are few artists in this group that have had the success and vision to be included here without the aid of color in their work; Joseph Clement Coll is one of those rarities. With few artists working at his level, he was one of the uncontested masters of ink work, known for bold compositions filled with action, great range of value, and top-notch draftsmanship. He was very influenced by Daniel Vierge's line work from Spain, exploring the black areas as focal points in work, rather than the brighter paper.

Apprenticed in the newspaper business, Coll worked for the *New York American* at age 17, and later for the *Sunday North American,* where his skills as an illustrator were discovered and encouraged. Most of Coll's work was in serialized newspaper stories—few of which have survived to the present—leaving his printed pieces harder to trace than many others of the period. In the last few years of his career, Coll landed work from magazines such as *Collier's* and *Everybody's Magazine.*

His first major assignment was for the *Associated Sunday Magazine,* when he illustrated Sir Arthur Conan Doyle's *Sir Nigel* for several months ending in April of 1906. Sax Rohmer's *The Insidious Dr. Fu Manchu* was a tale associated with Coll's dynamic illustrations for decades after its initial printing. He was known for capturing the spirit of drama and thrilling action in his art, making him a great choice for adventure fiction.

Appendicitis abruptly ended Coll's life in its prime in 1921.

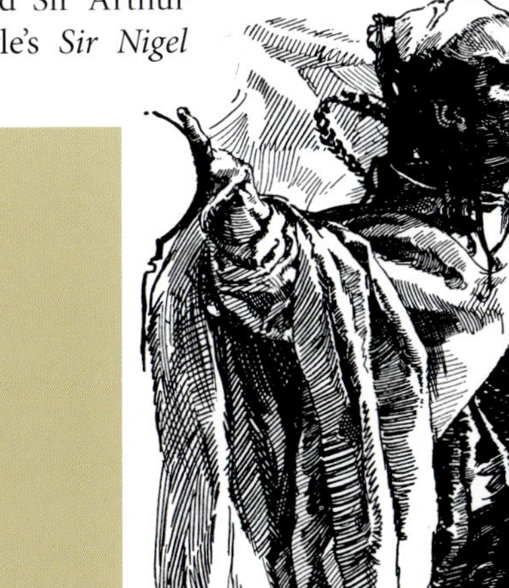

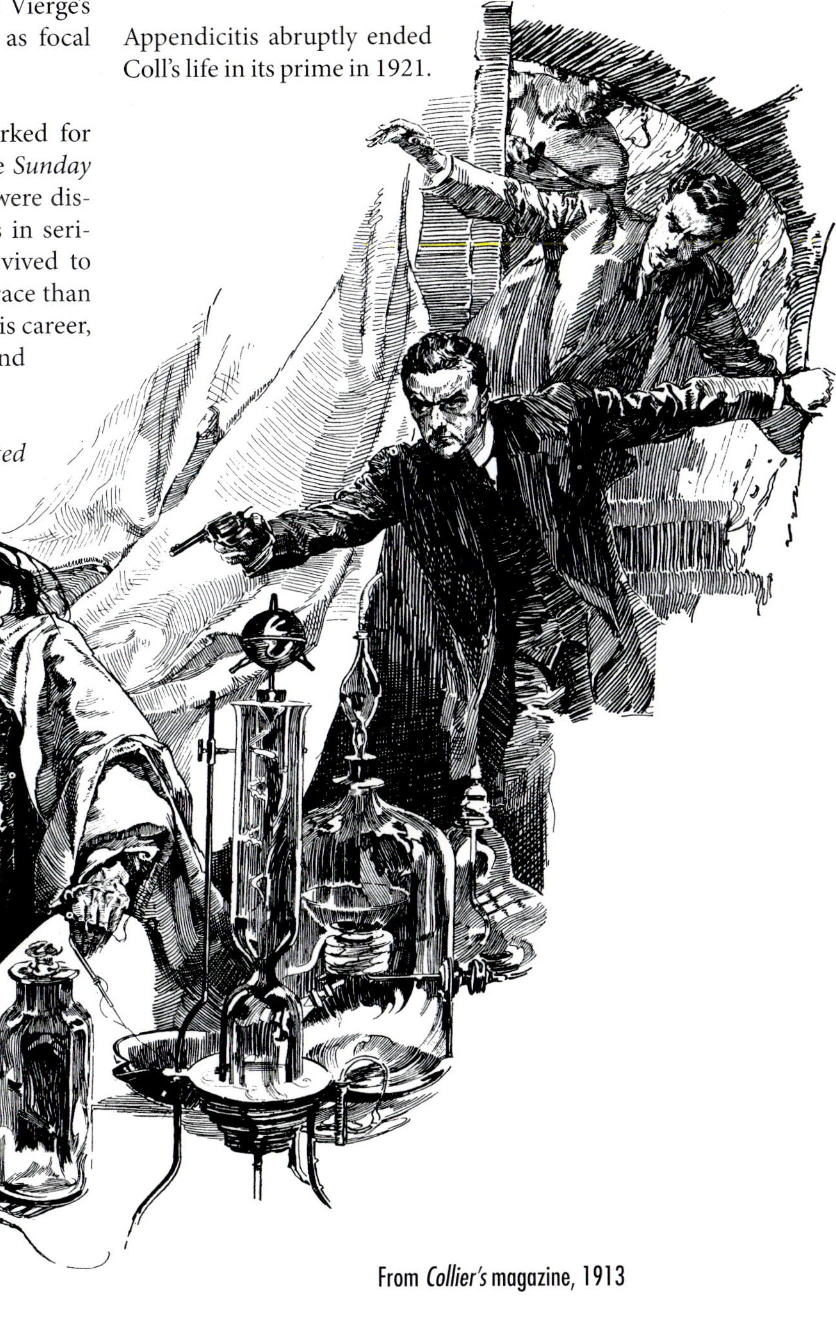

From *Collier's* magazine, 1913

Walter Crane
1845–1915, British

In 1862 the children's book industry in Britain was just beginning to find its way when Walter Crane began sharing his work with the world. Crane had apprenticed as an engraver for several years, but his natural ability to draw and compose didn't go unnoticed by his early employers. He had a special knack for creating imaginative scenes and drawing animals. Taking advantage of this ability, Crane found publishers who were more than willing to have him combine his skills with popular children's tales. In 1863 he was working with Edmund Evans, who would work with Crane for more than a decade, producing dozens of illustrated children's stories, mostly classic tales like *Jack and the Beanstalk* or *Beauty and the Beast.* Published in small, inexpensive, magazine-like formats known as "toy books," Crane's illustrated works were soon in most of the households in England, and grew in popularity. Crane's success in these endeavors gave him credibility for more serious publishing projects, and by 1900 he was lecturing as well as writing books on design and decoration. Later in his career Crane worked with noted designer William Morris to produce books that echoed the style of the late Renaissance, like his work on *The Story of the Glittering Plain,* Shakespearean subjects, and classic tales from ancient Greece.

Crane continued to work on books throughout his career, though his work grew more diverse. He also lent his illustration and design skills to political movements he supported, and to "practical" products like wallpaper or applied decoration. He presented work in gallery settings, and was fairly successful with it, unlike most other illustrator-painters. His painting *Neptune and his Horses* (1892) is considered an important piece of the period, along with many of the works of Crane's Pre-Raphaelite friends.

Crane had a great influence on the generation of illustrators that would immediately follow him, and much of his work remains in print today, still finding appreciative audiences.

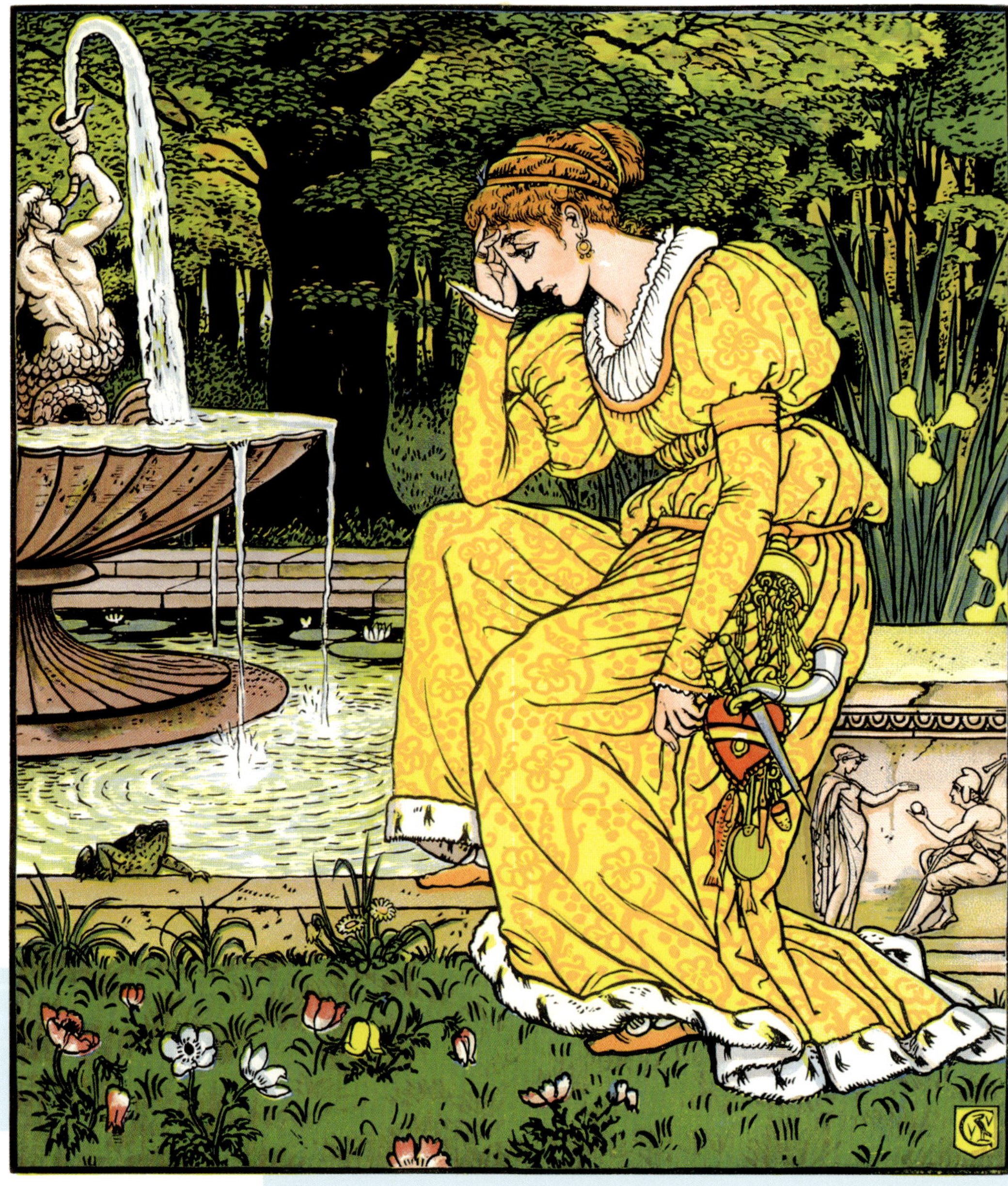

The Princess and the Frog, 1874

Crane, Walter

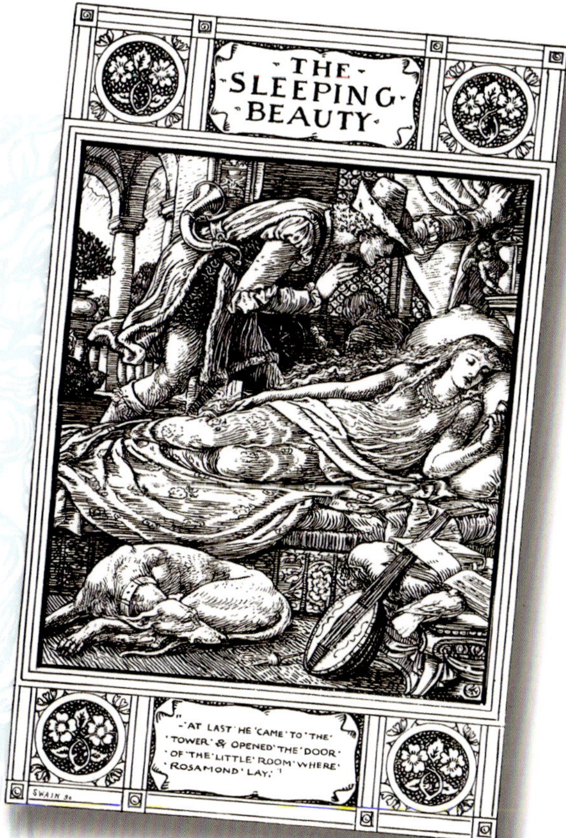

Crane's work spanned all the early eras of Golden-Age image reproduction, from wood-block engravings to multi-color blocks to full-color process reproductions.

Primarily remembered as an illustrator, Crane created decoration designs for wallpapers, tapestry, and ceramics—and also achieved success in gallery work.

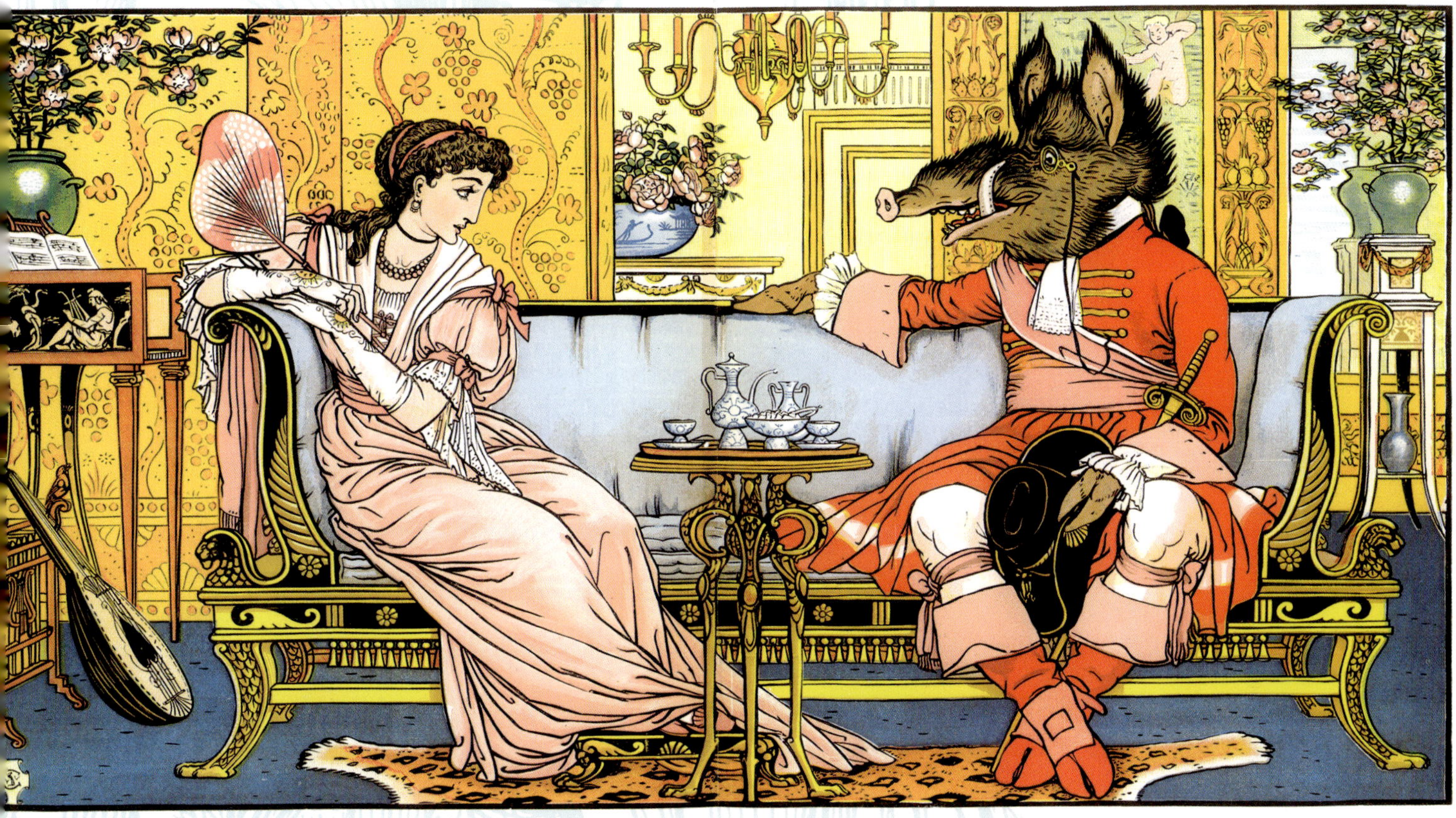

Beauty and the Beast, 1875

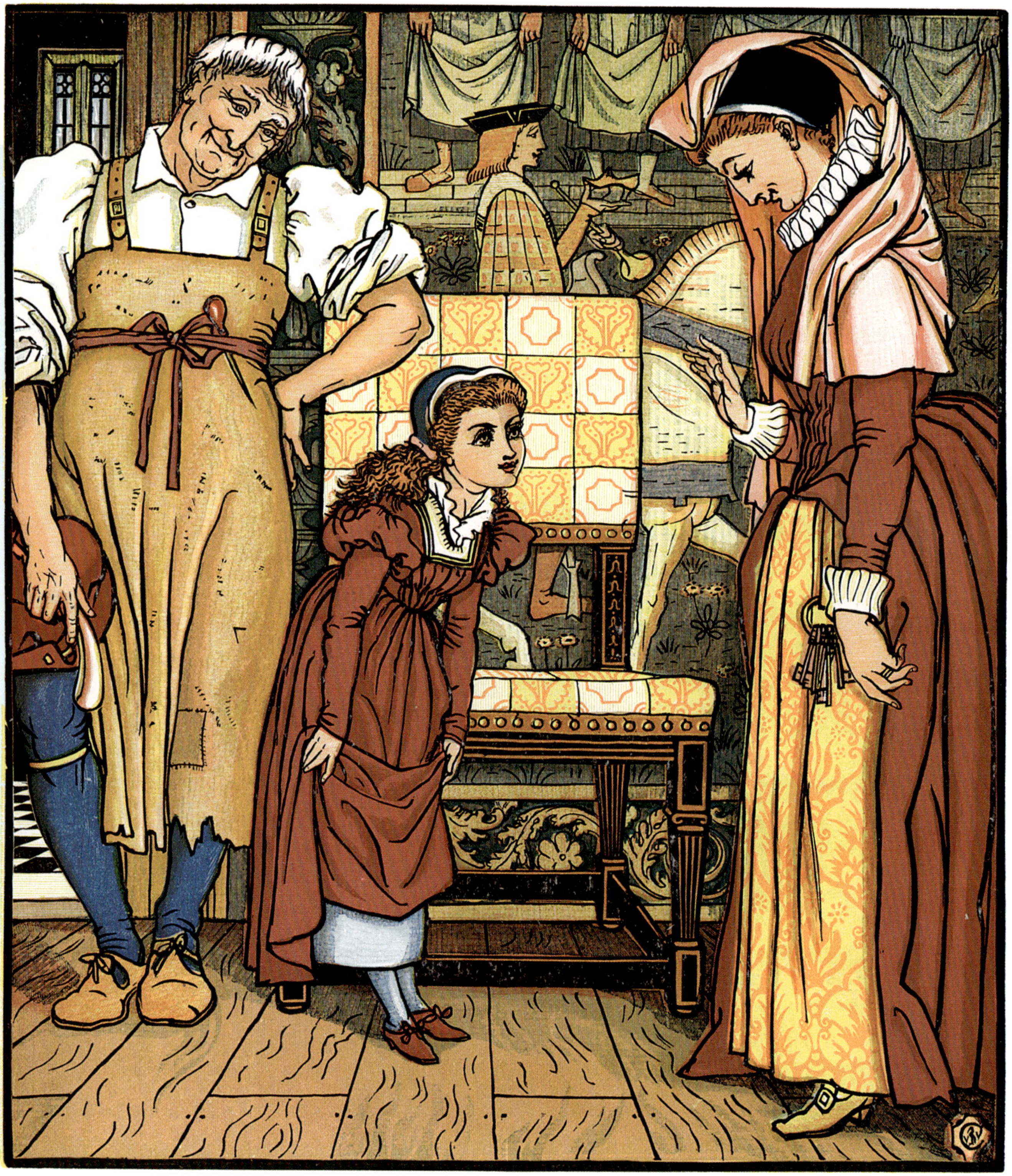

Little Goody Two Shoes, 1874

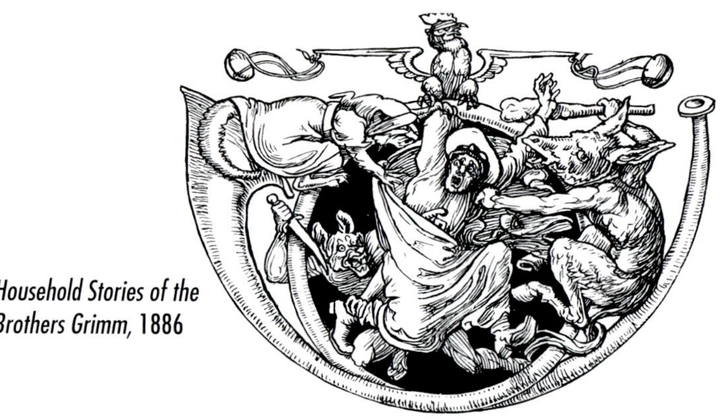

Household Stories of the Brothers Grimm, 1886

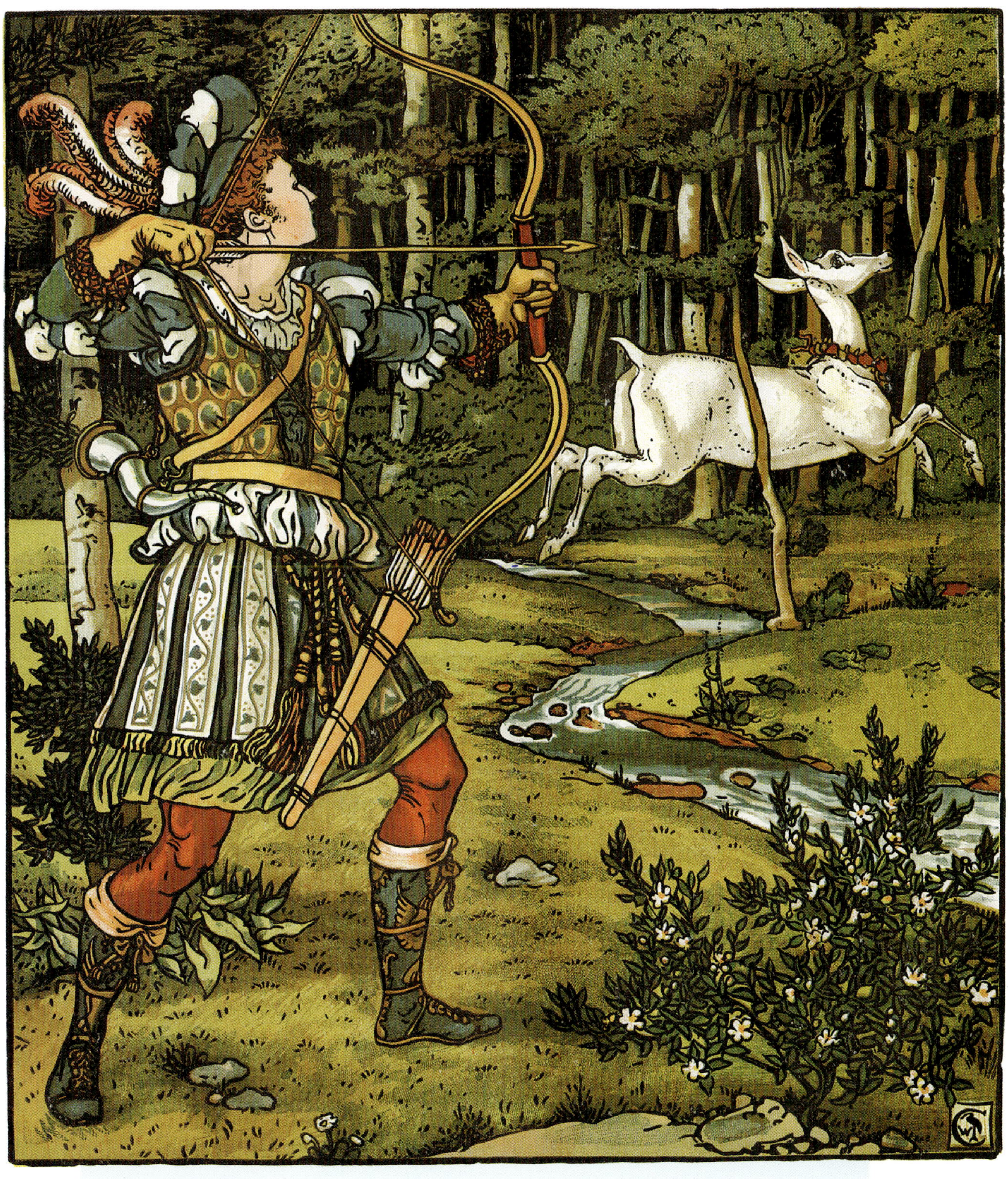

The Hind in the Wood, 1875

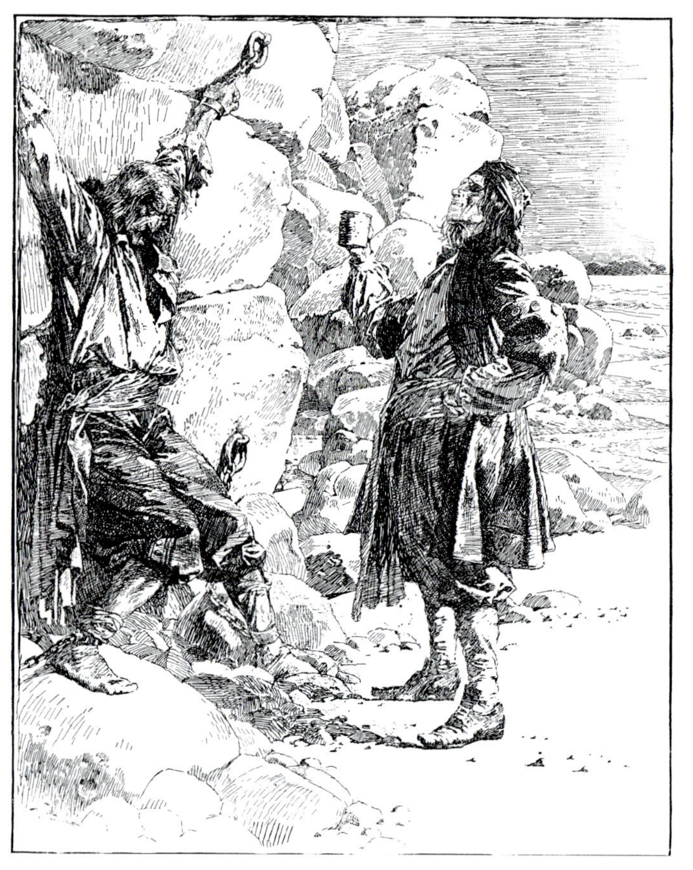

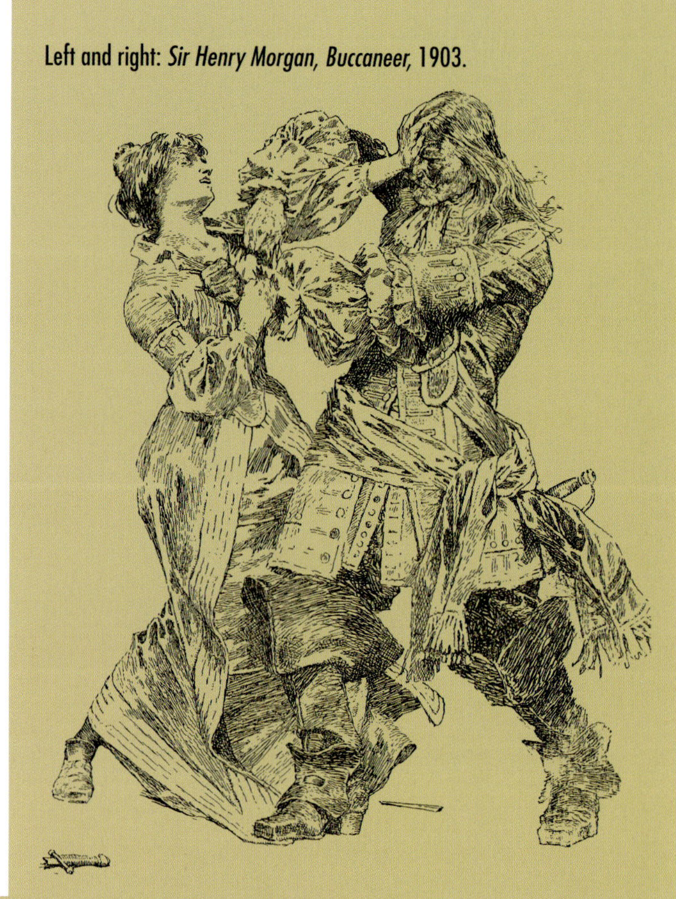

Left and right: *Sir Henry Morgan, Buccaneer,* 1903.

"…the best pen-and-ink artist in America."

—Charles M. Russell, speaking of his friend William Crawford

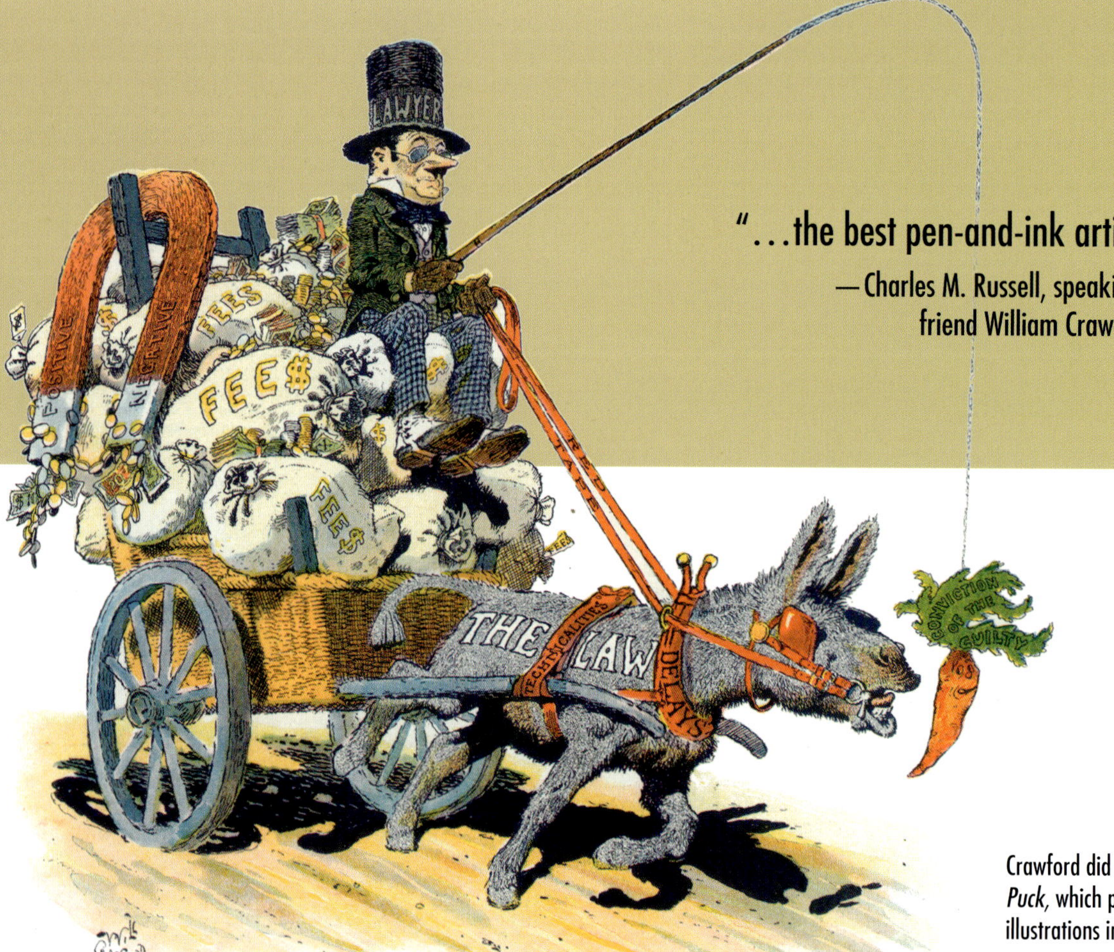

Crawford did a lot of political comic work for *Puck,* which printed many of its cartoons and illustrations in full color.

Crawford, Will

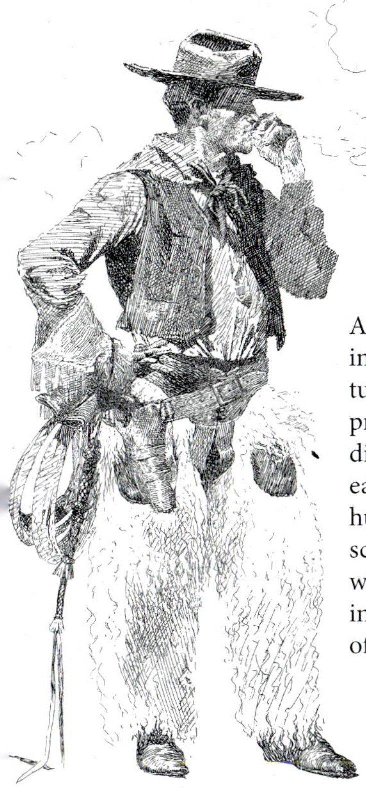

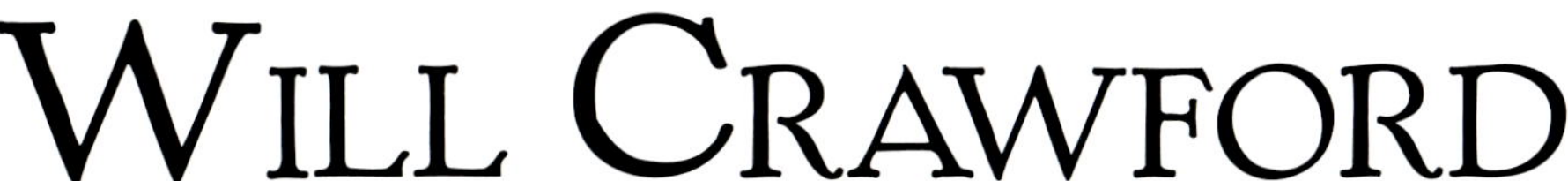

Will Crawford

1869–1944, American

Another amazing ink artist working during the twentieth century when line in print was so prevalent, Will Crawford had two distinct looks to his work. His earlier art brought out Crawford's humor—he enjoyed complex scenes that poked fun at history, which made his images popular in many papers and magazines of the day; *Life, Puck, Munsey's Magazine,* and *St. Nicholas* were all regular clients in his career. His more serious work was masterful in its value rendering, with Crawford relying only on the build-up of fine lines to produce his darker shadows. He wove a complex web of ink to attain a full-range work. Crawford was born in Washington, D.C., and spent time during his teen years working for Newark, N.J., newspapers. After moving to New York City, he added many of the papers and magazines there to his client list. An interest in the American West sent Crawford and John Marchand, his studio partner, there for research and relaxation in 1902. It was on this trip that the two struck up a friendship with the Western artist Charles M. Russell. The West had a lasting effect on Crawford, and Crawford's work and business acumen benefited Russell as well. The two remained friends for many years.

In 1914 Crawford moved from New York to New Jersey, and in the following years took fewer newspaper assignments, choosing more work in books. Less frantic deadlines and an opportunity to explore a more mature style suited him as he set himself up in a more relaxed community, in what was then considered "the country."

Despite a desire to lead a life more in tune with nature, his historic expertise led him to work in Hollywood late in his career. In 1939, at age 70, Crawford journeyed West again, to lend his eye and mind to the movie-making industry. However, Hollywood's tendency to bend facts to suit its needs didn't agree with Crawford, and after just a few years, and in failing health, Crawford returned to New Jersey. He died in 1944.

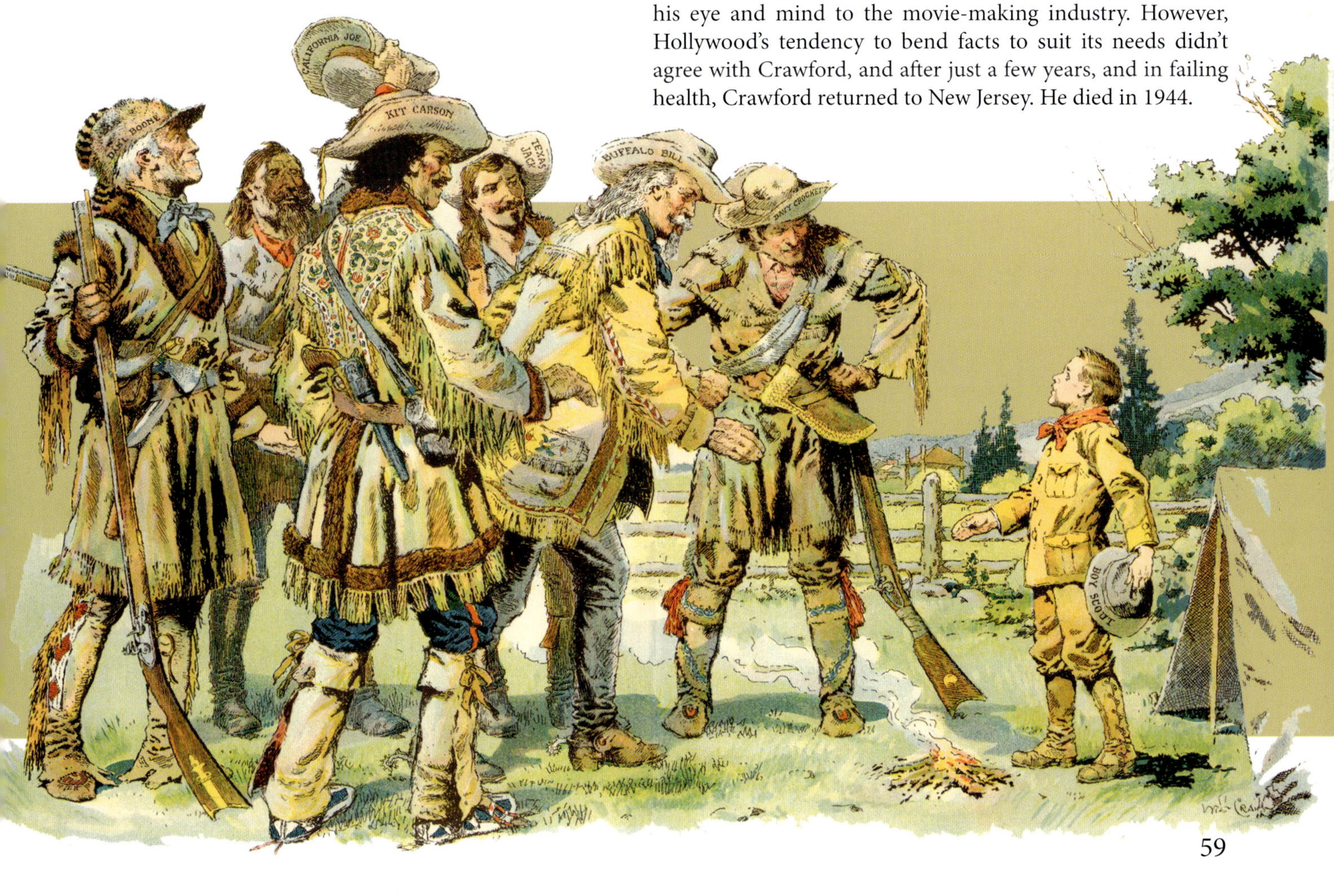

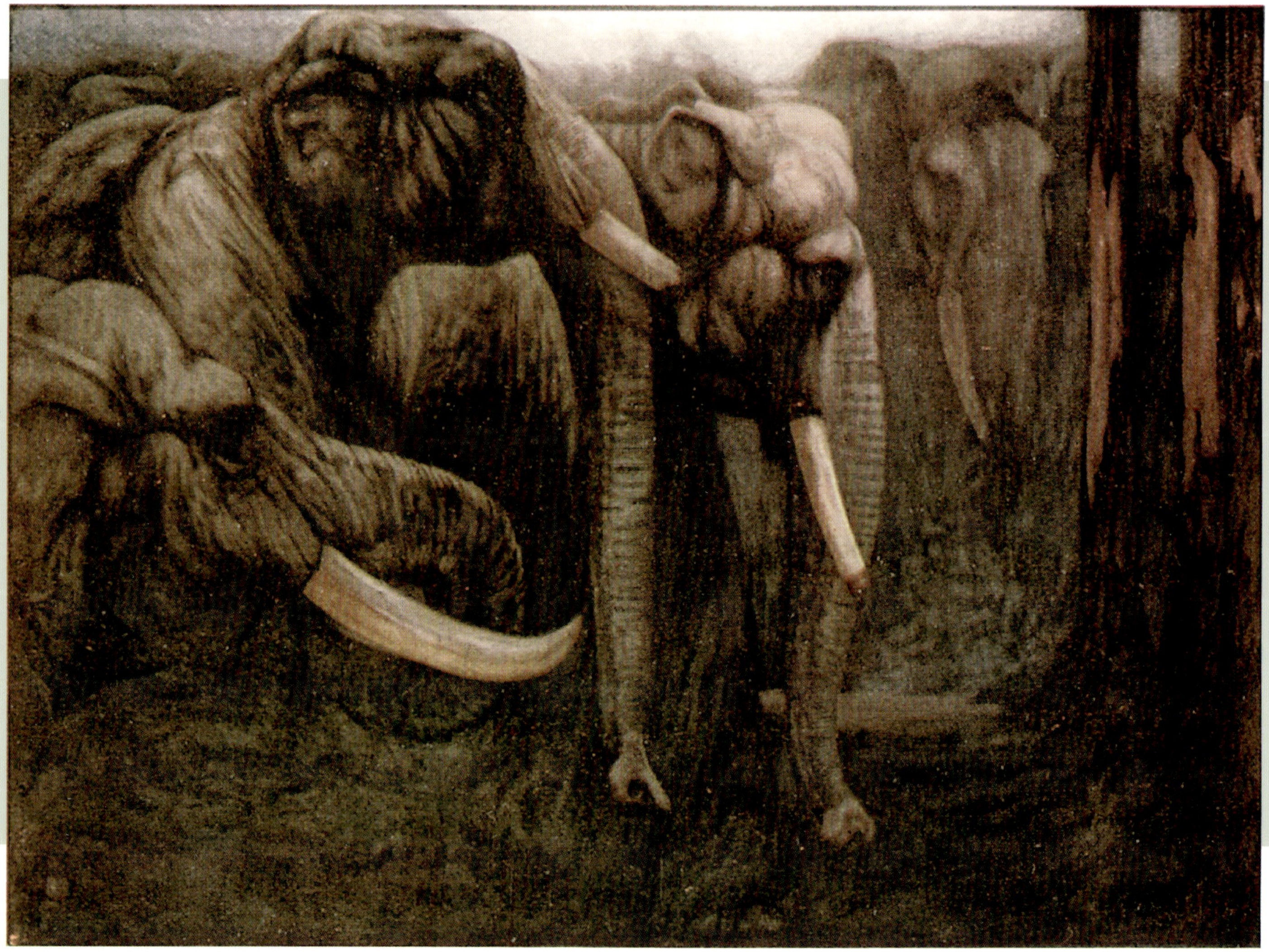

From Kipling's *The Jungle Book,* 1908, the last project the two brothers would work on together.

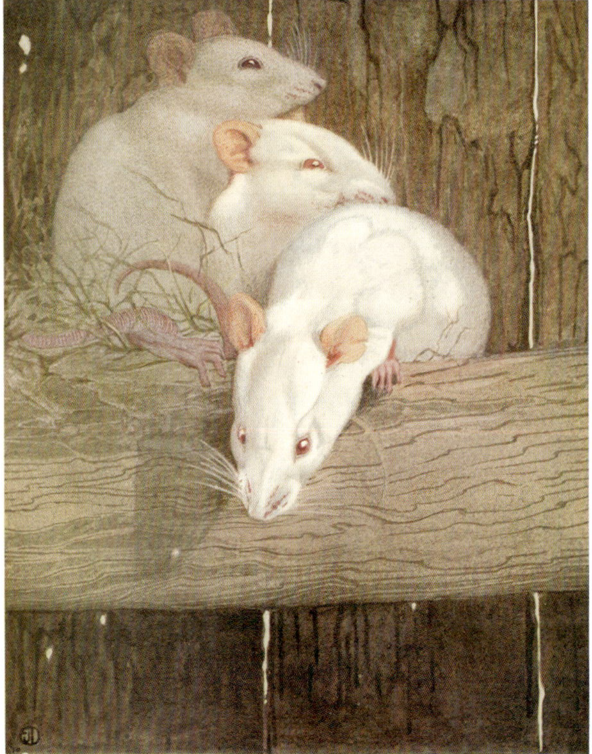

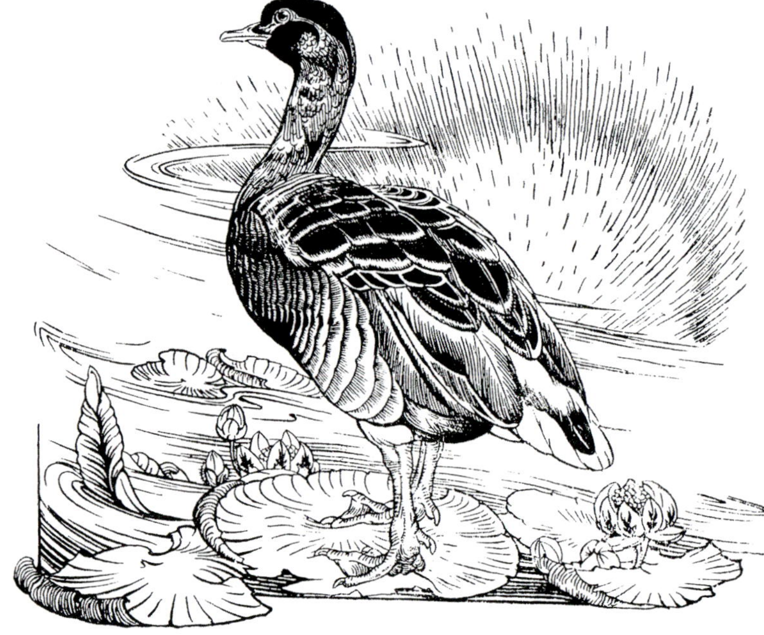

The Rat, from *The Book of Baby Beasts,* 1911.

Edward Detmold

1883–1957, British

At a very early age, the Detmold twins, Edward and Maurice, were inspired by the animals around them. An uncle used to bring them frequently to the London Zoo and the Natural Science Museum, where they would study the structure and movements of the animals. Their first book, *Pictures from Birdland* (1899), was more of a solid study of ornithology than a storybook, despite the fact that the artists were both in their teens when it was produced. The book used a limited form of color reproduction which, coupled with the influence of Art Nouveau posters that the boys admired, gave the images a strong graphic quality to complement the innovative designs.

With this success, the pair was asked to do artwork for Kipling's *Jungle Book,* and it looked as if the future was bright for the twins; plans were made to pursue other projects. But tragedy struck with Maurice's untimely (and somewhat mysterious) death in 1908. The loss was a severe one for Edward, who eventually proceeded with artistic work, but he grieved over the loss of his brother and artistic partner for the rest of his life.

Edward's work continued to focus on animals as a specialty, but ranged from the graphic designs of *Pictures from Birdland* to the near biological studies in *The Jungle Book, Aesop's Fables,* and *Fabre's Book of Insects.* A softer, more juvenile look was used for volumes of work on baby animals. Although designed for different audiences, all of the books required a deep knowledge of the animal world, and a scholarly understanding of anatomy.

In later years Detmold separated himself from publishing, and by the late 1920s he was leading a reclusive, retired life with his widowed sister in Montgomeryshire. After his eyesight began to fail, the depression it caused drove Edward to take his own life in 1957.

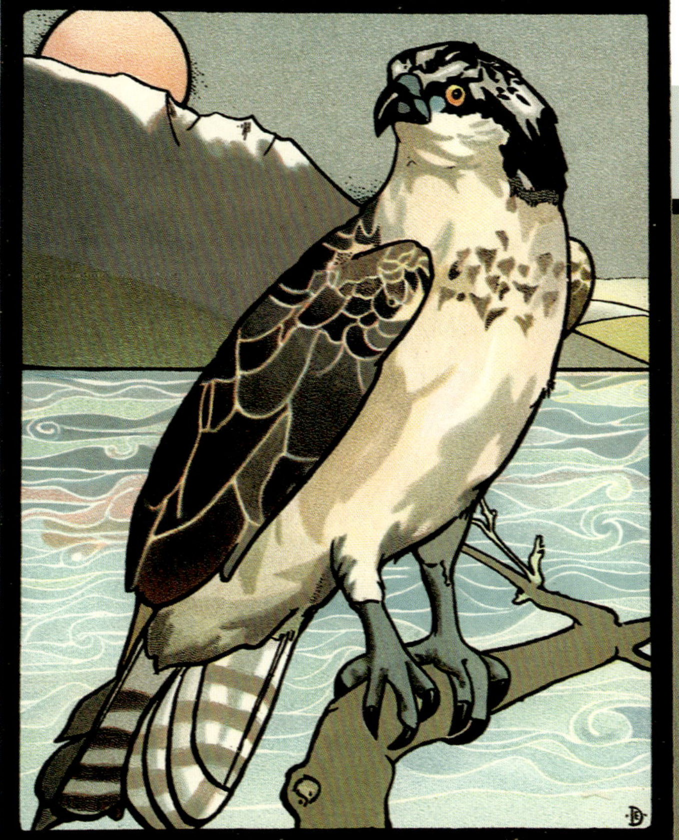

Produced when he was a teenager, *Pictures from Birdland* was a hint of the successful career that was to follow.

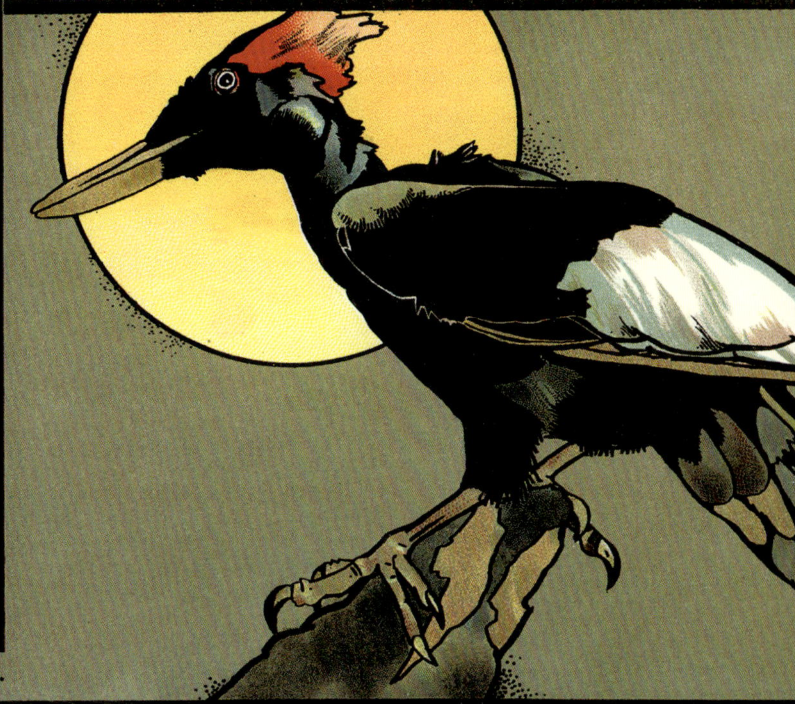

Edmund Dulac

1882–1953, French

Originally from the mountainous area between France and Germany, Edmund Dulac revisited those surroundings in the settings of the fairy tales he illustrated early in his career.

After some schooling in Paris, and after considering a law career, Dulac followed his more creative interests across the Channel to England, where some of the biggest book publishers in Europe were eagerly looking for talents such as his. It was England that won his heart—and in 1905, with a bright future in book illustration in front of him, he was hired by one of England's largest publishers, Hodder & Stoughton. By the age of 30, he had become a British citizen.

Influenced greatly by an early exposure to Eastern art, Dulac had a subtle edge in his work; and at the height of the British Empire, there was no shortage of Eastern subjects appealing to English-speaking audiences. Some of the books Dulac took on for his publisher included *The Rubáiyát of Omar Khayyám, The Arabian Nights,* and *Sinbad the Sailor*—all of which fed Dulac's interest in the exotic East. Earlier works were much in line with illustrators of the day, though Dulac's work was noted for his exceptional use of color. Later in his career, his work often reflected many of the characteristics of the Asian sources he used, both in style and color schemes.

From his entry into the market in 1905, and for the next two decades, Dulac's work in illustrating books was steady, and he sometimes completed multiple large projects in the same year. His works were called "jewel-like," his design sense delicate and refined, and Dulac was noted for the brilliant color that he used in his work. Most would conclude he was second only to Arthur Rackham in popularity during the gift-book era, though for many, Dulac was the foremost choice.

When book production began to cool in the 1920s, Dulac's career efforts became less visible. Dulac became an expert with engraved representation, creating designs for currency and stamps for many different European nations, including his native France and his adopted England. Occasionally, magazines like *American Weekly* and England's *Country Life* would carry his color work. A few book assignments came to him late in life, from the Limited Editions Club in New York. He died in 1953; his unfinished work on Milton's *The Masque of Comus* was published as his last commission in 1954.

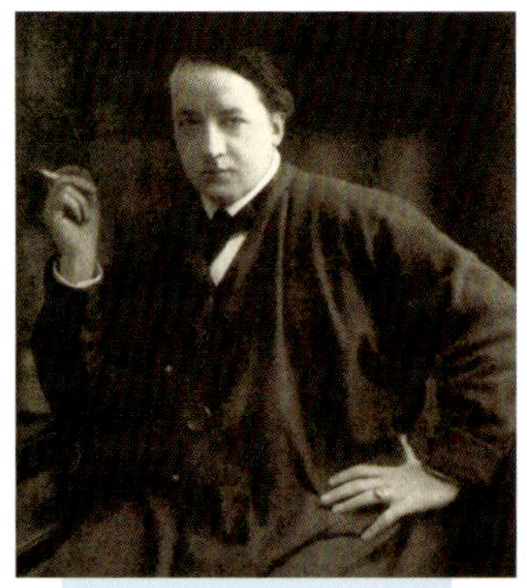

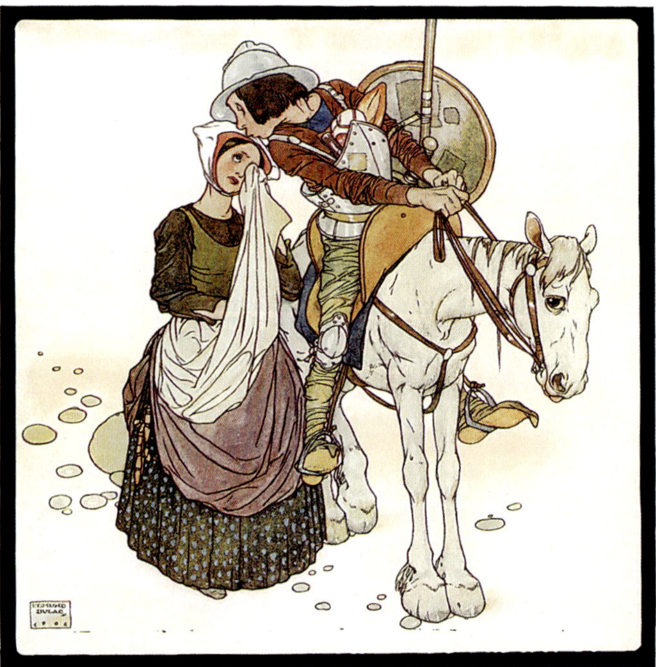

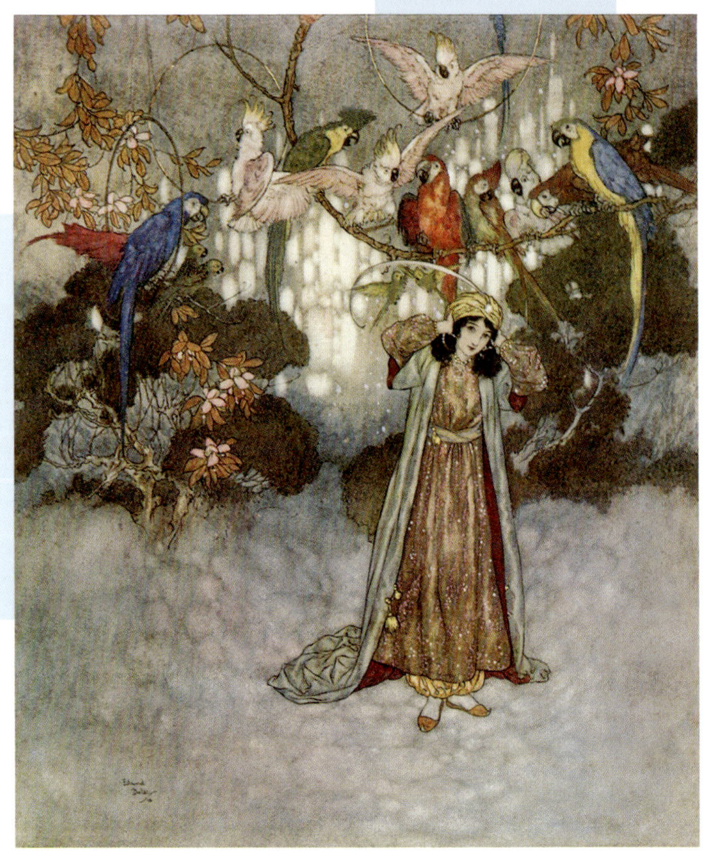

Dulac, Edmund

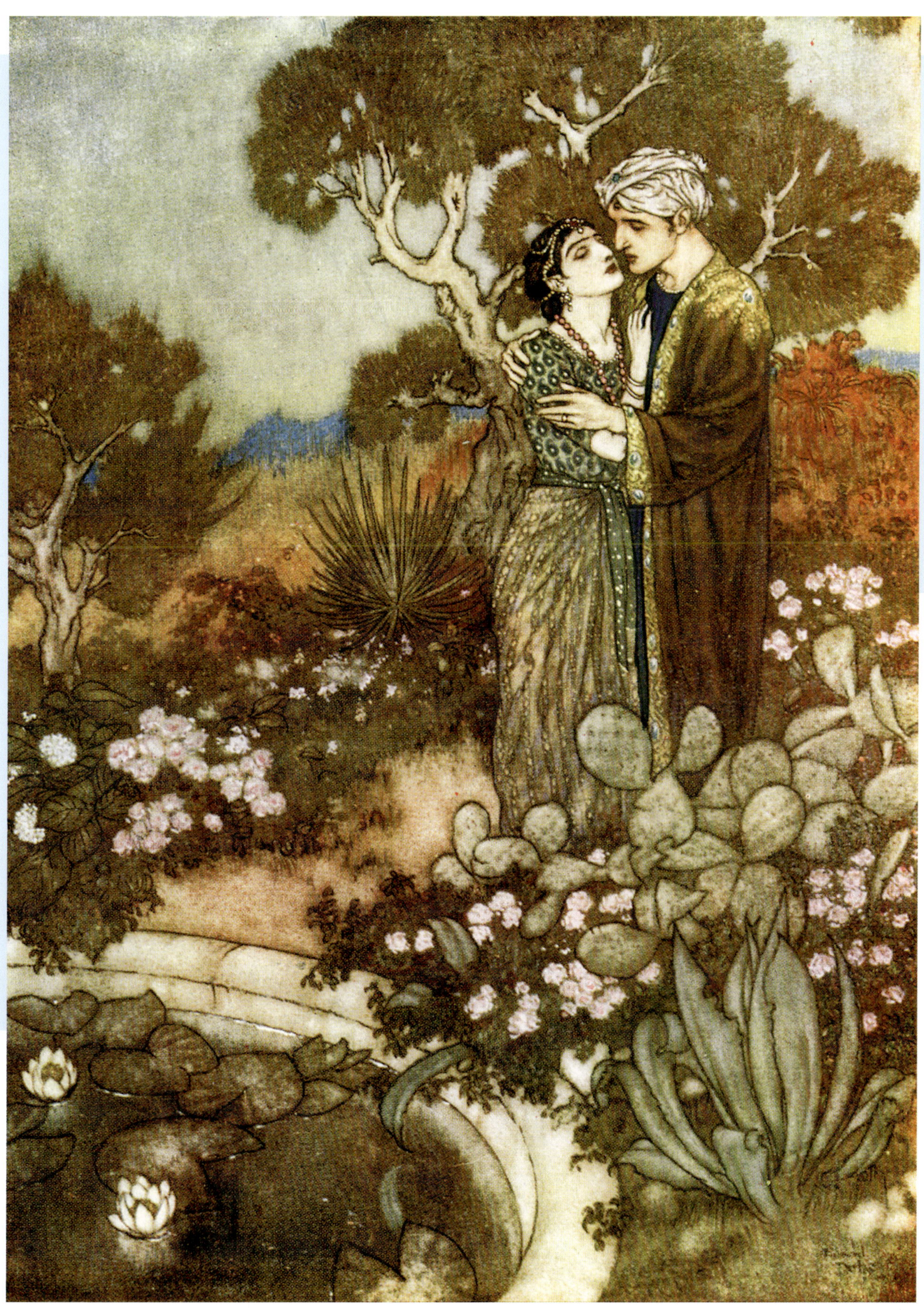

Dulac returned again and again to images with Eastern influence; his rich decorative style coupled with his full-spectrum color sense made him a natural choice for multiple editions of *The Rubáiyát of Omar Khayyám*. This image is from the 1909 edition.

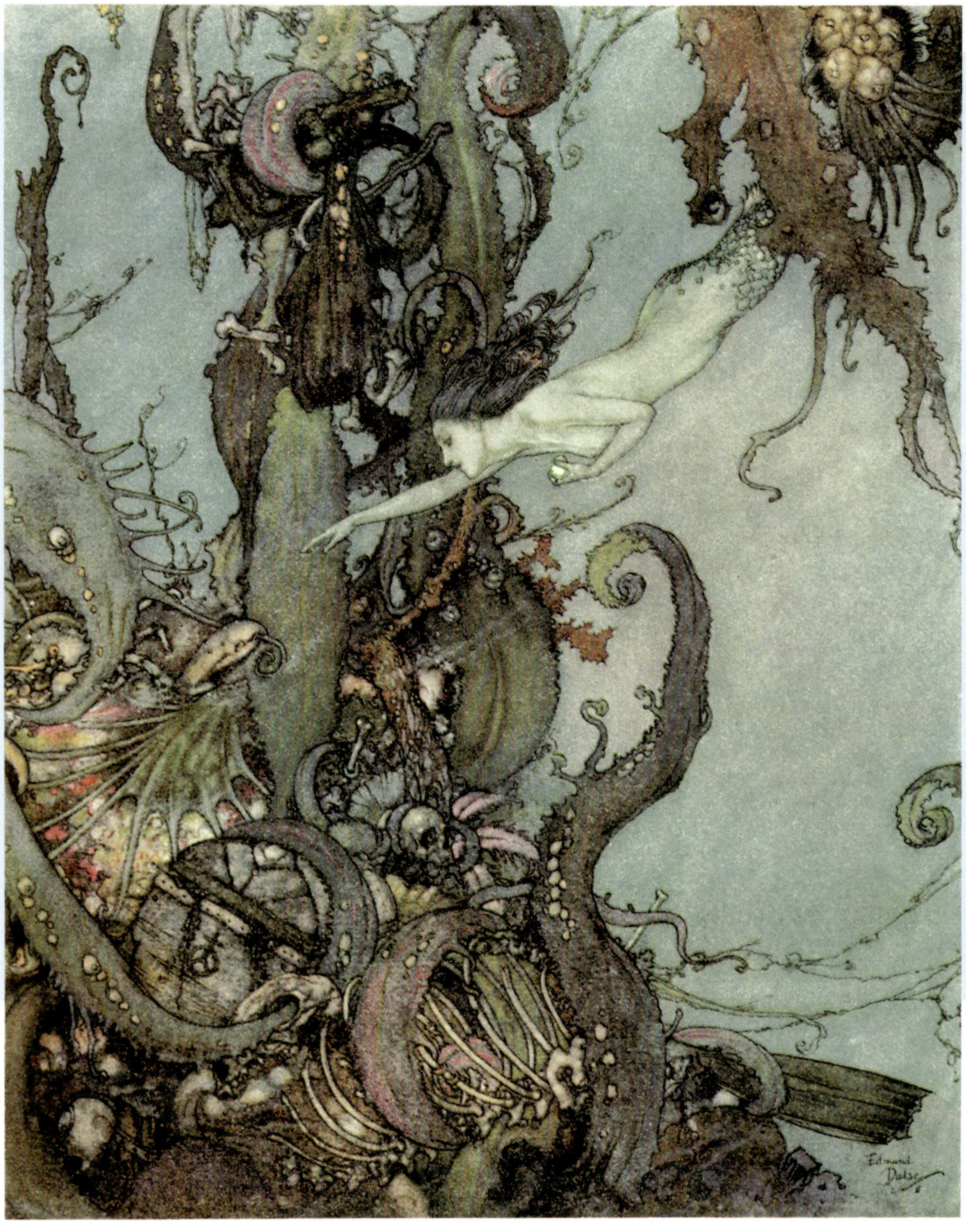

The "little mermaid" from Hans Christian Andersen's tales has rarely seen such an elegant treatment.

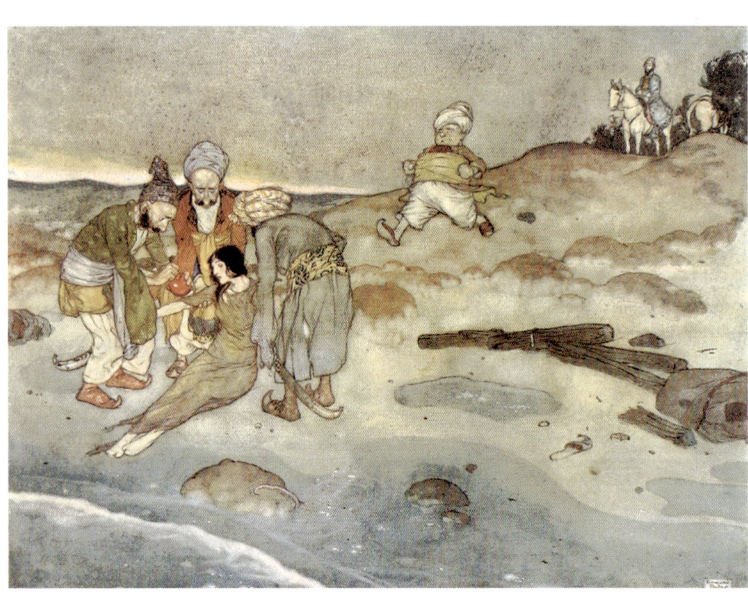

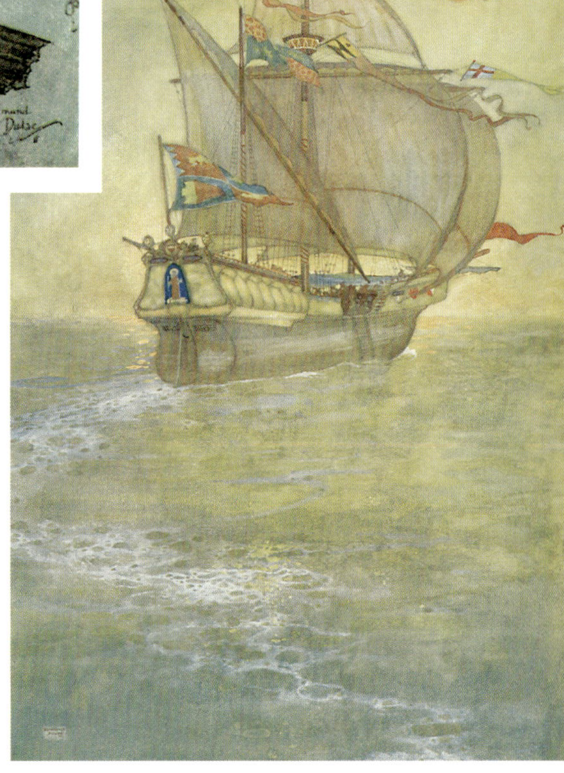

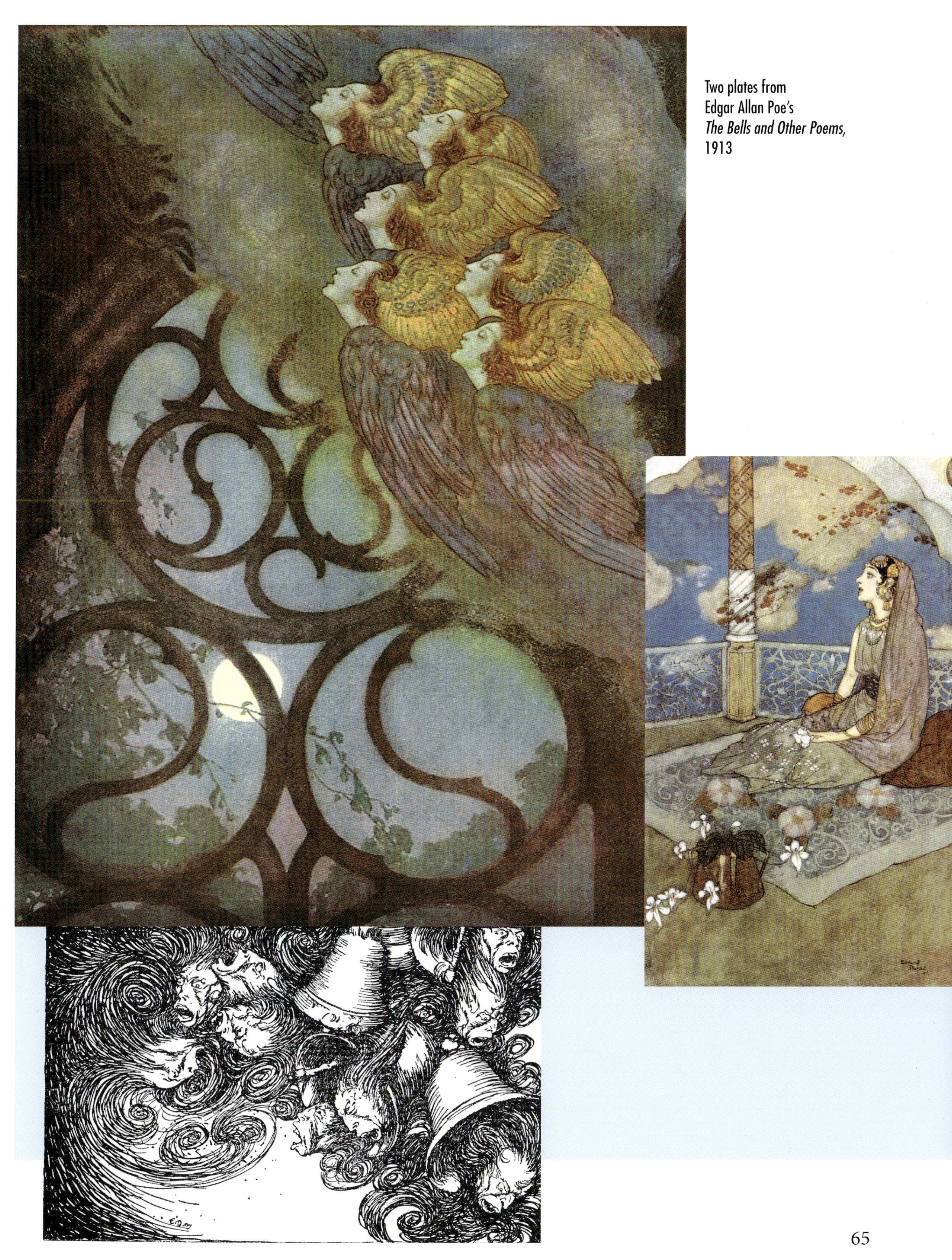

Two plates from
Edgar Allan Poe's
The Bells and Other Poems,
1913

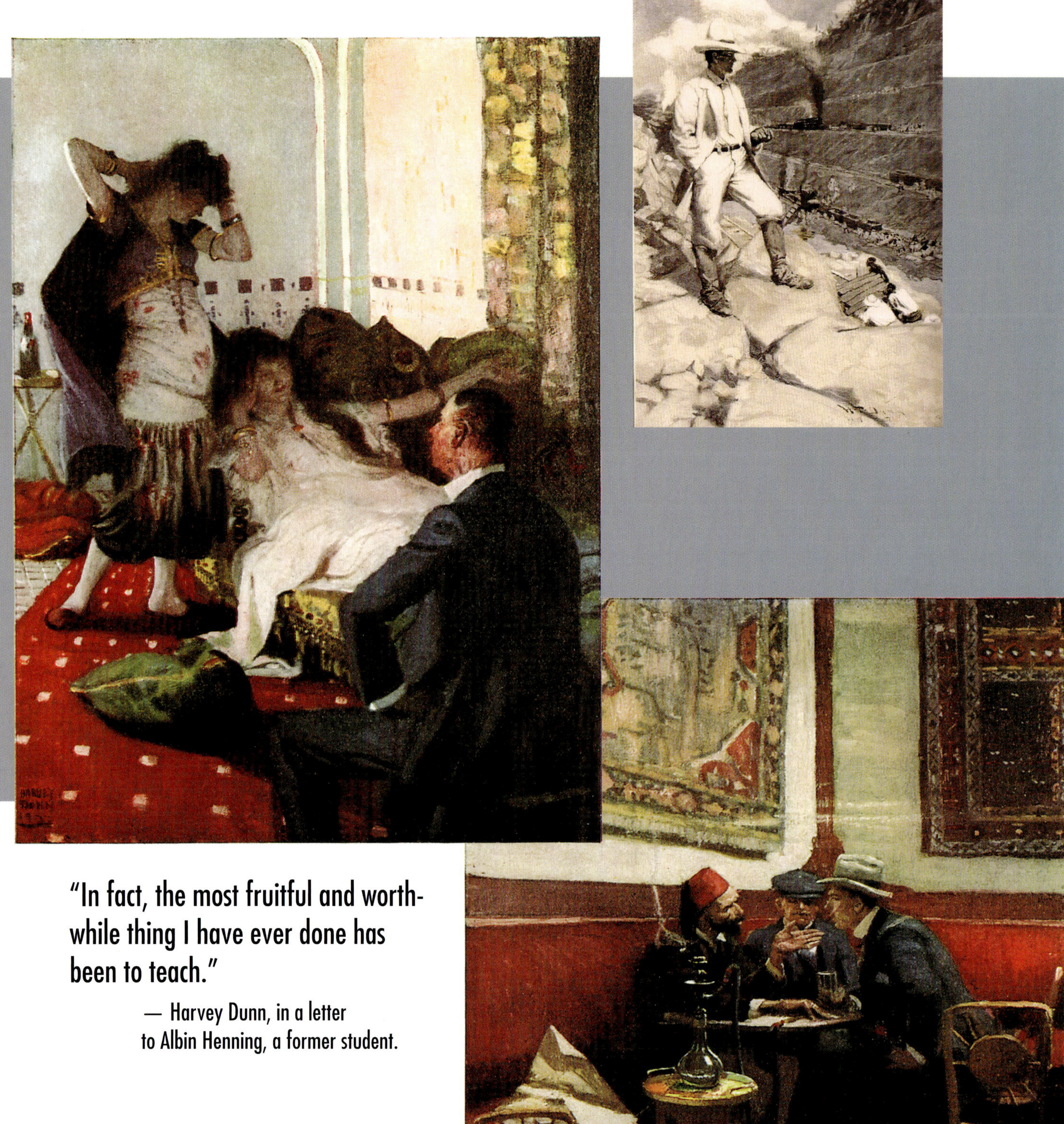

"In fact, the most fruitful and worth-while thing I have ever done has been to teach."

— Harvey Dunn, in a letter to Albin Henning, a former student.

Harvey Dunn
1884–1952, American

This Brandywine student traveled far to attend Howard Pyle's teachings in Delaware. Like many of his fellow alumni, his roots gave his work distinction and shaped his success—part of Pyle's "paint what you know" teaching. Dunn was born on a working farm in the plains of South Dakota. Being raised in such a sparse environment did not stunt his creativity; in fact, it fired his imagination for the world outside.

Dunn first attended a South Dakota prep school, where an art teacher recognized his abilities and directed him toward the Art Institute of Chicago. While Dunn was a student there in 1904, Howard Pyle presented a lecture that greatly influenced him. Soon after, Dunn was on his way to Wilmington to join Pyle's school, where he studied under him for nearly two years before Pyle encouraged him to set up his own studio.

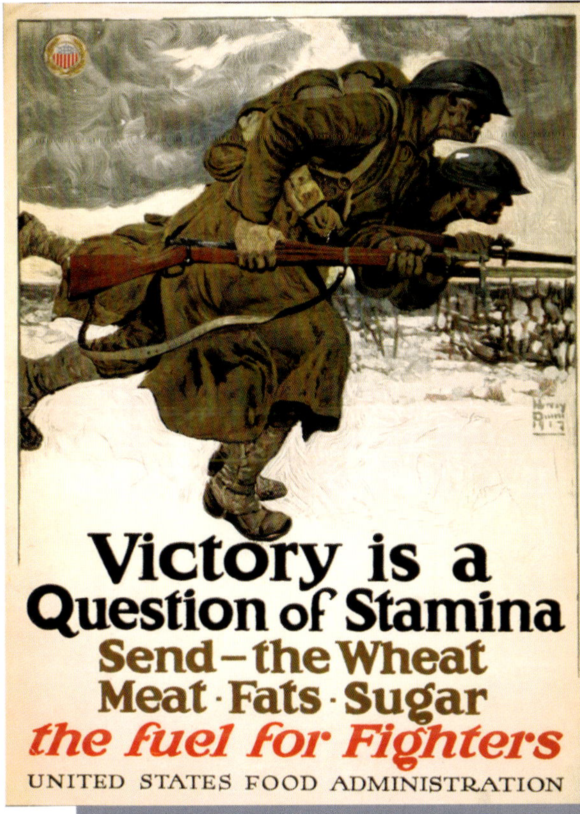

Dunn saw and lived the action firsthand as an official U.S. Army artist in World War I.

Early years brought assignments from clients such as *Outing, The Saturday Evening Post, Scribner's,* and *Harper's Monthly.* Dunn married Tulla Krebs in 1908, and N. C. Wyeth was his best man. Dunn began teaching while in New Jersey, opening the Leonia School of Illustration in 1914 with a great deal of inspiration from his time with Pyle. But the partnership he established to get it rolling proved difficult, and the school did not last. The year 1918 found Dunn contributing to the war effort as a war artist, traveling with active units and sketching on location. This had a deep and lasting impact on Dunn and his work for some time afterward. On his return to New Jersey, he went back to teaching as well as maintaining a steady output as an illustrator. In the years that followed, Dunn's teachings impacted a number of students who went on to become great illustrators in the next generation: Dean Cornwell, Saul Tepper, and Harold Von Schmidt, to name a few.

His teaching continued into his later years, at the Grand Central School of Art (which held classes in New York's Grand Central Station), the Art Students League, and from his own studio. After 1927 Dunn revisited the West annually, to recharge his artistic battery. He always returned with fresh ideas and renewed strength that affected his imagery. His later paintings frequently featured the West and the imagery of his youth on the plains. As Dunn turned more to easel painting in his twilight years, his devotion to illustration was still strong. He was also the president of the Society of Illustrators from 1948–1949.

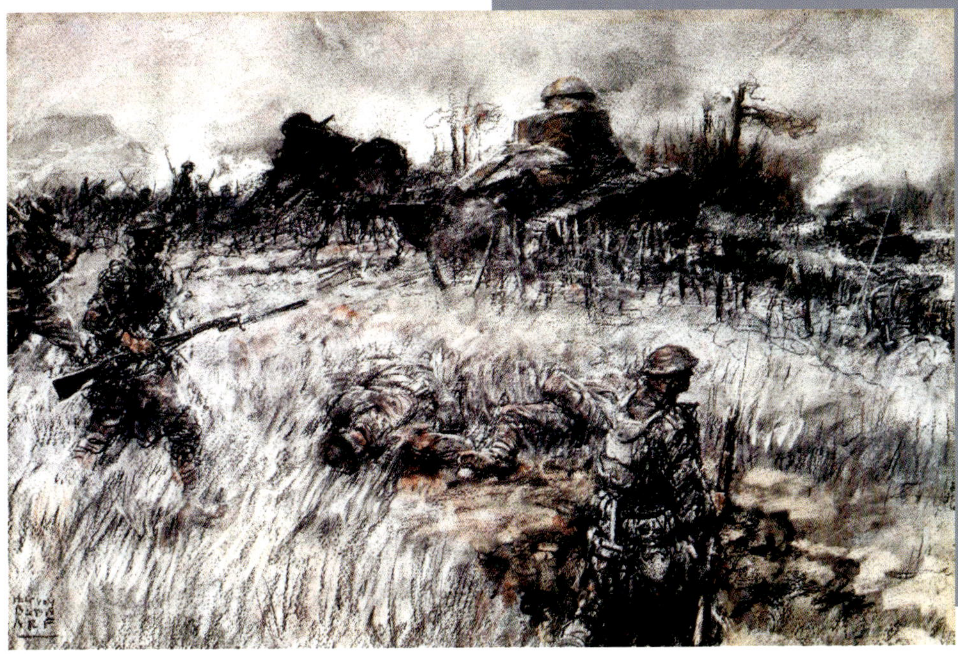

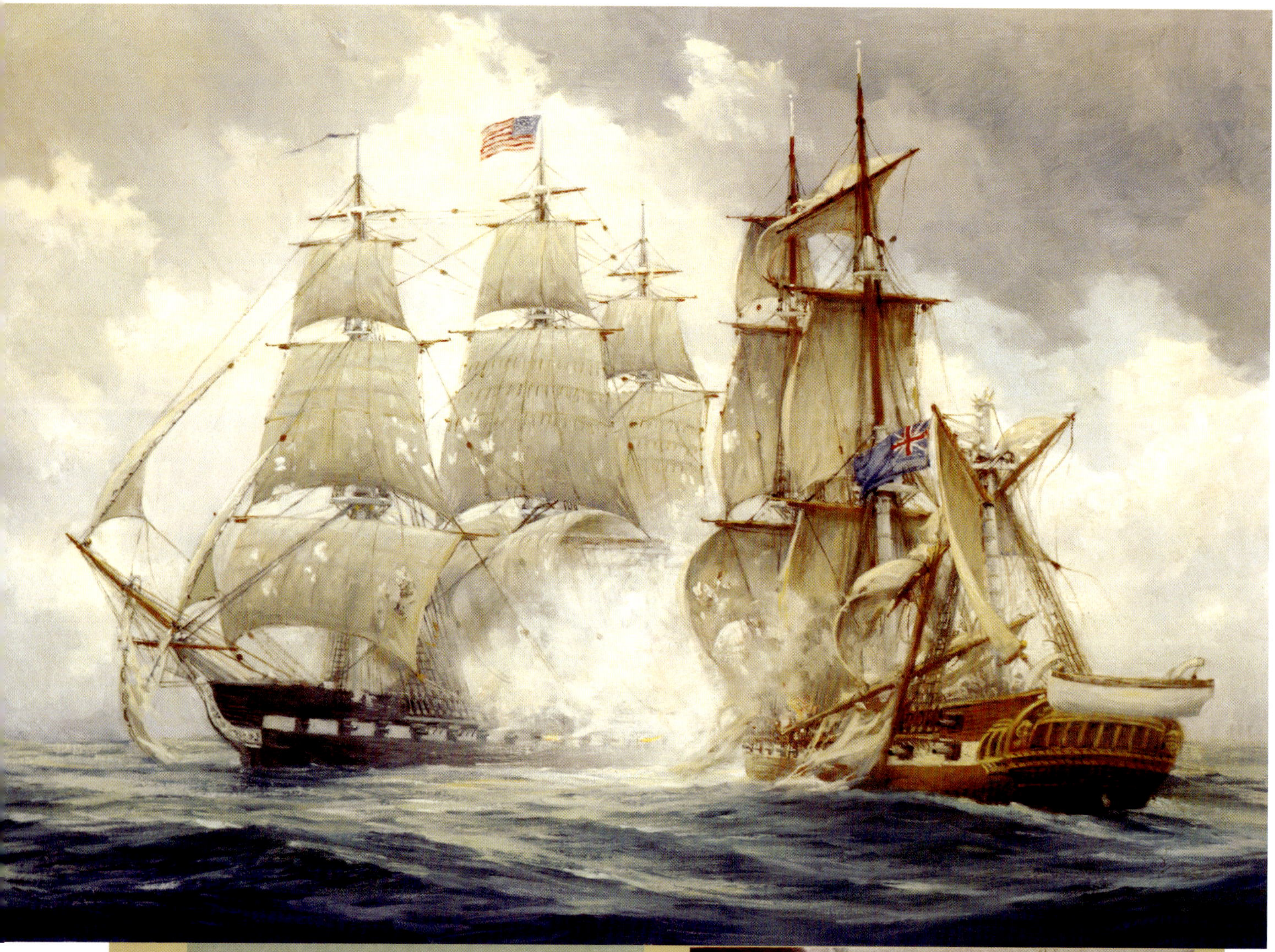

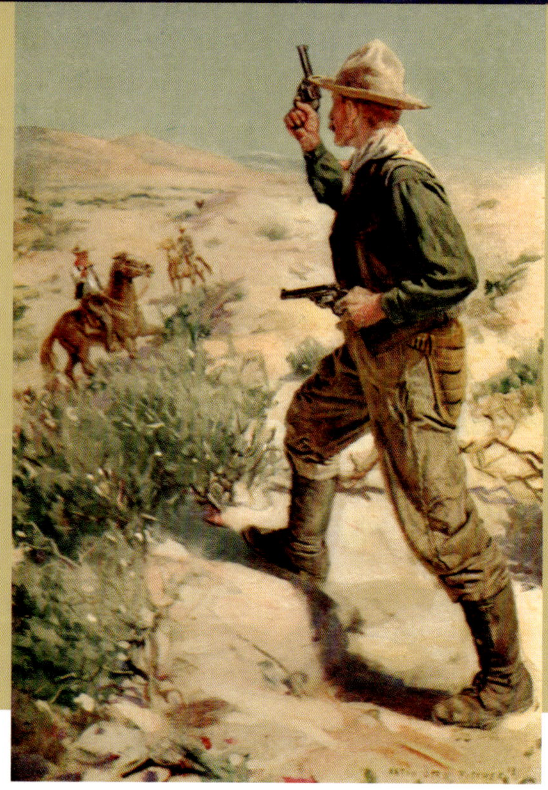

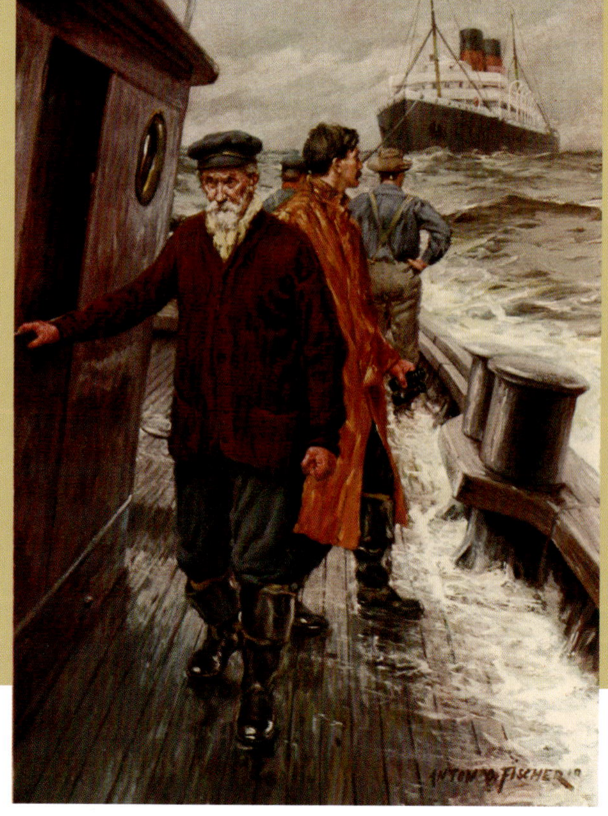

Fischer, Anton Otto

Anton Otto Fischer

1882–1962, German-American

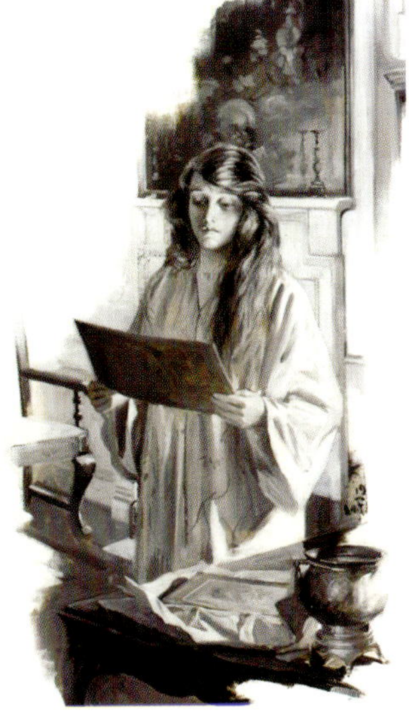

One of the great marine painters of the era, Anton Otto Fischer was born in Munich, orphaned at an early age and raised in an orphanage until the age of 15. The next decade was no easier for Fischer, although it undoubtedly helped shape him. He ran away from the orphanage, studied for the priesthood, and apprenticed with a printer before going to sea for eight years when he was twenty years old. For one 14-month period he lived in New York, where he worked with artist A. B. Frost as a handyman and a model. That time with Frost influenced his decision to leave the sea and pursue a career in art. Fischer brought some of his life experience to his painting with images of coarse men, difficult situations, and rough water. He had prepared himself well for a career as a marine painter.

Fischer was one of the best painters of marine subjects during the early part of the twentieth century. After finding his way to Howard Pyle's school of art in Delaware, Fischer had the good fortune to pair up with a writer whose stories spoke of the kind of life that Fischer had led. Jack London wrote numerous stories that took place in the wild North, and a great many at sea. In the next few years, until London's death in 1916, Fischer illustrated many of London's stories, in both magazines and books. This positive association elevated the demand for his work.

During World War II Fischer returned to the sea, and became an official war artist for the U.S. Coast Guard serving aboard the cutter *Campbell.* This was not only a chance to serve, but it also provided Fischer with a look at larger ships than the ones he recalled as a young man. Fischer's prowess at marine work kept him in demand, and he accepted private commissions—which he came to prefer over illustrations.

Fischer produced an autobiographical book of art and story called *Focs'le Days,* which *Scribner's* published in 1947, exploring memories of his earlier times at sea.

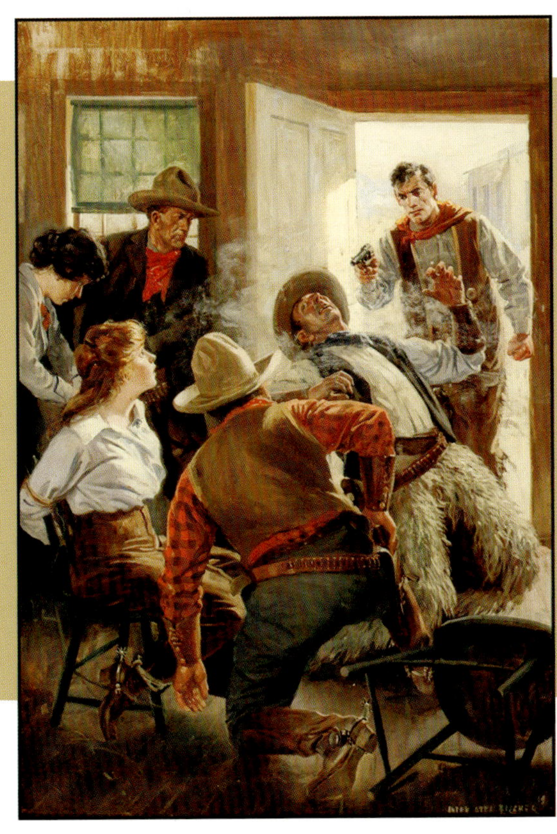

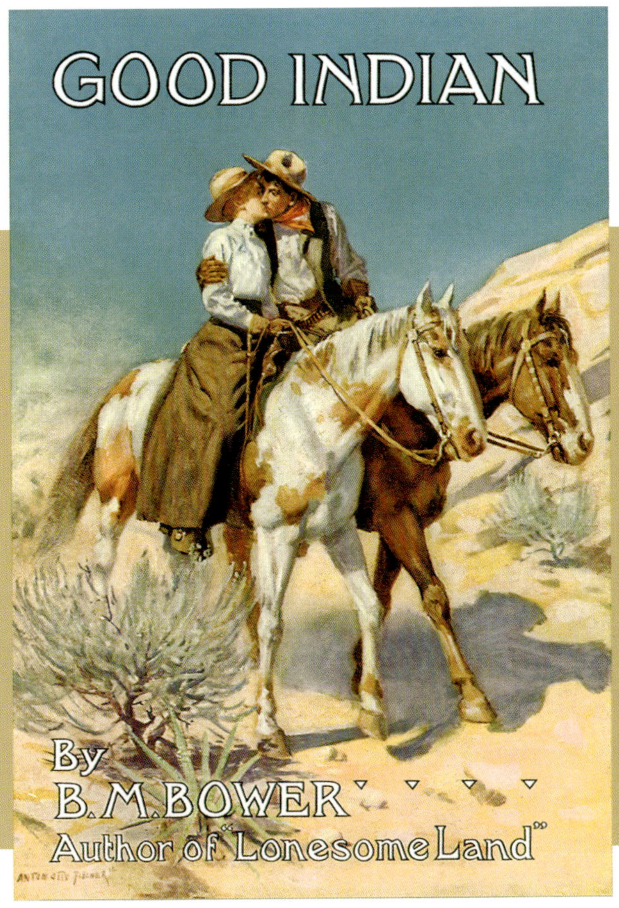

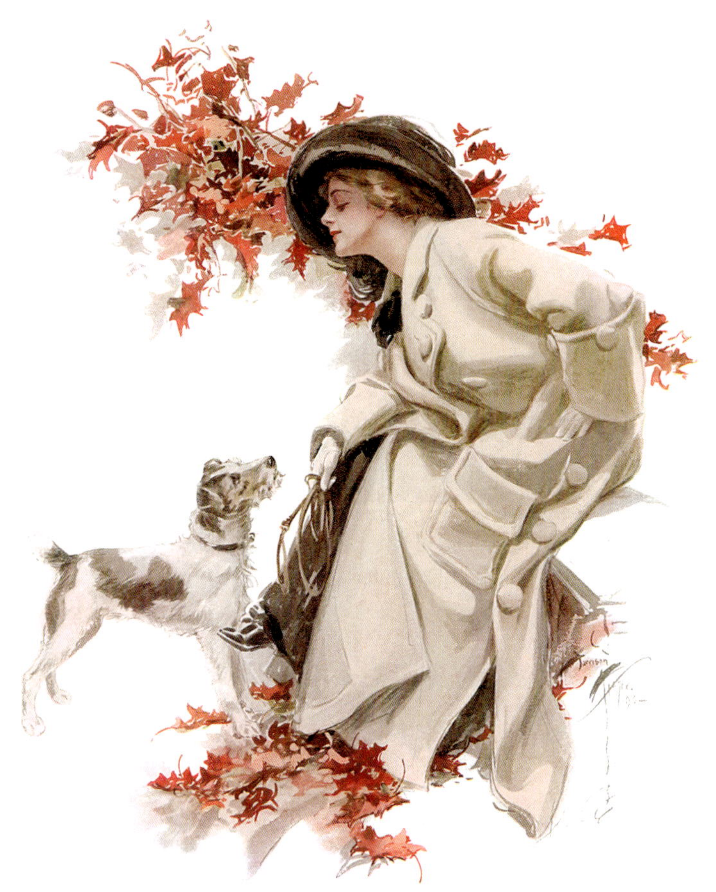

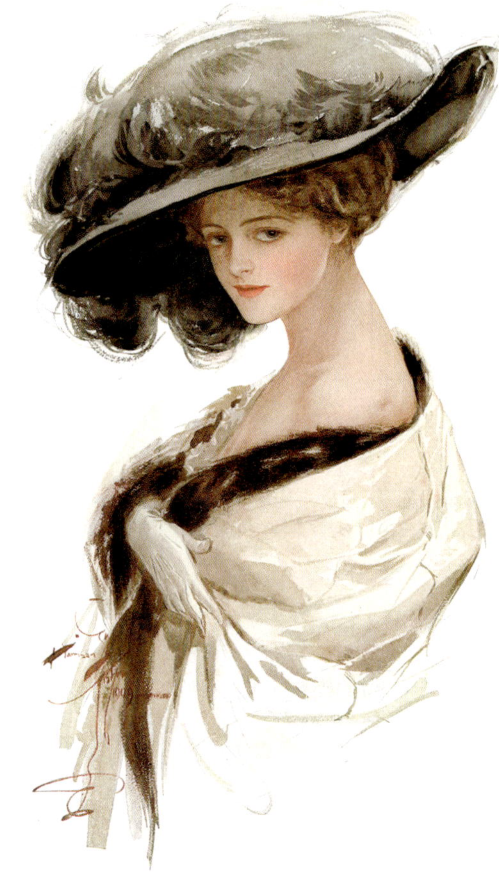

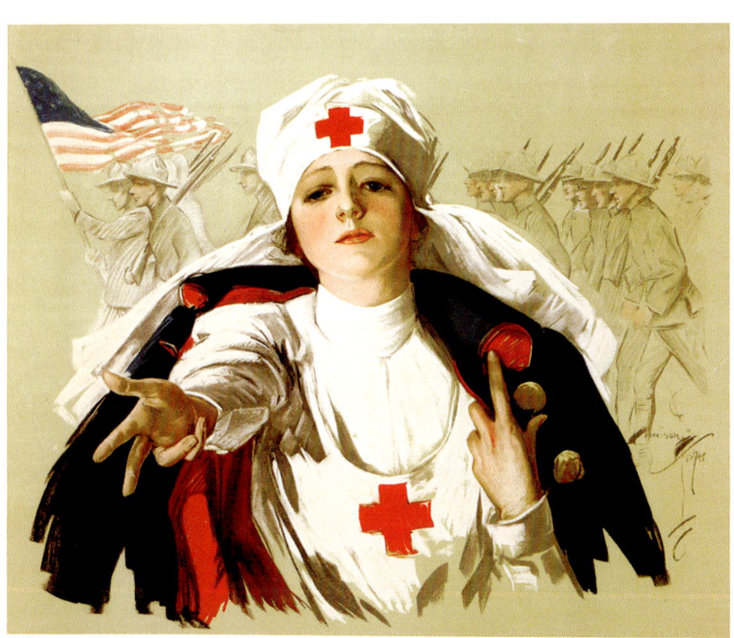

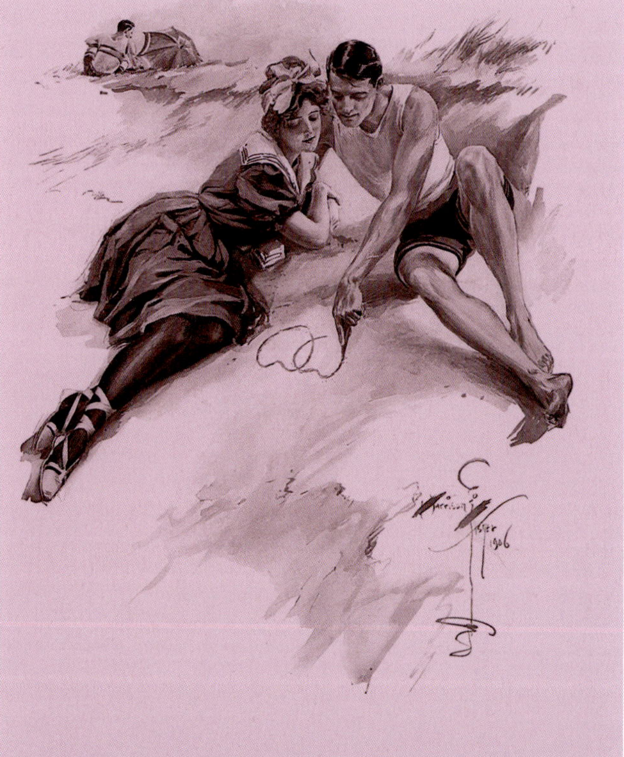

Like Flagg and Christy, Fisher used his popular "good girl" imagery to appeal to the public for help during World War I.

Harrison Fisher
1877–1934, American

Though he was Brooklyn-born, Harrison Fisher spent much of his younger years in the San Francisco area. Raised in a family supportive of a creative spirit—and showing promise from an early age—Fisher first attended art school there. In 1898 he briefly returned to the east coast, then traveled to England and France for more studies before landing his first employment as an artist for the newspaper owned by William Randolph Hearst on the west coast of the U.S. After a few years Fisher moved to New York, where Hearst's papers were based. Before long, it became evident that his striking images of women were his artistic strongpoint. Comparisons were made between his feminine icon and those of Charles Dana Gibson. Fisher's particular "model" did not have the high-society feel of Gibson's, but she was a bit more approachable, real, and seemed more likable. Legions of readers agreed, and Fisher's girls would soon be found on magazines, ads, and book covers for the first few decades of the twentieth century.

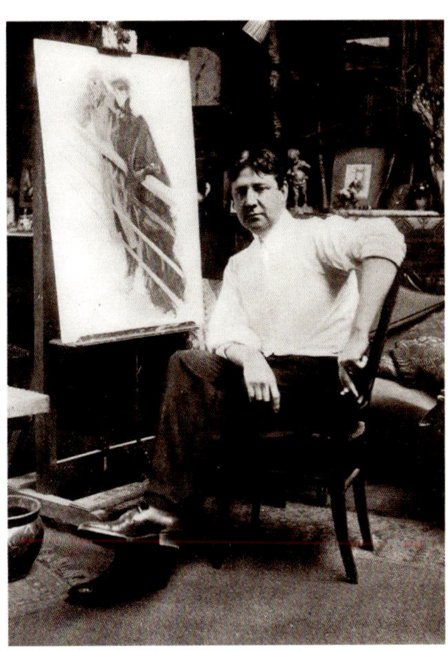

Fisher in his studio, 1905

In 1905, Gibson "retired" from illustration, and Fisher became known as "The Father of 1,000 Girls"—a title given to him in a 1910 magazine article. There were others who made careers out of painting women, but Fisher was likely the head of the class. He continued to lead the field for some time, and worked with clients at the forefront of publishing, like *Ladies' Home Journal, Scribner's, Cosmopolitan,* and *The Saturday Evening Post.* The consistent quality of Fisher's work, and the public's thirst for it, made him very successful and wealthy. Fisher's girls were in such public demand that books filled with his images sold well. *The American Girl* and *Harrison Fisher Girls* were among the titles that first sold as serialized magazine pieces, and later were compiled and bound for keepsakes.

Having completed over 80 covers for *The Saturday Evening Post,* and almost every cover for *Cosmopolitan* from 1913–1934, Fisher's archive was considerable. At the time, illustration art was not considered to have great value after it had served its intended purpose, and a relative who inherited his works burned over 900 original pieces of Fisher's art at his request. He died in 1934 after an appendectomy.

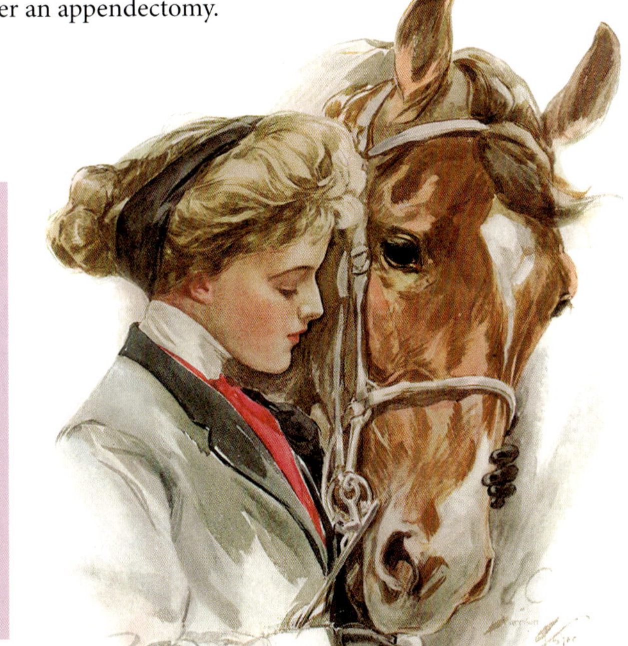

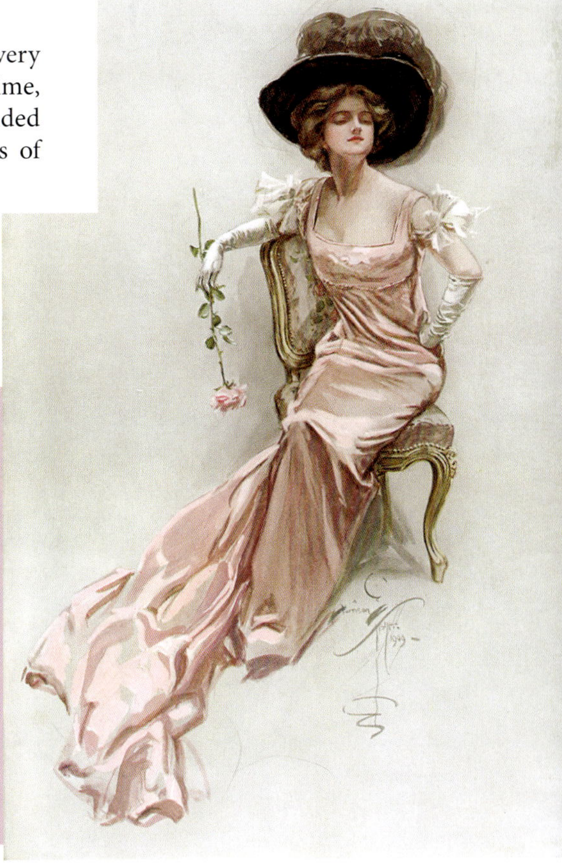

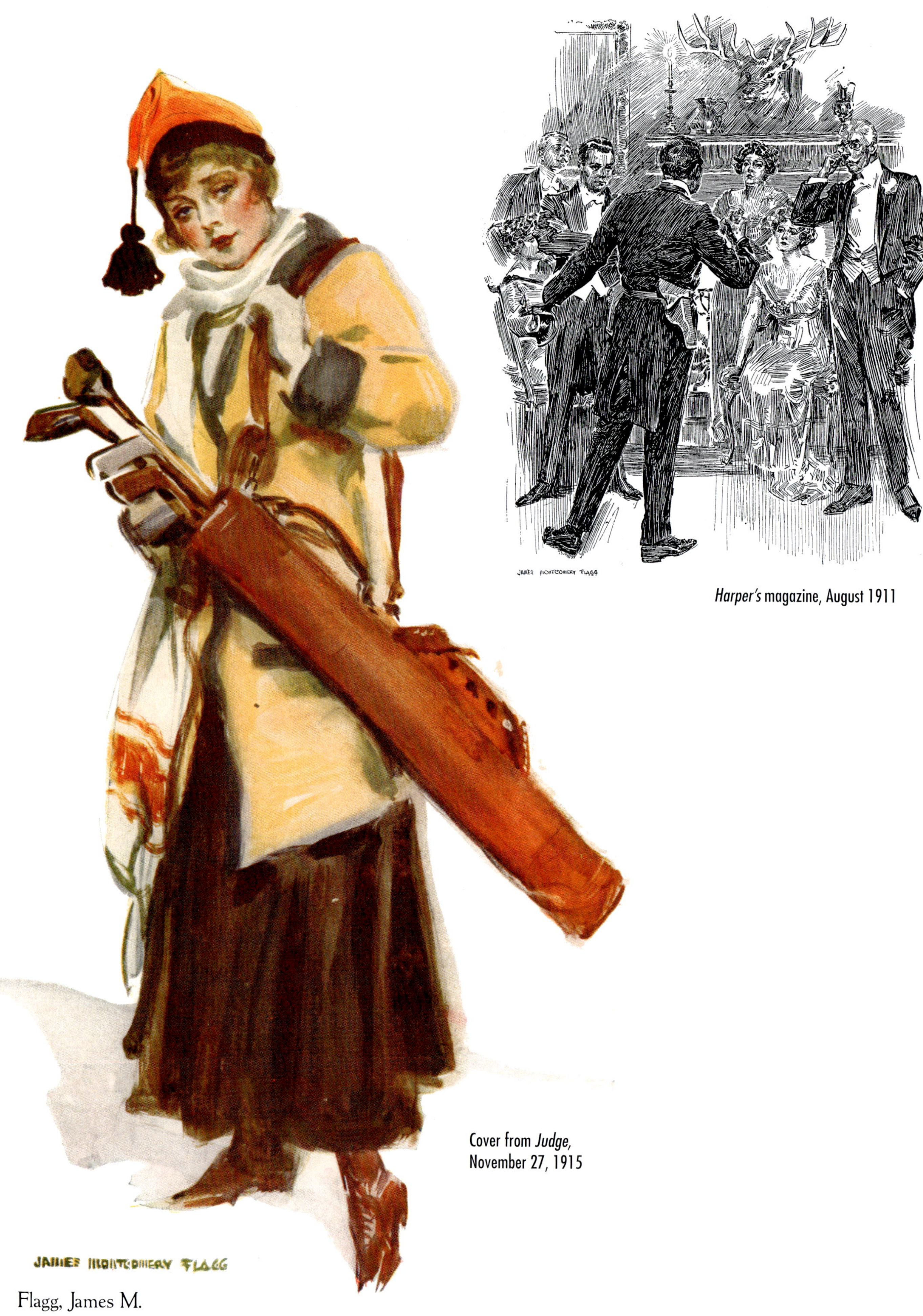

Harper's magazine, August 1911

Cover from *Judge*, November 27, 1915

Flagg, James M.

James M. Flagg
1877–1960, American

James Montgomery Flagg's career is largely remembered for *a single image*—both a blessing and a curse. His work was much more varied than the impression of any single work would lead one to believe. A solid draftsman, Flagg also had a humorous side to his work, and he was just as comfortable doing inked cartoon work as he was creating his society sketches and watercolors.

Flagg had an innate natural ability. Those around him could sense it in his work. Fast, confident, and sharp, he became one of the most successful illustrators of his day—and he worked for over fifty years. With his success came something of a celebrity lifestyle. The beautiful women he drew were all around him. He traveled frequently, seeking to add to his visual storehouse of knowledge. He was sought-after as an advertising spokesman and a beauty contest judge. But this vibrant life did not slow him down or reduce his work opportunities.

The image that has kept him in the mindset of Americans is a World War I poster Flagg produced to encourage enlistment. The title "I WANT YOU" under Flagg's arresting portrait of Uncle Sam pointing a finger at the viewer on a clean, white field caught the public's attention. It remains today one of the strongest, most recognizable images in the American iconography.

Flagg was an active member of many New York clubs, including the Society of Illustrators, where he frequently contributed to creating skits and shows for the members' entertainment. It allowed him to use his skills with another type of creative pursuit. He wrote, directed, and starred in a number of productions, some of them short comedic films.

While his career was active, Flagg enjoyed the social life it brought him. In advanced years, his eyesight began to fail, and he lost the ability to continue working. It put Flagg in a very depressed state, and his social life seemed to dissipate. He died in 1960.

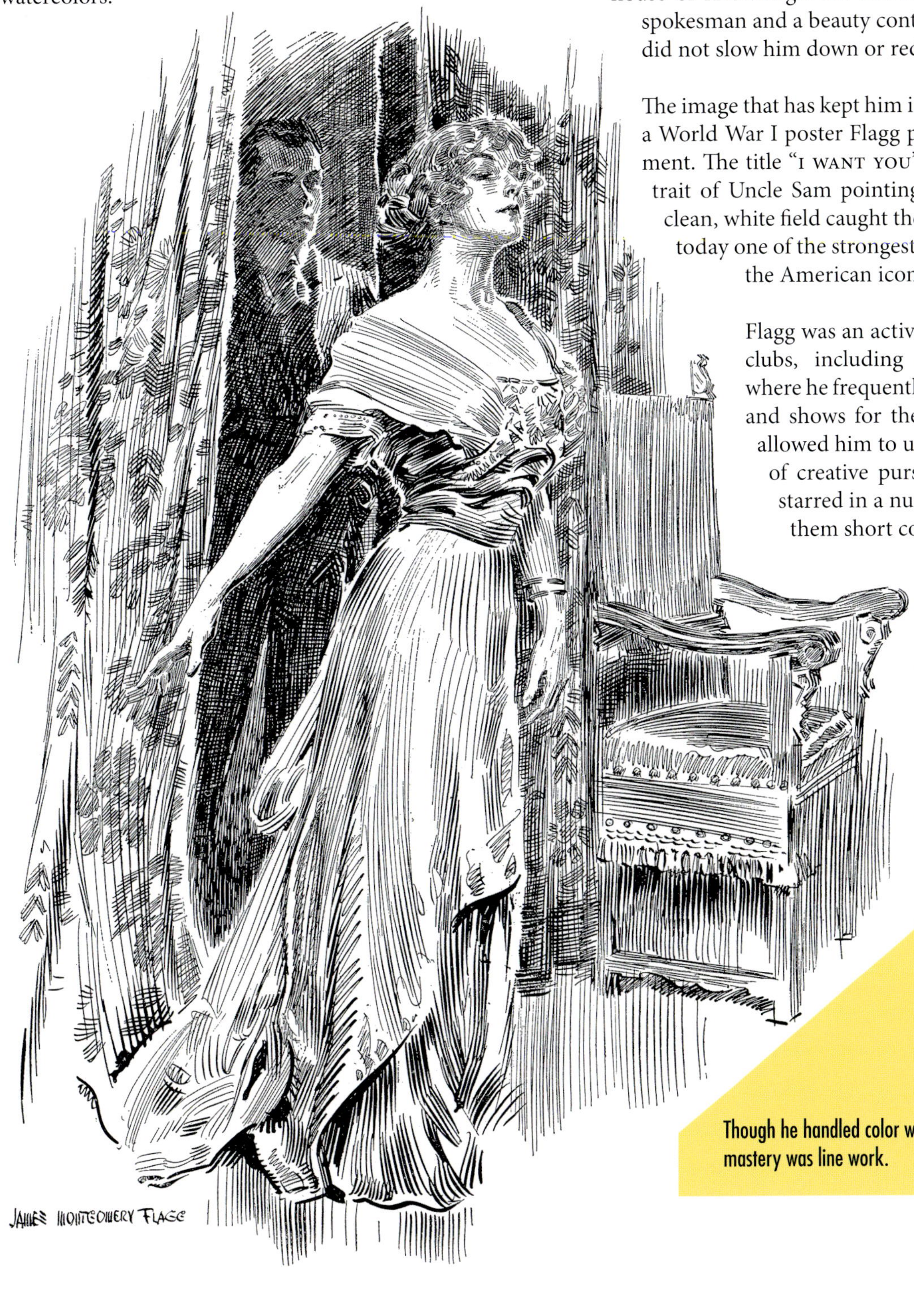

JAMES MONTGOMERY FLAGG

Though he handled color well and brushwork with flair, Flagg's first mastery was line work.

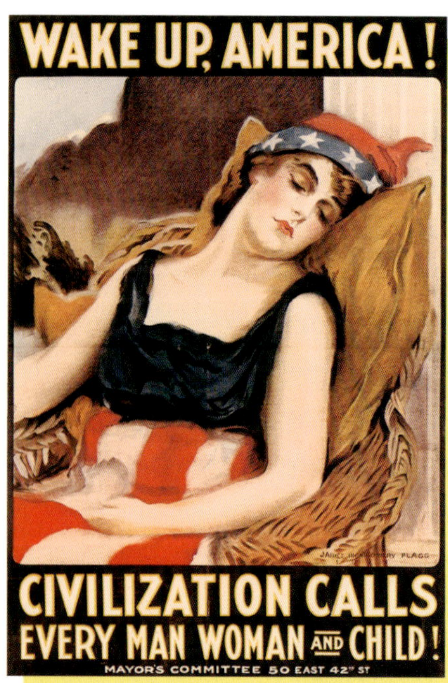

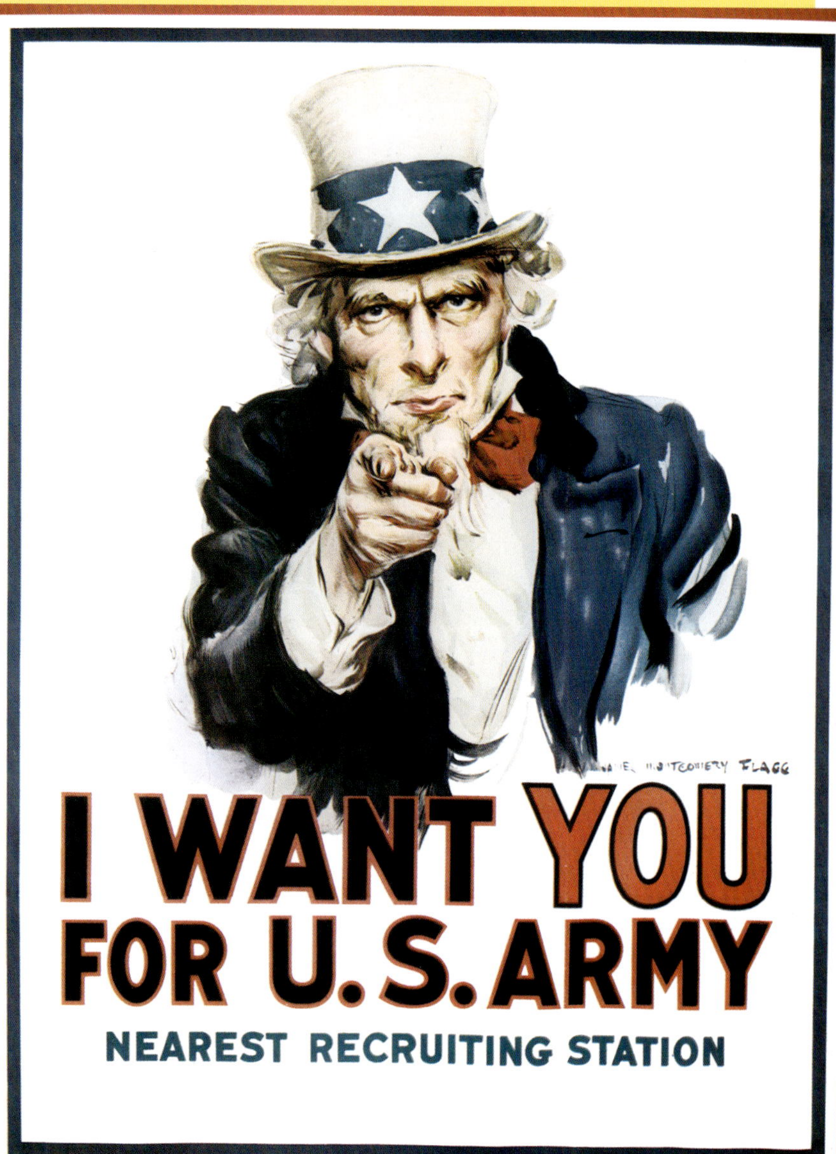

Over 4,400,000 copies of Flagg's "I WANT YOU" poster were printed during both world wars—Flagg modeled for the image himself.

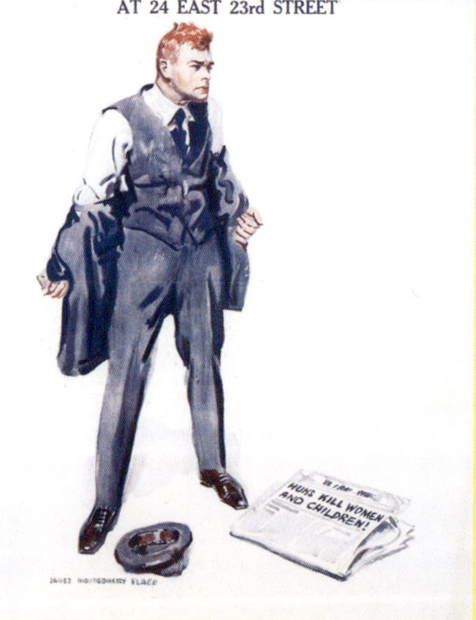

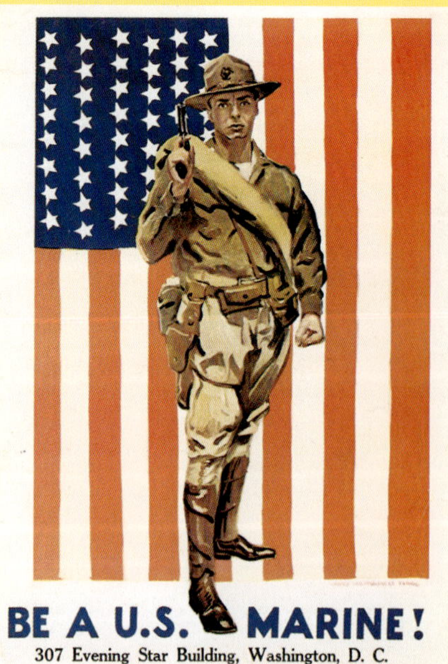

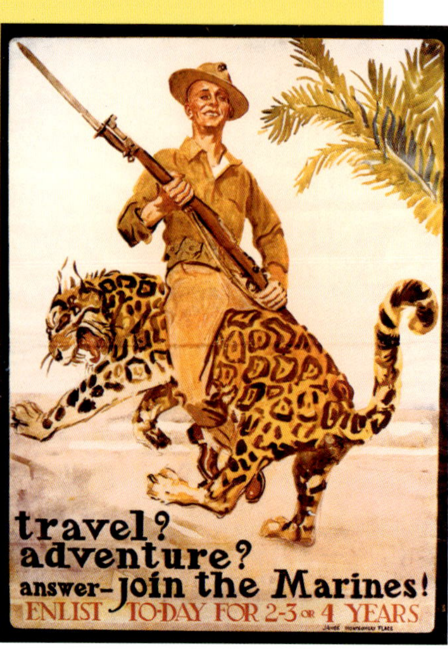

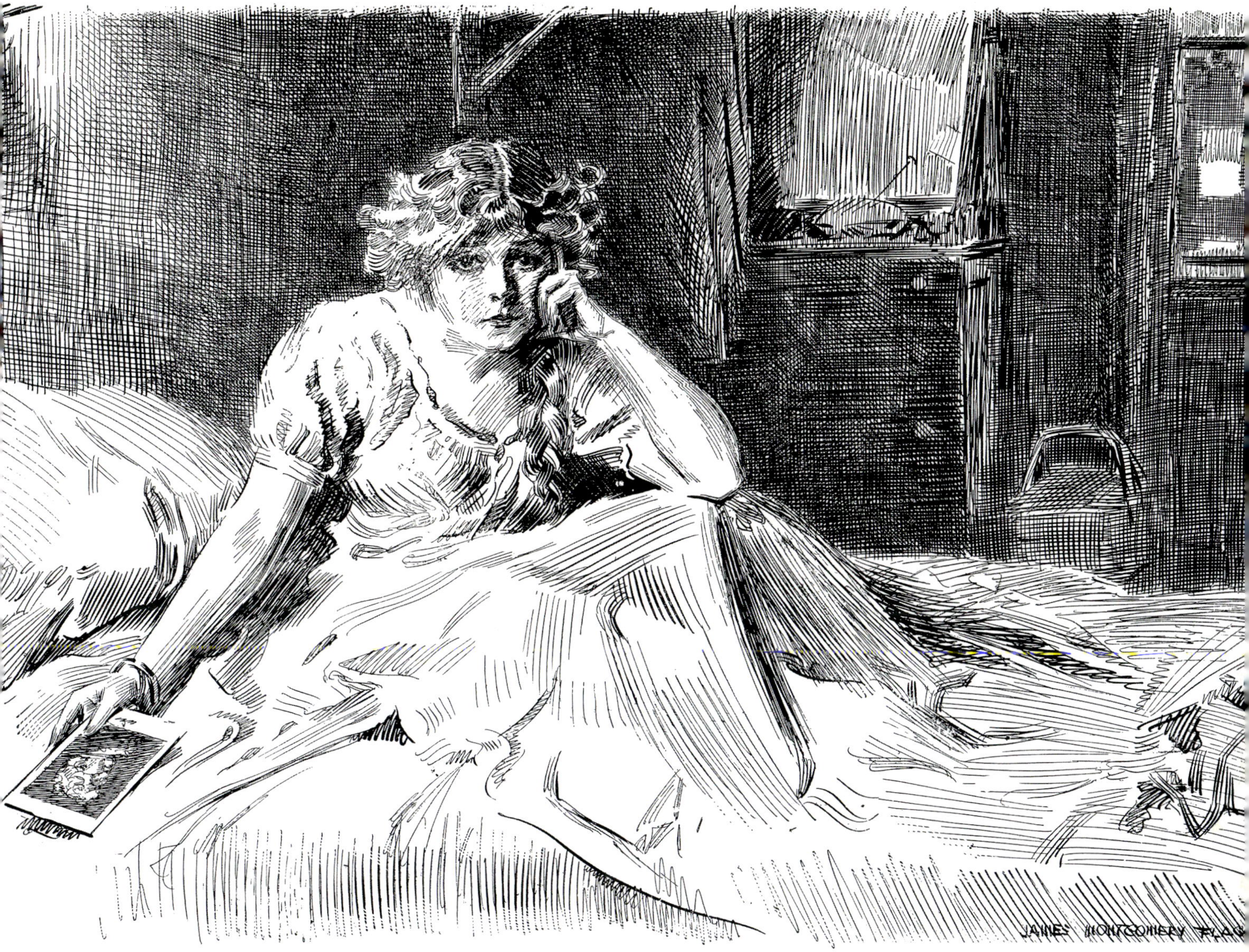

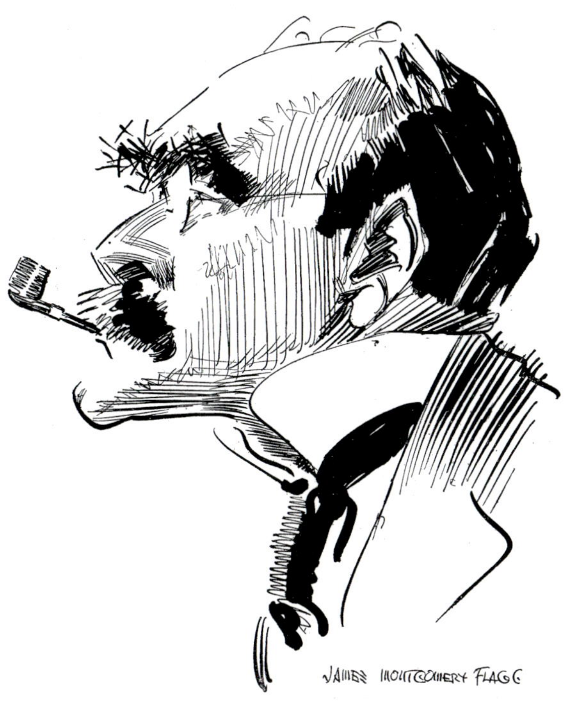

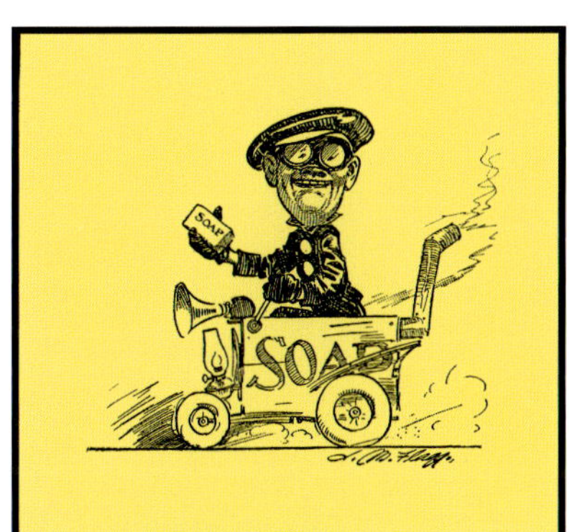

James M. Flagg on illustrators who worked from photographs: "[They drew] from the prints because it is so much simpler than troubling to learn how to draw."

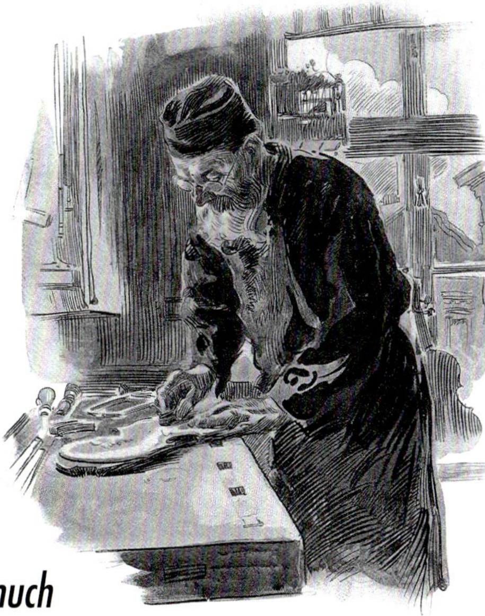

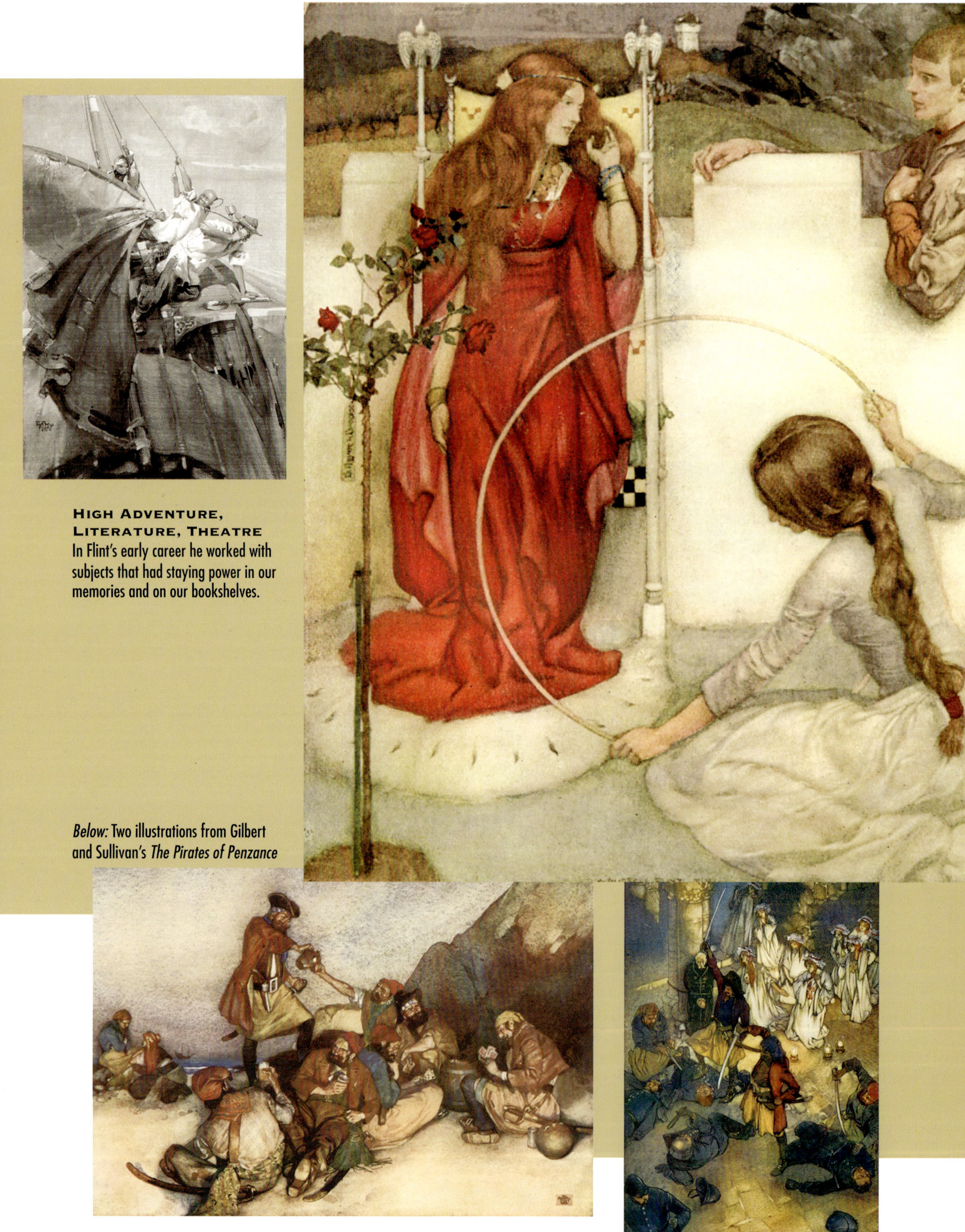

High Adventure, Literature, Theatre
In Flint's early career he worked with subjects that had staying power in our memories and on our bookshelves.

Below: Two illustrations from Gilbert and Sullivan's *The Pirates of Penzance*

Sir William Russell Flint
1880–1969, British

Entering the field of illustration just as the heyday of the gift book was beginning, Flint developed a unique level of mastery in his talents. He was a watercolor painter, illustrating such adventure tales as *King Solomon's Mines* by H. Rider Haggard in 1905 and magazine stories as well. He later achieved success illustrating more elaborate, sophisticated works of literature. Three large sets of volumes: Chaucer's works, Malory's *Morte D'Arthur,* and Homer's *Odyssey,* show Flint to be a master of the medium. Each set, containing 36 color plates or more, were showcases of his painting skill and elevated his standing in the public eye. Flint also illustrated editions of the plays of Gilbert and Sullivan. *The Pirates of Penzance, The Mikado,* and *Ruddigore* were among the titles for which he rendered imagery from 1909–1910, eight color plates in each. Flint worked on eight of the plays, published separately and in a two-volume set for a total of 64 color works.

In World War I, serving in the post of Airship Commander on HM Airship 24, Flint rose to the rank of Admiralty Assistant Overseer-Airships. Returning to painting after the war set him on a different path, and illustration gave way to work generated for galleries and prints.

The success he had in the medium was noticed by more than just casual readers, and Flint's popularity as a painter did not wane later in his career (as it did for many other illustrators). Flint found success in gallery work, showcasing images of southern European landscapes and the people who occupied them. In the 1920s and 1930s Flint spent a good deal of time in France and Spain, which fueled his work. The majority of his later works are female figures, in a wide range of exotic locales and costumes.

Flint produced work until the end of his life, though his career in illustration could largely be seen as limited to 1905–1921. His later works still carry the draftsmanship and attention to detail that made him a great illustrator, but the subjects were of his own choosing.

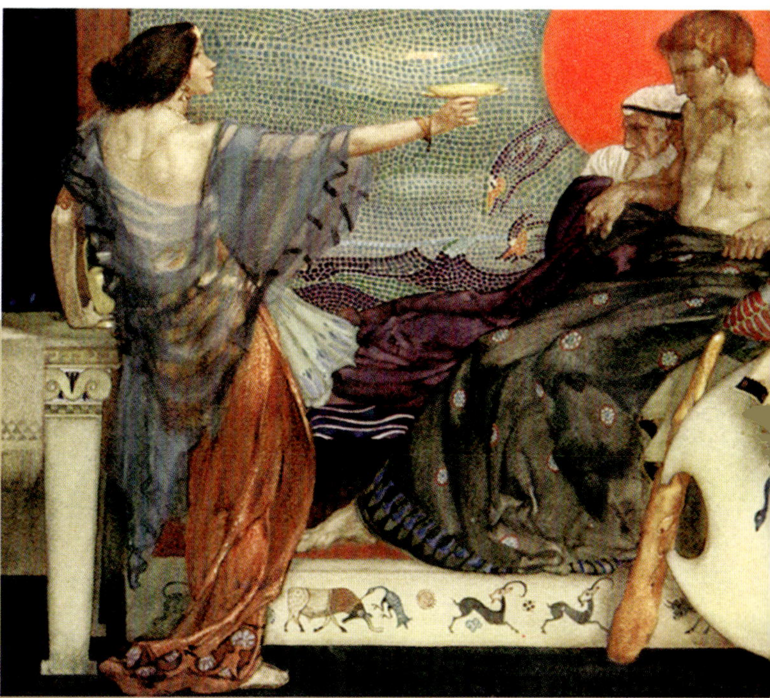

Flint was a twenty-year president of Britain's Royal Society of Painters in Watercolours, 1936–1956.

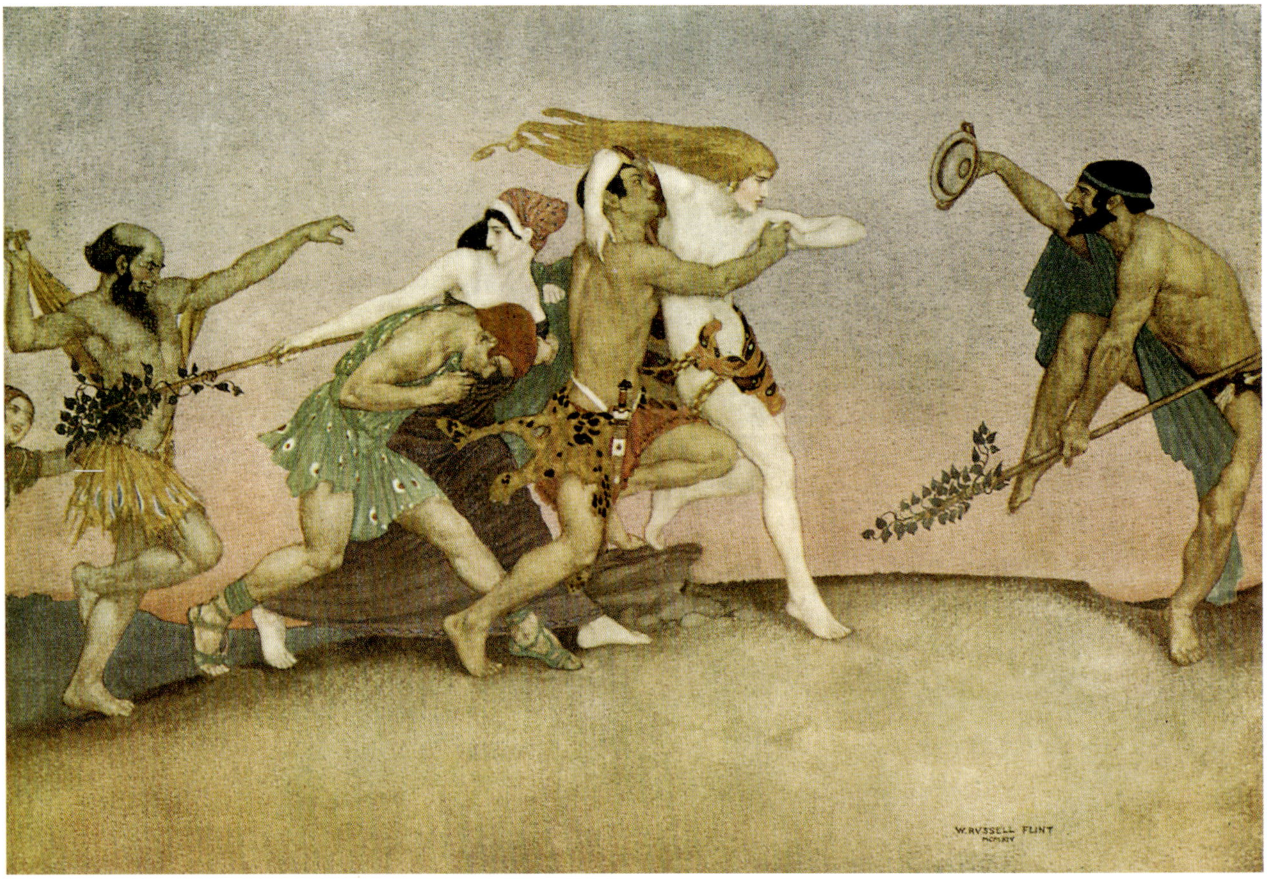

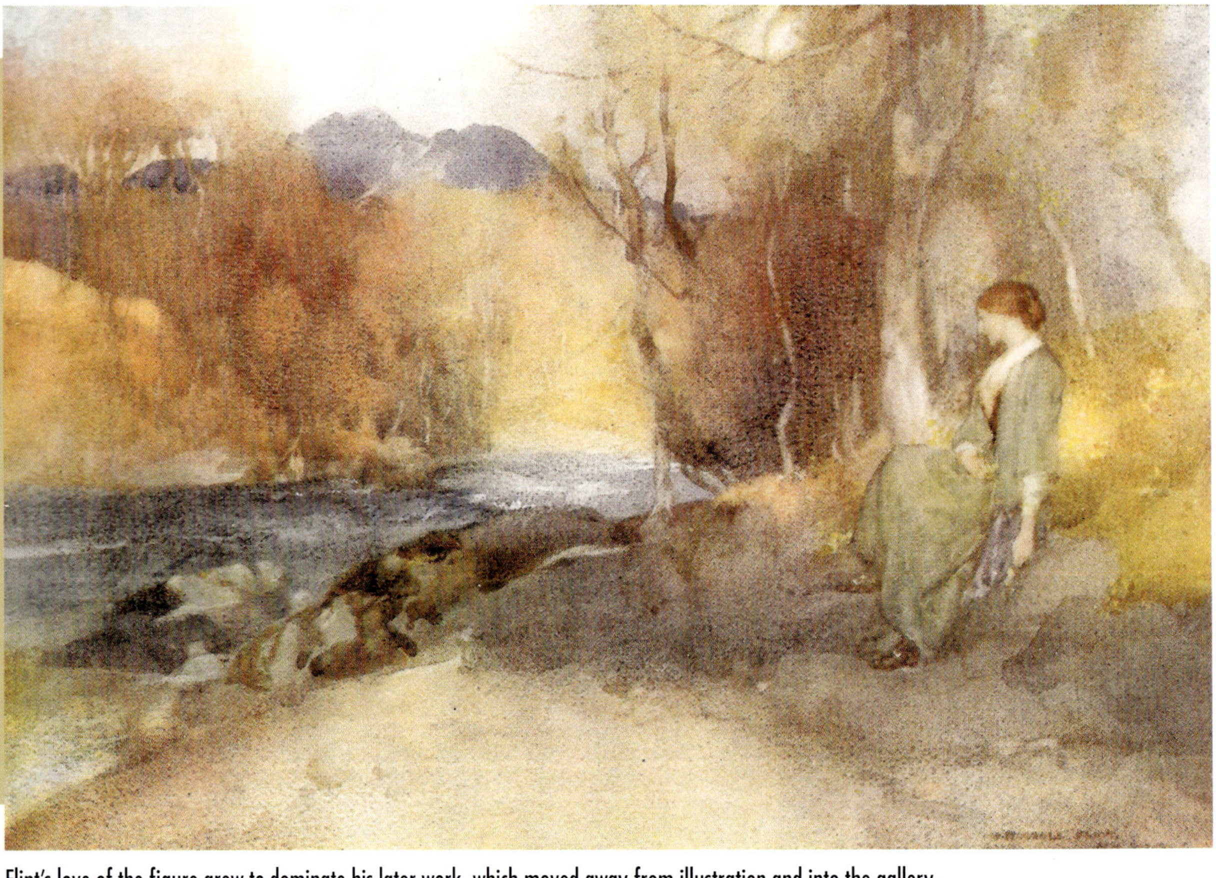

Flint's love of the figure grew to dominate his later work, which moved away from illustration and into the gallery.

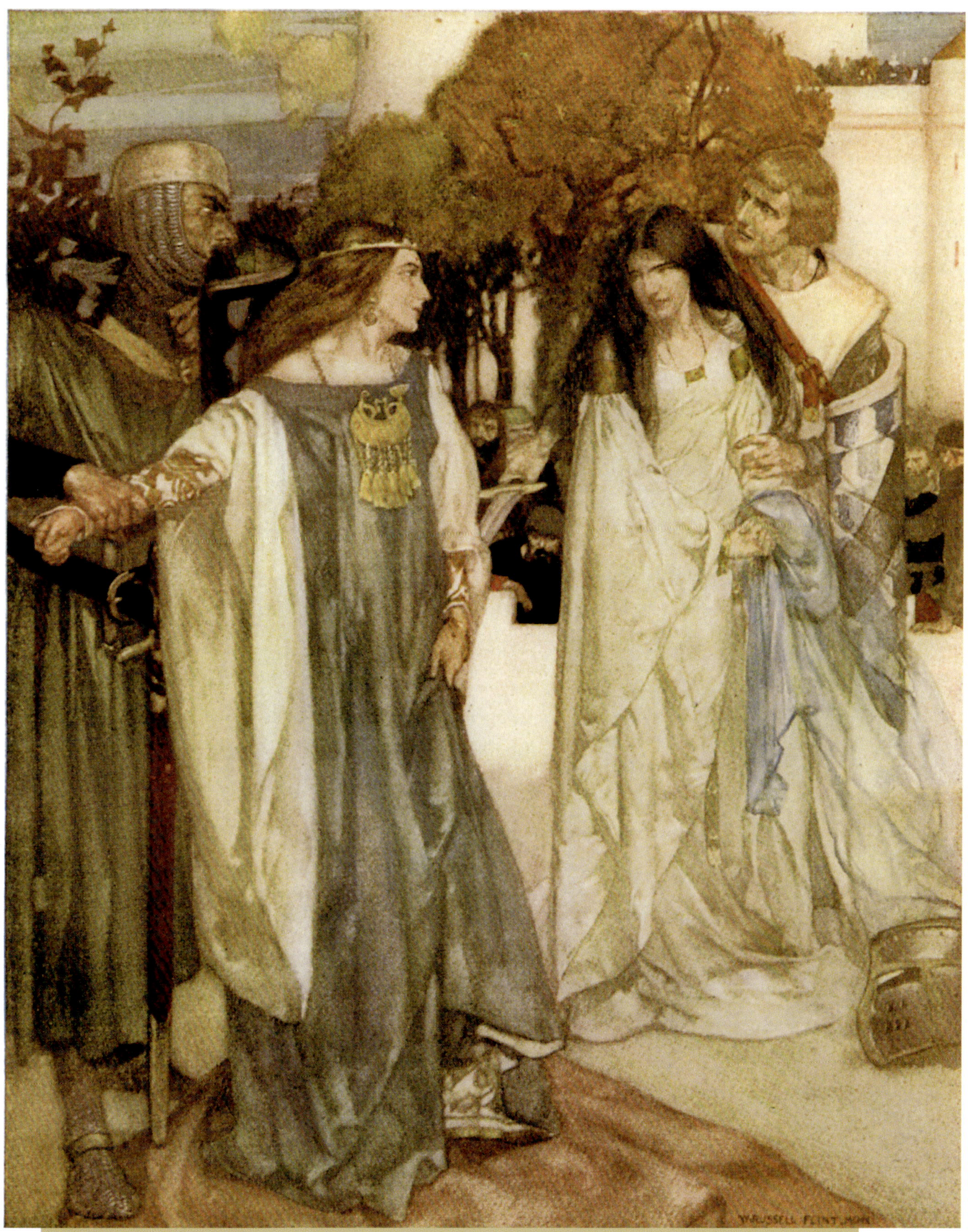

The 1910 two-volume set of Malory's *Morte d'Arthur* contains 36 superb color plates by Flint, among his best as an illustrator.

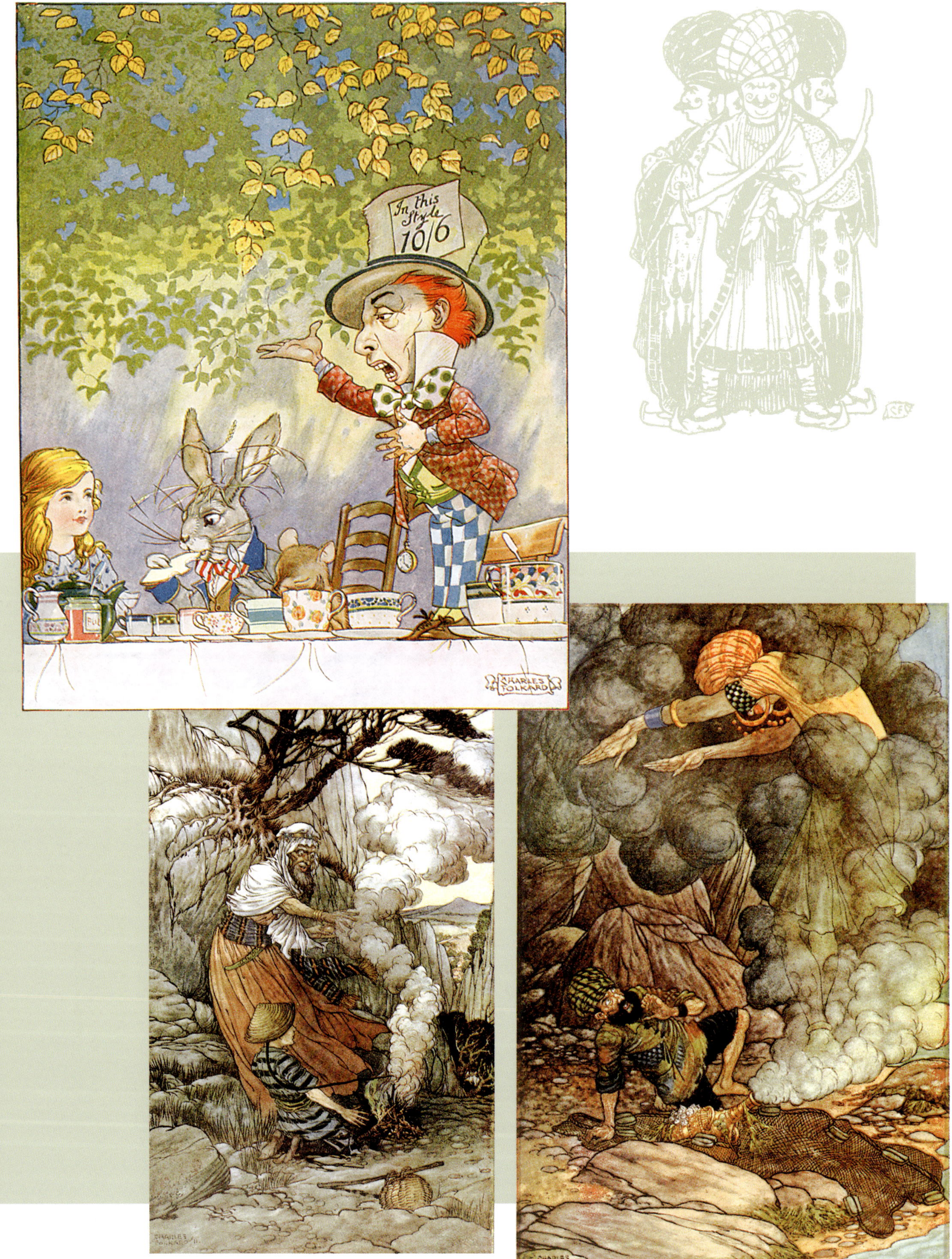

Folkard, Charles

CHARLES FOLKARD

1878–1963, British

Born in the South London neighborhood of Lewisham in 1878, Charles Folkard's penchant for drawing and design became apparent from an early age. Folkard at first tried his hand at being a stage magician, but the programs he designed and illustrated for his shows may have been more successful than his act. Following a period of magazine work with *Little Folks* and *Tatler,* Folkard landed his first big book assignment in 1910 for J. M. Dent, with a large gift edition of *The Swiss Family Robinson.* It was a good start for Folkard; he was particularly gifted for animal work, giving them expression and character. *The Swiss Family Robinson* led him to many more opportunities. His edition of *Pinocchio* the following year had over 80 images, including more than a dozen color plates, and it would remain in print for decades. Gift books of this sort were part of Folkard's output throughout his career.

The years to follow brought a pioneering addition to Folkard's illustration work. In 1915, after a few years of successful book illustration, Folkard premiered *The Adventures of Teddy Tail* in Britain's *Daily Mail.* This new idea of a daily "cartoon strip" met with immediate success, and other newspapers made efforts to produce a competing idea, giving birth to such characters as "Pip and Squeak," and "Rupert" the bear. *Teddy Tail* ran in the papers for decades, and four books were published featuring the strip's characters from 1915 to 1926.

A long-standing work relationship between Folkard and publisher A. C. Black started in 1911, and continued on deep into the 1930s. He produced many books with Black, including classics such as *Mother Goose's Nursery Rhymes* and a variation on *Alice in Wonderland,* but also ventured into more diverse titles like *The Magic Egg* and *The Troubles of a Gnome.* Folkard was still getting assignments more than a half-century after he began illustrating, a testament to the appeal of his style across generations. He passed away in February of 1963, days after completing an illustration.

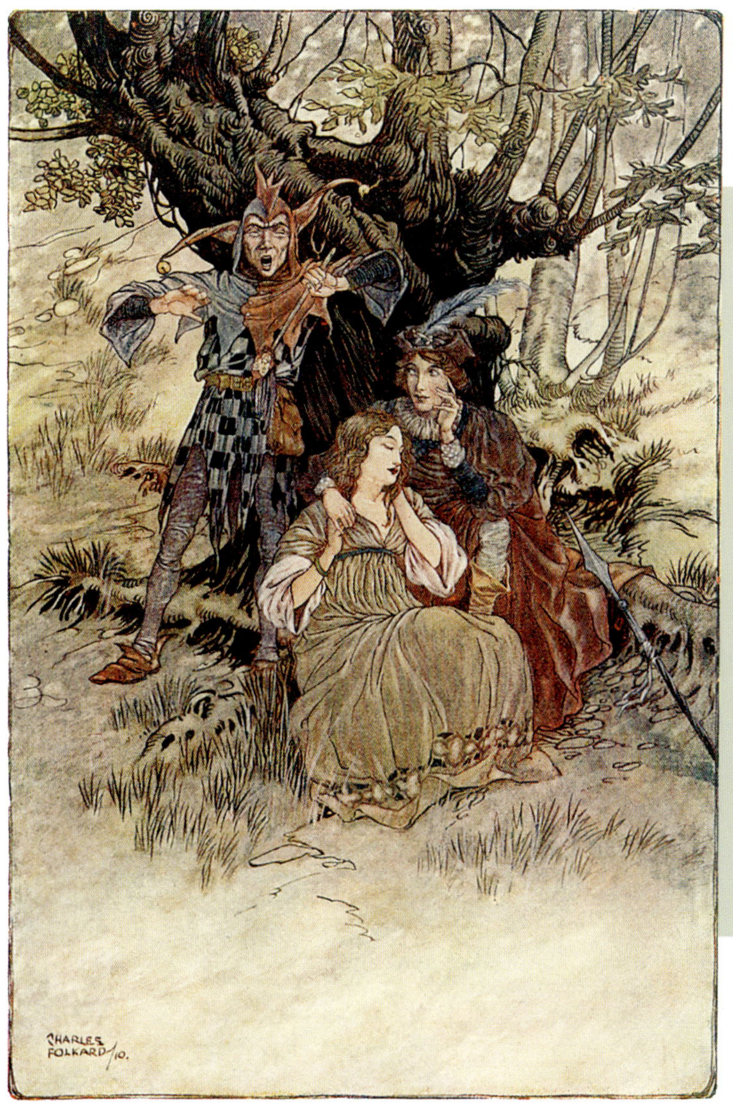

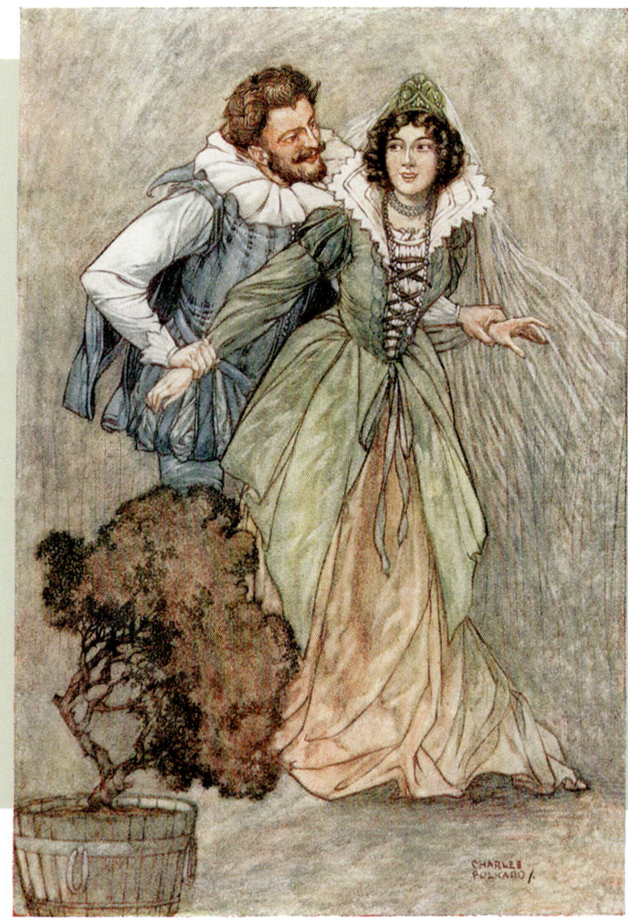

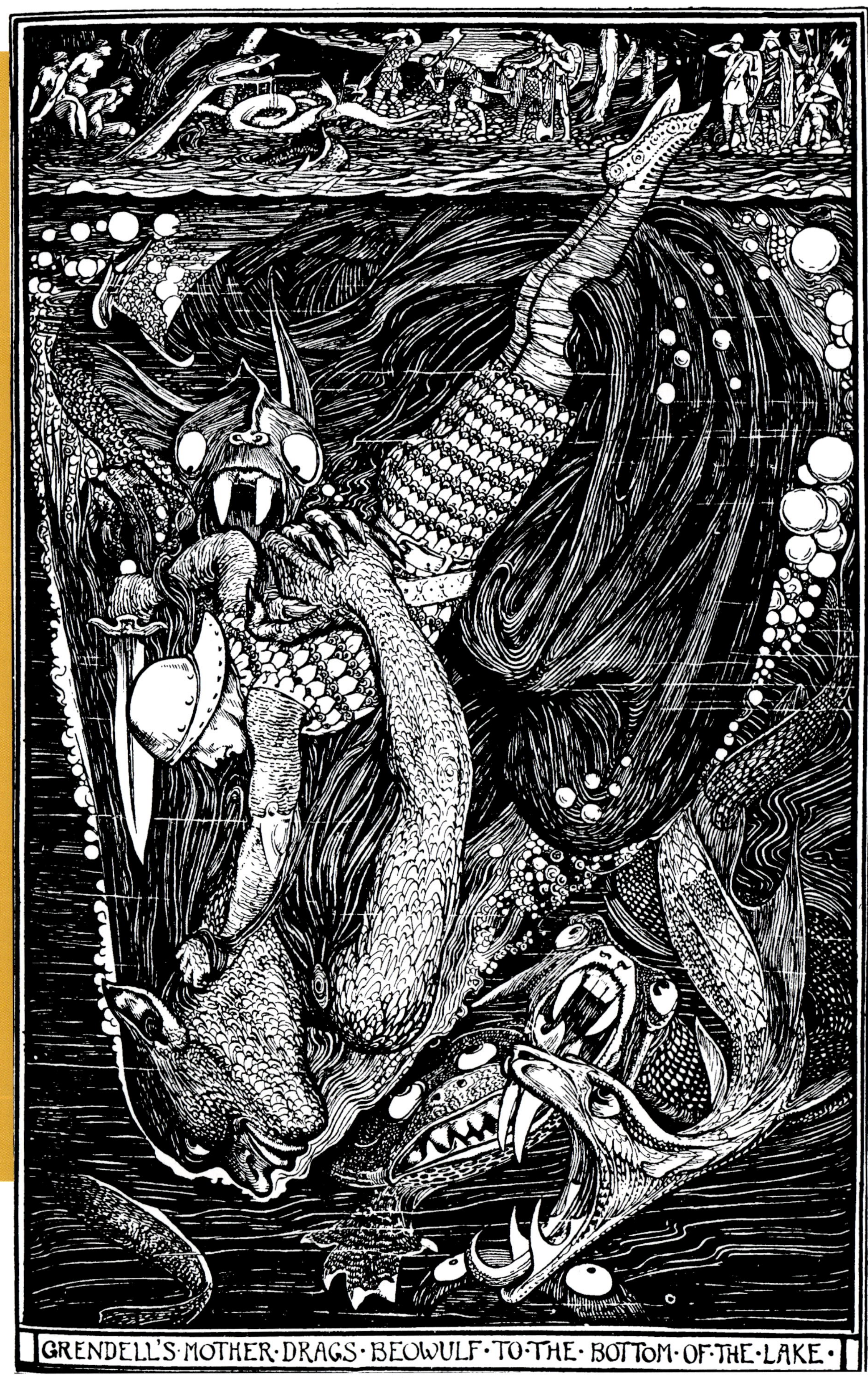

GRENDELL'S·MOTHER·DRAGS·BEOWULF·TO·THE·BOTTOM·OF·THE·LAKE·

Ford, Henry Justice

Henry Justice Ford
1860–1941, British

H. J. Ford's enduring imagery comes to us largely through his work in fairy tales. Ford got his start in London, where he was greatly influenced by the Pre-Raphaelites working there. He counted a good many friends among them, including painter Edward Burne-Jones. Many of the Pre-Raphaelites chose classic texts to inspire their subject matter, leading them to produce works of a highly illustrative nature. The two paths frequently intertwined, but Ford's successes came to him from his illustration work.

Andrew Lang was an important researcher and editor on the subject of fairy tales. In the late nineteenth and earliest part of the twentieth century, he collected folk and fairy tales from all over the world, assembling them in volumes that became identified by the color of their bindings. After working in collaboration with a few other illustrators on the first two books of the series (Lancelot Speed and G. P Jacomb-Hood), Lang and his publisher handed over all of the art for the third volume, *The Green Fairy Book,* to Ford in 1892. The art for a single volume was a considerable task, containing as many as a dozen full-color works and scores of full-page and detailed vignette line pieces. The partnership Ford developed with Lang proved to be a solid one—and Ford worked with him and his wife for the next eighteen years, producing another nine volumes for his colorful fairy tale series, and other volumes as well. *The Red Romance Book* in 1905 carried many English legends that were outside the realm of the fairy tale, and *The Big Book of Animal Stories* were two such volumes.

Ford began his formative work during the height of popularity of line drawing and it was there that he truly excelled. His full-page ink pieces are complex and rich, his figure work is exemplary, and he had the ability and imagination to add a universe of engaging creatures and little people. It was his understanding of tonal value relationships, and using them well in a picture, that made him such an outstanding inker.

Ford's partnership with Lang was also successful. He was steadily employed for years by the endeavors with Lang, and his images were seen by a great number of English-speaking people, on whom Ford's work made a lasting impression. After Lang's passing in 1912, Ford continued working with Lang's wife, Leonora, and completed a number of volumes. Ford's later works shifted away from fairy tales, where he illustrated titles such as *Introduction to American History* in 1916, and *Pilgrim's Progress,* which was his last book, in 1921.

In the twelve volumes of the "Rainbow" Fairy series, Ford was responsible for over one thousand images, about 80 of which were full color.

Lancelot bears Guenevere away, from *The Book of Romance,* 1902.

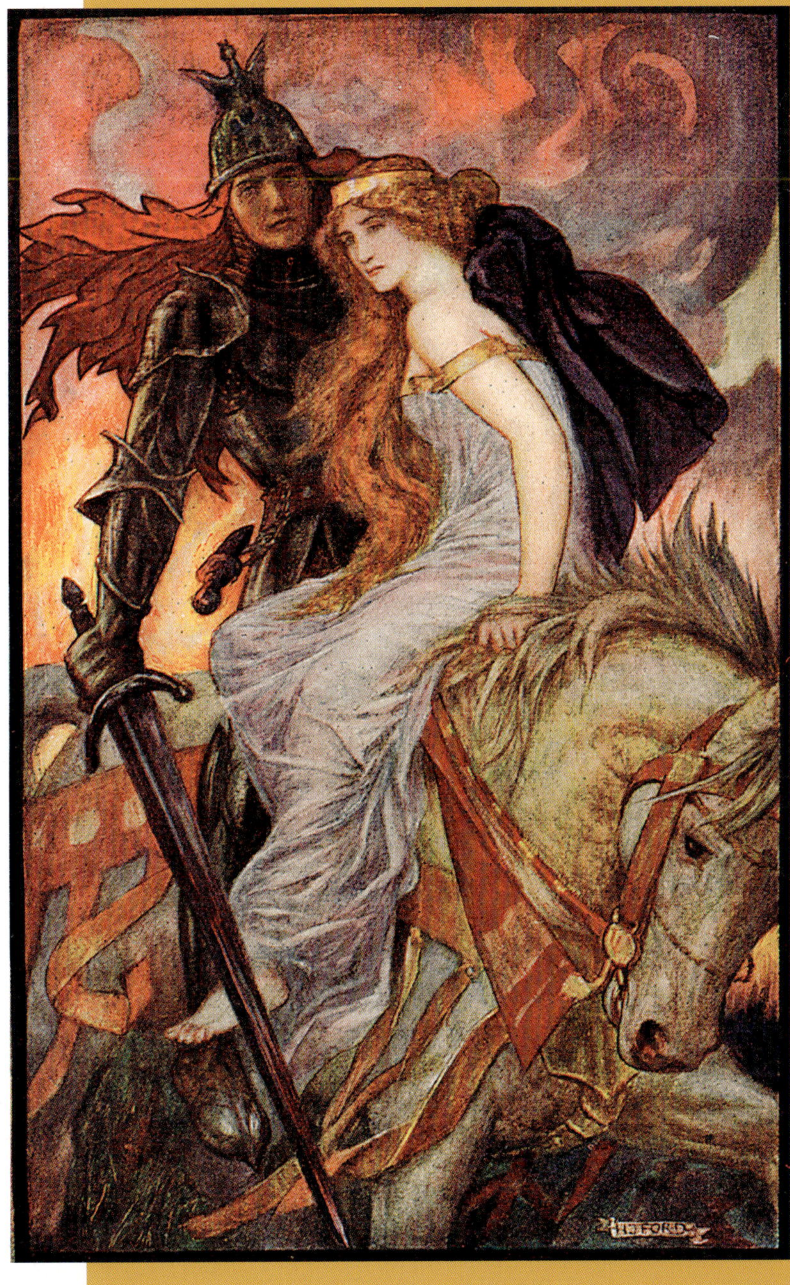

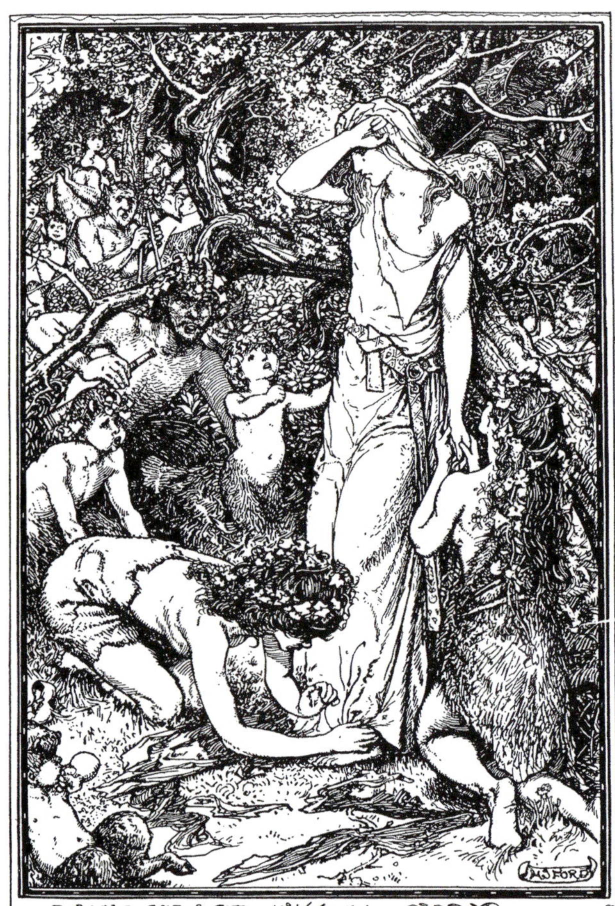

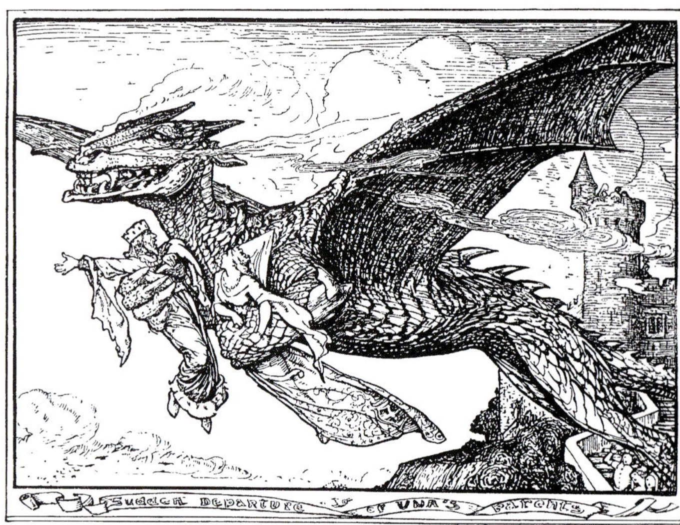

A father of modern fantasy art, Ford had a strong impact on generations of readers—even influencing some of the early creature design of *Dungeons and Dragons*.

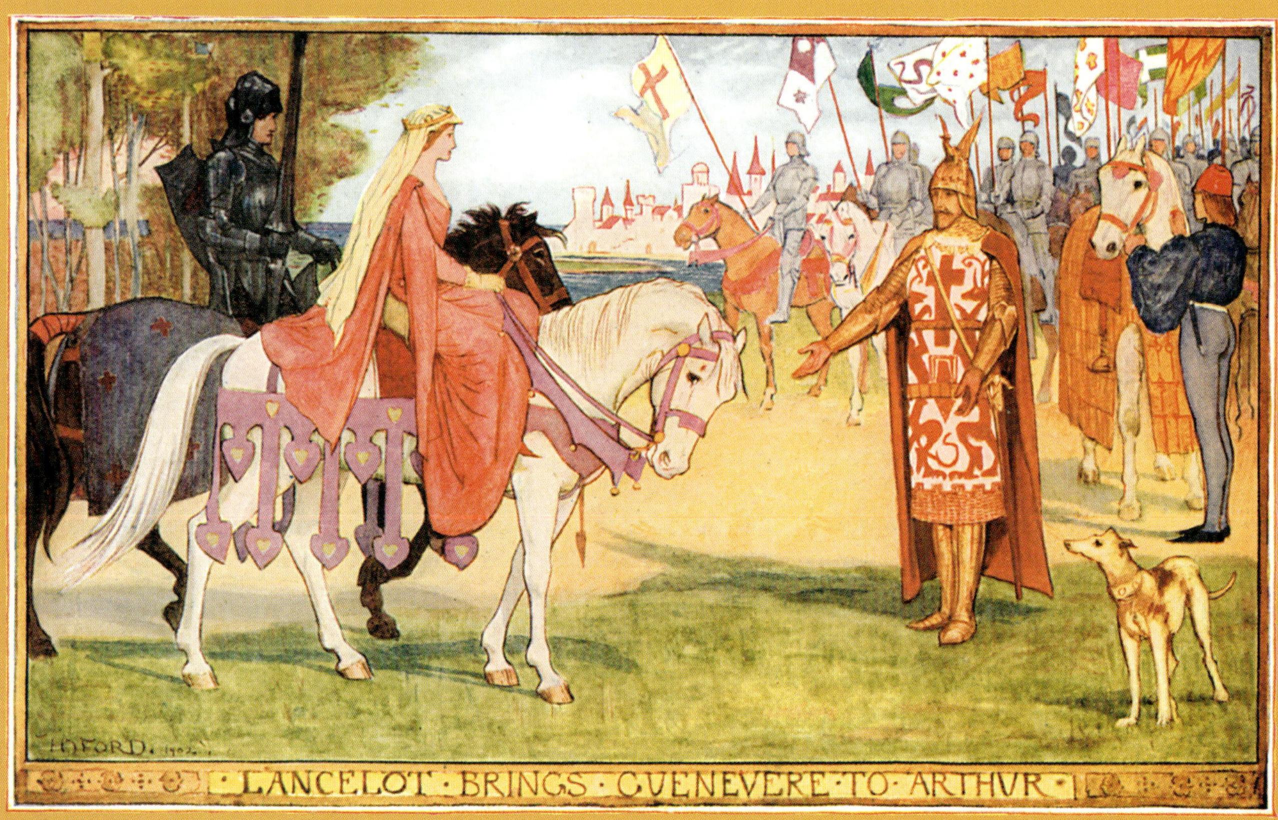

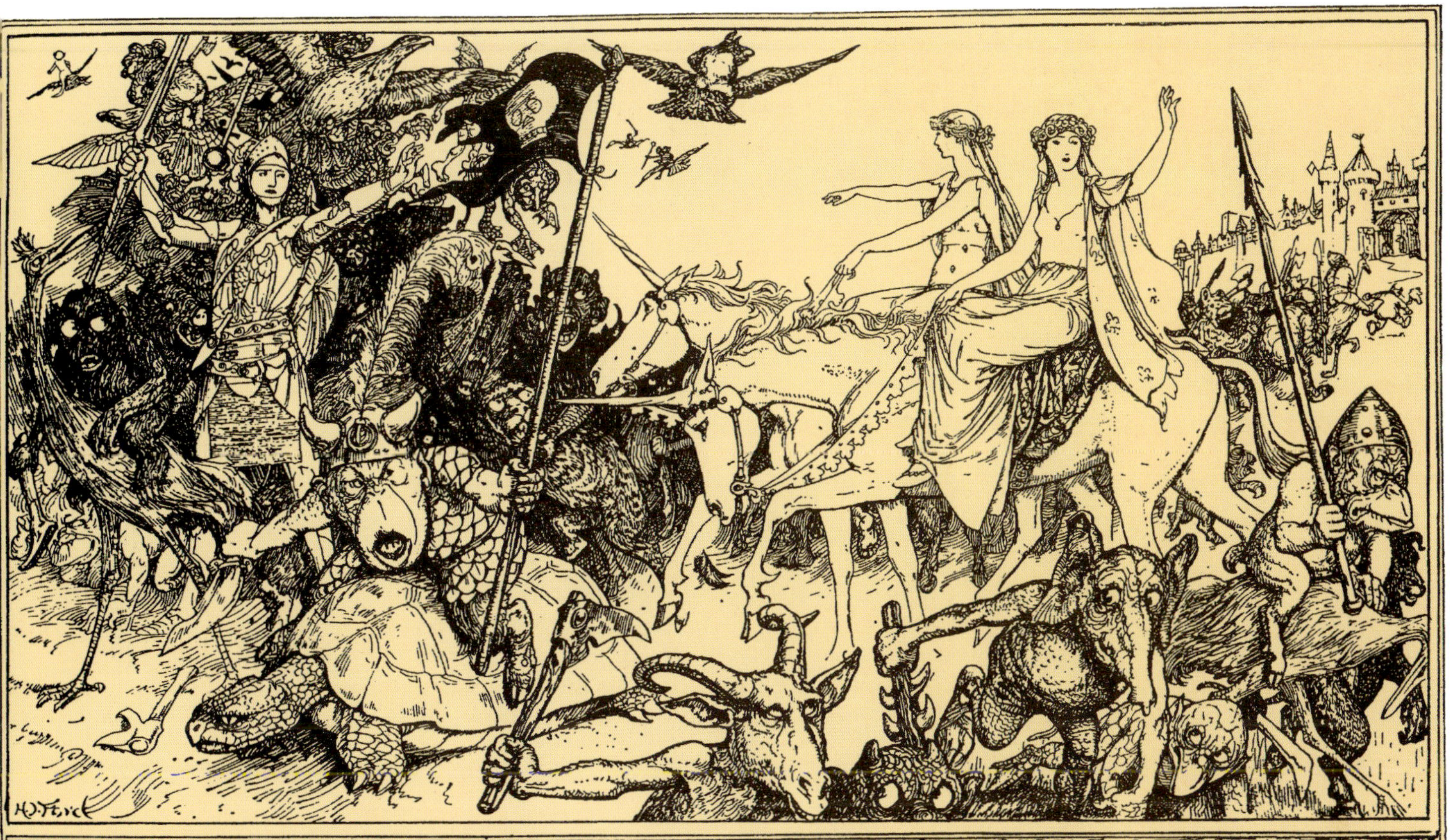

THE TWO DAMSELS RESCUE ROGER FROM THE RABBLE

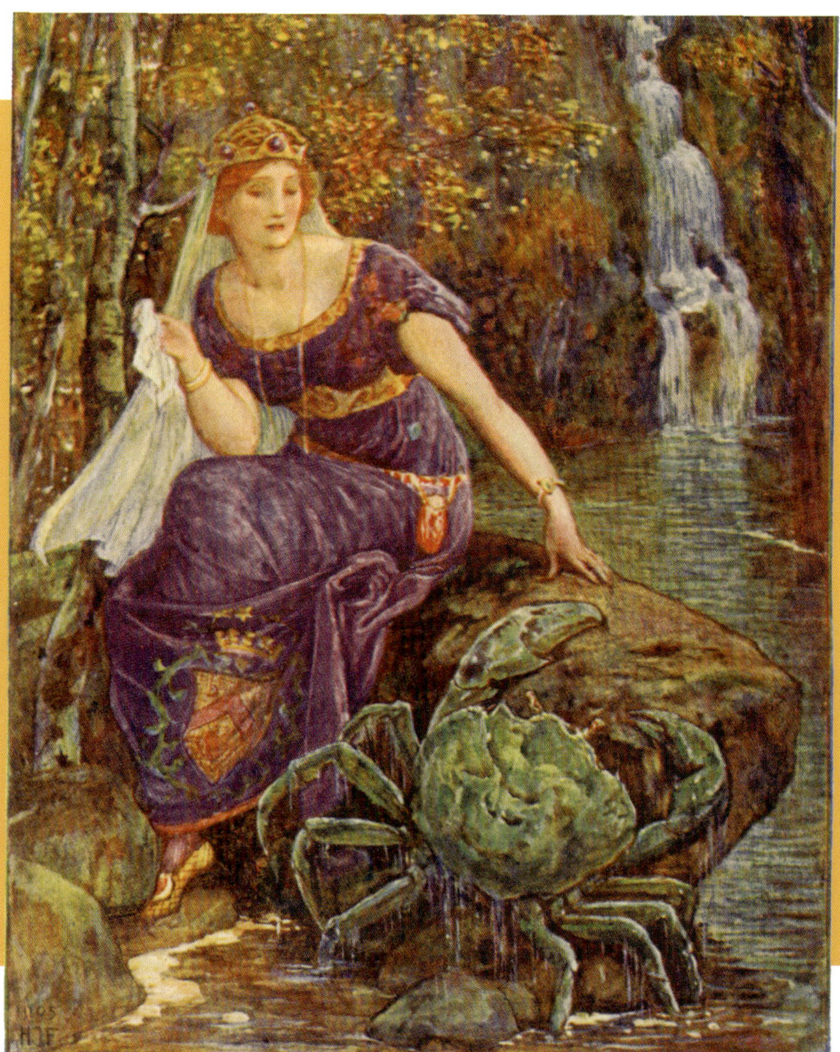

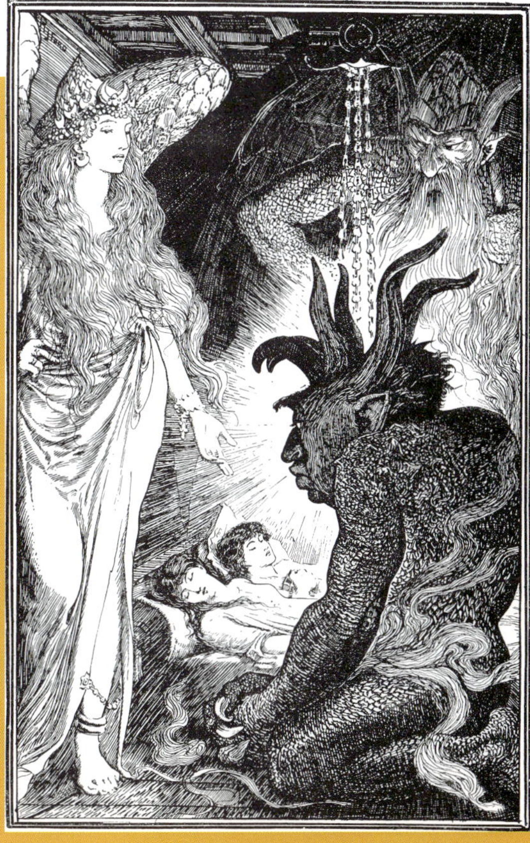

Arthur B. Frost
1851–1928, American

Born in Philadelphia, Arthur Burdett Frost began his creative path as an apprentice engraver and lithographer. He received little formal art training, but later in his career he was a student of painters Thomas Eakins and William Merritt Chase. Drawing what he loved, Frost became one of the best sporting illustrators of the late nineteenth and early twentieth centuries. His earliest success was a favor he did for a friend, drawing humorous cartoons for a book, *Out of the Hurly Burly,* by Charles Heber Clark. The book was very well-received, and the experience gave Frost the confidence to pursue a career in art. Humor remained one of Frost's strong points throughout his career, and it occasionally appeared in his sports work, most frequently, the golfing material.

The themes Frost seemed most focused on were scenes depicting outdoor life, sports, and a simpler lifestyle. In some ways he was the counterpoint to illustrators like Charles Dana Gibson and James Montgomery Flagg, who both focused on the exploits of city life and high society. In 1876 Frost worked as an artist at *Harper's,* alongside artists Howard Pyle, Frederic Remington, and E. W. Kemble. His contributions included *Tom Sawyer,* seven volumes of *Uncle Remus,* and some of Theodore Roosevelt's books on sporting and adventure in the wild.

A book of collected line pieces contained some of the earliest uses of sequential art panels, a forerunner to the comic strip. *Stuff and Nonsense* in 1884 contains many of these early stories, combined together in one volume. A second book by Frost, *Golpher's Alphabet,* was published in 1898.

Frost was red/green color-blind, but with the abundance of line-work assignments available to him in the late nineteenth century, this was not an impediment to becoming an illustrator. When he began to paint for prints later in his career, his pieces often had a neutral look, and he relied frequently on the labels on the paint tubes to place color correctly.

Frost went on to work and study in Paris between 1908 and 1916, and then returned to the United States, retiring to California in 1919.

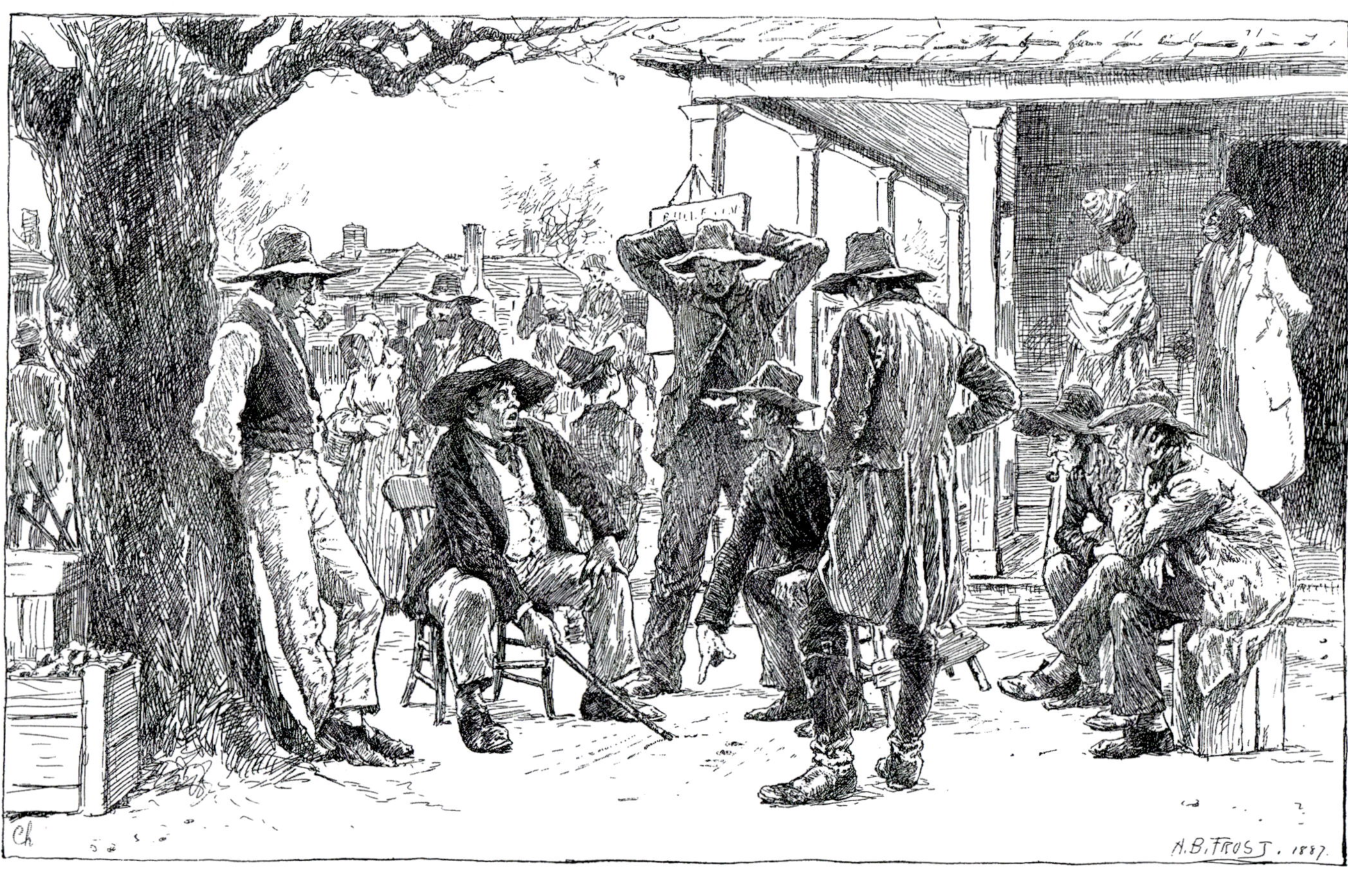

Frost, Arthur B.

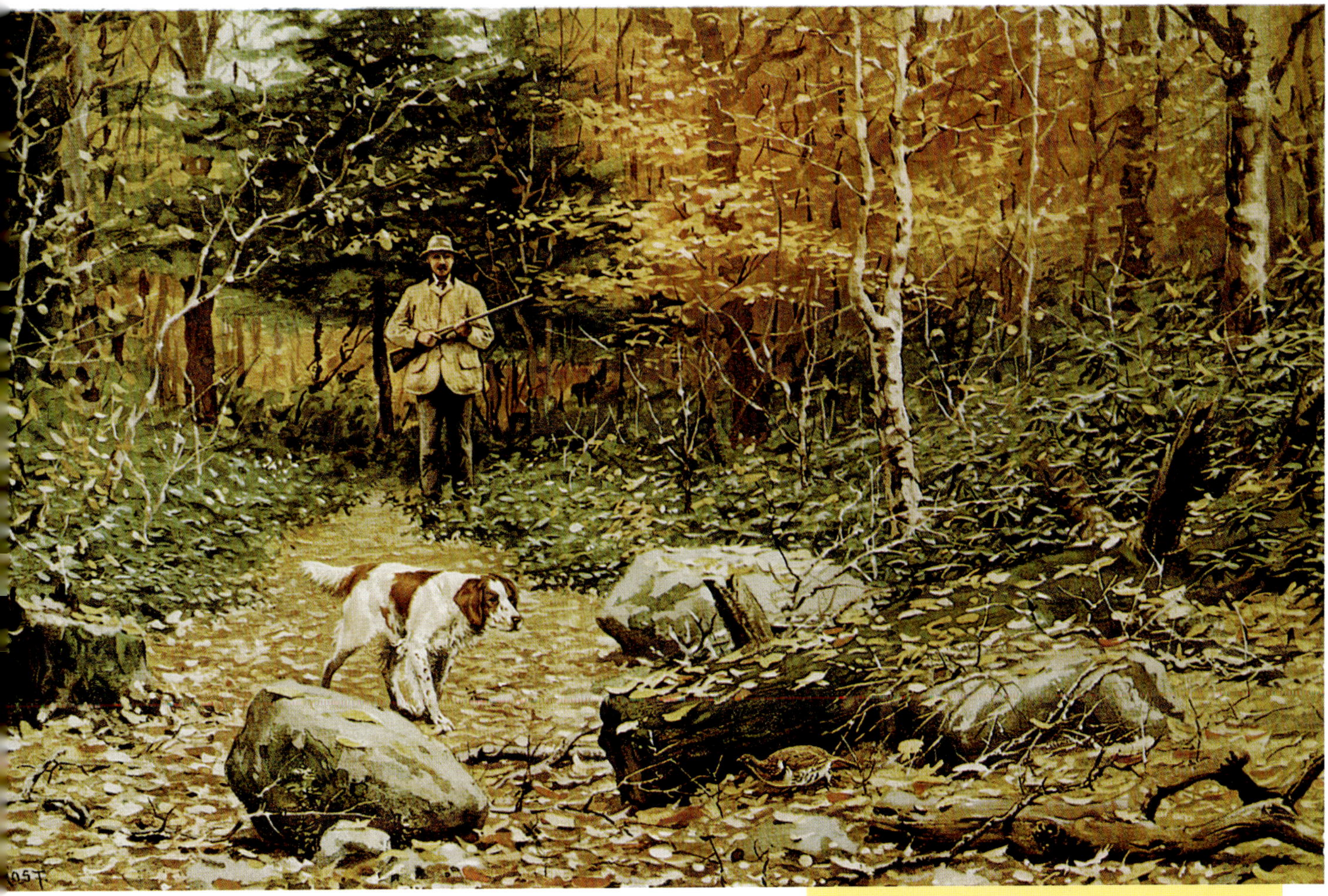

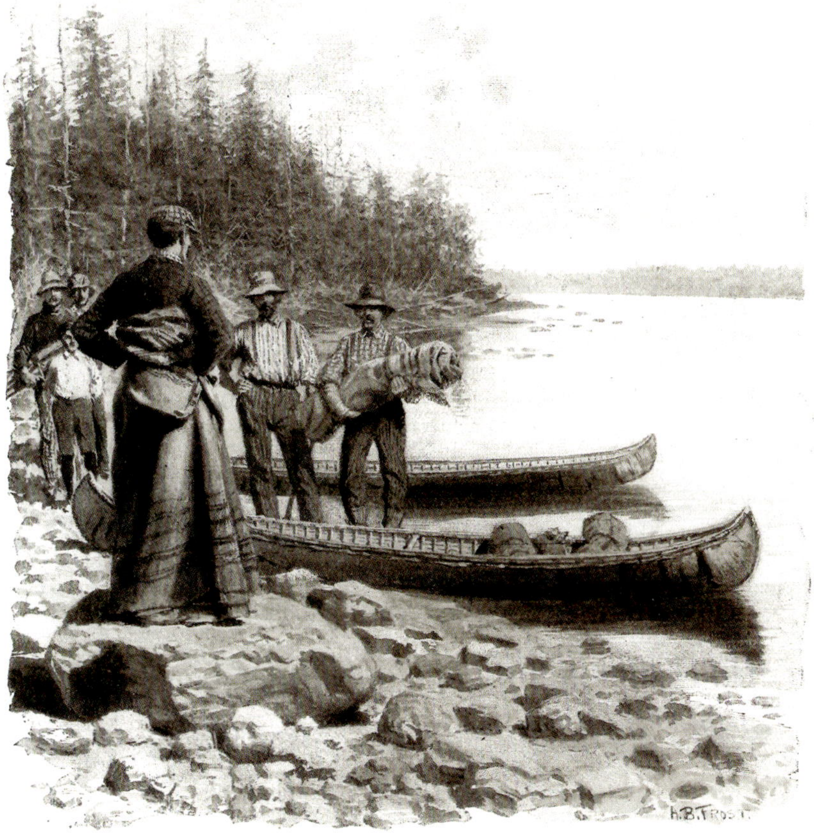

Two sides of Frost

He had both a straightforward realist approach, and also a humorous cartoon style, and called on both of them regularly.

The guides stood around, as solemn and respectful as judges.—Page 476.

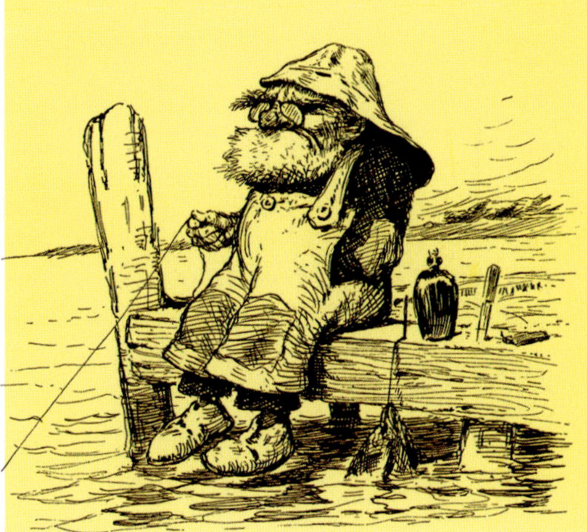

Charles Dana Gibson

1867–1944, American

If there was a king of line art in America at the turn of the century, it was probably Charles Dana Gibson. *Life* magazine certainly seemed to think so. In 1904, the magazine paid him an unheard-of salary of $100,000 to become their contributor for 100 illustrations over the next four years. Both his line work and his editorial observation of society were fluid and expressive. His ability to produce subtle tones from his instrument of solid black expression served as an example to others, and he was widely imitated. His sensitivity and wit in regard to the social standings of the day were sharp—his "writing" was as much a part of his success as his skilled draftsmanship.

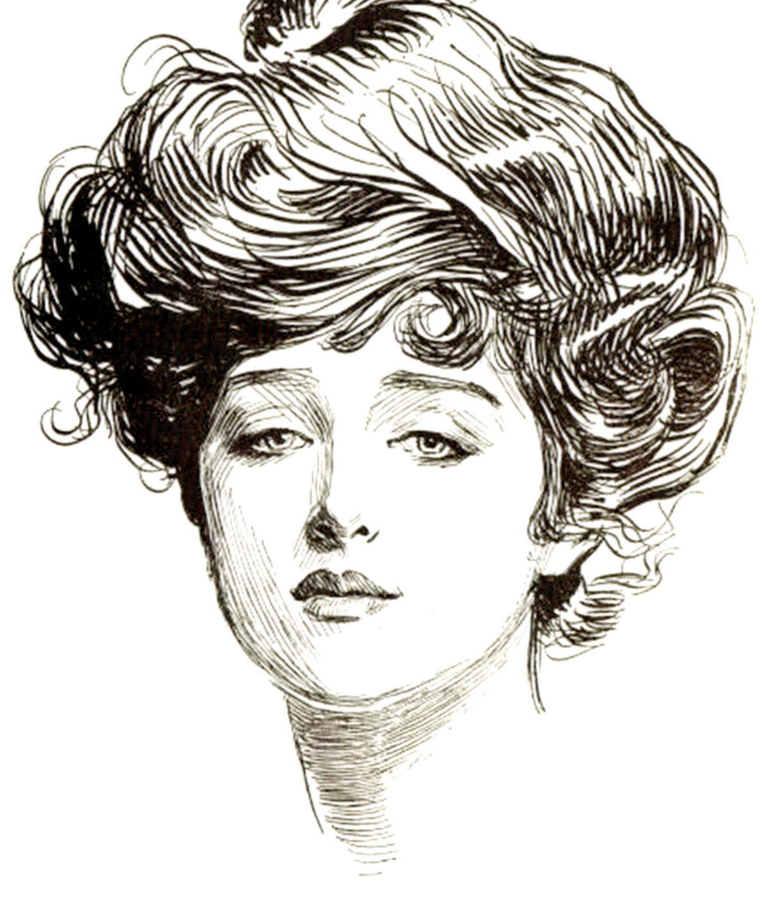

Gibson's earliest work was quite workmanlike; in fact, he had to persevere before he found a publisher that was willing to take a chance with him, and see the potential under his rough, raw ink work. *Life* was the first to recognize his talents, and as he honed his skills, more clients were added to the list. He worked for many of the premier New York magazines, and illustrated books like *The Prisoner of Zenda,* and a number of titles by Robert W. Chambers. He began drawing a cartoon, and it was this pairing of his own social observance and sense of humor with his skilled draftsmanship that made him an unparalleled commodity. It was the large ink splash pages that *Collier's* hired him for, and the way in which he made his fortune.

More than any other facet of his work, Charles Dana Gibson is best remembered for the "Gibson Girl," who starred in his large, single-panel commentaries. The character was an idealized figure of a woman; she was a singular treat for men's eyes, while, at the same time, scorned by elderly women. The Gibson Girl had a degree of self-awareness and symbolized the epitome of an independent American woman, which broke away from earlier traditions. Gibson's other notable character was "Mr. Pipp," an old curmudgeon whose sour attitude and over-bearing wife provided many comic situations for Gibson to exploit.

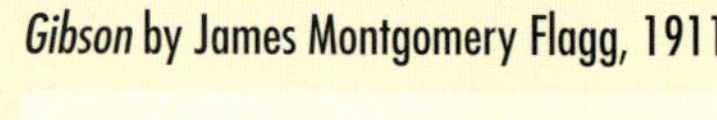

Gibson by James Montgomery Flagg, 1911

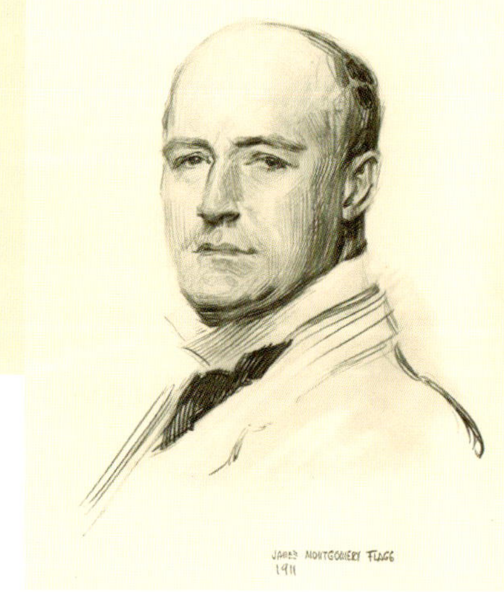

Gibson was a star of magazine publishing for two decades at a time when it was the most important form of news and entertainment the public could obtain. His iconic status began to fade in the twenties, however. While he worked to make the leap to oil work and join publishing's movement towards color reproduction, his later work was never embraced with the same fervor as his line work of the 1890s and 1900s.

Gibson, Charles Dana

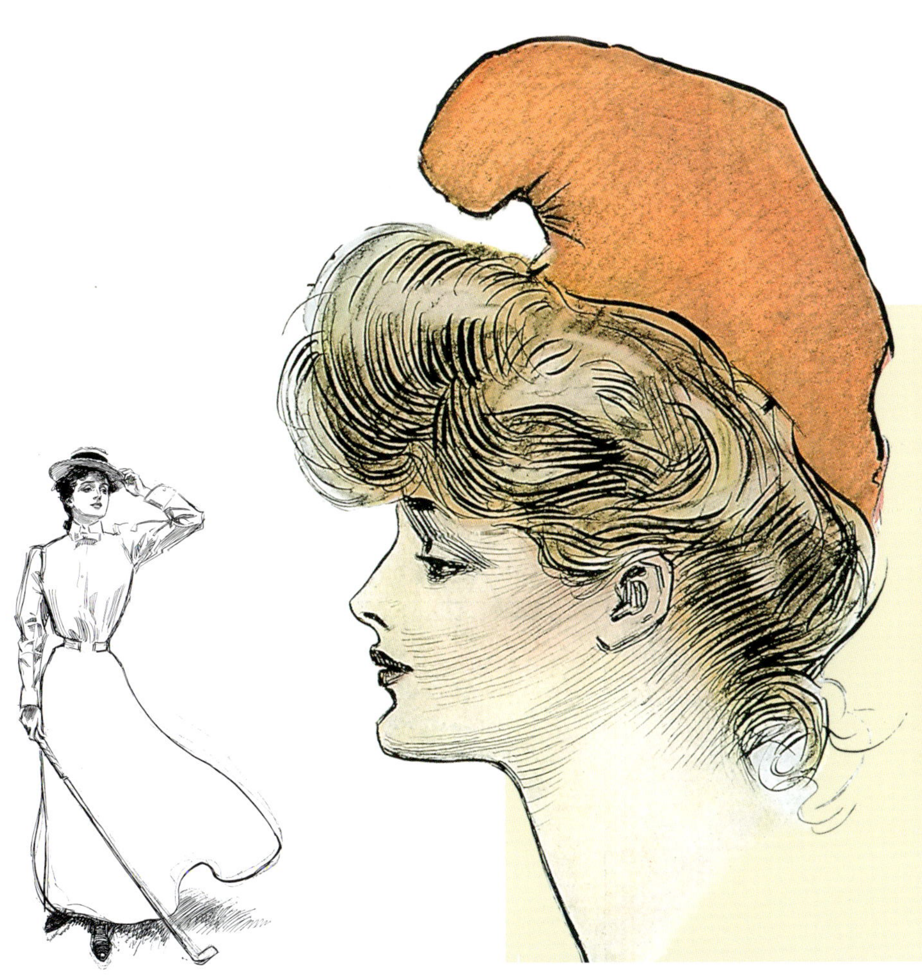

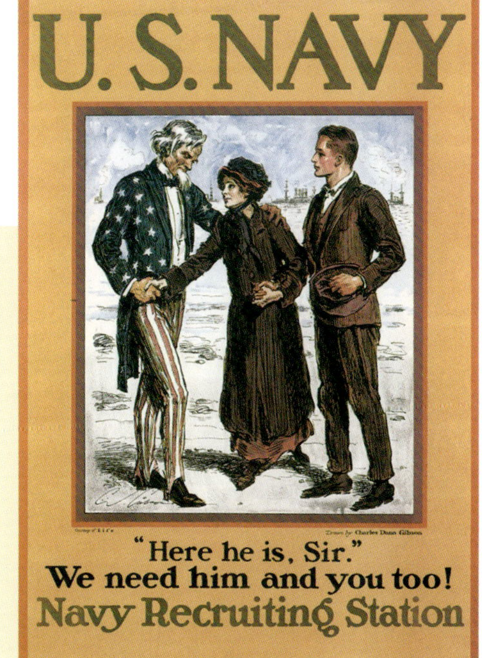

Past his heyday, Gibson was not beyond stepping up to do his part to help the effort in World War I.

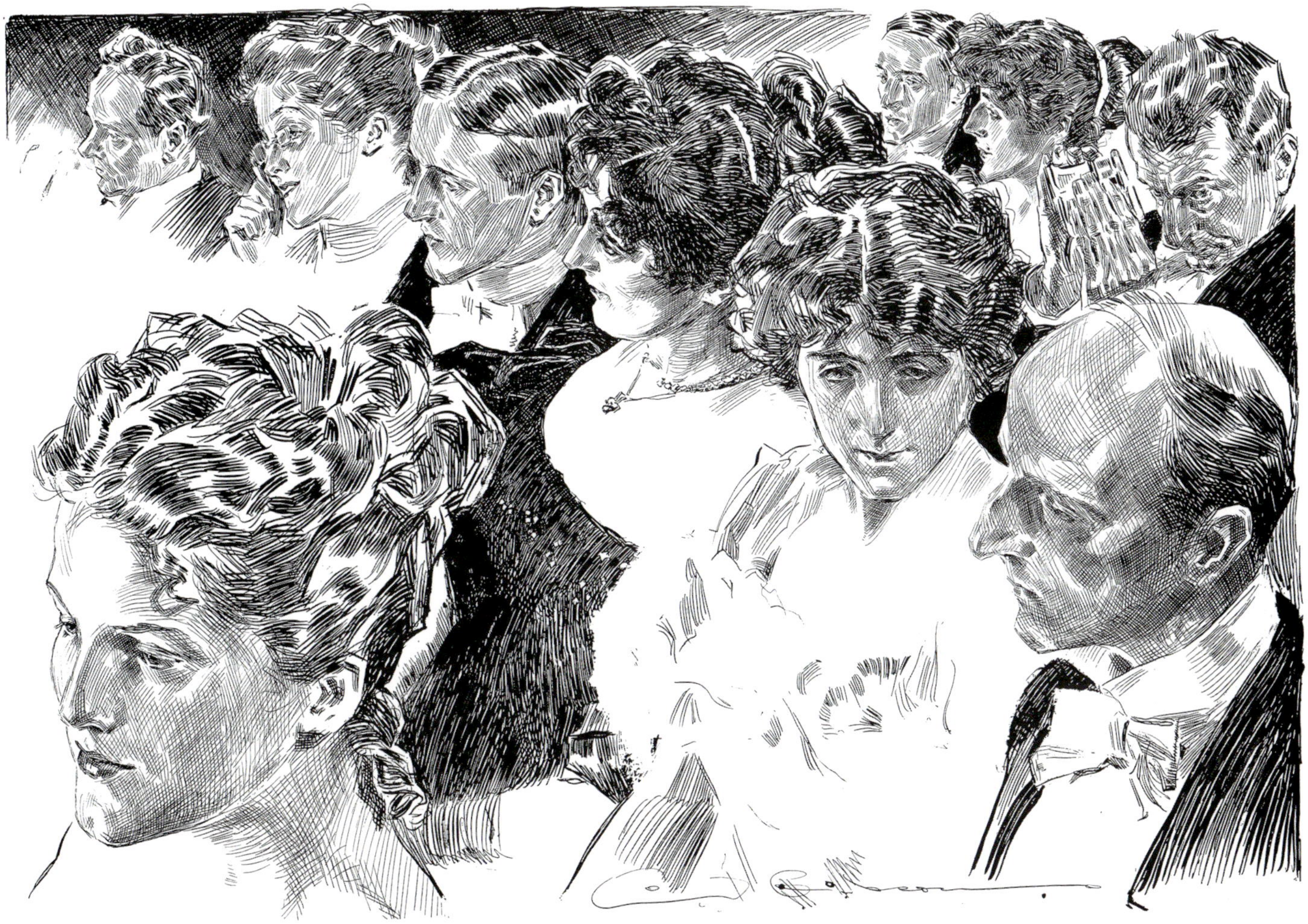

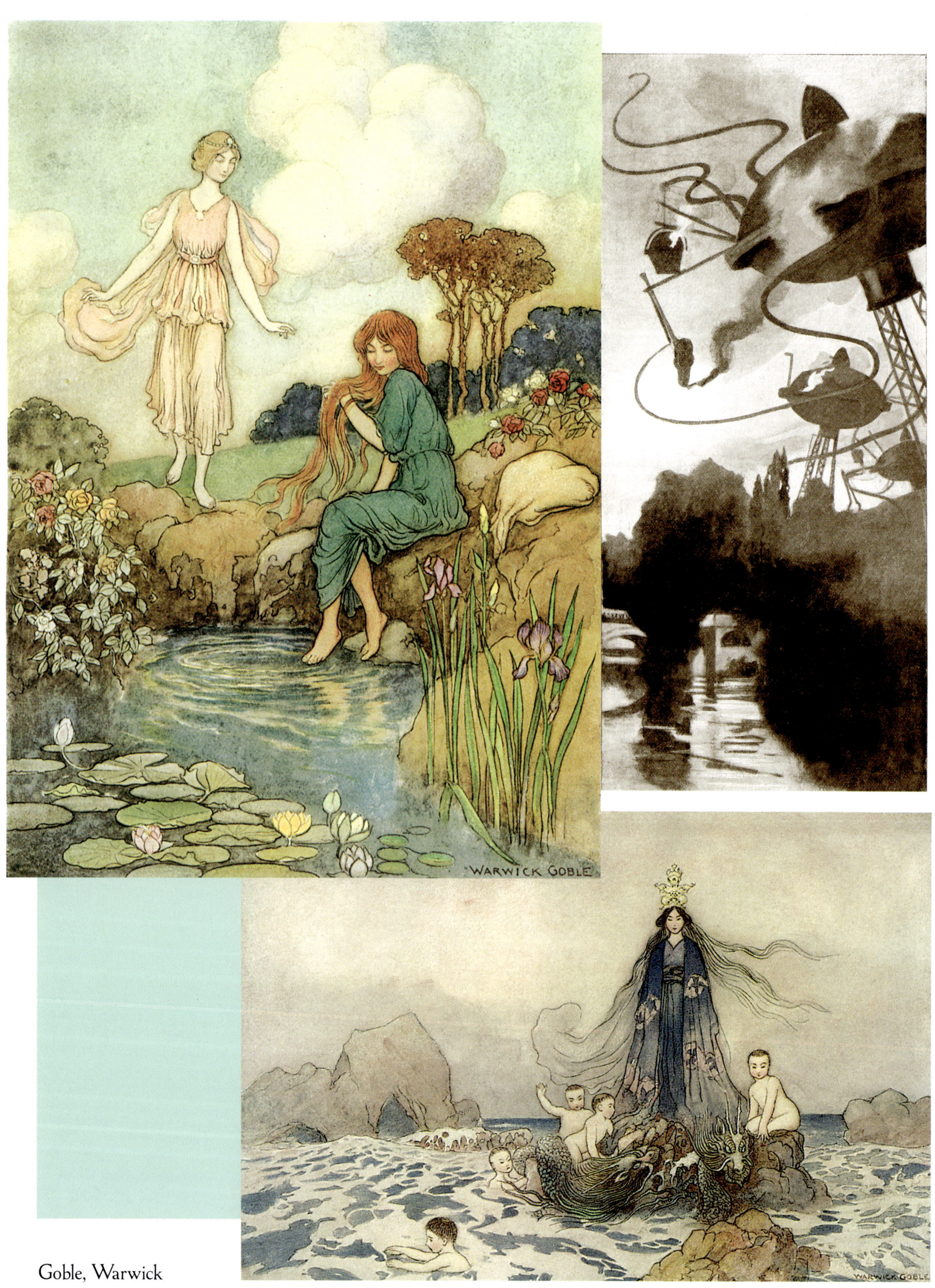

Goble, Warwick

Warwick Goble

1862–1943, British

Throughout the early part of his career, Warwick Goble competed with the biggest names in illustration for the best assignments in books and magazines. At his best, Goble's work rivaled qualities of the highly esteemed Edmund Dulac—and like Dulac, Goble had a strong interest in Eastern design and imagery, which influenced both the style of his work and the assignments he chose. He used a rich palette of color, great for exposing the exotic landscapes and fabrics of Eastern culture in all its beauty. Some of the titles that benefited from these Eastern inpirations included: *Stories from the Pentamarone* (1911), *Green Willow and Other Japanese Fairy Tales* (1910), and *Folk-Tales of Bengal* (1912). There were also moments when influences from his native England came through, such as in his 1912 edition of *Chaucer.*

Goble got his start in magazines during the 1890s. When the illustrated gift books began to make their appearance in the middle of the next decade, Goble recognized it as something appropriate for him, even though he had already reached the age of forty-four. He was hired by Macmillan in 1909 as the house resident gift-book illustrator. Active in books and magazines from his debut in 1890, his book production declined with the end of World War I. In his later years, Goble retired from illustration to spend time in more leisurely pursuits, such as cycling and travel.

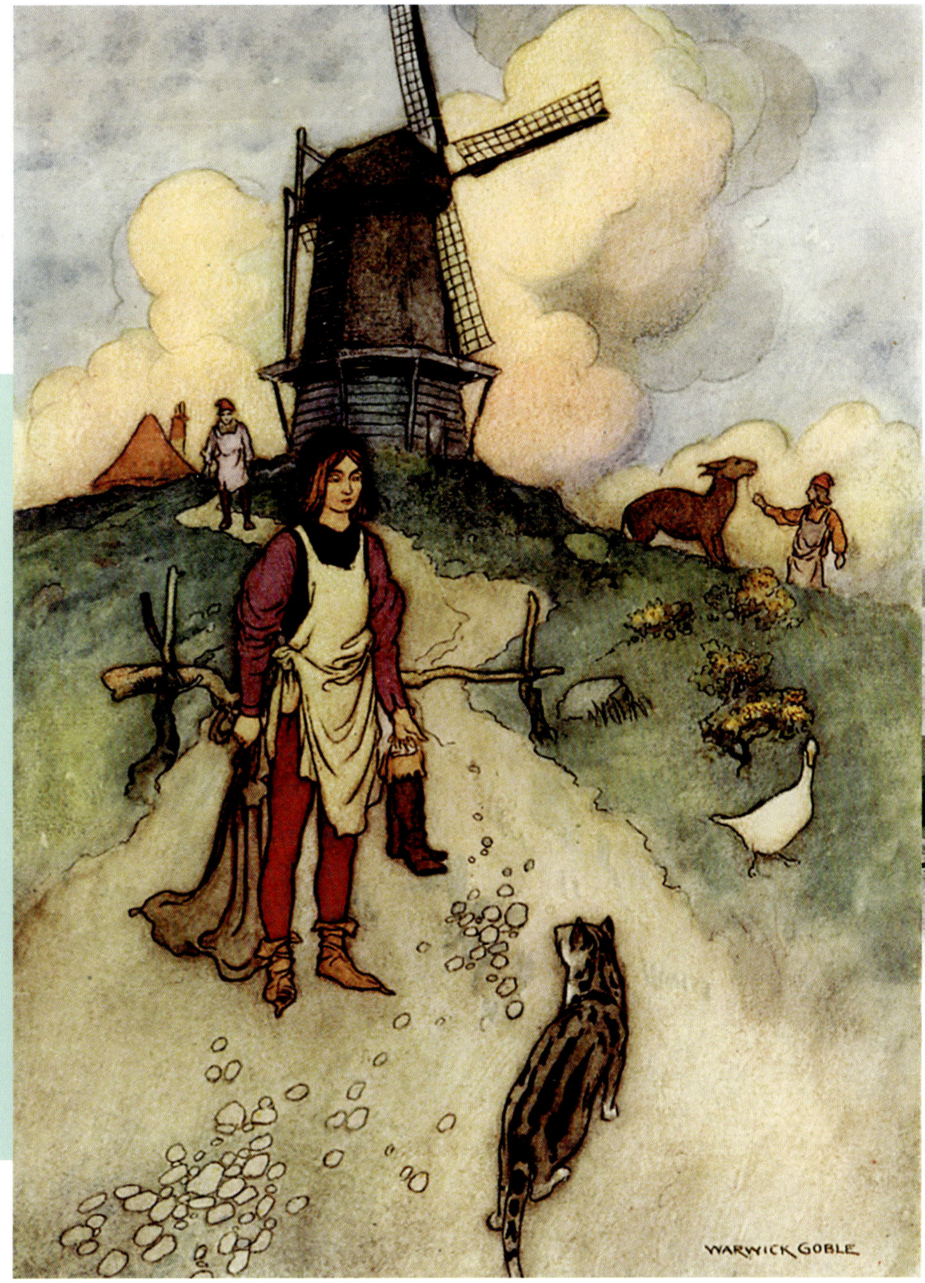

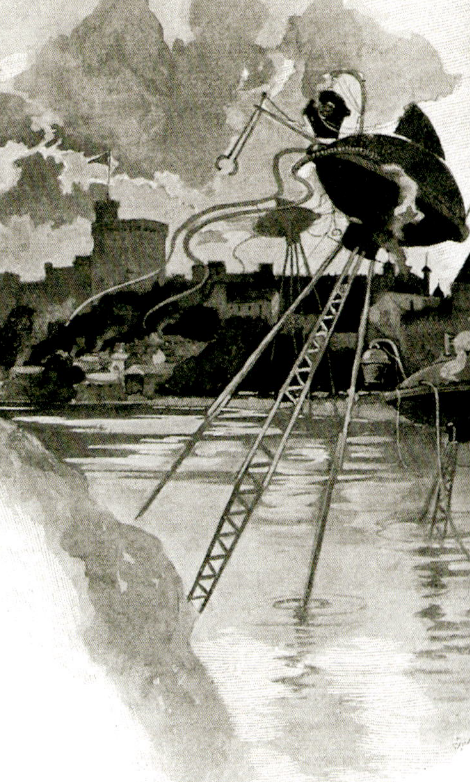

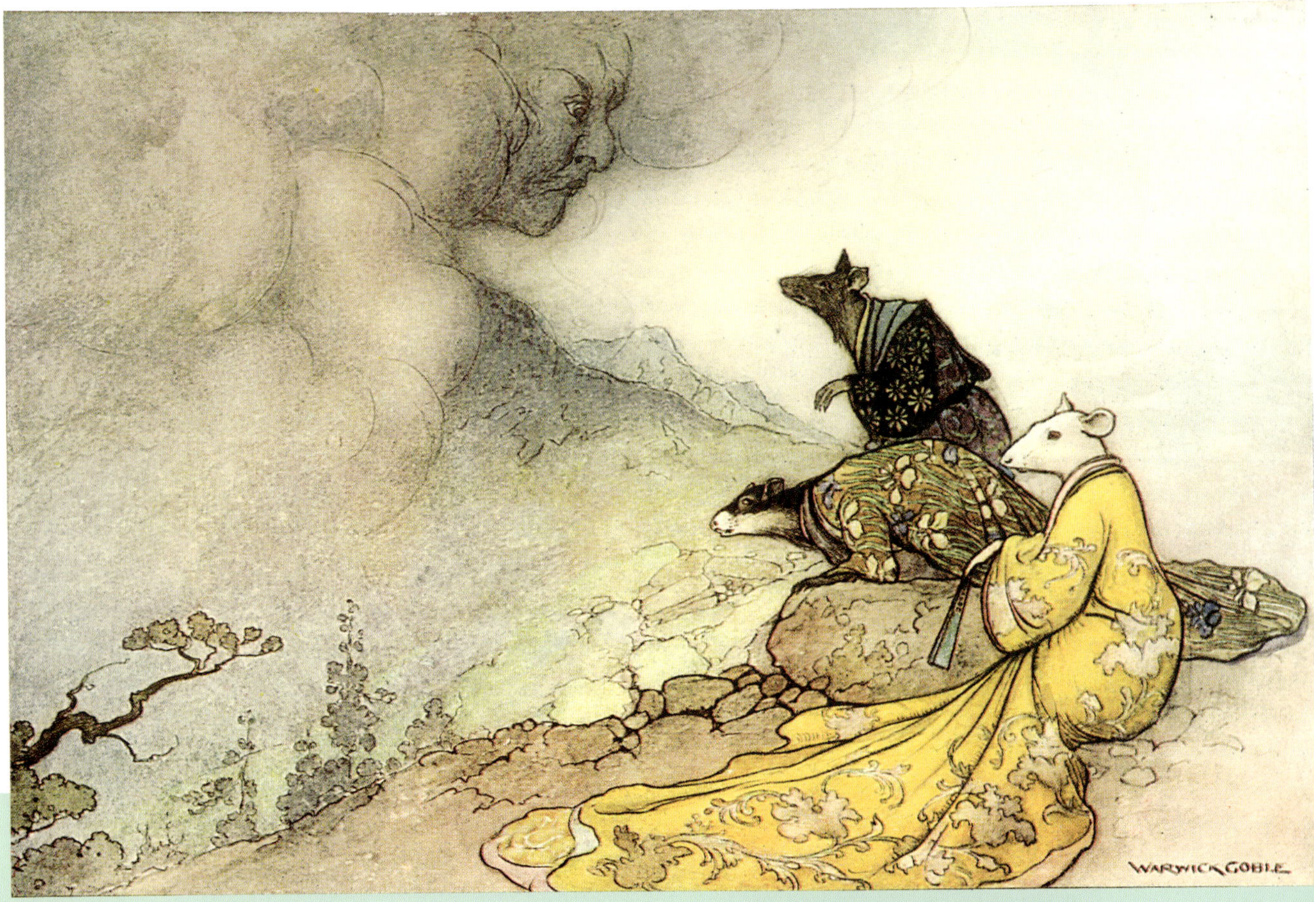

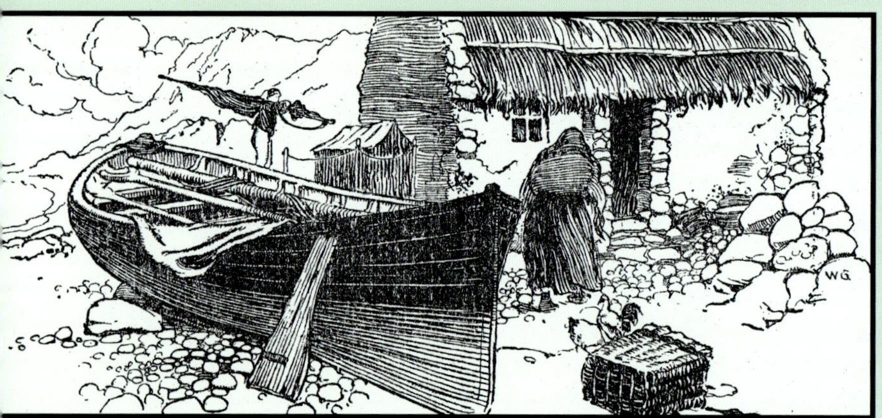

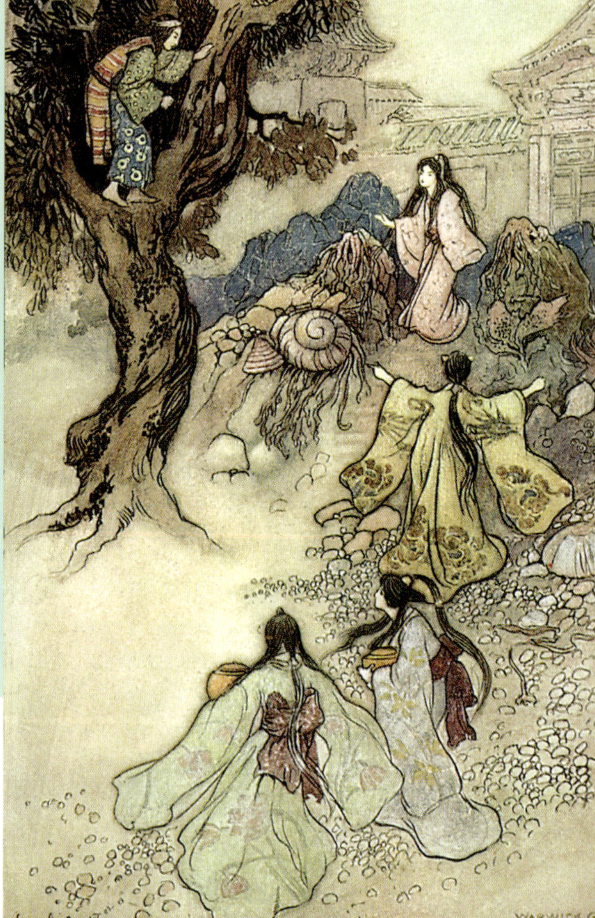

Goble was the first to illustrate H. G. Wells's *War of the Worlds,* in a serial magazine format for *Pearson's* in 1898. The serialization spread out over the course of months, and contained over 65 halftone drawings.

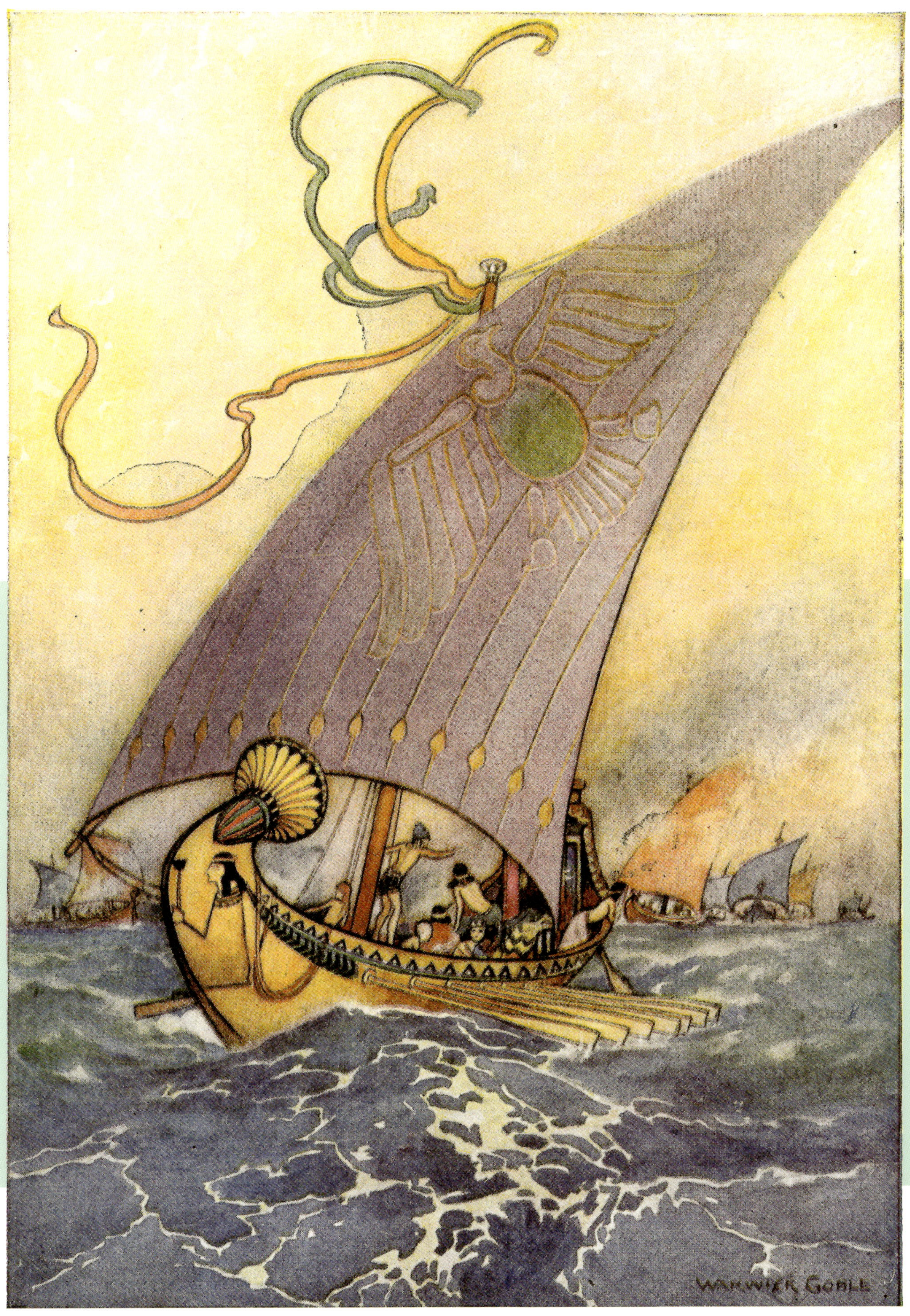
WARWICK GOBLE

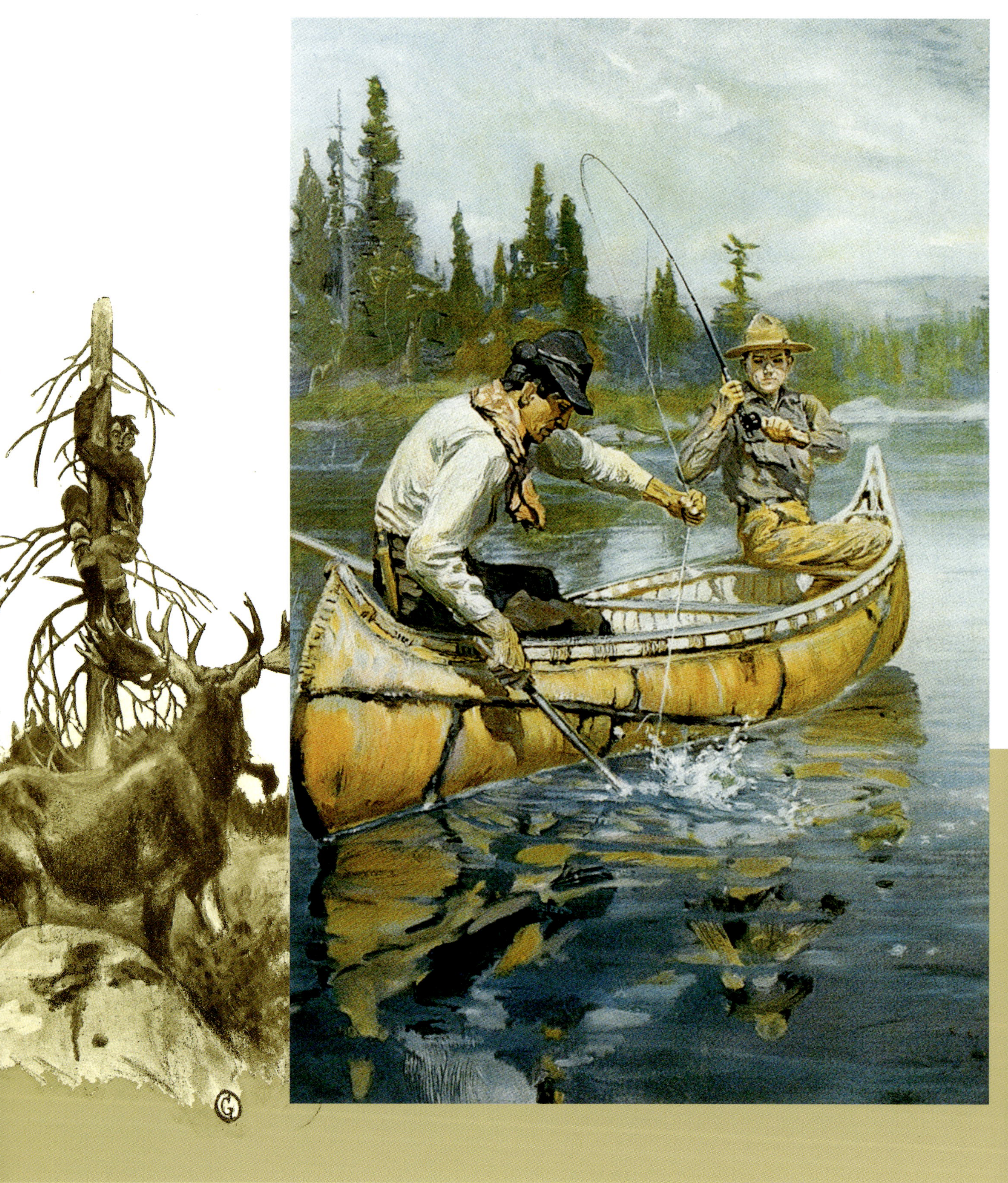

Goodwin, Philip

Philip Goodwin

1881~1935, American

One of the greatest purveyors of Western and cabin art in the early twentieth century, Goodwin became an artistic champion of the outdoorsman. A natural artist, Goodwin was already illustrating for publication as a young teen. He completed formal art studies at the Rhode Island School of Design and the Art Students League in New York before he found his way to Chadds Ford, Pennsylvania, and Howard Pyle's Brandywine School. Goodwin studied with Pyle from 1901–1903. By the age of 25, he had his own New York studio, and became a regular contributor for *Scribner's, Harper's, Outing,* and *Everybody's* magazines.

Hunting and fishing scenes were his forté, and there were plenty of venues for this work at that time to keep him and a few other specialists, steadily employed. Goodwin received a good deal of advertising work in that field, and had an especially long-running arrangement with Winchester Rifles and the Marlin Firearms Company. Following Pyle's model, he made time to visit the places he portrayed, traveling to the Maine wilderness and out West to the Rockies, in Colorado and Montana.

In his travels Goodwin befriended another notable artist in the genre, Charles Russell. The two often traveled together, and Goodwin experimented with sculpting as a result of his friendship with Russell.

Though originally used within a limited market, Goodwin's thematic work remains highly sought-after. Calendar illustrations he produced for tea manufacturers Brown & Bigelow are among his most often reproduced works. These pictures often show the sportsman in a moment of excitement, often caused by a chance encounter with a bear, moose, or some other large game. They have found their way onto a good amount of merchandise for the nostalgic outdoor look.

Goodwin's book illustration can be found in editions of Jack London's *Call of the Wild* and Theodore Roosevelt's *African Game Trails.*

Goodwin died of pneumonia at the age of fifty-four.

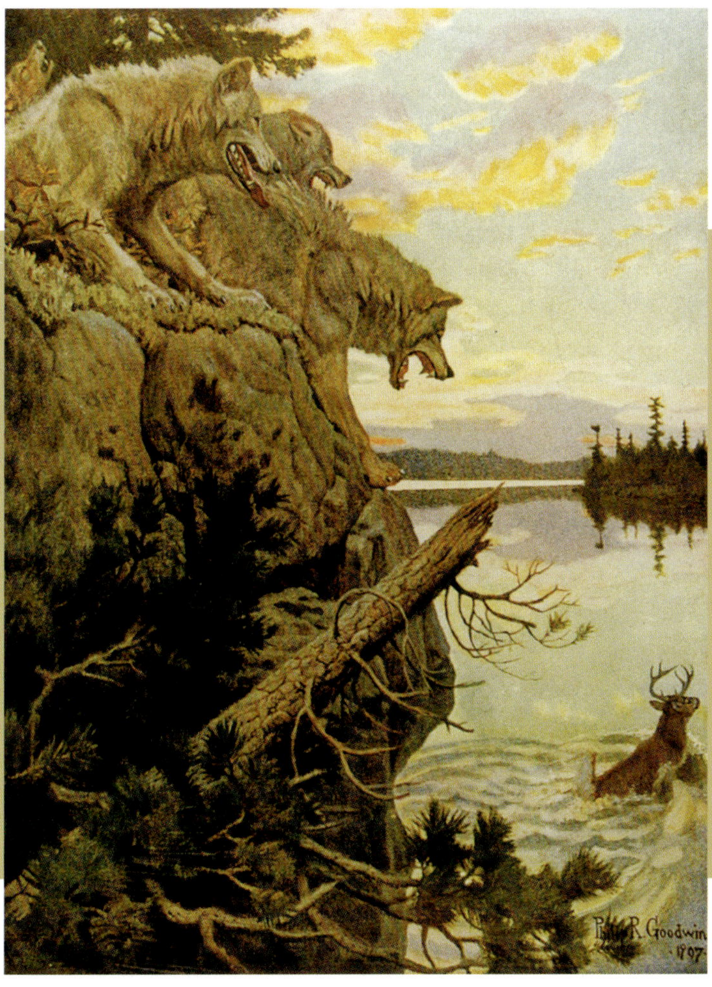

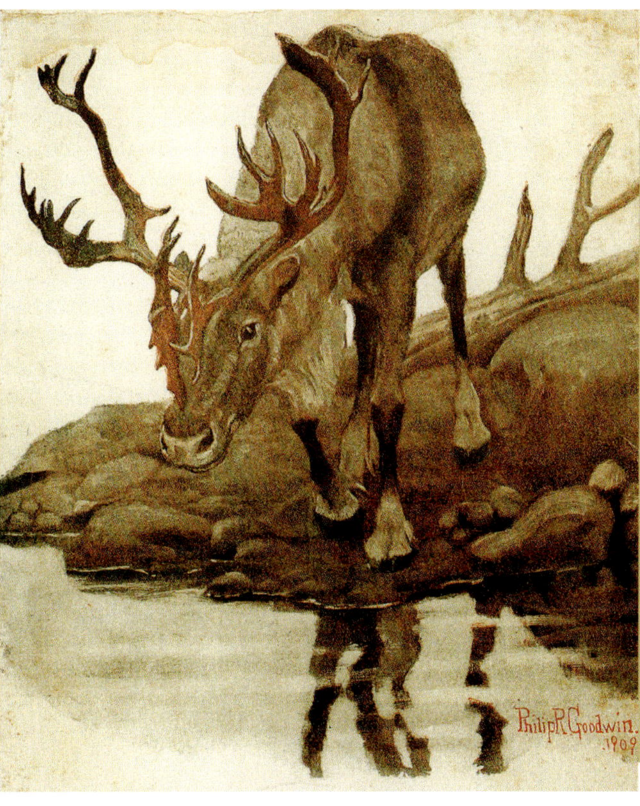

Gordon Grant

1875–1962, American

Grant's earliest works contain many widely different subjects—including social scenes, romance, and advertising. His childhood years were spent in San Francisco, California, and for schooling, he was sent to Scotland. This four-month trip halfway around the world via "the horn"—the southern tip of South America—greatly influenced Grant's interest in the sea and ships. This later became a specialty of Grant's, and in time, he was recognized for this talent. He studied at Heatherly and at London, and then returned to California for a job with the *San Francisco Examiner.* Grant became an artist/reporter working for both the *Examiner* and the *San Francisco Chronicle,* and before long, his drawings were being used by *Harper's Weekly* as well.

Grant developed strong ink skills during his newspaper days, a distinctive strength that would continue to serve him well throughout his long book and magazine career. Books such as *Sail Ho!, The Story of the Ship,* and *Greasy Luck* are full of Grant's signature ink style.

Along with artist/teacher Eric Pape, Grant was deeply involved in the preservation of the USS *Constitution,* and it was a print of Grant's, which sold by the thousands that helped raise considerable funds to lobby Congress and designate the ship a historic landmark. That effort alone helped solidify his reputation for marine work.

Unlike other marine painters of the time—Anton Otto Fischer, W. J. Aylward, and Henry Reuterdahl, to name a few—Grant's primary medium was watercolor, and after World War I, when attention on the sea turned away from warships to recreation and lighter discussion—his brighter, airier images were warmly welcomed after a decade of the weighty oils. He found both ample assignments and a great following with his marine work, and managed to get a number of book assignments on nautical topics as well as magazine covers.

Art publisher Watson-Guptill produced a sketchbook of Grant's work in 1950, a testament to both the strength of his developmental drawings and the popularity that Grant's work had attained.

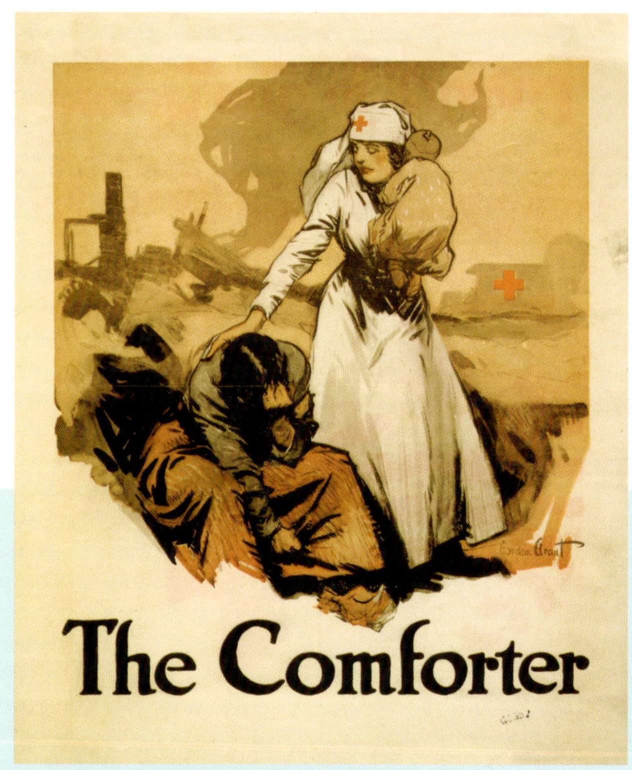

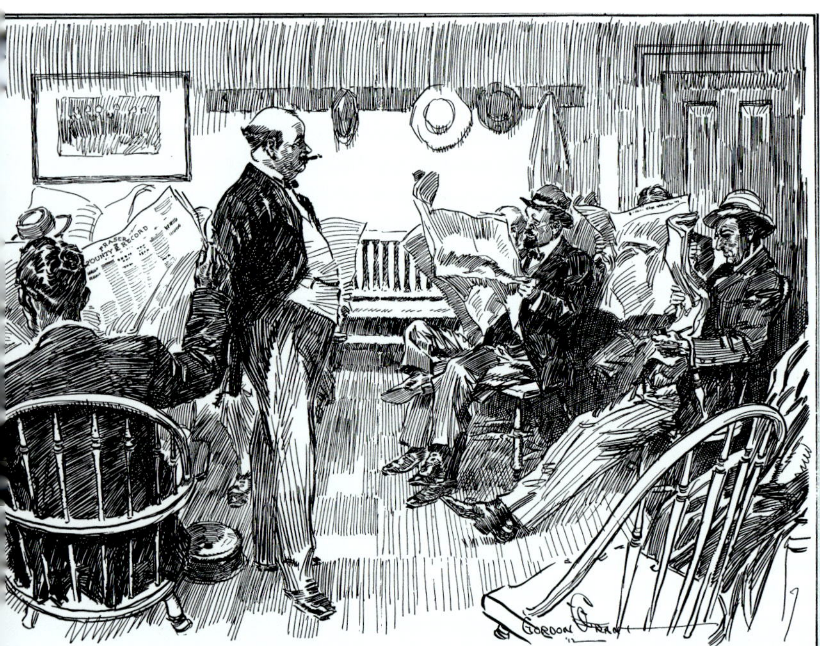

Though largely remembered for his excellent marine work, Gordon Grant woked for some time in much more general themes, including a good deal of regular work for *Puck.*

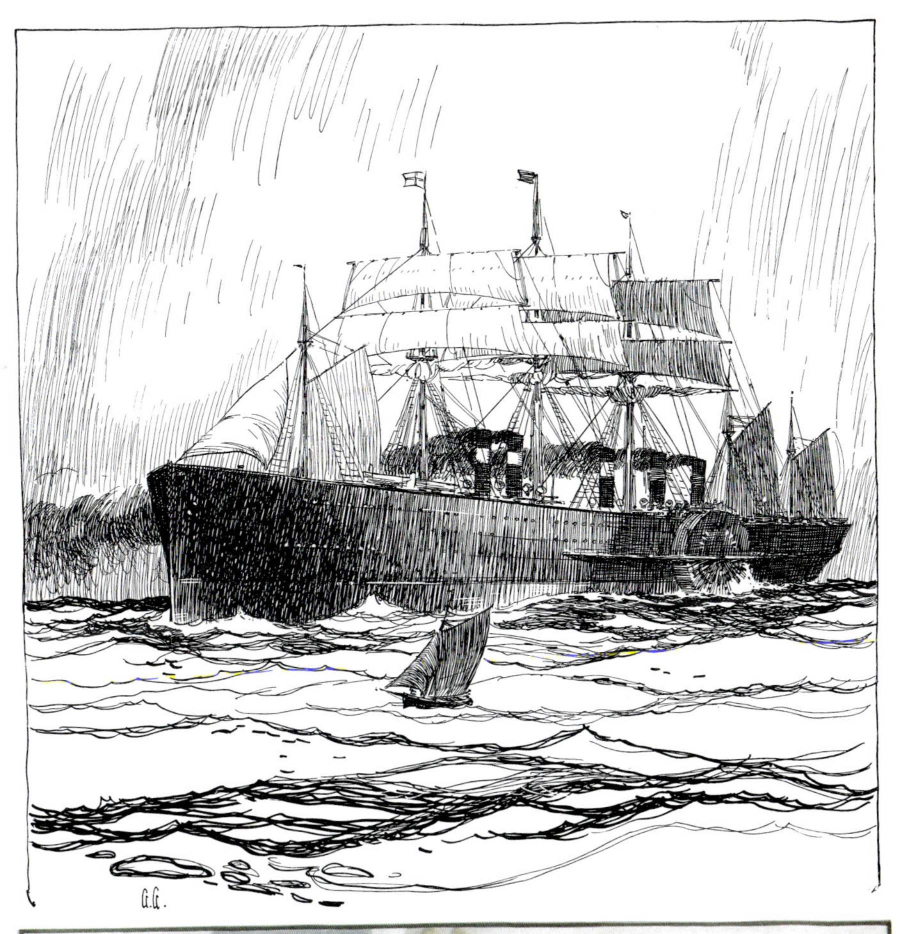

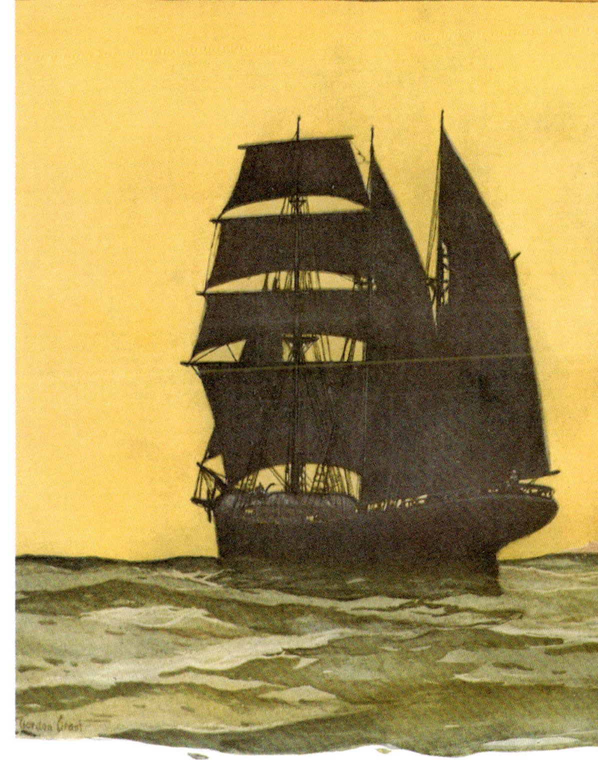

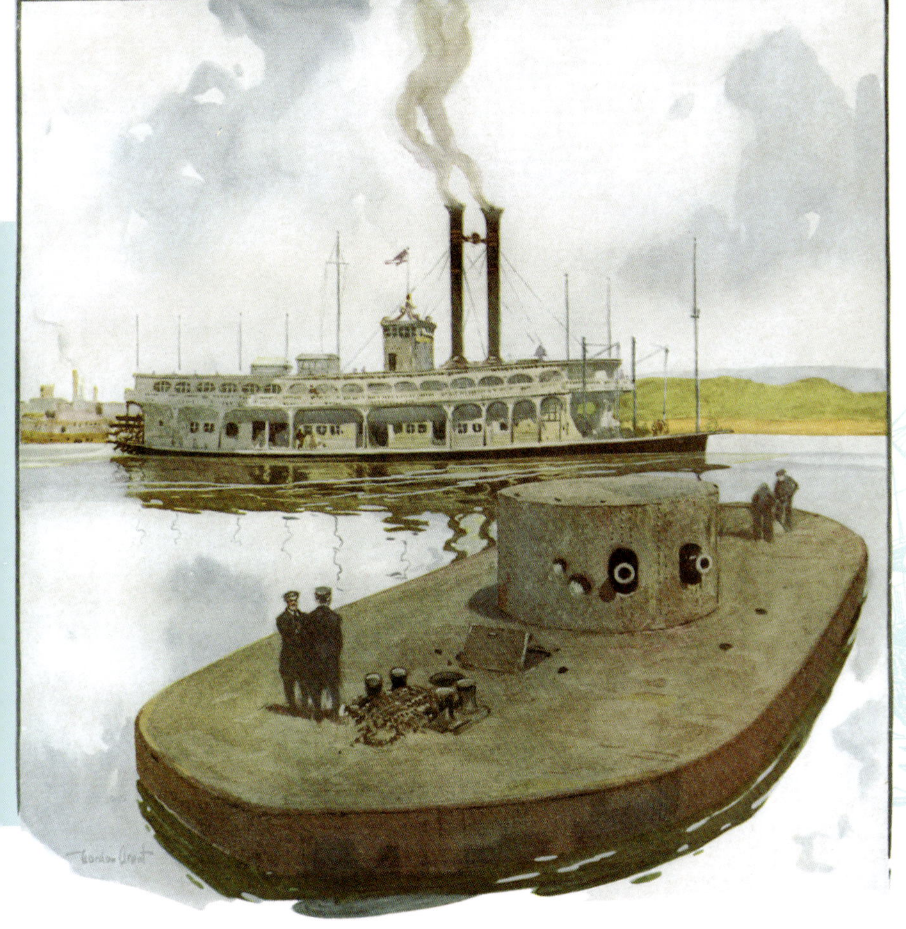

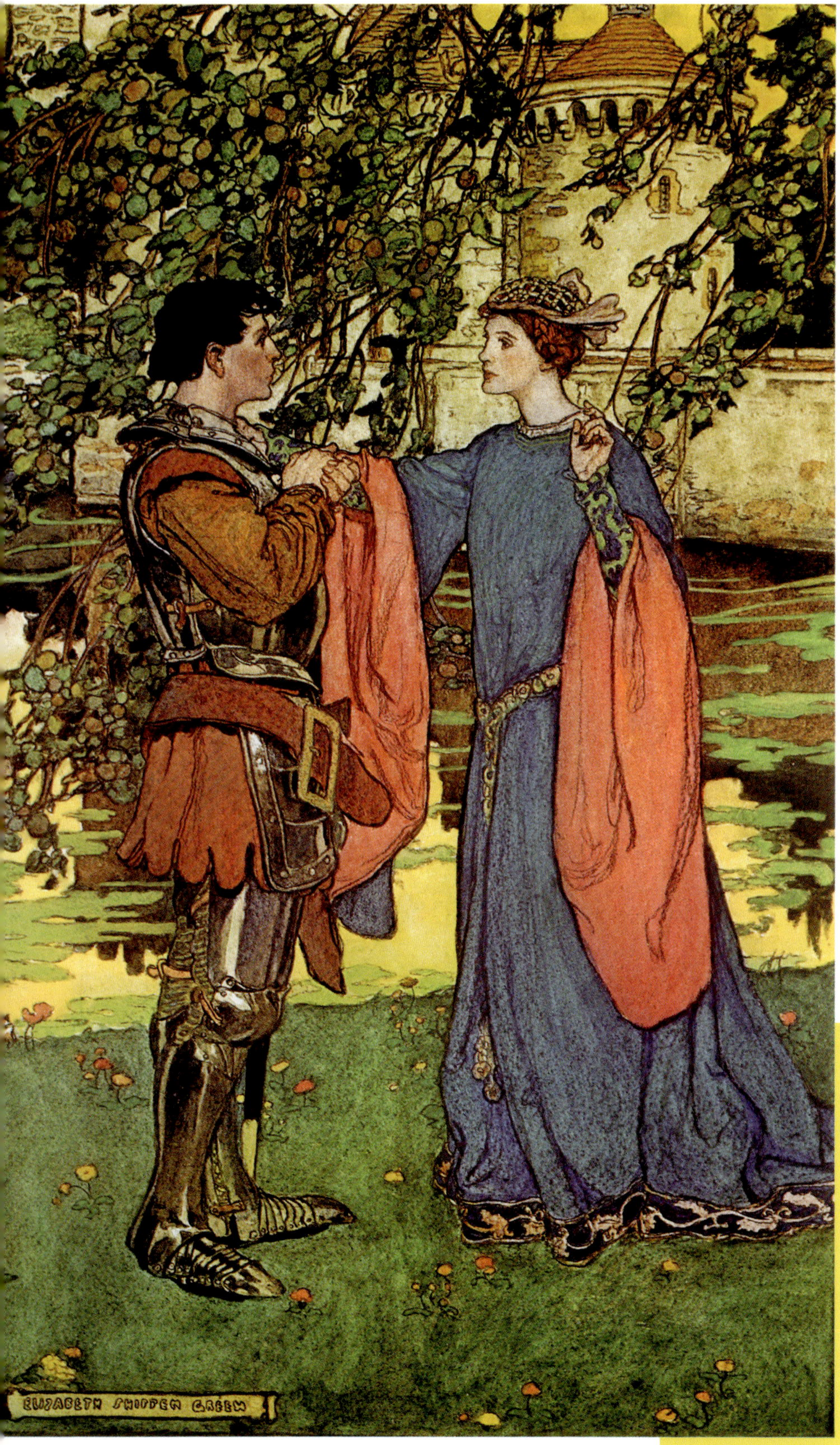

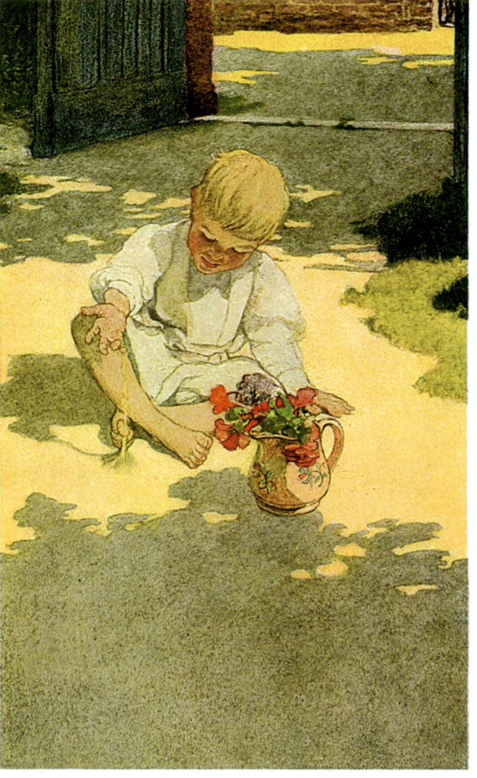

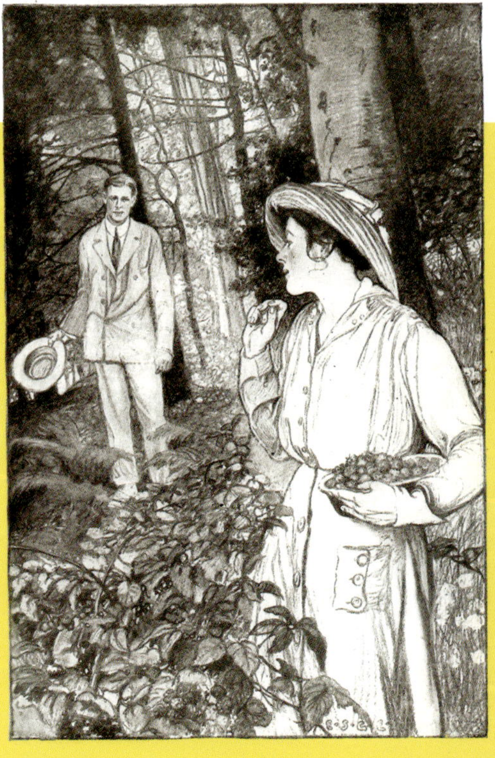

Green, Elizabeth S.

Elizabeth S. Green
1871–1954, American

One of the earliest successful women illustrators of the period, Elizabeth Shippen Green worked for numerous publications after her studies at the Pennsylvania Academy of the Fine Arts. In the early 1890s, she was working for Philadelphia newspapers, as well as producing advertising images for Strawbridge and Clothier. In the latter half of the decade, she began to attract attention as an illustrator for stories for adults and children.

It was around this time that Green also began studies with Howard Pyle at Drexel University. Throughout her life, she noted how influential she had found his philosophy on art. In Pyle's classes she met Jessie Willcox Smith and Violet Oakley, two trustworthy friends with whom she would share studio and home space for nearly a decade.

After working for a range of publications just after 1900—including *The Ladies' Home Journal* and *The Saturday Evening Post*—it was *Harper's Monthly* that was so taken by her work that they offered Green an exclusive contract in 1901. This relationship would be long-lasting, and continued to the end of 1924. While living with her studio mates, Green was introduced to architect and professor Huger Elliot. The two became engaged, though Green refused to marry while she was the sole support of her parents. The pair finally married in 1911, and soon moved throughout the Northeast U.S., where Huger held various positions in art schools, including an appointment as director of what is now the Philadelphia College of Art.

Green's earliest commercial work was very popular. Influenced by turn-of-the-century poster art, she developed a style with heavy charcoal lines, later filled in with vibrant watercolor, which produced a somewhat stained-glass look. It had the added benefit of meshing well with the less-than-perfect printing of the day, allowing for slight mis-registrations with little adverse effect. It remained the dominant style of her work for some time. In an attempt to gain more respect among her contemporaries, she moved toward oil painting in her later career, but never had the same success in that medium.

After her husband's death in 1951, Green returned to the Philadelphia area and resided near friends until her passing in 1954.

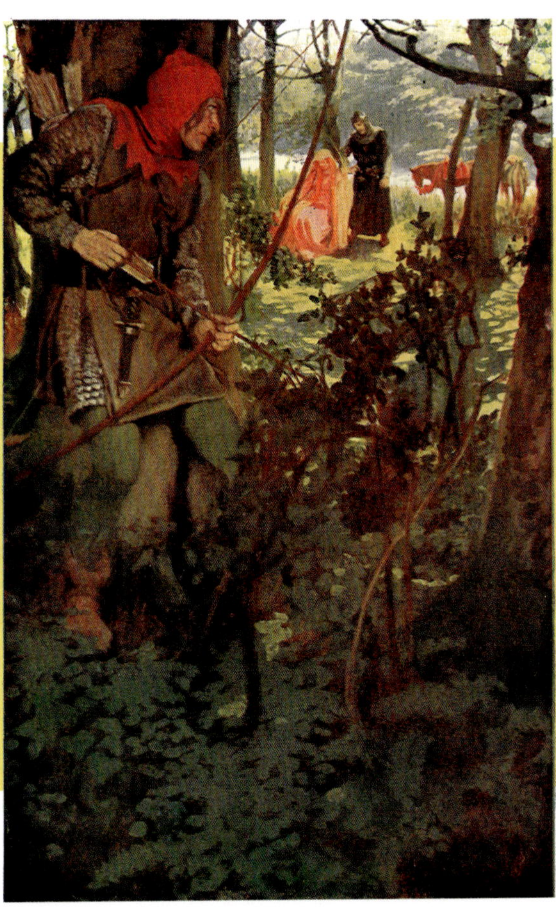

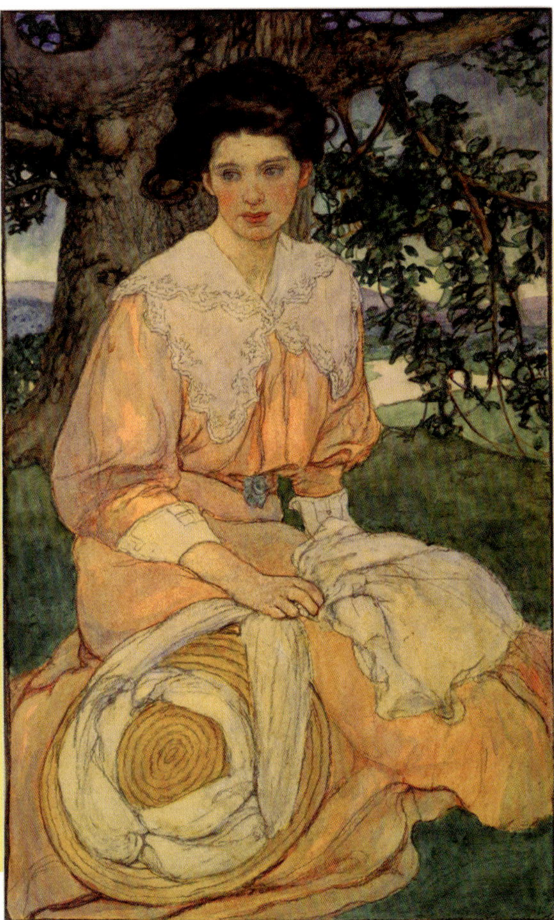

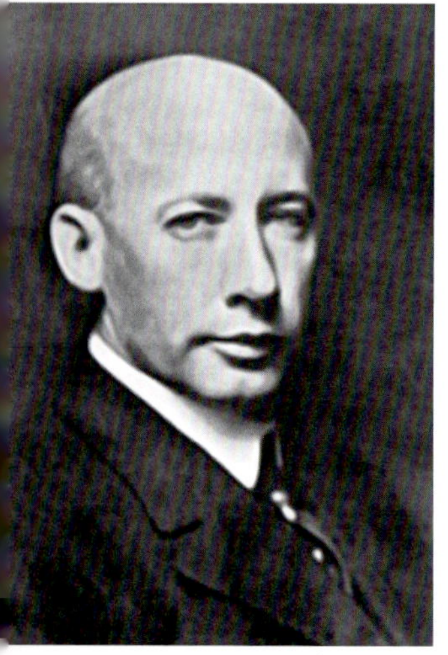

JULES GUÉRIN

1866–1946, American

In the field of illustration, artists—much like writers—often have subjects in which they achieve a high degree of expertise. Children's art, society figures, marine work, and westerns are all motifs that have dedicated followers.

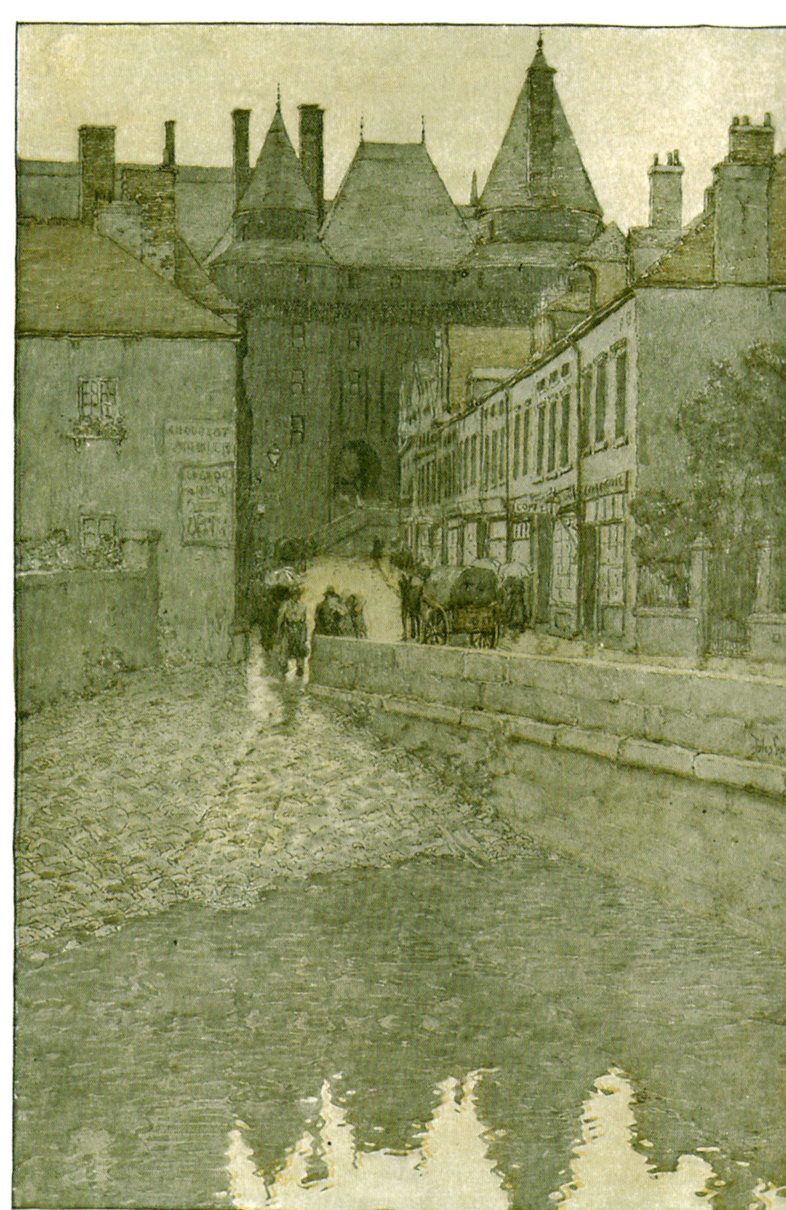

Guérin shared a studio space with Winsor McKay for a brief period in 1889. McKay went on to become a noted cartoonist and a pioneer in animation.

For Jules Guérin, his forté was in portraying physical settings. Guérin was a former student of architecture, and his understanding of buildings and perspective made his cityscapes and landscapes both believable and highly accurate. Guérin often worked directly with architectural firms, producing visionary renderings from their plans. What was different about Guérin's work was a subtle dramatic perspective, and the use of color to evoke the emotions of the viewer. His greater artistic sensitivity extended them far beyond standard architectural drawings. Few illustrators have made this topic as much of a specialty as Guérin did. His soft color choices produced an atmospheric effect and mood in his works, and created his unique recognizable style.

Guérin got his start in St. Louis, Missouri, and moved to Chicago to study art in 1880. While there, he developed a reputation with the area theaters, where he became well-known for his work on scenery backdrops and fire-curtains. After a move to New York in 1900, Guérin got a big break when he was awarded an assignment from the Senate Parks Commission. The high visibility of the work led to commissions from many private firms for similar pieces, and assignments for magazines such as *Scribner's* and *The Century.*

What may be the most important work in Guérin's career came in 1912 when he was asked by architect Henry Bacon to render drawings of the proposed Lincoln Memorial. When Bacon won the job, he rewarded Guérin with an assignment for two murals that now flank the giant sculpture of the sixteenth president.

In the coming decades, murals became a large part of Guérin's output. Many of them can still be seen in banks, railroad stations, and government buildings. One of his greatest was displayed at Penn Station in New York in 1911, but was lost when the building was dismantled in 1963. His mural at the Liberty Memorial in Kansas City, Missouri, can still be viewed by the public today.

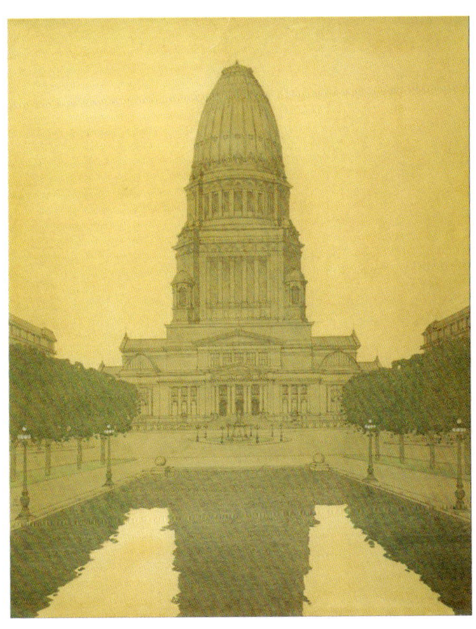

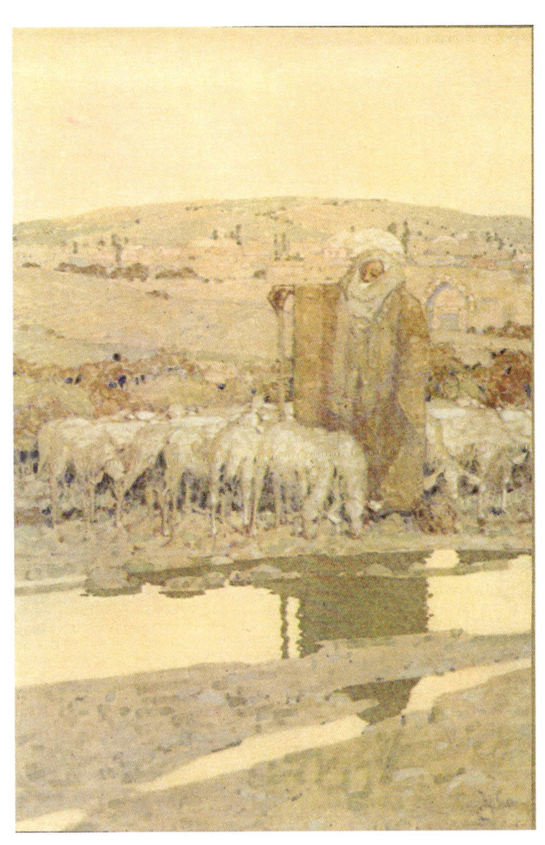

...he has preferred to see the city from afar in tranquility—as a spectacle, and not as a gigantic workshop.

—*Frank Jewett Mather, Jr.*

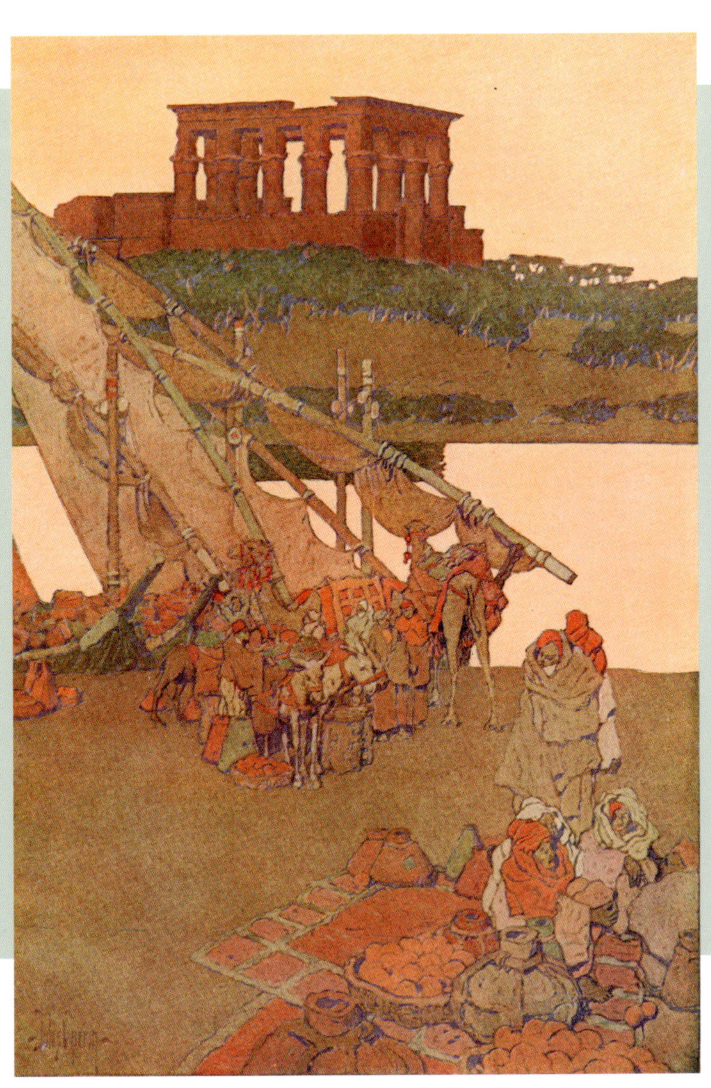

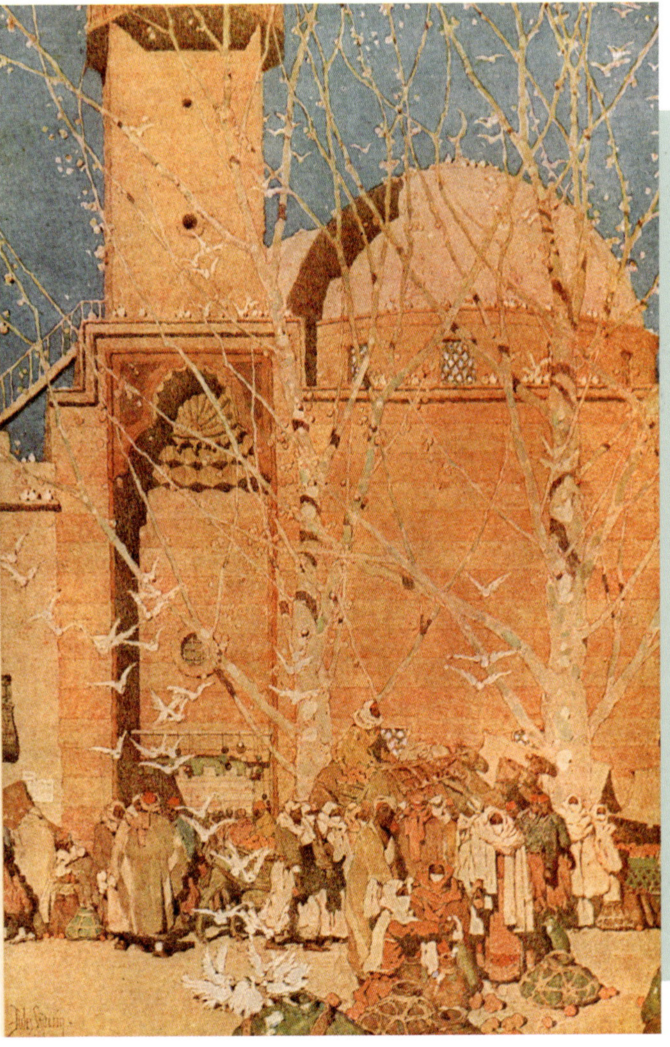

Florence S. Harrison

1877–1955, British

A ship captain's daughter, Florence Susan Harrison was born at sea aboard the *Windsor Castle* en route to Australia. In her early years, her family moved quite a bit. Most of her youth was split between Essex, England, and Bruges, Belgium. Her illustration career began in 1905, with books of her own children's poetry for Blackies, a Scottish publisher who employed her regularly throughout her career. Remembered largely as a children's book illustrator, Florence Harrison was known for a romantic element in her work, often tackling highly literary subjects like Tennyson's prose, or the poetry of William Morris. The strongest collections of her work come from books she illustrated from 1907–1920. In addition,

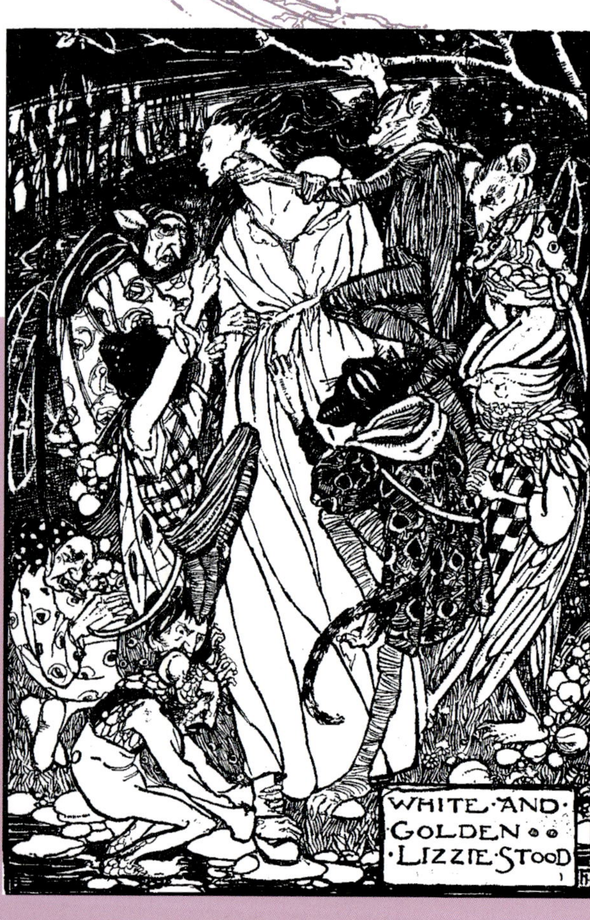

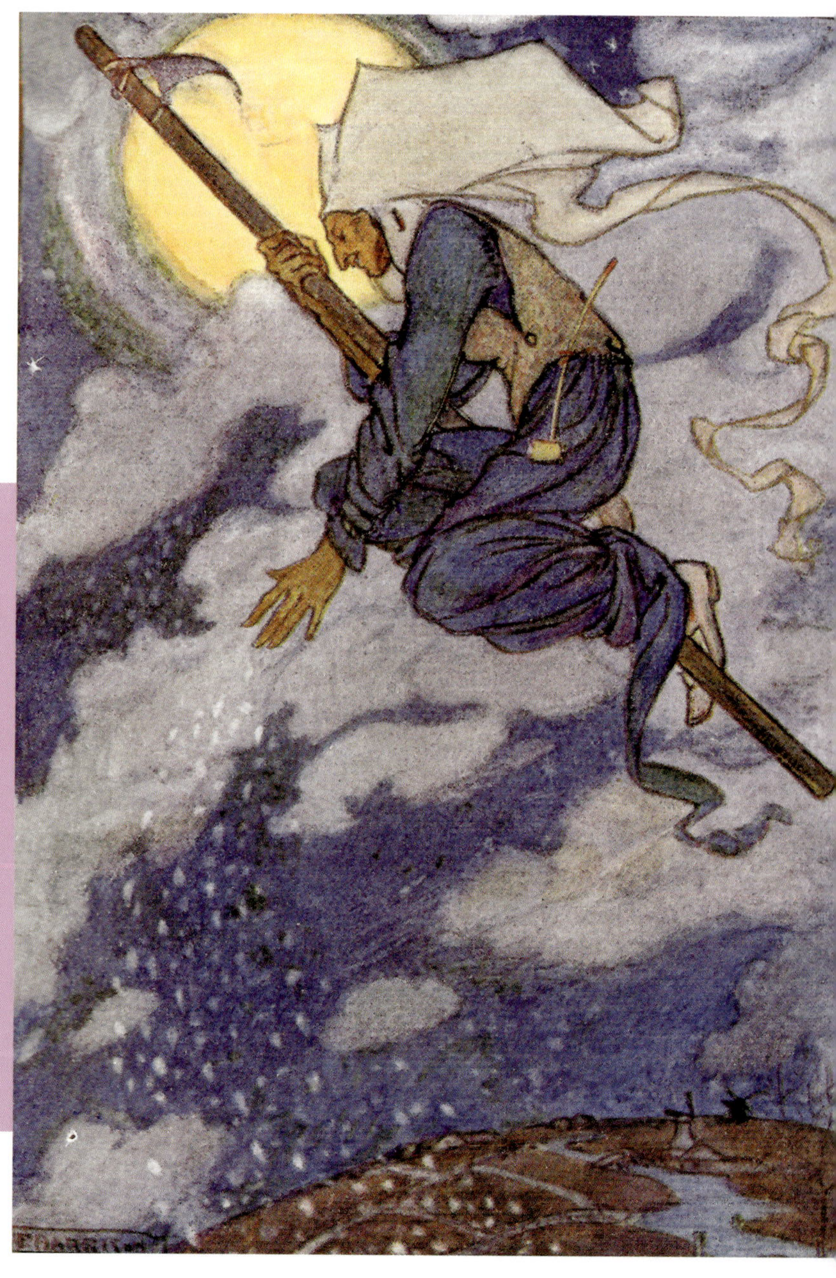

Harrison, Florence S.

she also illustrated books of her own poetry and fairy stories. Her figures were often wrapped in flowing garments with their long hair waving in the wind.

Having spent much of her teenage years and young adulthood in Bruges, Harrison drew inspiration from the setting as well as the art all around her. The combination of the city's rich medieval architecture and the influence of the Art Nouveau look of the period, along with Harrison's Pre-Raphaelite interests, all joined together to produce her unique personal style.

A regular contributor to Blackies' *Annuals,* Harrison could create a single piece of artwork, or produce a smaller group that allowed her to explore different themes. She continued to be one of the *Annual's* feature artists for over 30 years, until the books ceased production in 1939.

Today her works are highly valued by collectors, and original edition books of her plates are likely to be found at auction rather than at the secondhand bookshop.

At one time a biographer confused records of her works with those of artist Emma Florence Harrison, a mistake that misled others for years. Only recently was it discovered that the two were actually separate entities.

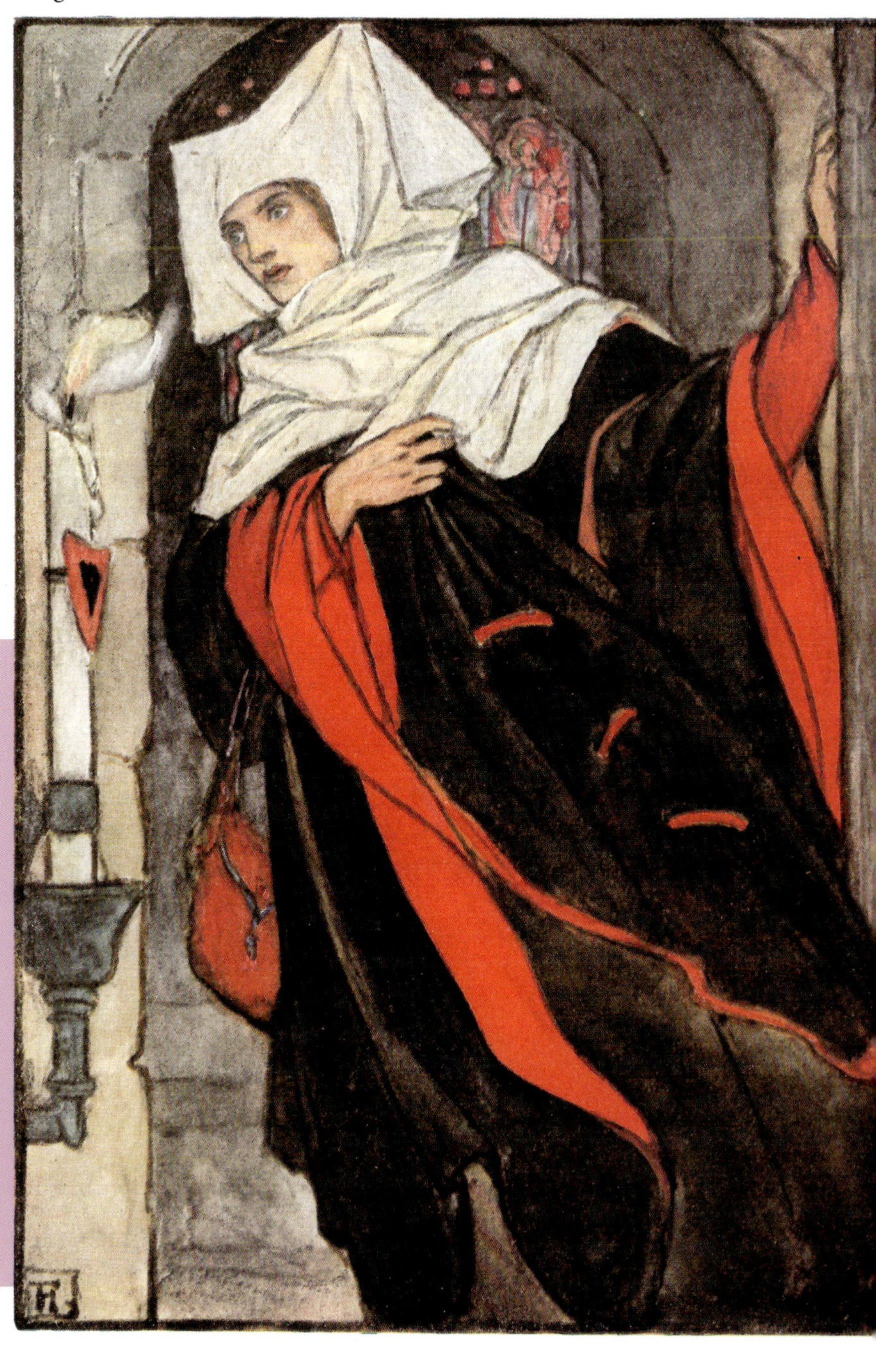

Vernon Hill
1887–1972, British

Although not a prolific illustrator, Vernon Hill exhibited a unique visual composite of illustration and design. His imagery was both intricate and highly stylized. His fantastic creatures and dreamlike settings made his work appropriate for strange fiction tales. In 1910 and 1911 he was selected to produce work for *The Arcadian Calendar,* creating strange and fantastic landscapes with somewhat nightmarish depictions of seasonal elements with the arts and crafts design look of the period. The look was very unusual, and the two calendars remain highly sought-after today.

His first major book work was *The New Inferno* in 1911. The tortured souls and alien settings were a good choice of material for Hill's vivid imagination. *Ballads Weird and Wonderful,* a collection of familiar English stories and folk tales set in ballad form, followed in 1912. Hill illustrated twenty-four plates, giving life to characters with a dark and stylistic vision. Another volume in 1922, *Tramping with a Poet in the Rockies*, was his last contribution to illustration, though the decorations he supplied for that volume were more in keeping with the designs he would sculpt in his future endeavors. Perhaps it was his experience as a private in World War I that shifted his creative output, but after the war, Hill's illustrations did not find their way to the public, with the exception of that one small volume.

Hill remained creatively active, but it was as a relief sculptor that his work would continue to be seen. Hill's three-dimensional visuals can still be seen today, as part of churches and public buildings in England. Guildford Cathedral, the Royal Air Force Memorial at Runnymede, and work on St. Columba's Church in London all feature Hill's sculpture in free-standing forms and as part of doors and other architectural details.

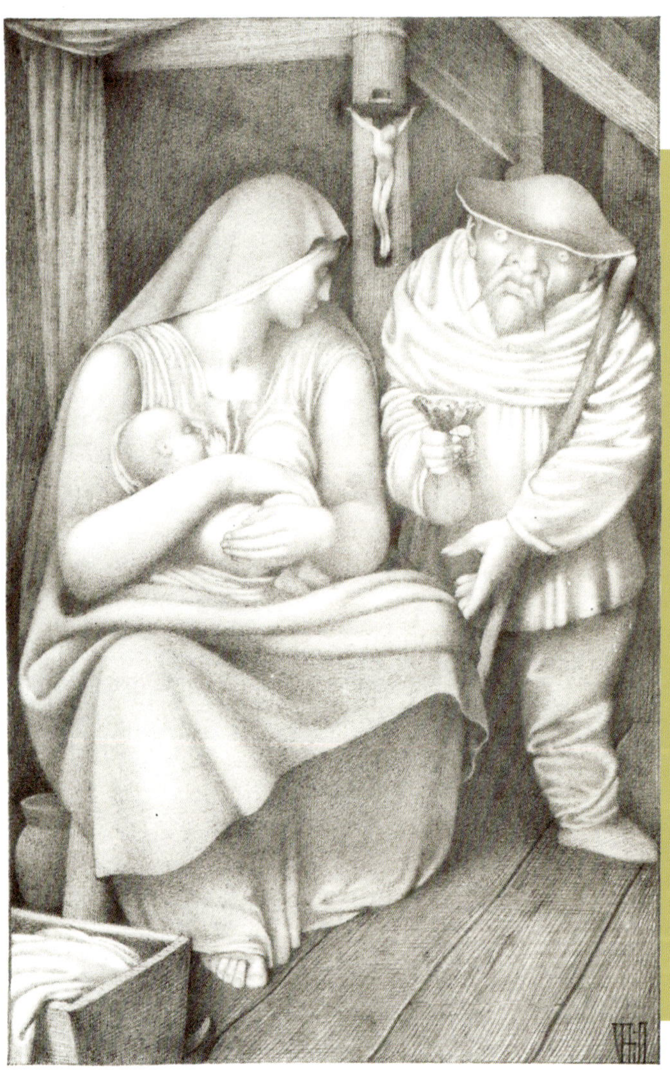

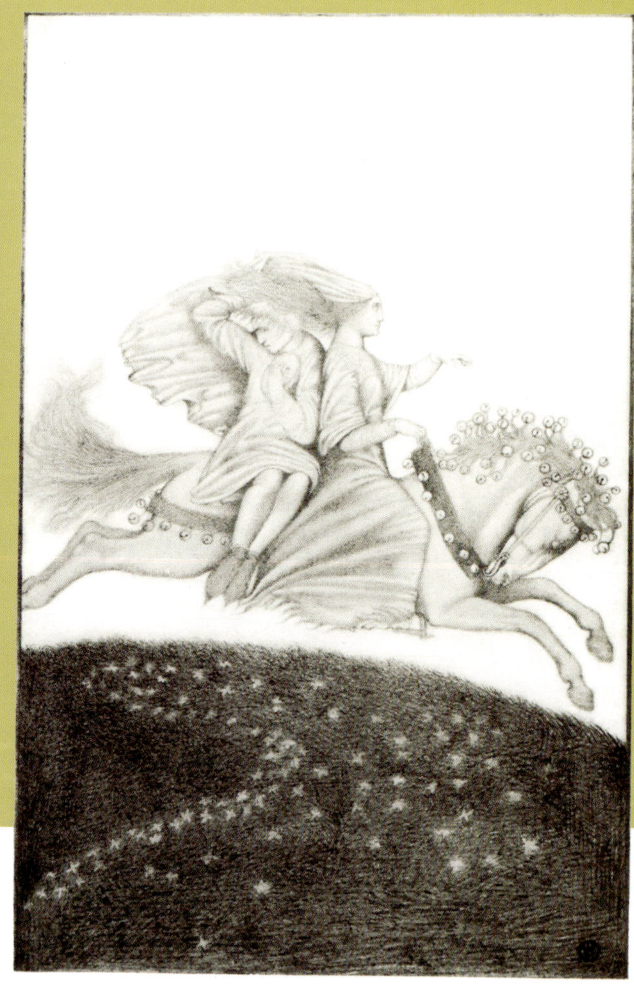

Hill, Vernon

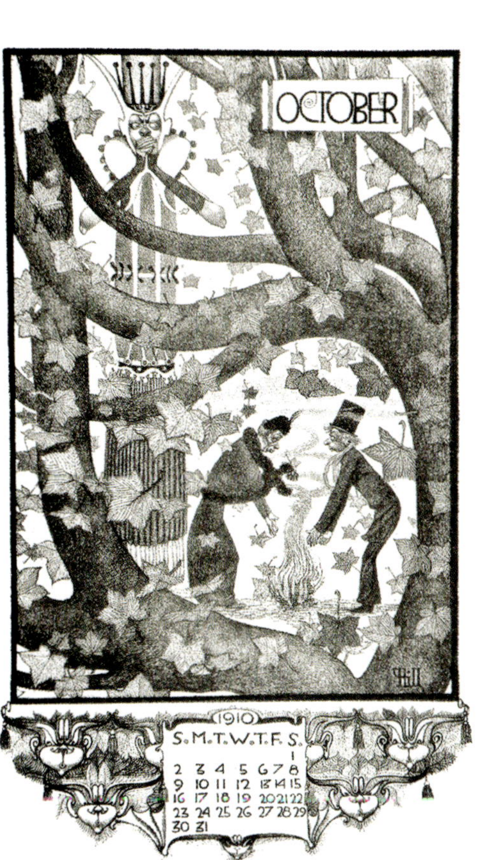
OCTOBER
1910
S.M.T.W.T.F.S.
1
2 3 4 5 6 7 8
9 10 11 12 13 14 15
16 17 18 19 20 21 22
23 24 25 26 27 28 29
30 31

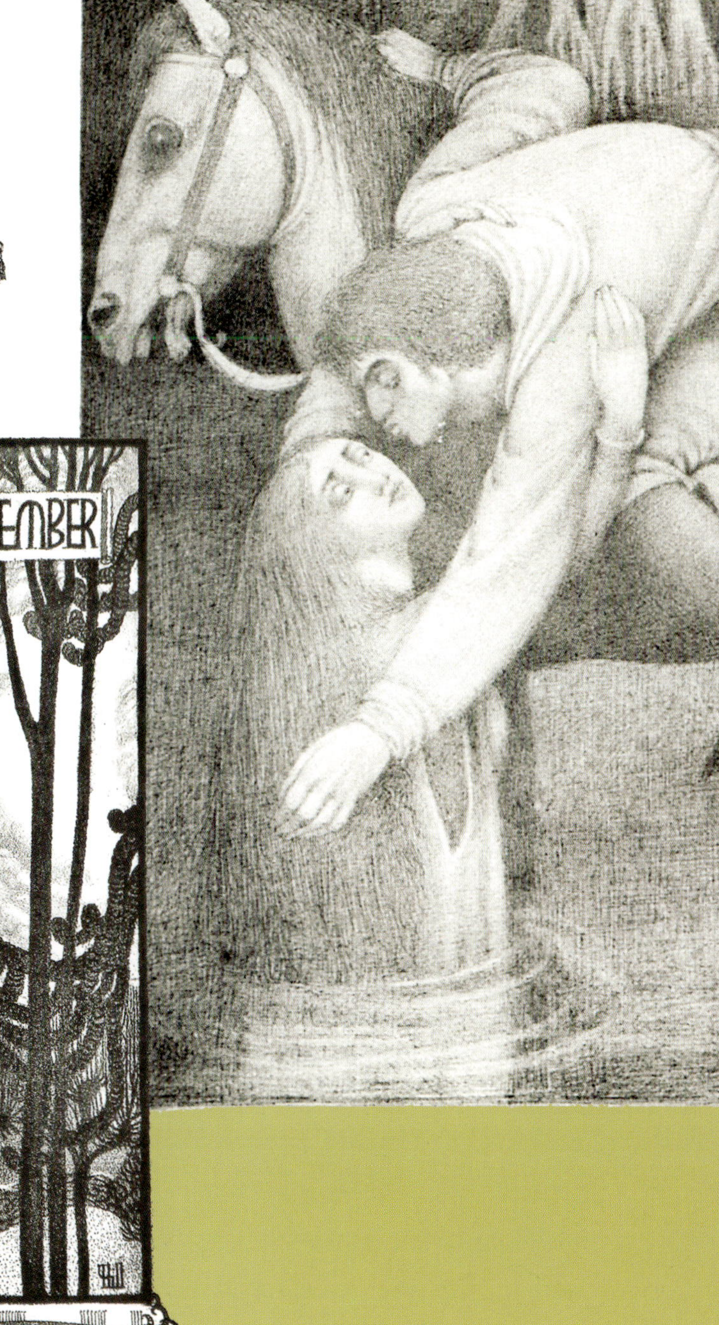

DECEMBER
1910
S.M.T.W.T.F.S.
1 2 3
4 5 6 7 8 9 10
11 12 13 14 15 16 17
18 19 20 21 22 23 24
25 26 27 28 29 30 31

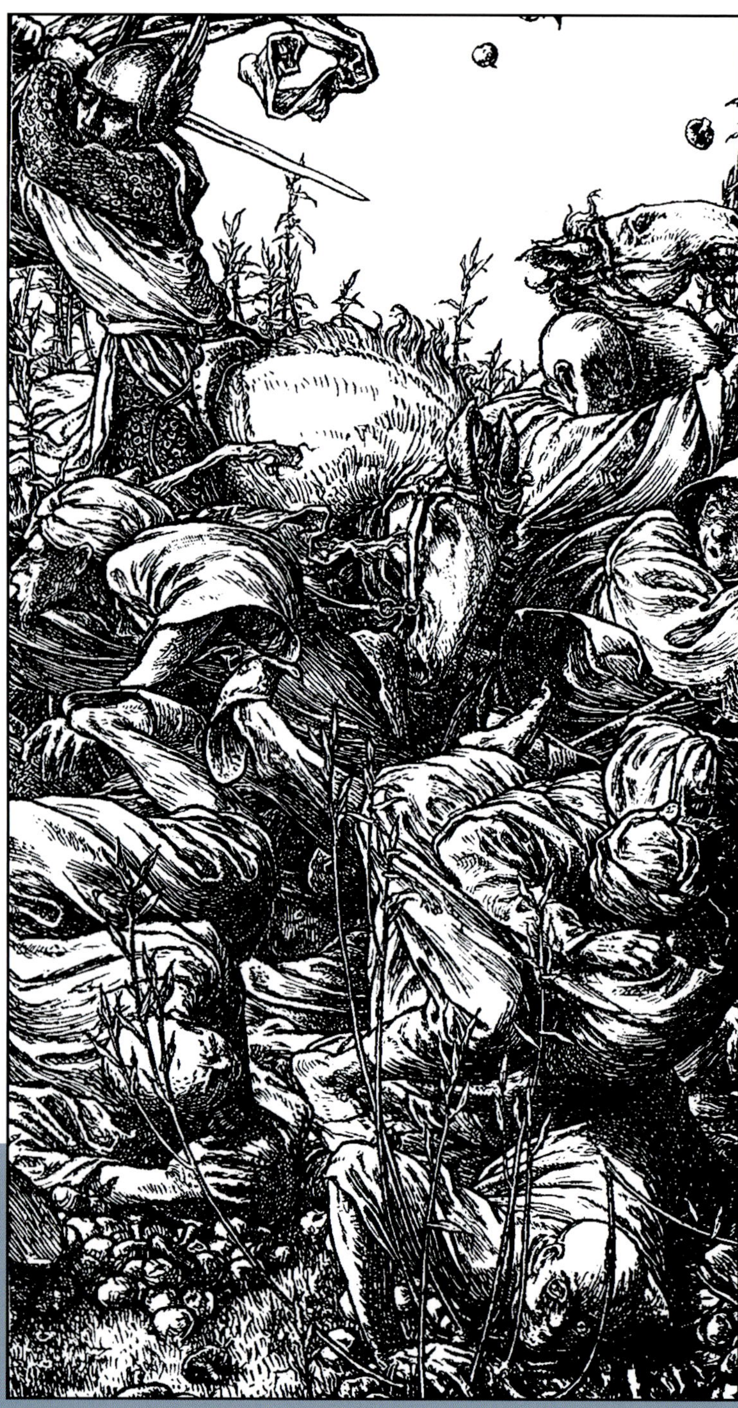

Clemence Housman, Laurence Housman's sister, went on to become a successful wood engraver, later engraving some of her brother's works.

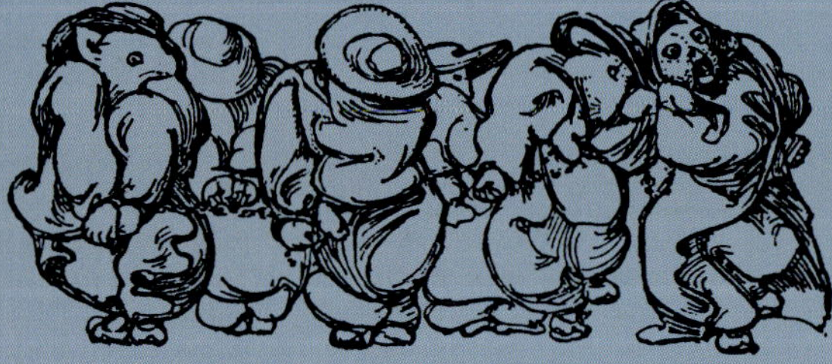

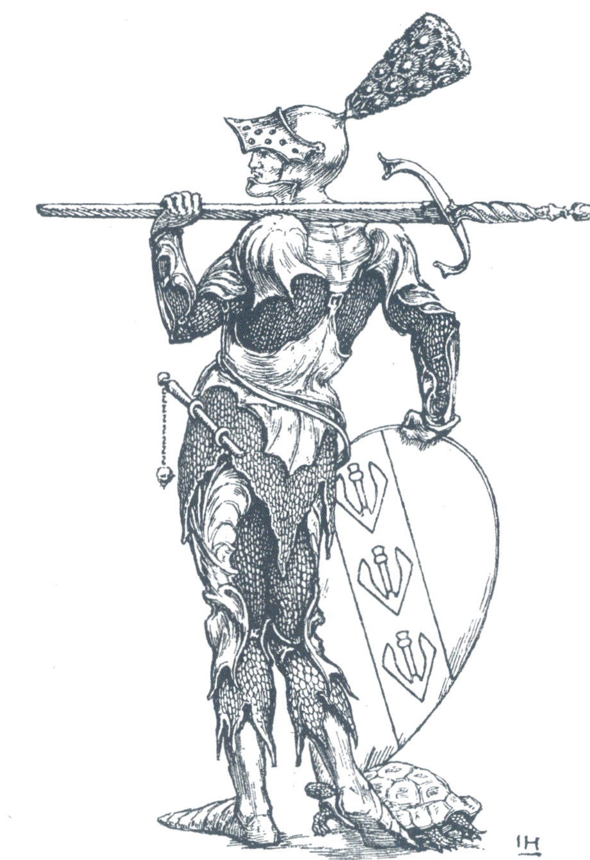

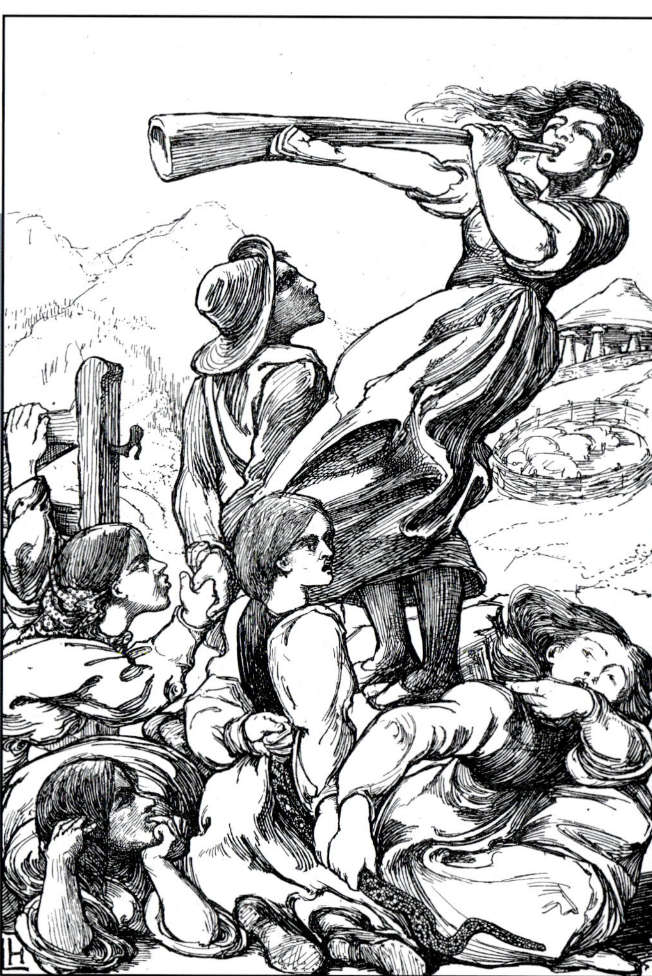

Laurence Housman
1865~1959, British

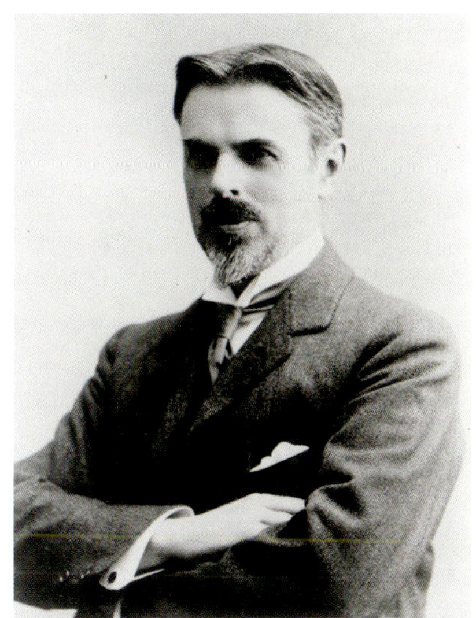

Early life was a struggle for Laurence Housman, who was one of seven children. His mother died when he was six, and his father raised them in poverty. Still, Laurence and his sister Clemence managed to study art in London in 1882, at the City Guilds Art School in Lambeth (then the Lambeth School of Art). After several years there, including some additional study at South Kensington, he began to get illustration assignments as early as 1888, and was given his first book work in 1892. In 1893 he began to work for publisher John Lane, primarily as a book designer, but also as an illustrator. Later that year, Housman would do some of his best-known work—an edition of Christina Rossetti's *Goblin Market,* which Laurence both designed and illustrated.

Laurence's illustration work combined many influences. The practical line training he received at City Guilds Arts and some instruction in wood engraving, both found their way into Housman's ink style. Housman was inspired by the Pre-Raphaelites for both his subject matter and for mood. He studied and admired the works of William Blake, Charles Ricketts, and Aubrey Beardsley. While Housman's work can be viewed as reminiscent of theirs, it has its own distinct visual identity.

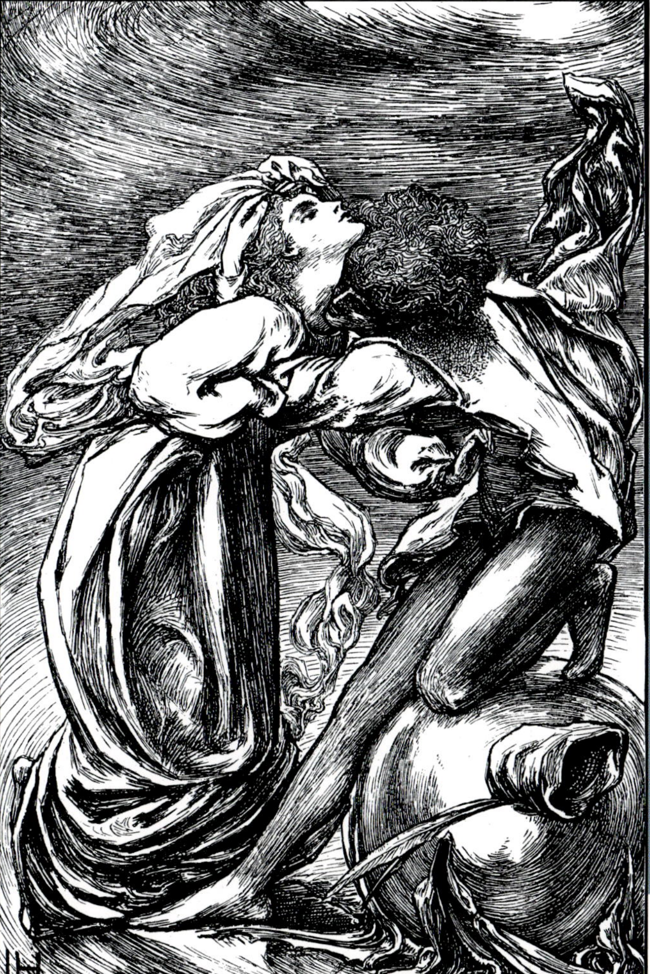

The incredible weaving of fine lines in his steady illustration work took its toll, as he eventually needed to abandon art due to his failing eyesight. As a result of Housman's deteriorating vision, he increasingly pursued his interest in writing. For some time in the late 1890s, he both wrote and illustrated his own works, and eventually became a moderately successful author and playwright. *Victoria Regina* was his best-known play; his written and illustrated books include *The Field of Clover* (1898) and *The House of Joy* (1901).

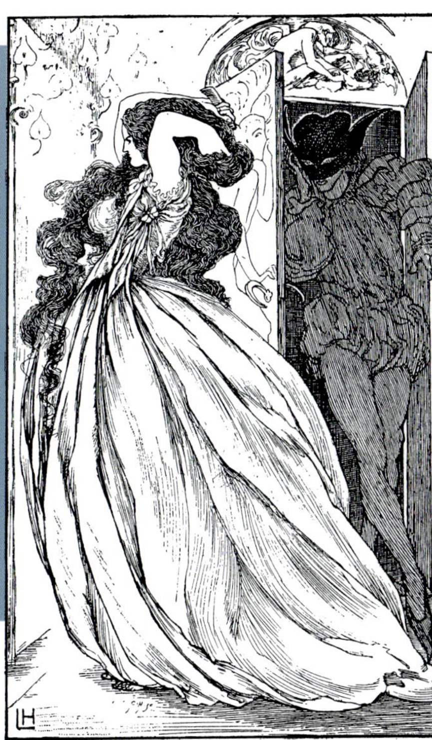

Arthur I. Keller

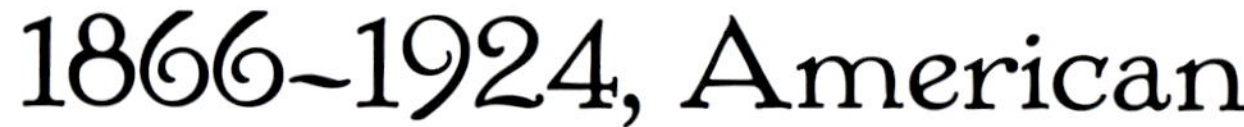

1866~1924, American

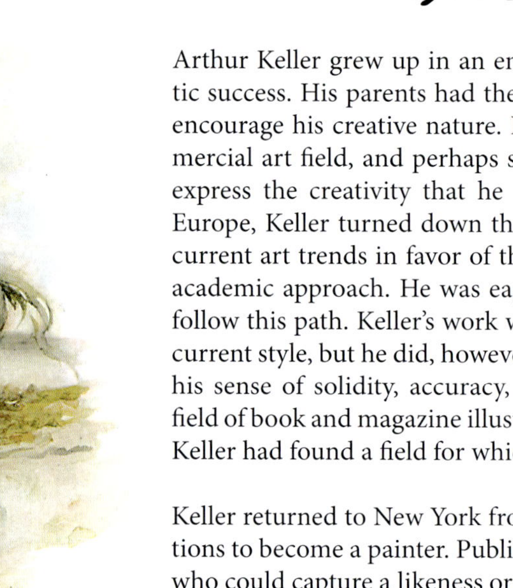

Arthur Keller grew up in an environment conducive to artistic success. His parents had the means to support him and to encourage his creative nature. His father worked in the commercial art field, and perhaps sought to encourage his son to express the creativity that he could not. While studying in Europe, Keller turned down the opportunity to further study current art trends in favor of the more classical studies of the academic approach. He was eager to return to the States and follow this path. Keller's work would not shift the direction of current style, but he did, however, find a market that embraced his sense of solidity, accuracy, and drama in the developing field of book and magazine illustration. Through circumstance, Keller had found a field for which he was perfectly suited.

Keller returned to New York from Munich in 1891 with ambitions to become a painter. Publishing was booming, and artists who could capture a likeness or convey realistic drama were in demand. Keller found paying work in illustration, which was much more to his liking. Keller went on to work for over thirty

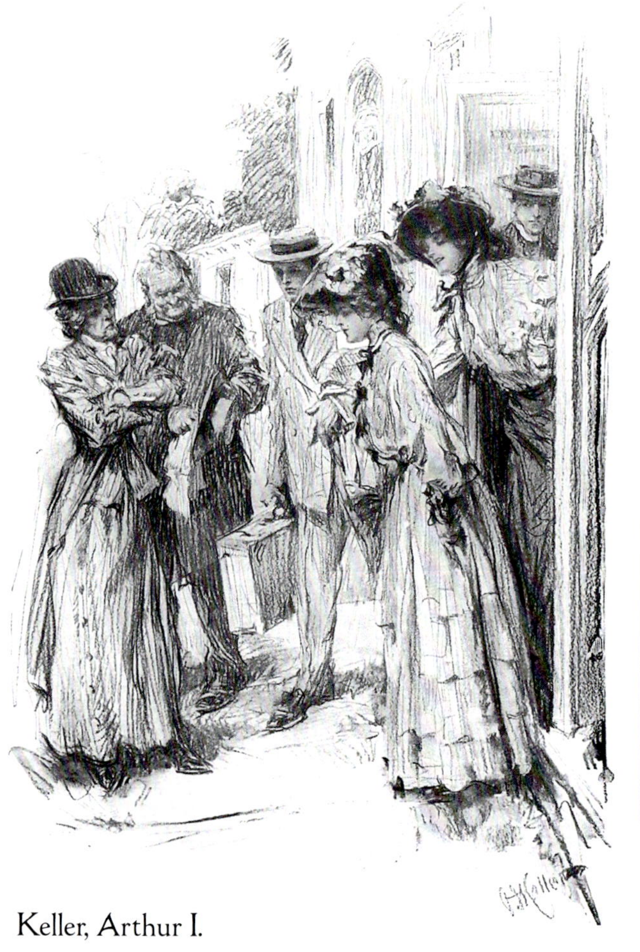

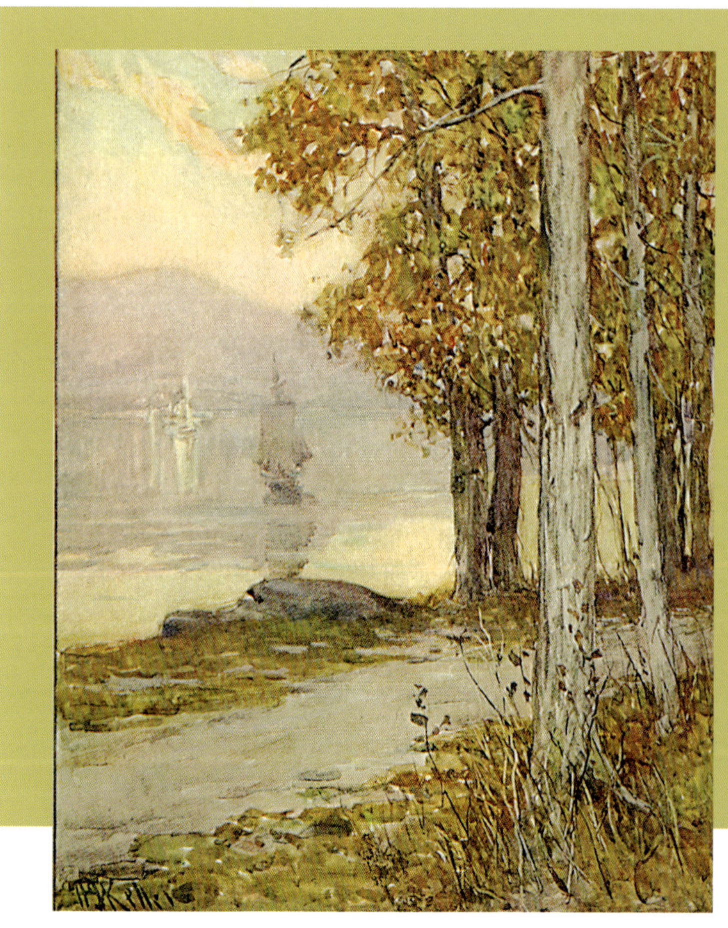

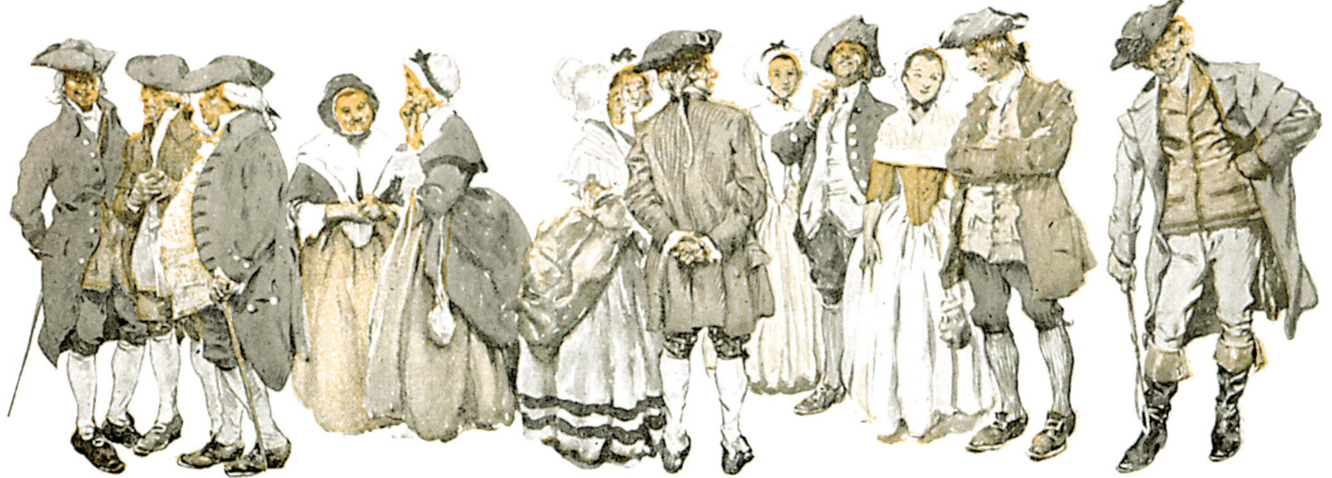

publications—including every major magazine of the day—and contributed to editions of books by leading authors, both new titles and the classics.

In 1903, Keller became president of the Society of Illustrators. He was highly respected by his peers and thought of as a well-rounded, fully capable illustrator.

One of Keller's strengths was his insistence on working from life; it gave his work freshness. In a collection of figure studies Keller published in 1920, his energy can be seen on each page, filled with everything from studies of single hands to full, costumed figures. When Calvin Coolidge became president in 1923, Keller journeyed to the Vermont farmhouse where he was sworn in to record the details of the space—not only to capture the drama of the midnight oath, but also to record it for its historical importance.

Keller died of pneumonia at fifty-eight.

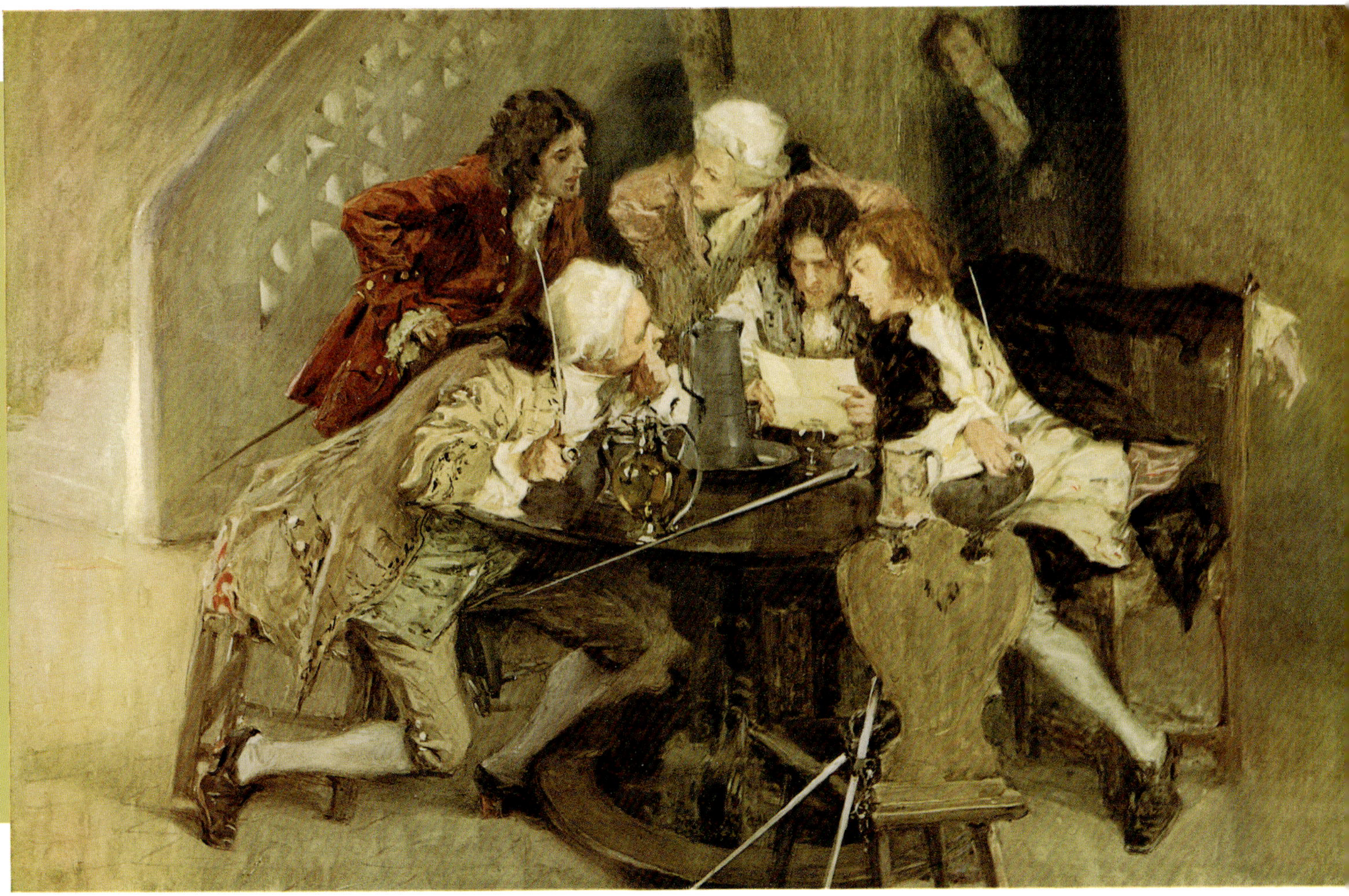

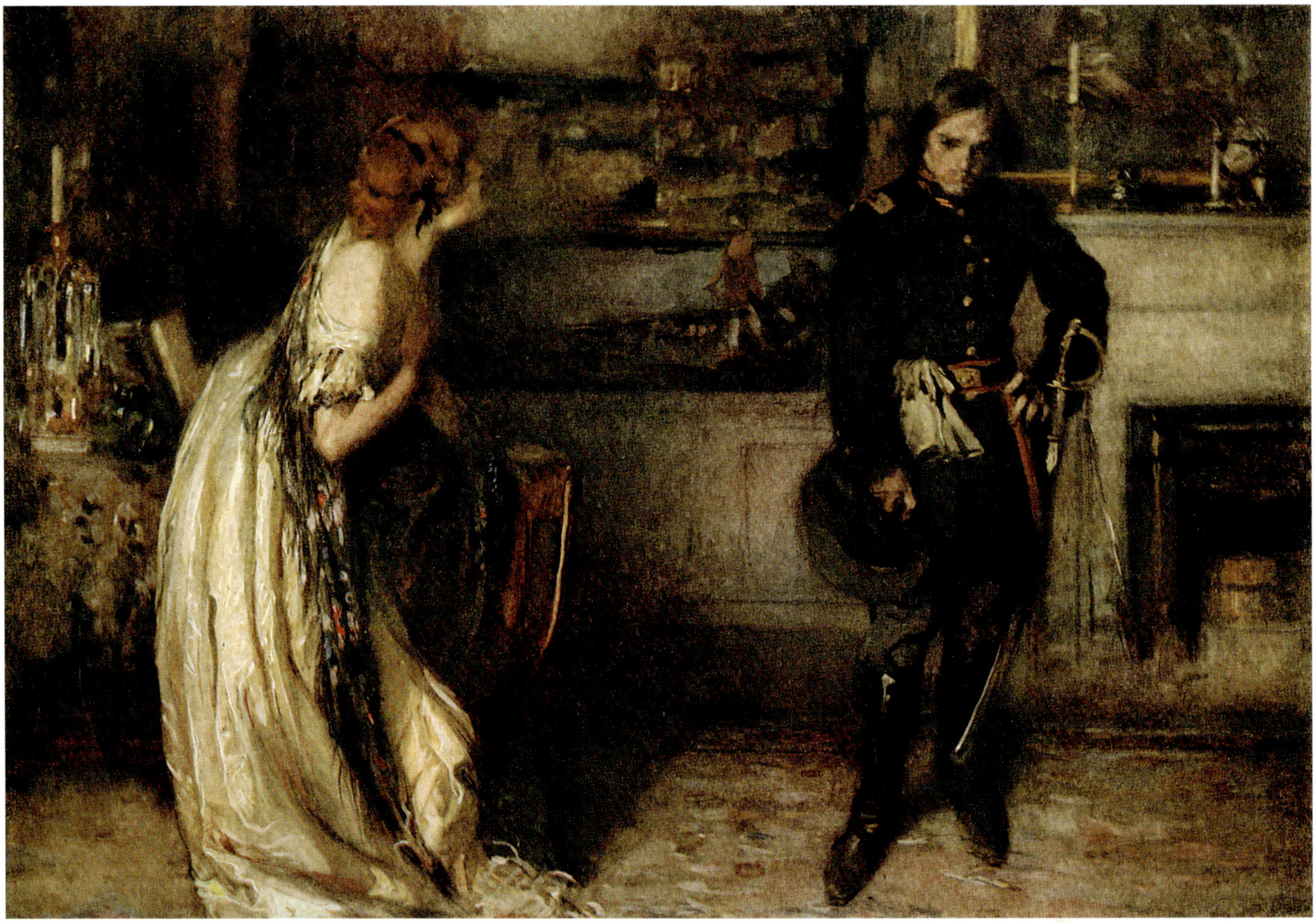

Keller studied at the Munich Academy of Art under Ludwig von Loefftz.

"He knew not time of day or season of year, once he became buried in a story for illustration."
Walter H. Dower,
Art Editor for *Ladies' Home Journal*
about Arthur I. Keller

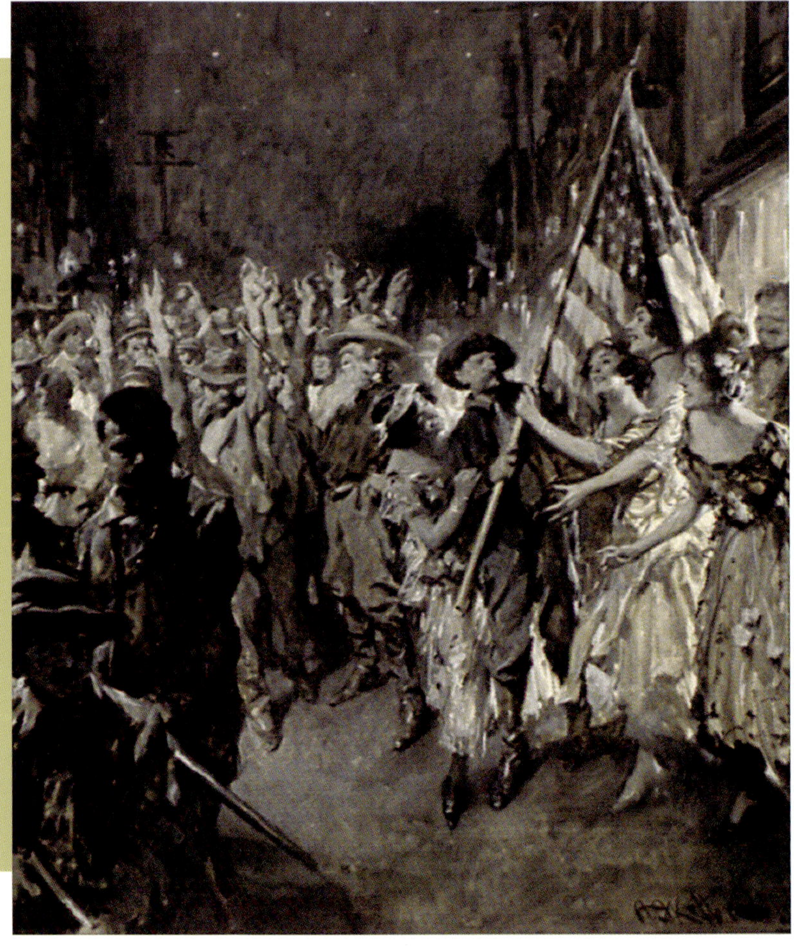

Keller, Arthur I.

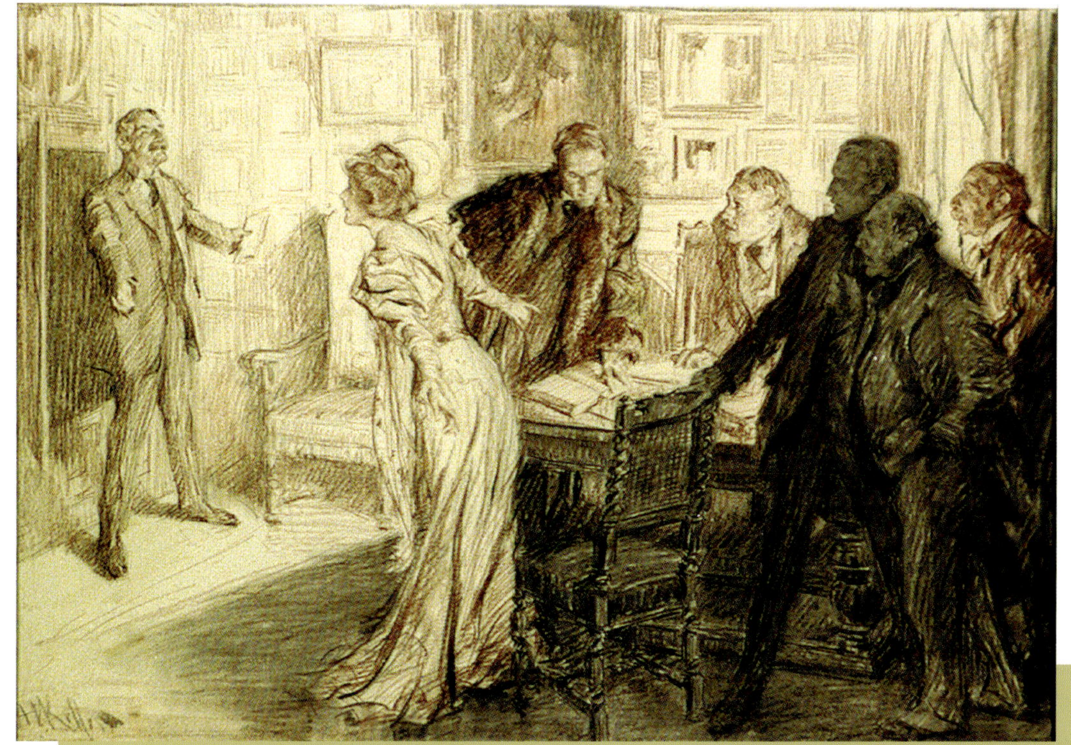

"...he was a high type of illustrator because of his sound grasp of the pictorial possibilities of a text and of his even excellence."
Frank Jewett Mather, Jr.

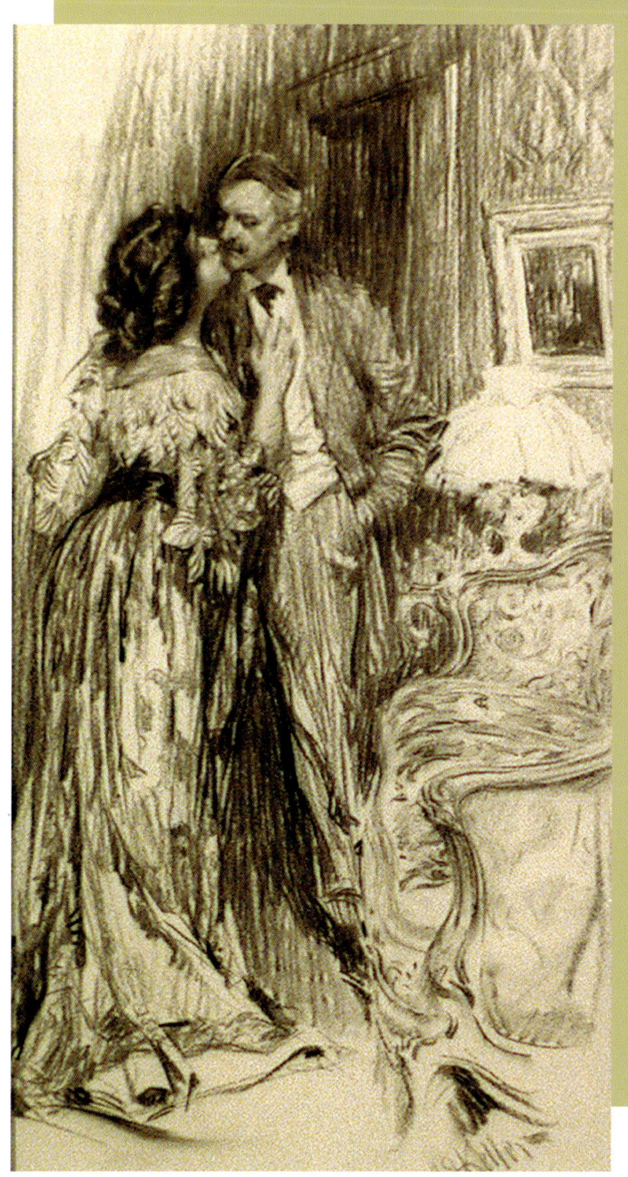

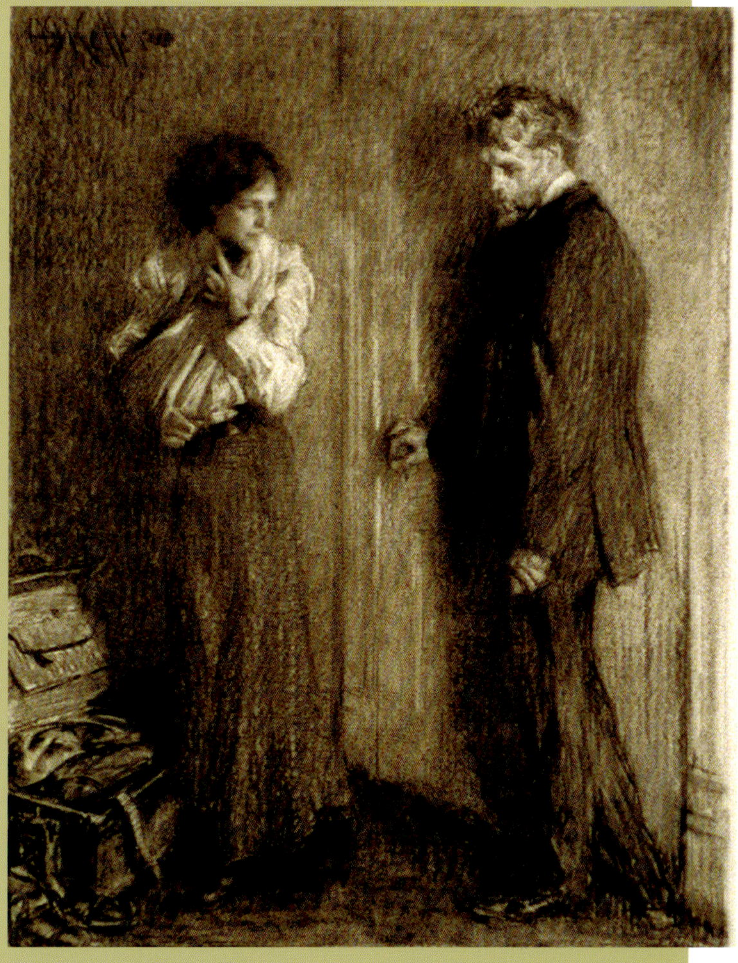

Personal Dynamics
Keller was adept at demonstrating tension between the sexes.

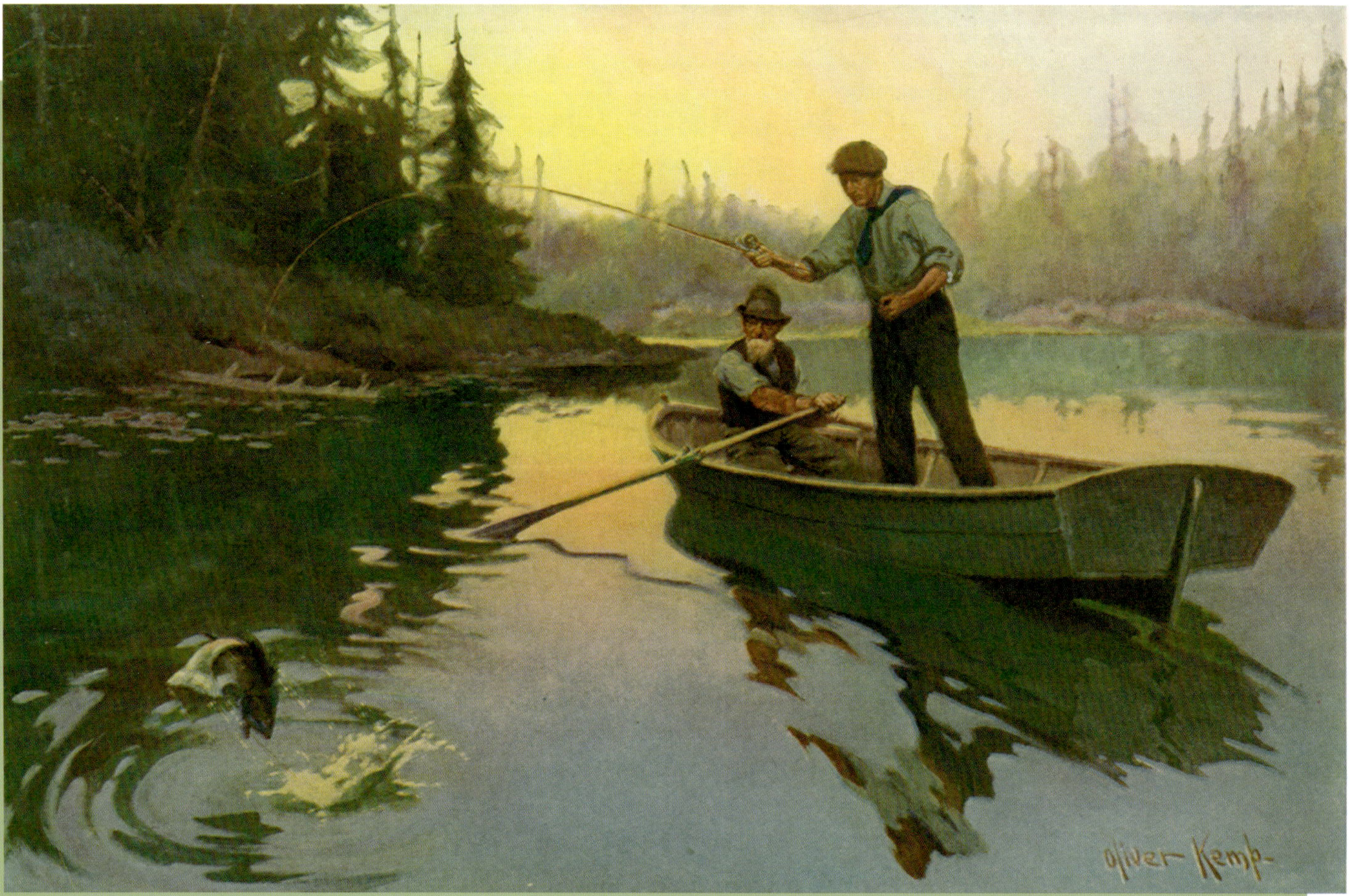

A Man of All Seasons
Deep summer woods, northern snows, or on the water—if it was outdoors, Kemp was at home with it.

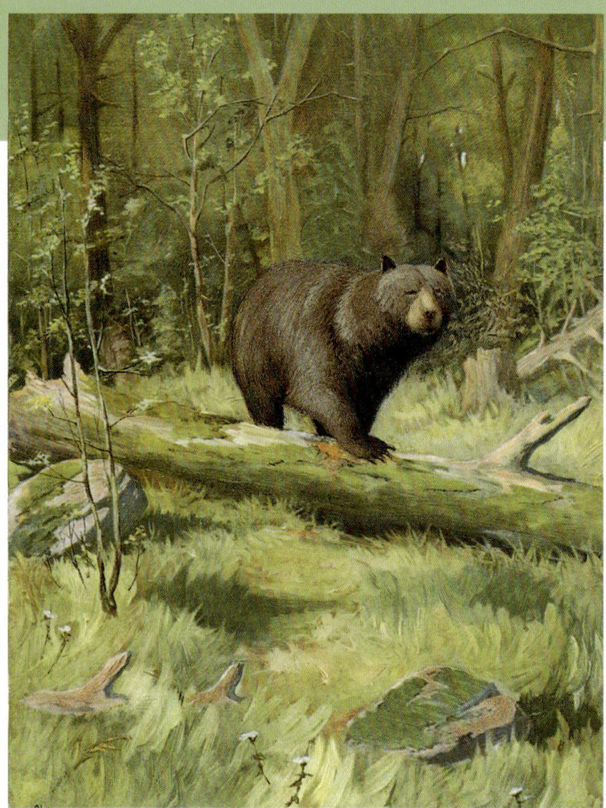

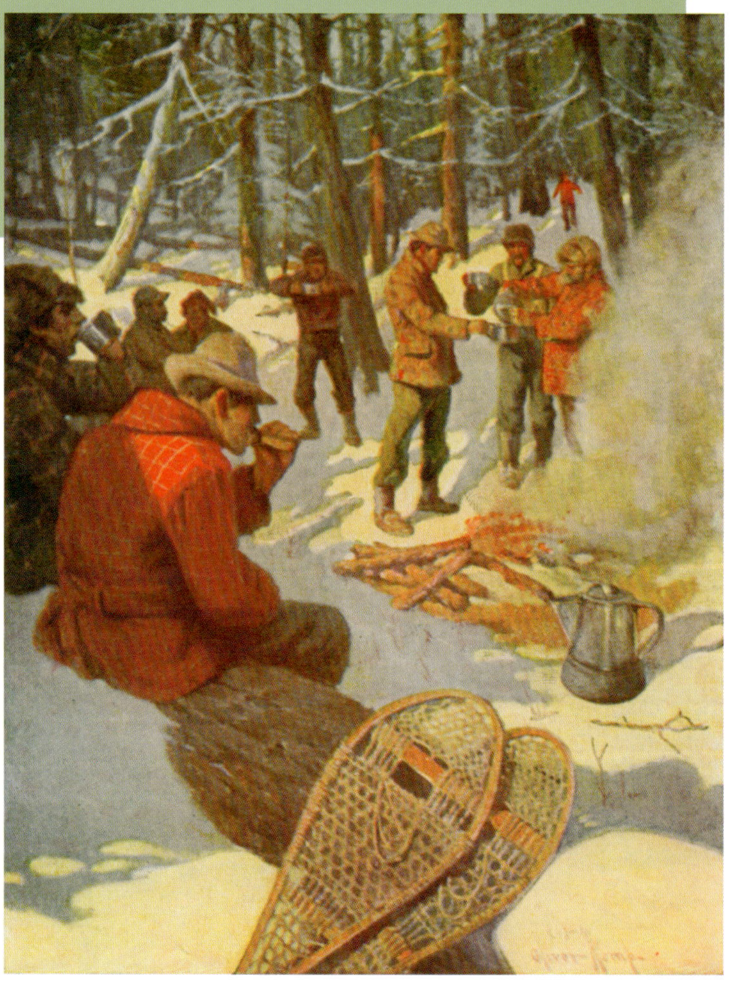

Oliver Kemp

1887–1934, American

An outdoorsman all his life, Oliver Kemp transformed his passion into the subject matter of his illustrations. His work was largely found in magazines such as *Outing, Red Book,* and *Collier's,* and he designed a large number of covers for *The Saturday Evening Post.* (By the end of Kemp's life in 1934, he had painted more covers for *The Saturday Evening Post* than any other illustrator up to that time. Later that record was surpassed only by the likes of J. C. Leyendecker and Norman Rockwell.) Interest in the West and the last edges of the frontier were still strong at the beginning of the twentieth century, and Kemp was one of the premier artists who fed that interest. His prowess with the art of nature landed him steady work covering the outdoors for the larger publishers, and also earned him the notice of companies that made wildlife products. Kemp attended some of Howard Pyle's lectures in Wilmington in the years between 1905–1907, and like many of Howard Pyle's Brandywine students, he subscribed to the value of traveling to a location to grant his work a level of credibility. He made nearly annual trips to the West and other wild locations to capture the landscapes and images of the people who lived in those areas. It inspired him to write about log cabin life in *Wilderness Homes* in 1908. He once survived a shipwreck in the Caribbean, and was stranded there for five days. Kemp enlisted in the service in World War I, where he achieved the rank of major.

Renowned for his depictions of camping, fishing, and hunting life, Kemp focused on the great outdoors, which remains his most popular imagery today. He managed to seek out teachers who would also be well-remembered. In addition to Howard Pyle, Kemp could also count James McNeill Whistler, Edward Austin Abbey, John Singer Sargent, and William Merritt Chase among his instructors over the years.

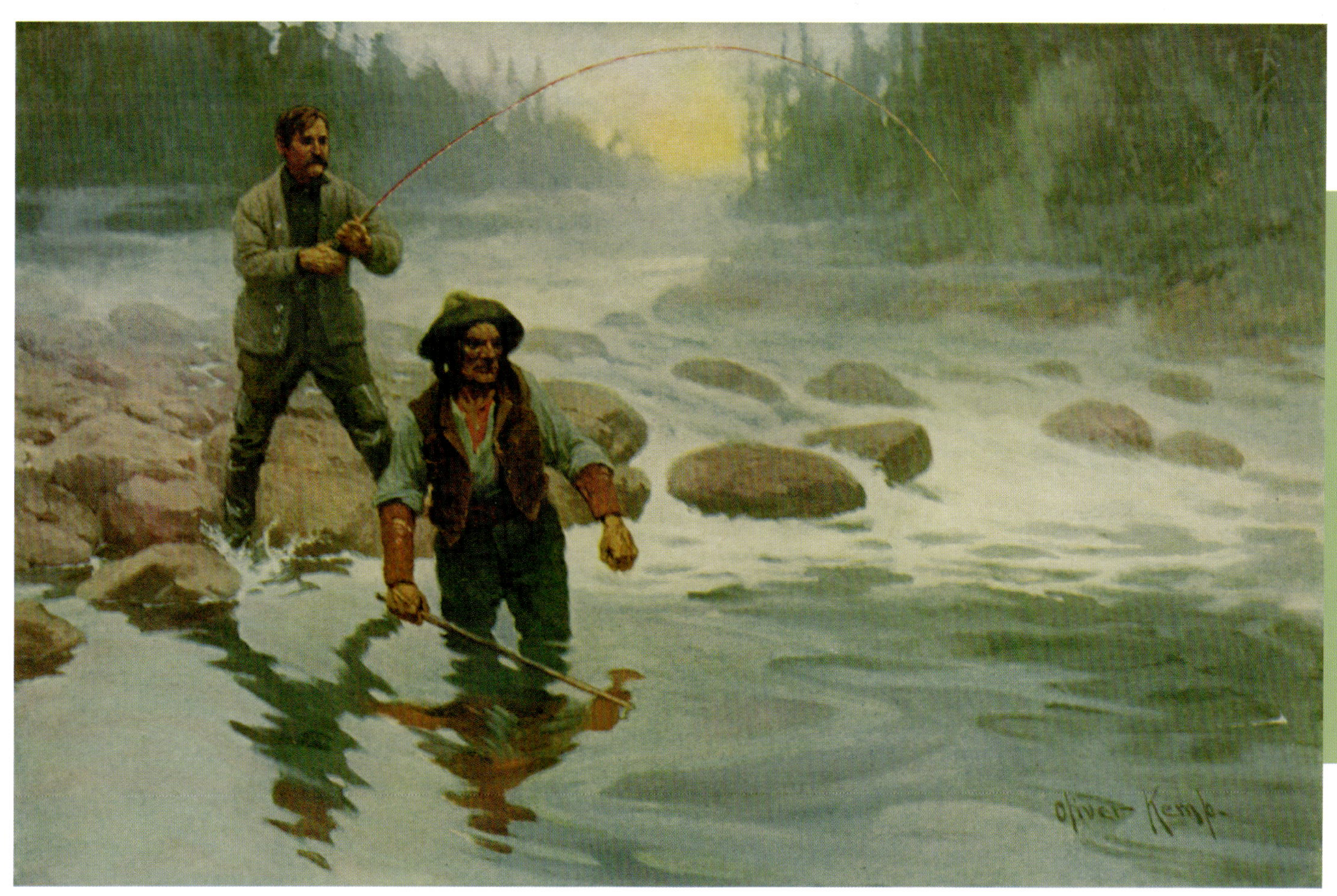

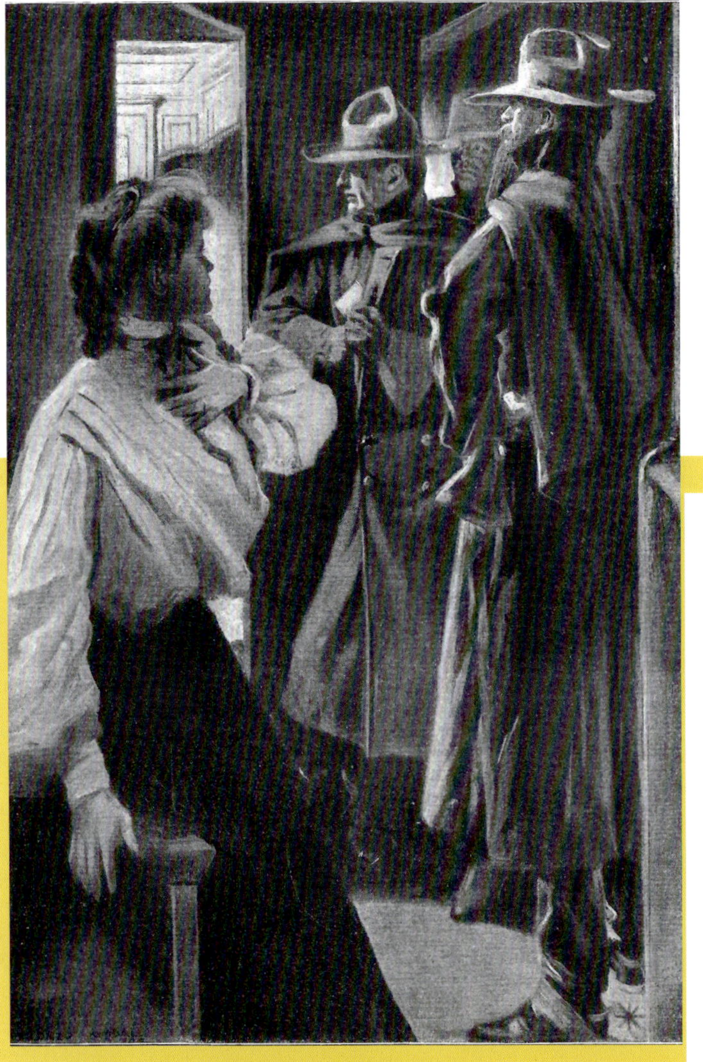

"It's a lot harder to start with the small magazines and work up, than it is to aim high in the first place."

"Life is a struggle to earn a living, I do enjoy the struggle."

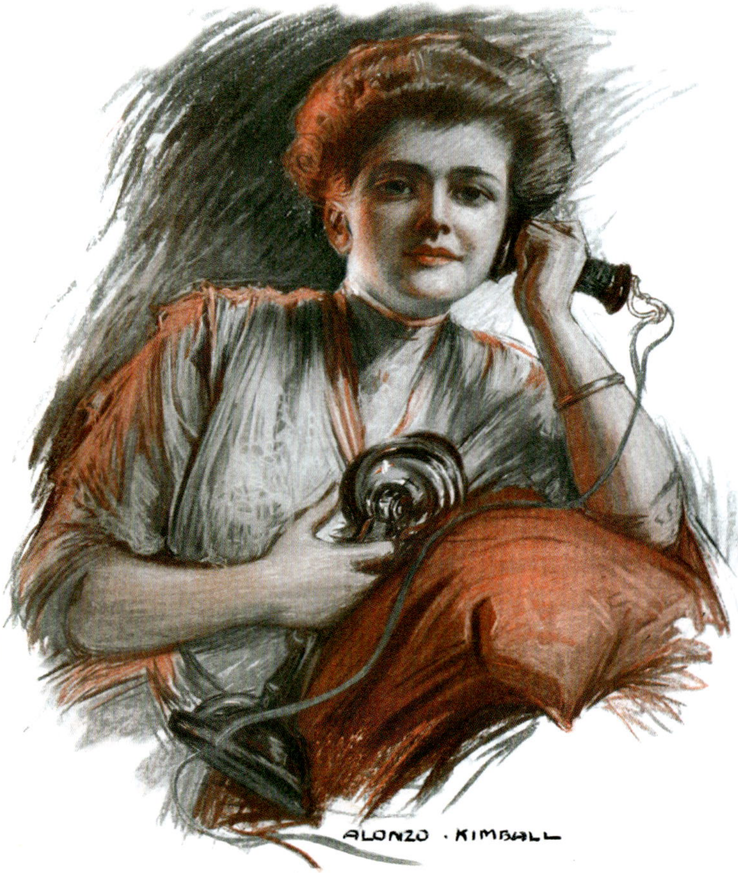

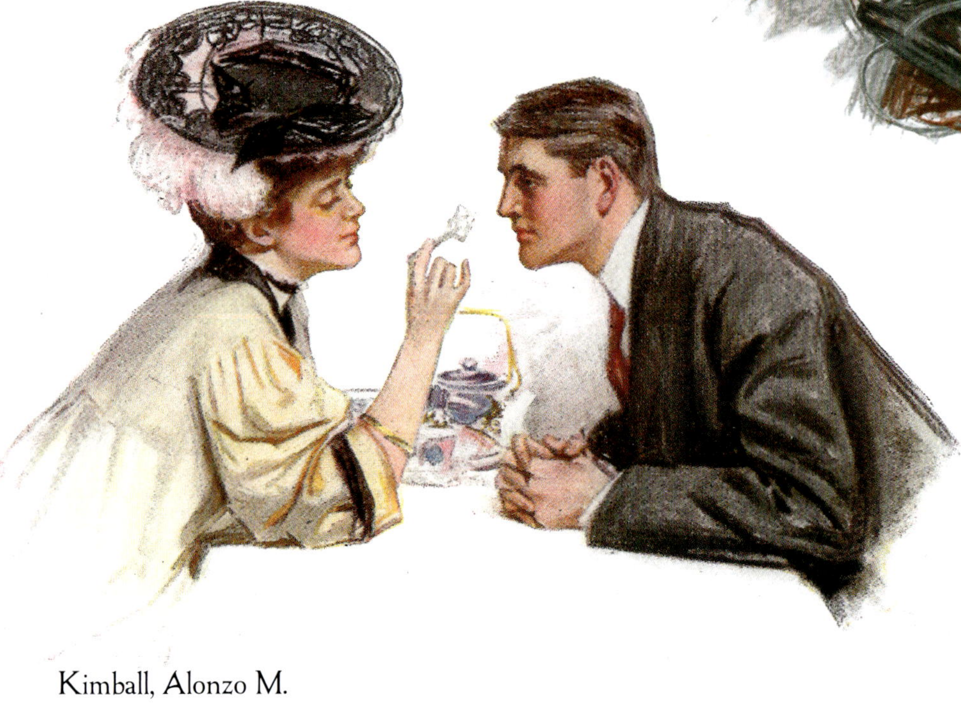

"Many artists have high principles and aims, but in actual practice fall short of them."

Alonzo Kimball.
From a written interview, 1902

ALONZO M. KIMBALL

1874–1923, American

Toward the end of the nineteenth century in the heart of the mid-West, it was Alonzo Kimball's grandfather that made local headlines as an early mayor of Green Bay, Wisconsin. As a promising art student, Alonzo M. Kimball left his family behind in Green Bay, and traveled to New York to spend a season at the Art Students League before journeying on to Paris, where he furthered his development at Julian's. Among his teachers there included one he cited as a significant influence: James McNeill Whistler. Kimball stayed in Paris for five years before he returned to America. Seeking illustration work in New York, Kimball set his sights on *Scribner's*, a publication he considered "about the foremost magazine, artistically, in America." *Scribner's* gave him his first illustration job, and kept him steadily employed for years.

Kimball's strength was in setting the stage for a story. He easily summoned a cast of characters and a variety of settings in which to place them, ranging from the home of a wealthy socialite to a backwoods farmstead. Kimball became a steadfast and reliable contributor to the pool of New York magazines, and garnered some fame there. Compared frequently to the biggest stars of the day, Kimball's work graced covers and countless pages for *The Saturday Evening Post, Collier's, Harper's,* and similar publications.

During World War I, Kimball sought to serve, and was granted the task of designing camouflage for the U.S. Navy, at times overseeing as many as 100 painters on a ship. Kimball later became known for his portraiture in the mid-West. After he left New York, he spent time in Cleveland, working for the Fuller and Smith advertising agency, and eventually settled in Evanston, Illinois.

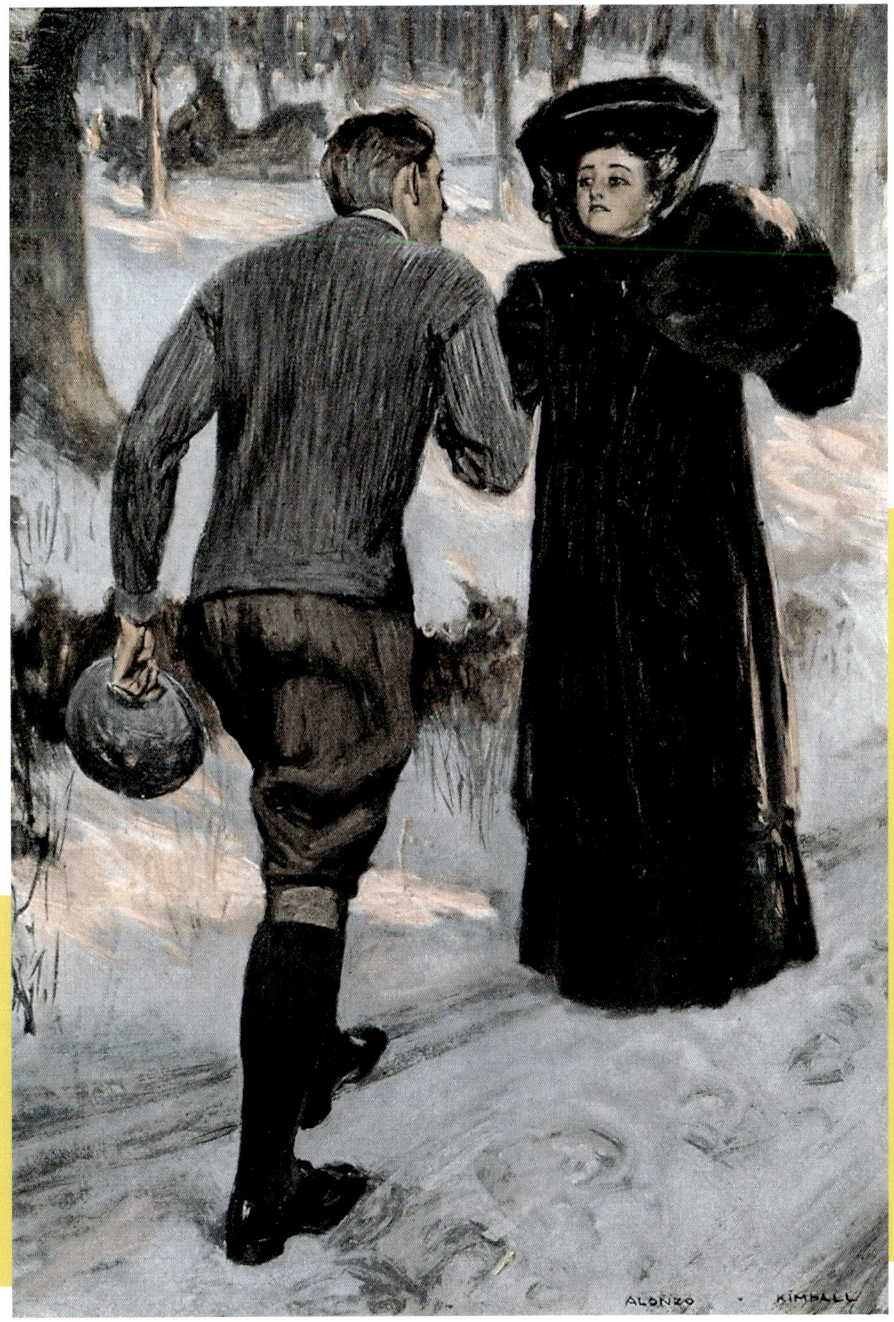

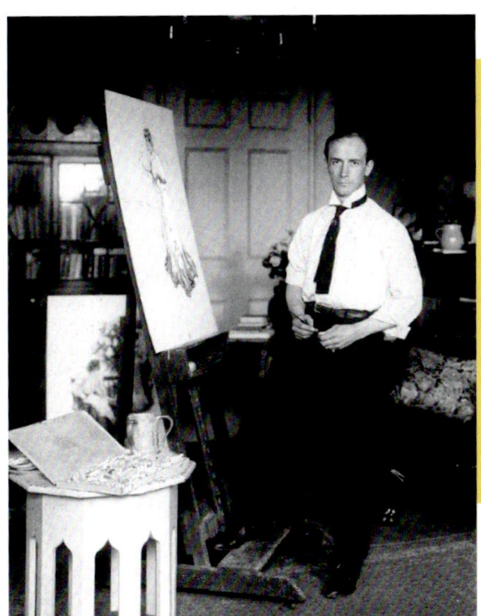

Kimball in his studio, 1905

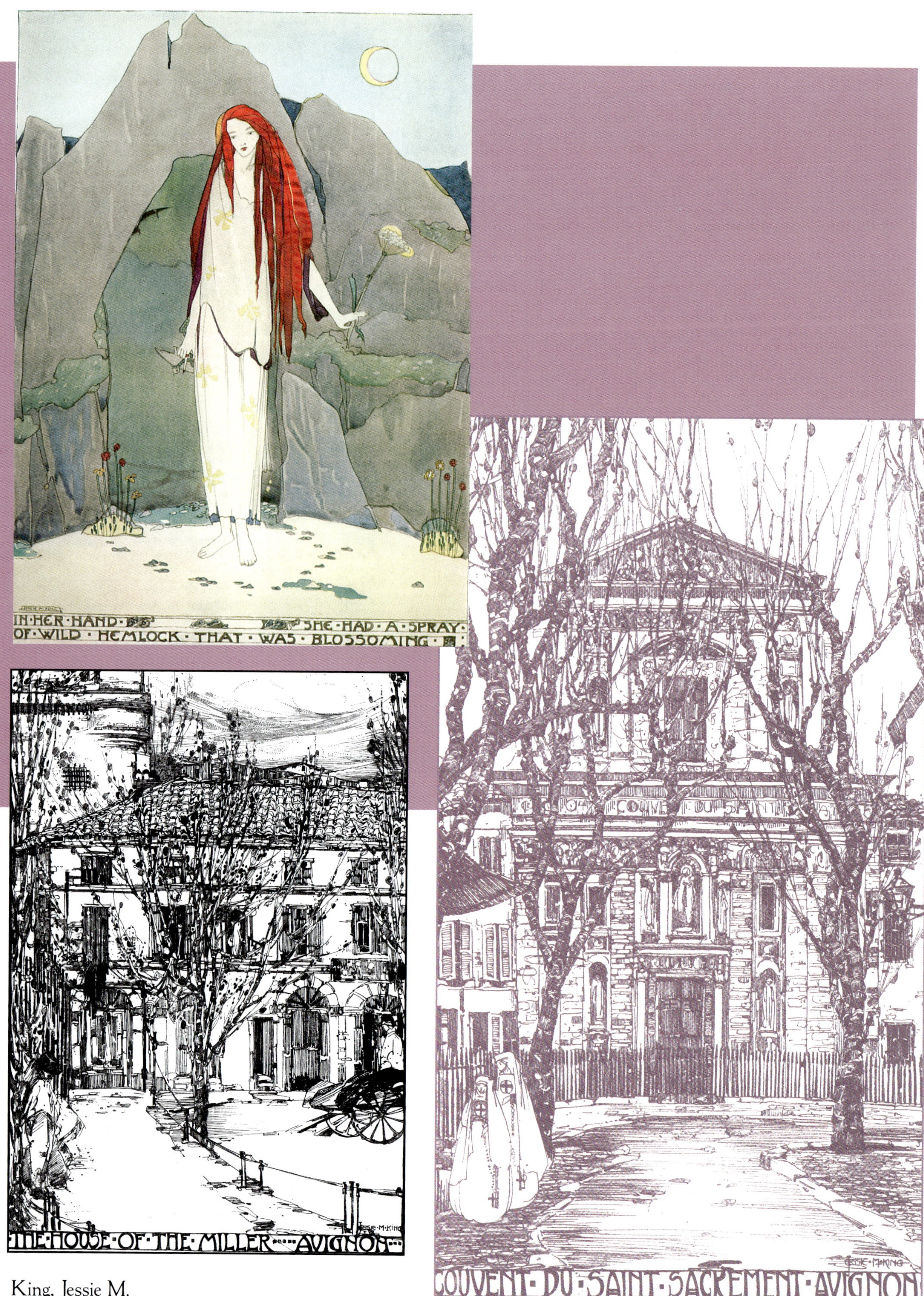

King, Jessie M.

Jessie M. King

1875–1949, Scottish

The daughter of a minister, Jessie Marion King was discouraged in her youth from pursuing a career as an artist. It was with the aim of becoming an art teacher that she began her schooling in 1891. Her own style and the strength of her design sense would soon become an overwhelming force, which led to a successful career in the arts. She continued to attend the Glasgow School of Art in 1892, and by 1898, she had received her first silver medal in the National Competition.

Her early work was in book decoration and design, and she divided her time between creating her own art, and teaching others. King's book designs showed influences from both the currently popular Art Nouveau movement and Renaissance art, particularly the Italian artist Botticelli. She toured Germany and Italy in 1902, which exposed her to both of those artistic styles.

King continued book design work throughout the next two decades. In her most notable volumes, she was responsible for not only the book's design, but the illustrations within them as well. King's illustration technique was highly unique and very identifiable. Volumes such as *The Defense of Guenevere* (1904), and Oscar Wilde's *A House of Pomegranates* (1915), reflected King's control of all the creative aspects of the book and became period gems that showcased her individual design style. After some years living and working in Paris, King returned to her native Scotland during the early stages of World War I, where she settled in Kirkcudbright, a community of artists, and started a center for women artists there. She remained a contributing force in the arts community until her death in 1949.

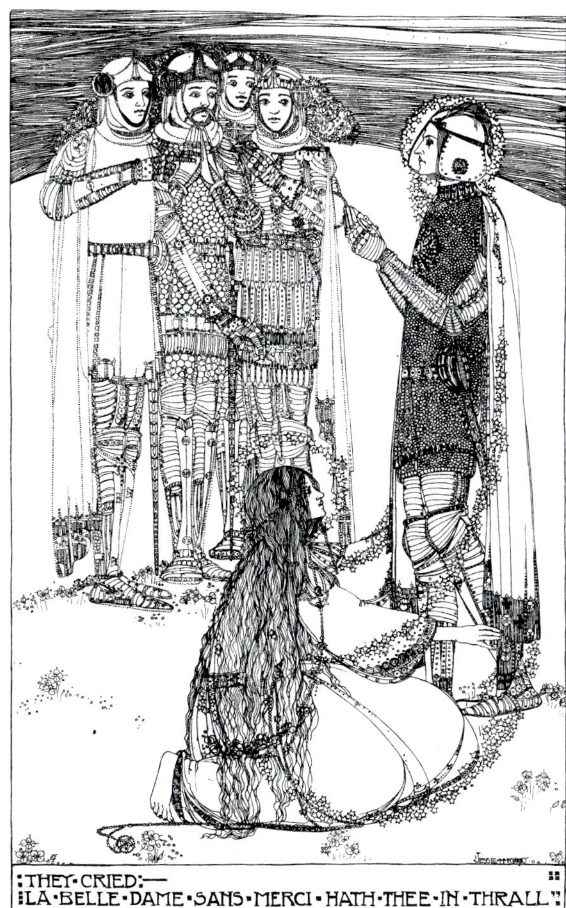

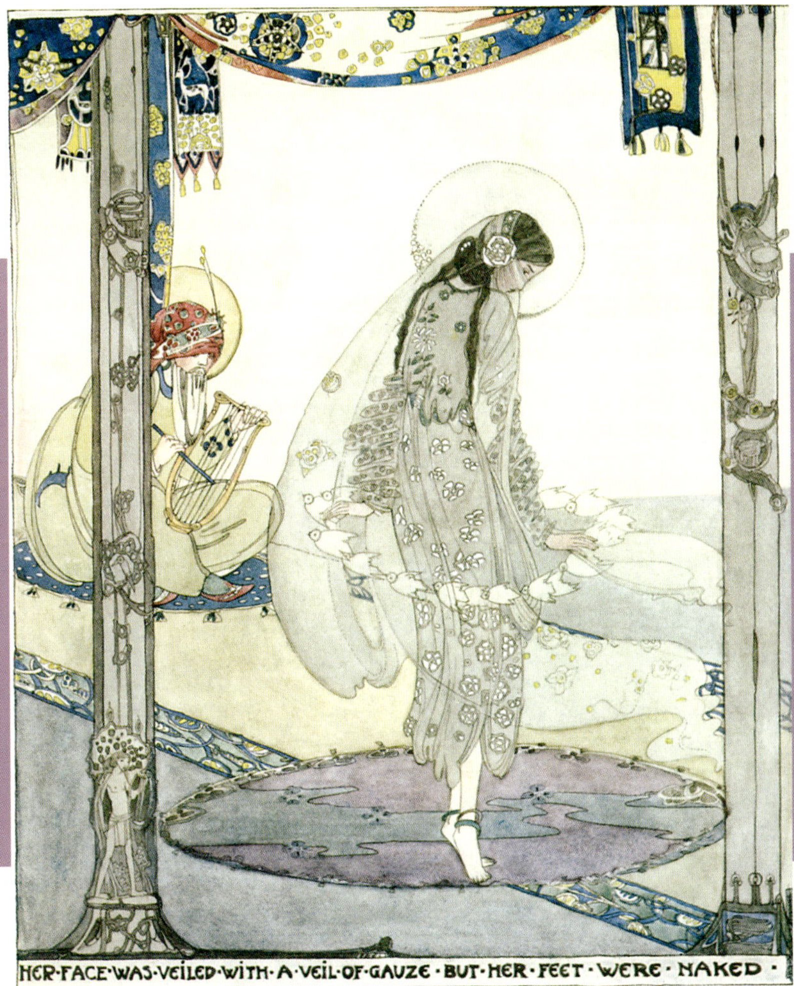

In a 1964 television interview Walt Disney said,
"Without the wonderful drawings of Heinrich Kley, I could not conduct my art school classes for my animators."

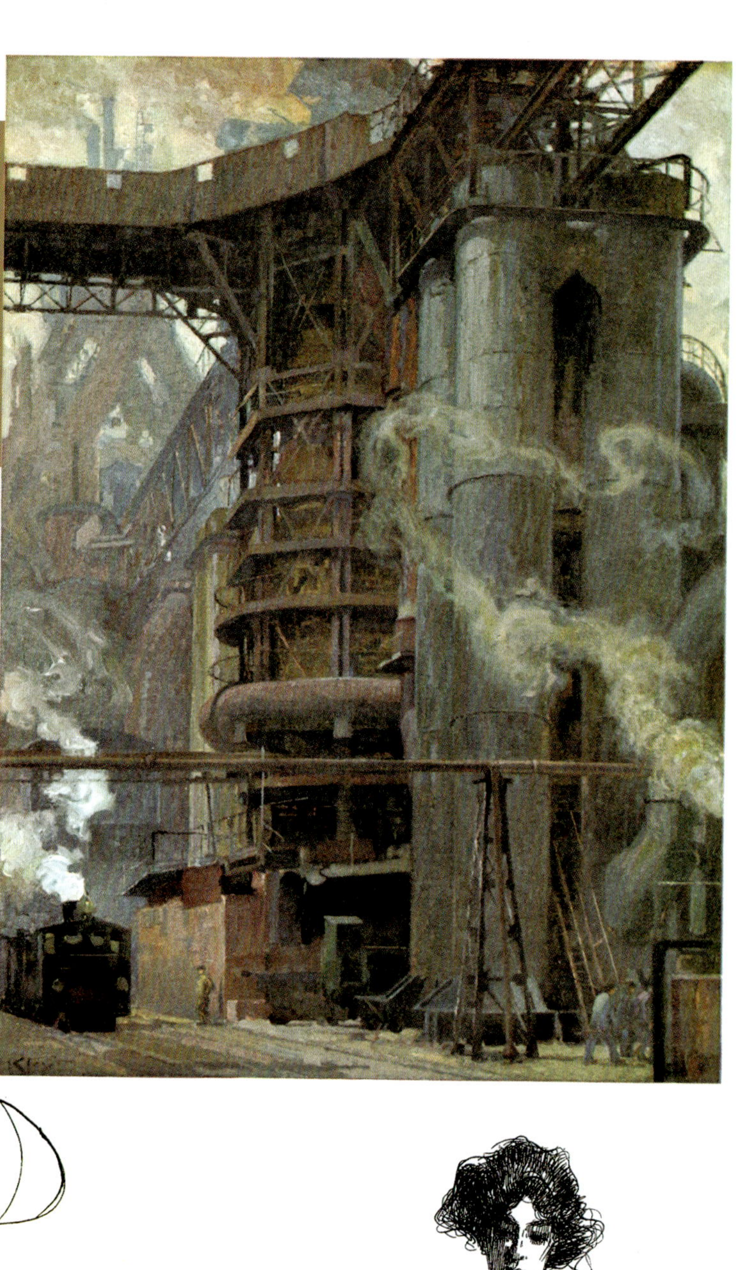

Kley had now become:

"Rubens corrupted by Rabelais."

from the Dover introduction to *The Drawings of Heinrich Kley*

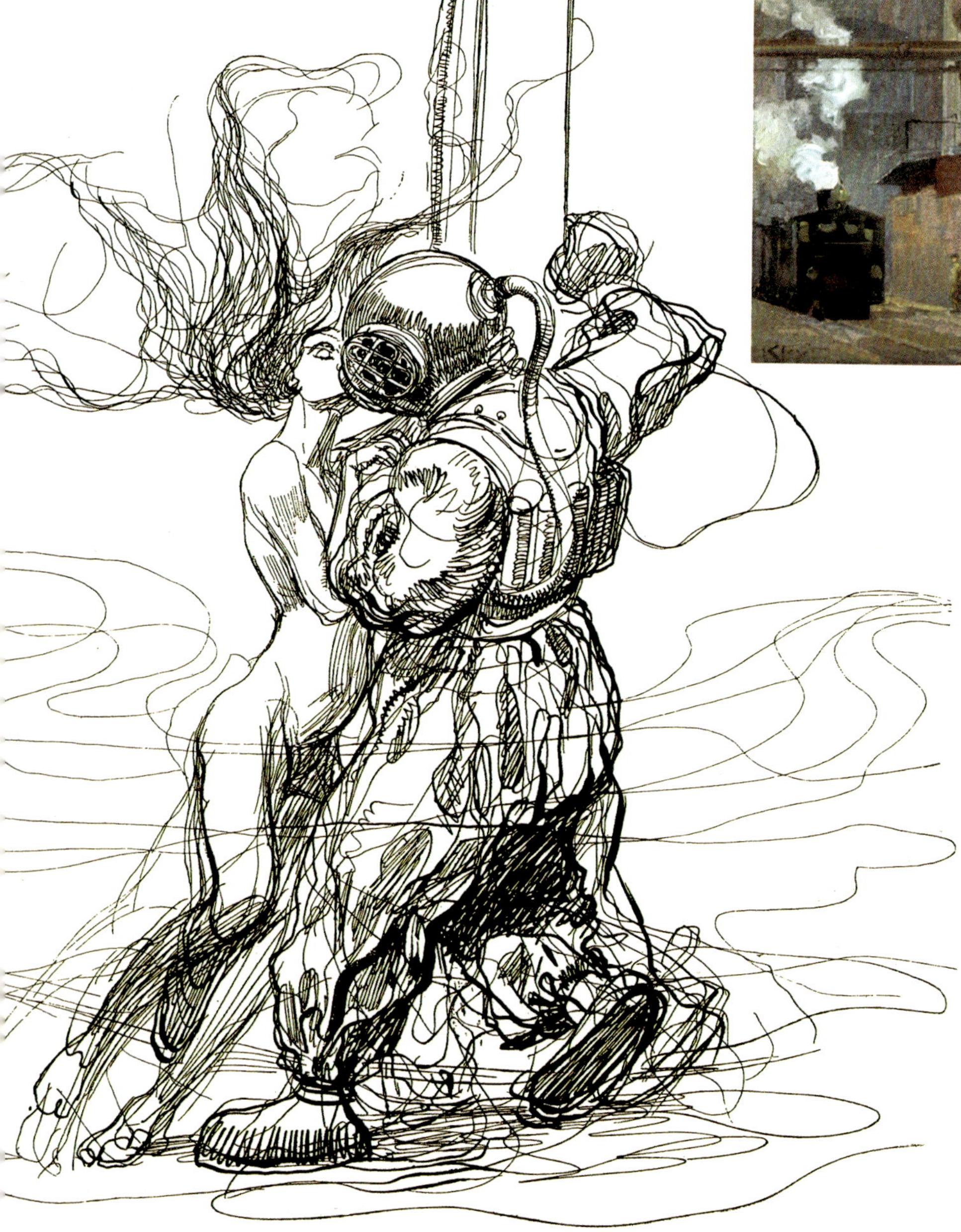

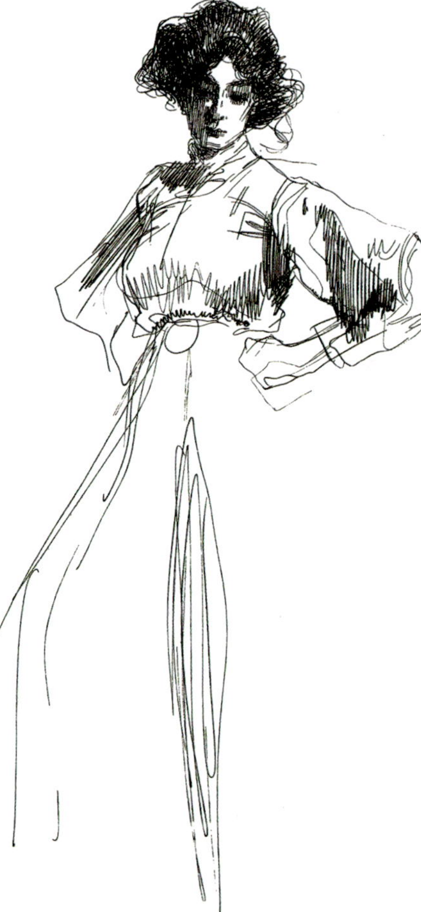

HEINRICH KLEY

1863–1945, German

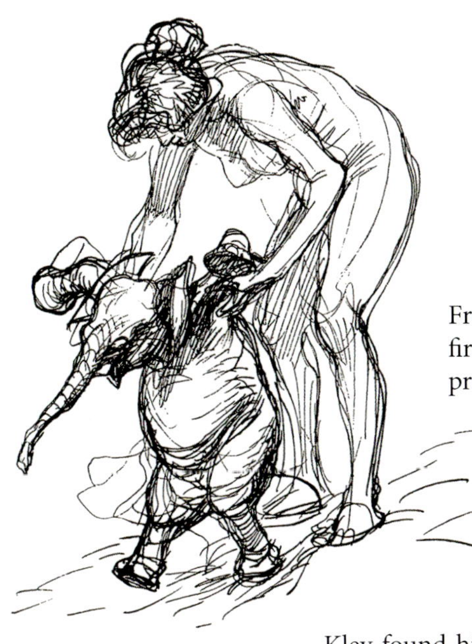

From his teens to the first few years of his professional career, Heinrich Kley proved himself technically adept, rendering everything from animals to industry with solid results. Kley found his strength in drawing the intricacies of modern machinery, a relatively new area of specialty. After studies both in his native Karlsruhe and later in Munich, he achieved early success in practical industrial illustration. When he added his own personal editorial opinions to his art, he produced work that was lasting and different.

Known for his masterful pen-work, Kley had become a regular in German magazines *Jugend* and *Simplicissimus* by 1908. His line work was loose and fluid, and his assembly of those lines produced a skilled representation, whether of a hardened soldier, a dancing tortoise, or a fair *fraulein.* Few artists could rival the freedom he seemed to achieve in a medium as rigid as ink. The style that Kley had exhibited in 1908 had all the markings of a talented draftsman, but with the additional touch of humor, which made his work rise above that of the more common illustrator. His art poked fun at the giants of industry, the elitist social class, and the pursuit of beauty. However, by 1920, he changed direction, pursuing the stability of more commercial work. It is the line work of this earlier period, however, visible to us through publications and republications, that necessitates repeated viewings. Kley is known to have also done book work, but only sparingly. His work never regained the popularity he held in the 1910s, and he passed away in Munich in 1945.

Kley's work was introduced at Walt Disney Studios sometime in the 1920s or 1930s. It was considered so influential, that some very strong parallels can be drawn between Kley's work and some of the early Disney film segments, most notably in *Fantasia,* where dancing alligators and hippos seem to have been born from Kley's sketches. In 2012 there was a special exhibition at the Walt Disney Family Museum, showcasing some of the original Kley artwork from the Disney archives that Walt himself had collected in the 1930s.

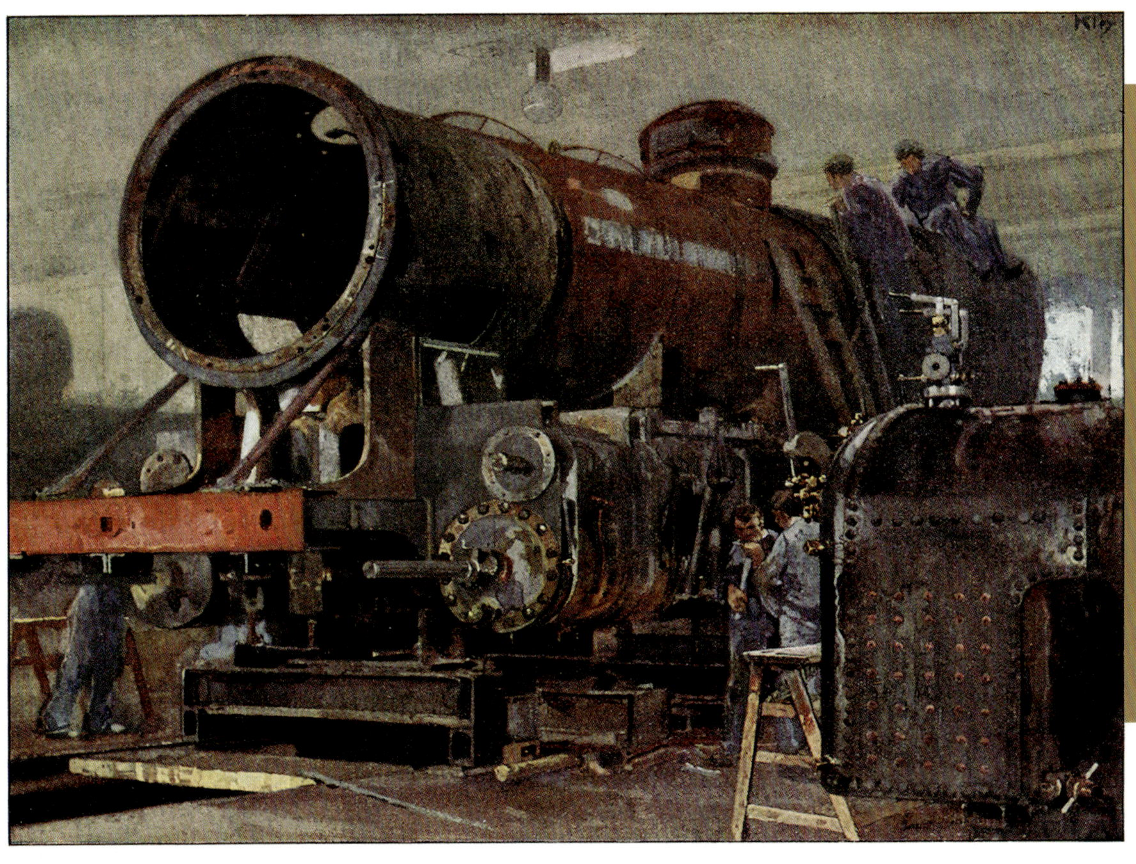

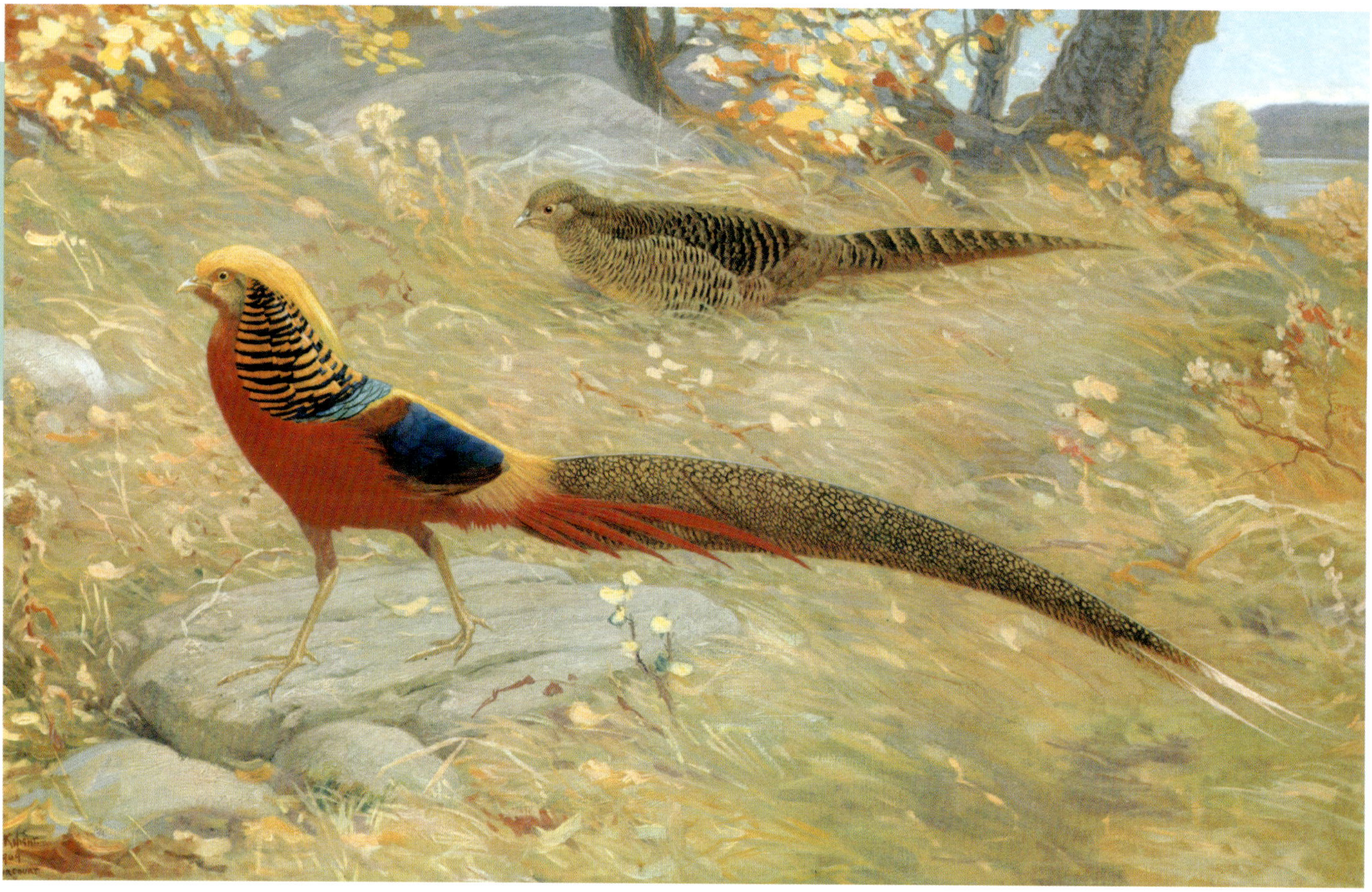

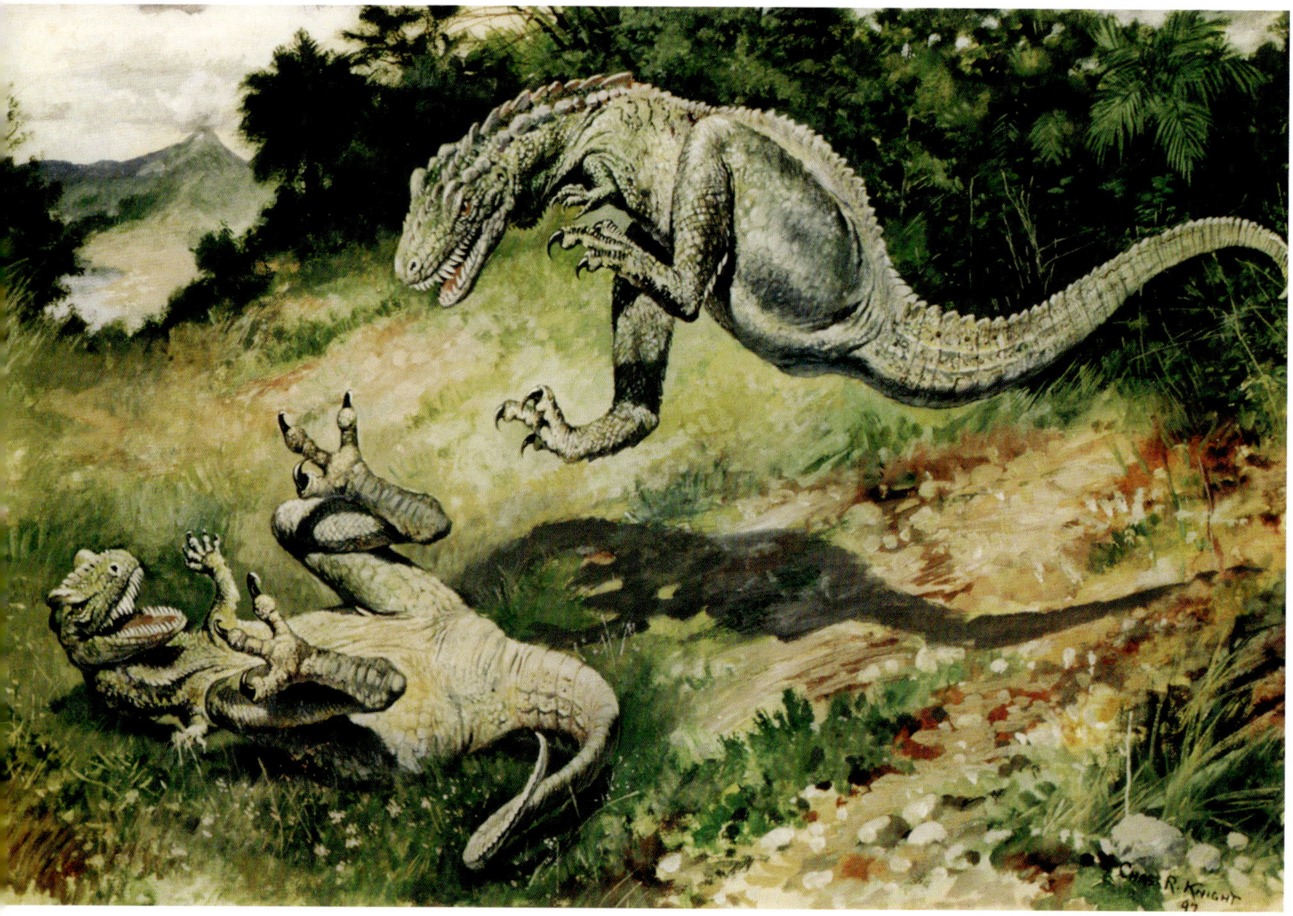

Knight, Charles R.

Charles R. Knight
1874–1953, American

A native New Yorker, Charles Knight was fascinated by the zoo as a child. His father took him there often, and before long, the passion he had for art and animals began to intertwine into a career. His earliest artistic efforts were practical and commercial. During the 1890s Knight worked with a church-decorating company, where he designed stained glass windows, then moved on to work as a freelance artist. He explored—and excelled at—depicting wildlife subjects, which he had embraced as a youth. He was soon sought after for his expertise in illustrating animals, and it became his specialty.

One of Knight's favorite pastimes was to visit the American Museum of Natural History in New York. He would often study the models there, and it was during one of these sessions that his work was noticed by Dr. Jacob Wortman, the museum director. Wortman thought that depictions of extinct animals and dinosaurs—which until now had only been seen in fossil form—might have great appeal to the museum's patrons. It was an opportunity that would alter the path of Knight's entire career. Wortman hired Knight to depict *Elotherium,* a type of prehistoric pig, and the results were well-received. Knight possessed the two things needed to perform the task exceptionally well—the knowledge of animal anatomy, and the imagination to apply practical ideas on the animals' diet and environment to his illustrations.

The success of Knight's work in New York caught the attention of other natural history museums throughout the country. In the coming years, he was asked to create murals and wall pieces for The Natural History Museum of Los Angeles County, famous for its association with the La Brea tar pits; the Field Museum in Chicago; the Carnegie Museums; and the Smithsonian. It also led to work at major zoos across the nation. As Knight's reputation for his animal work grew, he continued to find venues for his subjects in illustration as well. He contributed to collections of wildlife works, articles on various species for magazines like *Harper's* and *Collier's,* and later in his career, he would form a solid relationship with *National Geographic Magazine,* for whom he did work on subjects ranging from dinosaurs to early man.

His last museum mural was executed in 1951 for the Everhart Museum in Scranton, Pennsylvania. Knight passed away in 1953.

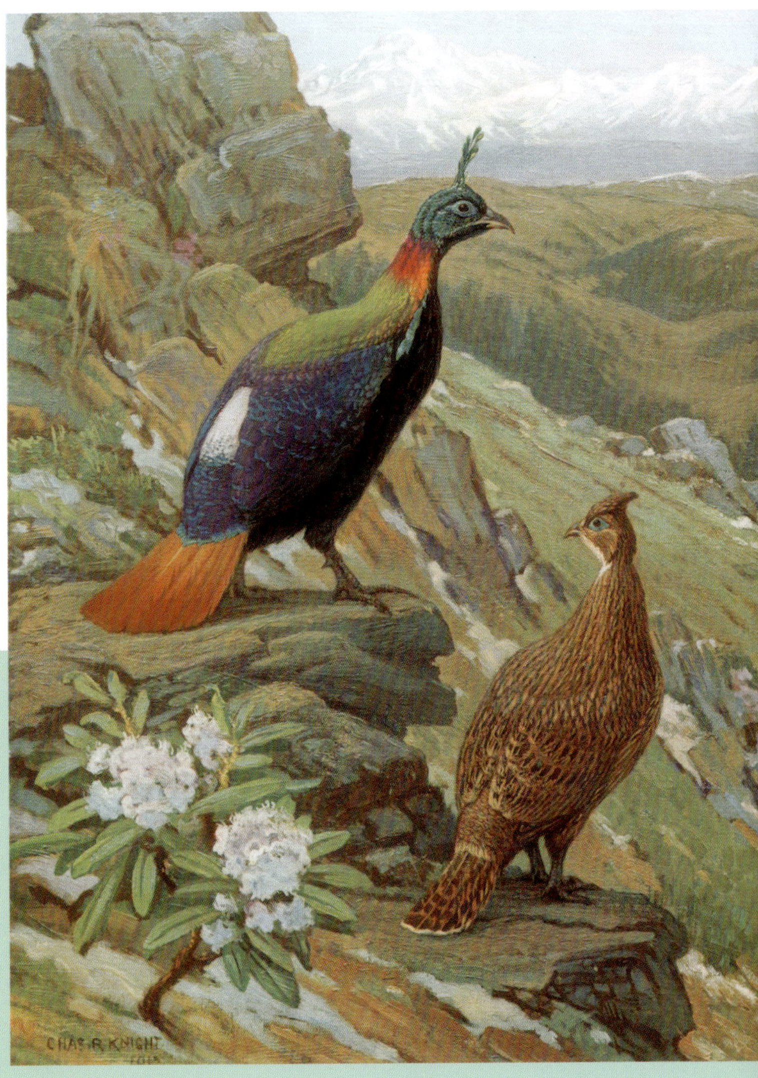

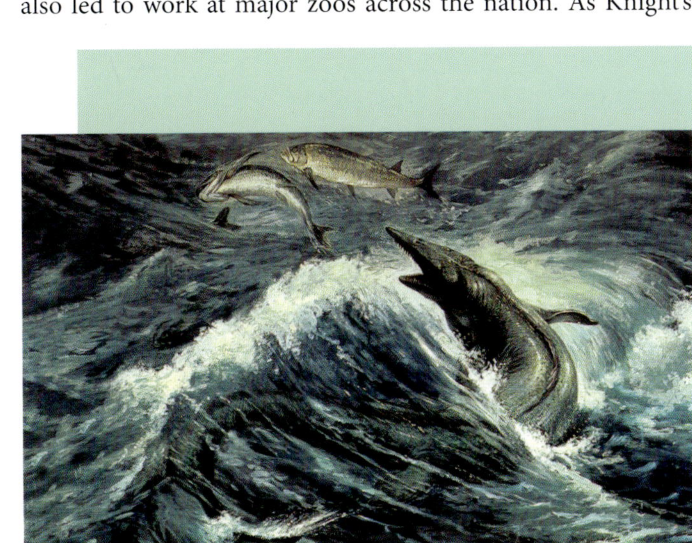

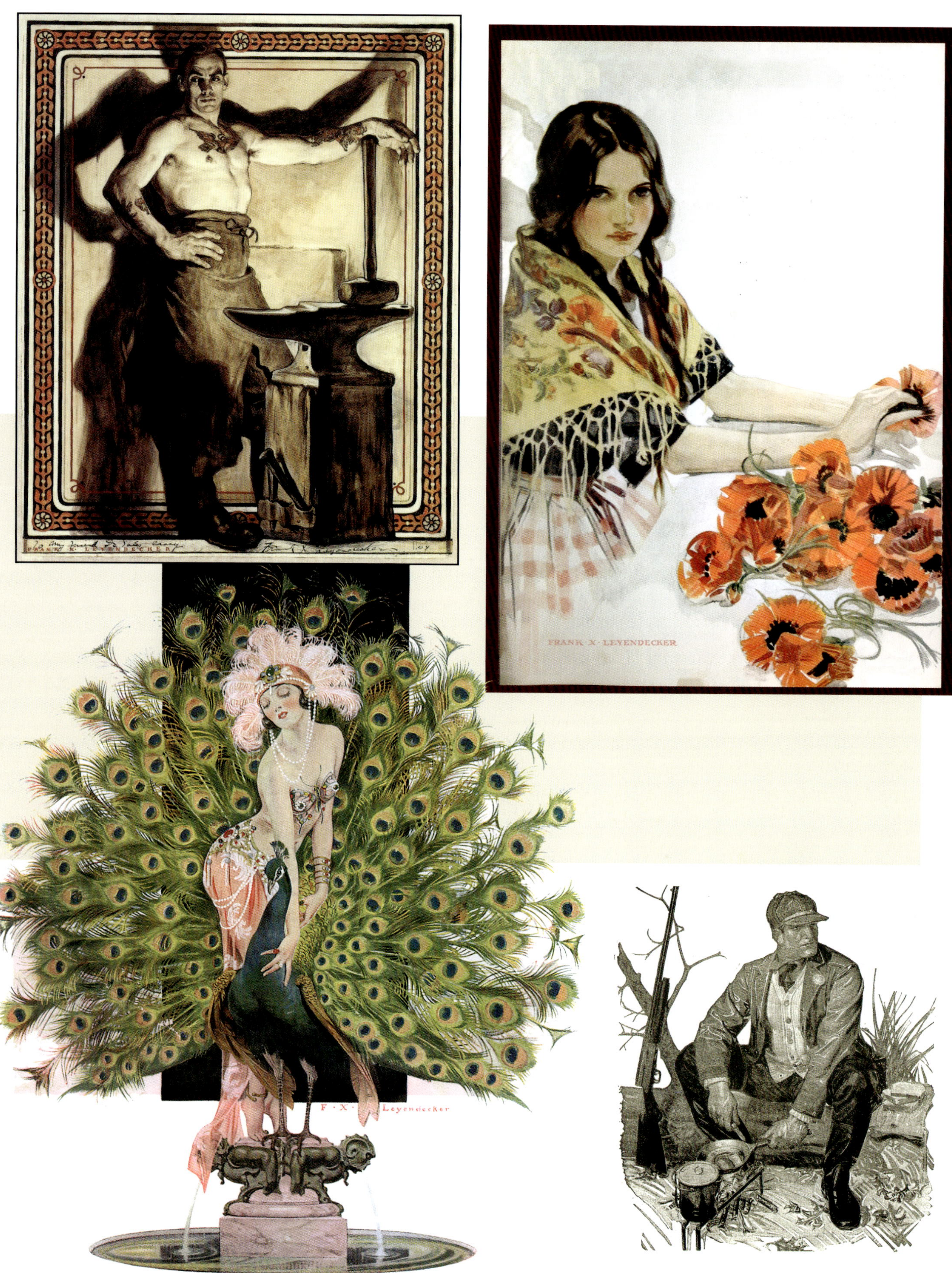

Leyendecker, Frank X.

Frank X. Leyendecker

1876–1924, German-American

Having an older brother who works in the same profession has both its drawbacks and its benefits. When that older brother is one of the biggest stars in that profession, and a major focus of the public's attention—it can certainly undermine efforts to make a mark there. Frank Leyendecker had that to bear. Frank came to America when he was six years old, and his brother J. C. was eight. The two were inseparable in most of their endeavors; both sought work in the growing field of illustration, both were immensely talented, and both had great success. When it came time to move to New York to further their work, they went together. The brothers bought a large house in New Rochelle, New York, in 1914, which would serve as their residence, as well as Frank's studio. It was also a backdrop for hosting some grand parties of the era.

Frank's work had a great attention to detail, while his brother's work tended to emphasize bolder images and shapes. His client list included *Collier's, The Saturday Evening Post,* and *Vogue.* While Frank's work shared many features with that of his brother's, the broad-stroked sculptural look that was J. C.'s signature style was more pronounced than Frank's. Frank pursued perfection in his work, and his tendency to place his own artistic satisfaction above the deadlines of commercial assignments cost him clients as his career progressed.

It was rare that Frank's work was not compared to that of his older brother—and more often than not, it was his brother J. C. who was preferred. Living under that shadow of his brother's success proved too much for Frank, and in 1921 he moved out of the New Rochelle mansion. A long struggle with drug addiction ended his life in 1924.

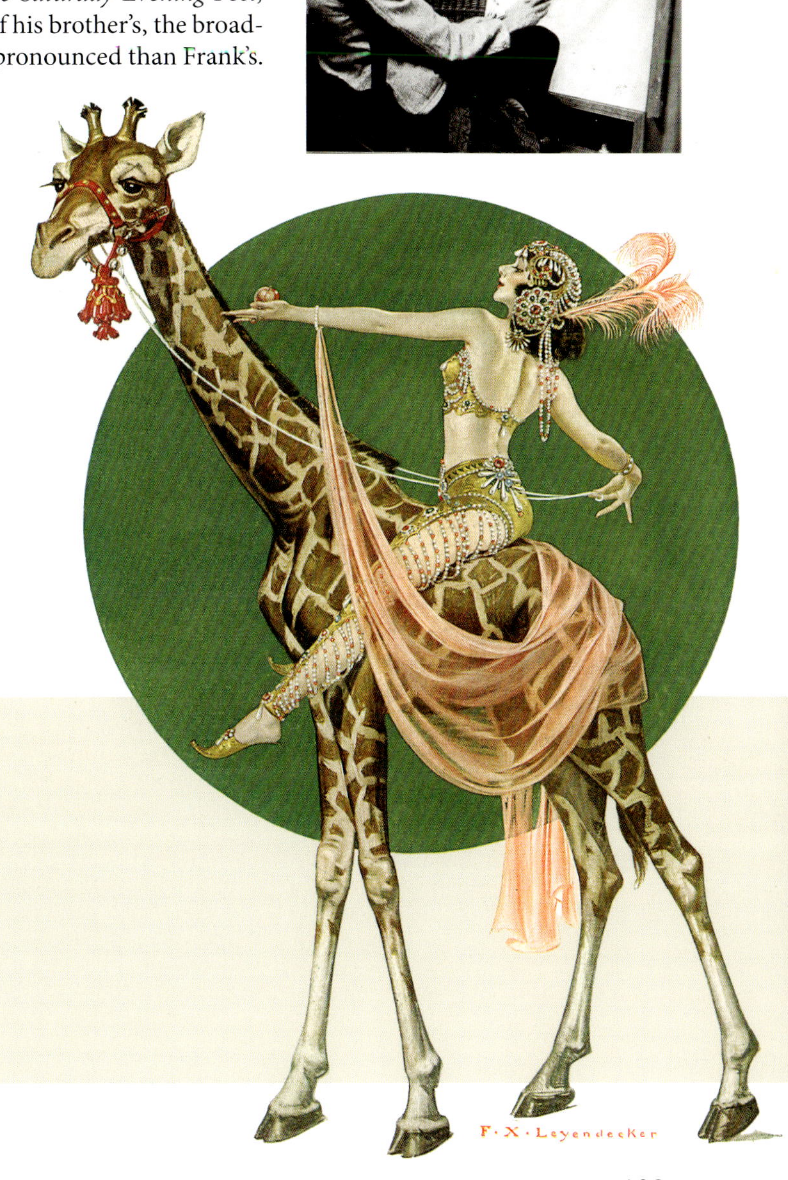

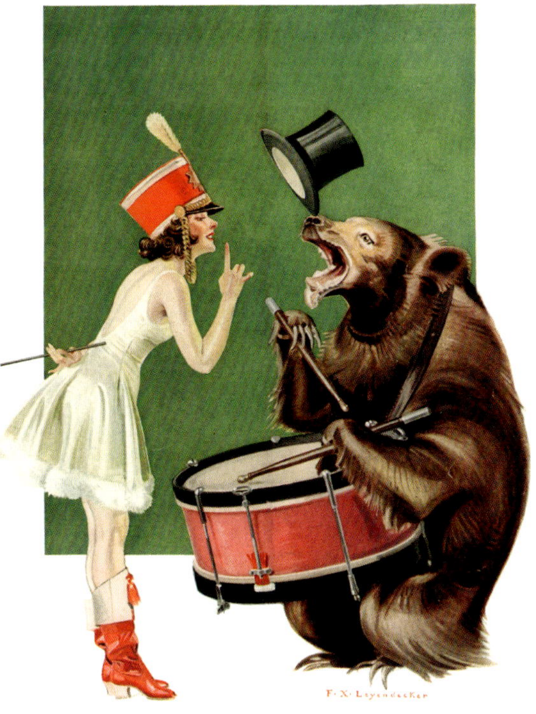

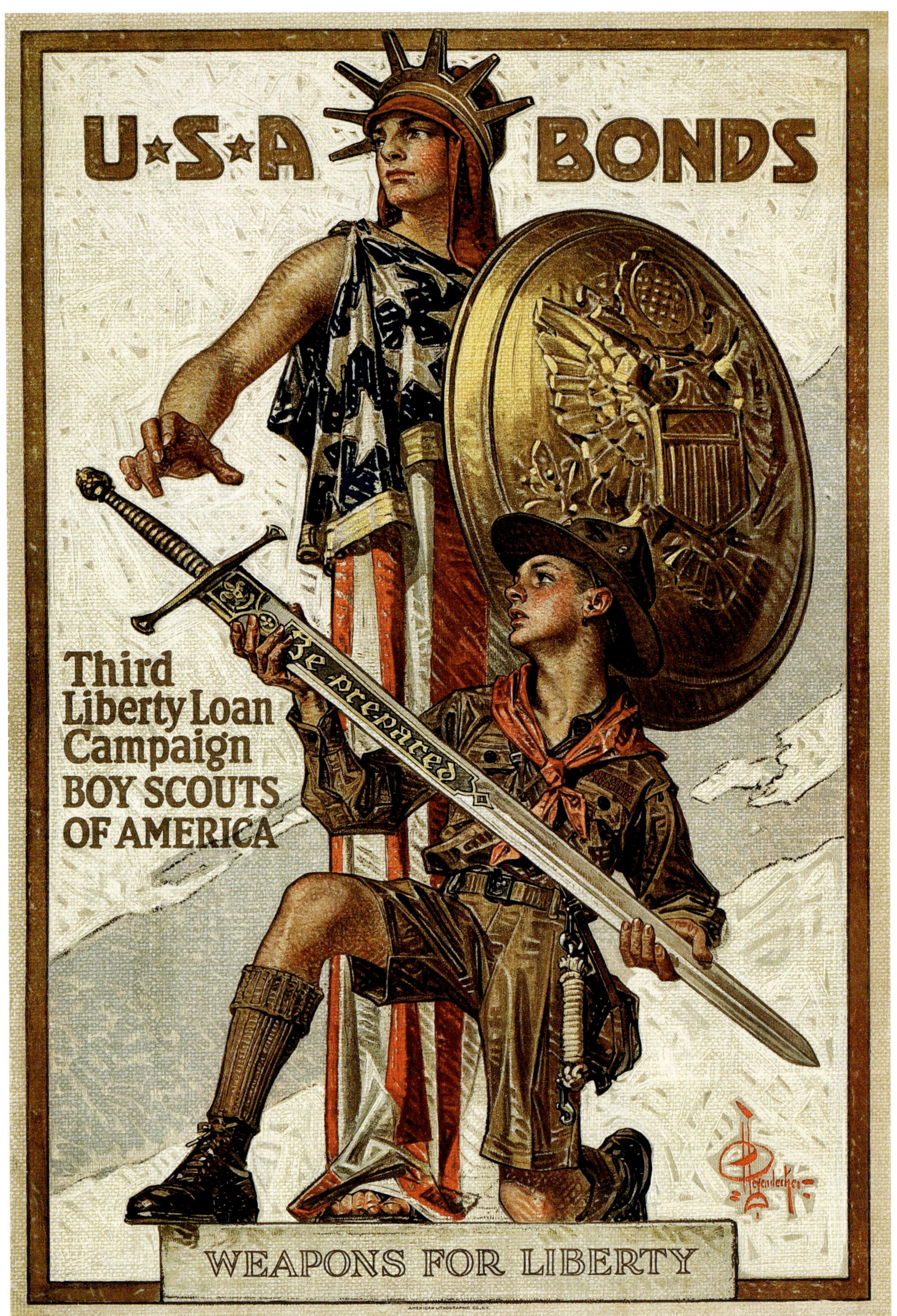

Leyendecker, J. C.

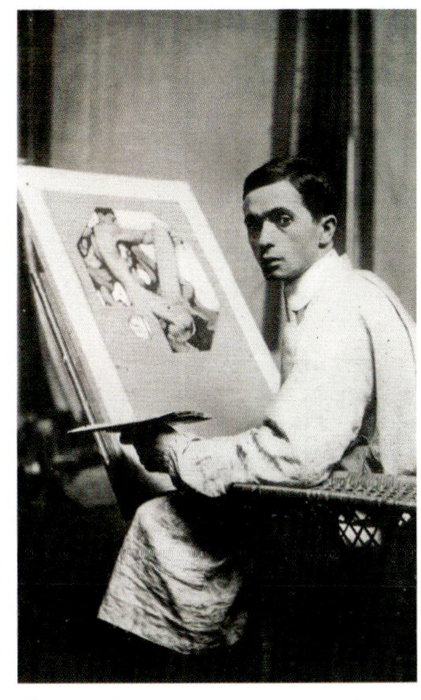

J. C. Leyendecker

1874–1951, German-American

Born in Montabaur, Germany, Joseph Christian (J. C.) Leyendecker and his brother Frank came to America as children with their family, settling in Chicago. J. C.'s earliest formal training was at Chicago's Art Institute, where John H. Vanderpoel was one of his instructors. After a year of further study in Paris, J. C. and his younger brother Frank began careers in illustration in the Chicago area, and by the time J. C. was twenty-five he had received his first cover assignment for *The Saturday Evening Post.* This working partnership would be one of the cornerstones of his career, as he would go on to produce 322 covers for *The Saturday Evening Post* over the next 44 years. Only Norman Rockwell would surpass that mark, and not for another twenty years.

The work J. C. and Frank pursued was in the periodicals of the day, and New York was the center of that publishing world. After moving there in 1900, both brothers gained additional clients in editorial and advertising work. J. C. became the better known of the two throughout the twenties. His work captured a slightly more heroic feel on his covers and advertisements, and his painting style gave him a more unique and identifiable look.

J. C. was just as successful in advertising as he was in magazines. He provided his strong visual identity for numerous accounts, and became indispensable to each of them. Interwoven Socks, Hartmax, B. Kuppenheimer & Co., and Cluett Peabody & Company were some of the accounts that J. C.'s visual "branding" would carry through the 1920s. The most important client in his career was most likely Arrow Shirt Collars. The images painted by the elder Leyendecker and his stark, elegant figures created a visual style that defined the iconography of the era. The success of the campaign made J. C. a wealthy man and a celebrity in his time, but being so identified with a specific decade has a downside when that decade is over and styles inevitably change. J. C.'s ad accounts and his cover commissions both dropped significantly in the 1930s.

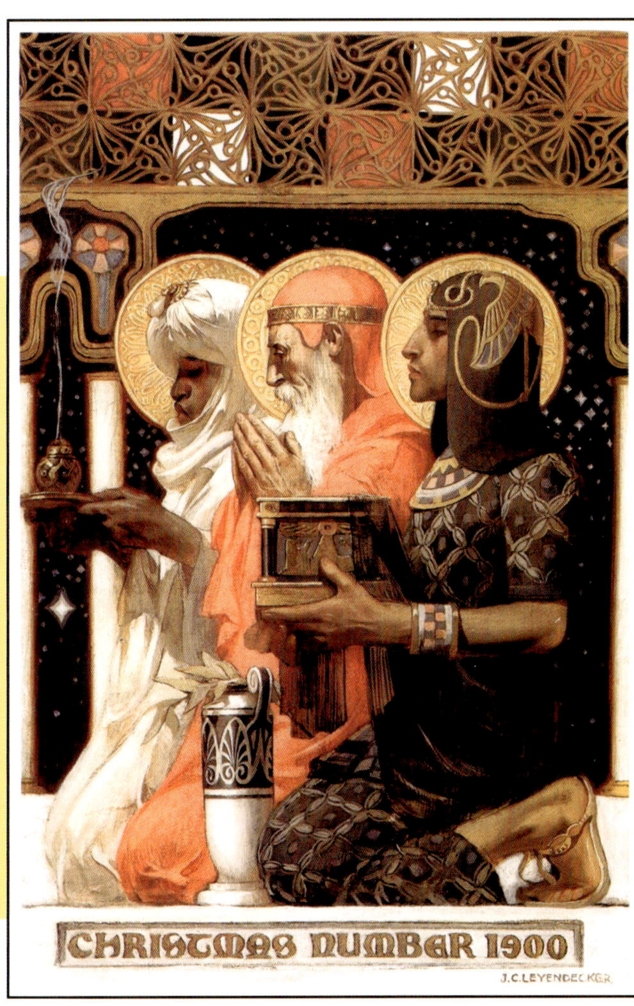

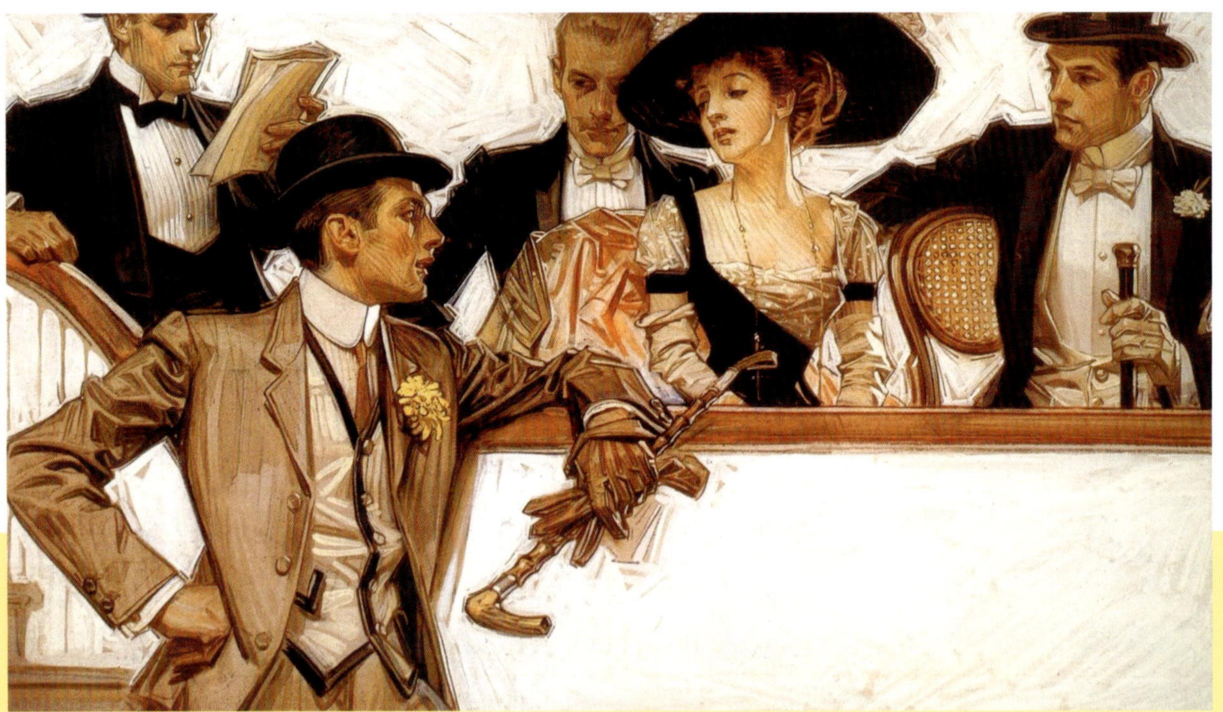

The Saturday Evening Post
Before Norman Rockwell became the visual identity of that prestigious magazine in the 1940s, J. C. Leyendecker was their most utilized cover artist. He painted 322 covers for them before his final one in 1943.

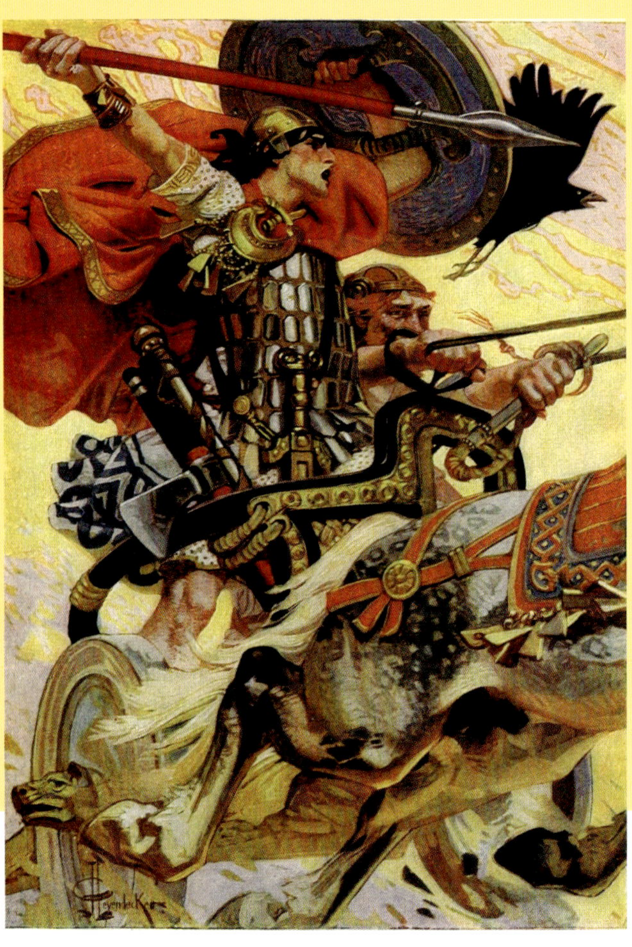

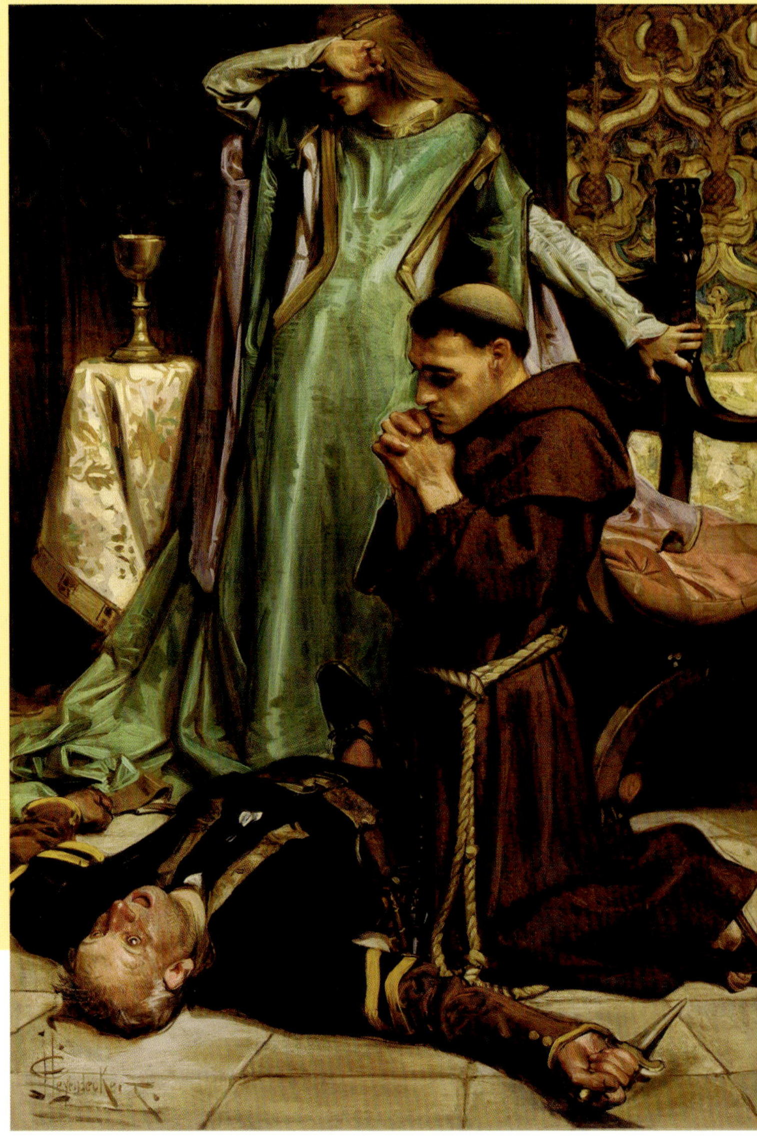

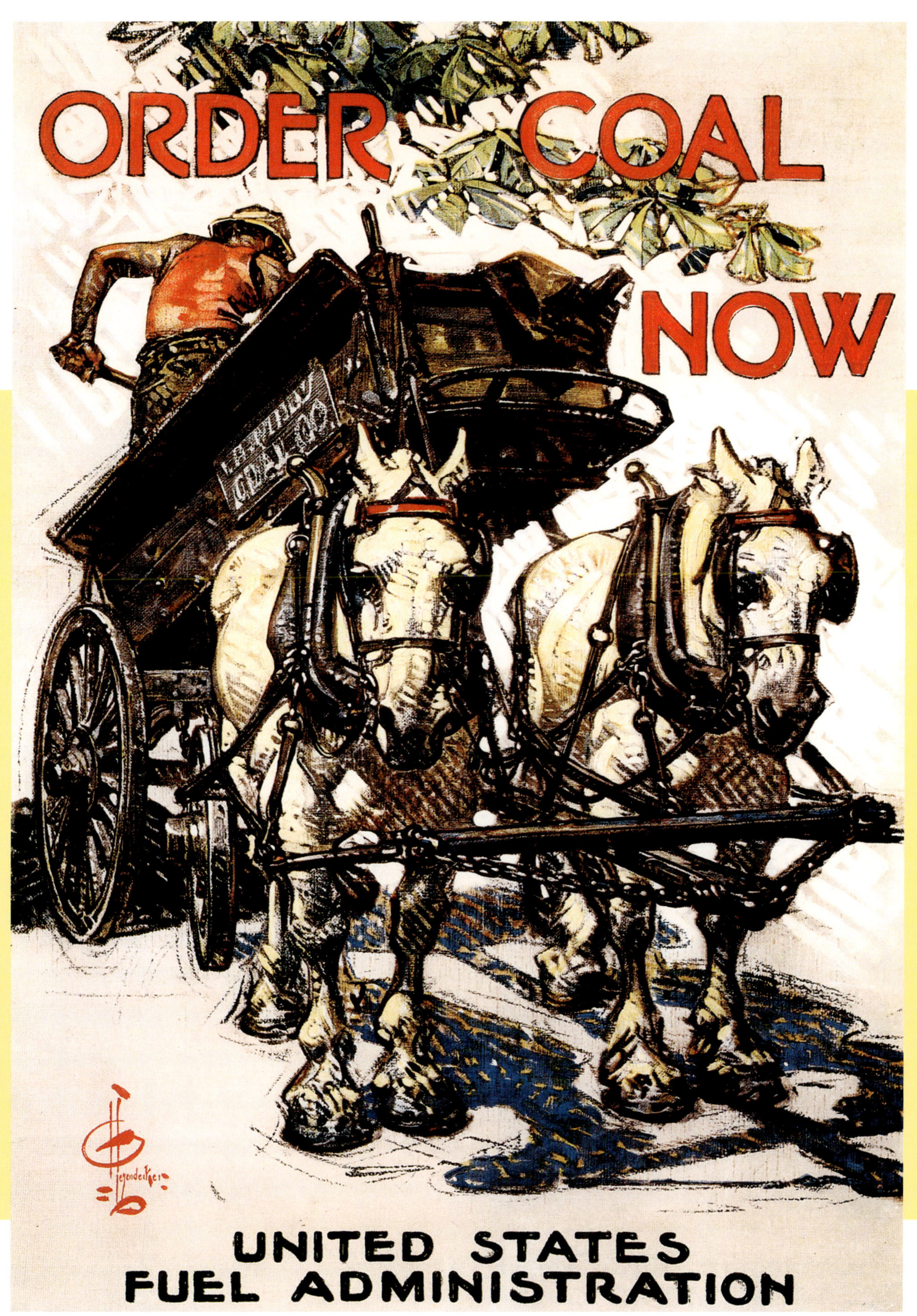

War Efforts
In his studio in New Rochelle, New York, J. C. produced a number of posters for the World War I effort; many of them still capture our attention and imagination a century later.

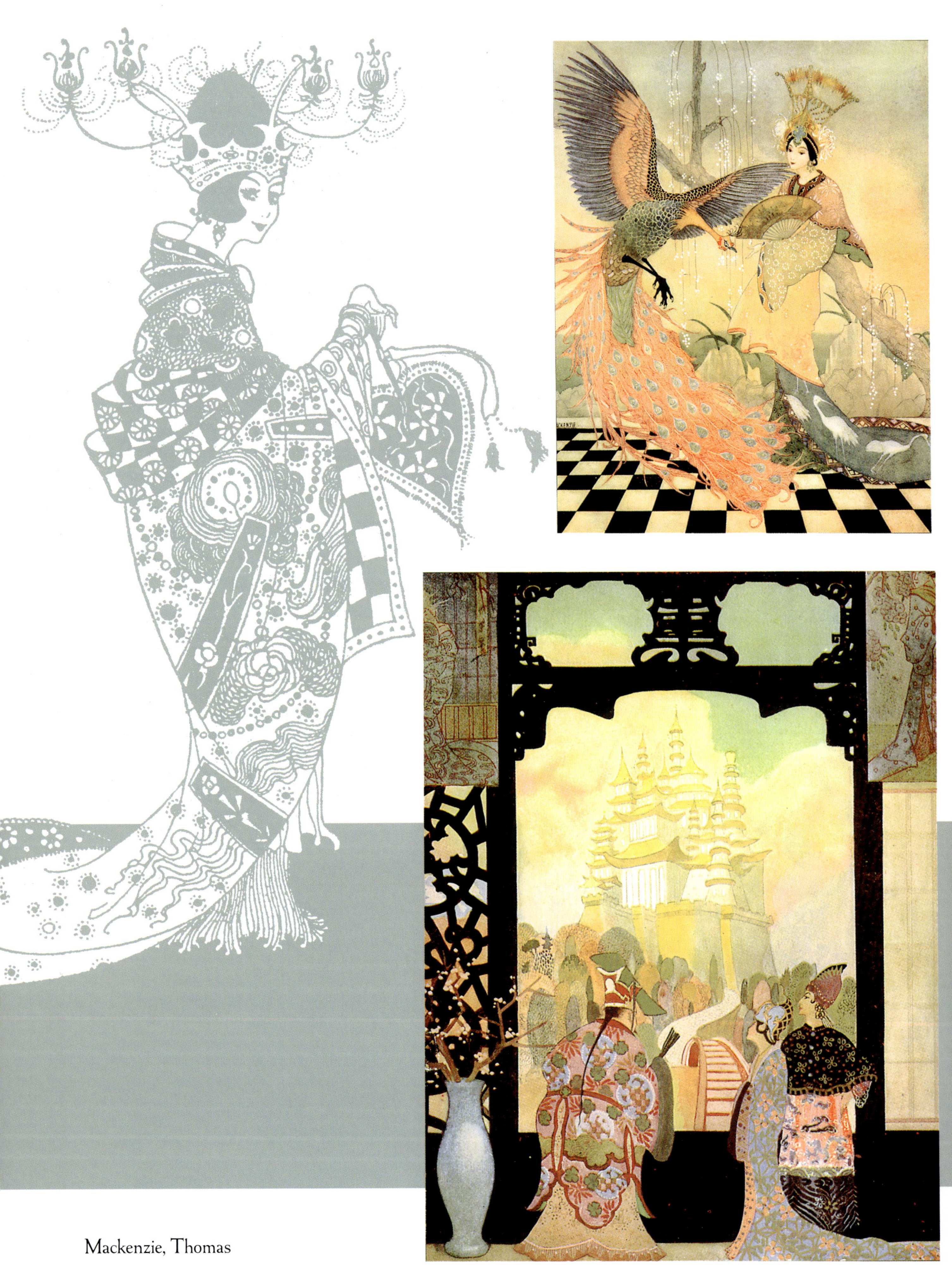

Mackenzie, Thomas

Thomas Mackenzie

1887–1944, British

Mackenzie's career in illustration began during the book publishing boom at the start of the century. His work was of the "Decadent" style, sharing attributes with the art of Aubrey Beardsley, Kay Nielsen, and Harry Clarke. Stylized figures, large black areas balanced with minute repetitious patterns, and an attention to design were all common qualities of his work. But Mackenzie stood out in another area. His watercolor work featured much of the same design as his line work, but with a mastery of the medium—smooth gradations and near flawless transitions that few others could match. As an illustrator, his work appeared mostly in books of children's tales; one of his earliest was James Stephens's *The Crock of Gold,* a collection of Irish fairy tales that featured Mackenzie's line work. Excellent examples of his color work can be found in *Aladdin and His Wonderful Lamp in Rhyme,* and *Arthur and His Knights.*

Although skilled as an illustrator, Thomas Mackenzie sought a reputation as a painter, and in 1929 he left England for France in search of that goal. It was not a successful quest, though, and Mackenzie's best-known works remain tied to his relatively short career in illustration.

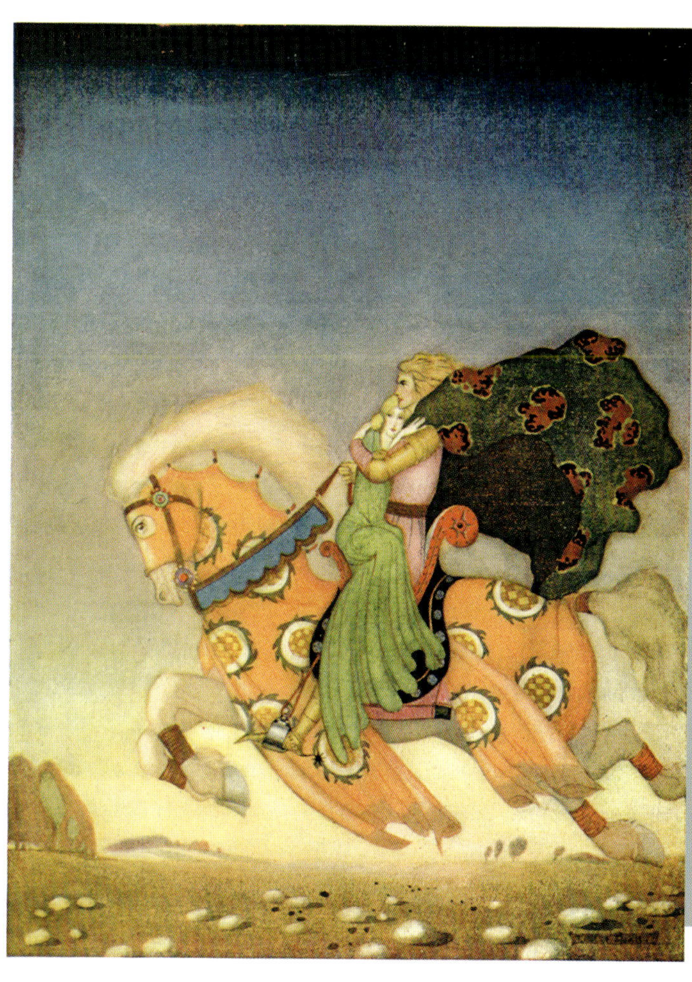

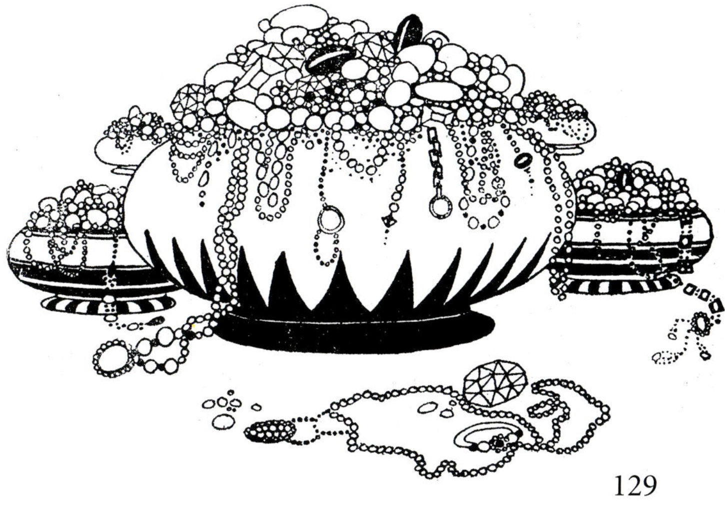

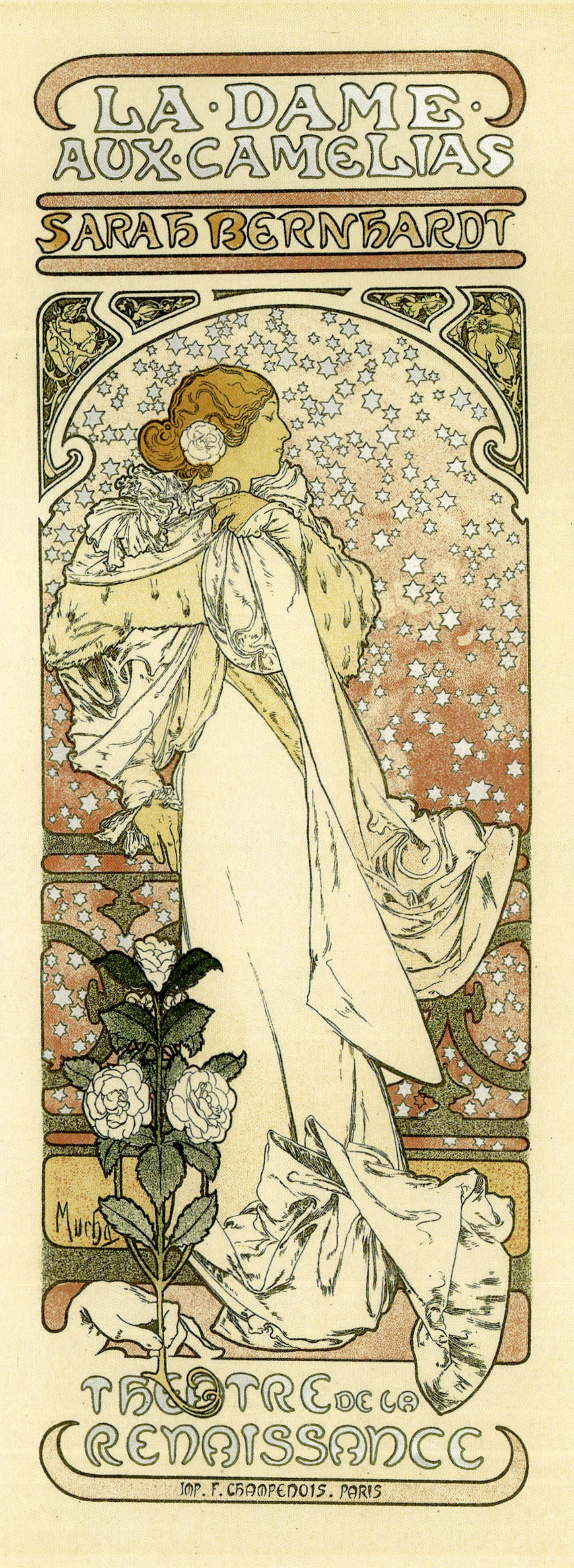

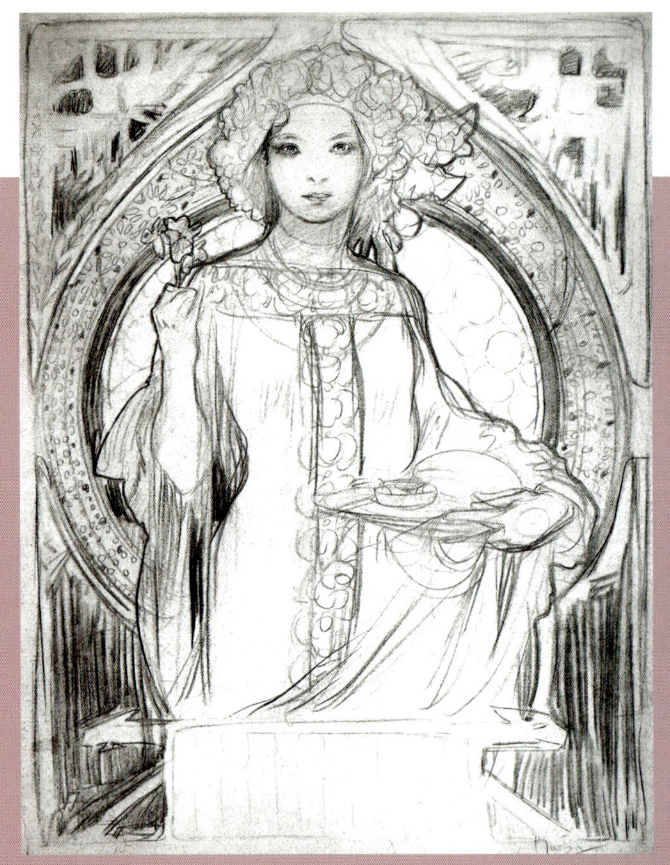

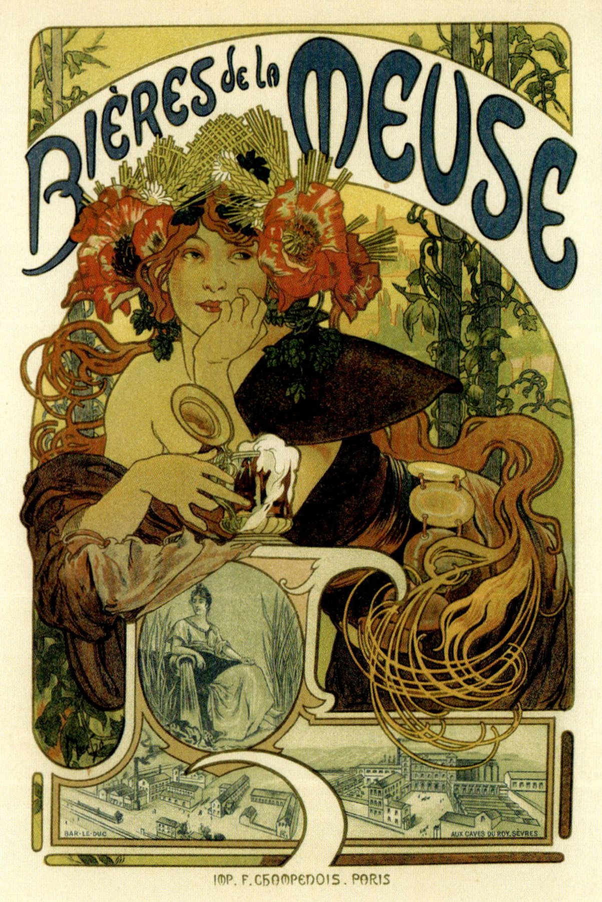

Mucha, Alphonse M.

Alphonse M. Mucha
1860–1939, Austrian

There are few designer-illustrators who have had as much of an effect on the visual sensibilities of their time as Alphonse Mucha. To this day, the impact of his design work reverberates through other artists' work. From his earliest professional days in Vienna, his illustrative and decorative imagery was so full of grace and style that he became the figurehead of the Art Nouveau period.

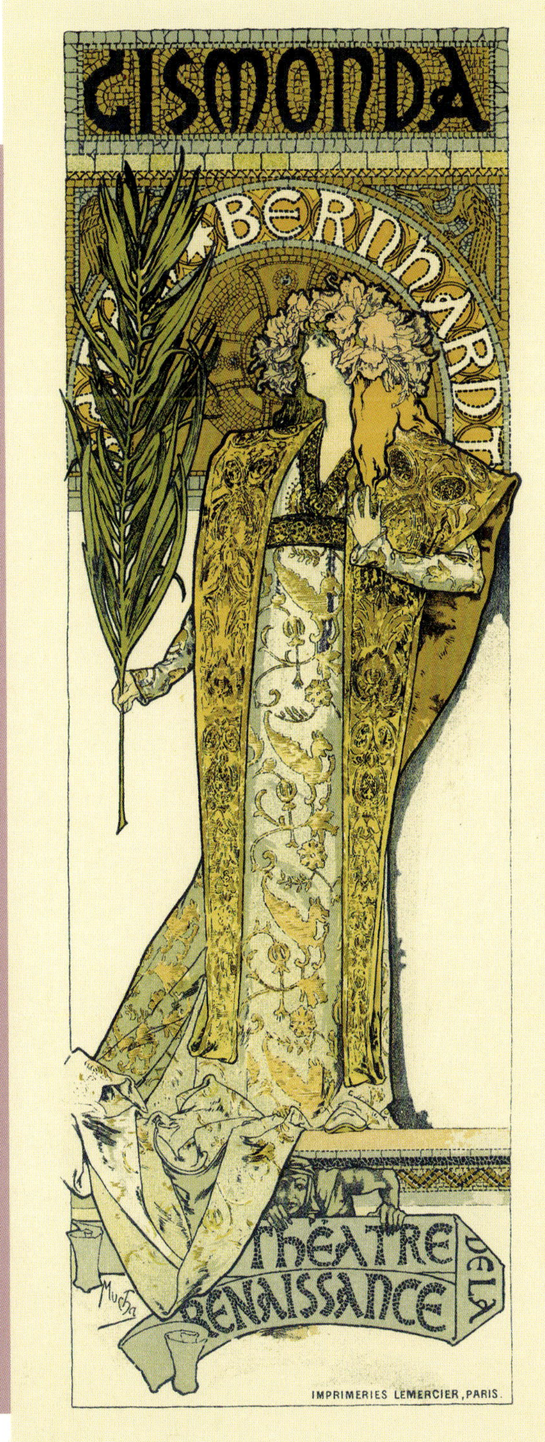

Mucha was artistically inclined from childhood. His schooling took place in the Moravian capital, and then he went to Vienna, finding work with a theatrical design company. In 1881 he returned to Moravia, where he was hired by Count Karl Khuen to decorate a castle with murals. The count was so impressed with the work that he became a patron, and sponsored more schooling for Mucha at the Munich Academy of Fine Arts. After two years of studies there, Mucha turned to Paris and the Académie Julian. When his sponsorship ceased, Mucha sought work from magazines and for advertisements, just scraping by, but he began to develop the look of what would become Art Nouveau.

In December of 1894 Mucha had been recently employed by a print studio when a job to design a poster became available. Within two weeks, he had produced a poster to advertise an upcoming production for the popular actress Sarah Bernhardt. It quickly became the talk of Paris—Mucha had taken his native design sense and wed it to the current art movements in Paris, producing his own unique look. Bernhardt was so pleased with the poster and its effect that she contracted Mucha for what would become a six-year arrangement.

The Art Nouveau movement would not have been the same without Mucha's involvement. His work was central to its appeal, and he was considered its master craftsman. Known for its natural flow and decorative graphic qualities, floral designs, and sweeping garments, Art Nouveau still appeals to a wide audience today. From Mucha's earliest poster work of 1895 into the 1920s, his name and the Art Nouveau style were synonymous. As the style began to fall from favor, Mucha's attention to graphic work declined as well, and he moved on to large-scale painting, which was his greater ambition. However, he would never achieve the same level of fame in this medium as he did with his graphic works.

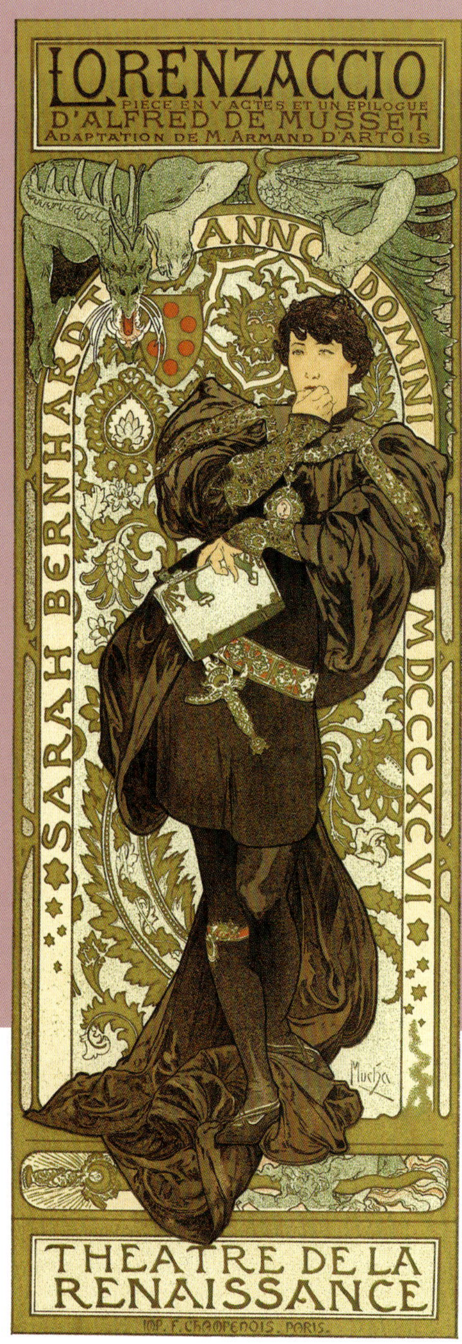

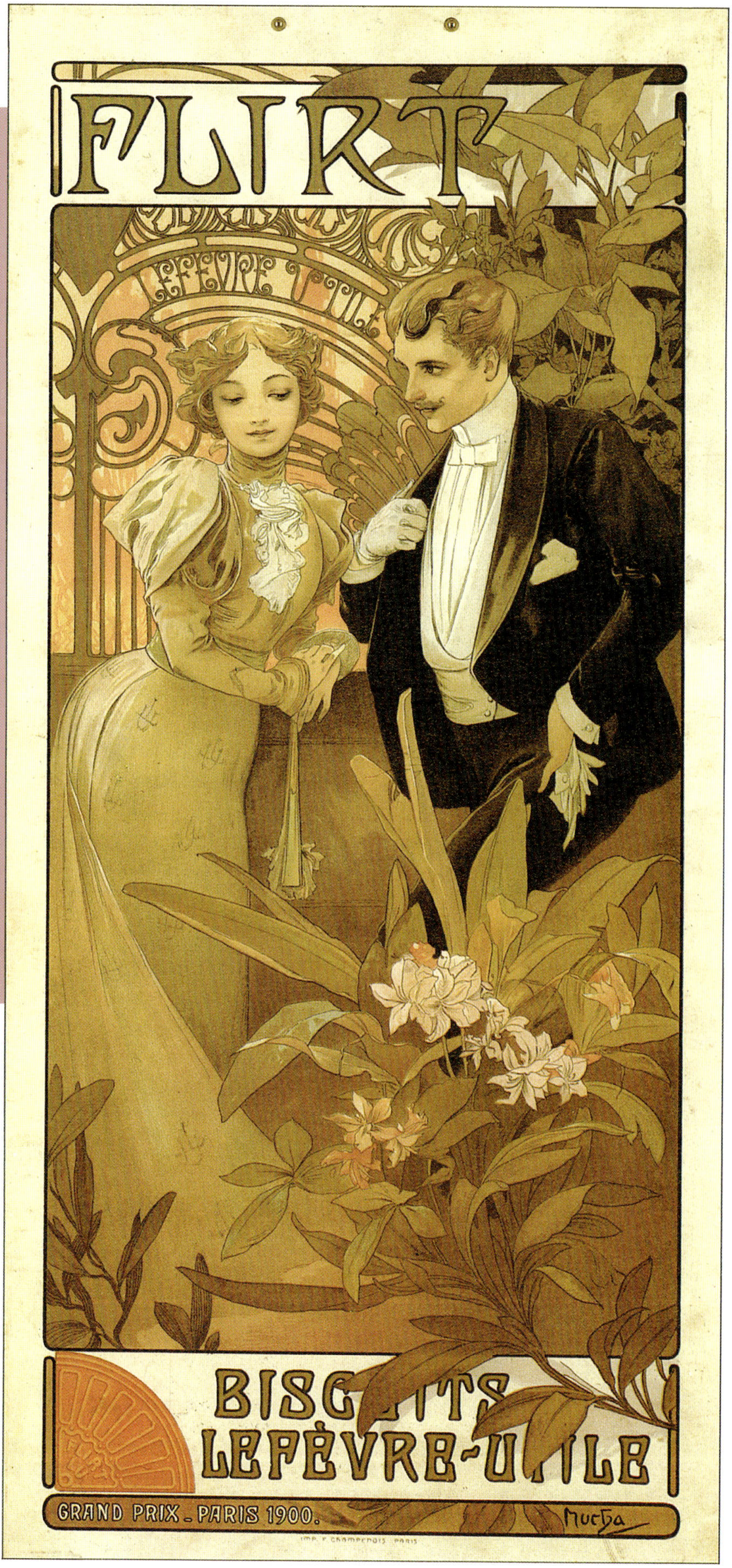

ELEGANCE AND ADVERTISING
The theatre, biscuits, chocolate, or wine—Mucha could make the mundane appear transcendent.

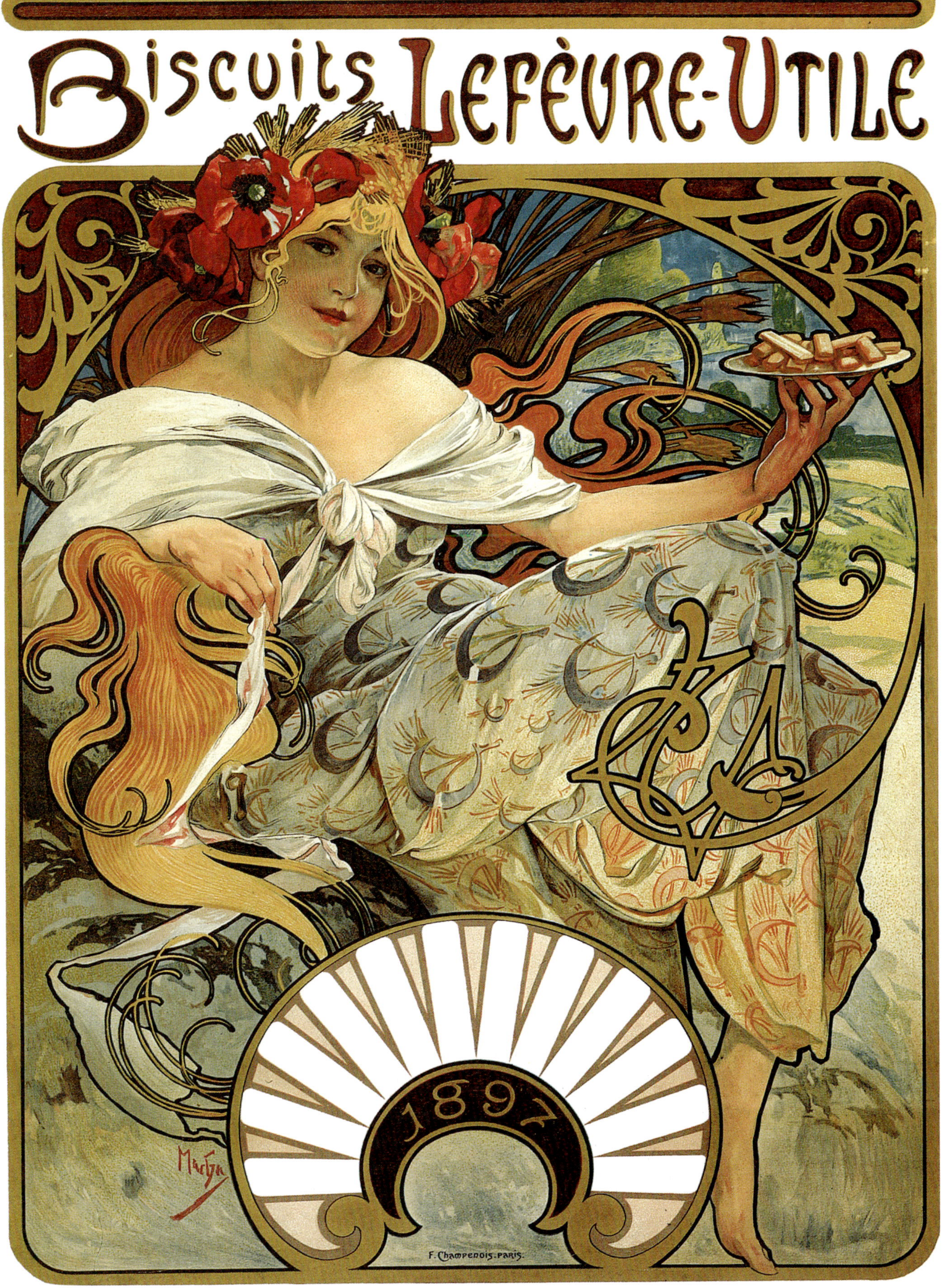
Biscuits Lefèvre-Utile
1897
Mucha
F. Champenois. Paris.

John R. Neill
1877–1943, American

A Philadelphia native from a large family, Neill began inking works for his high school newspaper in the mid-1890s. Subsequent training at the Pennsylvania Academy of Fine Arts was disappointing. He left after one semester, saying, "they have nothing to teach me." Neill found work doing court sketches for a Philadelphia newspaper, and honed his craft in the newspaper business for a few years. Over the next decade, Neill worked for various papers, mostly in Philadelphia, but also for a short time in New York.

His defining "break" arrived in 1904. Recognized for his expressive ink style, Neill was asked to work for Reilly & Britton, publishers for the second book in "The Wizard of Oz" series, *The Marvelous Land of Oz.* The original illustrator, W. W. Denslow, was not available so Neill was presented with the opportunity on the strength of the line work he'd done for newspapers, at first mimicking Denslow's style, and gradually—in later books of the series—showcasing his own expressive ink style. Neill's depiction of Dorothy's transformation from a very young girl to preteen years helped to keep the series growing with its audience. Though he continued working with newspapers for years, by 1911 Neill had made enough connections to become a full-time freelance artist for books and magazines. Neill would become known as the "Imperial Illustrator of Oz," working on 37 Oz titles over the next 39 years, including three Oz books that he wrote.

While his connection with the works of L. Frank Baum became the core of his career, Neill continued to work for many publications, including *Collier's, The Saturday Evening Post, The Ladies' Home Journal,* and *Century,* among others.

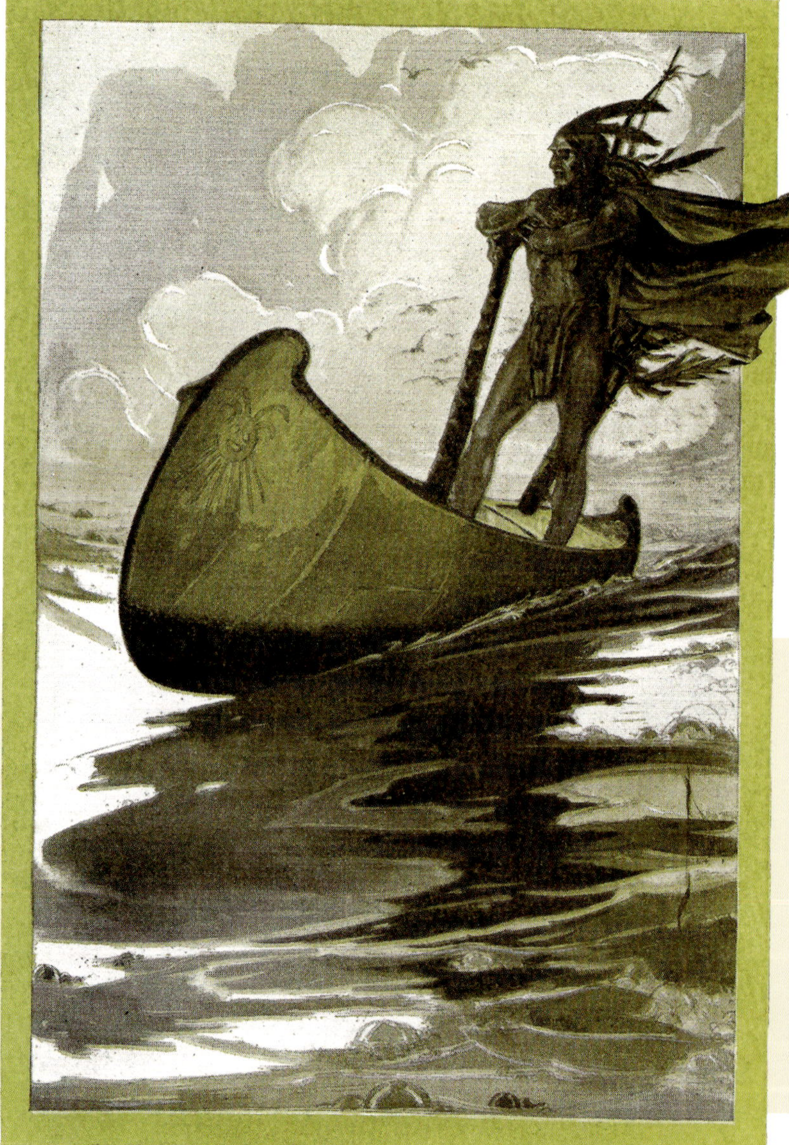

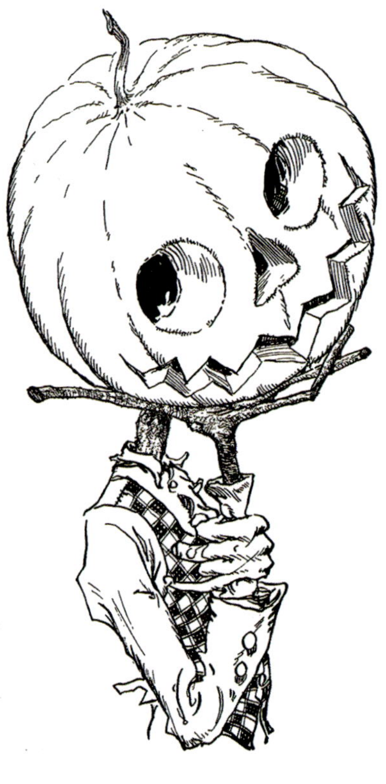

Neill, John R.

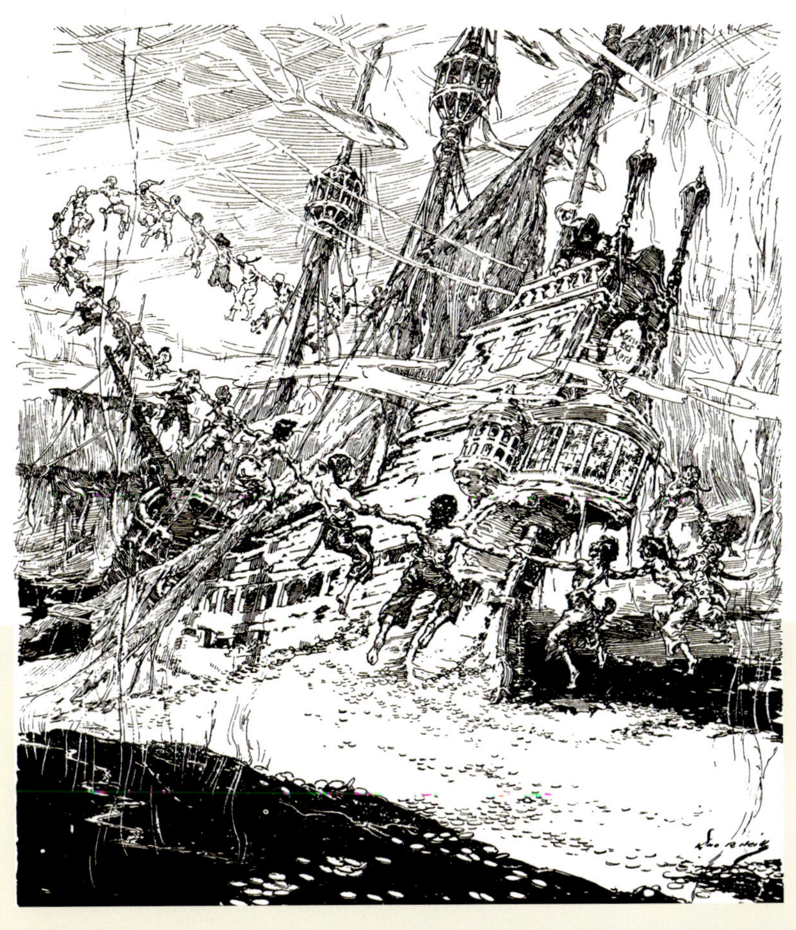

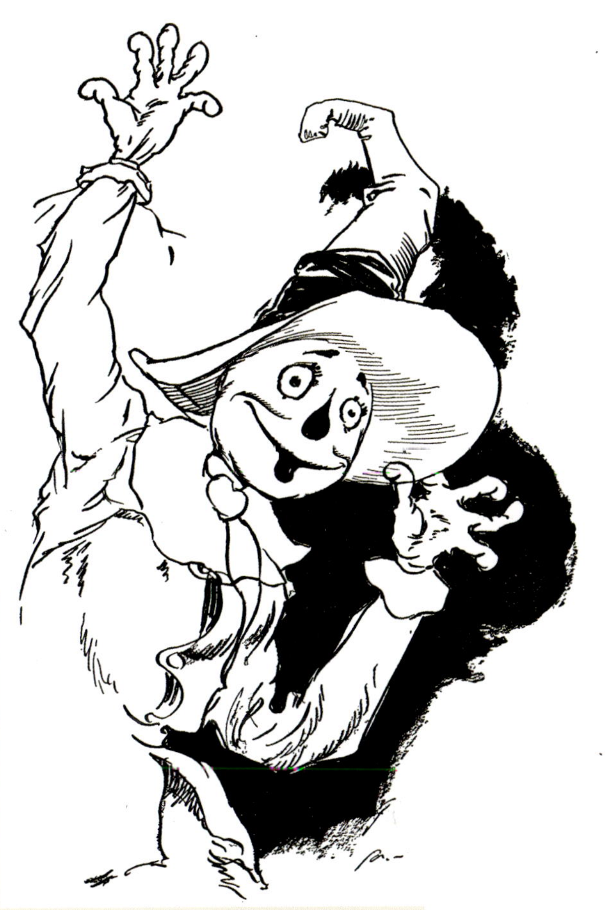

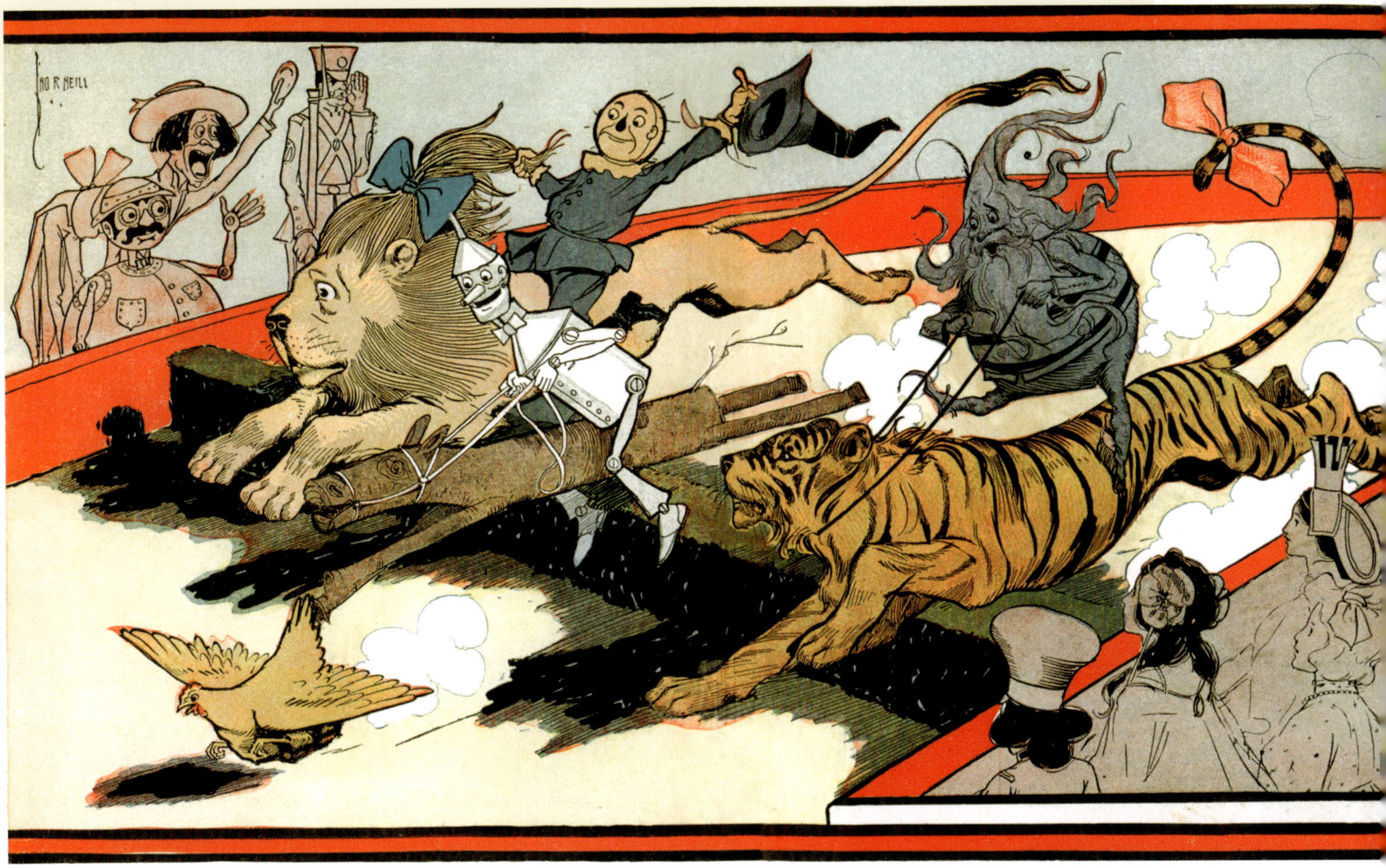

KAY NIELSEN
1886–1957, Danish

Kay Nielsen was perhaps one of the few Scandinavian illustrators whose work broke free of the boundaries of his homeland, and also received a great reception in the United States. Born into a family of theatrical artists, his style was a mixture of elements, combining some of the decorative design of Art Nouveau with the bold shapes of Art Deco. Leaving Denmark when he was seventeen, he spent seven years studying art in Paris. His success was bright but fleeting. From 1913–1930, Nielsen contributed to the illustration of at least five books: fairy tales, and similar children's stories. His masterpiece is considered by most to be one of the pillars of the twentieth-century gift book market—*East of the Sun and West of the Moon* by George Webbe Dasent. Nielsen's edition was put out by Harrap in 1914, and featured 25 color plates and numerous drawings.

Following World War I, Nielsen combined his talent as a designer with the knowledge of the theater learned from his parents. Until 1923 he was the chief stage designer at the Danish State Theatre.

Nielsen and his wife moved to the United States in 1936 to pursue opportunities in theater design. In California, the growing industry for image makers was in the field of animation, and Nielsen contributed his sketches later that year, at Walt Disney Studios. Some of his influence can be noted in scenes from the 1940 animated film *Fantasia*. Animation was very demanding in its nature, and artists who had grown accustomed to the pace of book work usually did not last long in the field of animation.

In the early 1940s he was hired to paint large murals for schools in Los Angeles. The murals were well-received, and Nielsen hoped it might be a precursor to better times. His health was already frail by then, and it soon deteriorated further. When he died in 1957, he had been struggling for years to find work. Over forty canvases of unpublished *Arabian Nights* images—most of which were done when he was working on *Aladdin* for the Danish Theatre in 1923—were fortunately rescued by his neighbors, though they were not published until 1977.

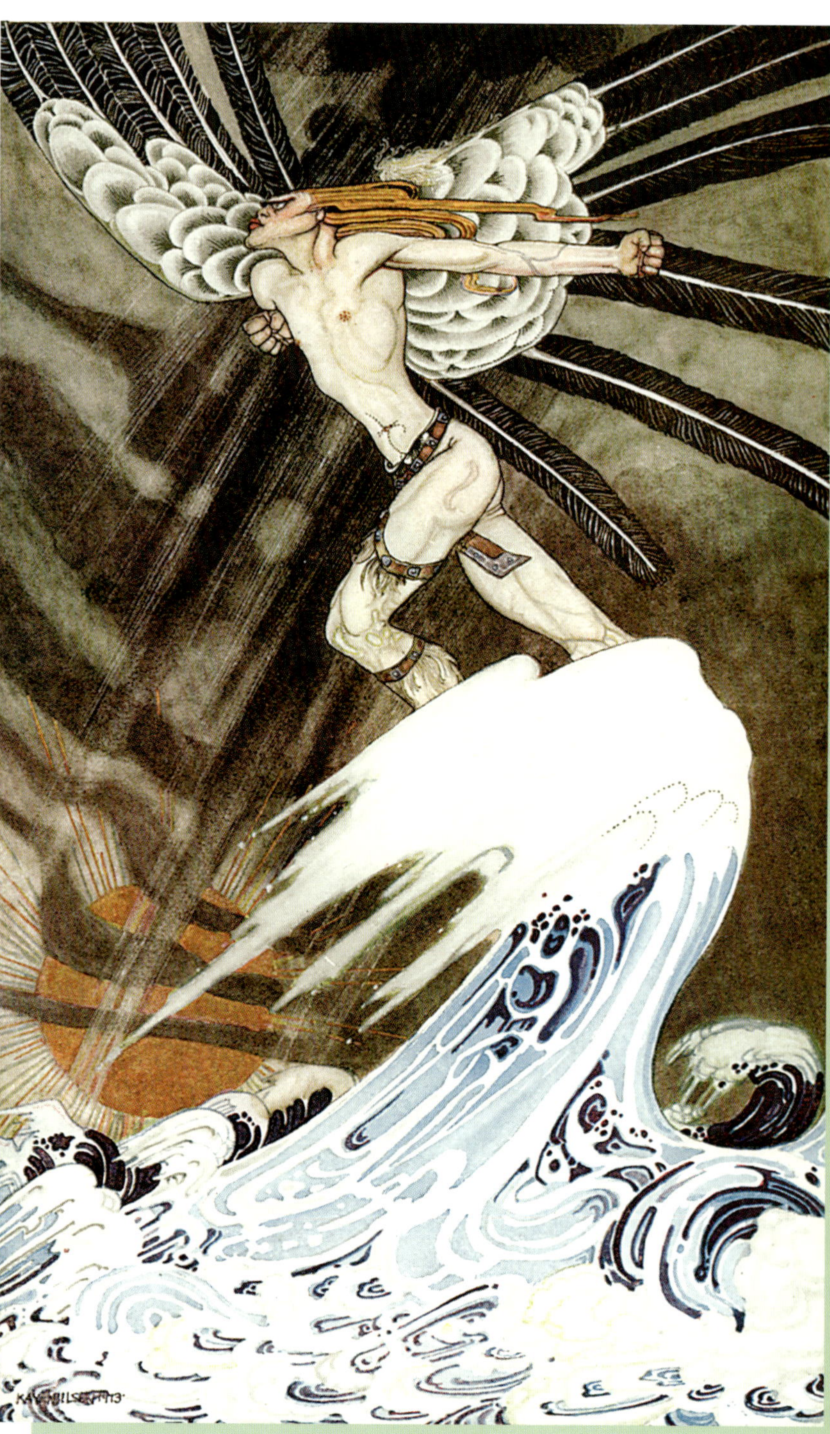

From *East of the Sun and West of the Moon*, 1914.

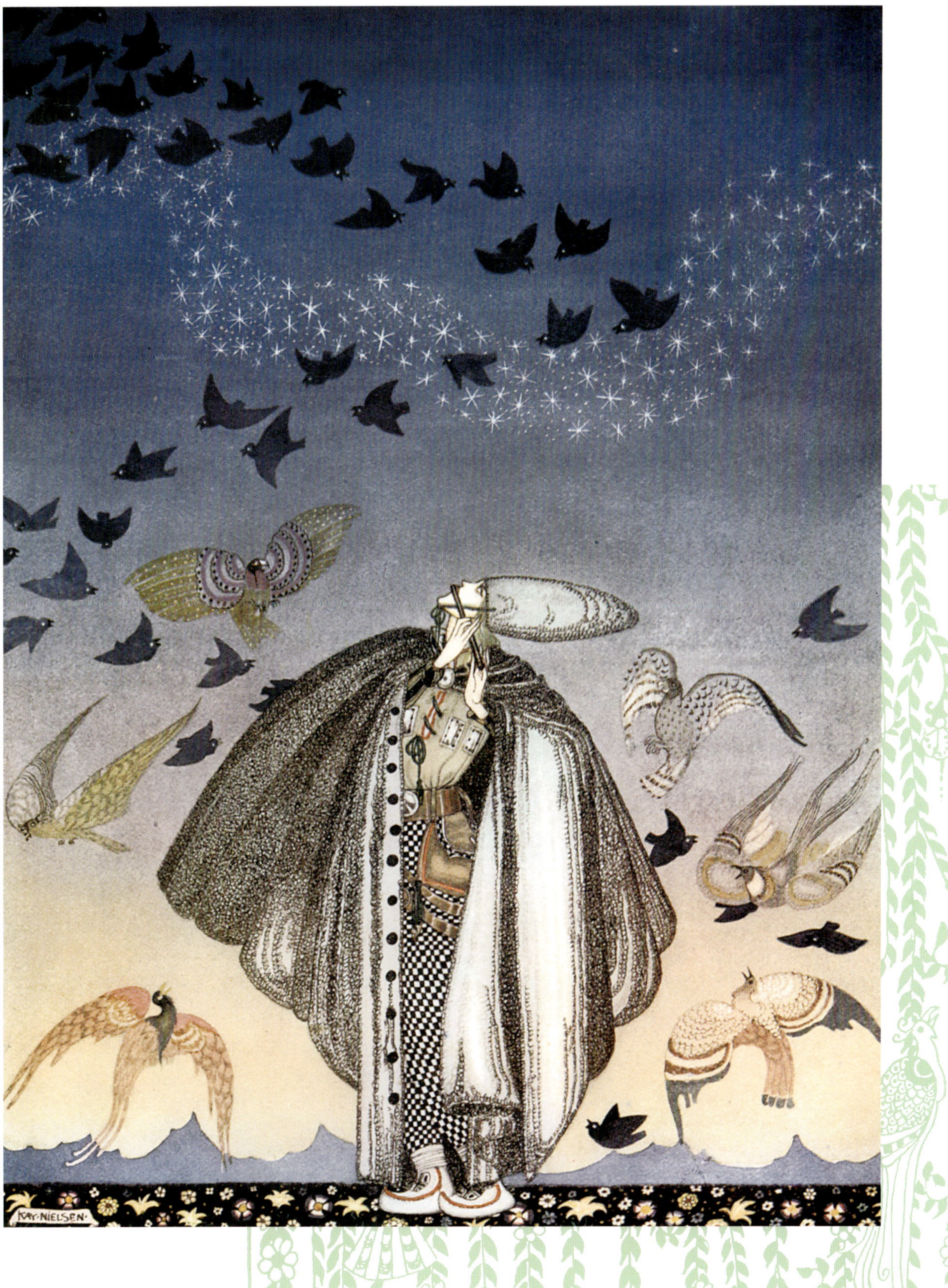
KAY·NIELSEN·

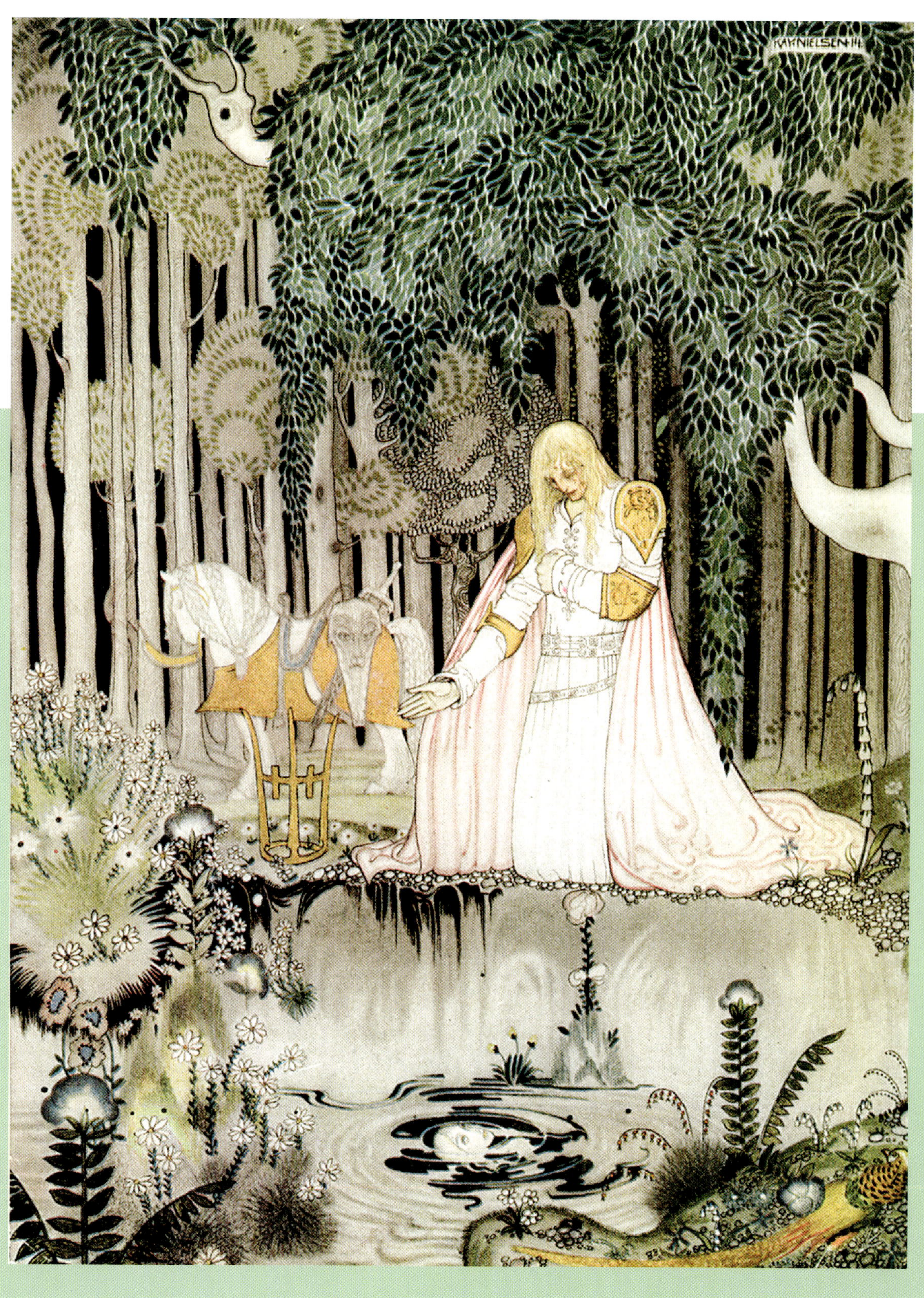

From 1918–1922 Nielsen completed a series of settings for The Royal Theater in Copenhagen, which included *Aladdin, Scaramouche,* and Shakespeare's *The Tempest*, among others.

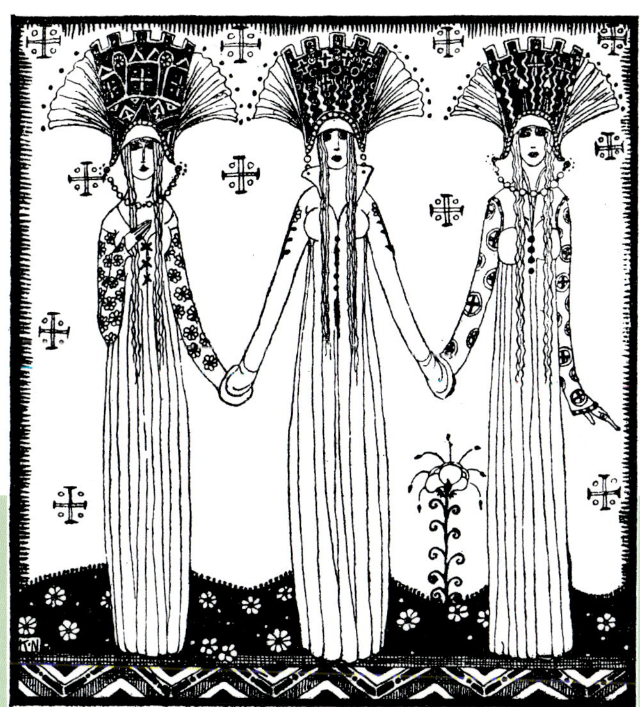

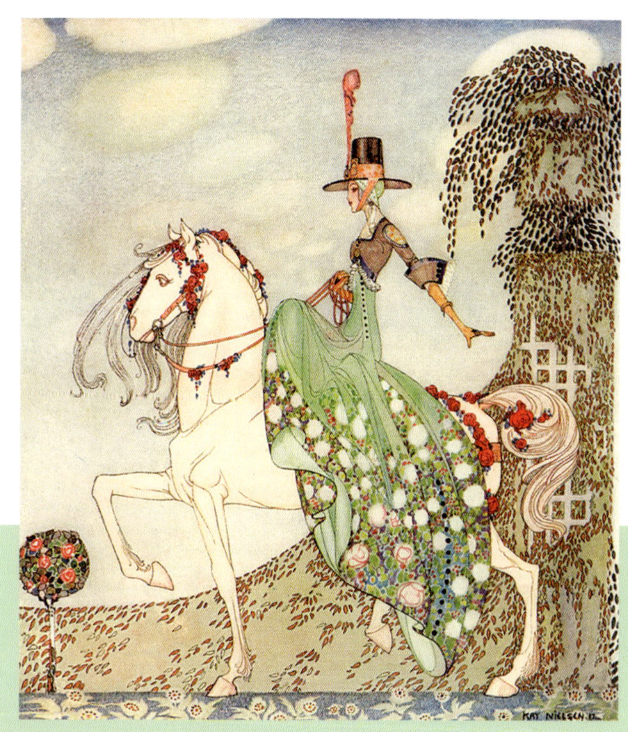

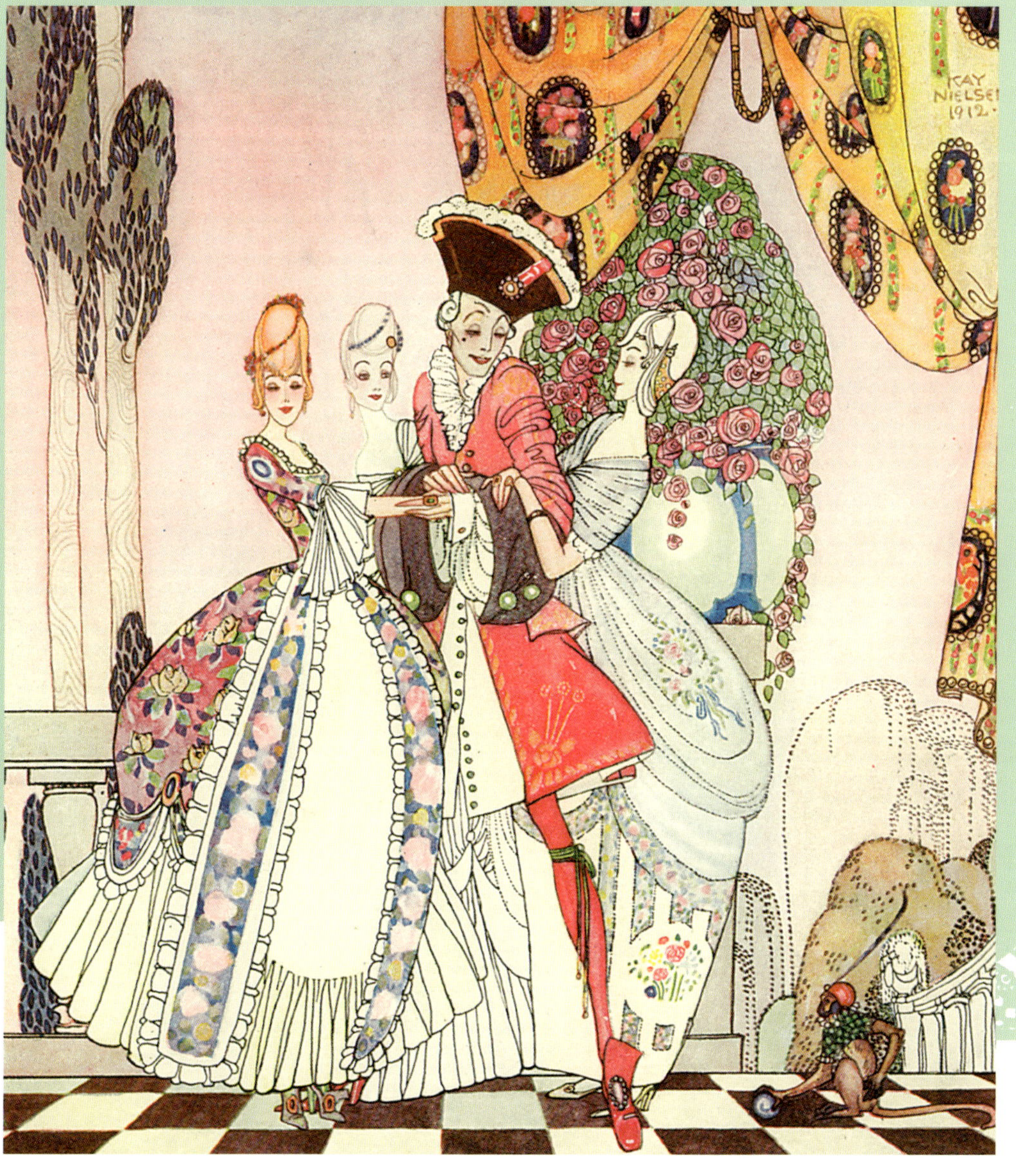

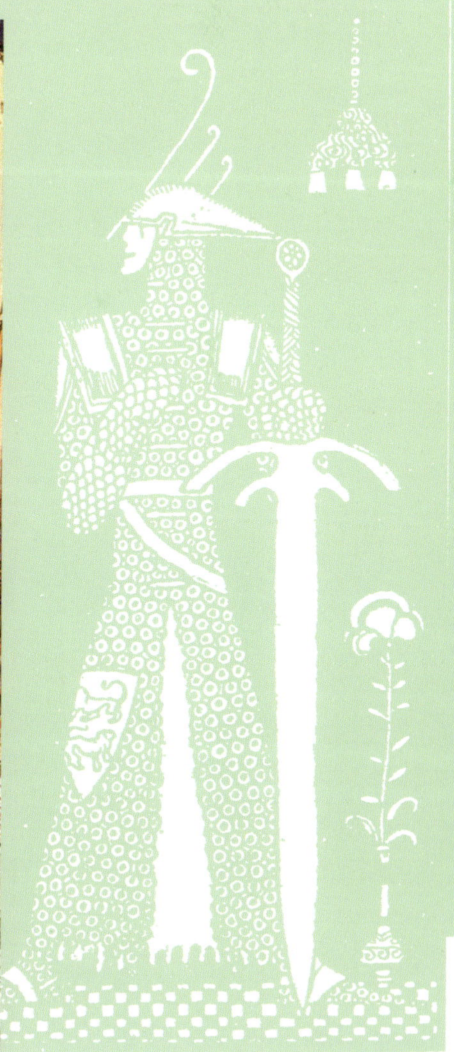

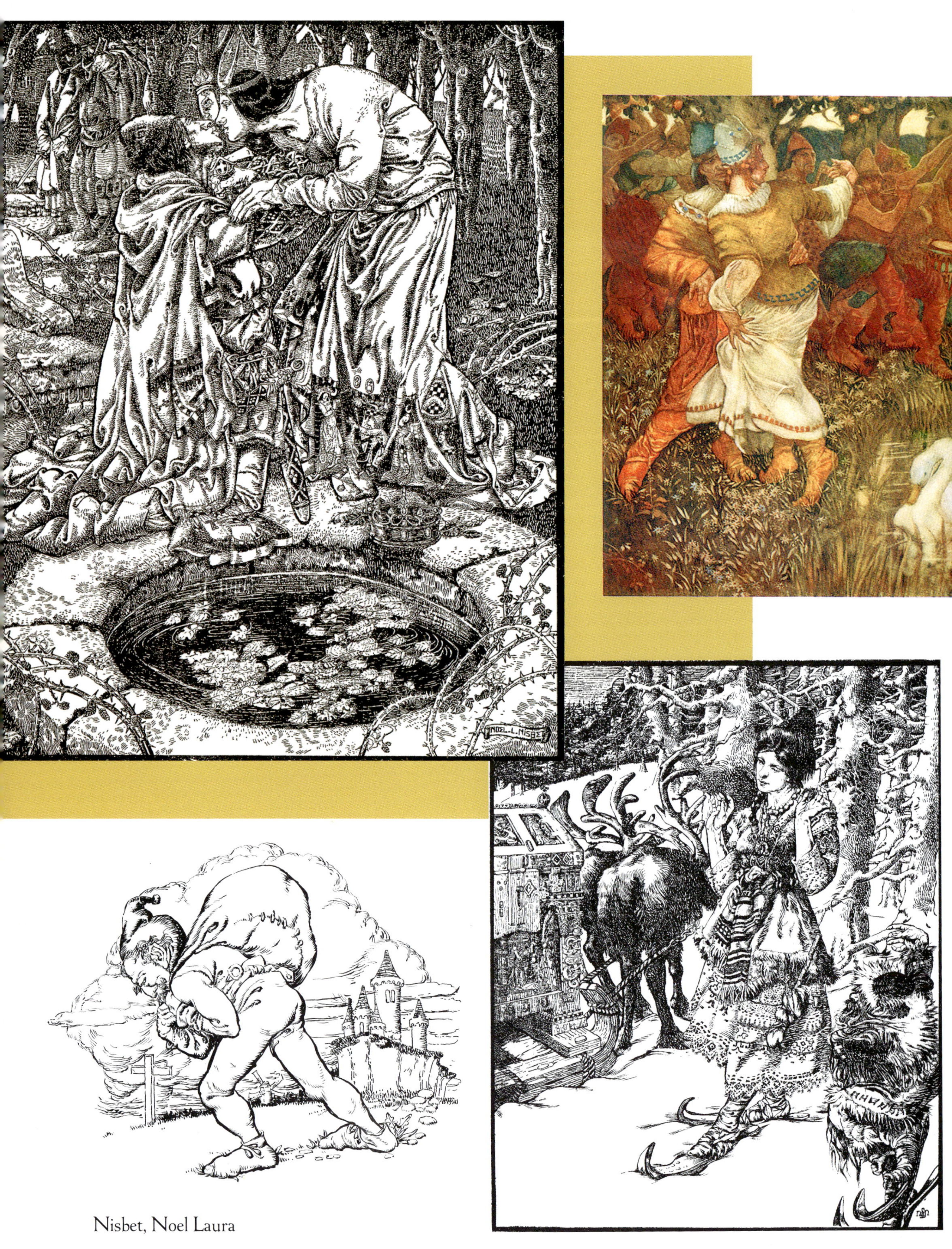

Nisbet, Noel Laura

Noel Laura Nisbet

1887–1956, British

Noel Nisbet's illustration work can largely be relegated to a handful of books she worked on from 1913 to 1917. She had a long and productive artistic career afterwards, but her later work took on a more personal note, often with religious and allegorical themes. Her beginnings in British book work—fairy tales, mythology, and folk stories—coupled with the style of her artwork, label her among the last of the Pre-Raphaelites. She recounted, "I was fortunate in my early days, in being brought up in imaginative surroundings and an atmosphere of books, for my father was a writer of romances, a painter, and a poet."

She was the youngest daughter of author/artist Hume Nisbet, and grew up in an environment that certainly nurtured creative ideas. She studied at the Clapham School of Art, and won numerous awards there. In 1910 she married fellow Clapham student Harry Bush, with whom she would spend her life and share her studio. She exhibited regularly at the Royal Academy from 1914 to 1938.

Though not well known, Nisbet's illustration work is worthy of attention; there were few artists of her time who produced comparable line work pieces. Her method was to plan a line piece with the thoroughness of preparing a painting, regarding texture and value placement. The finished works seem more similar to complex Renaissance woodcuts than early twentieth-century illustrations. Her color work often carried a full range of hues from the palette, allowing even the darkest scenes to carry a thread of vibrance through them.

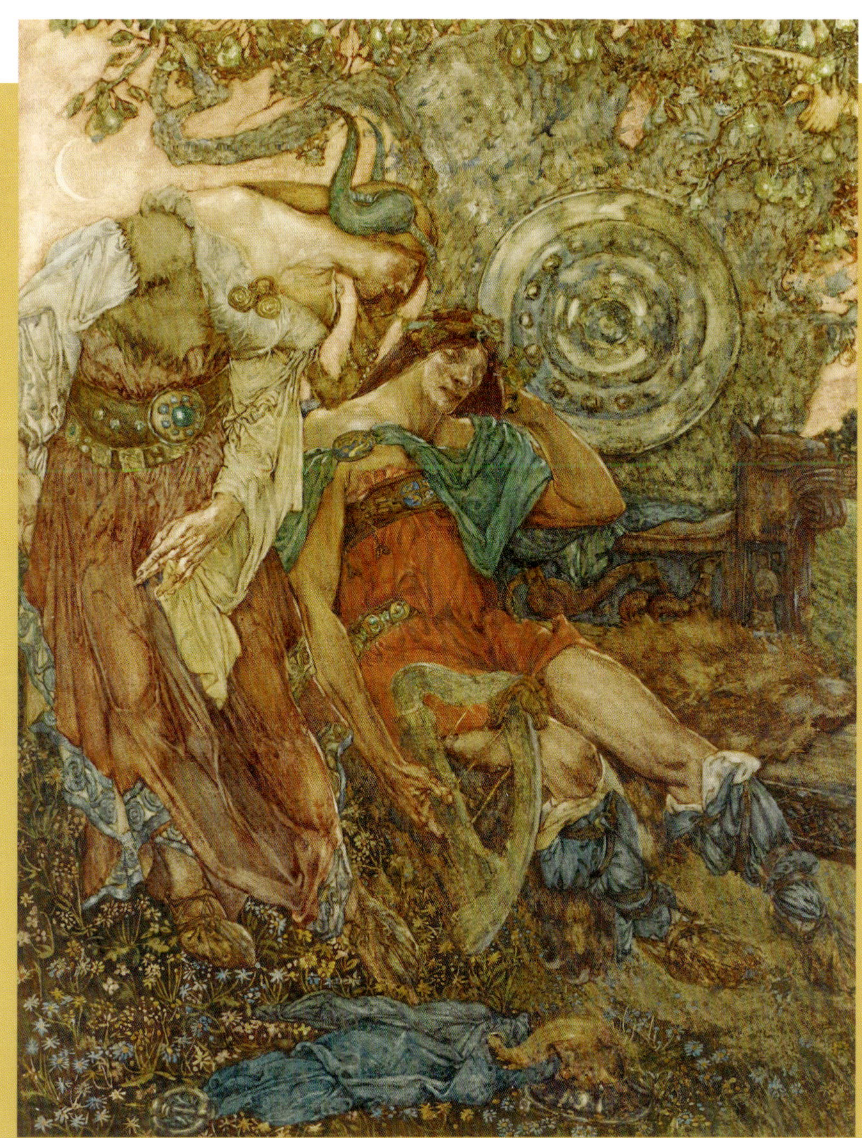

Illustrating titles not as well known may have kept Noel Nisbet from the commercial success that her peers were enjoying. After 1918 she turned her efforts to more personal work.

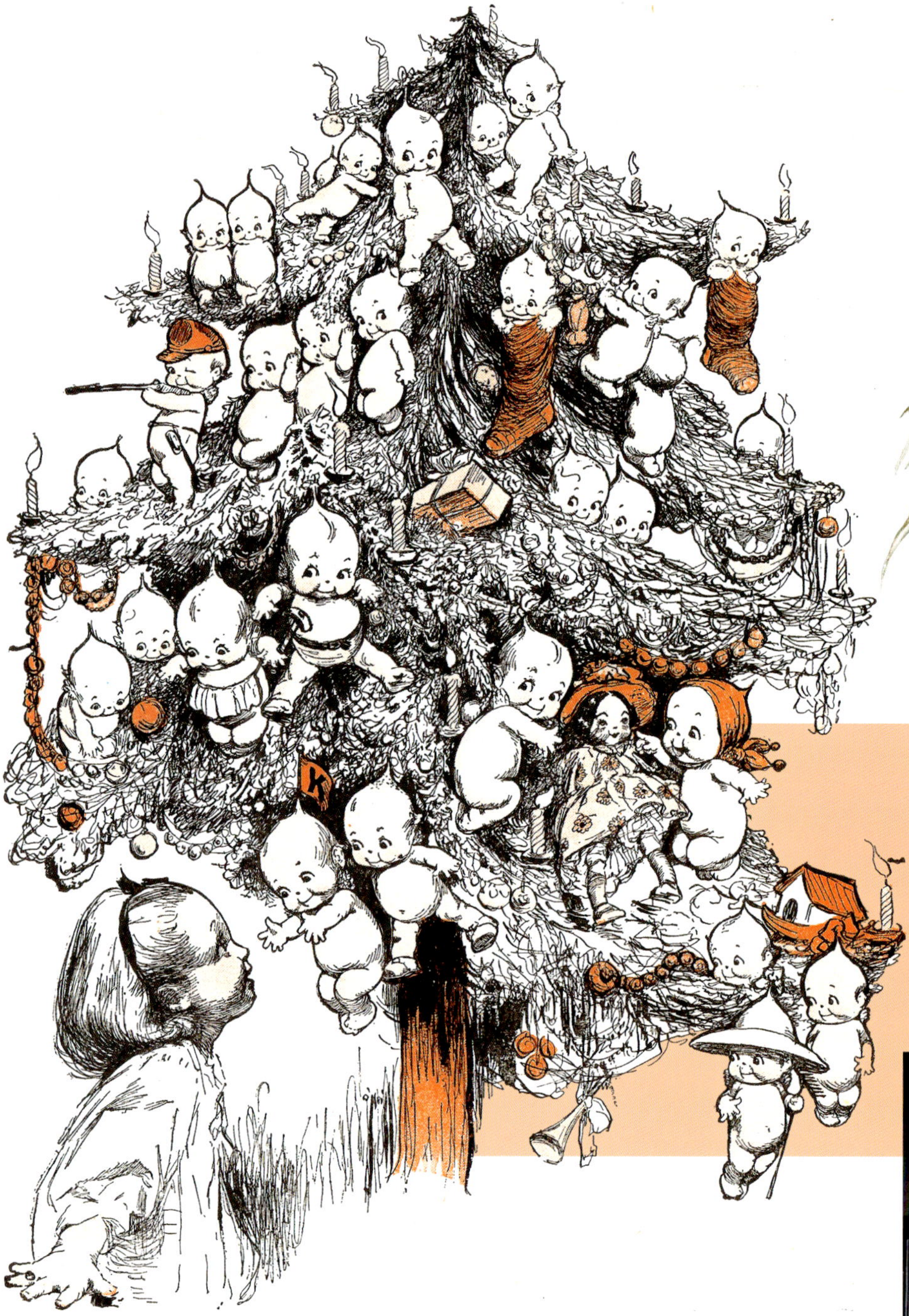

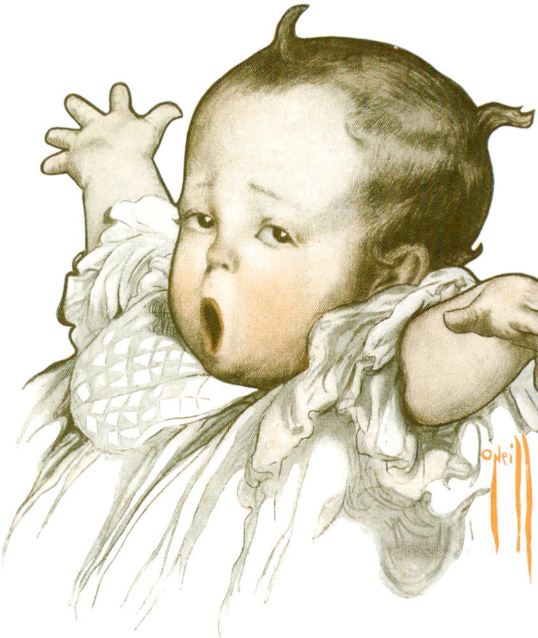

The Mother of Kewpies

Few artists would be as successful as O'Neill in developing an intellectual property. Her creation of the "Kewpie" dolls for books and advertisments made her wealthy.

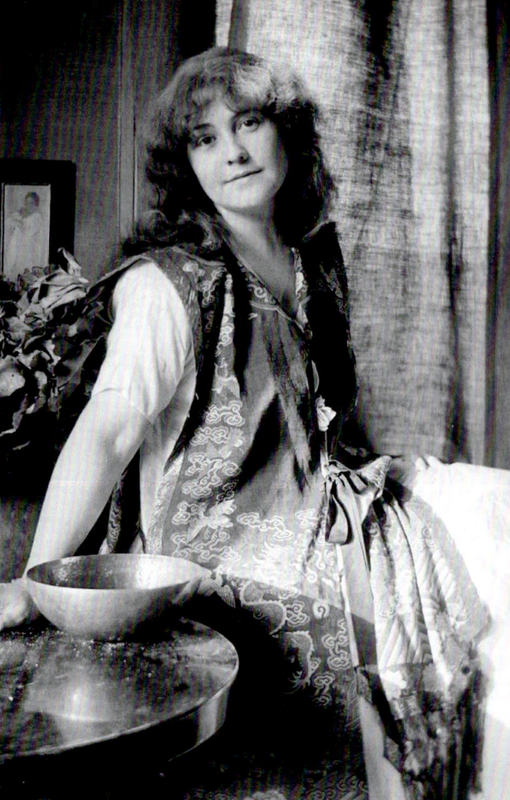

O'Neill in 1907

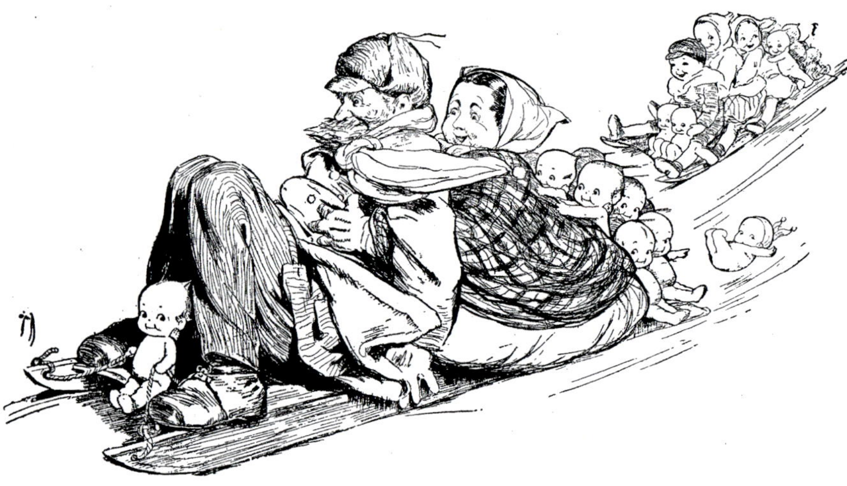

Rose O'Neill
1874–1944, American

Though originally from eastern Pennsylvania, Rose O'Neill was raised in Nebraska, where she got her start as an illustrator. Recognized early for her talent and ability, by the age of 15 O'Neill was working for numerous publications, both regional and national. The income was welcomed by her family, and in 1893 her father brought Rose to New York, where she had more chances to prosper. Left in the care of an order of nuns, the then-19-year-old impressed many publishers, and sold existing work she'd brought with her, as well as securing new commissions.

One of the first magazines to give O'Neill steady work was *Puck* magazine, where from 1896 to 1903 she was a regular contributor. She soon became recognized as America's first female cartoonist. Her work was consistent, earning a reputation for her appealing characters and cute children. Her successful achievements led to her becoming an important voice in the changing role of women in society, and she was a visible and vocal leader of the suffragist movement in America.

O'Neill's success, coupled with her striking appearance, brought her many suitors. While visiting family back in Omaha, she met Gray Latham, a charming playboy who loved the fast lifestyle that O'Neill's income afforded. The couple were married for only a short while before O'Neill realized how much of her money he had, in fact, stolen from her. There was only a brief period where she signed her work "Rose Latham." After her divorce in 1901, the editor with whom she worked at *Puck* began sending her gifts—at first, anonymously—and married O'Neill the following year. After a few years, and some collaborative books, that marriage ended as well. O'Neill remained single for the rest of her life.

During the years leading up to World War I, her iconic "Kewpie Dolls" took shape. First appearing in 1909, the cute little characters with the signature hair and dimples began to appear in numerous books and advertisements, ultimately making O'Neill a wealthy woman. In 1913 a German doll manufacturer licensed the design for a porcelain doll, which, along with other smartly marketed merchandise, was quite successful. O'Neill invested in real estate, buying homes in multiple corners of the United States, and a villa in Italy as well. She returned to her Missouri home, Bonniebrook, in 1937 and was active in the arts until her passing in 1944.

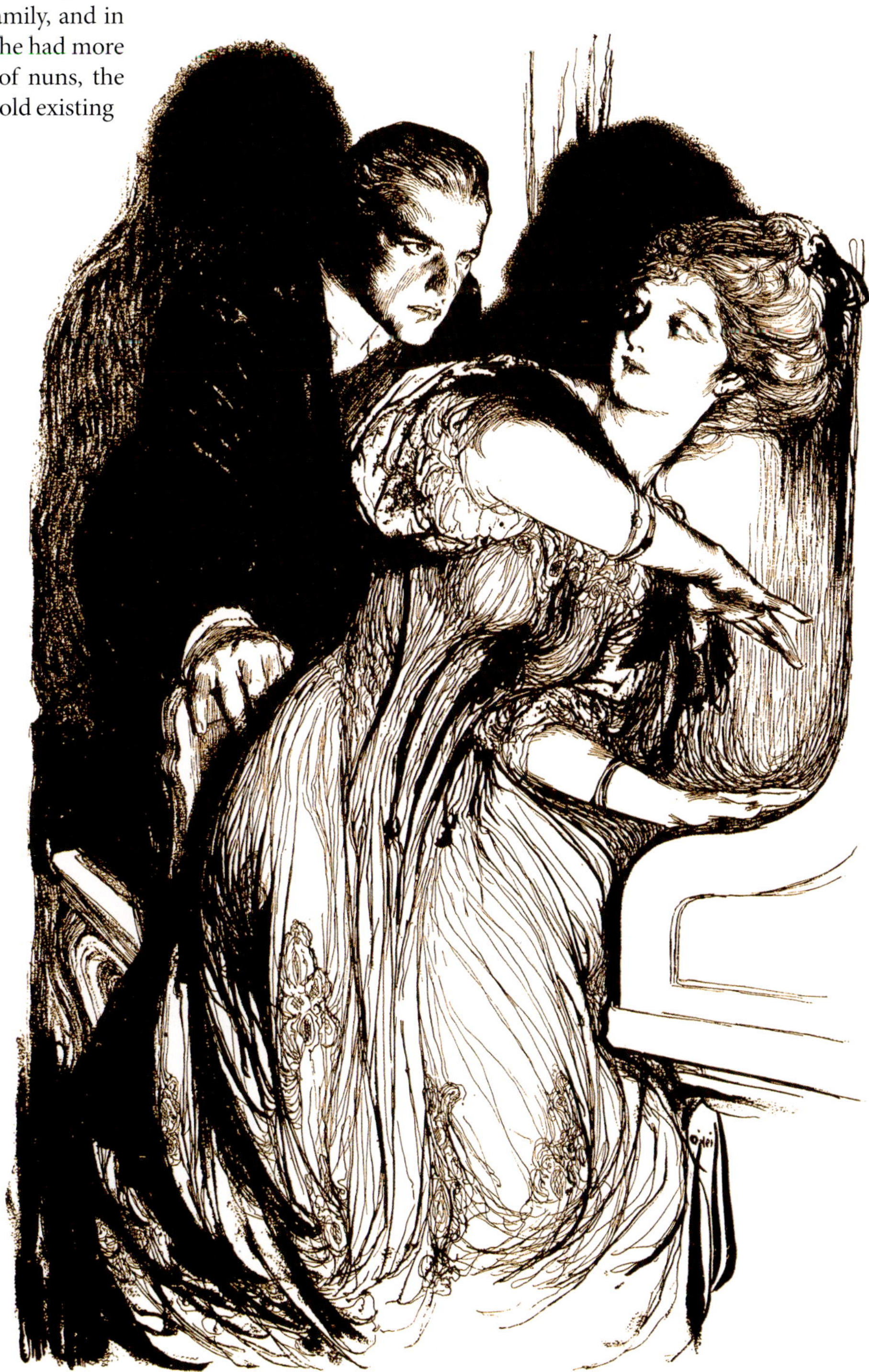

Thornton Oakley

1881–1953, American

Unlike most artists who enter the field of illustration, Thornton Oakley had another career path behind him before he enrolled in study with Howard Pyle. Having already earned a degree in architecture, Oakley's first field of study contributed to his success as an illustrator. Oakley gravitated toward industrial themes, such as large machinery, working yards, and railroads. Growing up in Pittsburgh in the shadows of steel mills gave him a respect for their size and power. His understanding of perspective and his ability to execute accurate technical renderings with conviction gave his work a solidity that was greatly appreciated by his clients.

Oakley came to study under Howard Pyle in 1902, immediately after he received his architecture degree. He continued to study with Pyle at his Brandywine Valley-based school for three years, after which he immediately began receiving assignments from *Leslie's* and *Collier's*, with *Century, Harper's Monthly,* and *Scribner's* following. His illustration career was off to a solid start.

Like Pyle, Oakley had a great interest in teaching, and allowed that to become a large part of his life. He was the department head of illustration at the Philadelphia Museum School of Industrial Art for all but two years between 1914 and 1936, and taught at the University of Pennsylvania as well. Guest lecturing was something he did with some regularity, and he was also a sought-after jury member for special art exhibitions.

With a specialty in machinery and industry, it became a natural fit for Oakley to do a large amount of work for the war effort, especially during World War II. Clients later in his career included railroads, utilities, and the growing oil industry. The murals he painted for Philadelphia's Franklin Institute from 1938–1939 are still visible there today.

Oakley held a lifelong respect for Pyle. In 1951, forty years after Pyle's passing, Oakley donated a large collection of Pyle-related materials—both published and personal—to the Free Library of Philadelphia. Shortly before Oakley's death in 1953, he presided at a memorial exhibition at the Philadelphia Art Alliance, where many of Pyle's former students spoke.

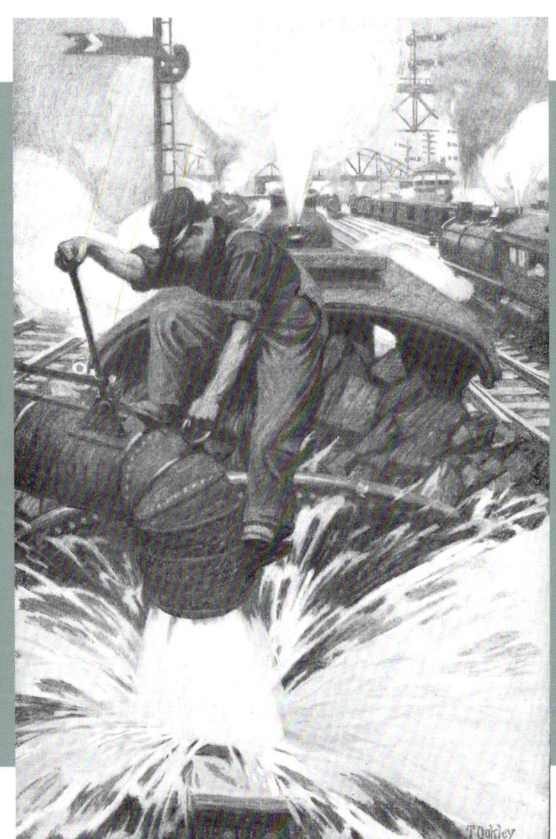

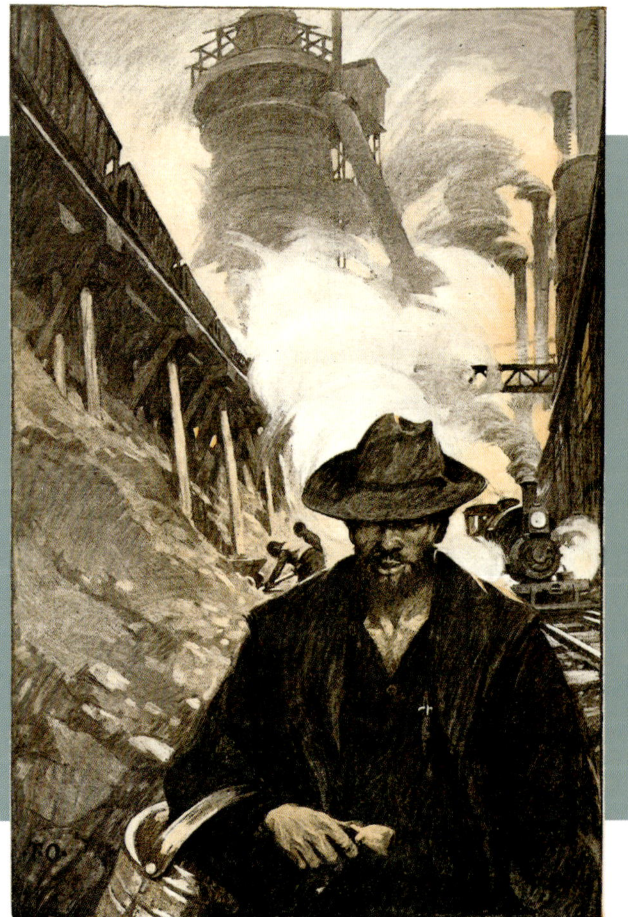

Oakley, Thornton

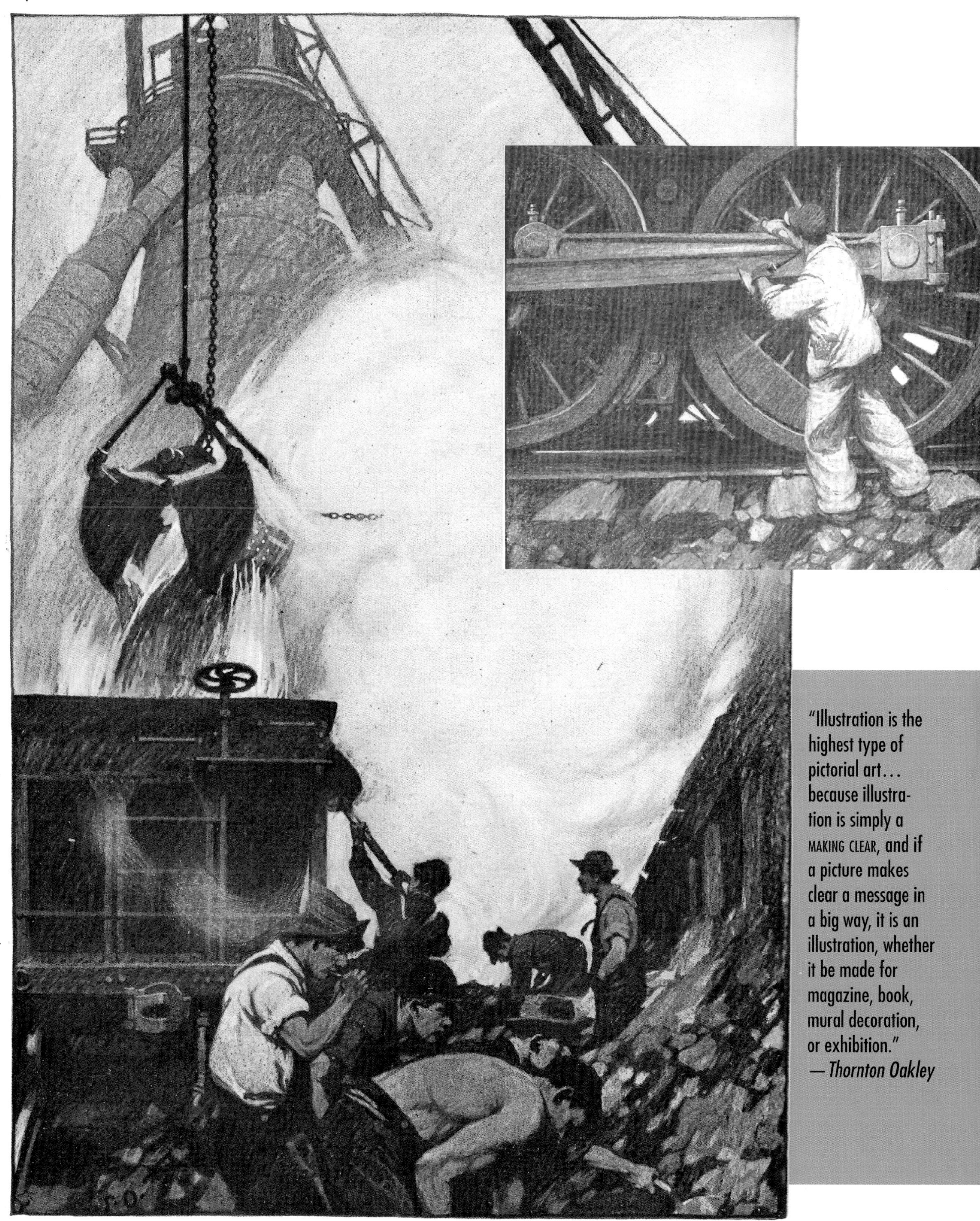

"Illustration is the highest type of pictorial art... because illustration is simply a MAKING CLEAR, and if a picture makes clear a message in a big way, it is an illustration, whether it be made for magazine, book, mural decoration, or exhibition."
—Thornton Oakley

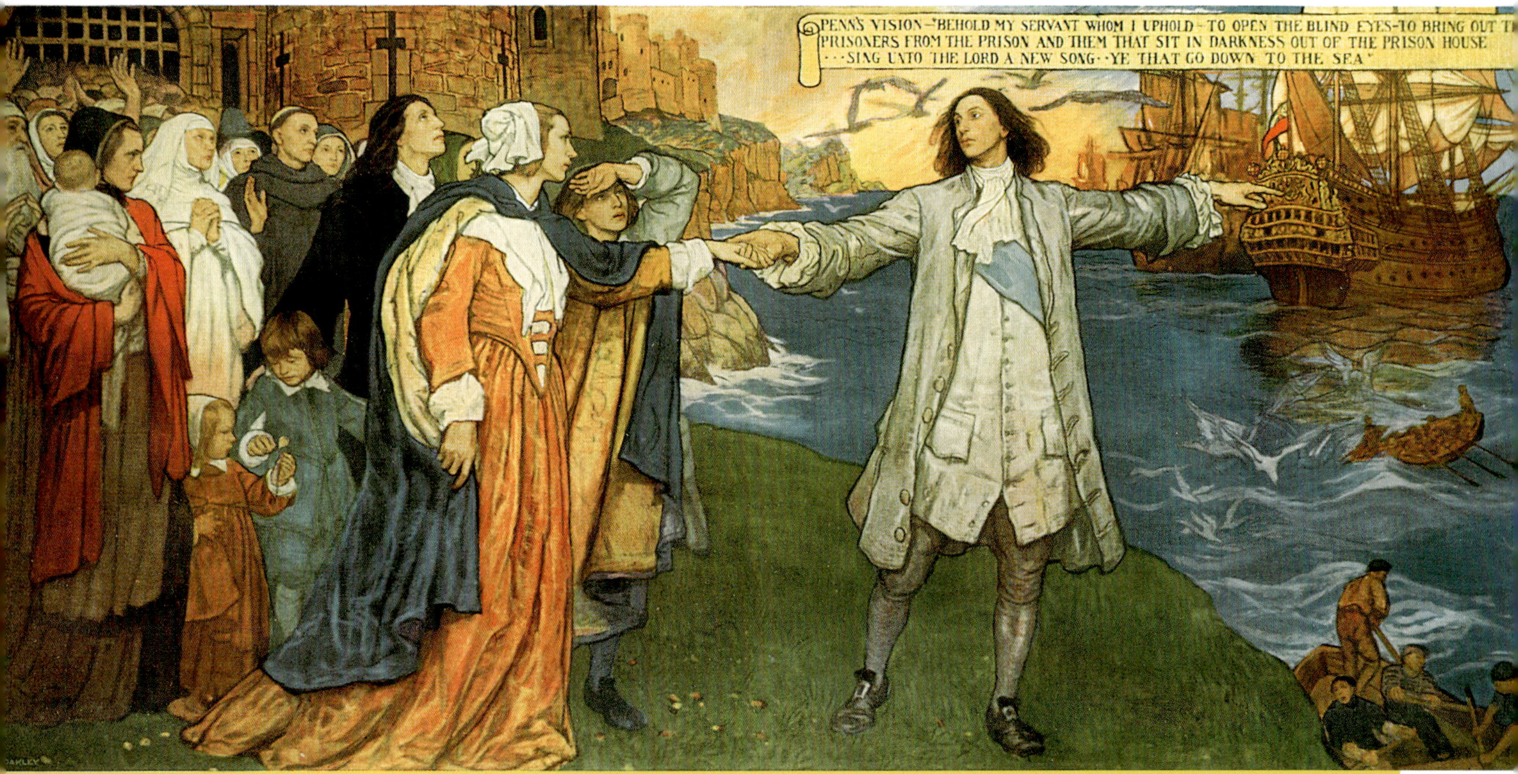

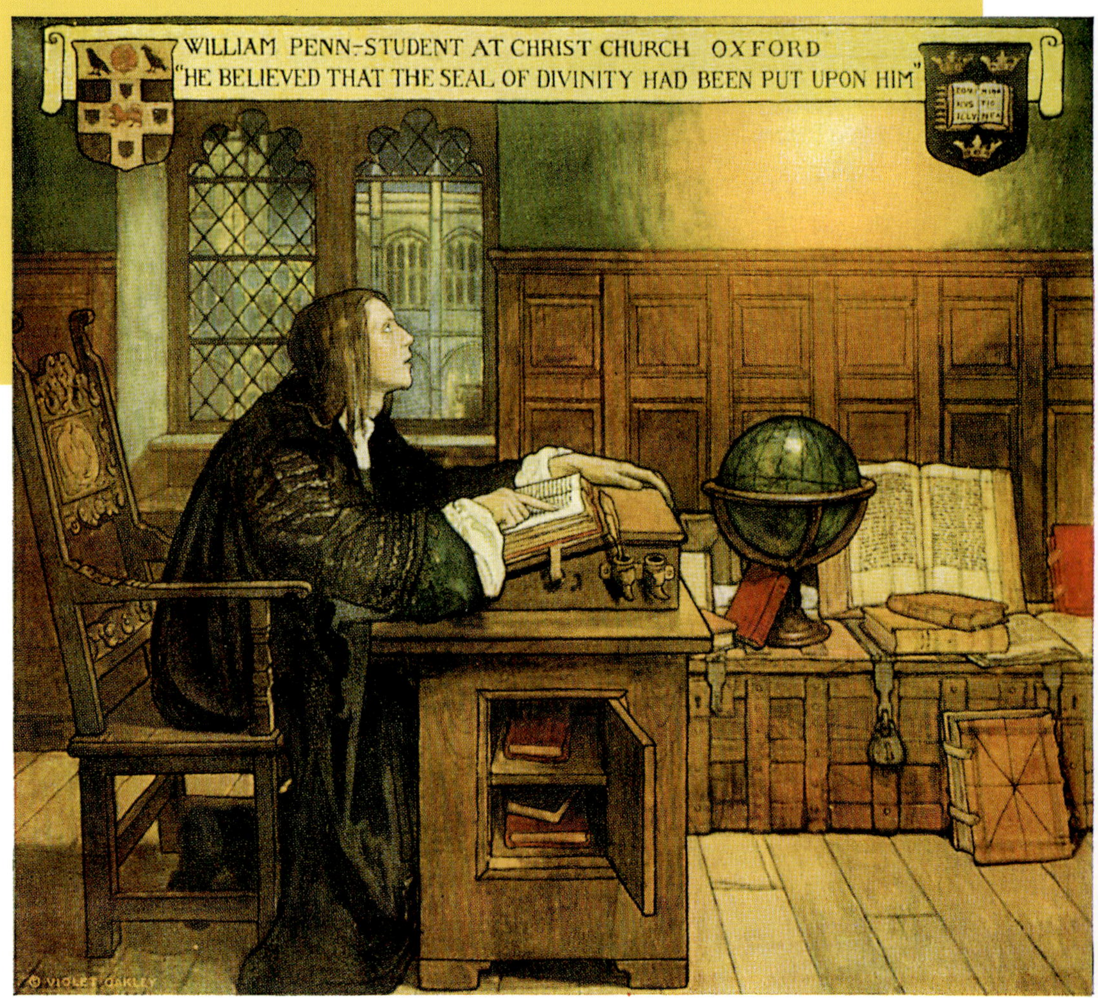

Oakley, Violet

Violet Oakley

1874–1961, American

Self-portrait from 1900

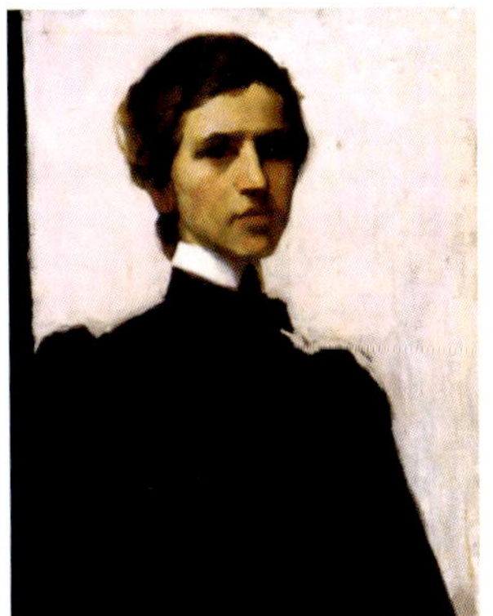

An early student of Howard Pyle, Violet Oakley benefited from his classes at Drexel University as early as 1898. Violet rose above the level of her peers in the class, and landed a steady amount of magazine work in high-profile national publications. But Pyle recognized her ability to handle larger projects. Perhaps it was the level of comfort she had with large forms. He felt stained-glass design was something at which she would excel, and she soon received her first large window commission for an Epiphany Window for the Church Glass and Decorating Company in New York in 1899. Stained-glass design became part of her artistic output throughout her life.

Violet was awarded a mural commission at the new Pennsylvania State Capitol in 1902. The decision to award Oakley the prestigious assignment was not without some controversy; heroic imagery in public mural work was not considered a task for a woman at that time. It was a challenge that Oakley accepted and successfully accomplished. She took over a larger part of the assignment after the passing of Edwin Austin Abbey in 1911. The work, which included part of Abbey's plan as well as material of her own design, led to a great deal of national press coverage, and future employment for nearly twenty years.

Oakley is known as one of the "Red Rose" girls. With fellow Pyle students Jessie Willcox Smith, Elizabeth Shippen Green, and friend Henrietta Cozens, Oakley first shared quarters at the Red Rose Inn while studying with Pyle. They would later find property together, which they called *Cogslea* (Cozens/Oakley/Green/Smith). It became their combined studio, home, and a joint workspace, where they would support and inspire each other.

A large number of important works at the League of Nations in Switzerland followed her mural work at the Pennsylvania State Capitol, and she also worked on windows and murals at the Alumni Hall at Vassar College.

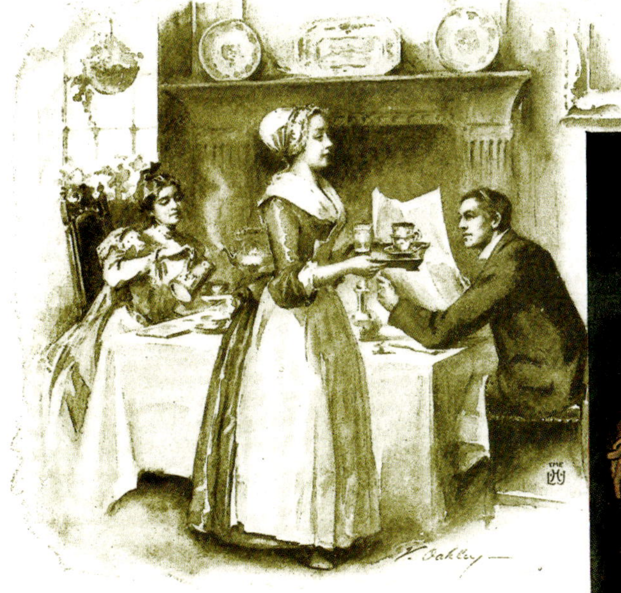

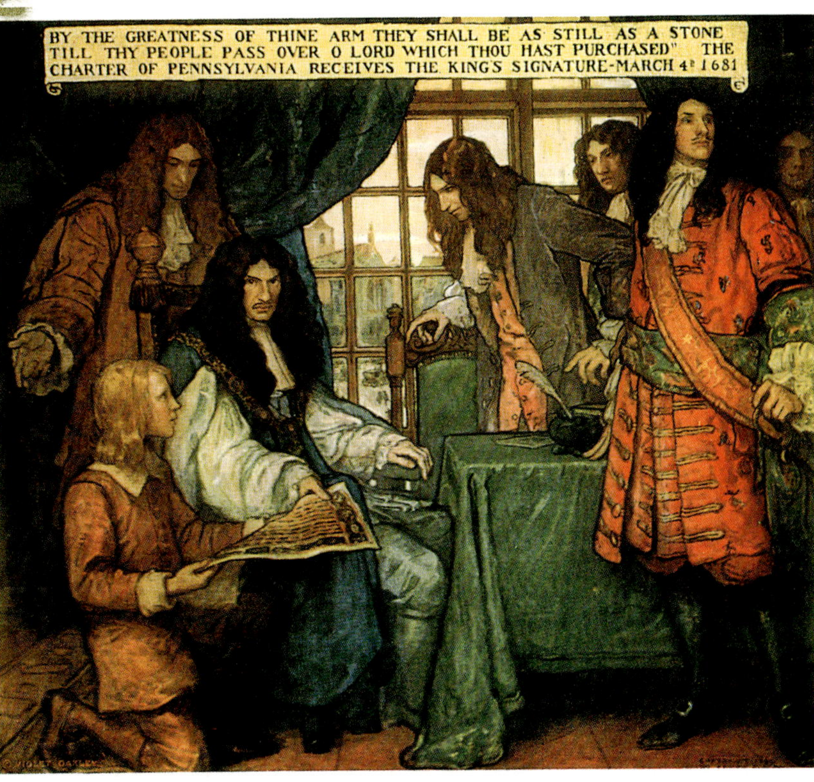

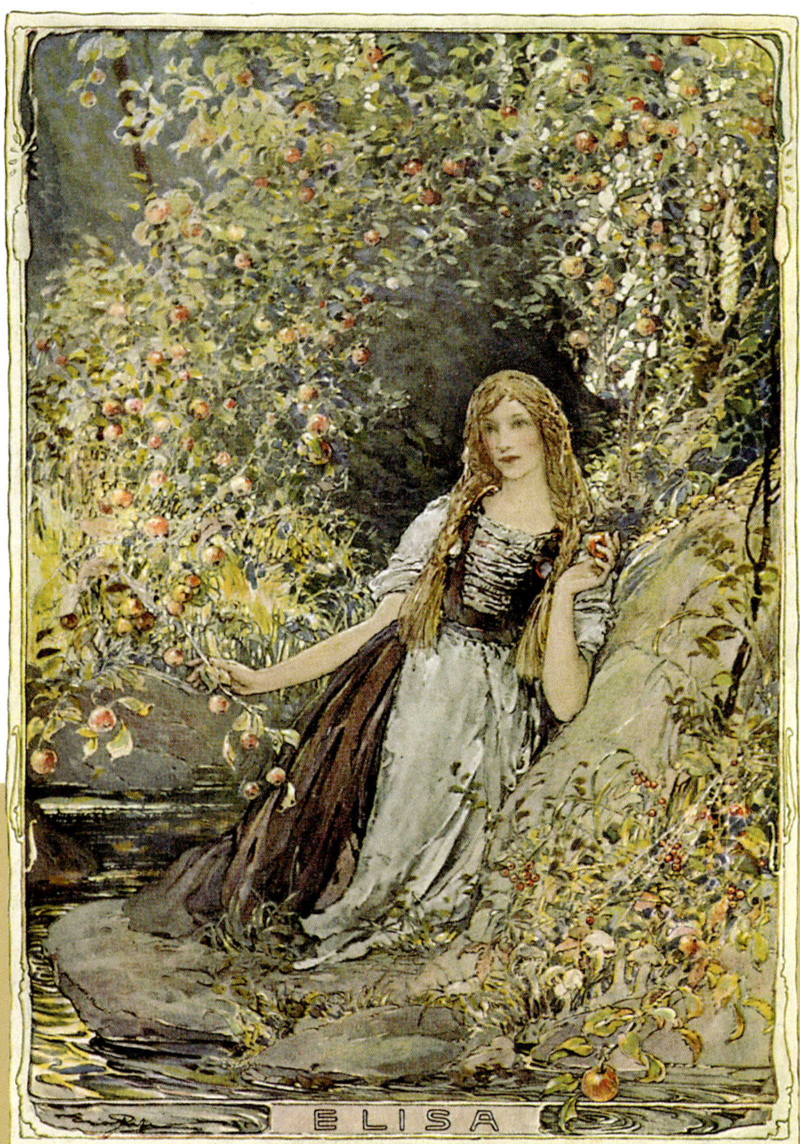

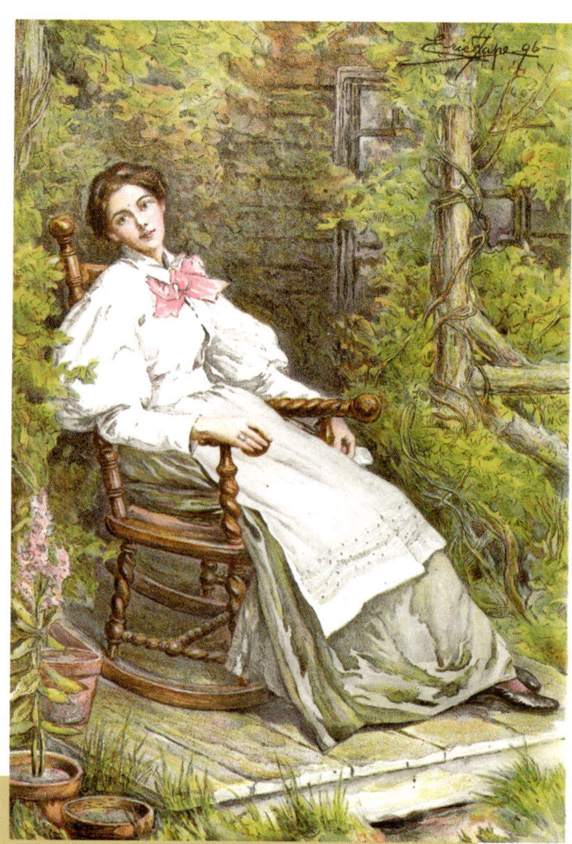

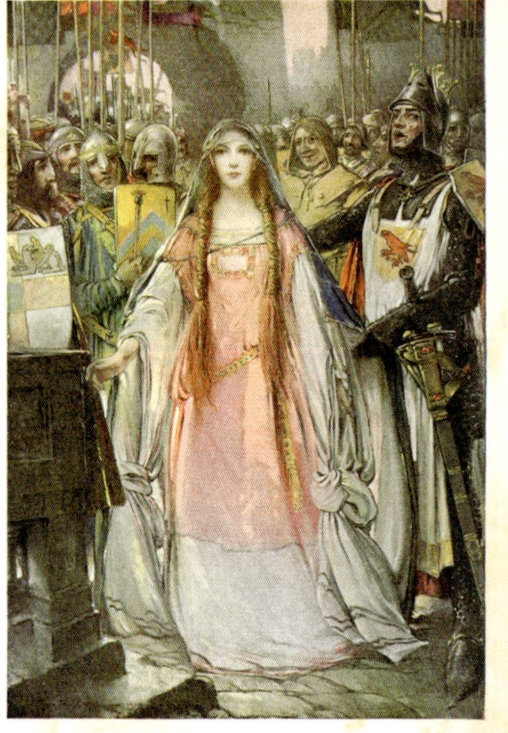

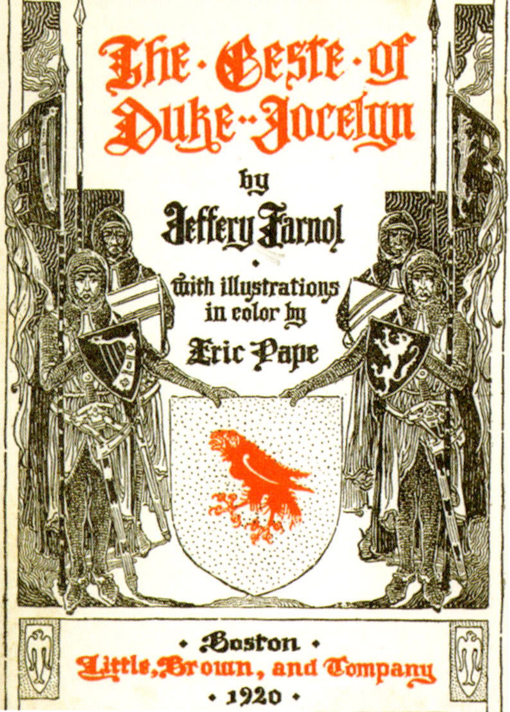
The Geste of Duke Jocelyn

by

Jeffery Farnol

with illustrations in color by

Eric Pape

Boston

Little, Brown, and Company

1920

Pape, Eric

Eric Pape
1870–1938, American

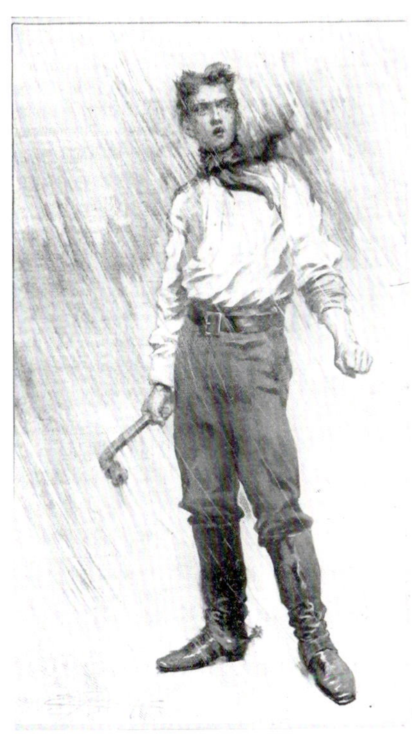

Born in San Francisco, California, Eric Pape's earliest studies were at the San Francisco School of Design. He sought further studies in painting, and with three other friends from California, Pape set off to Europe. Pape studied at the École des Beaux Arts in Paris, and at the Académie Julian as well. He toured much of Europe before journeying to Egypt where he lived for two years and painted in a studio once occupied by noted artist John Singer Sargent. He was soon well on his way as a gallery painter, exhibiting in Cairo, Europe, and America.

On his return to the United States in the mid-1890s, Pape settled in New York, and sought to start a career in illustration there. He was soon working on new books by leading authors—the latest titles from Henry James, Robert Louis Stevenson, and H. G. Wells. Pape also succeeded as a gallery painter, and occasionally had shows in city museums.

Toward the close of the century, in 1898, Pape decided to open an art school in Boston. The Eric Pape School of Art was in operation for fifteen years, and was at one time one of the largest art schools in the country. N. C. Wyeth was among the many students who received some training there.

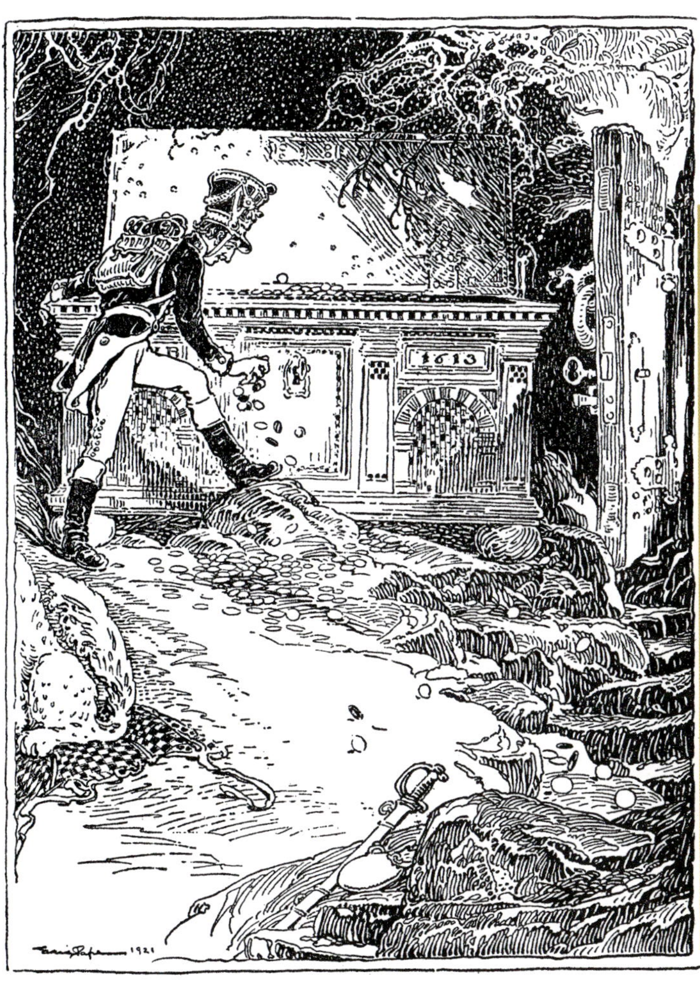

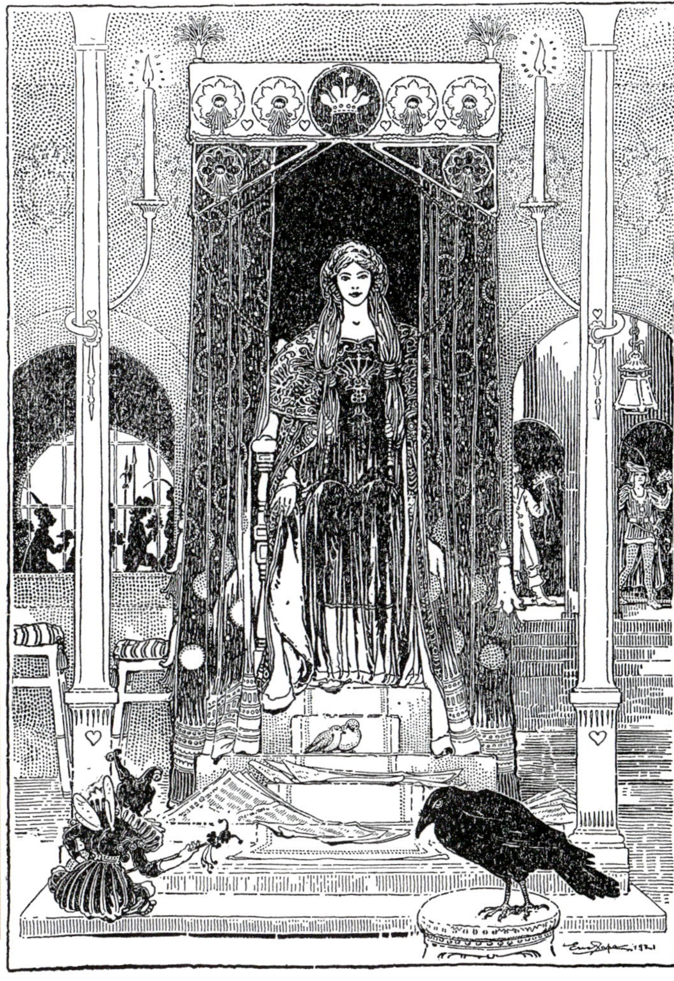

Frank C. Papé
1878–1972, British

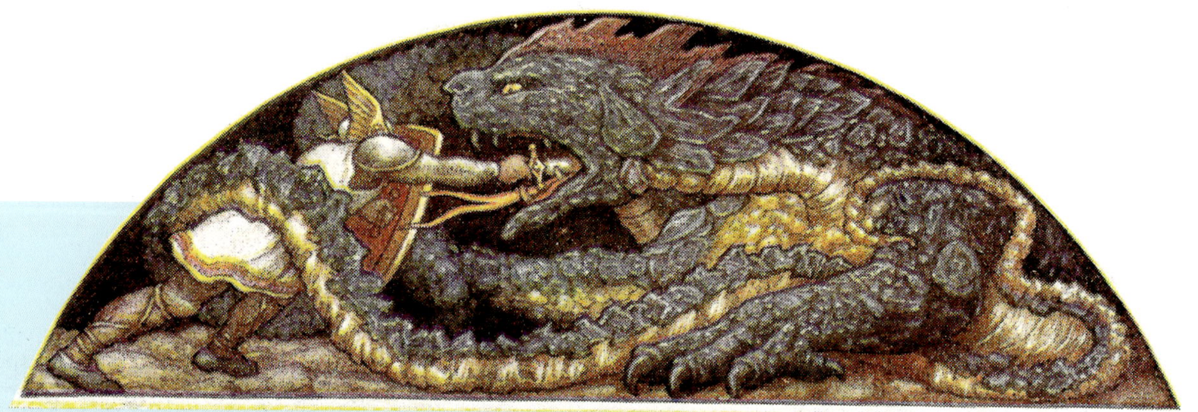

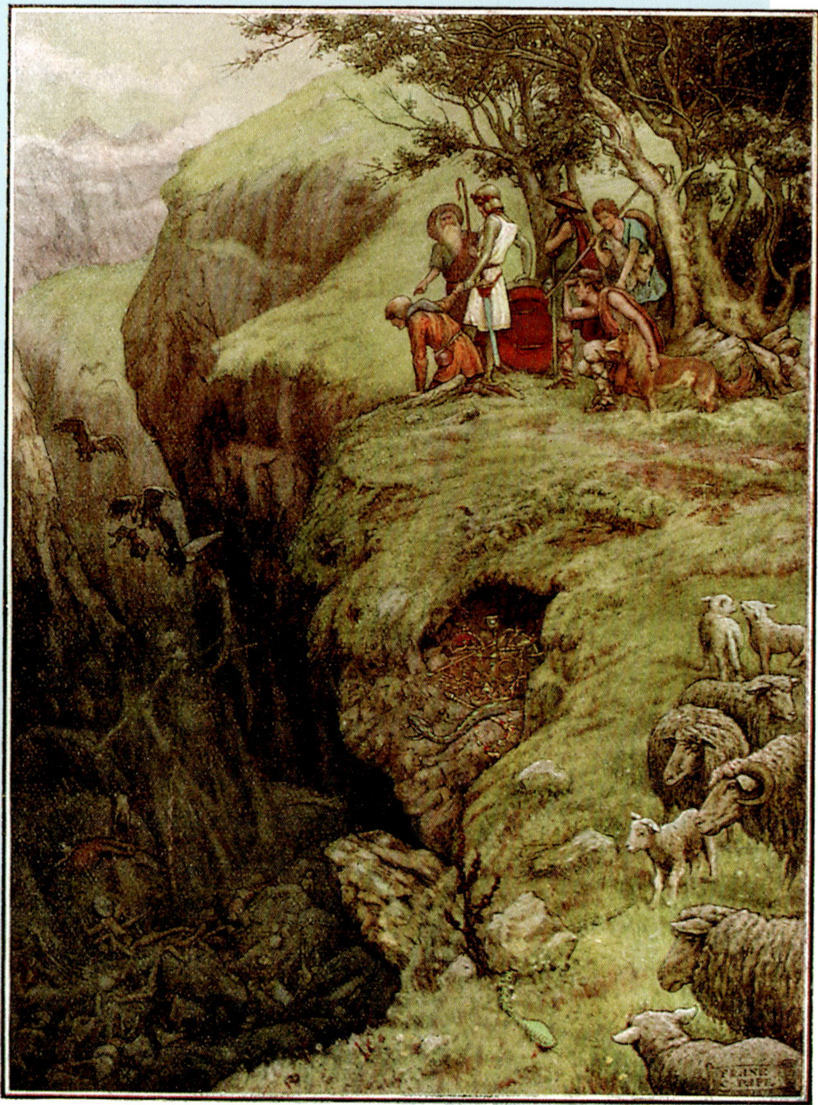

Born in London in 1878, Frank C. Papé came of age during the publishing boom of the Golden Age. Prior to the outbreak of World War I, his art was peppered with the fairy-tale work that was plentiful at the time. The subject was a good match for Papé's vivid imagination, and he would never stray too far from fairy tales as creative material. The first two color illustrations here, from *A Russian Story Book* in 1916, show a mature and refined color sense.

In 1921, Papé did line illustrations for author James Branch Cabell's *Jurgen.* This wild tale involved a time traveler's exploits with various women through time and history—it was radical for its time, and quite controversial. The near banning of the book, combined with the quality of Papé's fine line illustrations, made the book a huge success when it finally made it to market. The attention given to Papé's work was considerable, and the acclaim steered Papé to stick with line as his signature style for years to come. He became Cabell's steady partner, later working on *Something About Eve* and *The Cream of the Jest.* Anatole France was another name associated with illustrations by Papé, with volumes like *Penguin Island* and *The Revolt of the Angels,* which featured his illuminations.

In the years following World War I, the jobs for book illustration began to decrease, and Papé found staff work with a children's newspaper column out of Wisconsin called *Raymond Coffman's Uncle Ray's Corner.* Though it didn't have the same

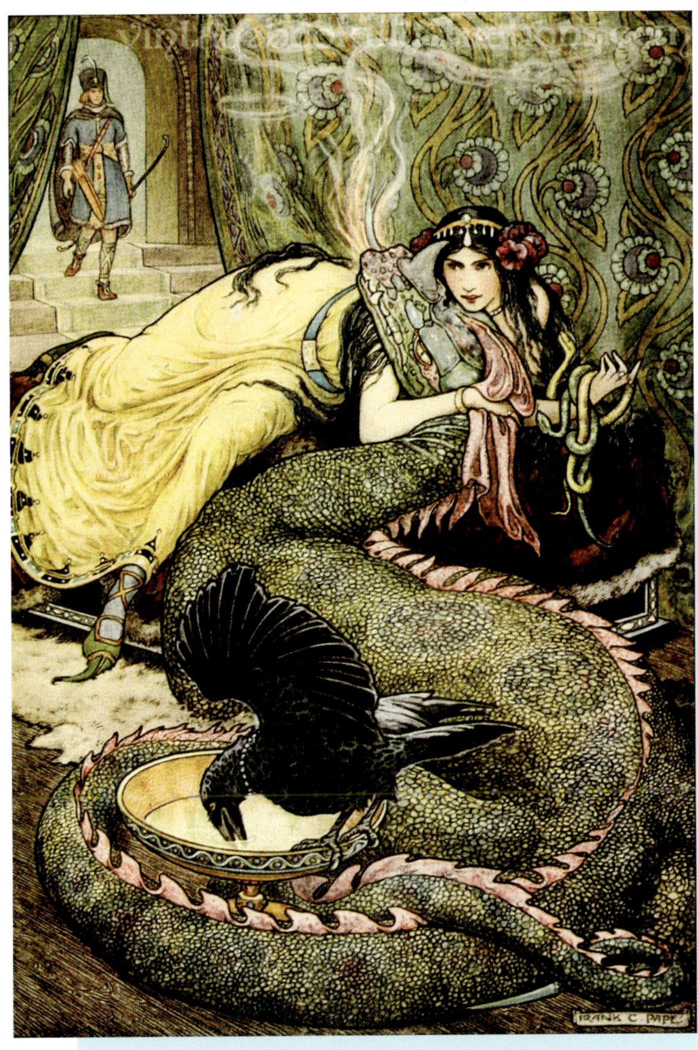

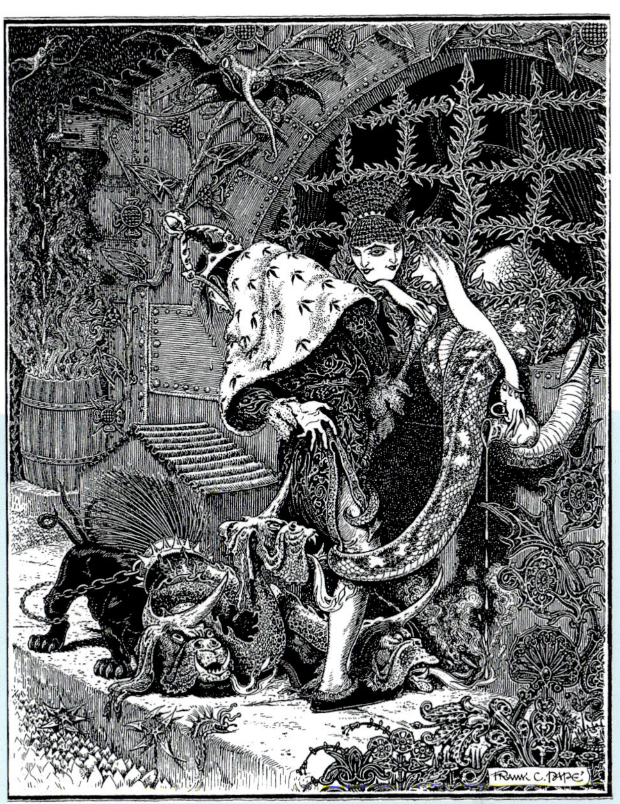

COMPLEXITY AND ELEGANCE
Few artists approached Papé when it came to detail. Whether he was drawing the scales of a dragon or an involved traditional border, Papé was a master of intricate design.

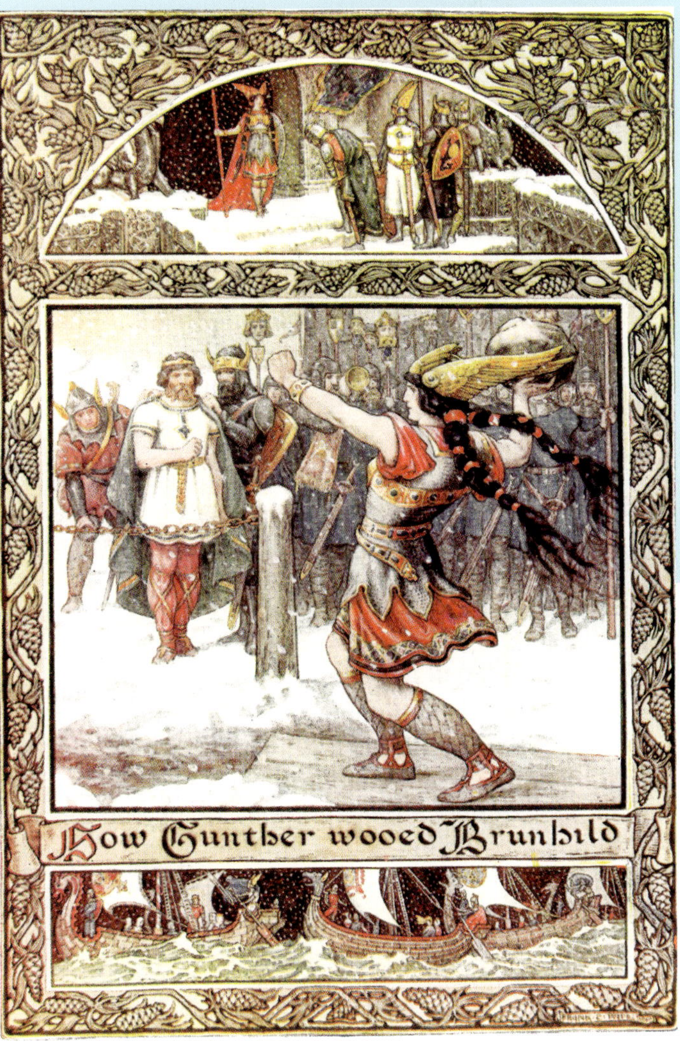

prestige that book work did, it was steady and secure, and Papé worked with Coffman for the next three decades. Sometime after 1935, Papé found additional weekly employment while continuing his work with *Uncle Ray's*. He also served as an art director for a children's magazine in Chicago.

Papé's career explored many aspects of publishing and creative imagery, but it was the illustration he produced, characterized by imagination and humor, that he would be known and best remembered for.

Maxfield Parrish

1870–1966, American

Born Frederick Parrish in the Philadelphia area, this fresh-minded, young creative artist sought out Howard Pyle to seek his advice on a career in illustration. Parrish was already published at that time, and though the two had some small exchange, and Parrish attended some of Pyle's classes at Drexel University, Pyle's influence was minor. He told Parrish that he "had nothing to teach him," implying that Parrish was already proficient in the arts.

Parrish chose his middle name, Maxfield, to identify his work. Its unique character was well-matched with the highly recognizable style that Parrish developed during his half-century-long career. Influenced by poster designs of the period, his earliest works were bold and graphic, mixing referenced figures with flat decorative patterns in an often humorous way.

Illustration work was plentiful, but Parrish longed to work undisturbed and without commercial restrictions. He sought a quiet location, and before the turn of the century, Parrish and his wife relocated to Cornish, New Hampshire. Its rolling landscape and the support of many of the local artists provided Parrish with the right environment for his work to prosper. Maxfield Parrish became virtually a household name in the 1920s, when it was estimated that nearly 25% of the homes in America contained a Parrish print or calendar. While Parrish produced book and magazine work in his early career, his art was very different from other illustrators of the time. He was one of the first true proponents of the use of photography for the creation of reference material, both for live models and for landscapes. He constructed some of these from complex models, using mirrors for bodies of water, and controlling every aspect of the lighting and shadows. Parrish was also well known for a certain shade of blue that permeated his color work. His underpaintings were often done in blue, the root color of shadow, and built up with other colors.

His later years were spent creating his own images for prints and calendars, rather than art-directed images for magazines and advertisements. This freedom gave Parrish the ability to pursue subjects of supreme interest to him. He continued working into the 1960s. His influence is still very strong in illustration and the decorative arts.

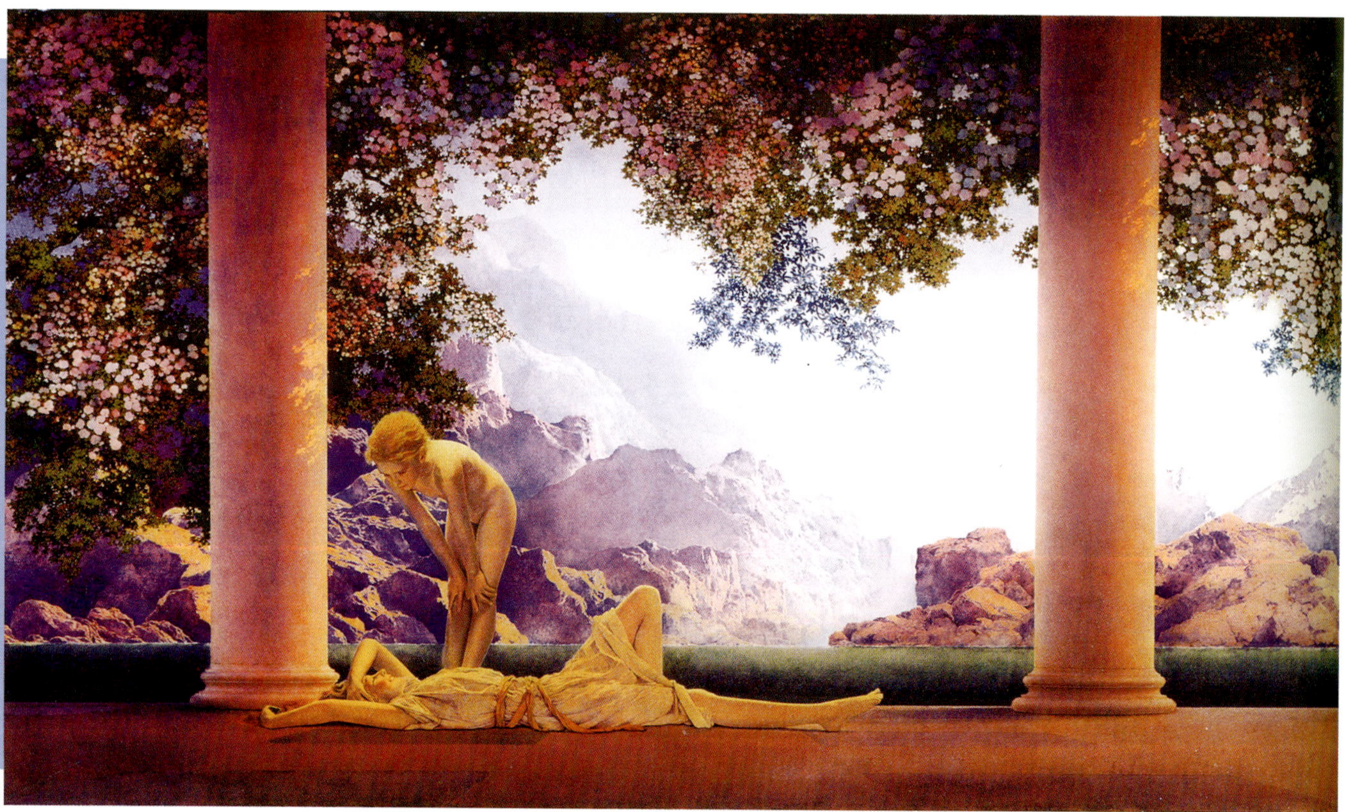

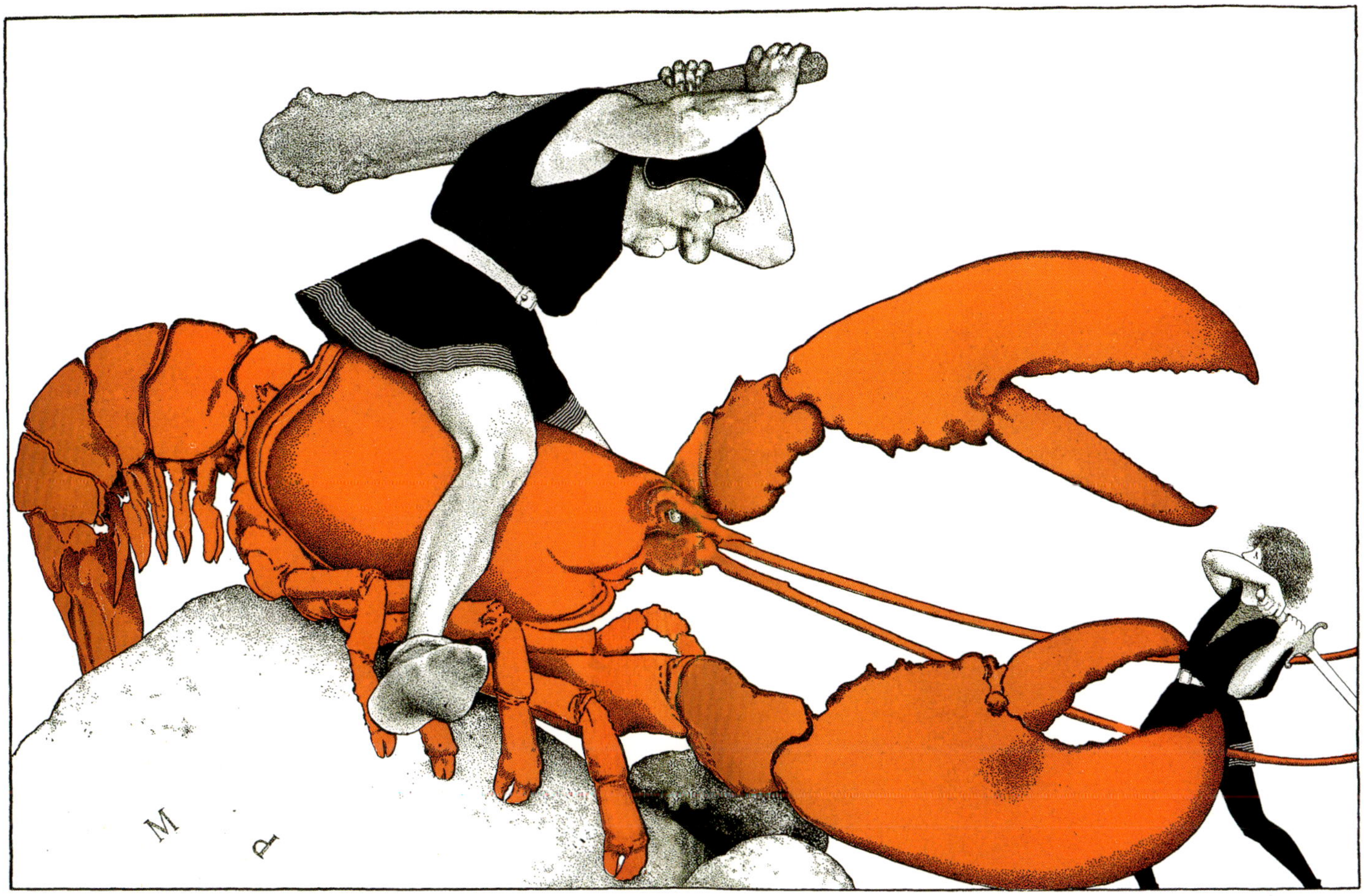

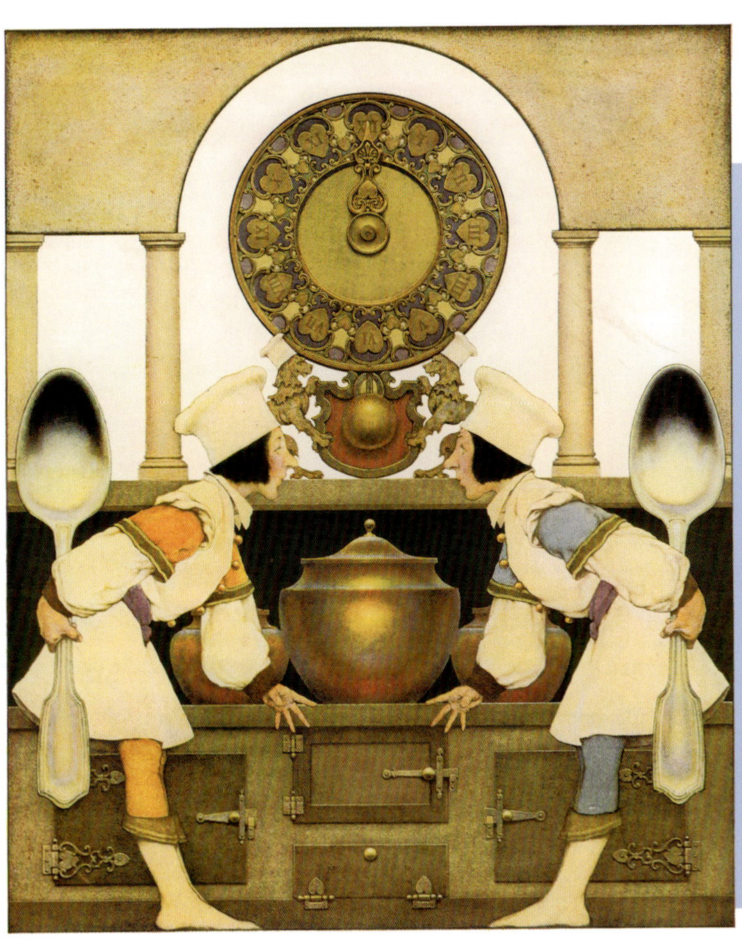

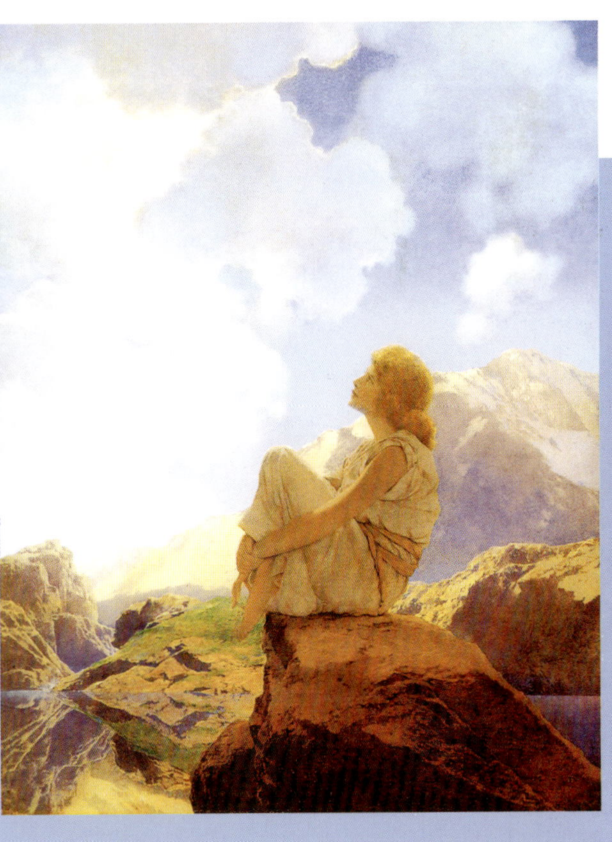

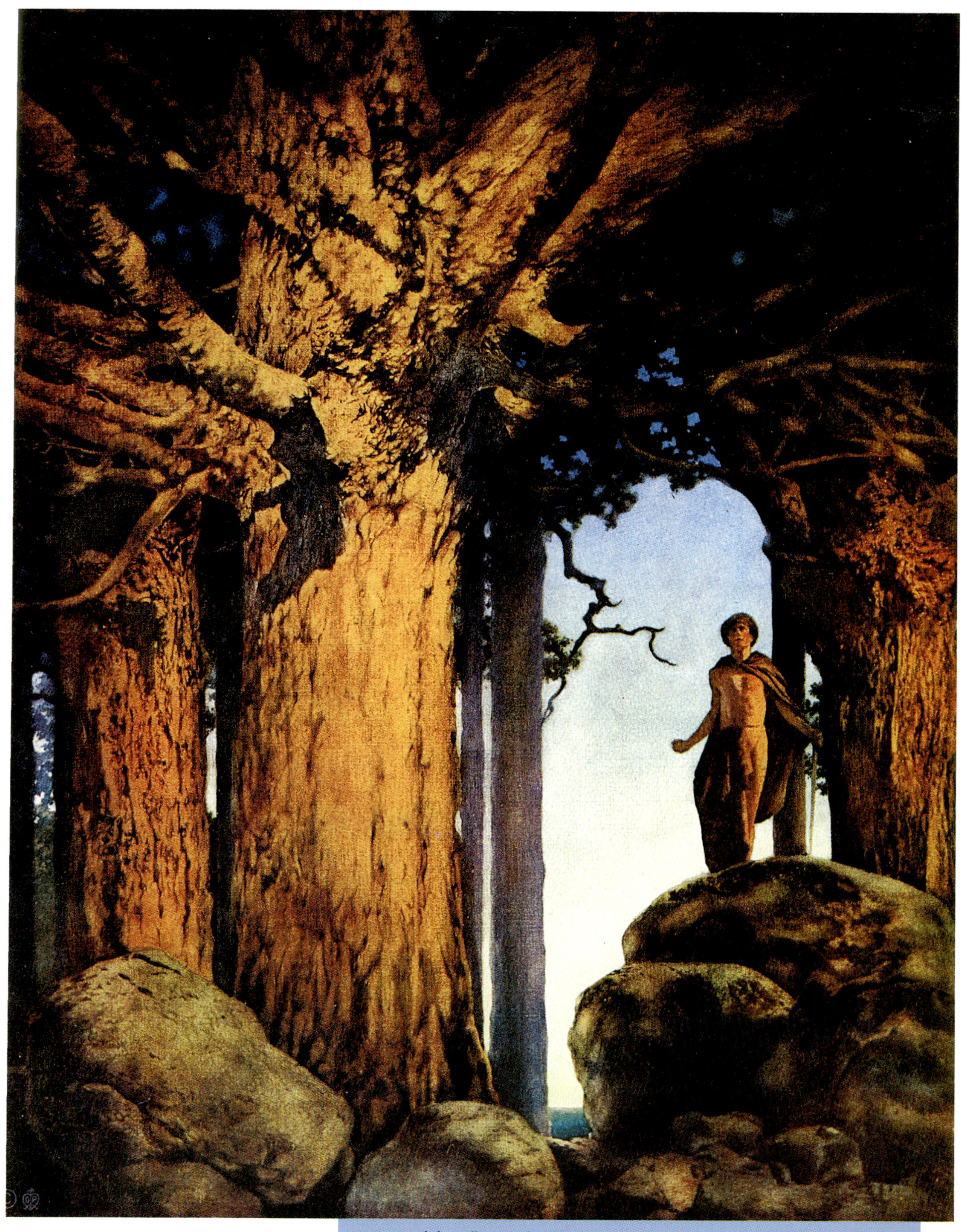

Jason and the Talking Oak, 1910

Parrish, Maxfield

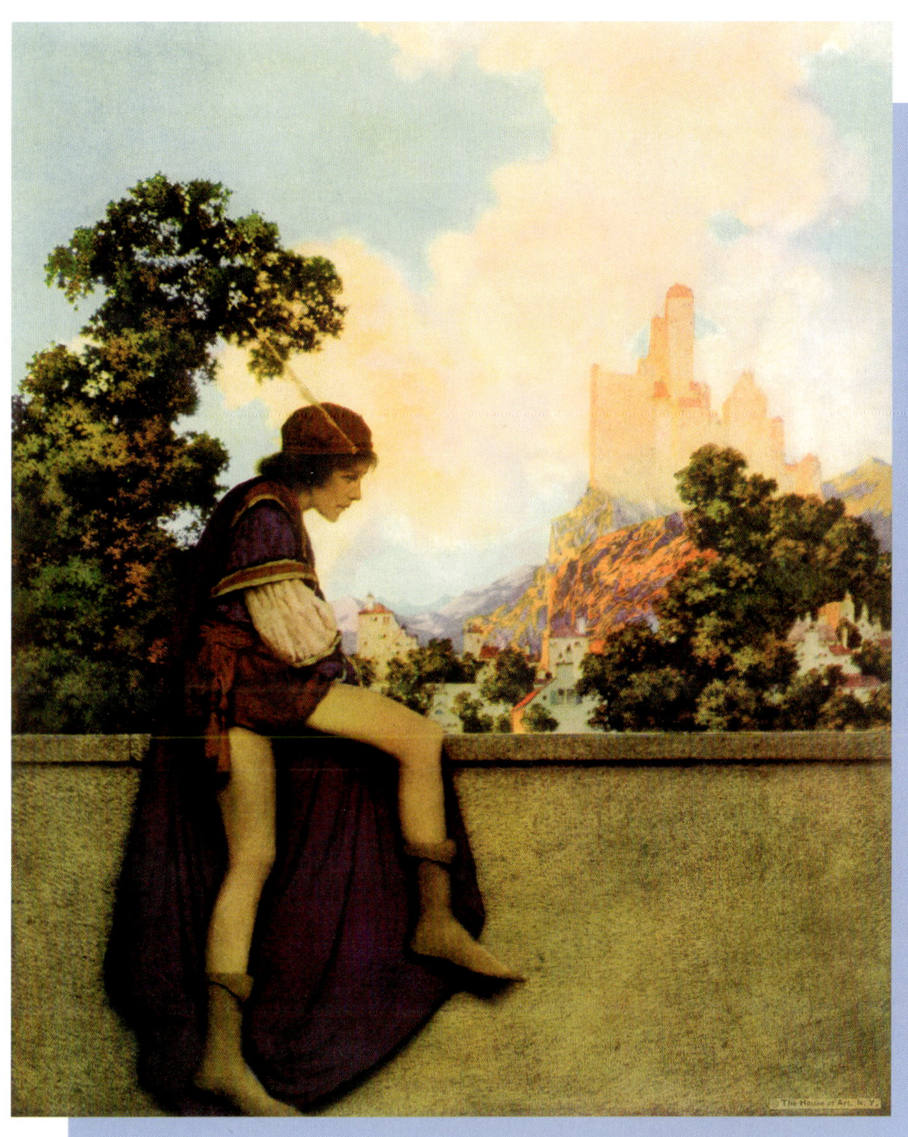

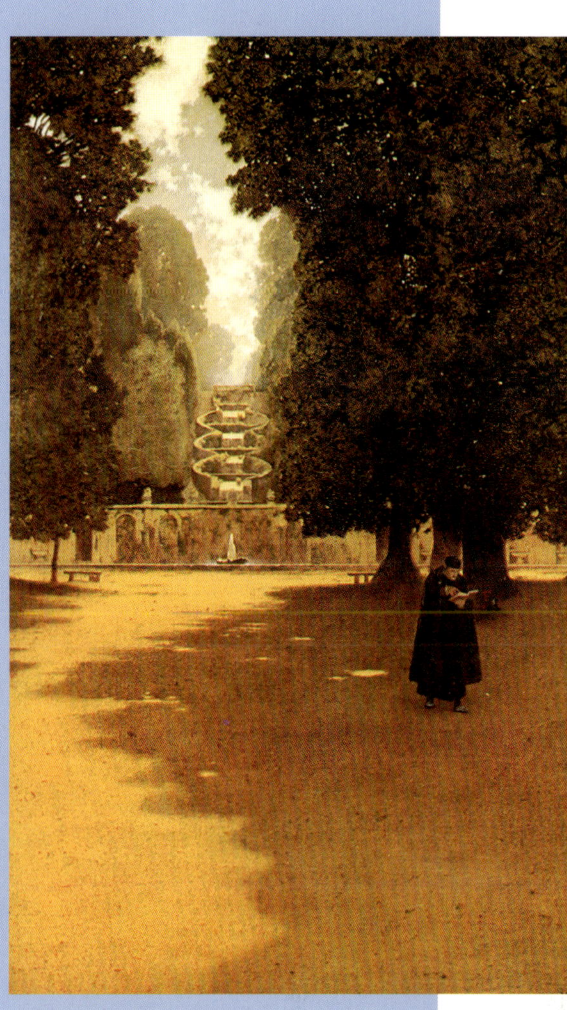

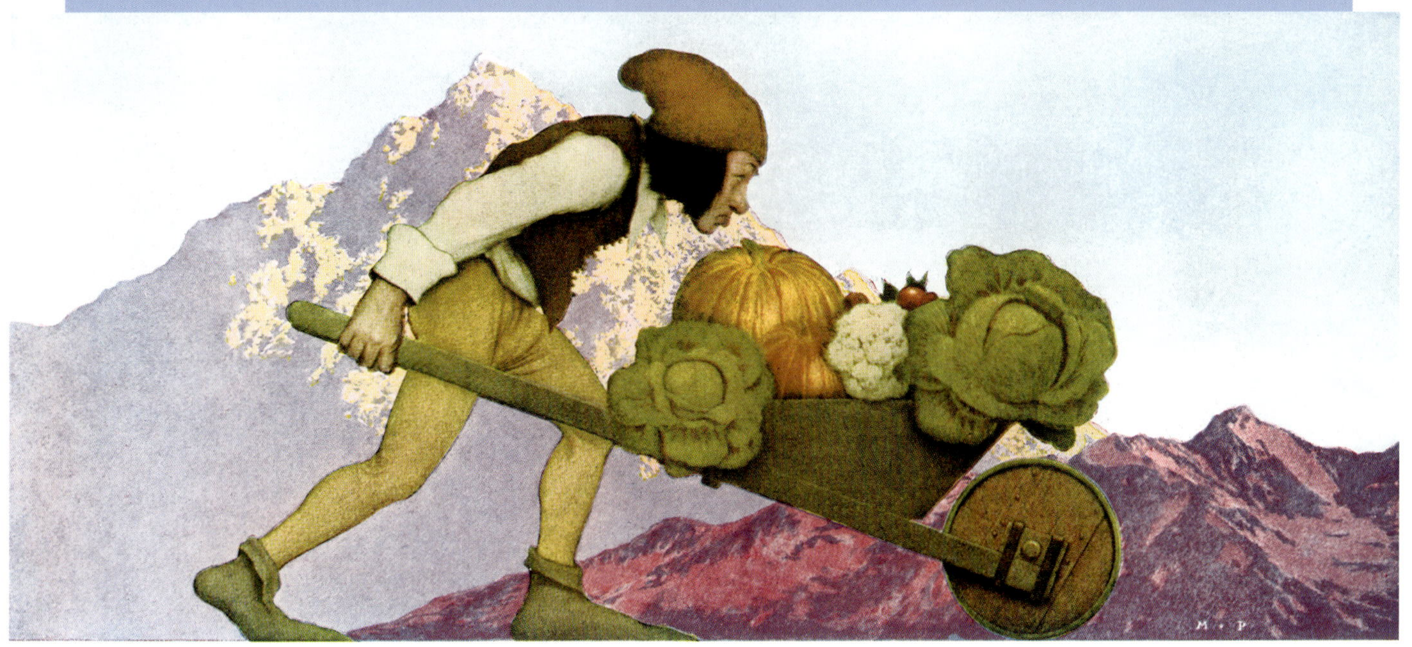
M • P

Herbert Paus
1880–1946, American

Showing artistic promise from a very early age, Herbert Paus was encouraged by his parents, and received some private instruction with local Minneapolis artist Burt Harwood. The elder artist later helped Paus land a job with the *St. Paul Pioneer Press,* where he began his career in commercial art as a cartoonist. Paus went to Chicago to seek more formal training, and began working with books and magazines while employed with an engraving firm. That same firm soon sent him East to New York, where they were setting up a new office. The move opened up possibilities in the booming world of New York publishing and advertising, and it was not long before Paus opted to be a freelance illustrator. His background in graphics and sharp design sense made his images well-suited to posters, covers, and advertisements. He was a regular contributor to *Collier's, The Ladies' Home Journal, Life,* and *Country Life,* and had a stable of commercial clients and occasional book work as well.

When the United States became involved in World War I, Paus was recruited to work with the Division of Pictorial Publicity. He embraced this role with enthusiasm, and his posters became largely identified with the war effort. His bold style acquired a strong and positive association, which in turn gave him even greater popularity in the advertising market.

Paus was very successful depicting machinery in his work, which brought him many large accounts from commercial and industrial clients. From 1927 to 1931, he was the only artist to produce cover work for *Popular Science Monthly,* making his style even more identifiable with the cutting-edge technologies of the period. What separated Paus's work from other illustration of the time was his use of bold color, combined with solid forms and eye-catching design. His work touched upon the style of the times, offering a keen sense of the current trends, without yielding the draftsmanship in which Paus excelled.

A CHAMPION OF THE VIGNETTE
Paus often used the form to create a more interesting and graphic shape for his work, giving it a stronger presence on a clean background.

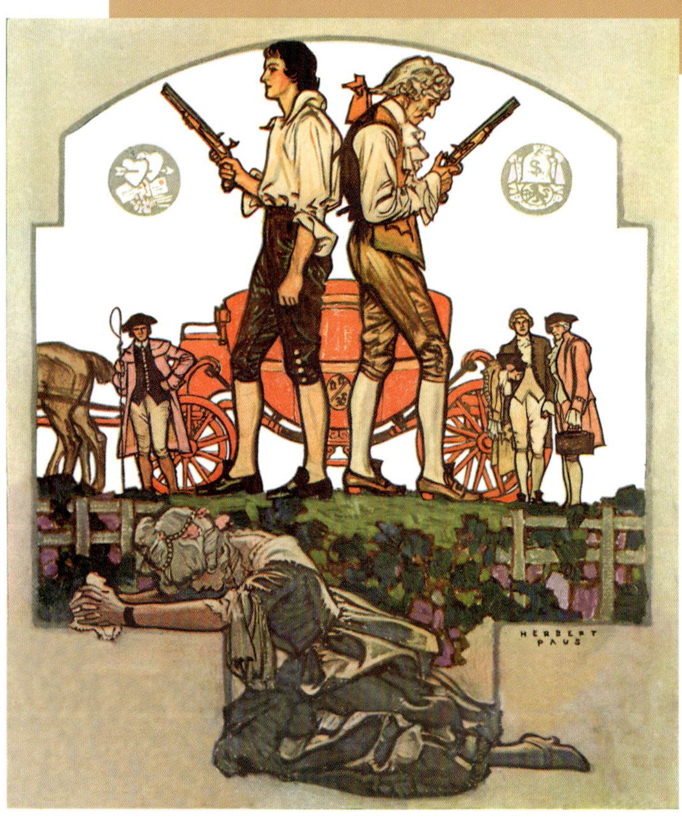

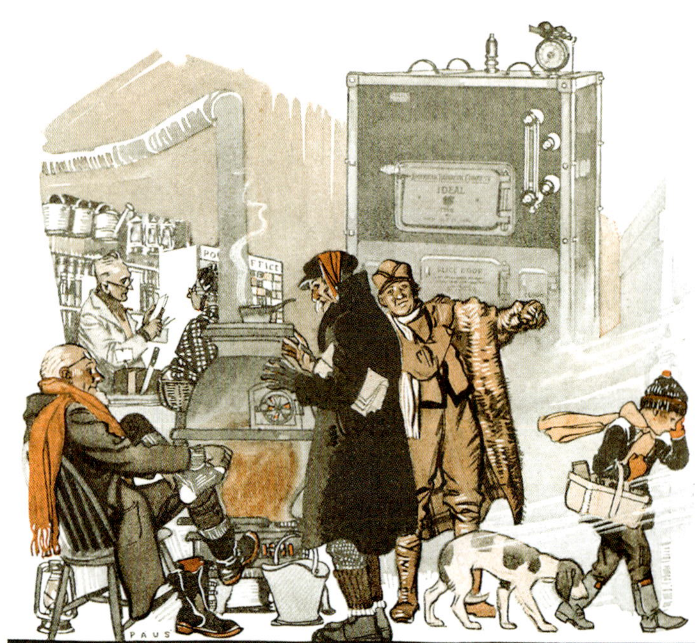

Paus, Herbert

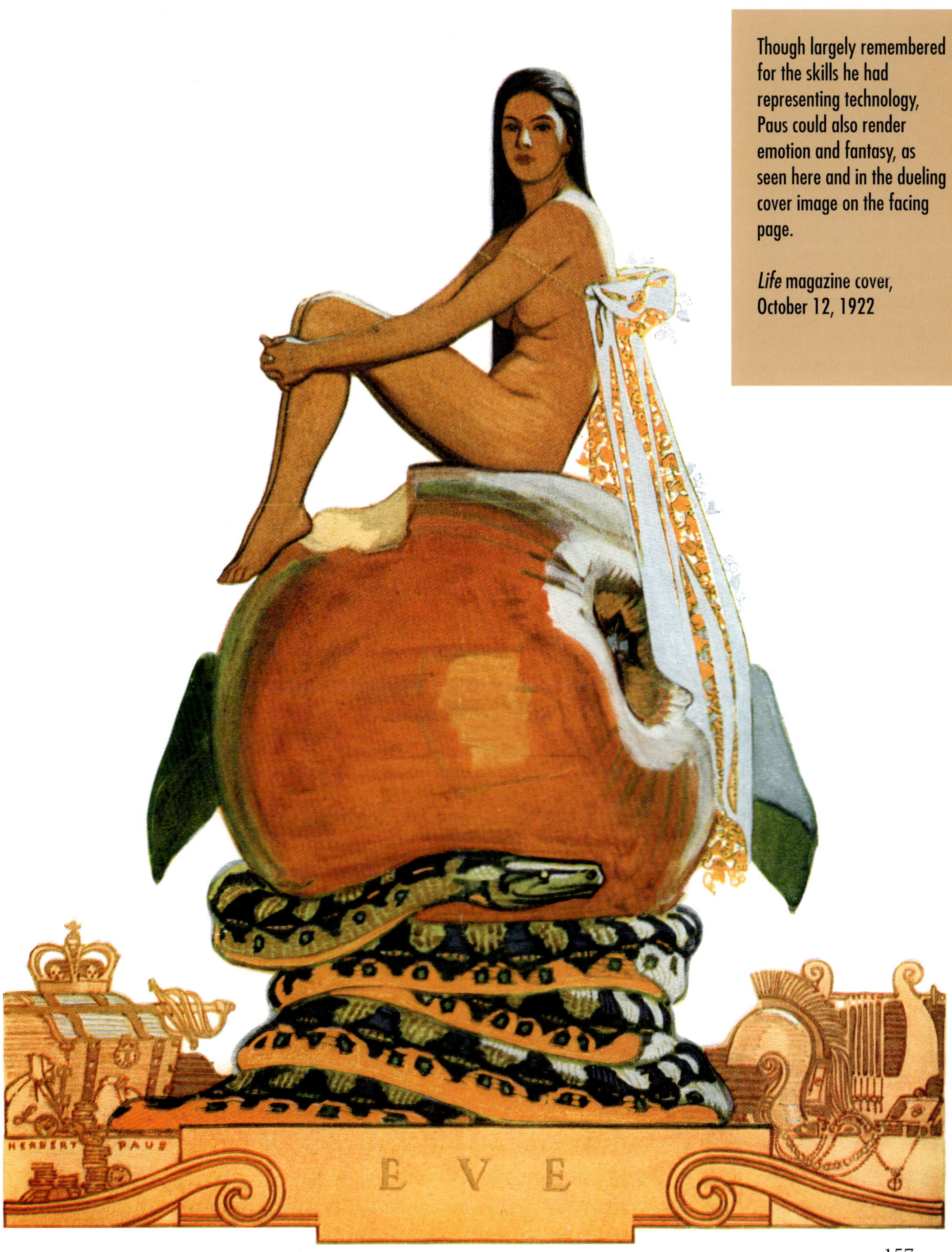

Though largely remembered for the skills he had representing technology, Paus could also render emotion and fantasy, as seen here and in the dueling cover image on the facing page.

Life magazine cover, October 12, 1922

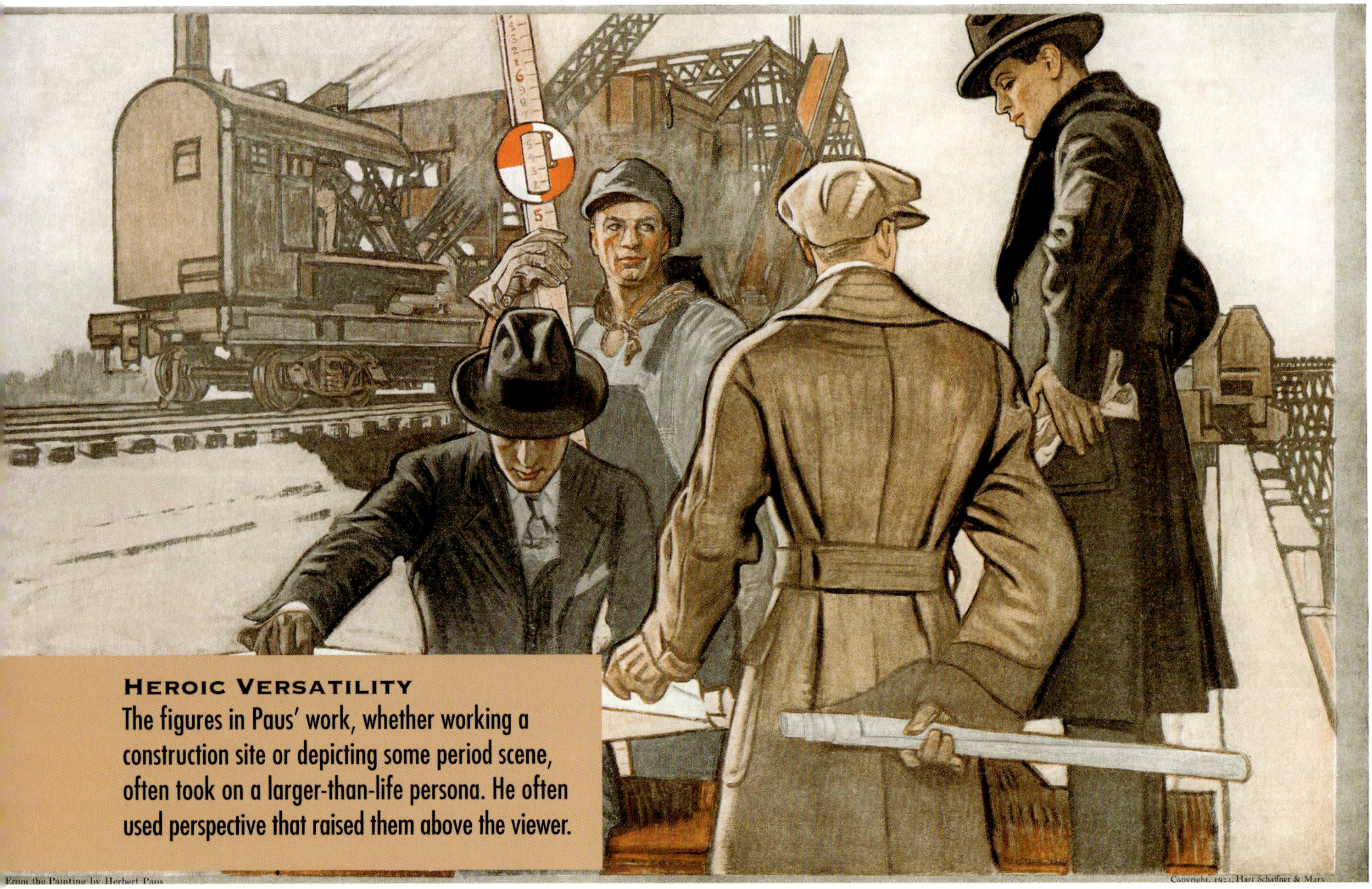

Heroic Versatility

The figures in Paus' work, whether working a construction site or depicting some period scene, often took on a larger-than-life persona. He often used perspective that raised them above the viewer.

From the Painting by Herbert Paus

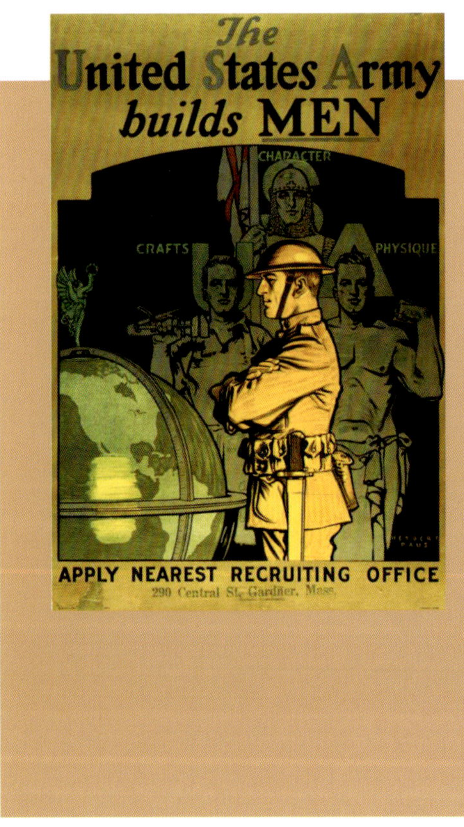

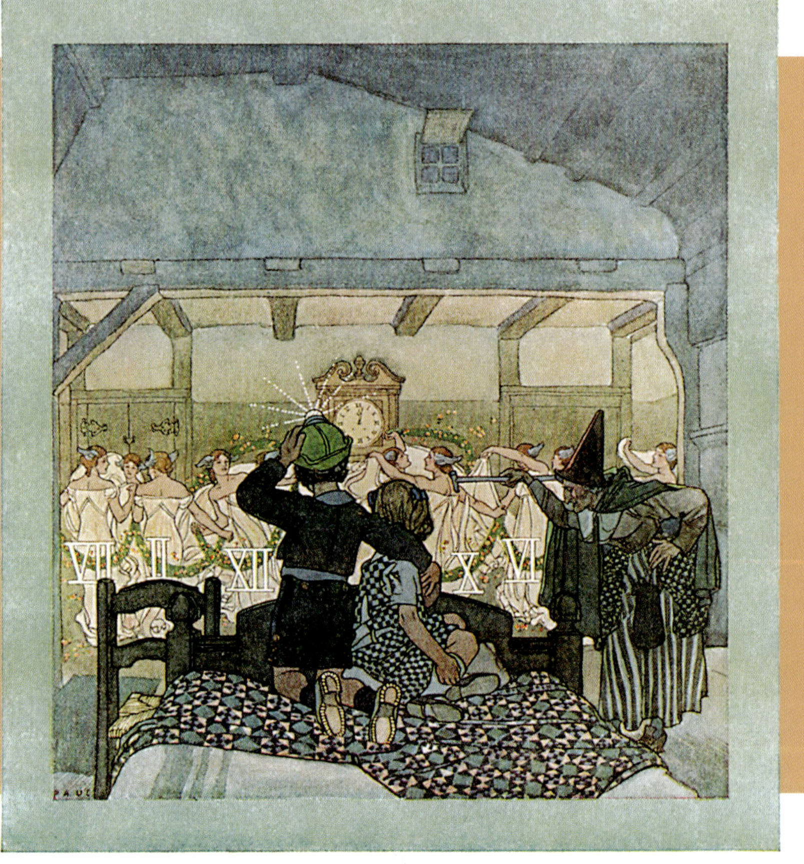

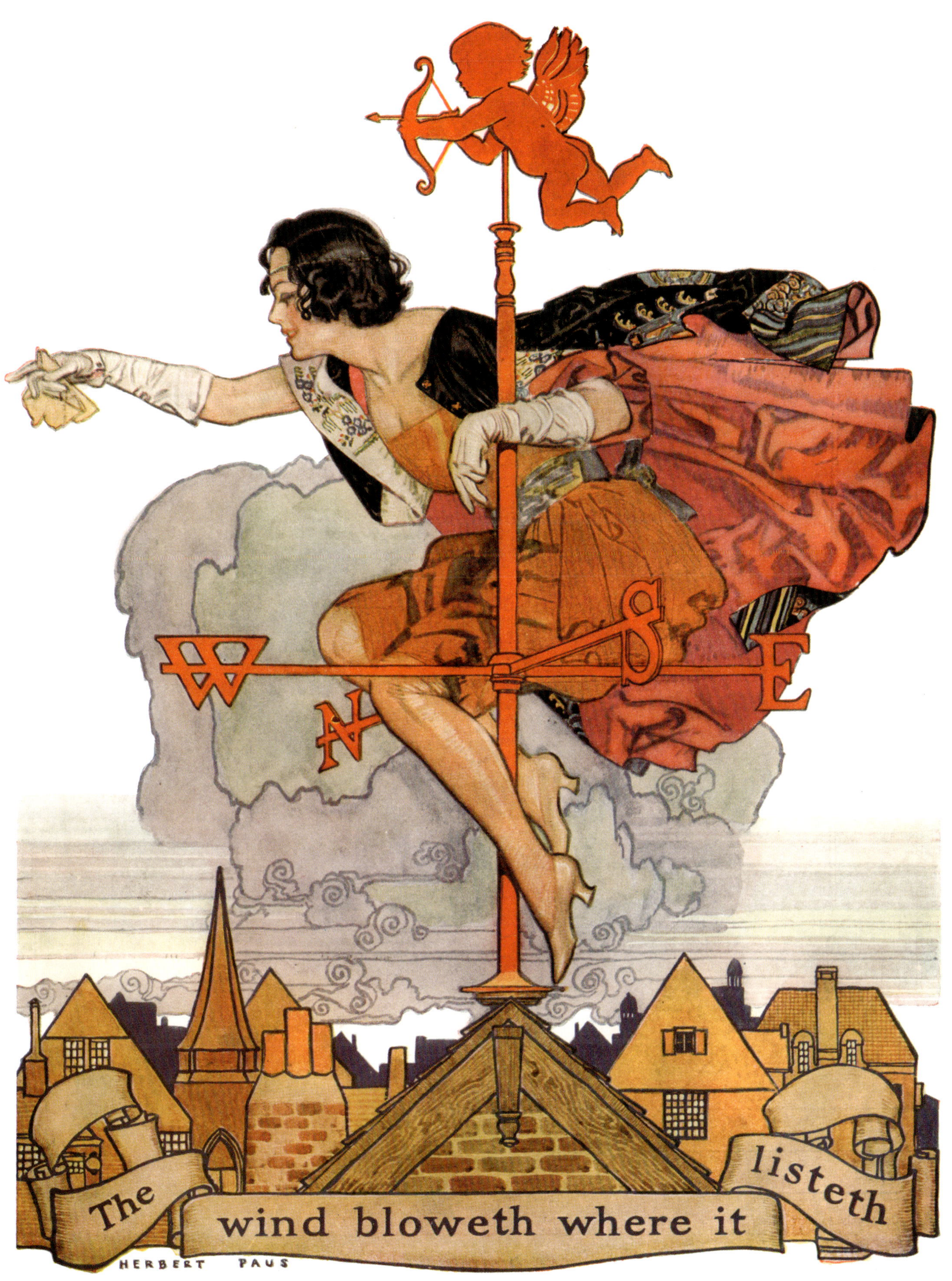
W
N
S
E
The
wind bloweth where it
listeth
HERBERT PAUS

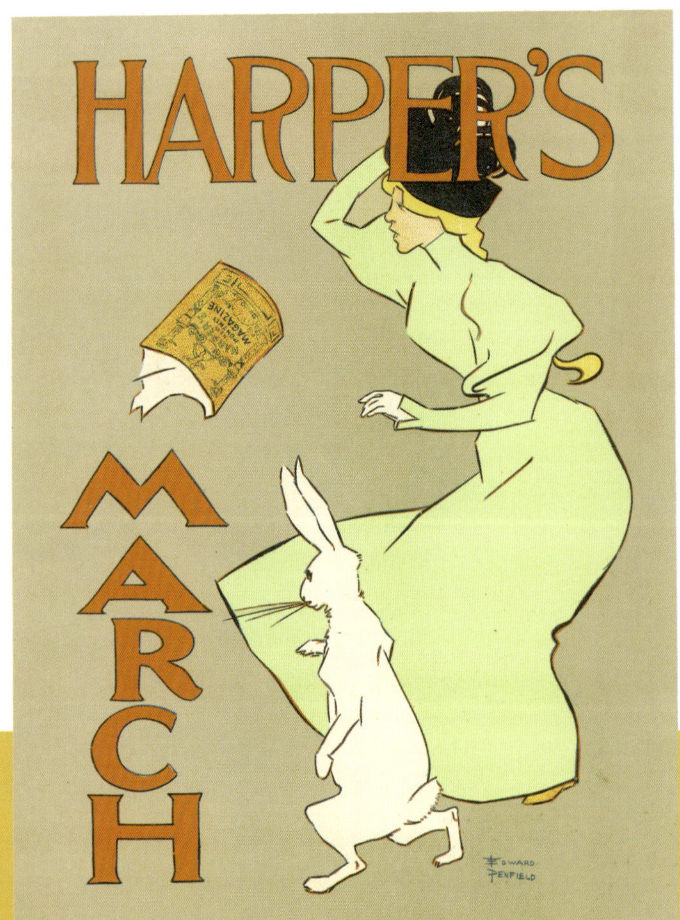

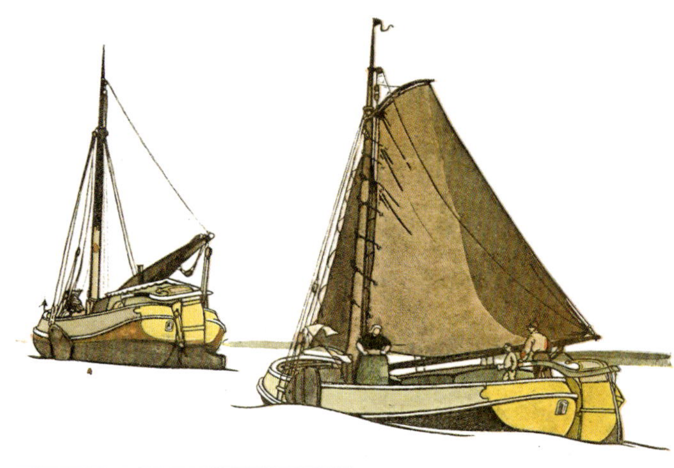

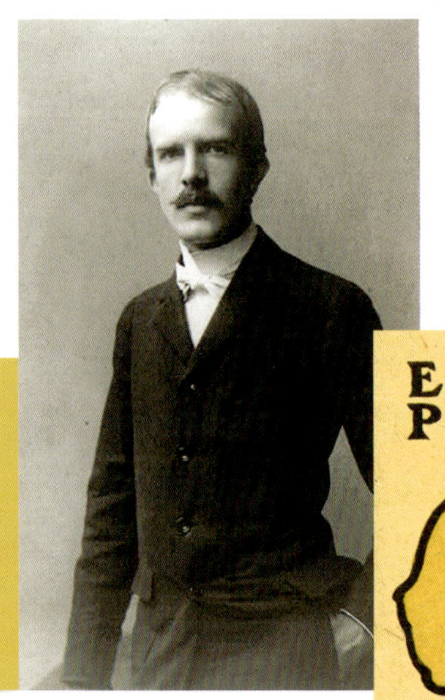

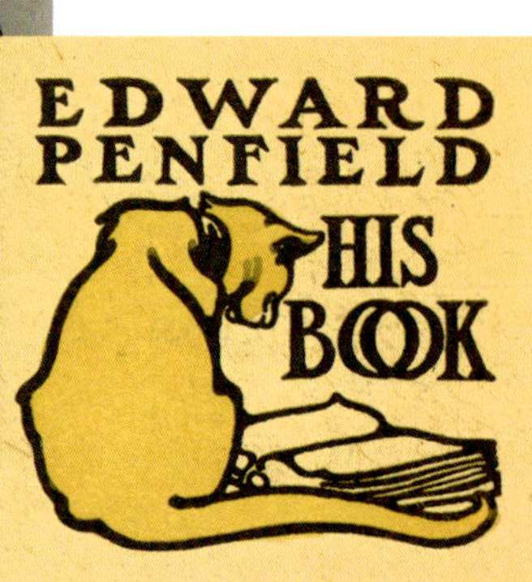

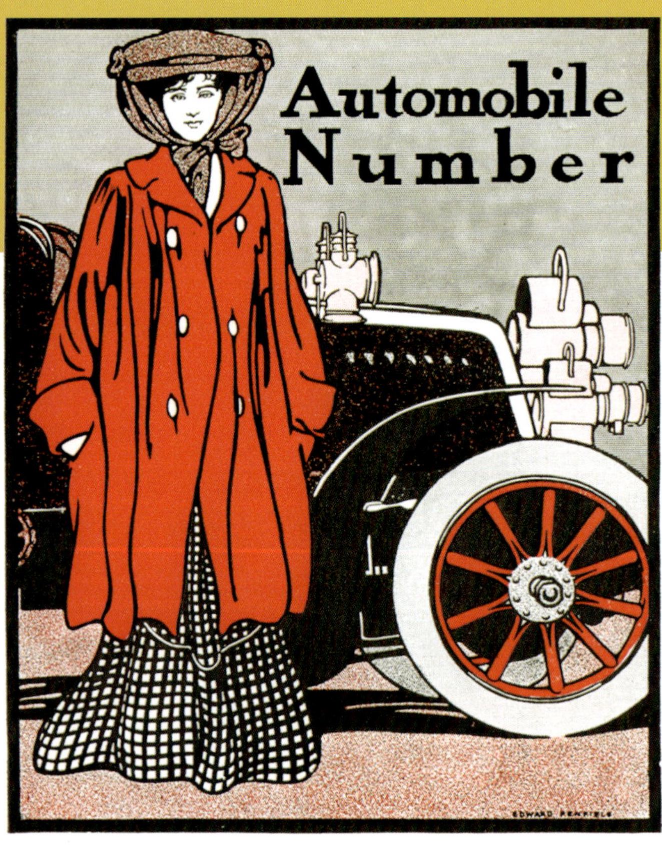

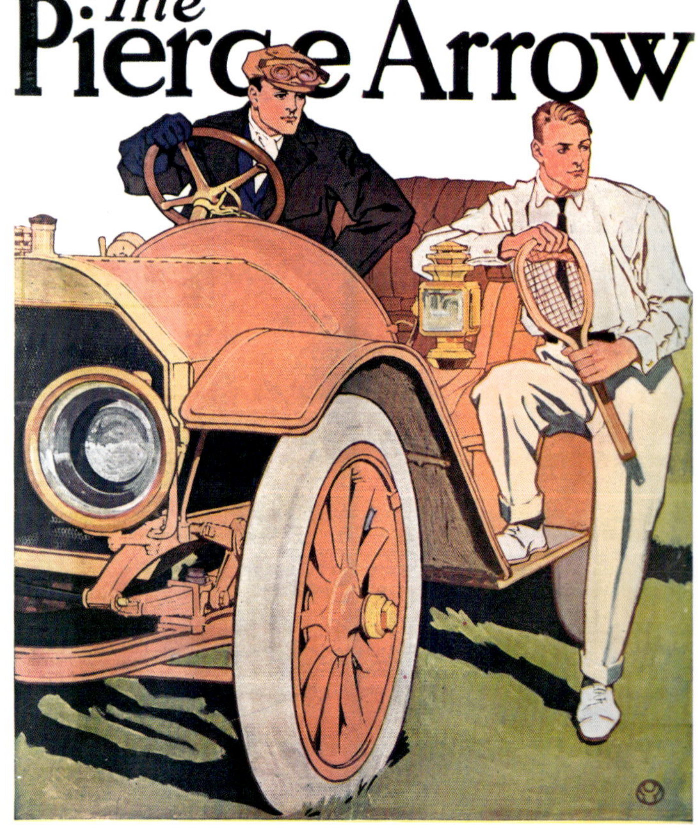

Penfield, Edward

EDWARD PENFIELD

1866–1925, American

As a student in New York's Art Students League, Edward Penfield was studying under noted painter George de Forest Brush when his work caught the eye of the *Harper's* art editor. He was eventually offered a position on staff, working in the art department at one of the biggest magazine groups in New York. In the middle of a deadline pinch, Penfield offered to complete a poster design for the next day. This set Penfield on a path to become a leading figure in American poster design.

His style was simplified, graphic, and strong—often with large areas of flat color surrounding the subject, with an organic, wandering line. It effectively communicated an idea at a glance as well as utilized the current print capabilities. It was a perfect pairing of strength to objective. Influenced by European poster artists, Japanese woodcuts, and American illustration, Penfield tied those looks together into something that was new and entirely fresh. His success at *Harper's* eventually led to his promotion to art editor there, where for a decade his eye and imagery infused *Harper's Weekly, Harper's Monthly,* and *Harper's Bazar* with style.

After ten years Penfield left *Harper's* to stimulate his creativity. In the years that followed, Penfield traveled to Europe, where his studies and notes on life in Holland became first a series of illustrated articles for *Scribner's,* and in 1907, a successful book. That project led to a sequel, *Sketches from Spain*, in 1911.

Success in varied areas made him a desirable freelancer, allowing him a greater range of clients. His talent for poster design was called upon during World War I as well, when Penfield produced many strong and memorable images for various war offices. With the popularity of the poster declining, Penfield adapted well, and his work shifted toward more magazines. Covers for *The Saturday Evening Post, Collier's,* and *Life,* among others, became part of his portfolio. Advertisers liked the impact of his images as well; he had a particularly strong campaign with Pierce Arrow automobiles. The strength and directness of his poster art was still evident later in his career, even though more detailed styles of illustration became fashionable.

Penfield was also active in various art organizations. One of the earliest presidents of the Society of Illustrators, he also taught at the Art Students League, where he first was discovered.

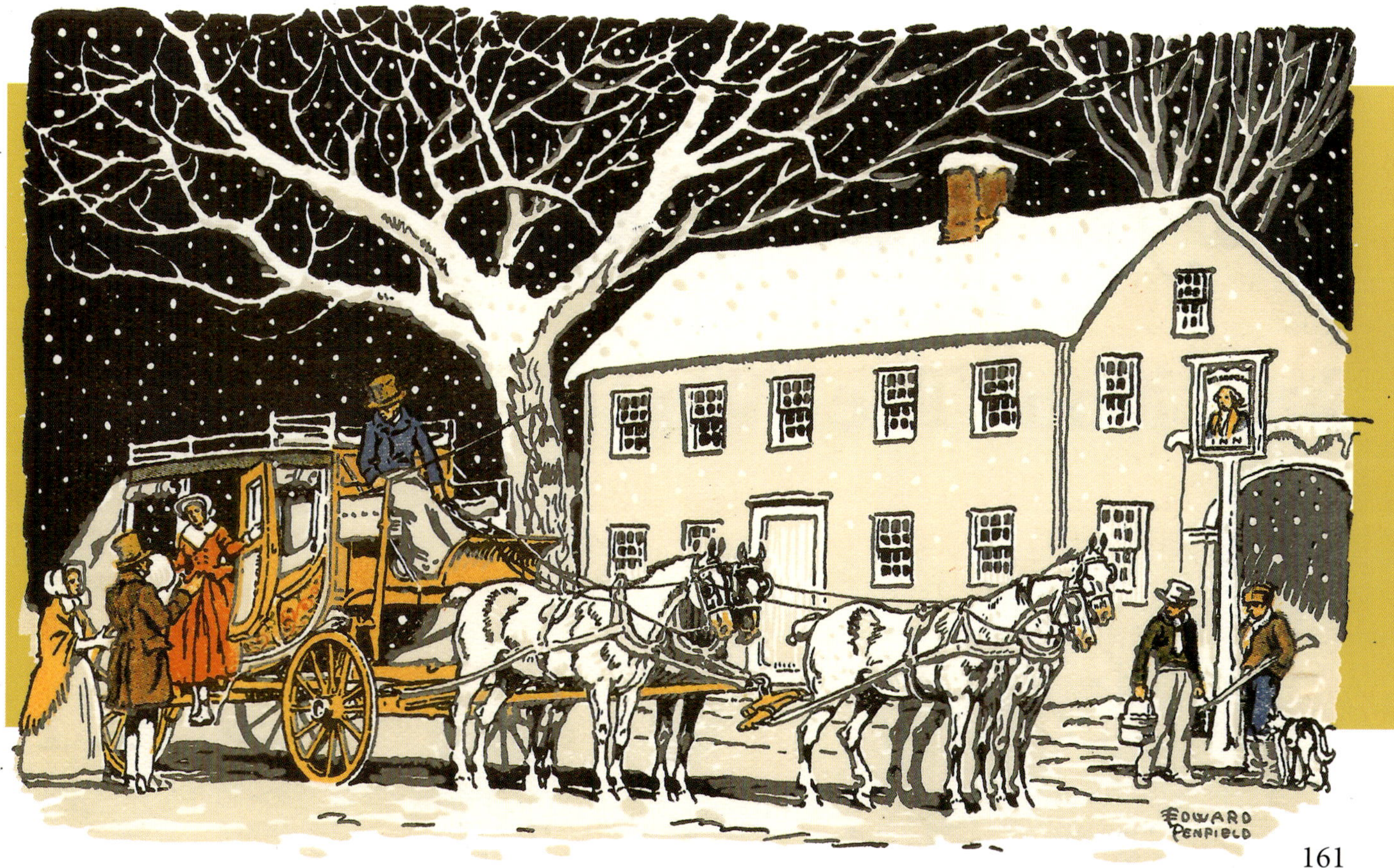

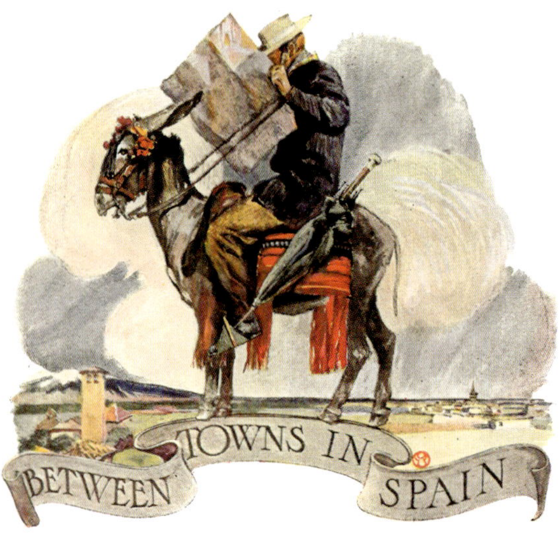

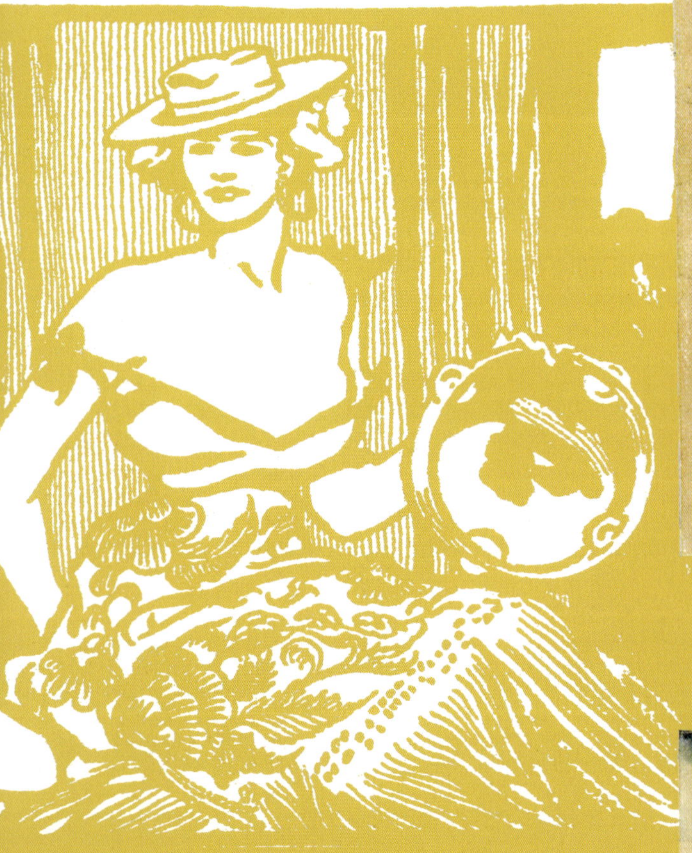

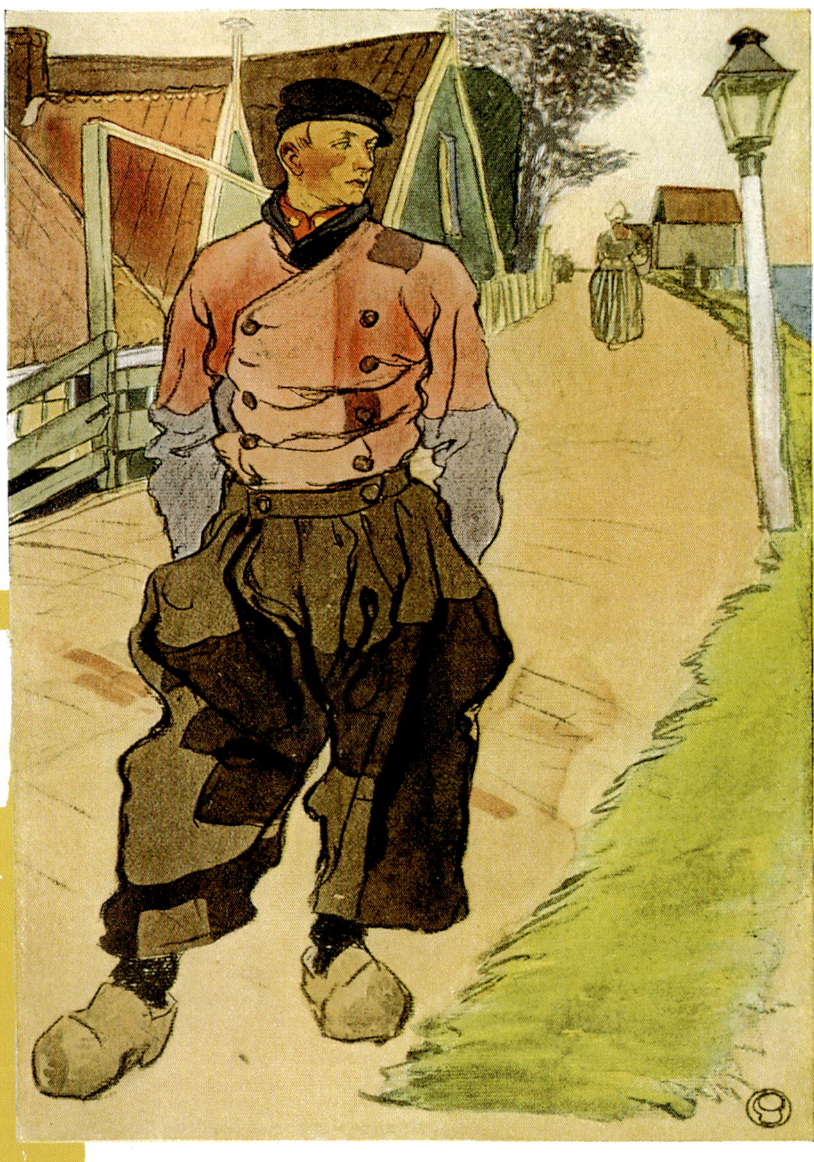

Penfield the Explorer

The two volumes Penfield produced about his tours through Holland and Spain provided him with great material for writing and art.

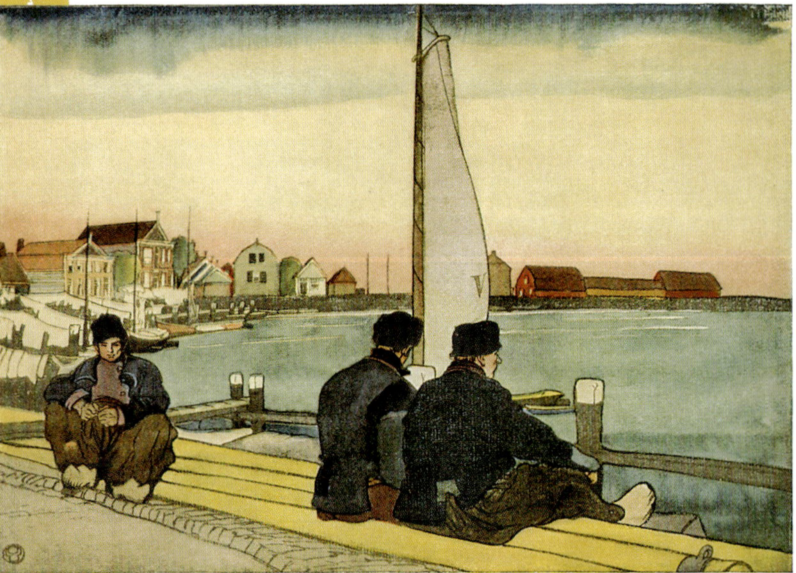

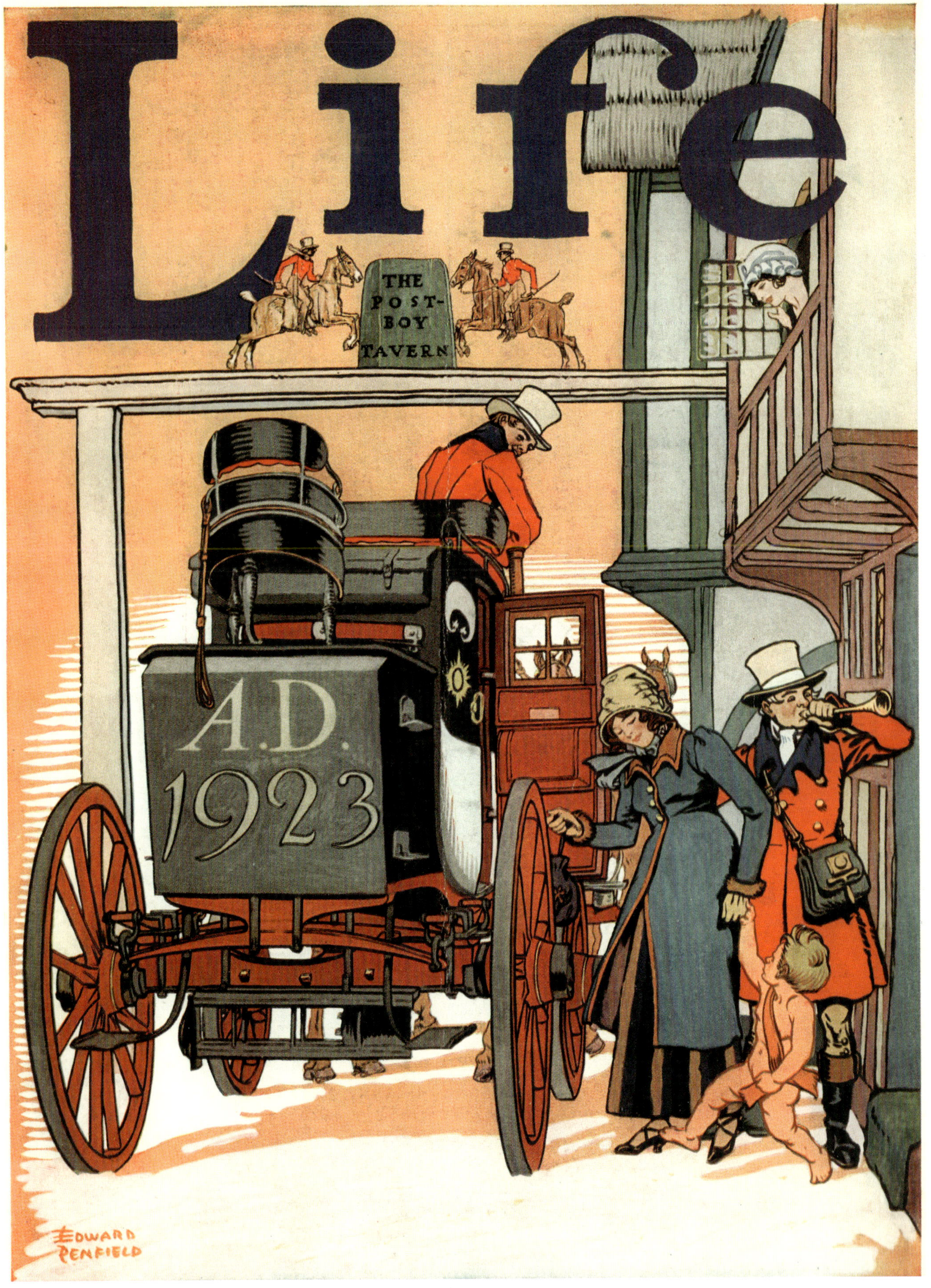
Life
THE POST-BOY TAVERN
A.D.
1923
EDWARD PENFIELD

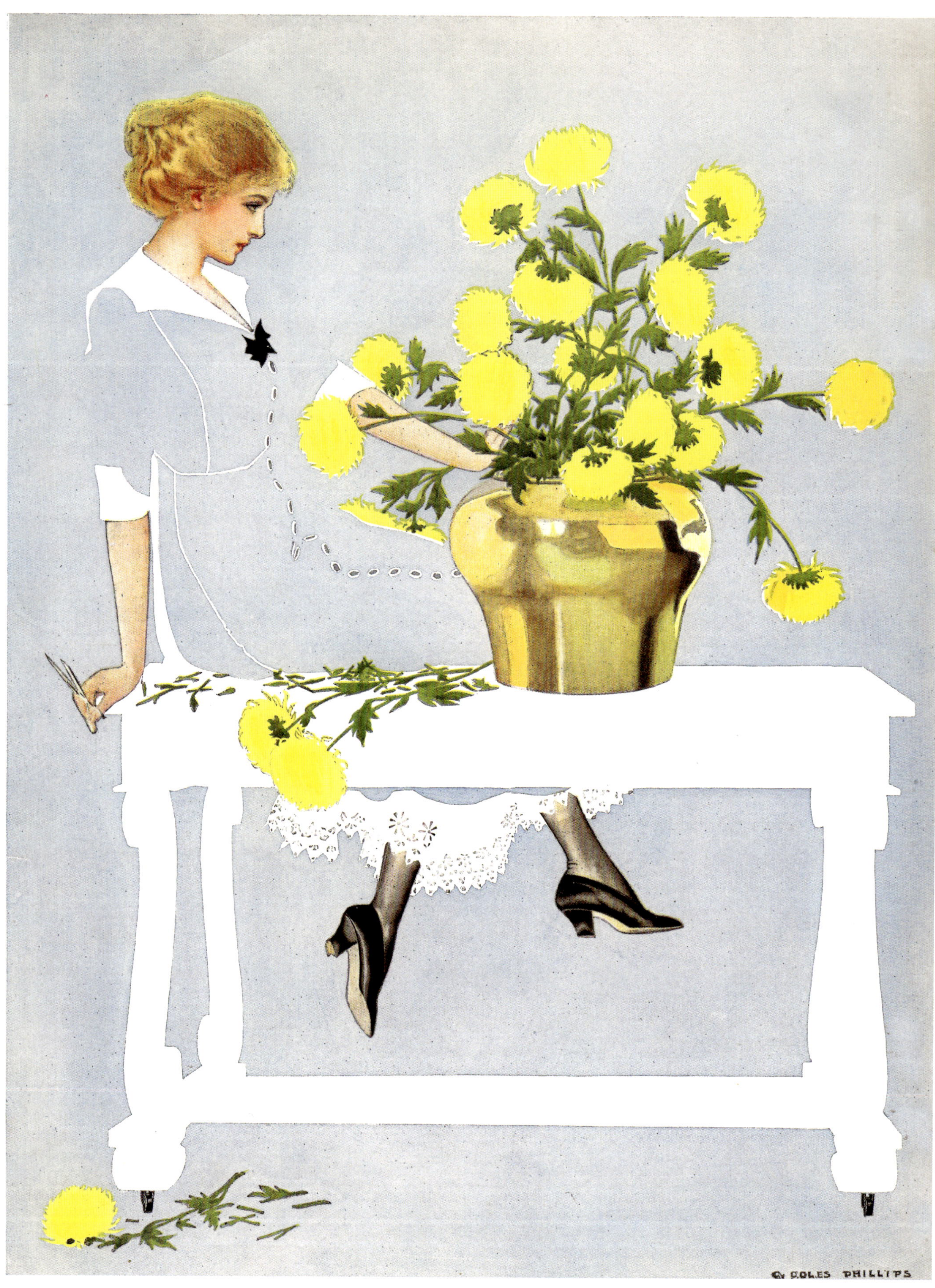

Phillips, C. Coles

C. Coles Phillips

1880–1927, American

Confident that he could thrive in the field of art, C. Coles Phillips left Kenyon College in Ohio after his junior year and headed for New York, determined to follow his dream. Phillips brought a letter of recommendation from his employer, the American Radiator Company in Ohio, to the New York office of the same company. It got him a job there, first as a clerk, then in sales. However, his time spent in a non-art job was brief. After a few months of studies at the Chase School of Art, he opened his own illustration studio. Phillips became quite skilled at navigating the waters between art and industry. Among his first employees was a fellow classmate, Edward Hopper, in the earliest days of his career. Though work for the small agency was satisfactory, it was an opportunity with *Life* magazine that really put Phillips's illustration career on the fast track.

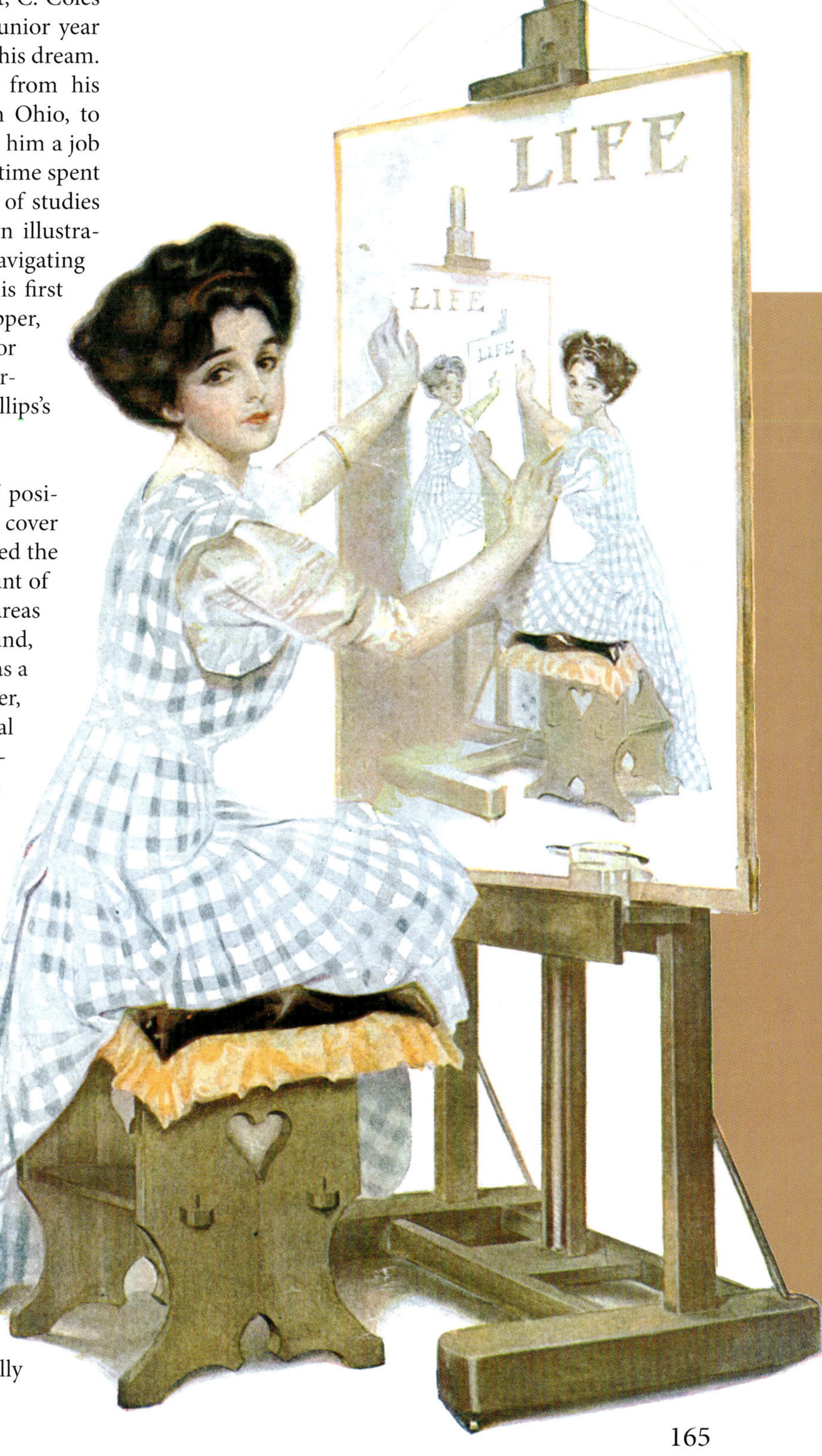

When Phillips was twenty-six, he took a staff position at *Life*. In May of the next year he created a cover painting with an optical effect, one that compelled the viewer to study the image for a prolonged amount of time. It used color and texture to blend large areas known as "positive" into the picture's background, making it appear negative. This became known as a "fadeaway." The technique was an attention-getter, and a boon to the magazine. It had the additional benefit of allowing *Life* to maintain two- or three-color covers, with no expense for photographic separations, when other magazines were paying for full color. The look became Phillips's signature style, and also spawned some imitators. He employed this technique in both his editorial work with magazines, and the many advertisers that sought his design savvy and rendering skill. In addition, Phillips's penchant for depicting attractive women made his work some of the earliest "pin-up" imagery.

In 1912 *Good Housekeeping* magazine hired Phillips as their sole cover artist, attesting to the power of his imagery over the public at the time. The next decade was prosperous for him, and Phillips had plentiful magazine and advertising work. In 1924 his health began to fail, and he was diagnosed with tuberculosis. The disease eventually took his life; Phillips died at the age of forty-six.

THE FADEAWAY

A technique which Phillips mastered — his joining the foreground and background — produced an effect that led the viewer to linger over the covers he presented, often resulting in increased sales.

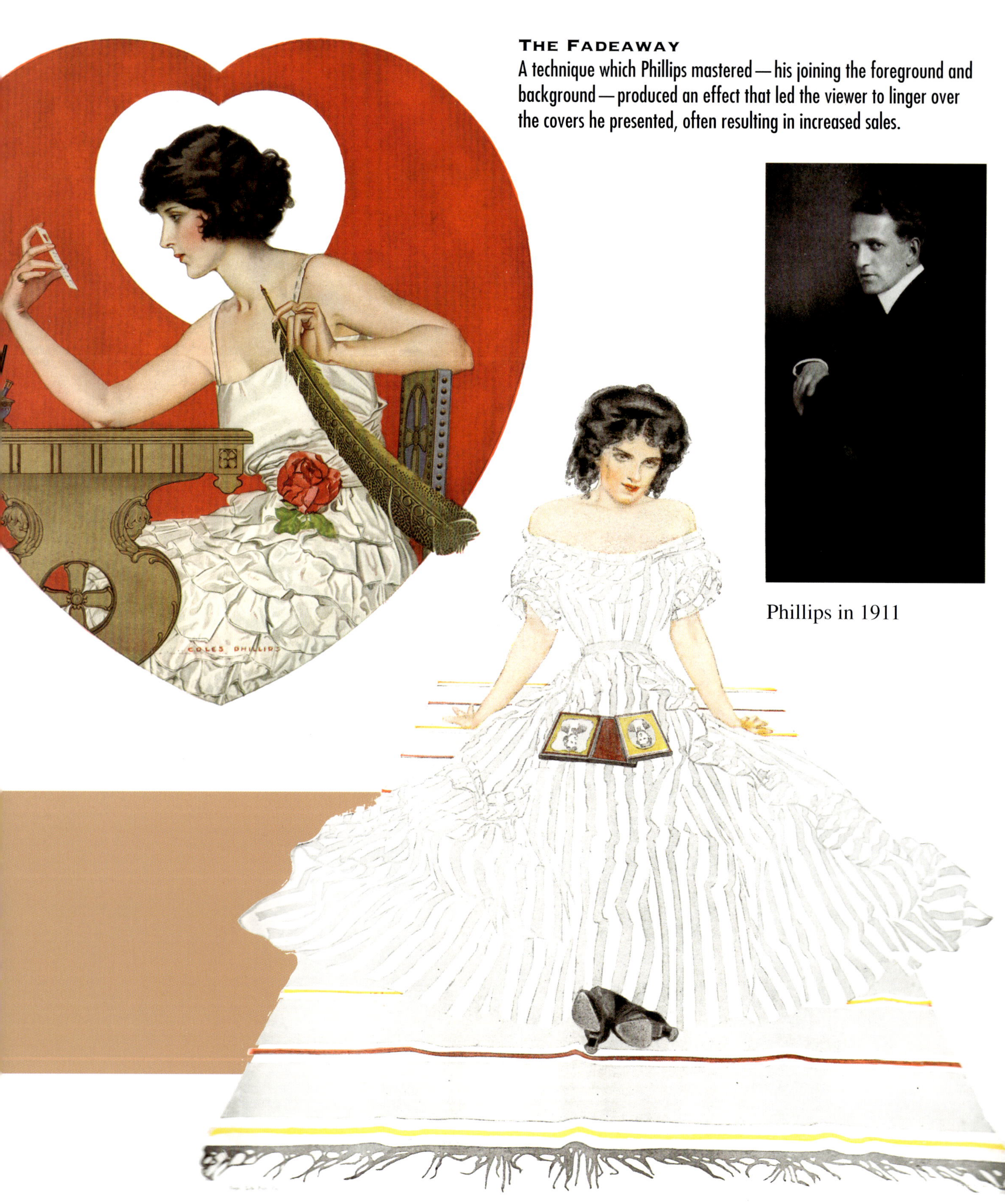

Phillips in 1911

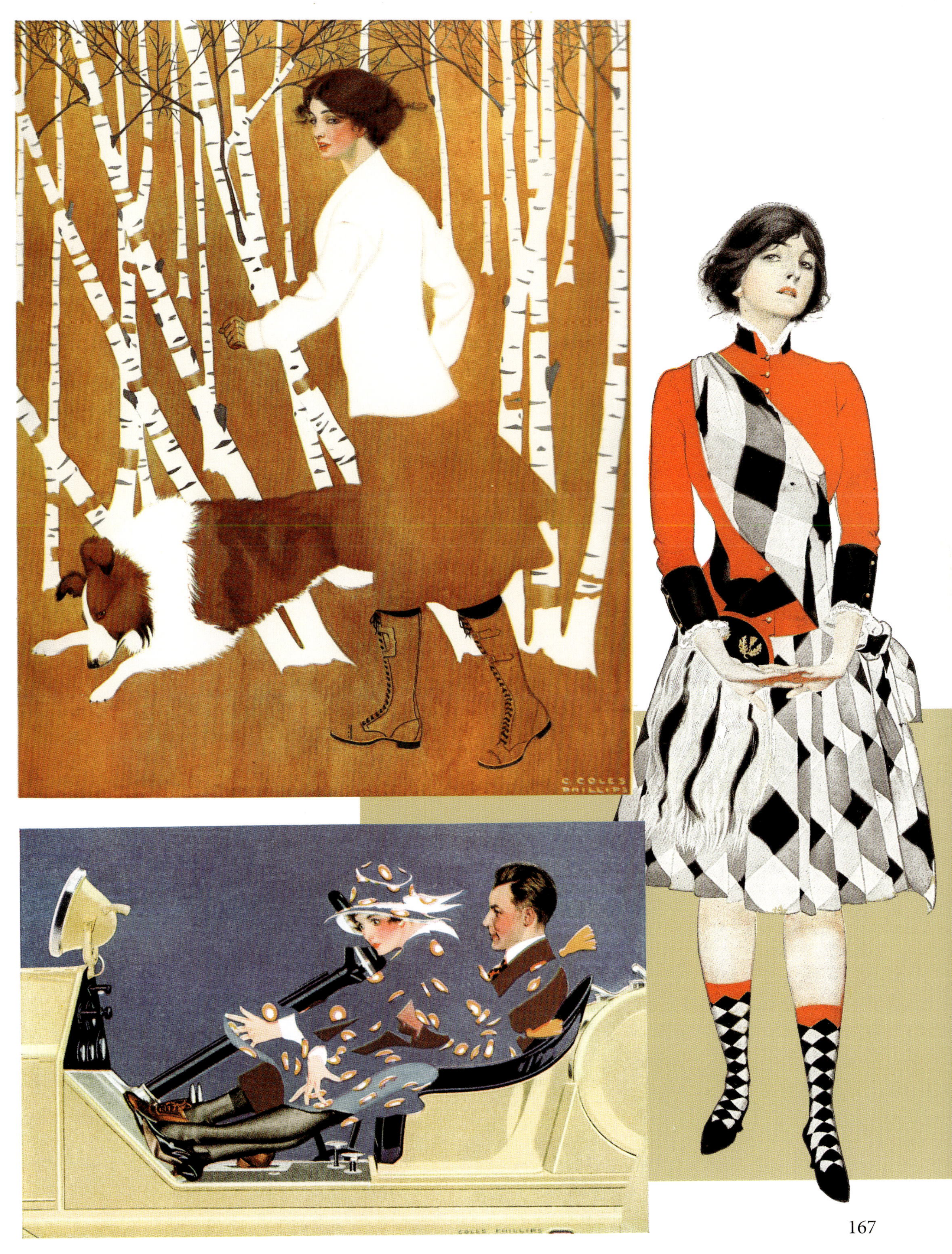
C. COLES
PHILLIPS
COLES PHILLIPS

Willy Pogány
1882–1955, Hungarian

Willy Pogány's output during his career was matched only by his appetite for new creative endeavors. During the near sixty years that spanned Pogány's working life, he was a book illustrator, muralist, film art director, ad man, author, portrait artist, and more. Few of his colleagues could approach the amount or the diversity of creative outlets that Pogány mastered in his lifetime.

Among Pogány's earlier works are a number of illustrated books that were praised for their design and production. These volumes are still considered works of art in their own right today. Four in particular—*Tannhäuser, Parsifal,* and *Lohengrin,* followed by *The Rime of the Ancient Mariner*—are considered to represent the peak of Golden Age book production, and are highly valued by bibliophiles and illustration fans today. While the more typical subjects of fairy tales and mythology dominated his work, he also illustrated titles as diverse as *Alice in Wonderland* and Browning's *Sonnets for the Portuguese.* On more than one occasion, Pógany had the opportunity to depict tales from his own cultural heritage, as in 1913's *Hungarian Fairy Book,* and later, *Magyar Fairy Tales,* in 1930, both of which he illustrated for his sister, Nandor.

As the political climate in Europe progressively grew unstable leading up to World War I, Pogány chose to try his luck in America, and immigrated to New York in 1915. Though he found book work there, it soon became apparent that the war's effect on social attitudes and interests had shifted the needs of the market for illustration. Always one to take advantage of change, Pogány kept an eye on the up-and-coming markets, seeking new avenues for his creative work. Several New York theaters and hotels have preserved Pogány's mural work, including the August Heckscher Children's Theater, the Bernard B. Jacobs Theatre (née Royale), and the Eldorado Hotel. Pogány kept his hand in book illustration when he could get work, but also became a regular contributor to a number of weeklies and illustrated magazines of the day. He continued working up until his death in 1955.

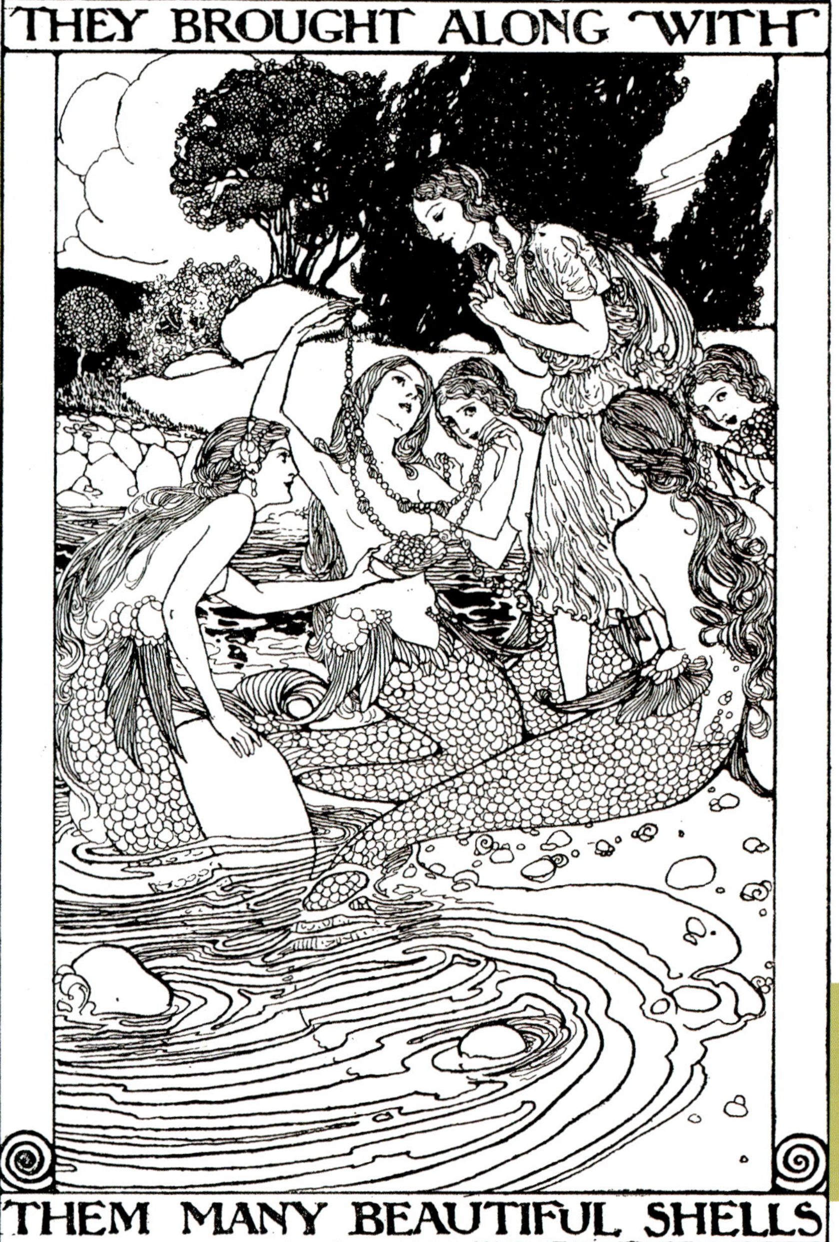

Pogány, Willy

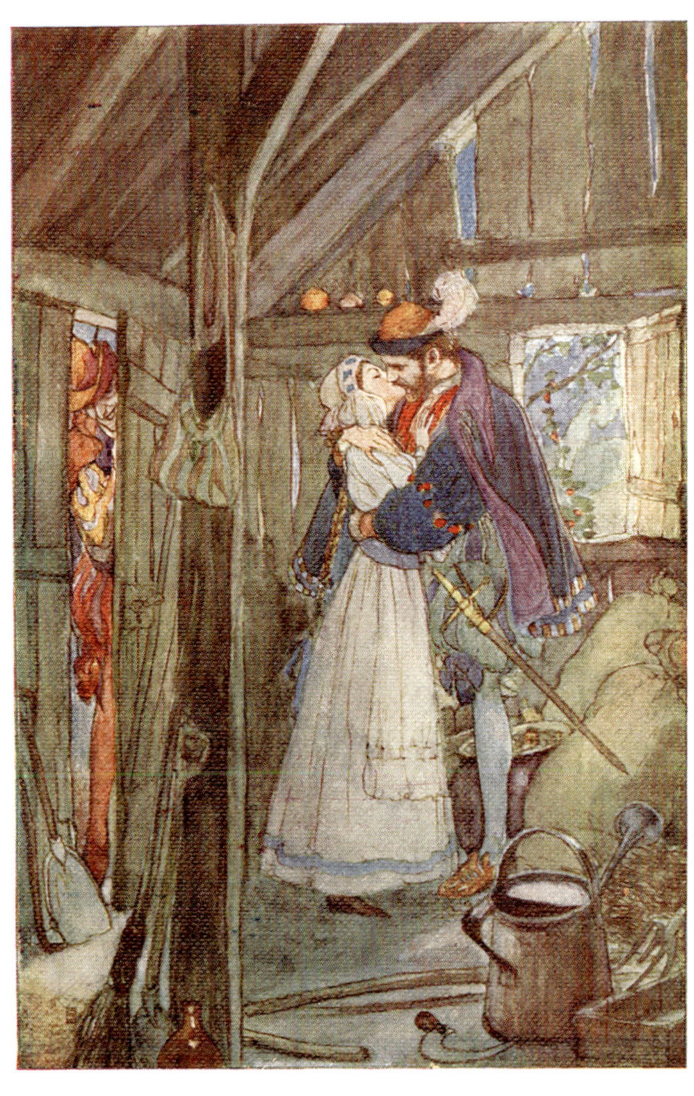

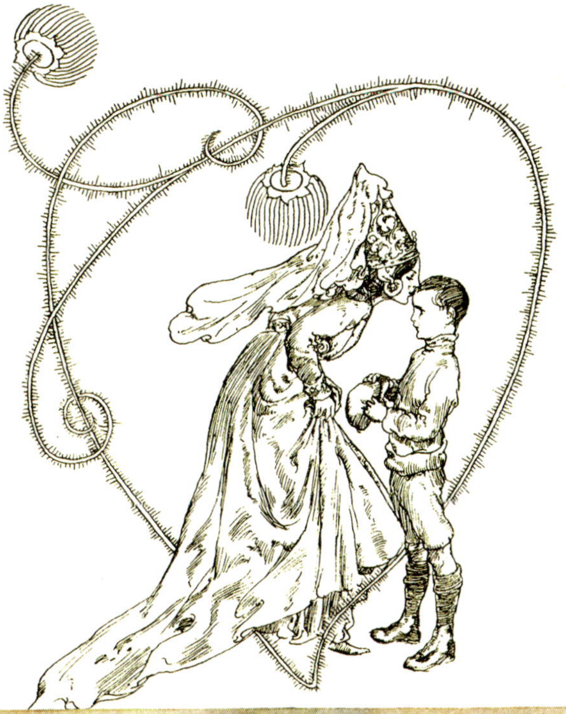

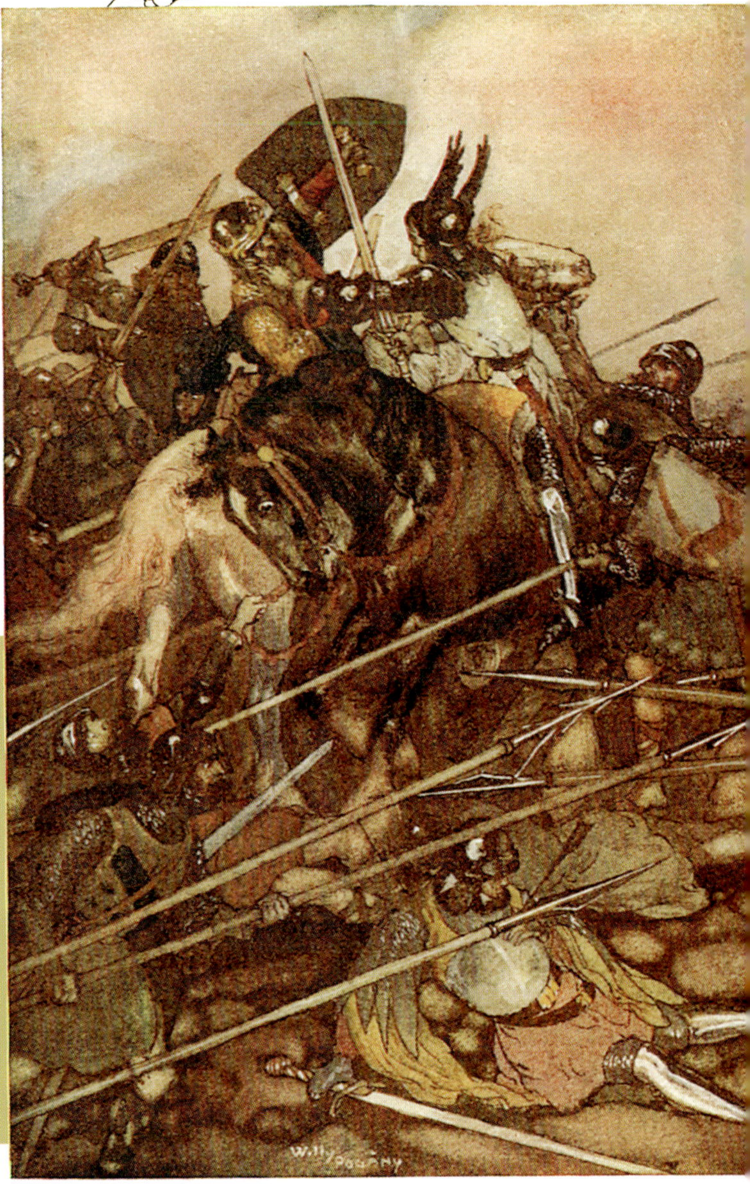

Bane of the Aesir
A chapter heading from Padraic Colum's *The Children of Odin*

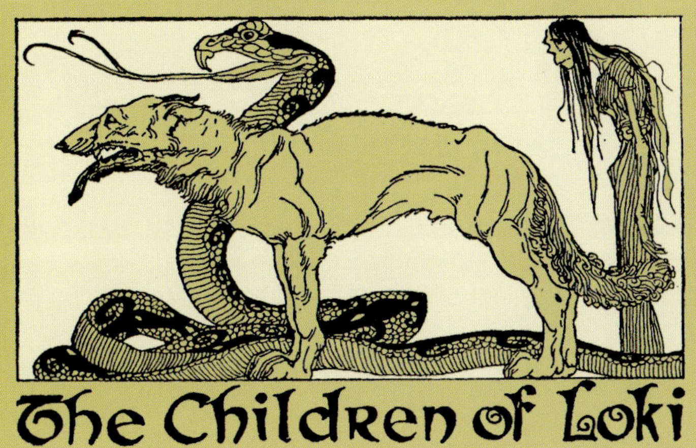

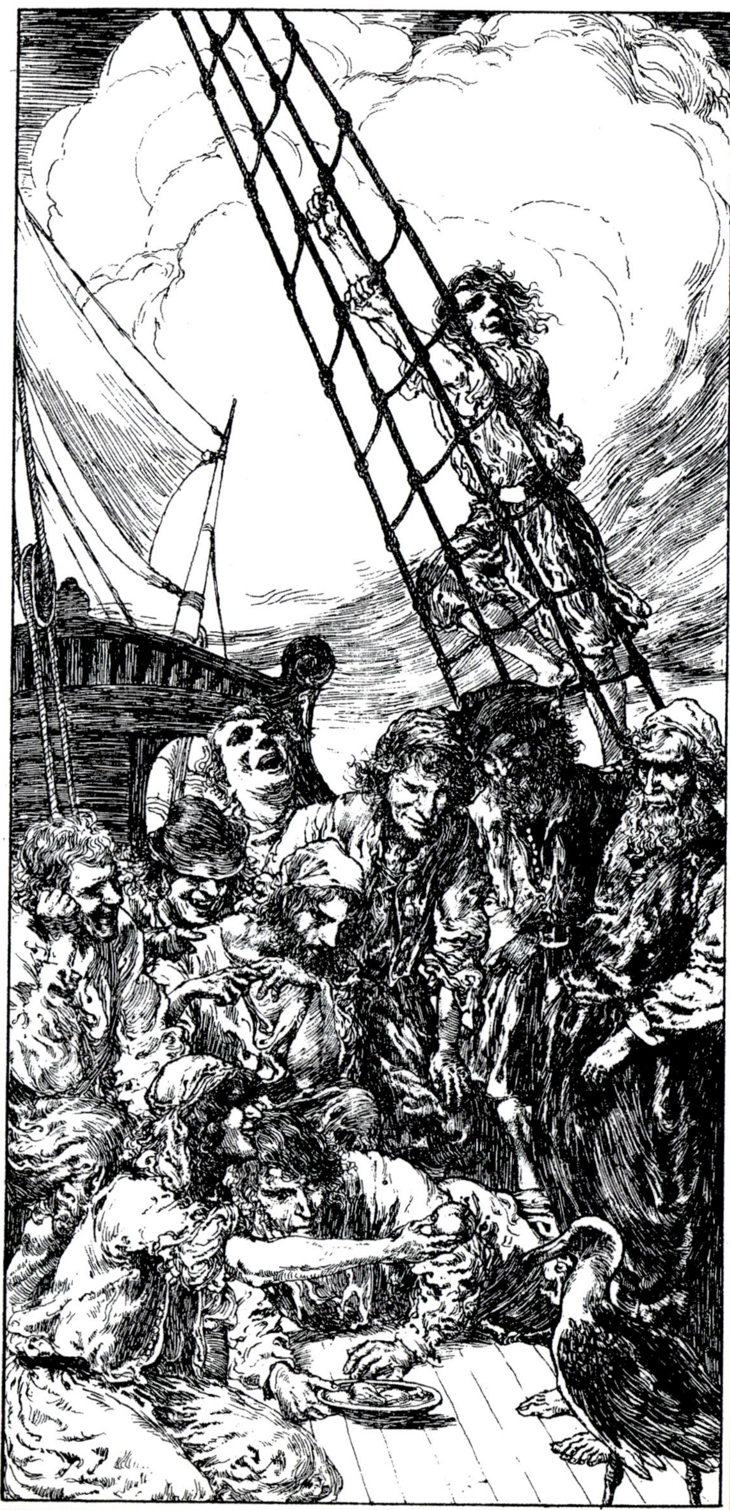

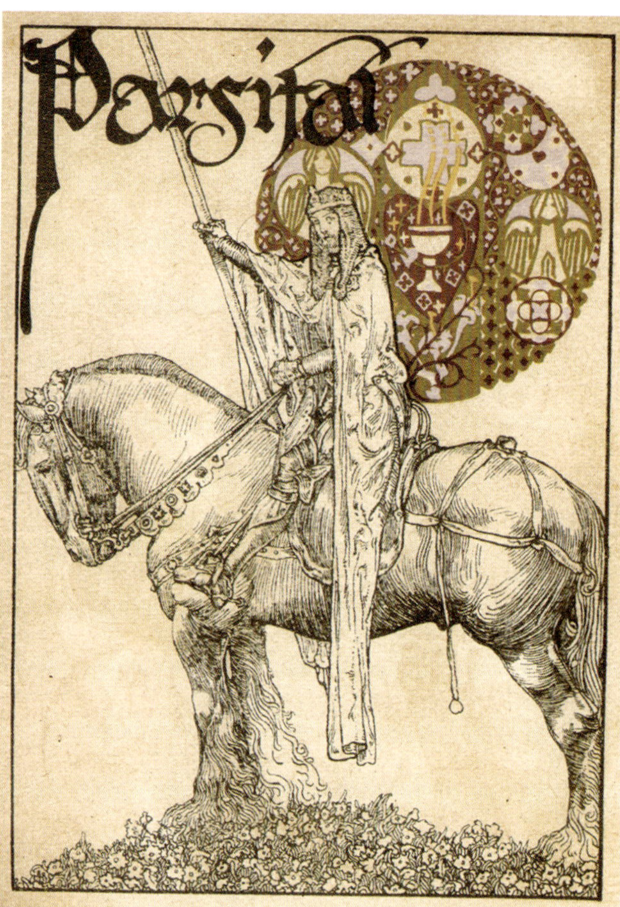

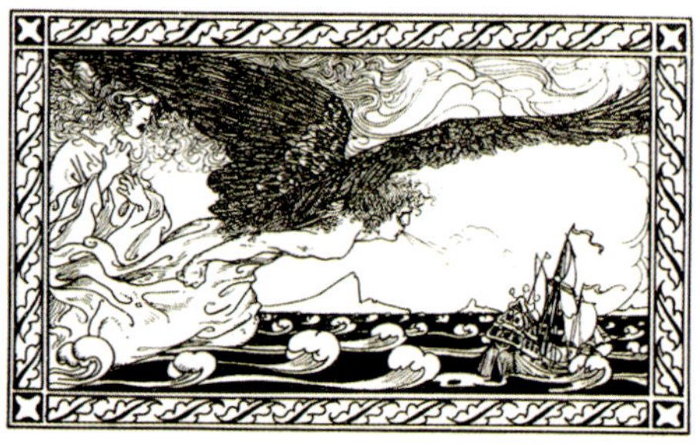

Argument

How a Ship, having passed the Line, was driven by storms to the cold Country towards the South Pole; and how from thence she made her course to the tropical Latitude of the Great Pacific Ocean; and of the strange things that befell; and in what manner the Ancient Mariner came back to his own Country. 1798

A TESTAMENT TO THE RANGE OF HIS DESIGN SKILLS.
Not only did Pogány design and illustrate, he also created the calligraphic text in many of his volumes.

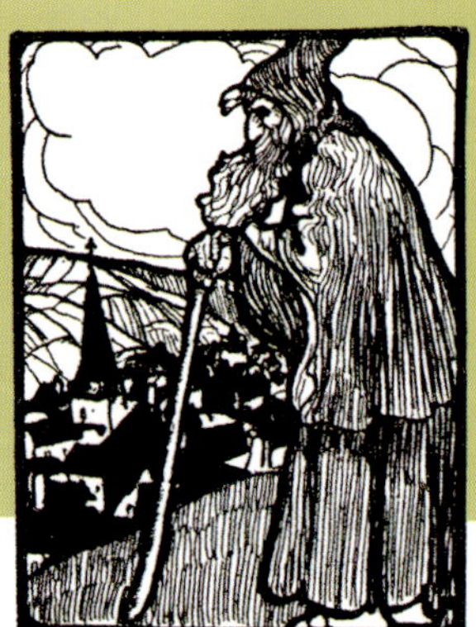

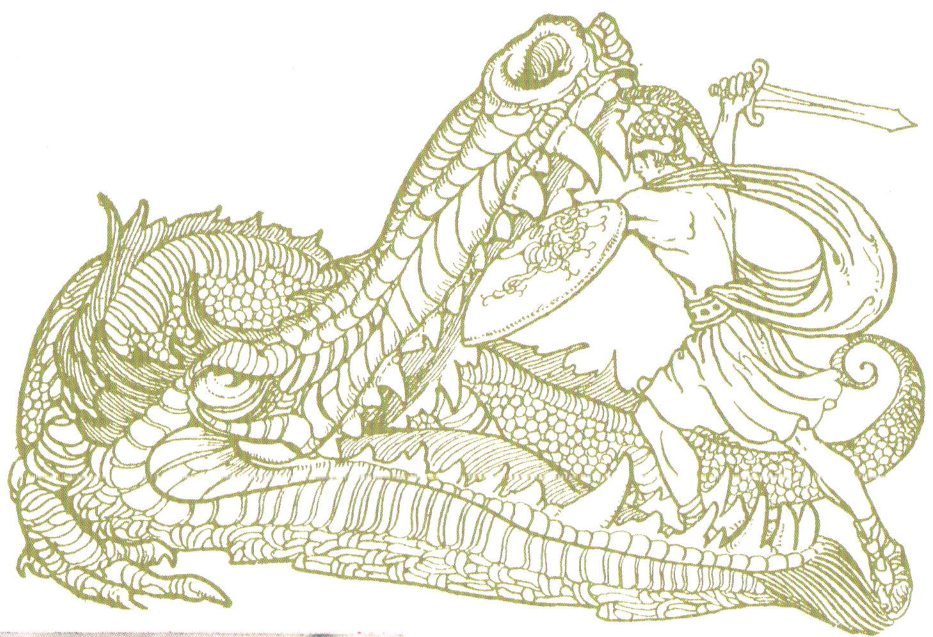

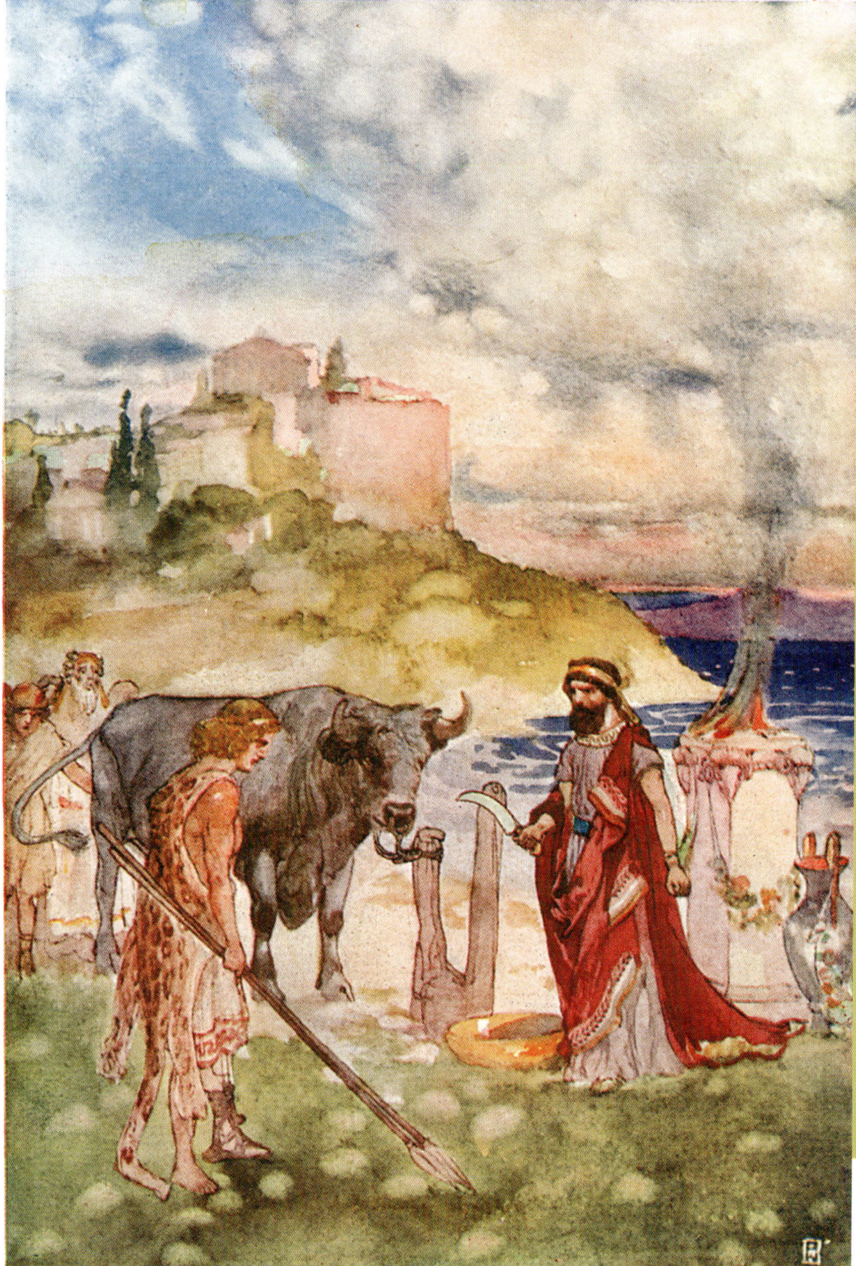

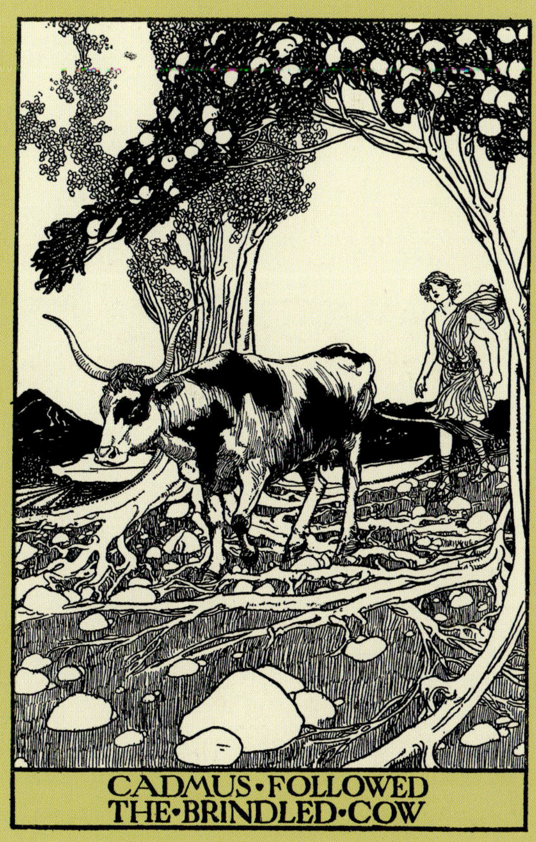

CADMUS·FOLLOWED THE·BRINDLED·COW

Norman Price

1877–1955, Canadian

As a young boy, Norman Price was captivated by the illustrations he saw in *Harper's, The Century,* and *Scribner's.* That passion for art never left him, and in fact, it motivated him to join the ranks of those same illustrators. Born in a small town outside of Toronto, Canada, Price's creativity extended to music as well, and until he was 25, he trained to be a concert pianist. Seeing no future in that, he chose to embrace illustration. Along with two other artists, Price left for London to study art and find employment in London's booming publishing market.

His studies in London took place at the Westminster Institute of Art and the Goldsmith's Institute. Soon thereafter, an ambitious Price founded Carlton Studios, named for the cottage he and some colleagues were renting at the time. In 1909 he spent a brief stint studying in Paris and then moved back to North America in 1911, to go to the publishing capital of New York.

Price found success in New York illustration. With real strength in historical work, and a penchant for accuracy, he acquired many long-lasting clients, including some of those same magazines he admired as a child. Opening a new branch of his own Carlton Studios, he gathered both commercial accounts and editorial work in New York. The book work often reflected his strength, allowing him to explore the historical subject matter he both enjoyed and excelled at. His specialty was American history, and after the passing of Howard Pyle, he became one of the most sought-after illustrators for pirate-related subjects.

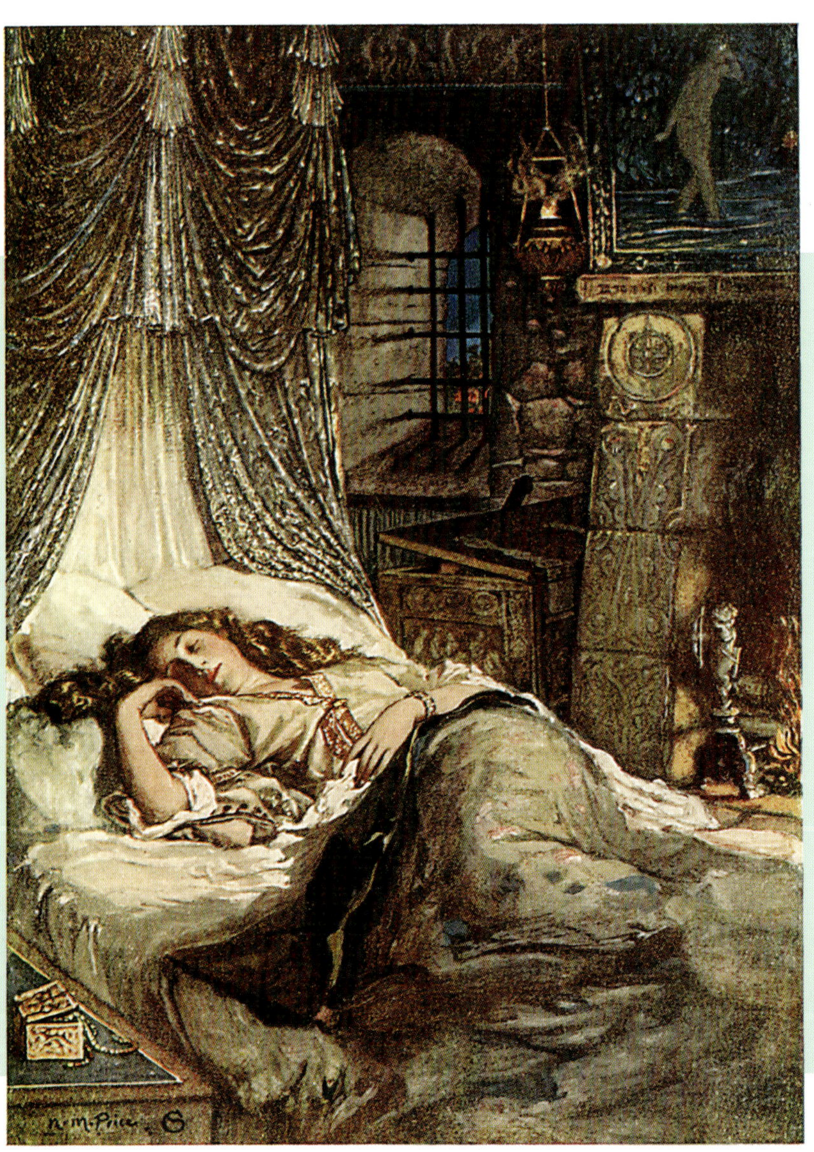

Price, Norman

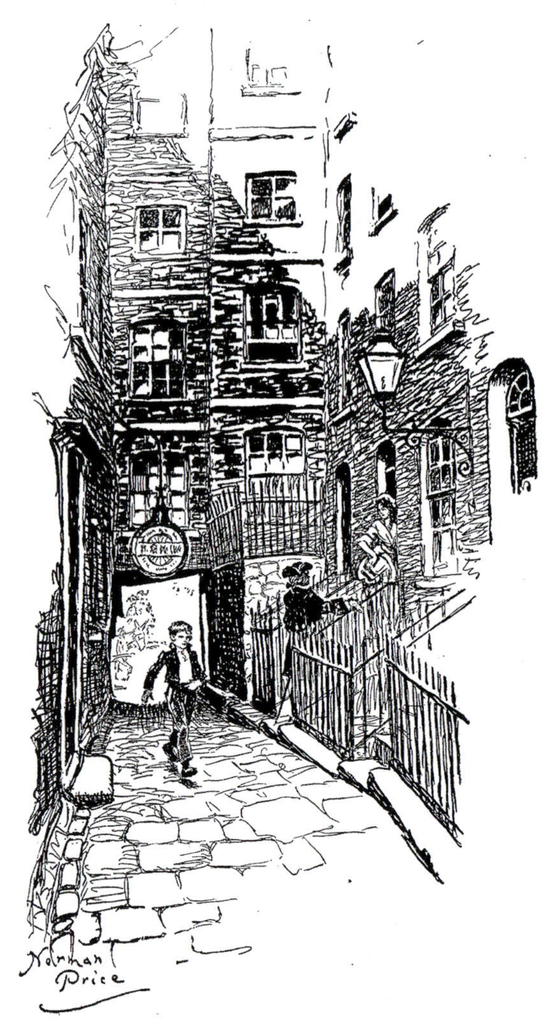

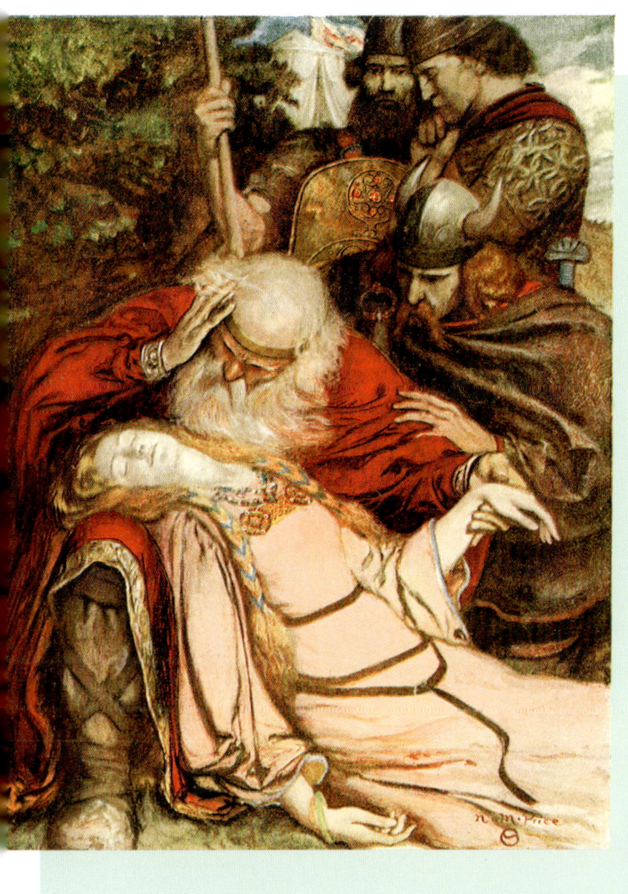

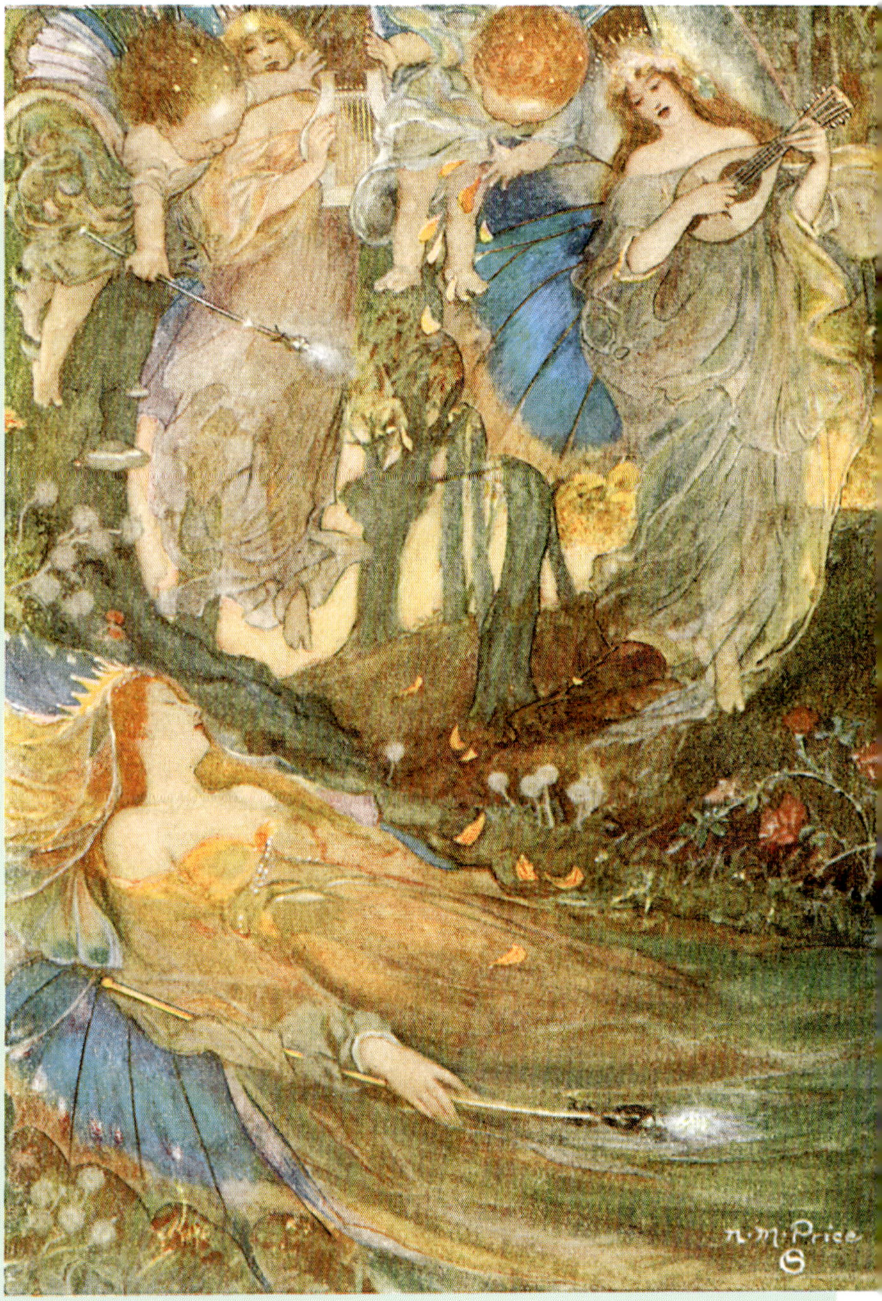

"His medium seems to be a matter of no serious consequence, for one has seen charming drawings in pen and ink, in wash and in a rich profusion of oil or watercolor."

—C. Matlack Price, *The International Studio*

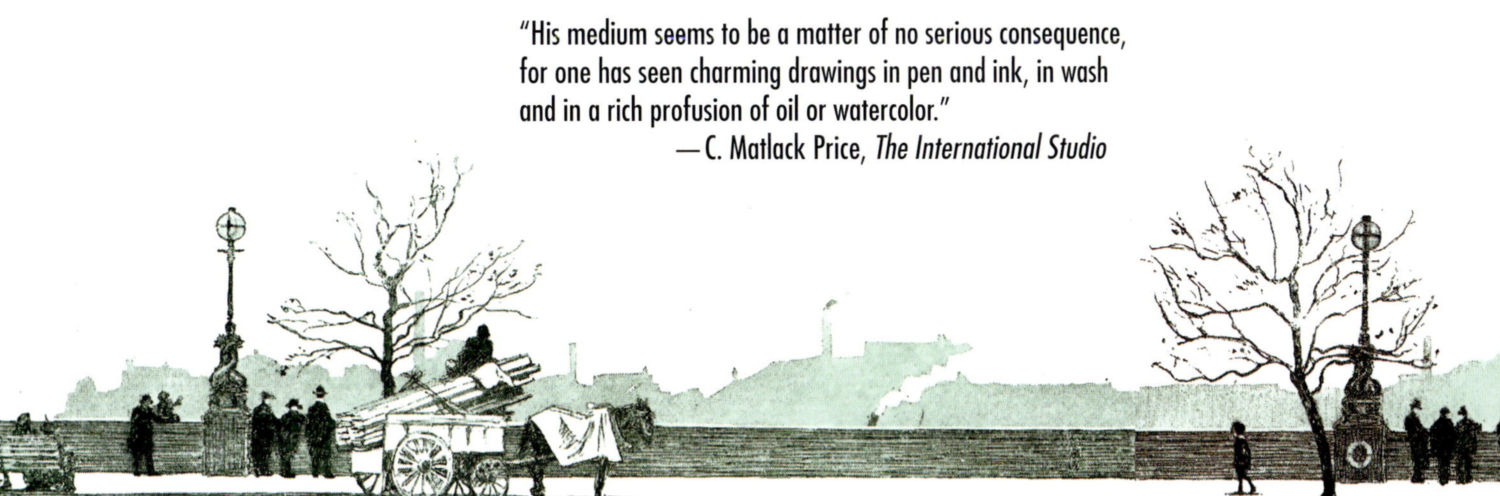

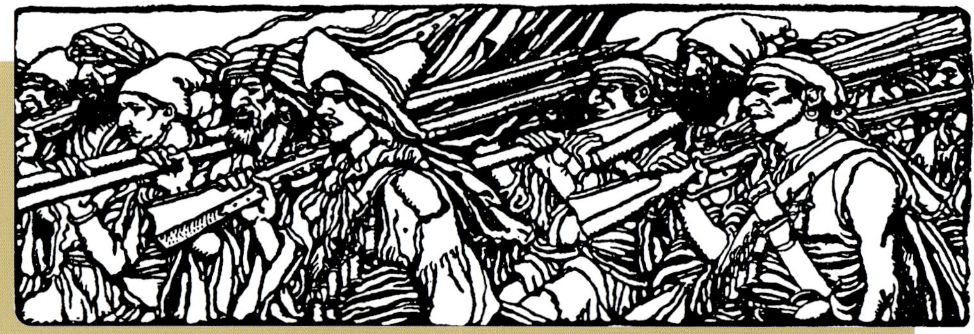

A TRIP TO JAMAICA

In 1889, Pyle journeyed to the island to research *pirates*—the reference and the information he obtained there made him an authority on the subject for the rest of his career.

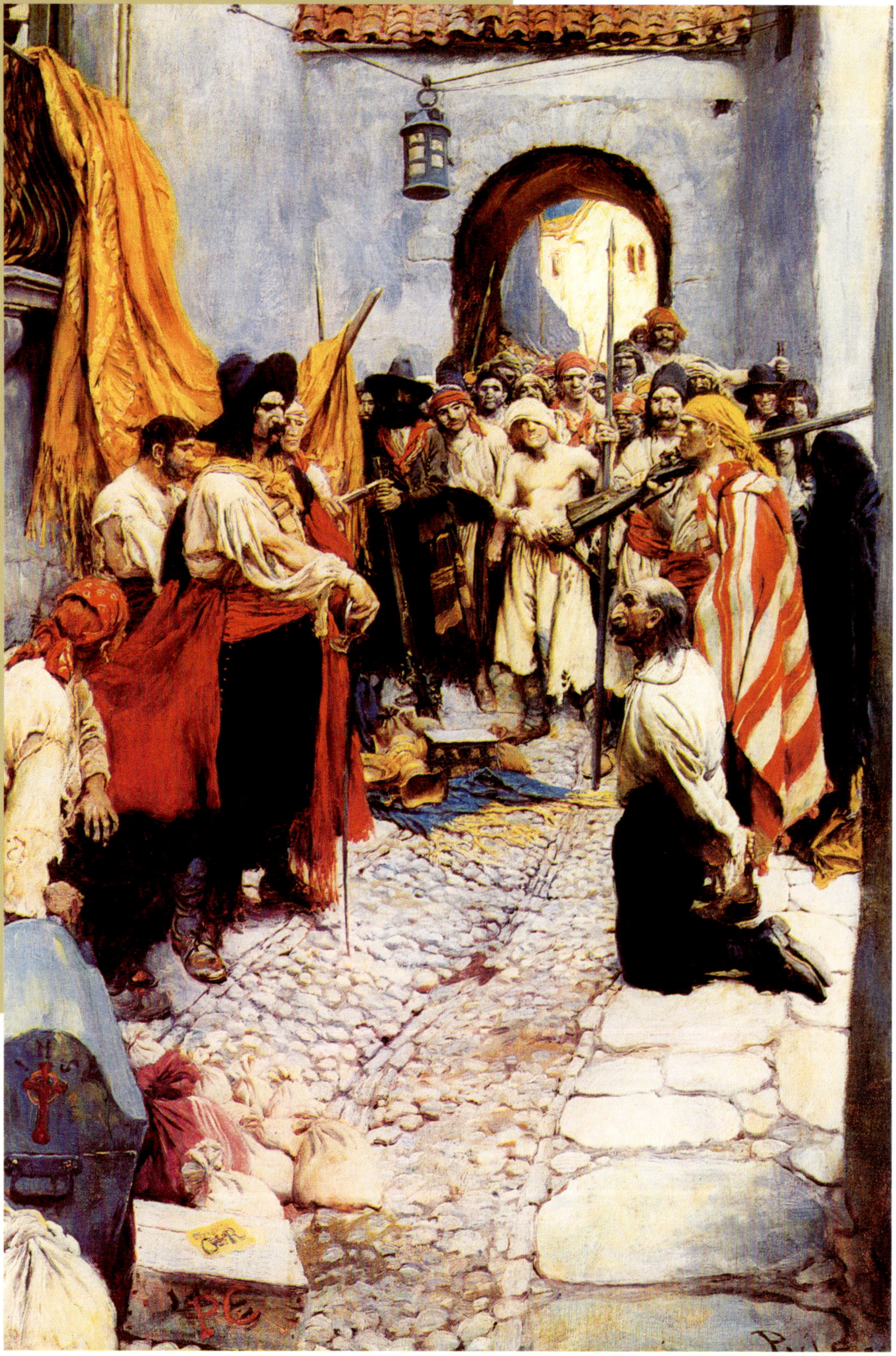

Extorting Tribute from the Citizens
The Fate of a Treasure Town,
Harper's Monthly, December, 1905

Howard Pyle

1853–1911, American

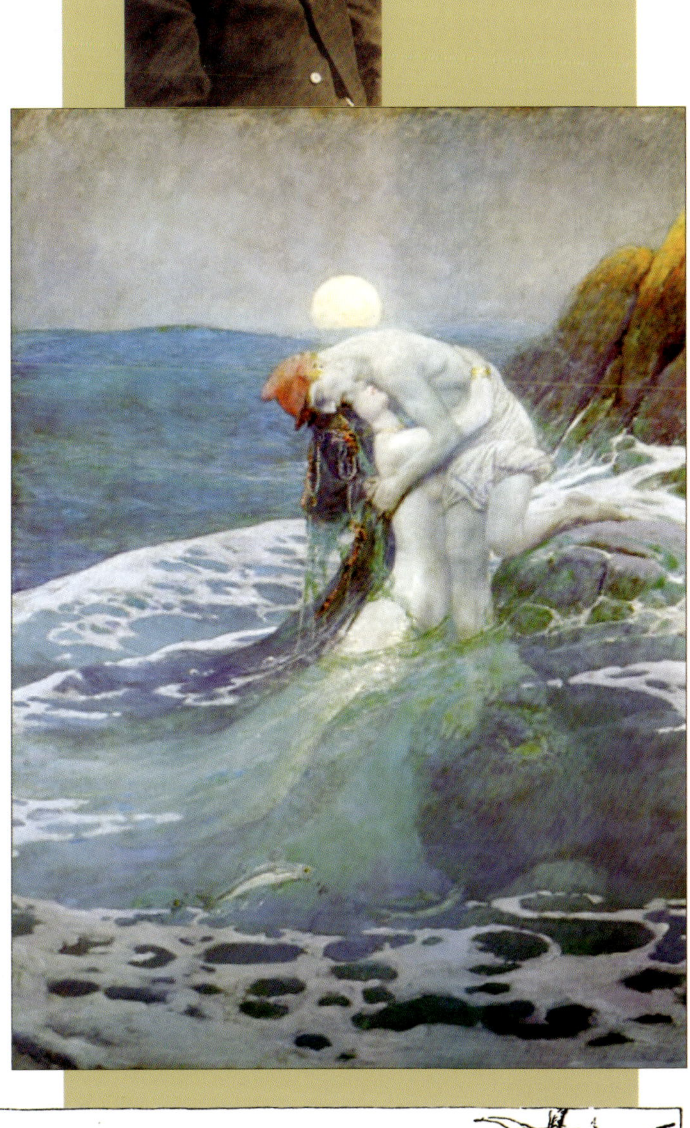

So much of the art form of illustration has been shaped by the efforts of Howard Pyle that he is often referred to as the father of American illustration. Pyle's areas of specialty were American historical and medieval periods (which were very popular in the fiction market at the time), and pirates. It is largely from Howard Pyle's own research and imagery that we have our current visual idea of what a pirate looks like.

Based in the Wilmington, Delaware area, Pyle worked with publishers in both Philadelphia and New York. After a successful entry into the field at the close of the nineteenth century, Pyle was positioned to be one of the biggest stars in an emerging profession, not only as an illustrator, but as an author as well. Not finding enough material to fuel his artistic passion, he found that writing and illustrating together allowed him the freedom to choose his own subjects. He would go on to produce numerous children's books and adventure stories, most in the earlier part of his career, as well as to become a regular contributor of articles for many of the magazines.

Pyle willingly shared his success, and began teaching in the Philadelphia area at Drexel University in 1894. His lectures were well-attended, often by young artists coming from great distances and looking for a chance to benefit from his experience. Pyle's frustration with a lack of real commitment from many students led him to an experiment which changed the field in the United States, and the art world still feels the ripple effect today. In 1900 he left Drexel and shortly afterward founded the Howard Pyle School of Art. Taking on students only after personal interviews, each was hand-selected by Pyle after showing the necessary promise that he felt was needed to shape them into a professional. Students that went through Pyle's program were among the best American illustrators of the day, and many were so impressed with Pyle that they became strong teachers of the craft as well. Classes during the year were held in Wilmington, while summer studies were held at a mill in Chadds Ford, Pennsylvania, on the Brandywine River. It is this river and the surrounding valley that gave its name to the "Brandywine school," Pyle's particular style of illustration.

J. W. Aylward, Harvey Dunn, Frank Schoonover, Stanley Arthurs, Violet Oakley, Thornton Oakley, and N. C. Wyeth were just a few of the pupils who passed through Pyle's tutelage and became stars of their own generation.

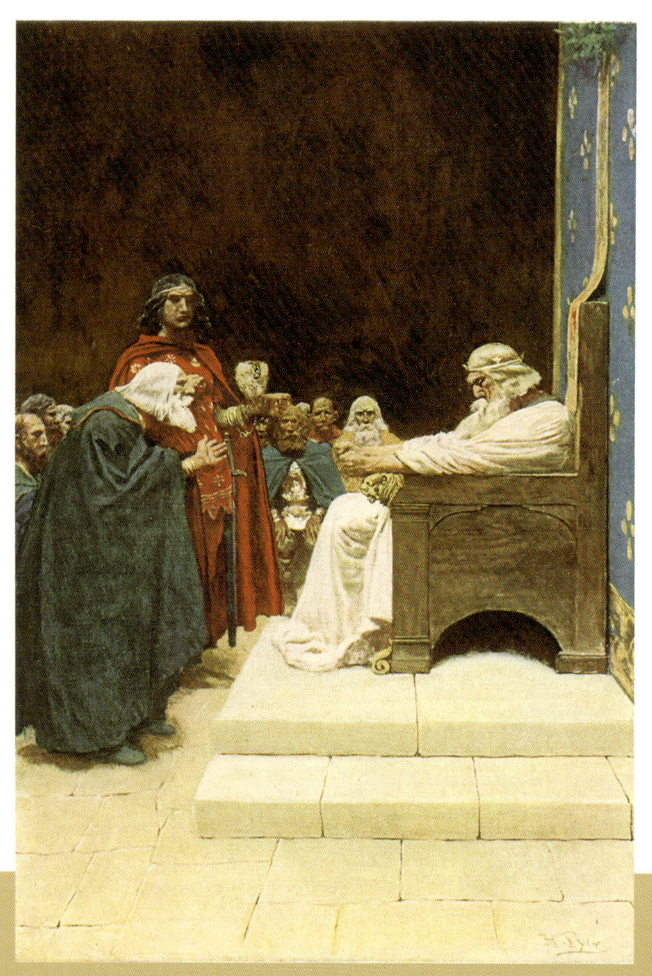

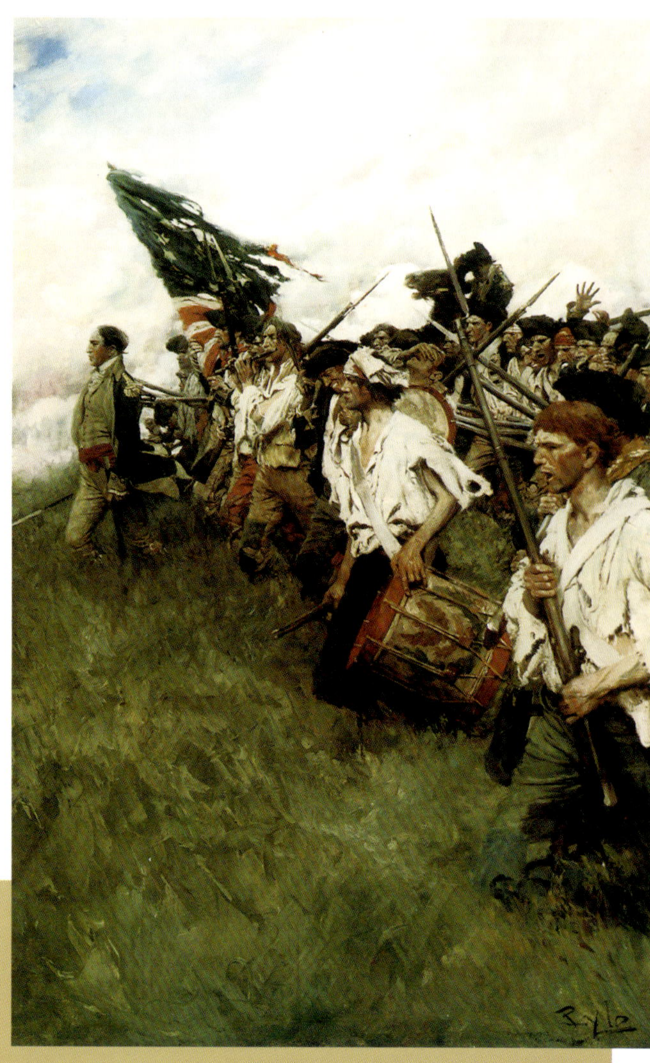

POCKETS OF RED
Pyle effectively used the color red to bring attention wherever he wanted it.

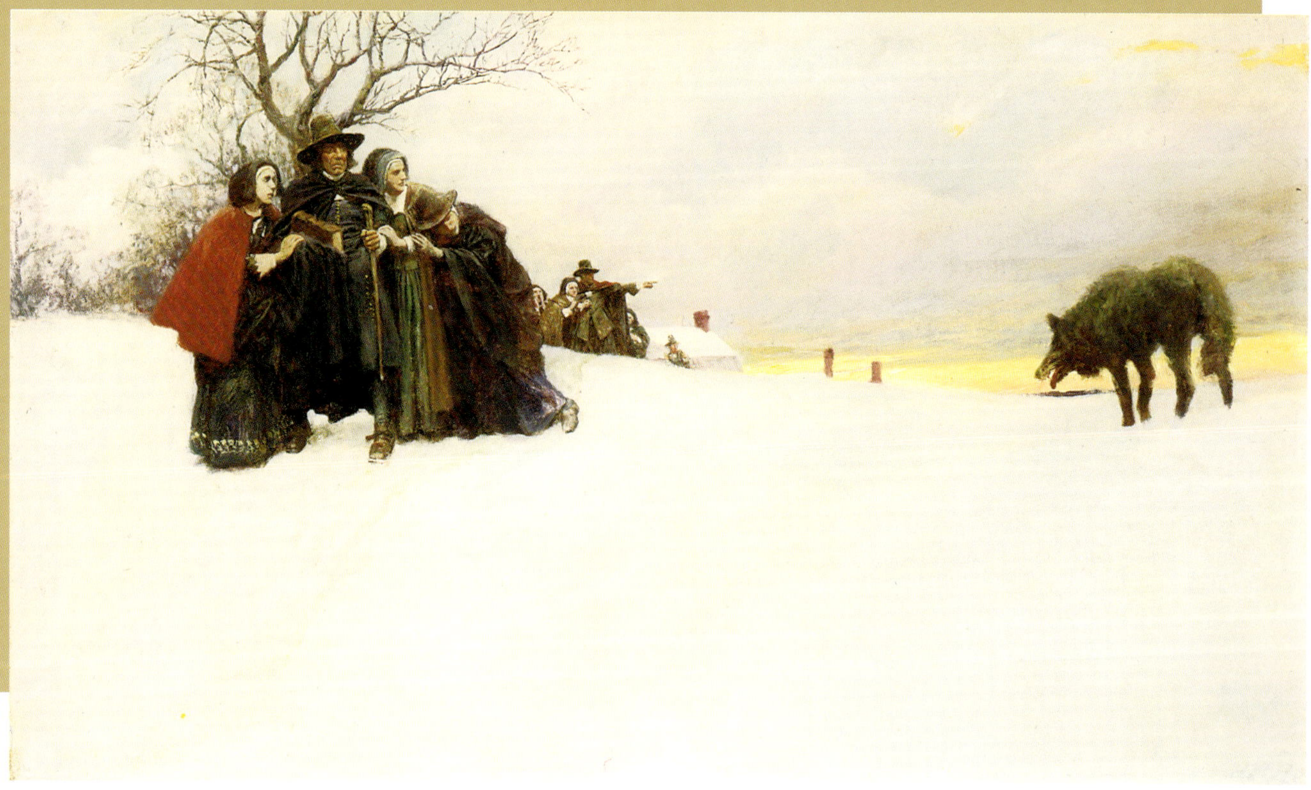

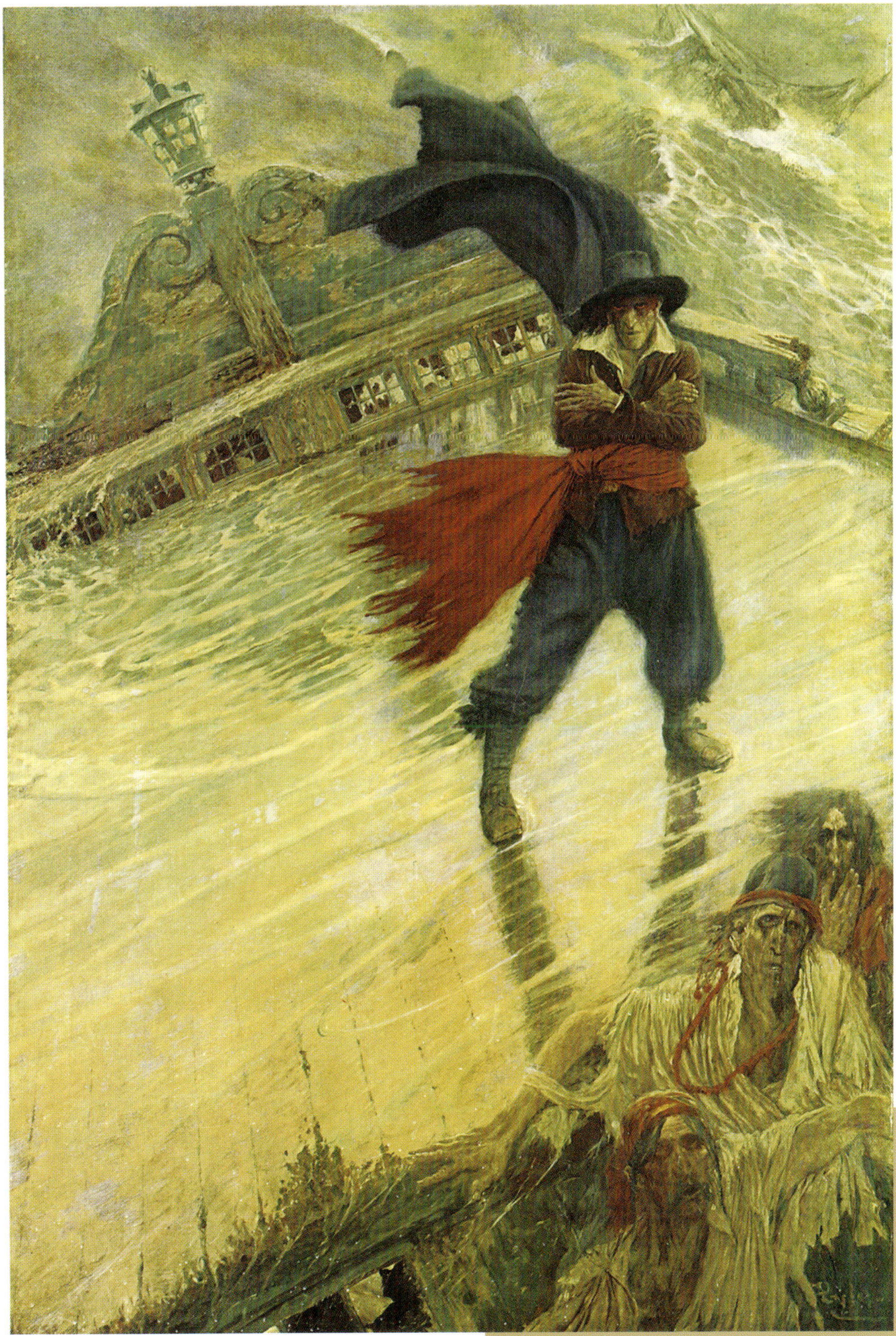

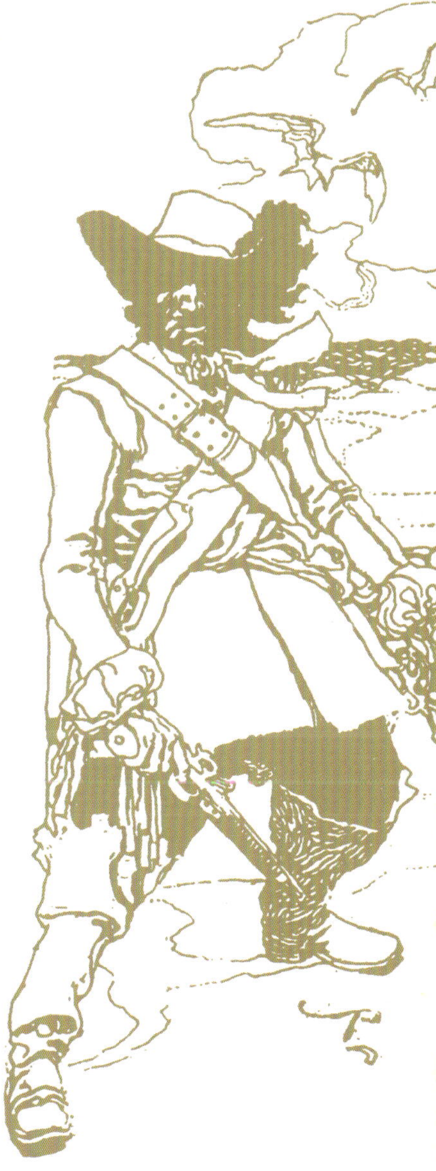

"Project your mind into your subject until you actually live in it."
— *Howard Pyle*

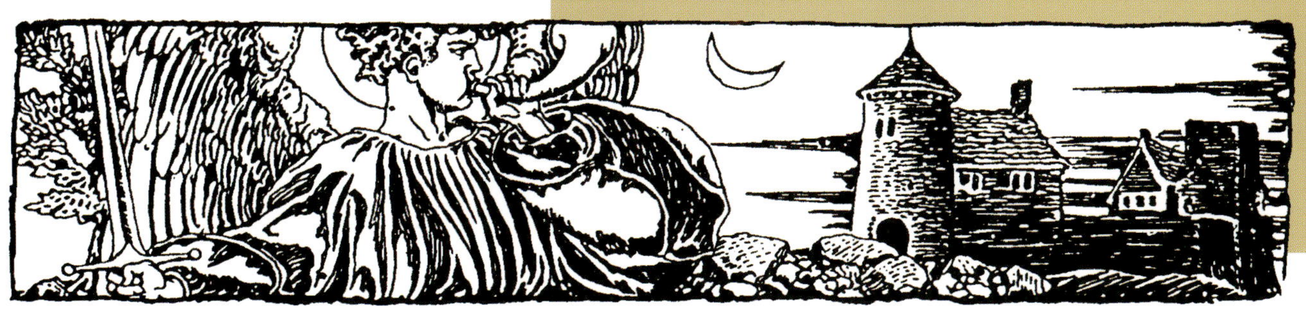

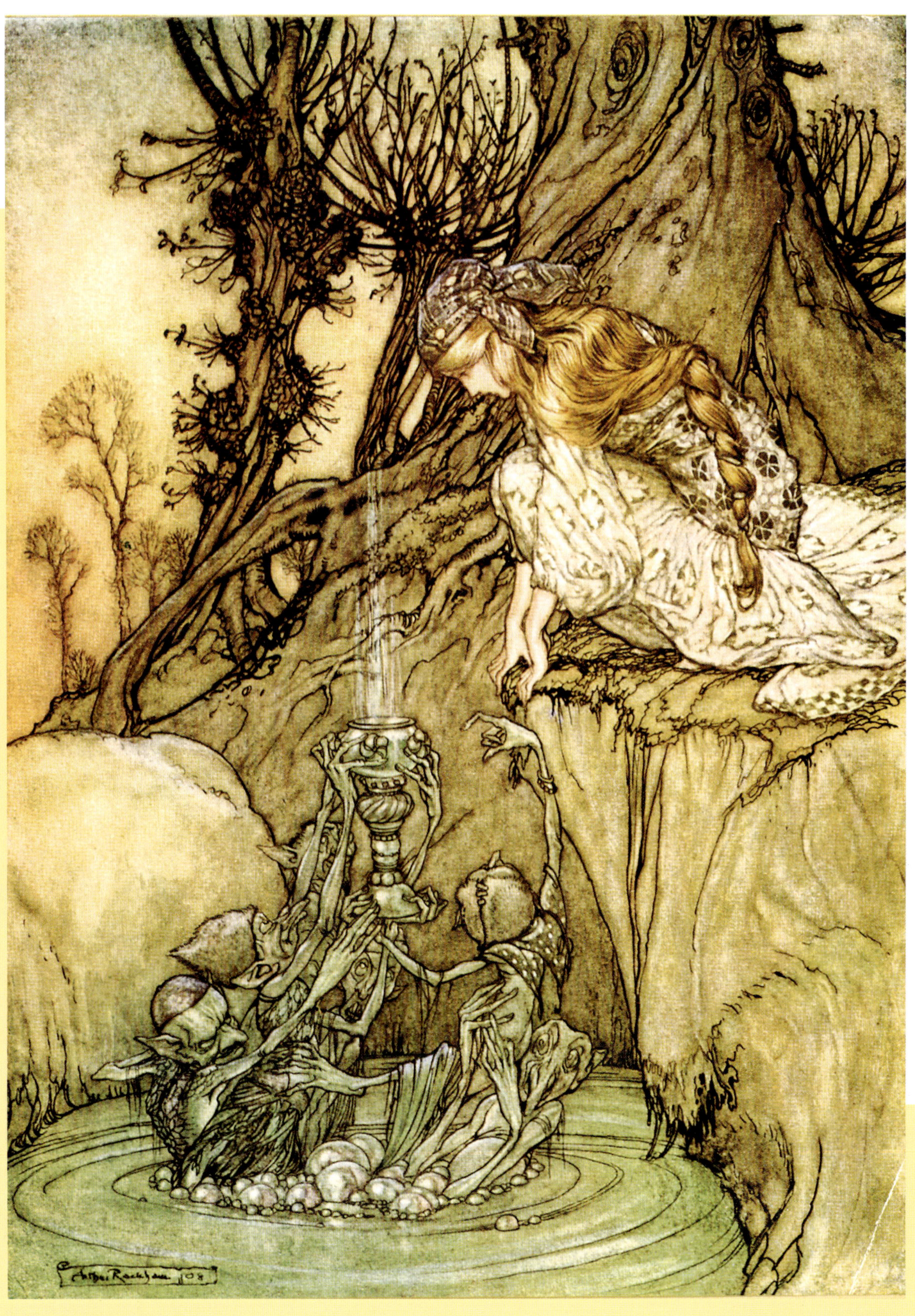

Rackham, Arthur

ARTHUR RACKHAM

1867–1939, British

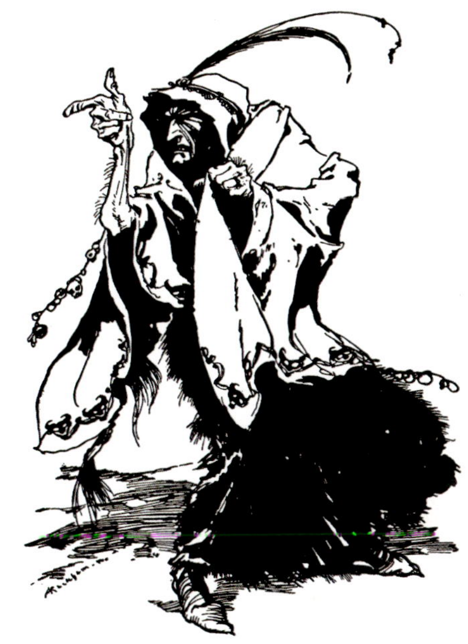

By all accounts, Arthur Rackham was a practical man, unusually so considering his fame would come as an illustrator of fairies. Born in a London suburb, his earliest ventures into an artistic career were close to home, and far less fanciful than his later work. He also cautiously maintained his job as a clerk for years before pursuing an illustration career. When he did focus his career exclusively to art in 1893, his initial impact was minor. It would take a few years for Rackham to find his style, and a market that embraced it.

In 1905 publisher William Heinemann proposed a project that would change illustrators' careers for nearly a generation. Full-color printing was just becoming affordable, and the publisher found Arthur Rackham's style to be an ideal pairing with a classic American tale—*Rip Van Winkle* by Washington Irving. It was published with 51 tipped-in full-color plates that followed the text block. It was a huge success, and became the outstanding "gift book" of the holiday season. This inspired a new era in publishing—gift books from various publishers became the pride of their annual publishing seasons, and the pinnacle of an illustrator's portfolio. Arthur Rackham produced one of these titles nearly every year after that first book, long after his contemporaries had moved on to other areas in illustration.

While many artists of fairy tales and fantasy had to diversify into other fields as the age of the gift book came to a close, Rackham was secure in his market. His ink-heavy style drew fans in adult markets as well. With projects as varied as Shakespeare titles, Poe's tales, or *The Compleat Angler,* Rackham was not solely a children's book illustrator; he was an artist for all people who loved what his drawings brought to the story. Most titles throughout his career were produced by William Heinemann, Hodder & Stoughton, and George Harrap.

Late in his career Rackham traveled to the United States for the first time, and was astounded to find that the American audience welcomed him with great fanfare. His last project was one he had longed to do for most of his life. In 1936 he was given a contract and an opportunity to illustrate *The Wind in the Willows* for the Limited Editions Club of New York. He completed the 16 plates shortly before his death in 1939.

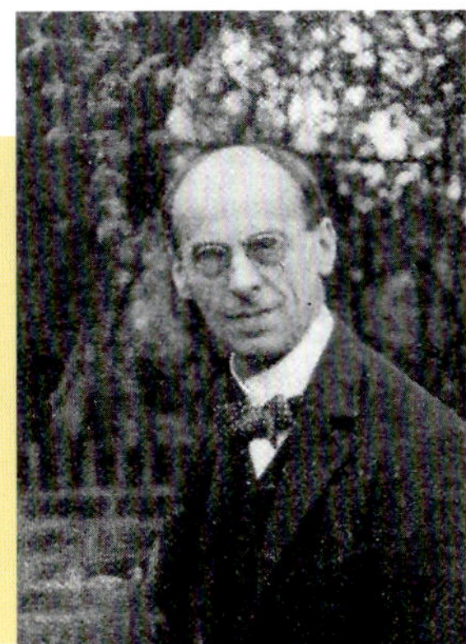

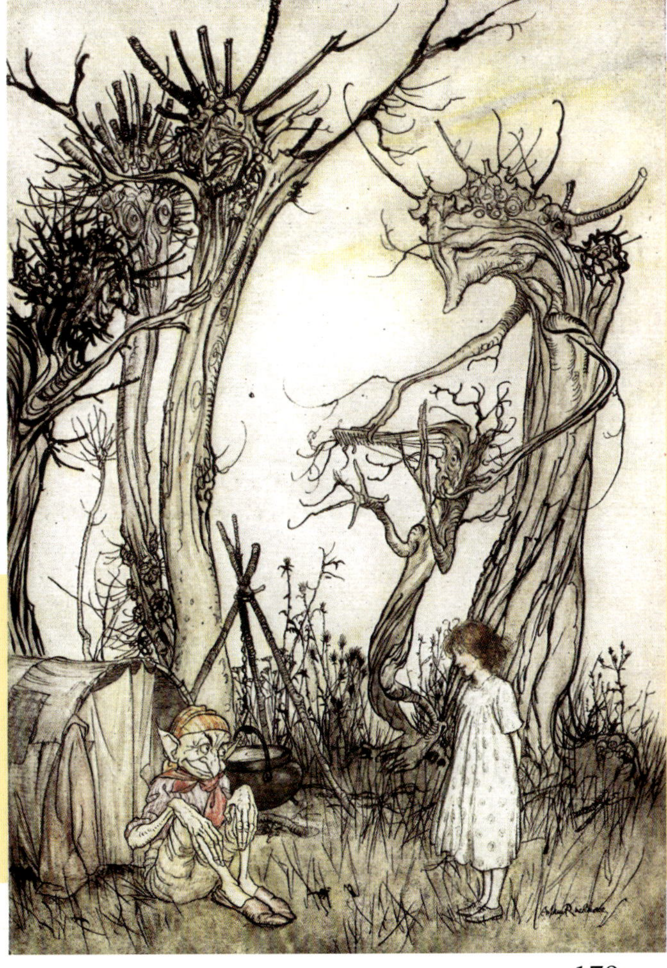

THE MASTER OF THE FAIRY TALE
The winding, organic line was Rackham's greatest ally.

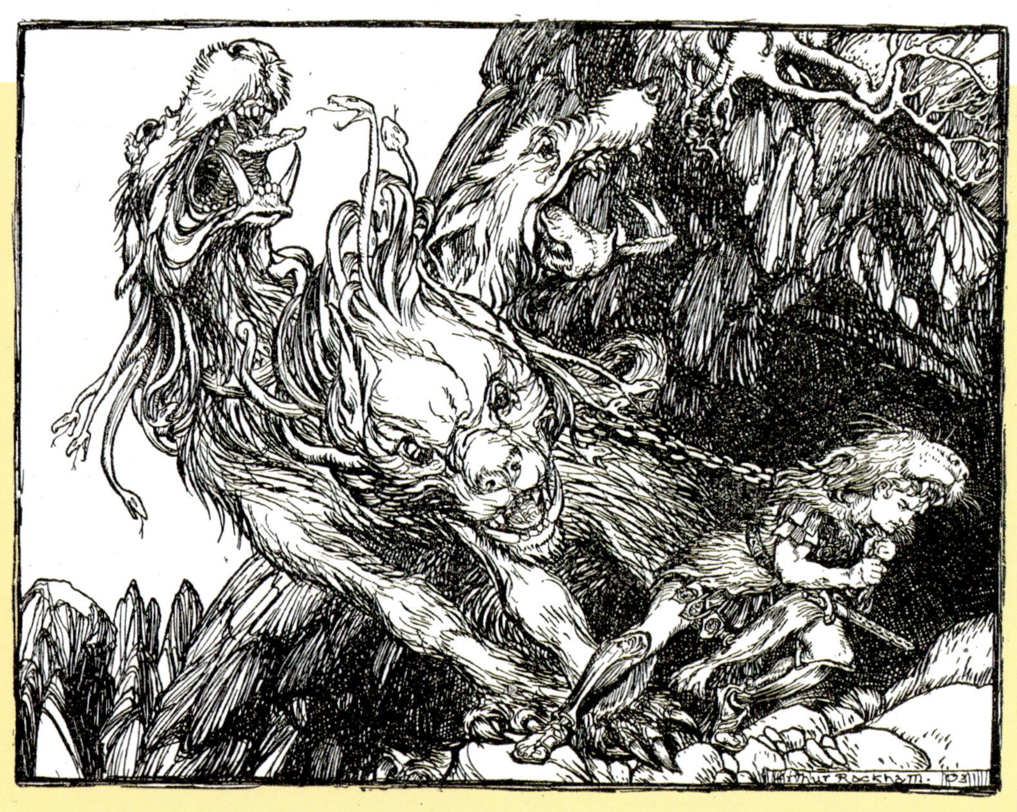

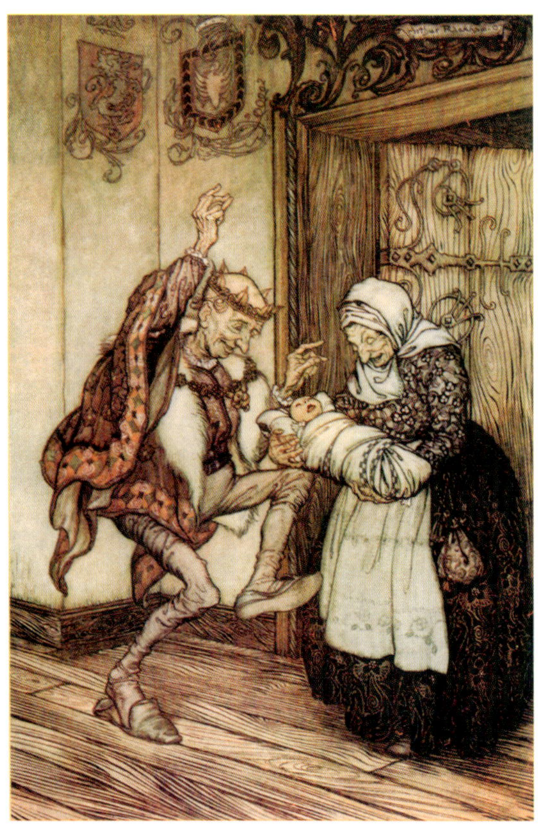

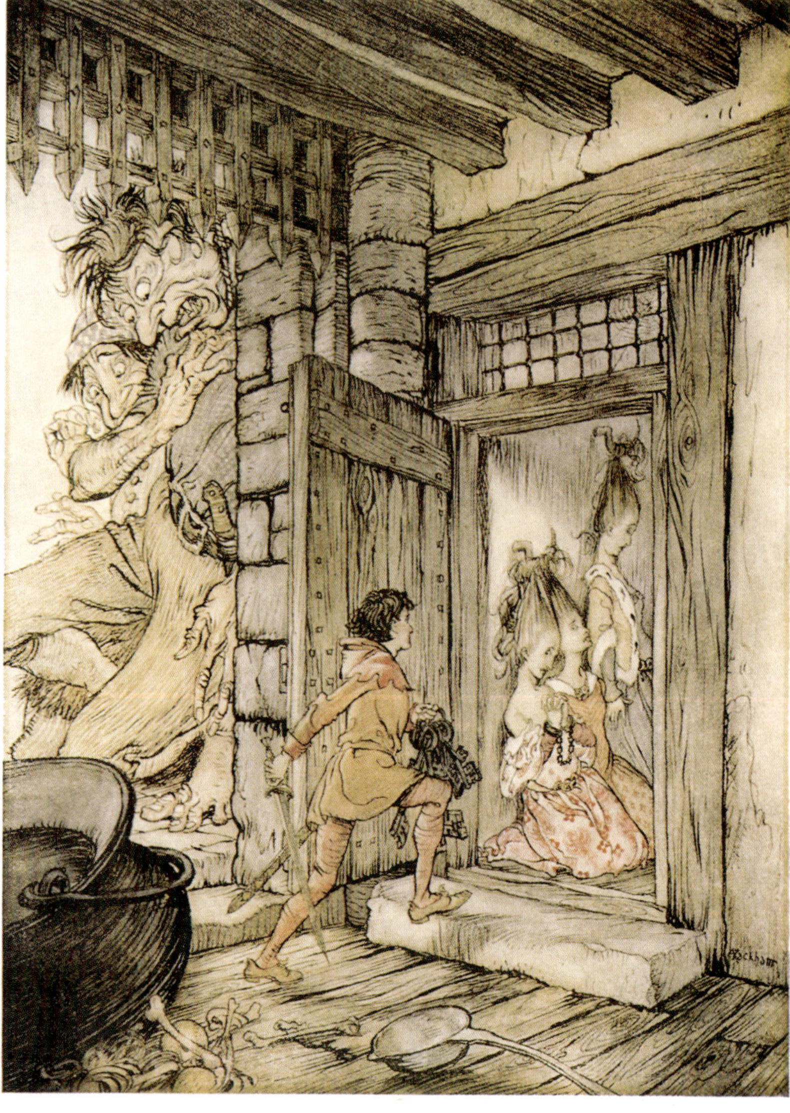

Rackham, Arthur

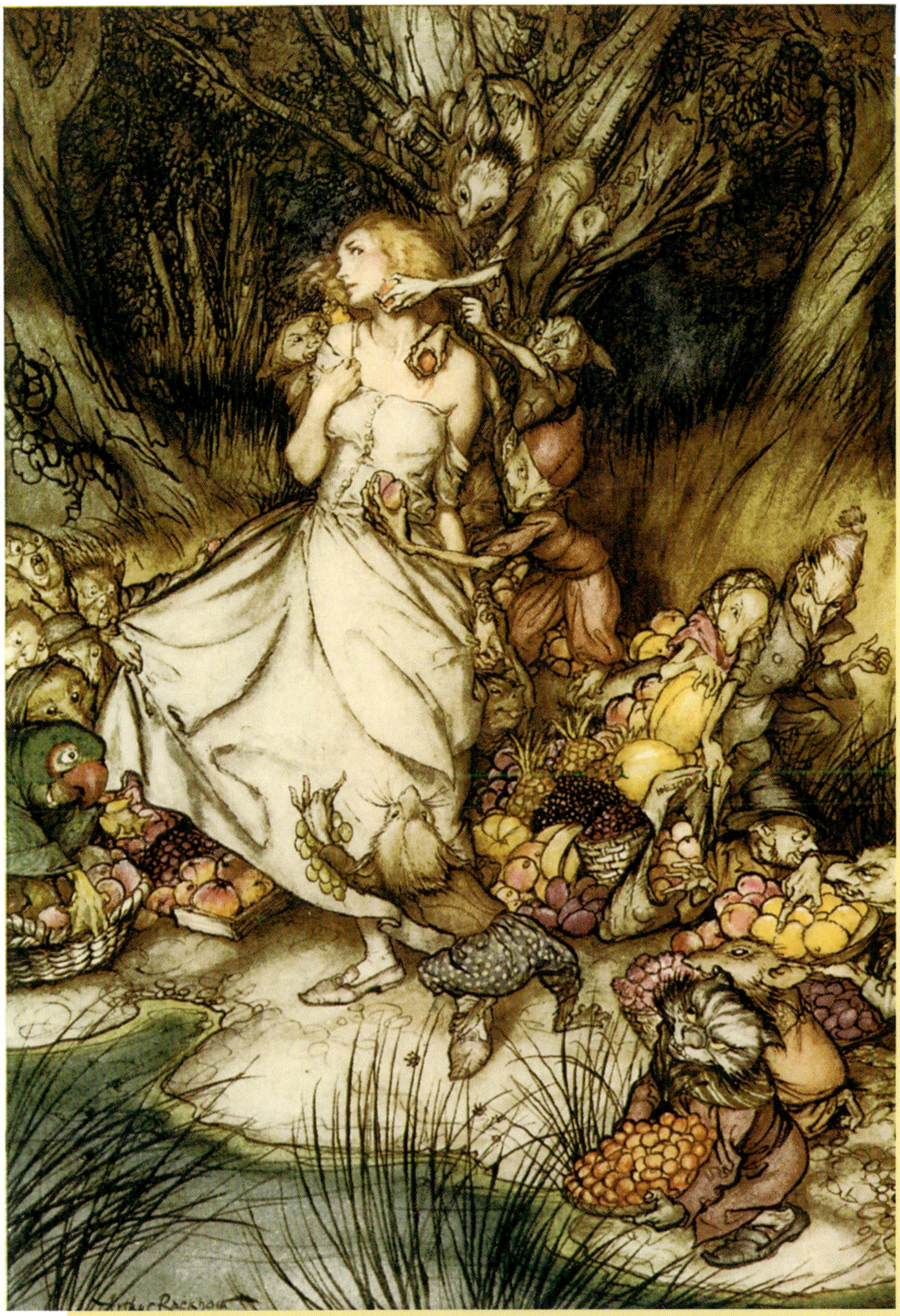

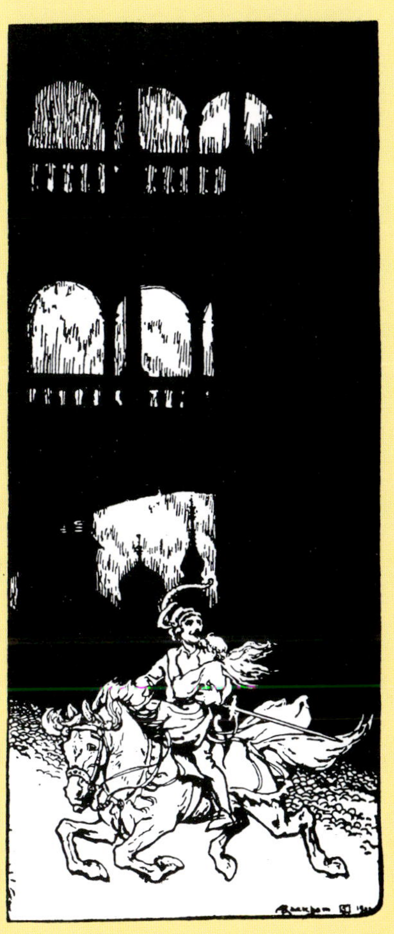

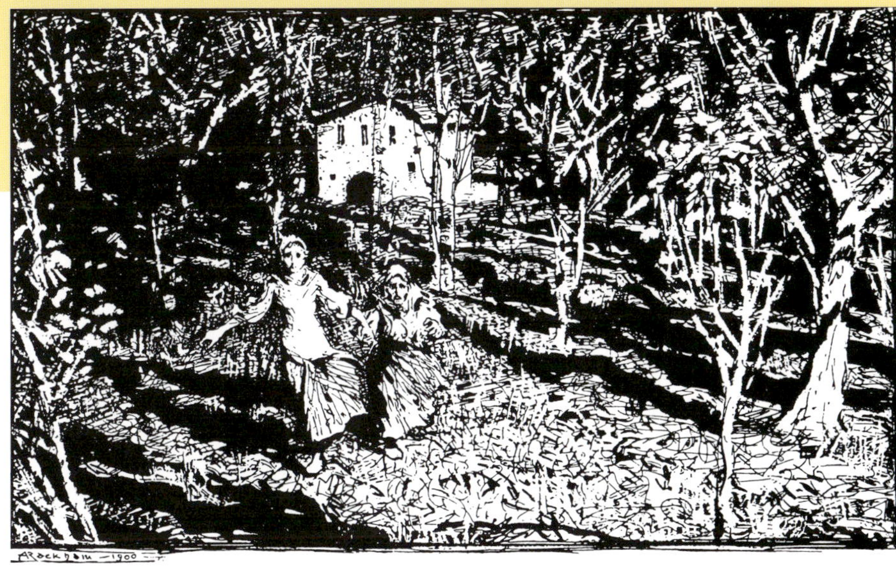

Stephen Reid
1873~1948, Scottish

Born of humble beginnings in the farmlands of Scotland, Stephen Reid developed as a painter from his early childhood. As a young adult he worked for four years in his uncle's office, and then spent a year studying art near home before leaving to attend the Royal Scottish Academy in Edinburgh. After three years there, with letters of introduction, he set out to London in 1899 to make his way as an artist.

Reid's earliest assignments were line works in magazines, with occasional color work for children's books. He also spent some time teaching life drawing at King's College in Kensington alongside Eleanor Fortescue Brickdale and Byam Shaw. Topics that recurred in his book illustration work included Celtic mythology, pirates, and the works of Shakespeare. Always attracted to historical subjects, he began working with much larger projects during World War I, focusing on more serious historical subject matter. He continued to pursue that work later in his career, frequently exhibiting historicals, landscapes, and portraits at both the Royal Academy and the Royal British Academy.

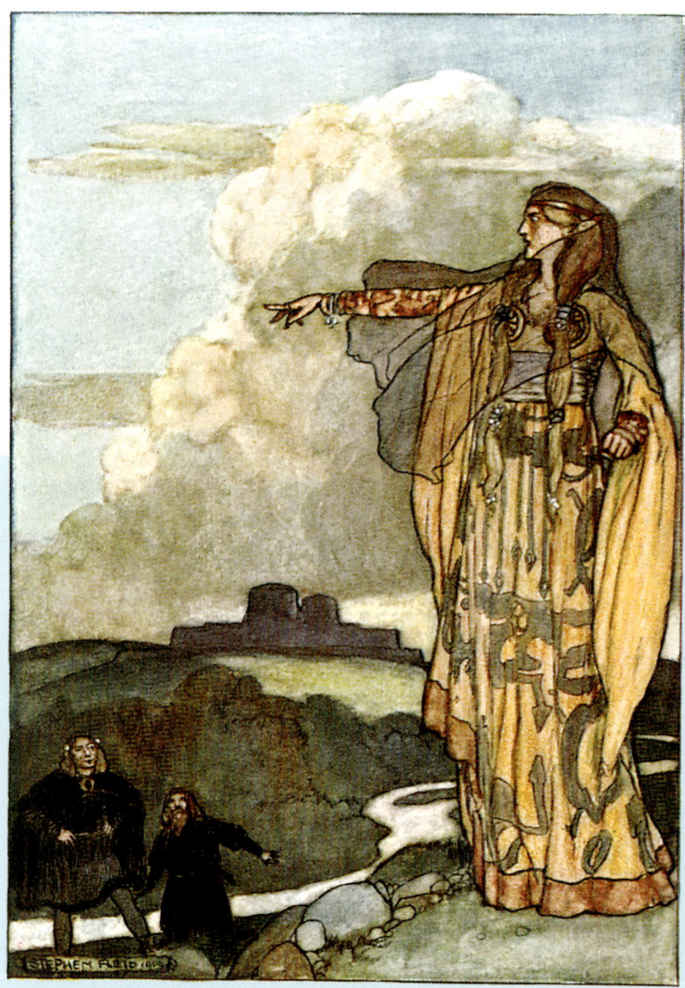

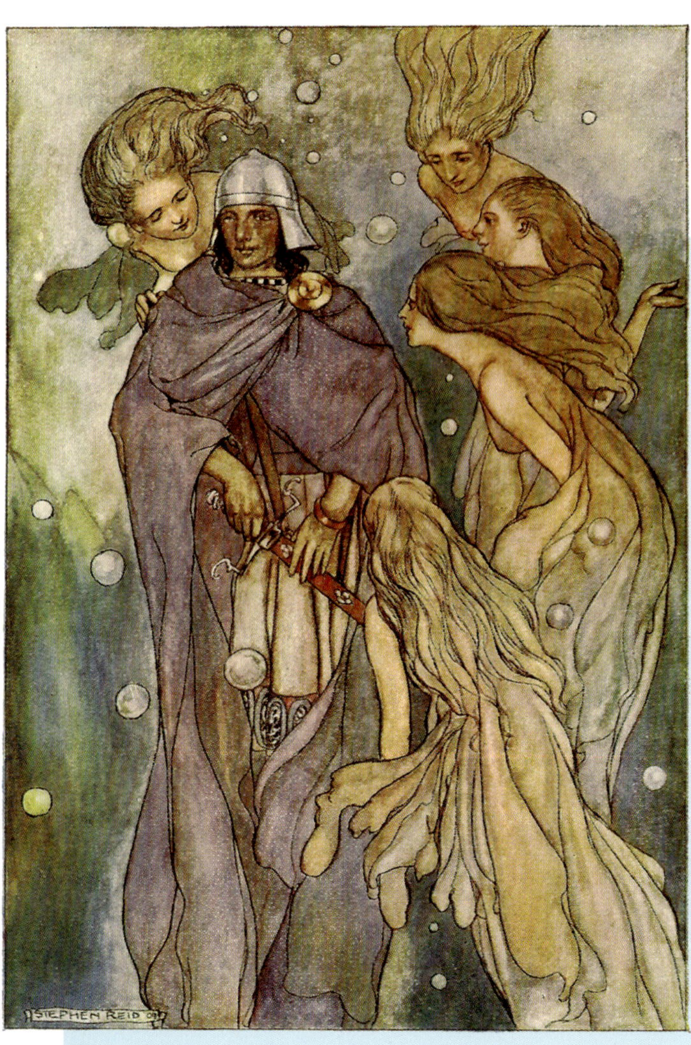

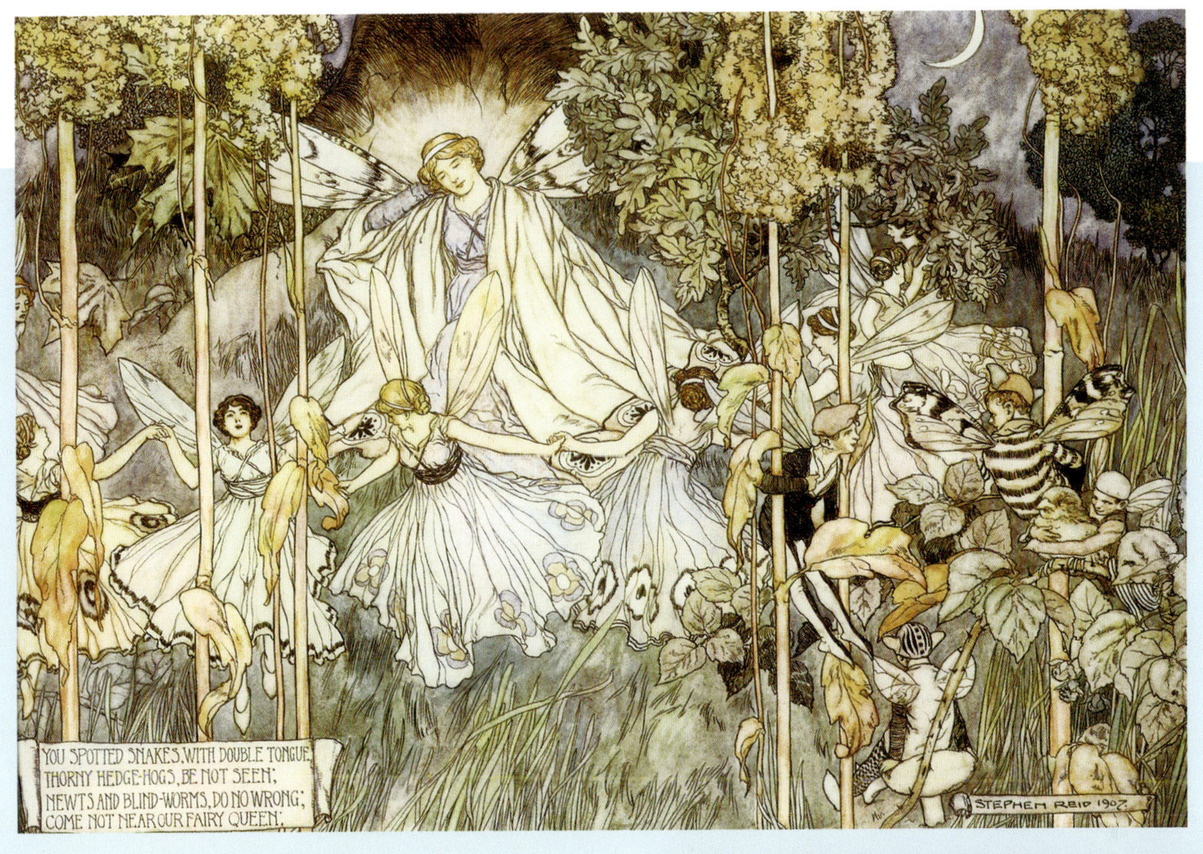
YOU SPOTTED SNAKES, WITH DOUBLE TONGUE,
THORNY HEDGE-HOGS, BE NOT SEEN;
NEWTS AND BLIND-WORMS, DO NO WRONG;
COME NOT NEAR OUR FAIRY QUEEN.
STEPHEN REID 1907

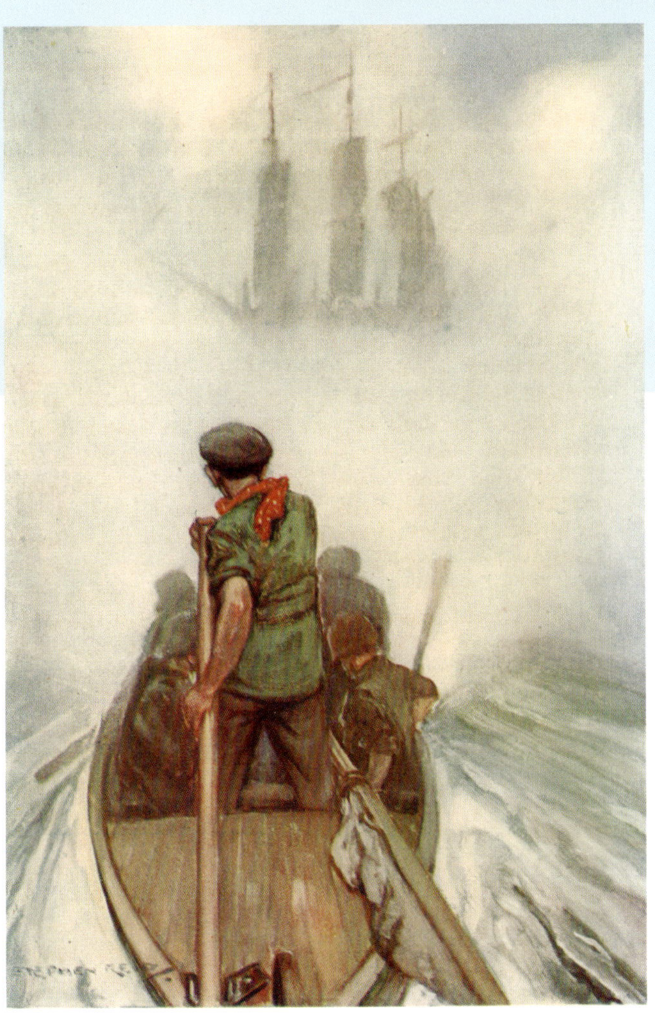

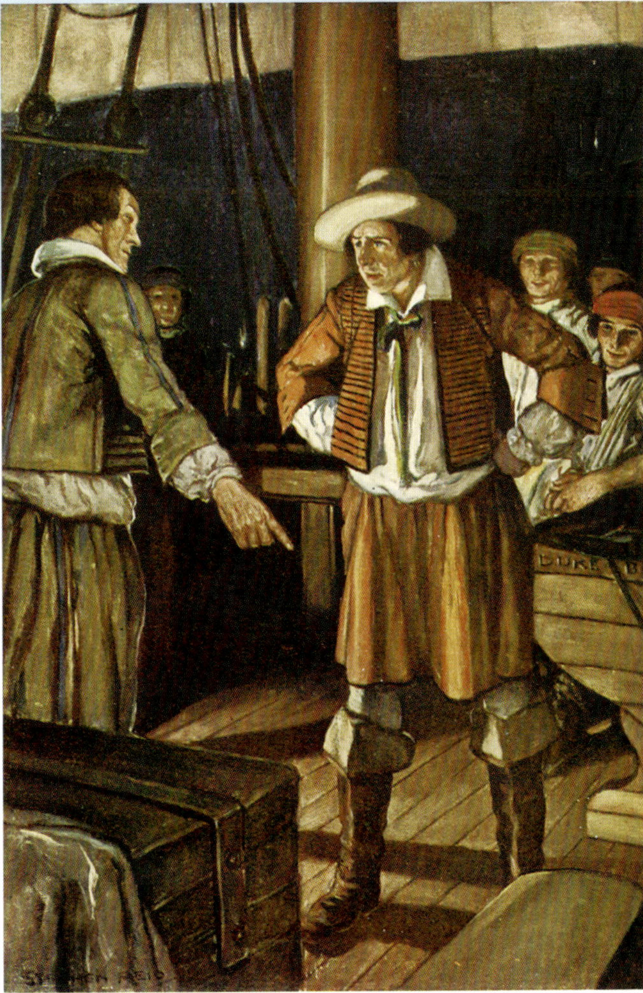

Frederic Remington

1861–1909, American

The son of a newspaperman-turned-military hero, young Frederic Remington was a rough-hewn sort, more likely to cause fights than to contemplate art. In pursuit of fortune he headed West after failed stints at both military school and Yale Art School. Remington soon realized that the West was vanishing, and that so much of what he loved about the ruggedness and wild nature of it would be gone in the short years to come. He applied his fledgling skills to capturing and recording the West as it was. Though not an immediate success, he improved his abilities with some persistence, and the publications in the East and their readers soon embraced his vision. First-hand knowledge of his subjects and a nearly unmatched mastery of drawing horses made him the premier Western illustrator of the day.

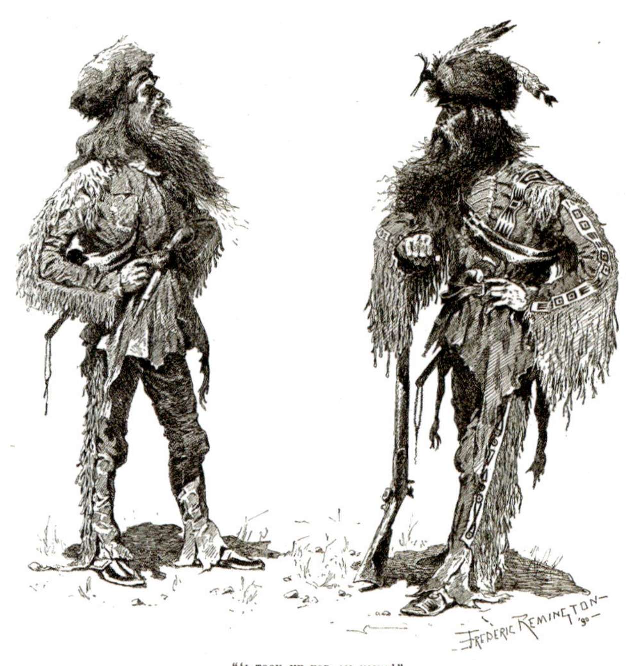

"'I TOOK YE FOR AN INJIN.'"

His earliest assignments were sketches done on location for publications such as *Harper's Weekly,* or *Frank Leslie's Illustrated Monthly,* and Remington gradually went on to work with most of the major publications of the day. One departure from Western themes was the coverage Remington provided for the Spanish-American War, particularly the Rough Riders, with which Theodore Roosevelt was associated. That was the basis for a friendship between the two men, who shared many characteristics, among them, their mutual love and fascination for the frontier. Remington produced a number of books and magazine articles with Roosevelt over the next several years.

An exclusive contract to work with *Collier's* in 1903 lasted little more than a year. Other illustrators began competing with Remington for the same subject matter, and Remington's disapproval of their work soon soured him from illustration. He devoted the remainder of his years to exhibitions of his paintings and sculpture.

As adept at sculpture as he was at painting, Remington produced many fine bronzes in addition to his drawings and oils. Just as he was beginning to gain acceptance in fine art circles, his life was cut short in 1909 when he was stricken by acute appendicitis.

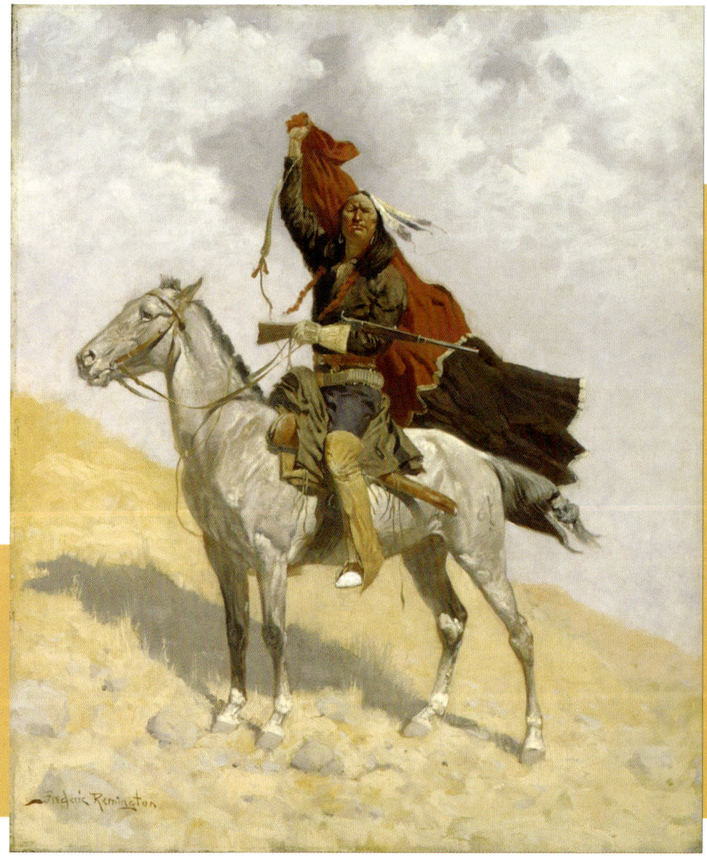

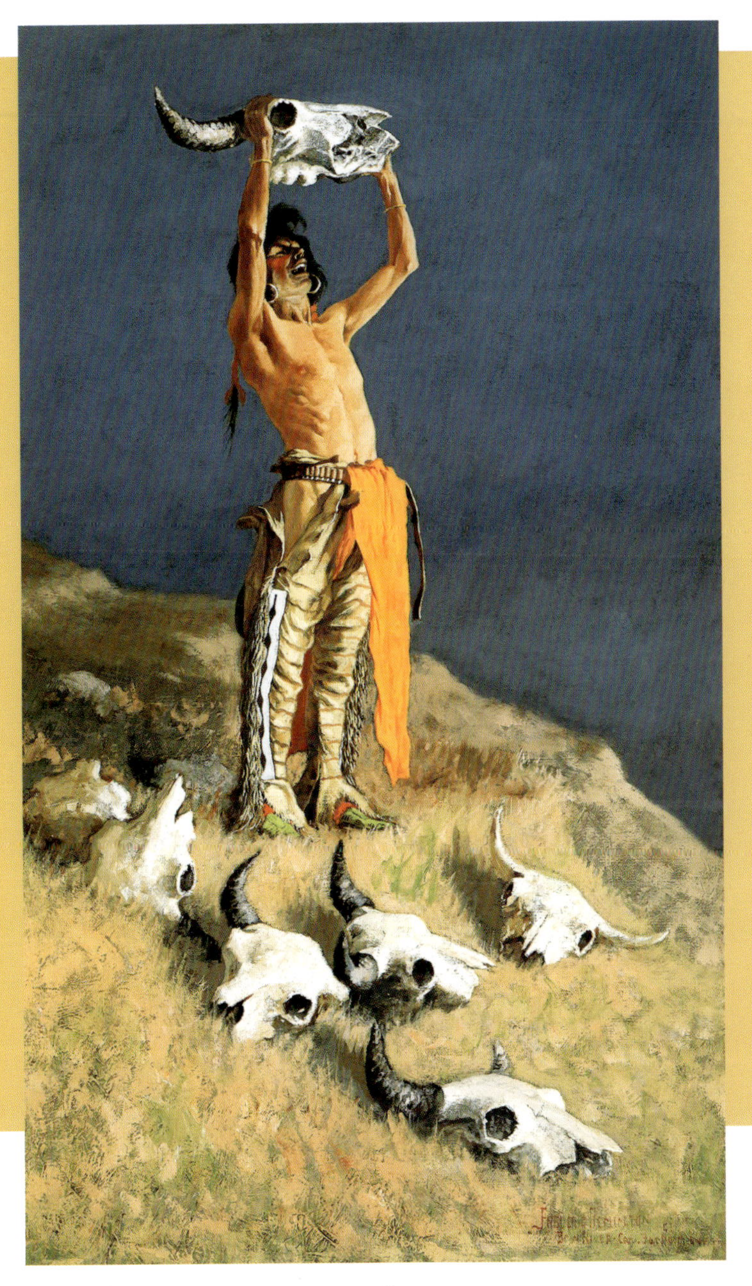

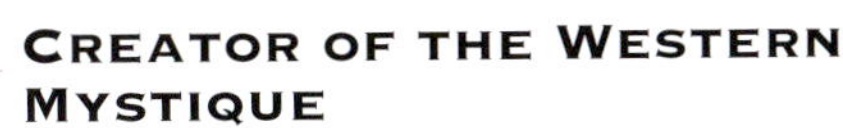

CREATOR OF THE WESTERN MYSTIQUE

In line and in color, Remington defined the West for most of America and the rest of the world.

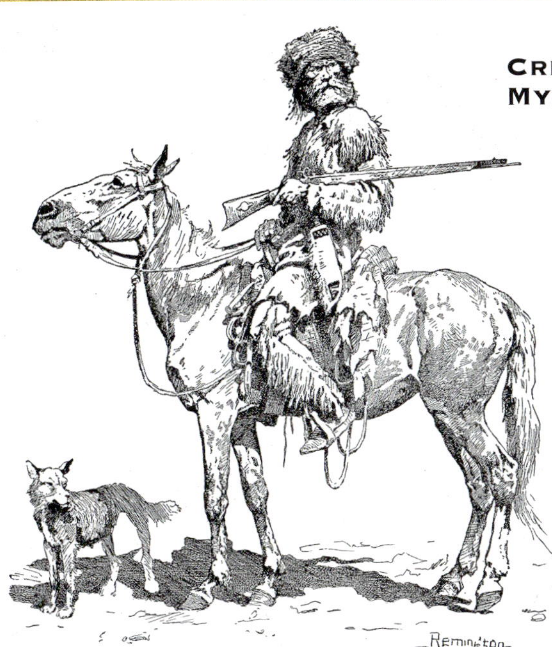

Henry Reuterdahl

1870~1925, Swedish-American

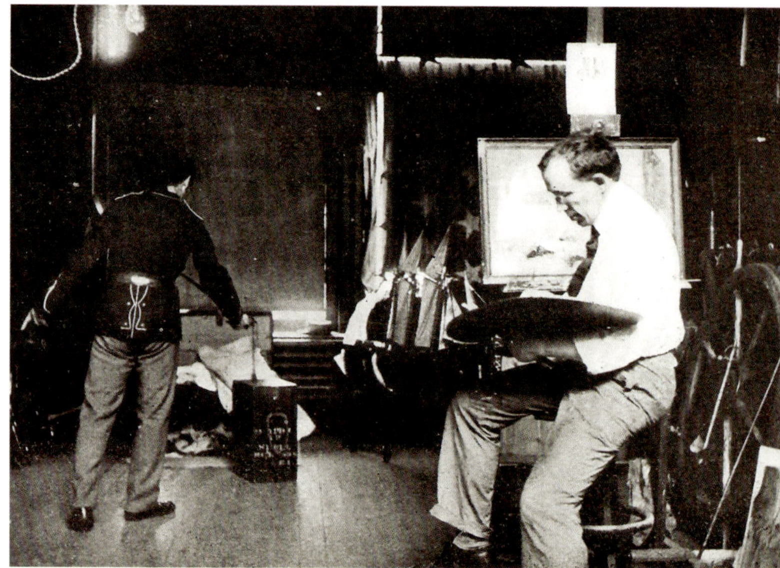

A self-taught artist, Henry Reuterdahl began securing illustration work in his native Sweden while still a teenager. At the age of 23, Reuterdahl was given an assignment to produce illustrations at the World's Fair in Chicago. Finding the United States to his liking, he stayed, marrying and settling in Weehawken, N.J., just outside of New York. During the Spanish-American War, he served as an illustrator-correspondent, providing striking art for the periodicals back home, and writing on the subject as well. Traveling with the Navy, he developed a specialty depicting marine work and rendering ships. *Collier's Weekly* magazine took notice of his artistic eye for ships, and shortly after the Spanish-American War, sent him to Europe to produce a series of works called "Navies of the World." Working extensively on naval voyages, Reuterdahl covered the American fleet first-hand. In 1908 Reuterdahl wrote an article that was quite critical of the navy's make-up and methodology, which led to some wide-scale changes for the navy, from the way it conducted promotions to ship construction.

He was later assigned to the battleship *Minnesota,* and during World War I, he became commissioned as an officer in the Naval reserve, and was placed in charge of making posters to promote the navy's efforts during the war. His later works are known for their rich color and lush oil-painting style, and are widely prized not only for the accuracy of the rendering but also for the emotion they portray.

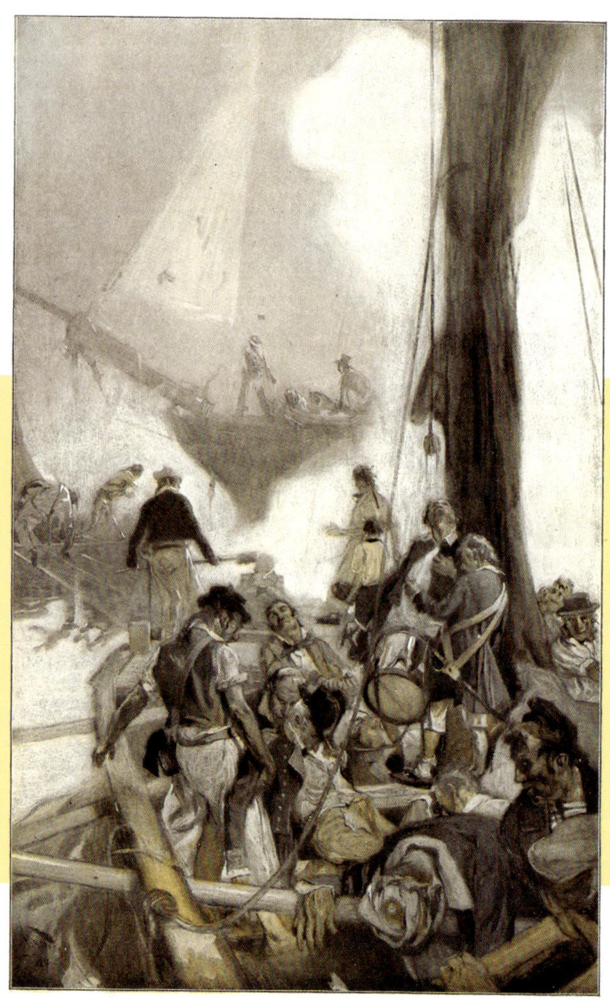

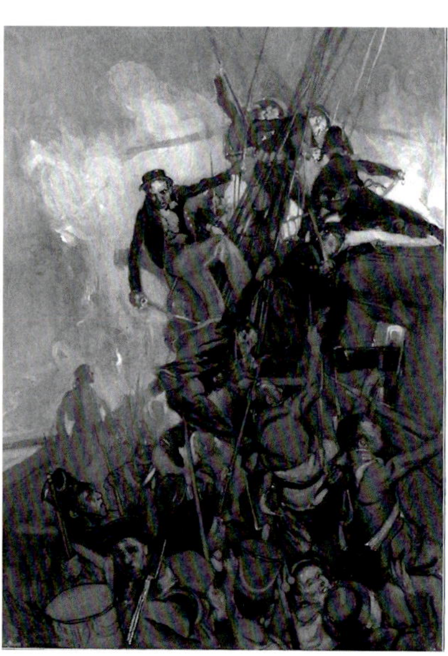

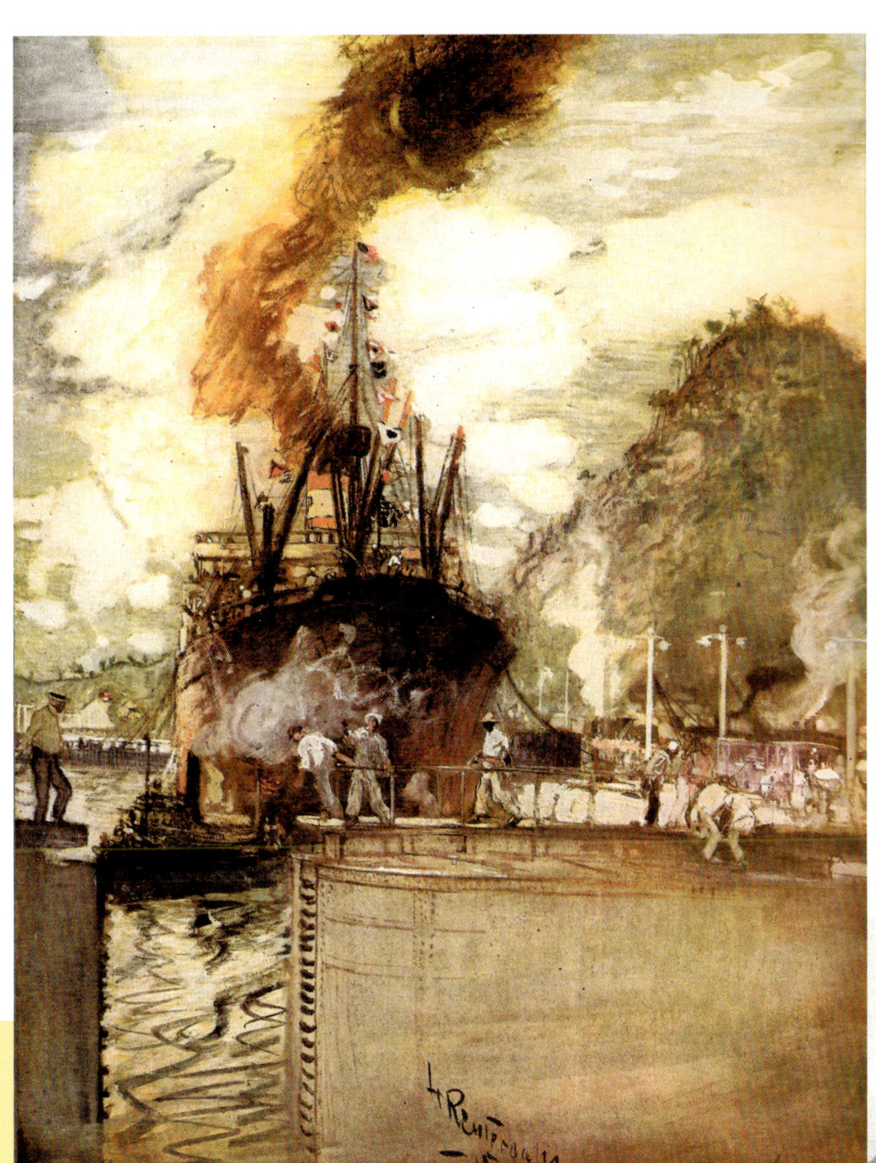

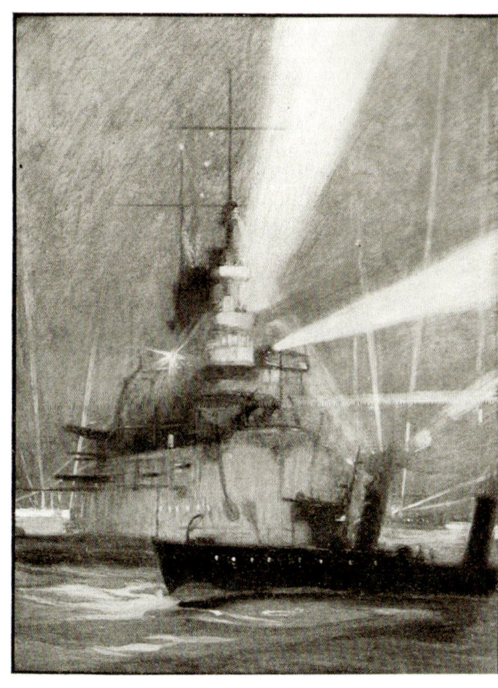

Our Navy at Searchlight Drill

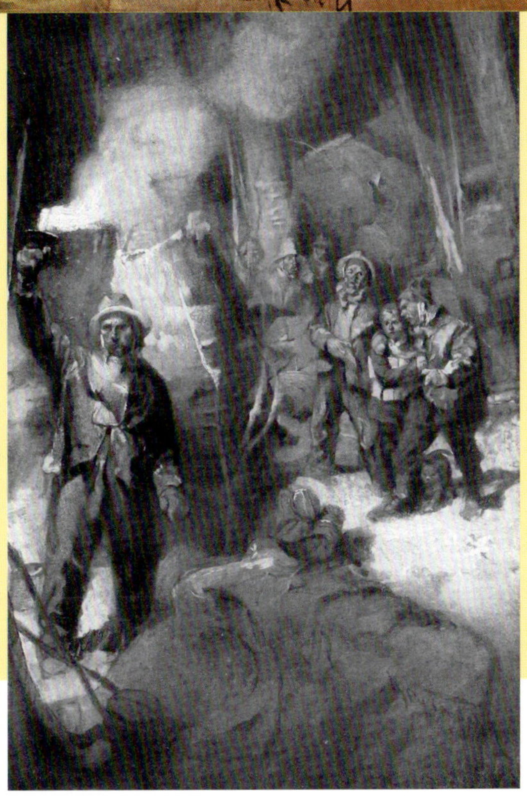

Louis Rhead

1857–1926, British

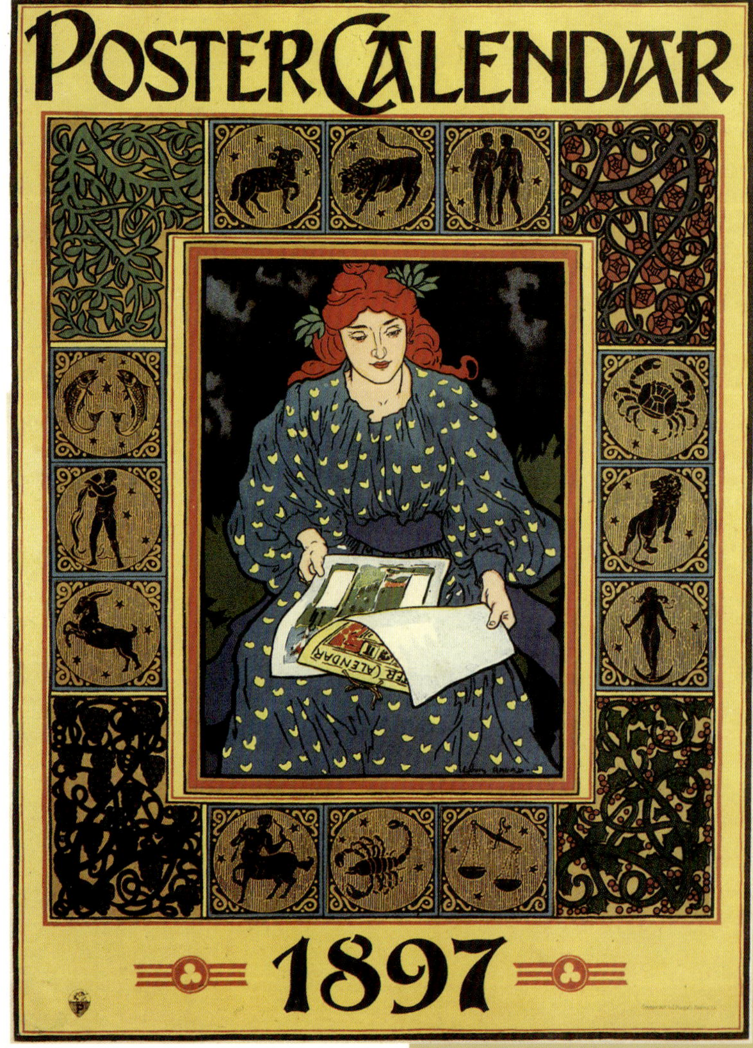

Born into a family of ceramic artists, Louis Rhead showed exceptional artistic talent early on, and was sent to study in Paris from his home in England at the age of 13. More study followed after he returned to England, and by 1881, Rhead left the family business of ceramics and began a career in publishing at Cassell in London.

Rhead was not at Cassell long before he caught the attention of a New York publishing firm, D. Appleton. He accepted a position as art director with them, and settled down in New York, where he brought an element of Parisian Art Nouveau to an eager American audience.

During the 1890s, the poster became a popular medium, and Rhead took advantage of the trend. He became one of the leading figures of the American Art Nouveau movement, and during most of that decade, his graphic work regularly appeared in association with *The Century Magazine, Harper's* publications, and *Scribner's,* among others.

When poster work began to decline, Rhead found new direction in the growing market for book illustration, where he became a regular contributor to the genre of children's classics. He regularly produced volumes for *Harper's* with numerous line illustrations, sometimes recalling the graphic styles of his earlier poster designs, including *Treasure Island, Robin Hood,* and *Robinson Crusoe.* Though some of his later volumes featured color versions of his line works, Rhead was more comfortable with black and white.

Rhead's second passion in life was angling. It was not long after the turn of the century that Rhead's artistic talent and his interest in fishing merged. In the latter part of his career, he not only illustrated numerous books on the subject, but became an expert author as well. Illustrations centered around fishing were featured in his own books, and in the early sporting magazines of the day, such as *Outdoors* and *Field & Stream.*

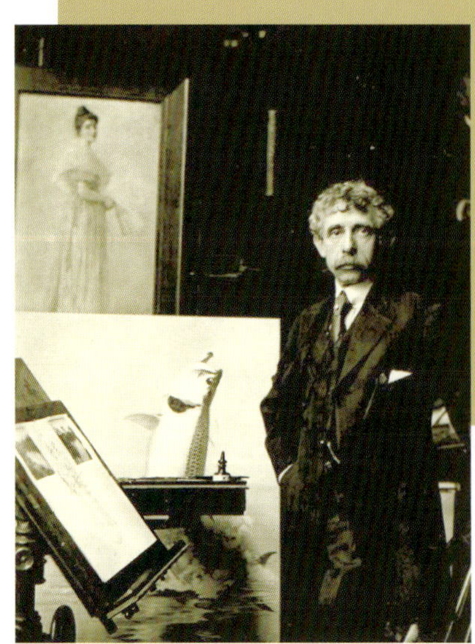

In 1926 a fishing adventure ended Rhead's life. After an hour-long struggle with a 30-pound snapping turtle, Rhead landed the turtle, but the strain proved too much for him and he suffered a heart attack. Two weeks later a subsequent heart attack ended his life at age sixty-eight.

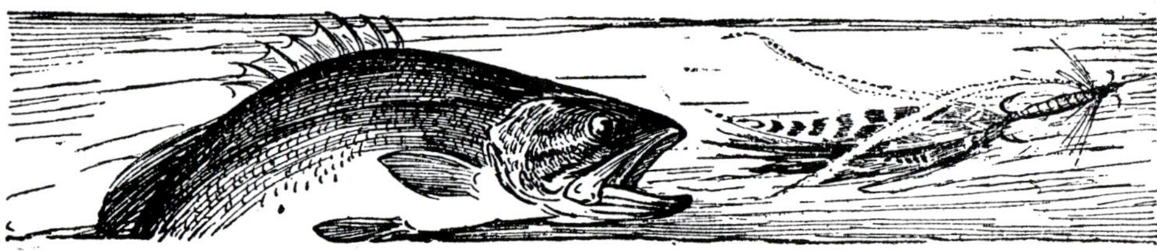

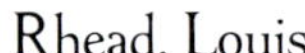
Rhead, Louis

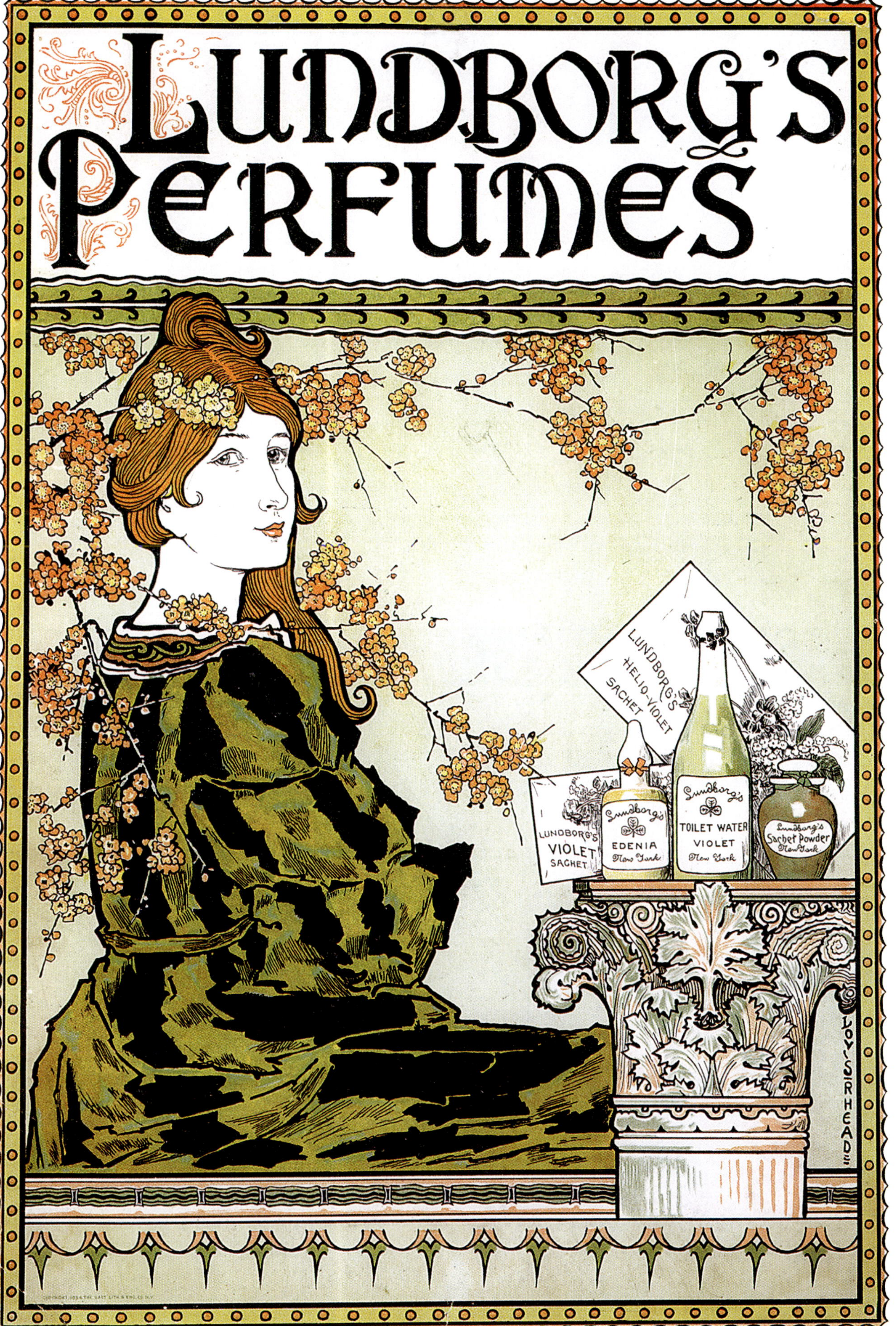
LUNDBORG'S
PERFUMES
LUNDBORG'S
HELIO-VIOLET
SACHET
LUNDBORG'S
VIOLET
SACHET
Lundborg's
EDENIA
New York
Lundborg's
TOILET WATER
VIOLET
New York
Lundborg's
Sachet Powder
New York
LOUIS RHEAD

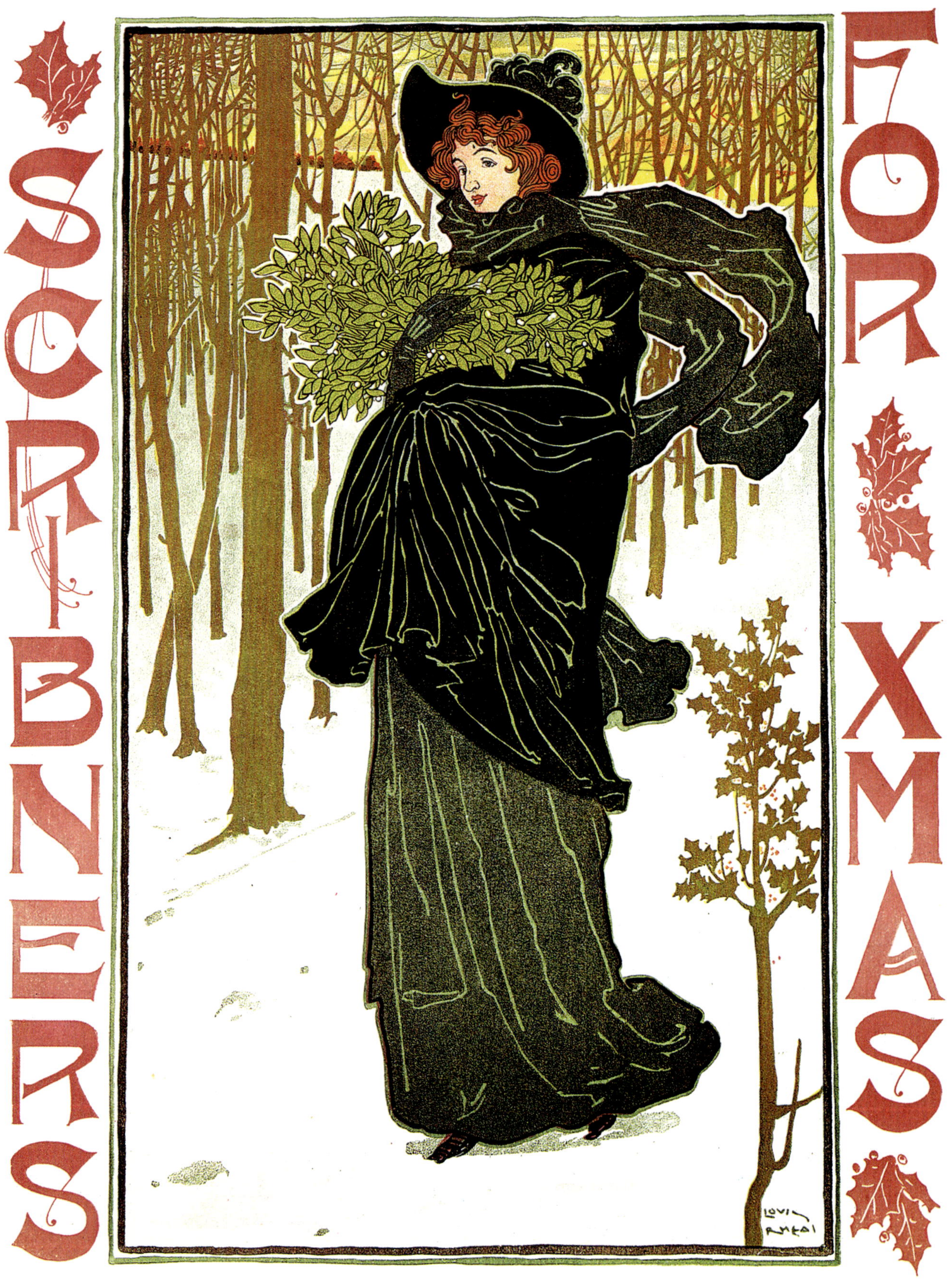

Rhead, Louis

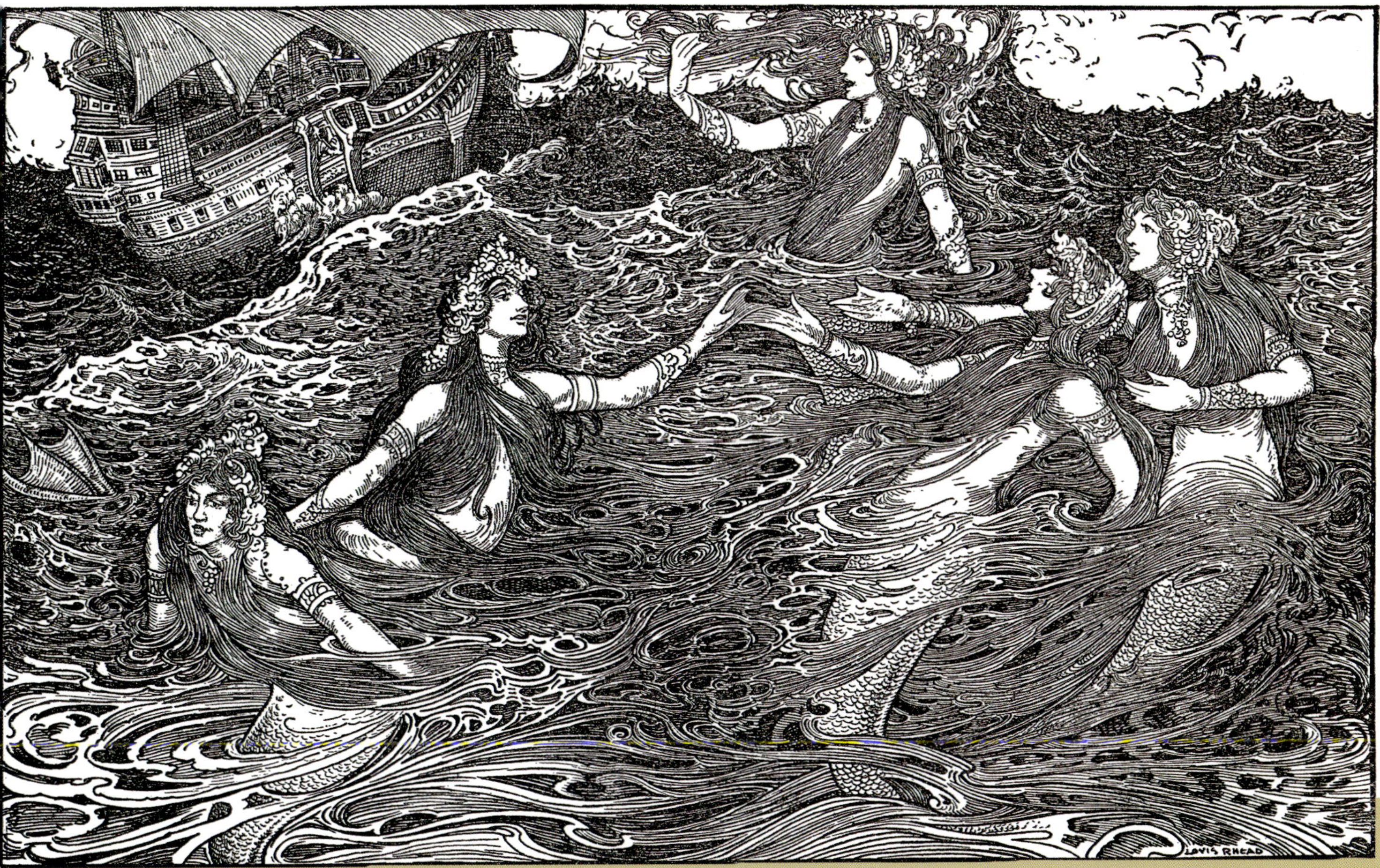

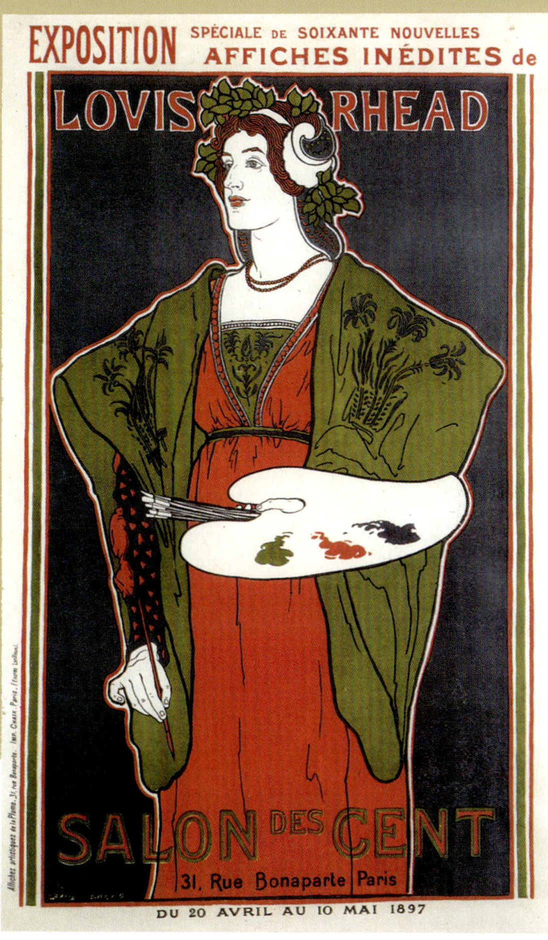
EXPOSITION SPÉCIALE DE SOIXANTE NOUVELLES
AFFICHES INÉDITES de
LOVIS RHEAD
SALON DES CENT
31, Rue Bonaparte Paris
DU 20 AVRIL AU 10 MAI 1897

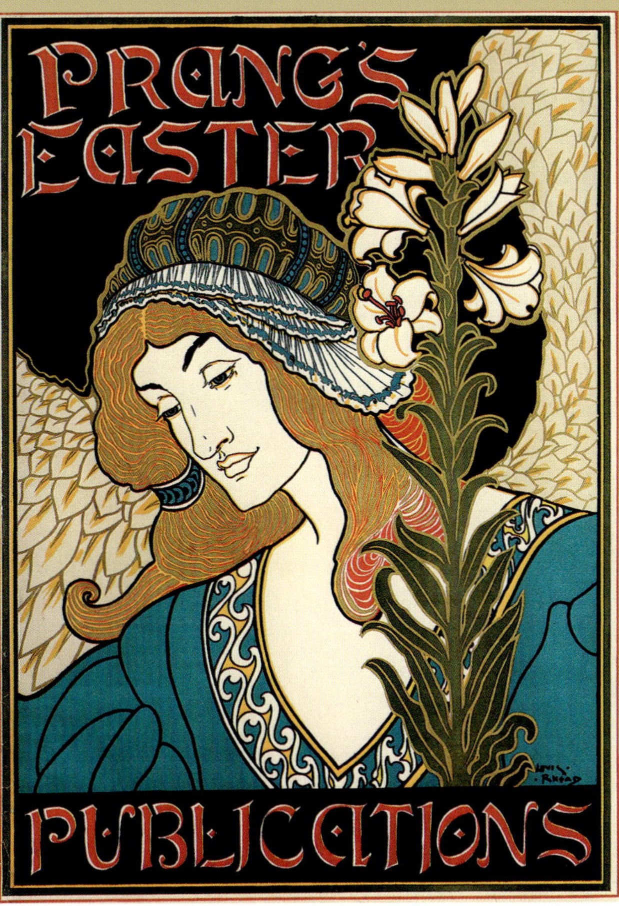
PRANG'S
EASTER
PUBLICATIONS

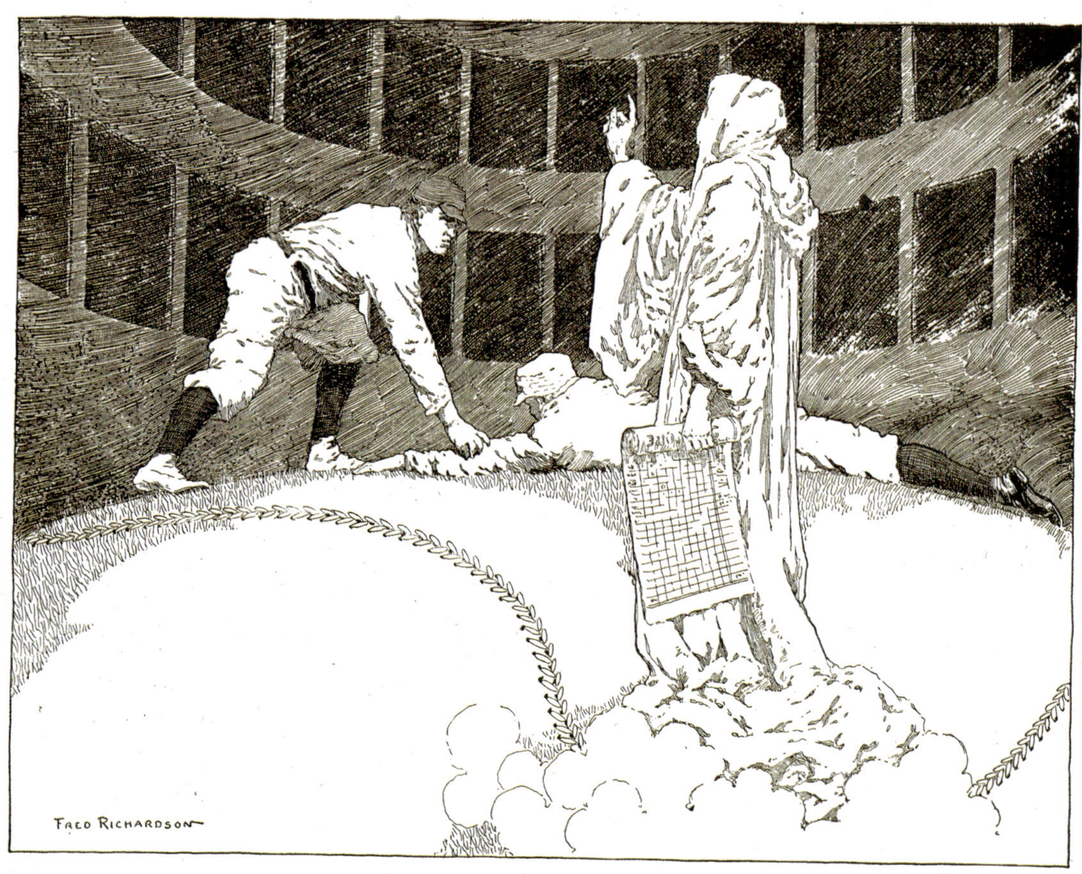

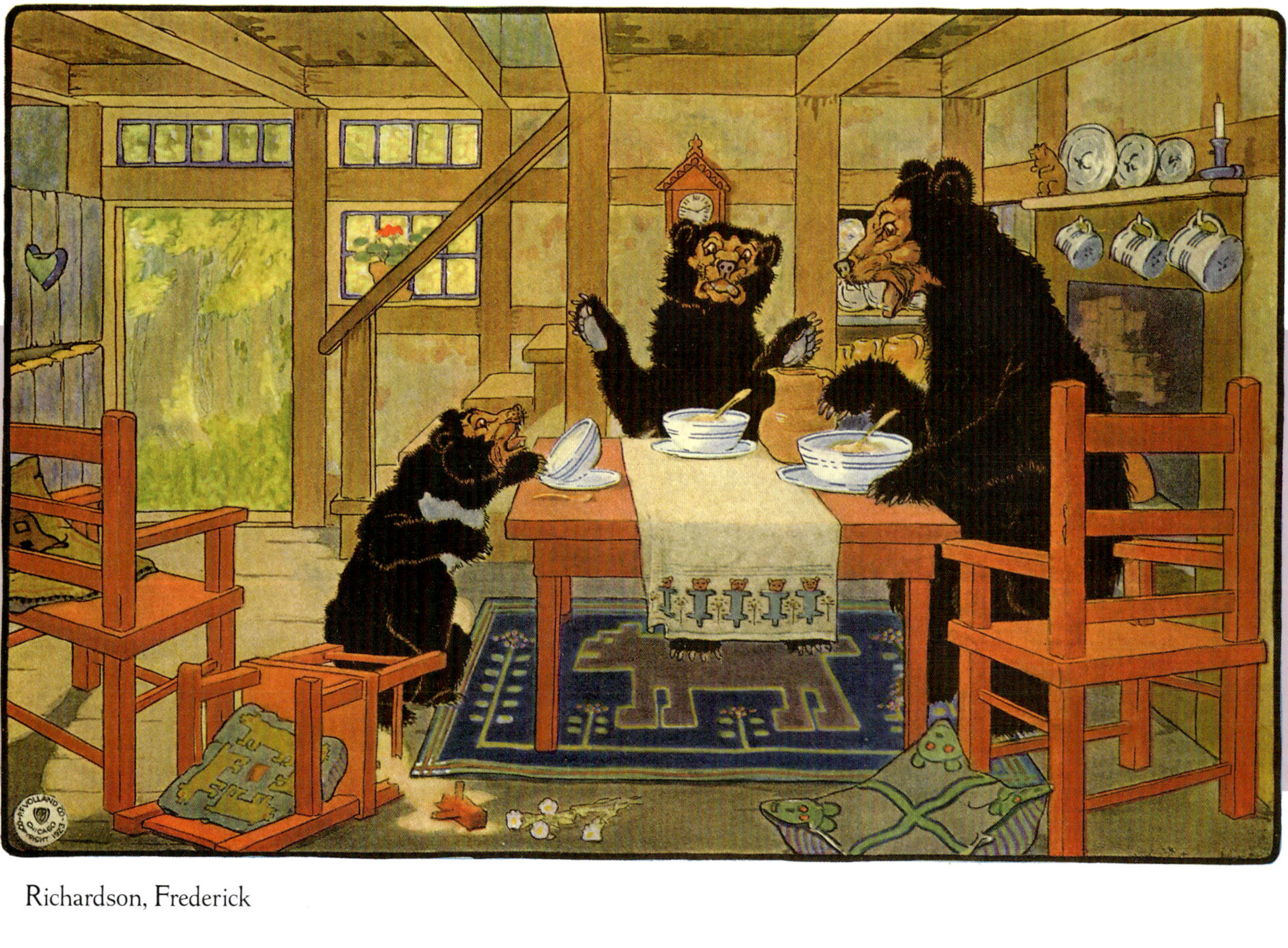

Richardson, Frederick

Frederick Richardson

1862–1937, American

After studying in the Midwest at the St. Louis School of Fine Arts, and at the Académie Julian in Paris, Frederick Richardson returned to his roots in Chicago and taught at the Chicago Art Institute. He spent seven years there, before moving on to become a newspaper illustrator. He took a position with the *Chicago Daily News,* and was notably adept at covering a wide range of needs for the paper. He created images for editorial stories, recorded important events, such as the World's Columbian Exposition in 1893, and also contributed to the children's pages with cartoons and illustration. His work gained such a following that in 1899, Lakeside Press published *Book of Drawings* to capitalize on the popularity of his ink works created for the paper.

In 1903 Richardson left Chicago for the publishing houses of New York in an attempt to find more work in children's books. His elaborate pen-and-ink style and ability to imagine creatures of all sorts led him to many fairy tales, and he worked on some of the great fiction classics of the period. Titles by Andrew Lang, L. Frank Baum, and Nathaniel Hawthorne were among his list of favorites. Richardson's ability to tailor his style to suit the specific requirements of the assignment, adding cultural flair or a period charm to a story that needed a more exotic image to best capture the emotions of the plot was relished by his employers.

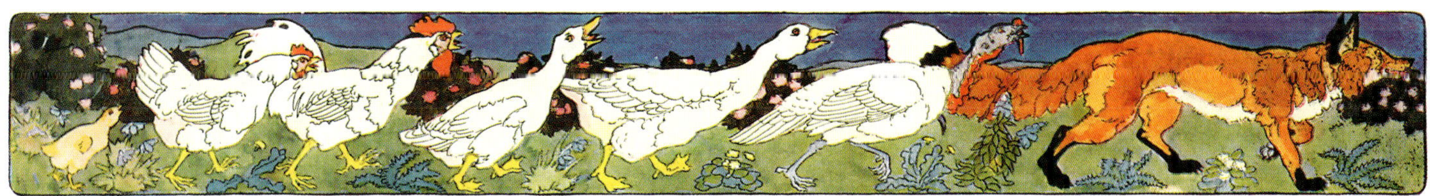

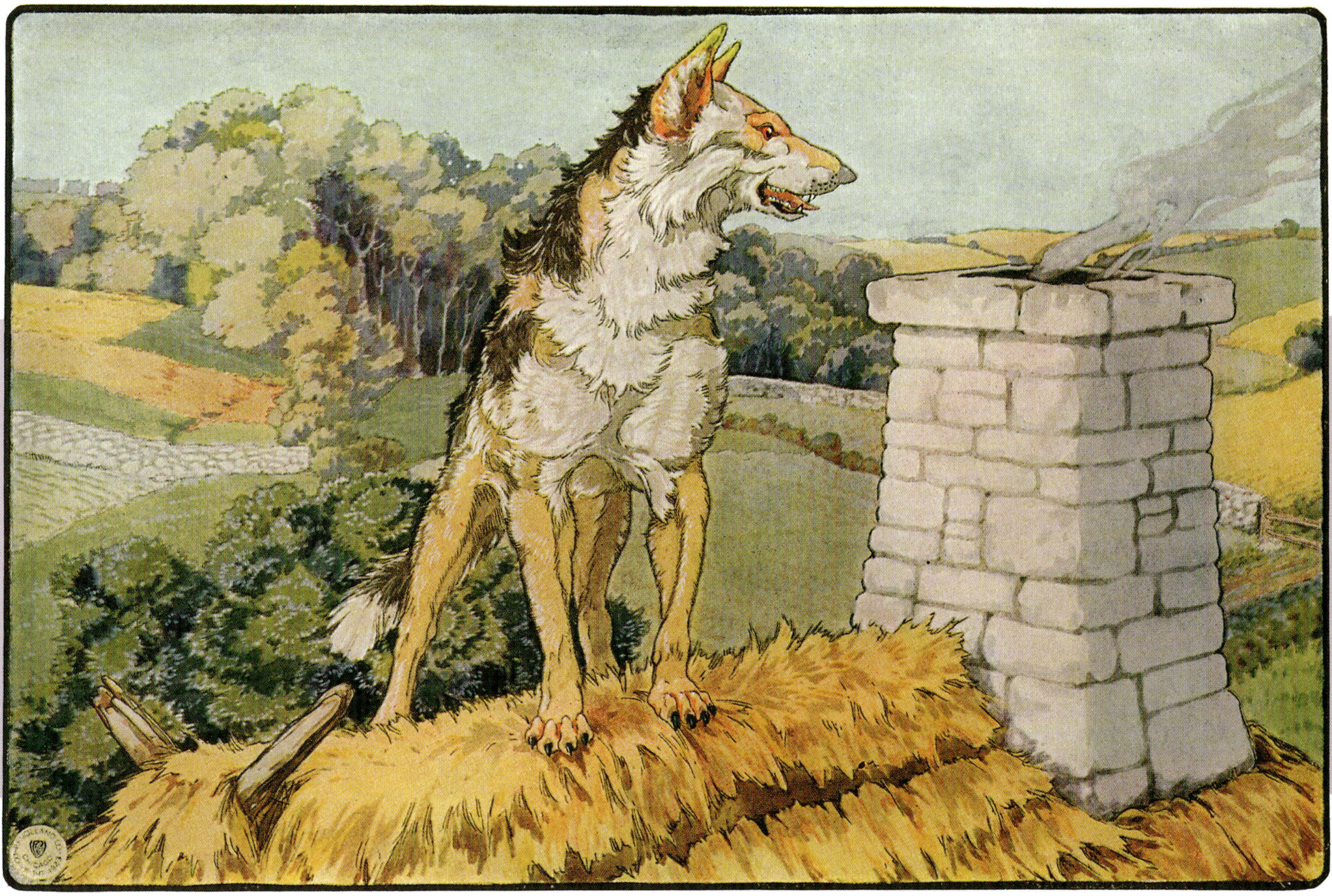

Charles Robinson
1870–1937, British

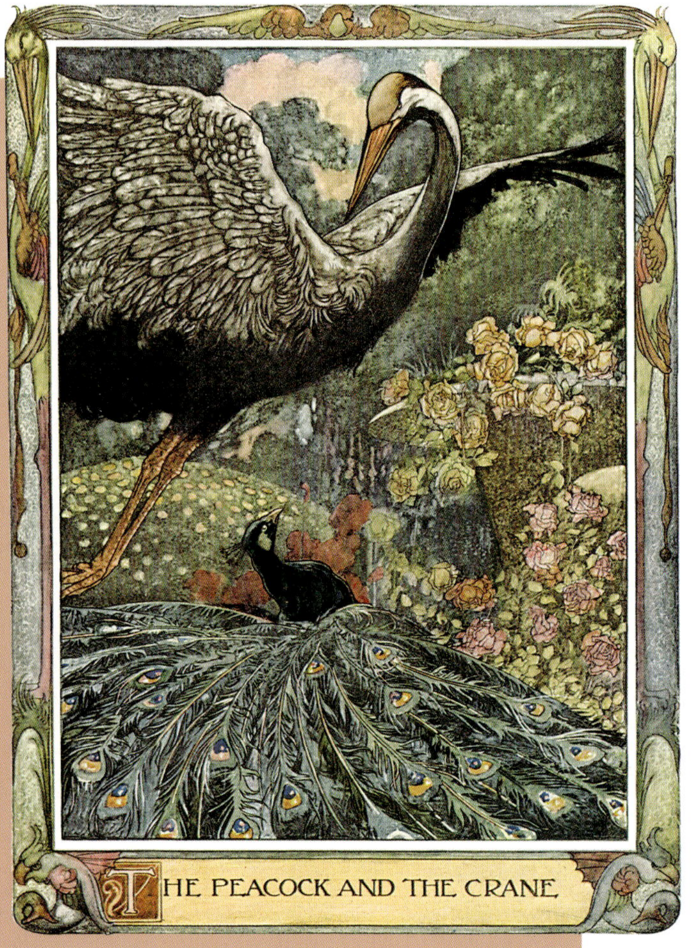

In a triumvirate of artistically successful brothers, Charles was the middle child. His elder brother, Thomas Heath Robinson, went into the family business of producing images for a growing market of printed materials, books, and periodicals. Charles—and later, William Heath Robinson—continued in the family business of illustration.

Charles would be considered by most critics to be the most accomplished painter of the three. His sensitivity to color was a true gift in a field where exploring full color for illustration was a fairly new idea. His work captured a moody, emotional quality that was missing from commonplace illustration. For these reasons, Charles went on to be the most successful book illustrator of the three.

Charles was largely self-taught with a lot of family influence, and began working professionally by 1895. His earliest book was *A Child's Garden of Verses,* which contained over 100 ink drawings. In a short span of time he was producing many plate volumes with scores of line drawings as well. Among the notable books Charles worked on was a set for Blackie and Son, called *The Big Book of Fairy Tales, The Big Book of Fables,* and *The Big Book of Nursery Rhymes.* Not only did these three volumes collectively contain over 60 color plates of his work at the pinnacle of his output, but each also held upwards of 100 line pieces, scattered liberally throughout. With art on nearly every spread, they are a distinct pleasure to leaf through.

Charles worked on books throughout his career. After World War I, when book production declined and many other book illustrators found work in magazines and elsewhere, Charles held fairly well to his station in books, and was one of the very few to continue receiving commissions from that shrinking market. Outstanding examples of Charles's book work can be found in Oscar Wilde's 1913 *The Happy Prince and Other Tales,* or 1915's *The Songs and Sonnets of William Shakespeare.* His death in 1937 was sudden and unexpected, when he passed away while working on a ship model, one of his favorite pastimes.

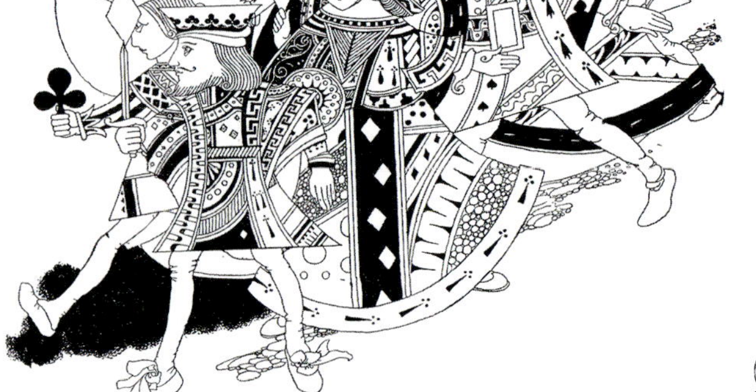

Robinson, Charles

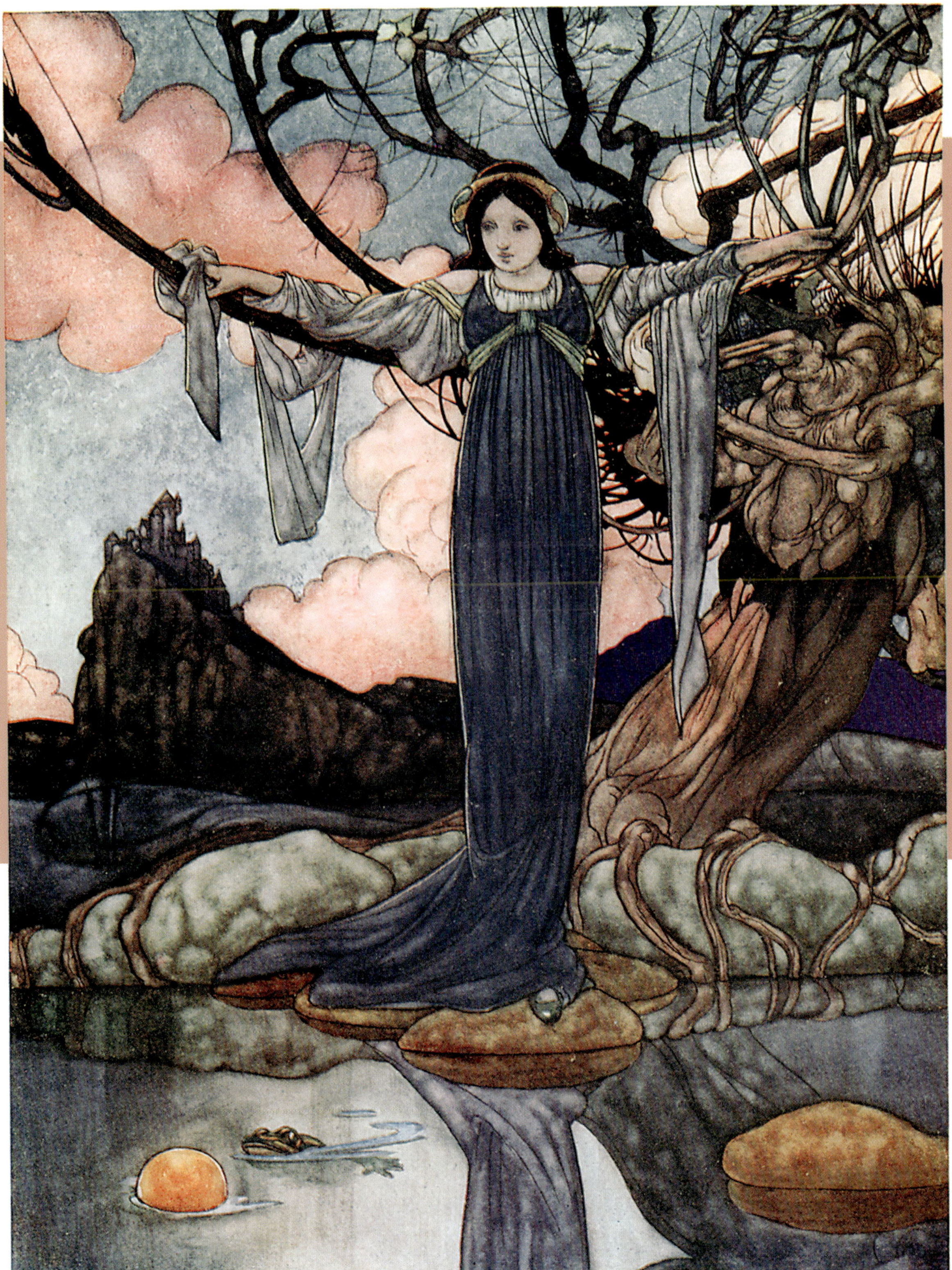

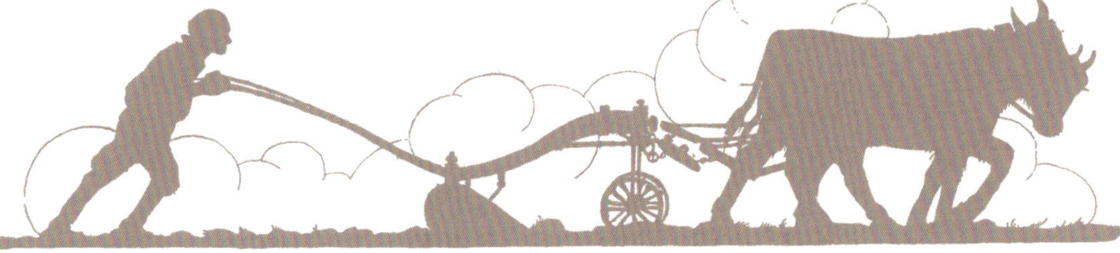

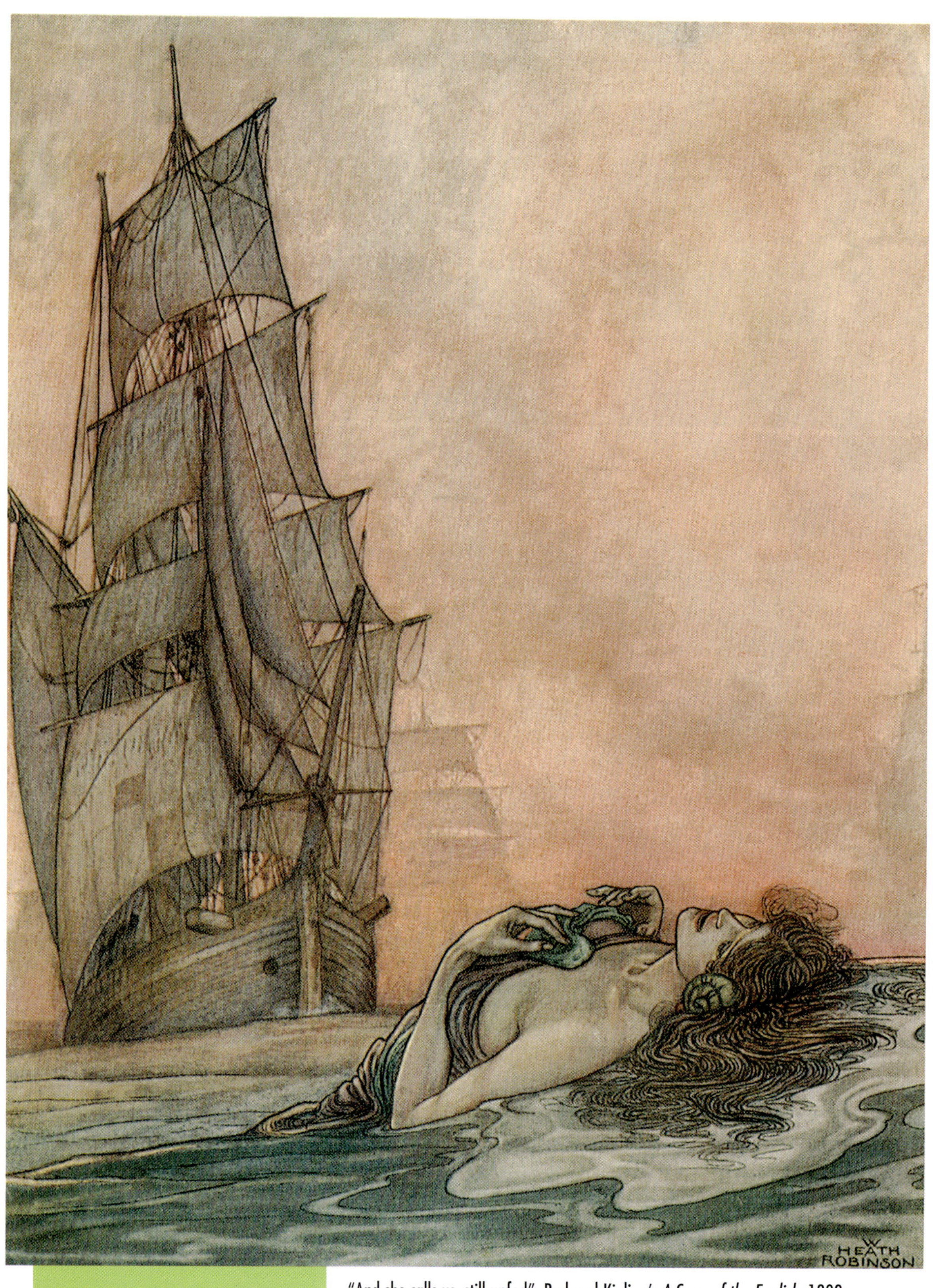

"And she calls us, still unfed". Rudyard Kipling's *A Song of the English,* 1909

WILLIAM H. ROBINSON
1872–1944, British

Born into a third generation of engraver-illustrators, and with two older brothers preceding him into the illustration field, William H. Robinson had a solid foundation to launch him into the Golden Age of illustration. When William first began his career in the arts, he had hoped to become a landscape painter. The challenges of a less commercial path into the arts quickly made an impression on William, who acknowledged that drawing for magazines was a much better means of earning income. His love for landscape remained, and is evident in much of the illustration he did during his entire career.

William was the youngest of three brothers. His oldest brother was Thomas Heath Robinson, who entered the illustration field in 1895 doing line work for tabloids and magazines of the day. His other brother Charles was just two years older than William; Charles had a career in book illustration. Their father had been an engraver by trade during his whole career. William learned from his whole family, who provided him with a nearly unparalleled support structure. Thomas preferred historical pieces, while Charles was becoming a major force in children's book illustration. William seemed to find his stride while working on serious, contemplative works such as Shakespeare's *The Tempest* or Kipling's *A Song of the English*—but it was his humorous side that would persevere, and earn him his reputation.

Early in his career, William worked in the same circles as his brothers, creating book and magazine illustrations. William had a flair for adding a touch of humor into his characters. From the cherub-like children in Kingsley's *Water Babies,* to the crazy characters of his own written works, or the unusual background extras in *Rabelais,* William could create unfolding stories in a single image through gesture and expression. Readers and publishers wanted more of the cartoon style which used complex ideas to lead the viewer to the punchline. His humor separated him from others in the field, and by the time the Golden Age was drawing to a close, it saved William's career. In the third decade of the century, when book assignments began to dwindle, the sharp wit of a humorous W. H. Robinson cartoon, and the distraction it provided, was in high demand, and it provided William with lasting employment long into his later years.

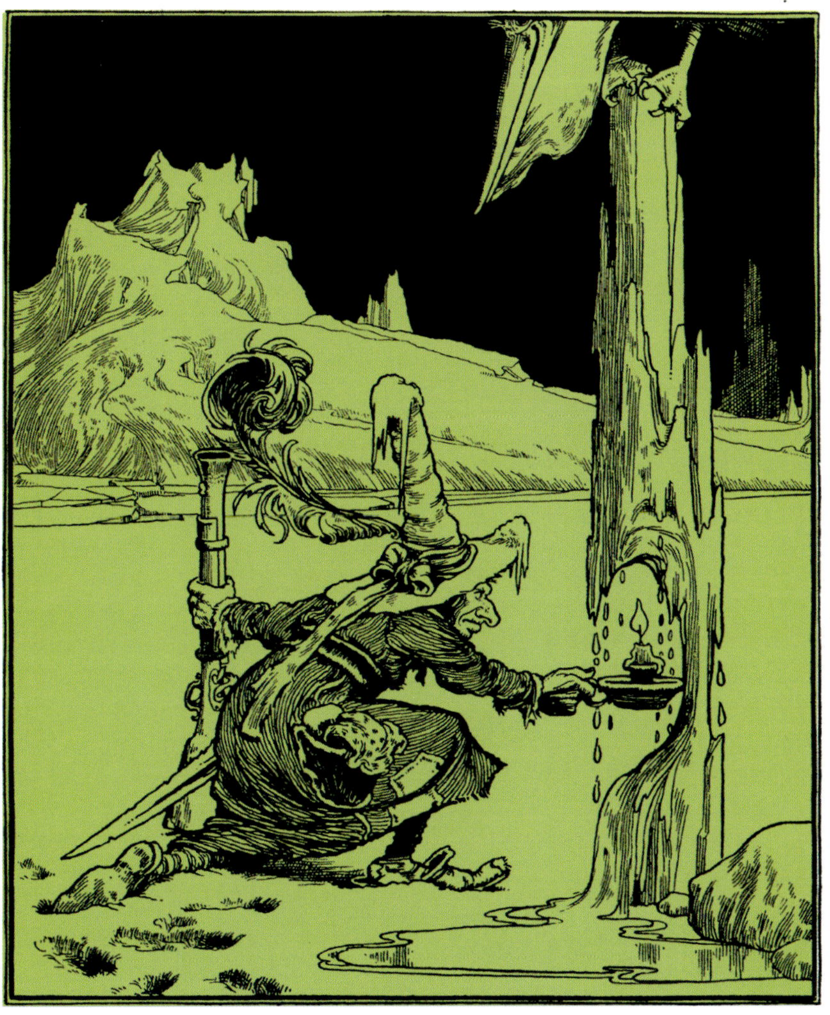

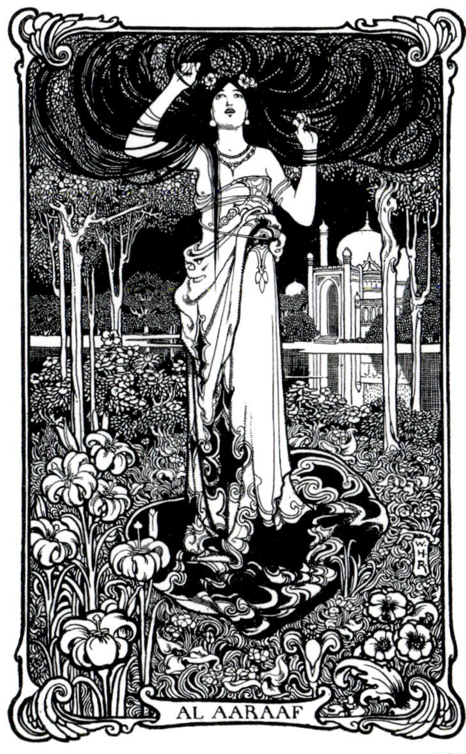

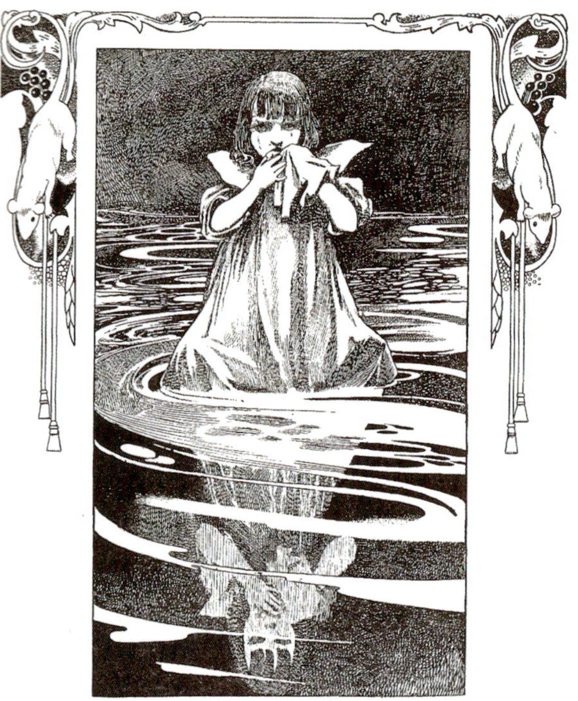

There was a large pool all around her about four inches deep and reaching half down the hall

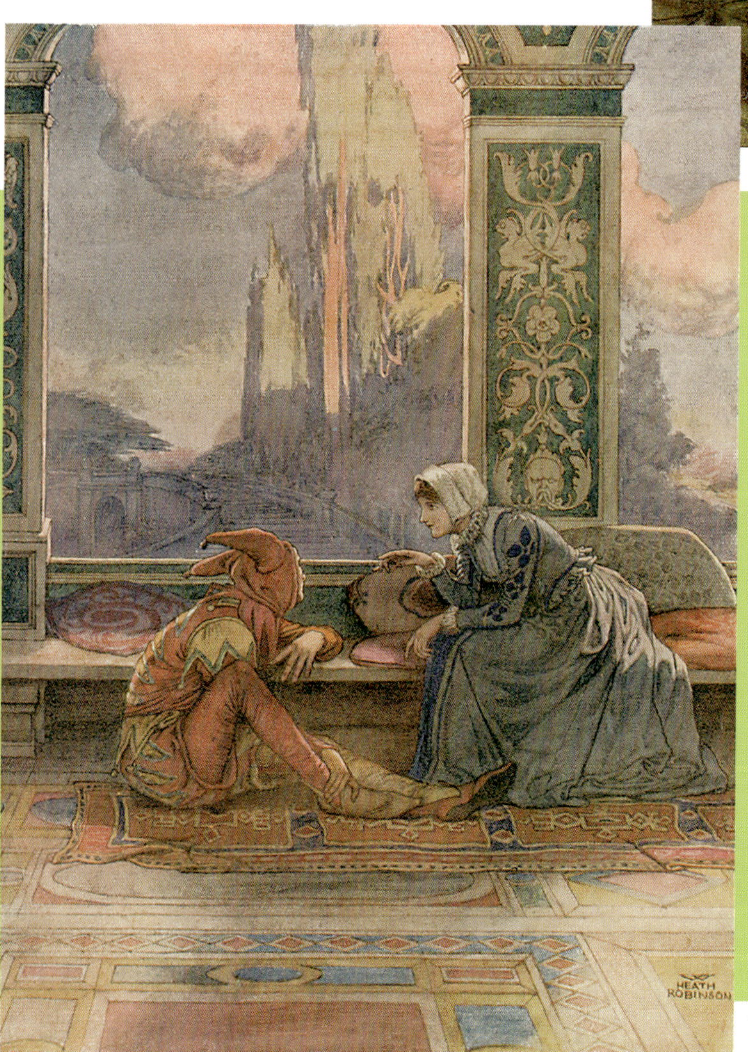

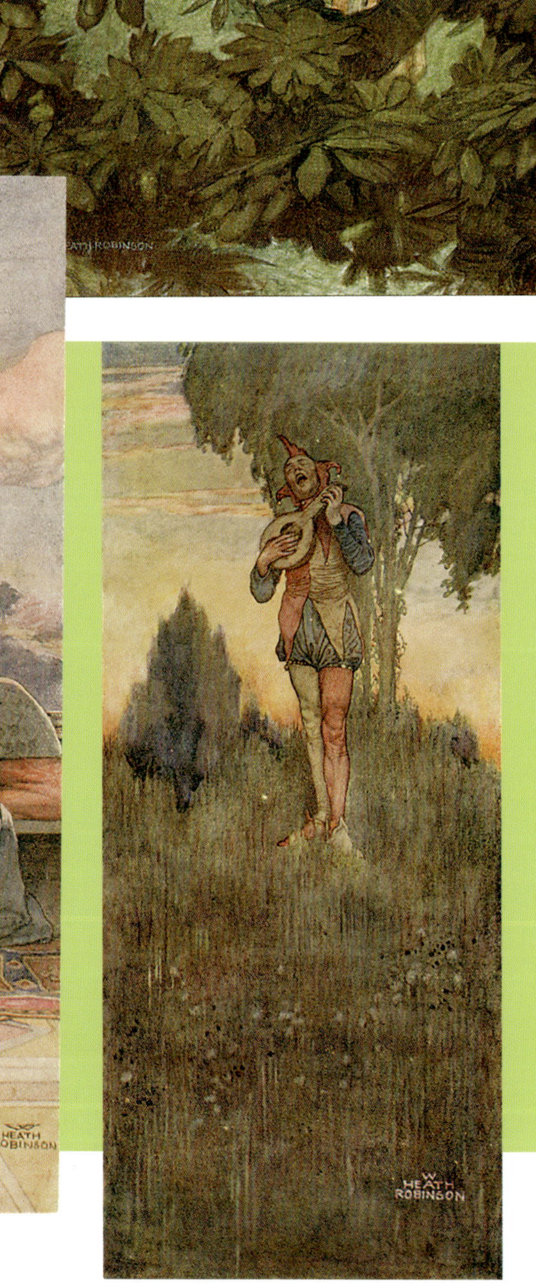

Robinson, William H.

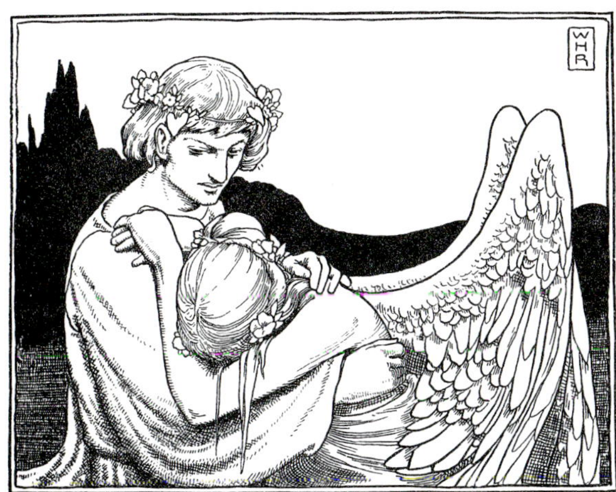

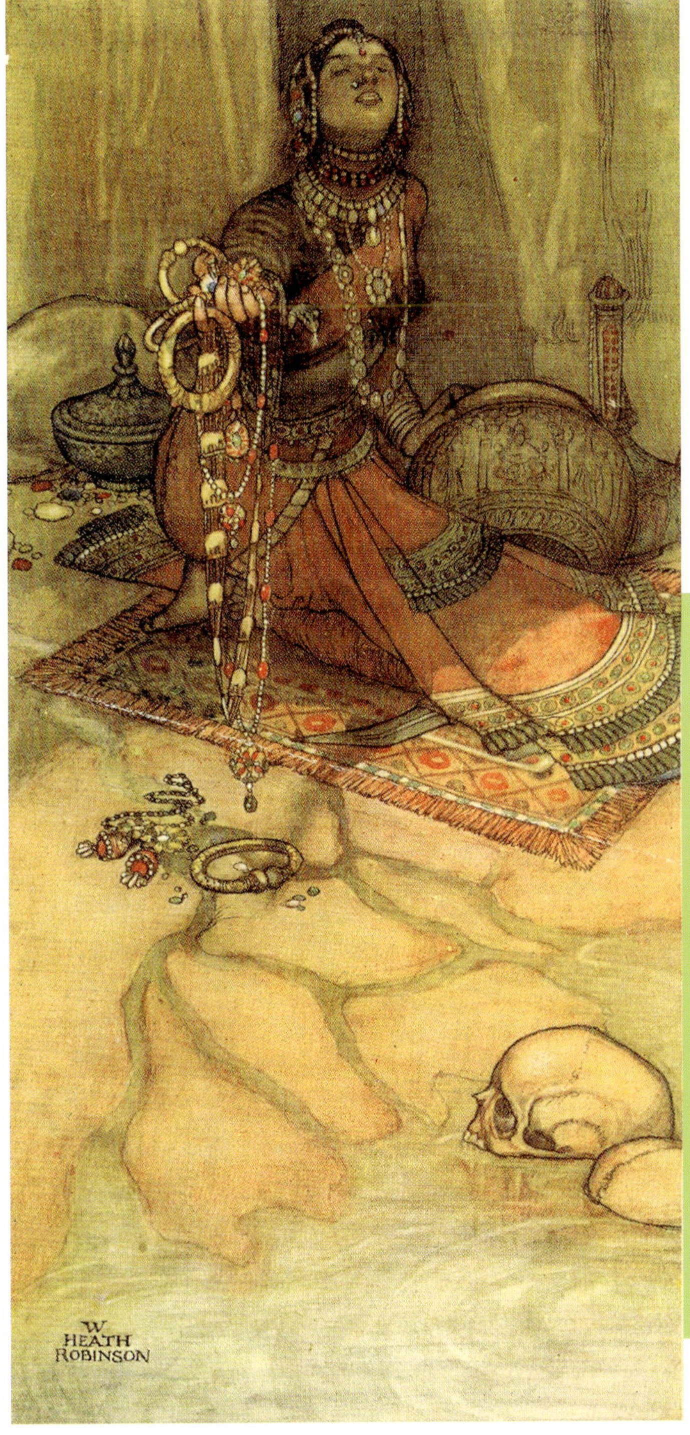

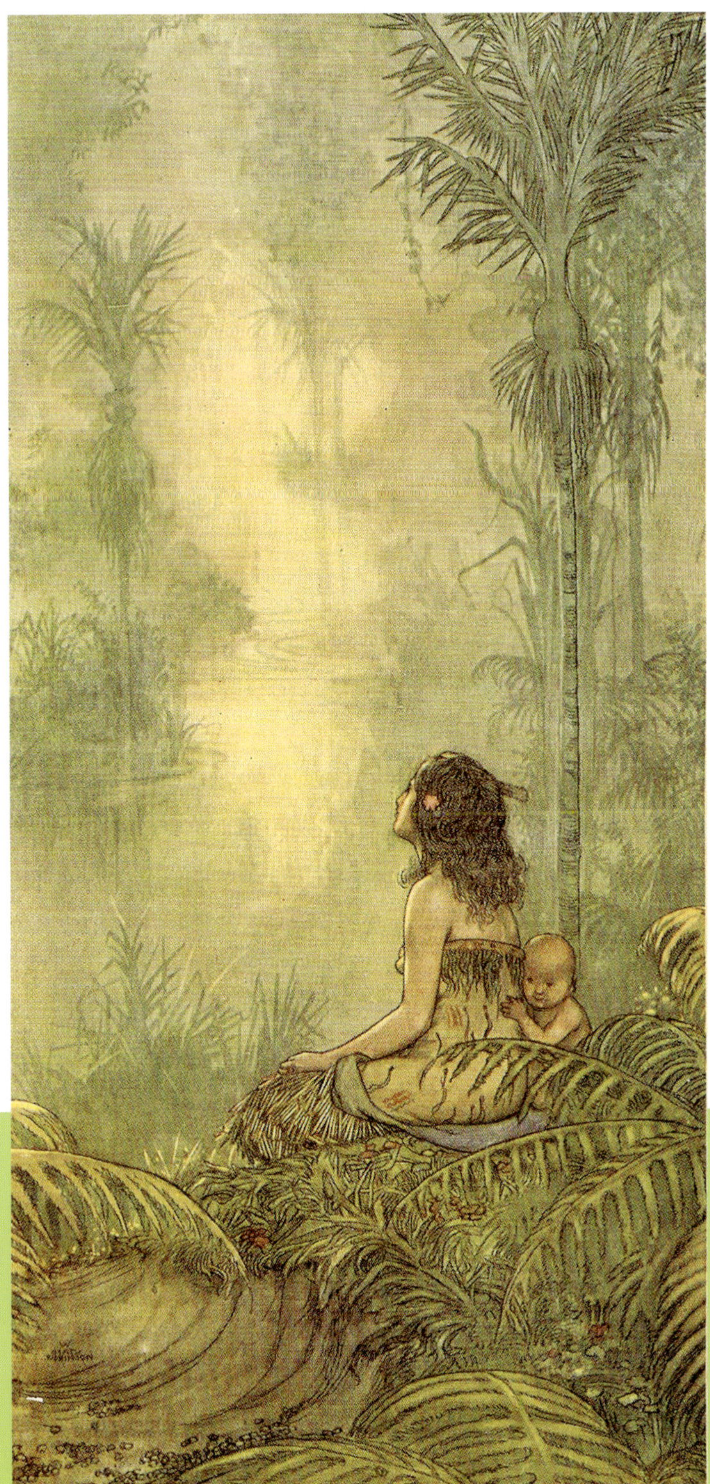

William Heath Robinson was the youngest of three successful illustrator brothers.

A strong career in illustration was followed by an even stronger one in cartooning. His command of line work was his visual strength.

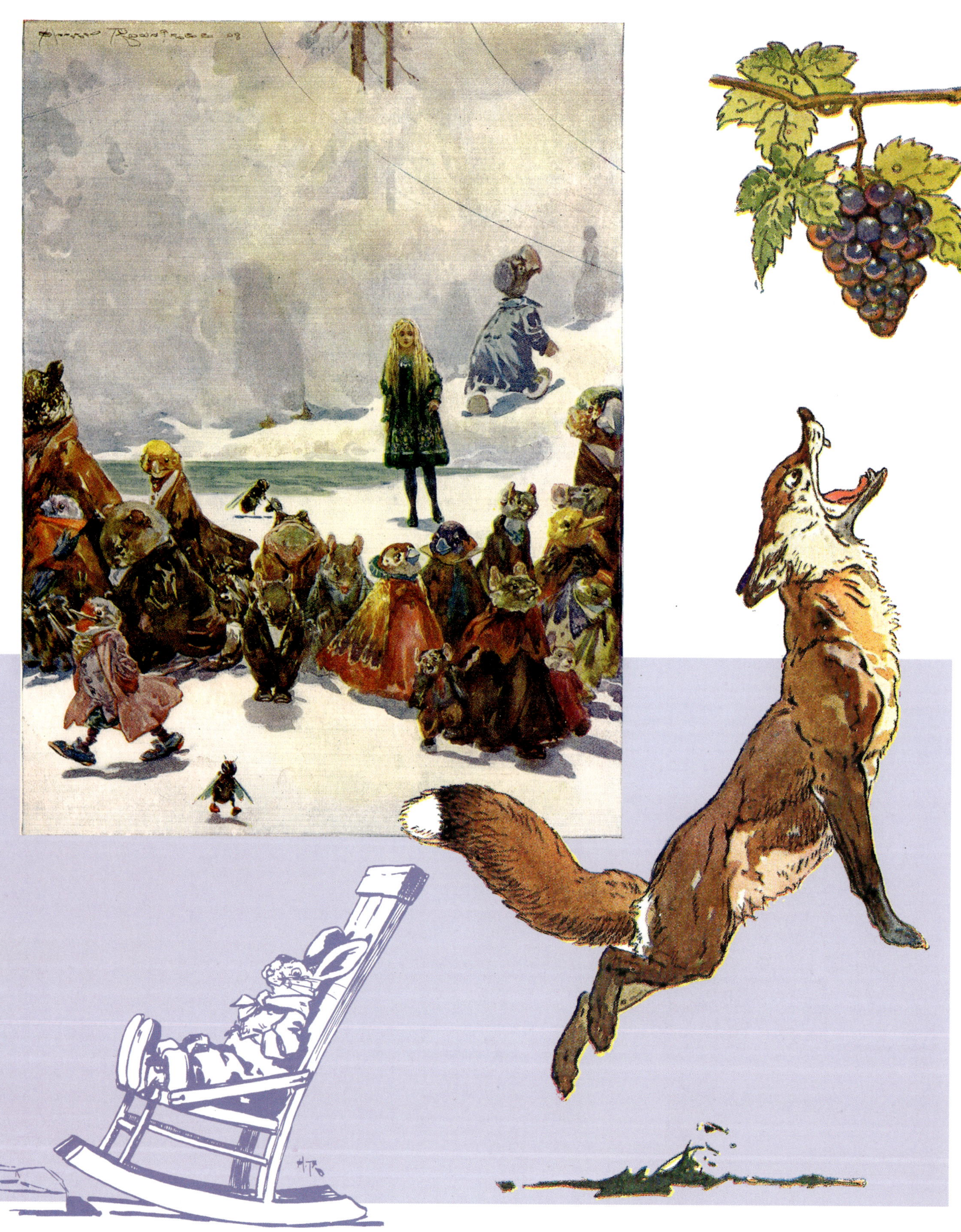

Rountree, Harry

Harry Rountree
1878–1950, New Zealander

Although Harry Rountree spent his childhood in New Zealand, by the time he was 23 he had traveled halfway around the world to London, in an attempt to pursue a career in illustration. His earliest attempts were not all that successful. While he did get some published work in *Punch, The Sketch,* and other magazines, it was not until he had an assignment to illustrate an animal that he achieved some success. This was to become his area of specialty from that point forward. His illustrations of animals had two aspects that endeared them to an audience—they were technically well-rendered, and at the same time, still retained some humanlike emotion. Some illustrations, particularly his birds, were beautifully true to form. What was unusual about Rountree's animal portrayals was his ability to imbue them with character and humor, without losing all resemblance to their real counterparts. Rountree excelled at this balance, and his assignments soon reflected the recognition of his talent. After 1903 and his success with magazines, there was no limit to his achievements in both book and magazine publications.

An outstanding collection of his work was his edition of Lewis Carroll's *Alice in Wonderland.* While one of many editions released in 1908 (when the British copyright expired), it was one of the most lavish volumes, featuring over 90 color images by Rountree, who had ample opportunity to show his expertise with animals. Other volumes that displayed Rountree's work with animal subjects included 1906's *Uncle Remus,* and his version of *Aesop's Fables.*

After art, Rountree's second love was golf, and he found a chance to work that into his illustration career as well, producing a classic volume for the British golf world in 1910. *The Golf Courses of the British Isles* has 64 color plates, beautiful examples of Rountree's watercolor mastery. During World War I, Rountree served as a captain in the Royal Engineers, and after the war he continued to be productive in both book and magazine publishing until 1942.

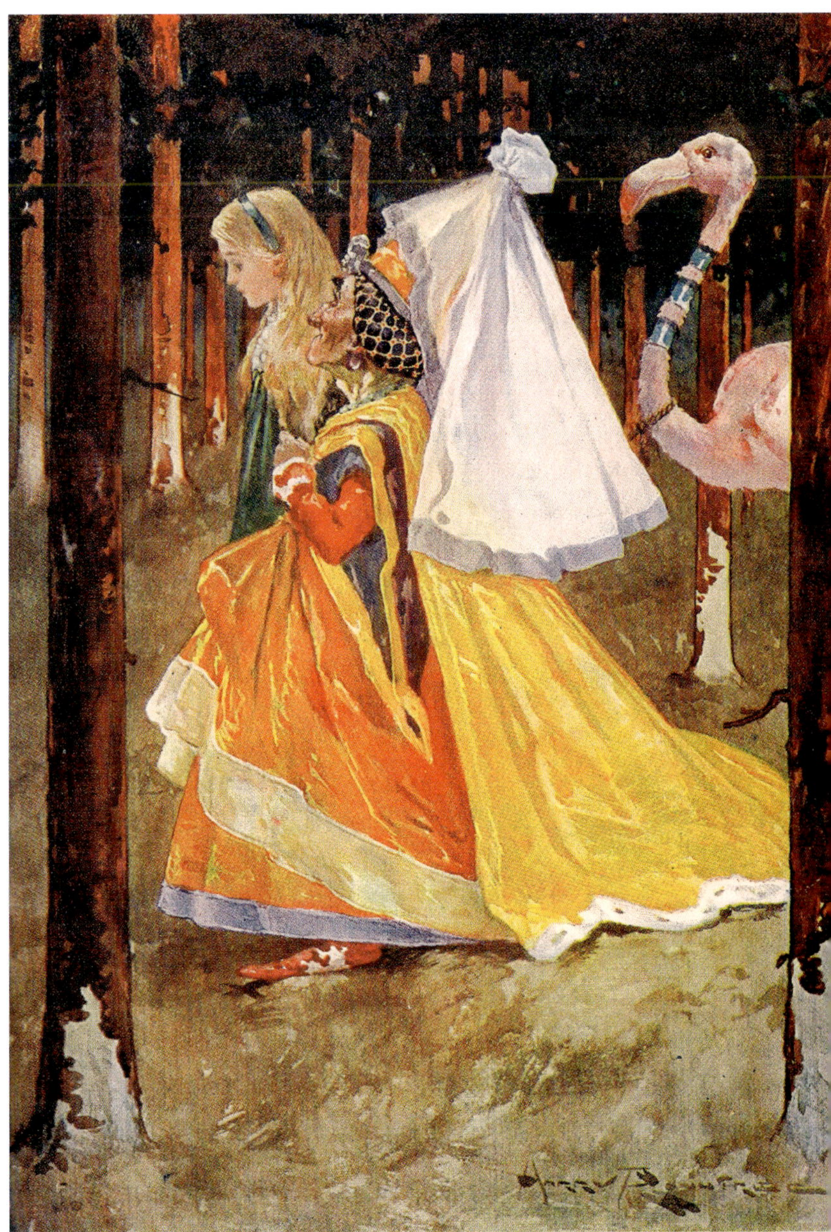

Frank Schoonover

1877–1972, American

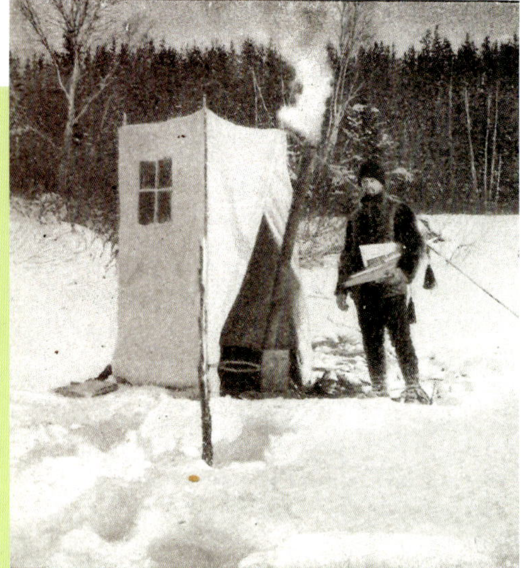

This quiet, studious New Jersey native decided to pursue a career in illustration rather than enter the ministry. While studying art at Drexel, Frank Schoonover became a follower of Howard Pyle, and became one of his most successful students. In the summers of 1898 and 1899, he continued with Pyle at his Chadds Ford, Pennsylvania, summer sessions. He was a class monitor, and benefited from the mentorship that Pyle shared with his hand-picked scholars. After studying with Pyle, Schoonover settled in the Wilmington area, and remained there for the rest of his career.

Schoonover's experiences led to a unique specialty. Like his instructor Howard Pyle, Schoonover preferred to gain first-hand knowledge of an environment to achieve full mastery. While he would spend a great deal of his time with Western themes, Schoonover's first explorations were to the North. An avid outdoorsman his entire life, Schoonover ventured twice through the Canadian wilderness—first by snowshoe, and later by canoe. He became an expert in depicting adventures in this region. The people who lived there, the tools for survival, and the beautiful landscape all found their way inside the pages of Schoonover's sketchbooks. That kind of information gathering became typical of his work throughout his life. Schoonover made trips to Europe, the Gulf area of the United States, and to the West—with the research always helping to produce better illustrations.

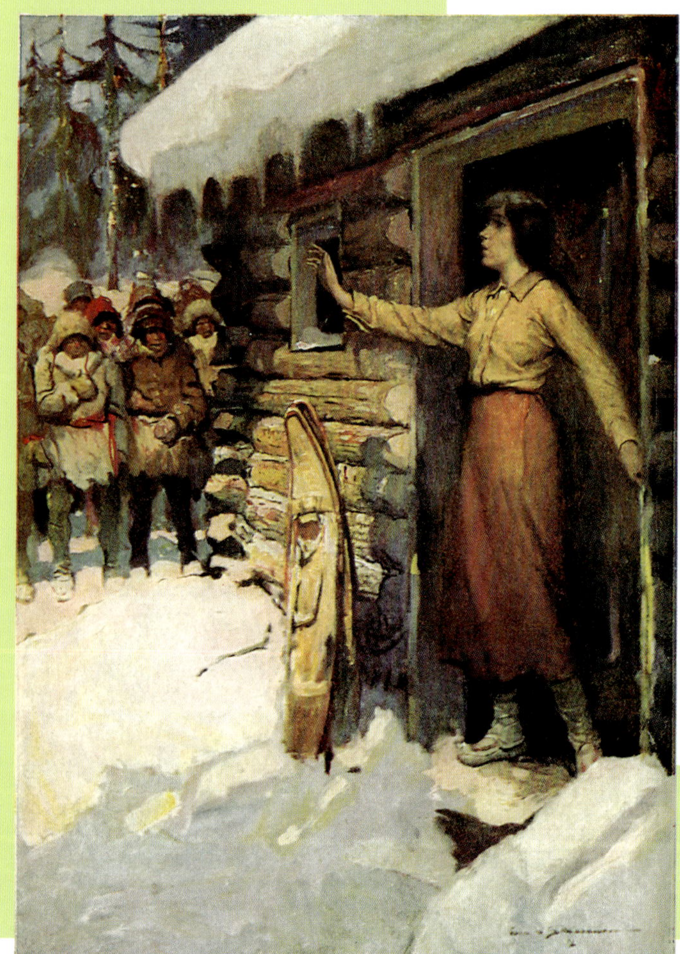

Schoonover spent time in Scranton, Pennsylvania, during a coal miner's strike; Richmond, Virginia, for a story on tobacco fields and their owners; and Butte, Montana, for work on a long magazine serial on the fight over the Minnie Healy copper mine. This travel reflected the dedication Schoonover put into his research and his image-making. As his reputation grew, he went on to work for many major magazines, and *Outing* became one of his earliest employers. He received many opportunities for Western stories, and later book work followed, including an unusual arrangement in the 1920s, in which Harper & Brothers had Louis Rhead produce scores of line drawings for children's classics, and paired them with cover plates by Schoonover. *Treasure Island, Robin Hood,* and *Grimm's Fairy Tales* are just a few of these books.

Active well into his later years, Schoonover enjoyed landscape painting, and began teaching in earnest in 1942, at a point in life when most are considering retirement. He taught classes until 1968, and died at the age of ninety-five.

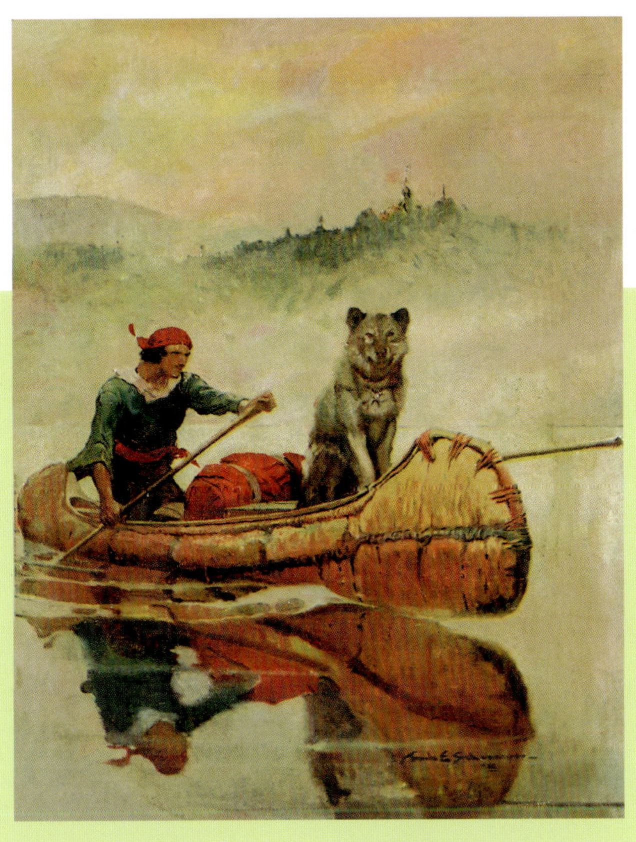

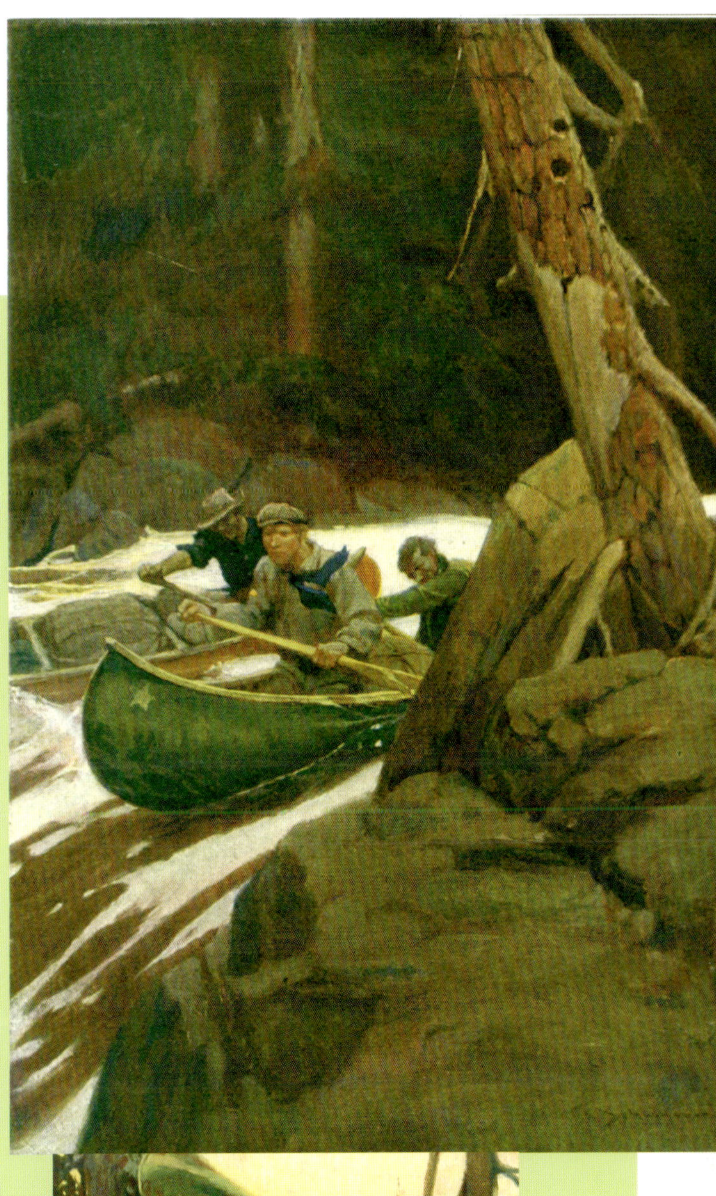

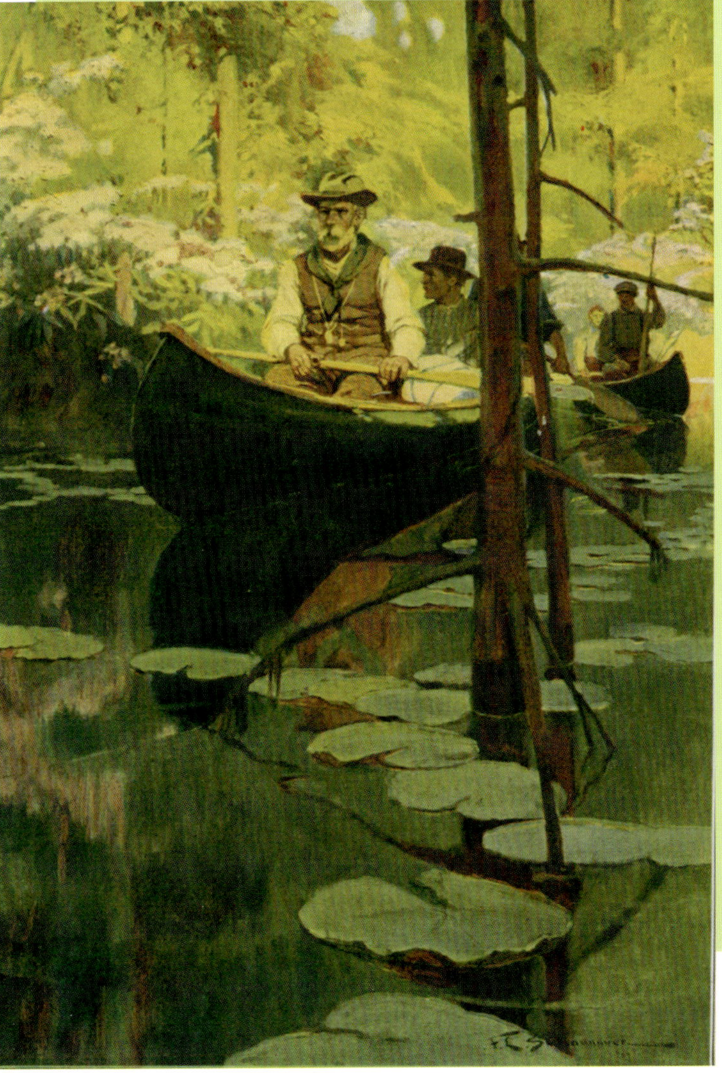

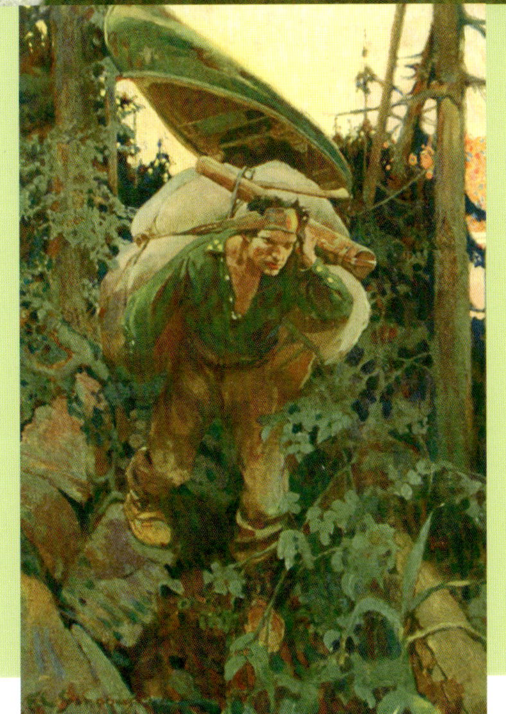

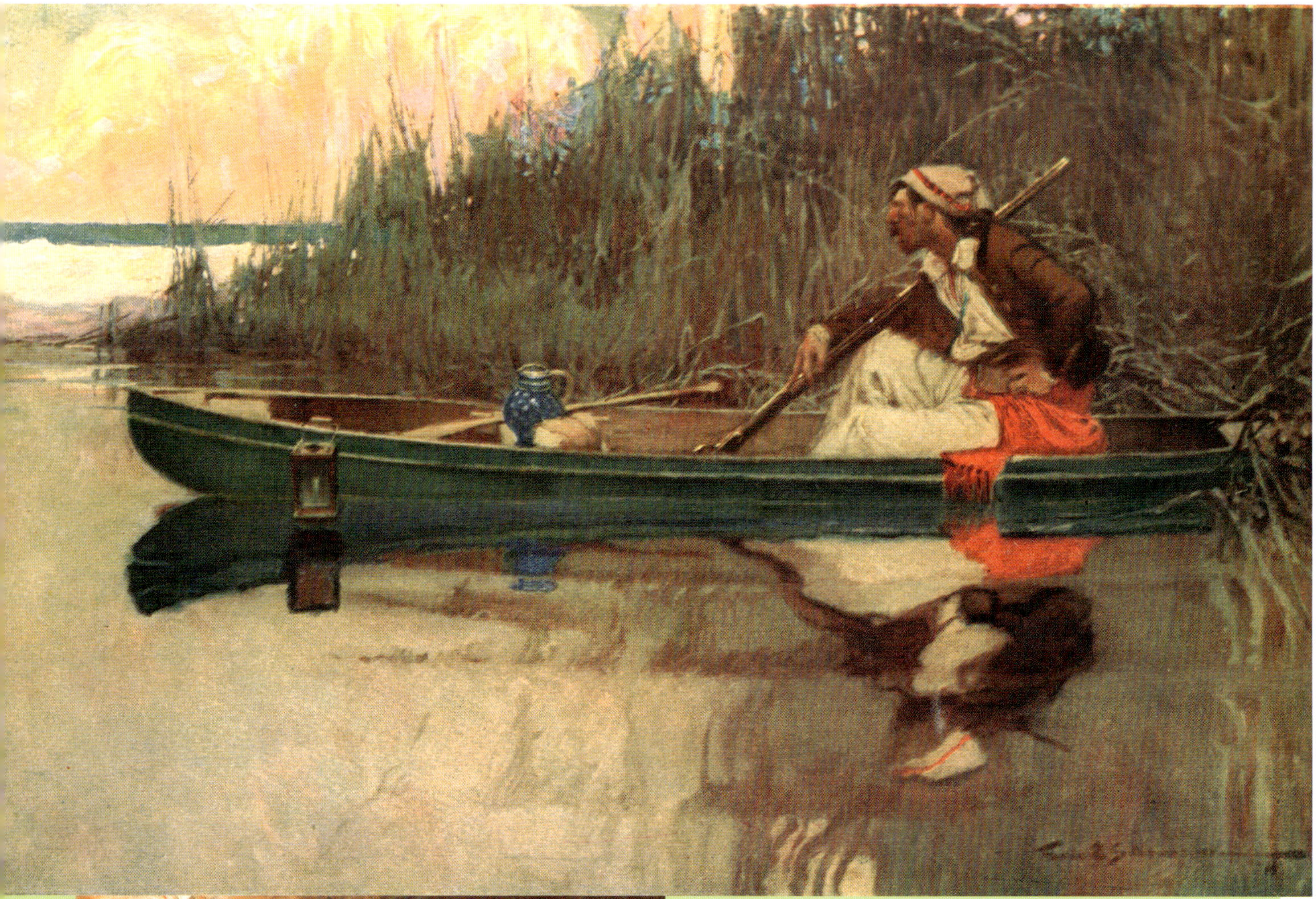

Schoonover provided the final details on Howard Pyle's "The Mermaid" (see page 175)—a painting that had been left unfinished since Pyle's fateful trip to Italy in 1911.

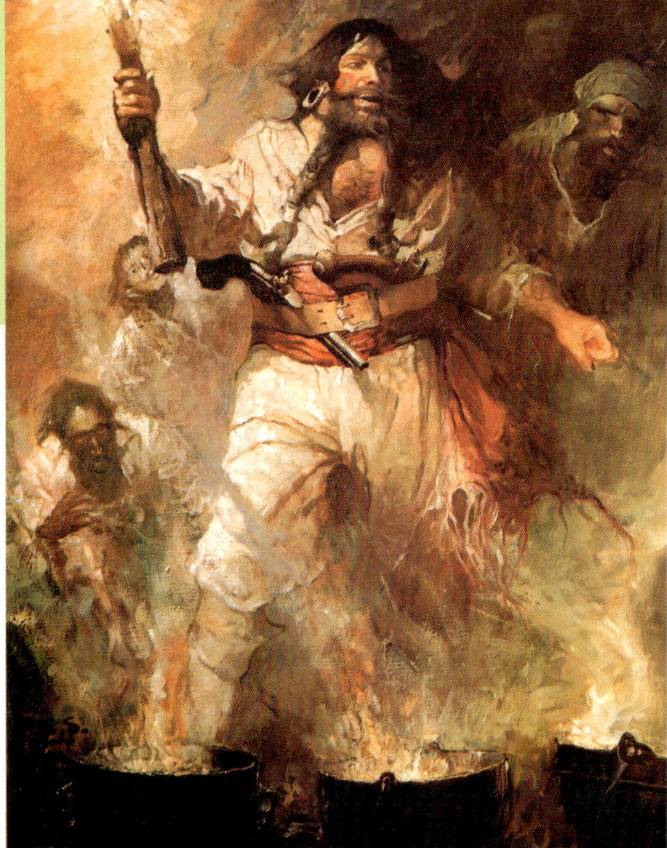

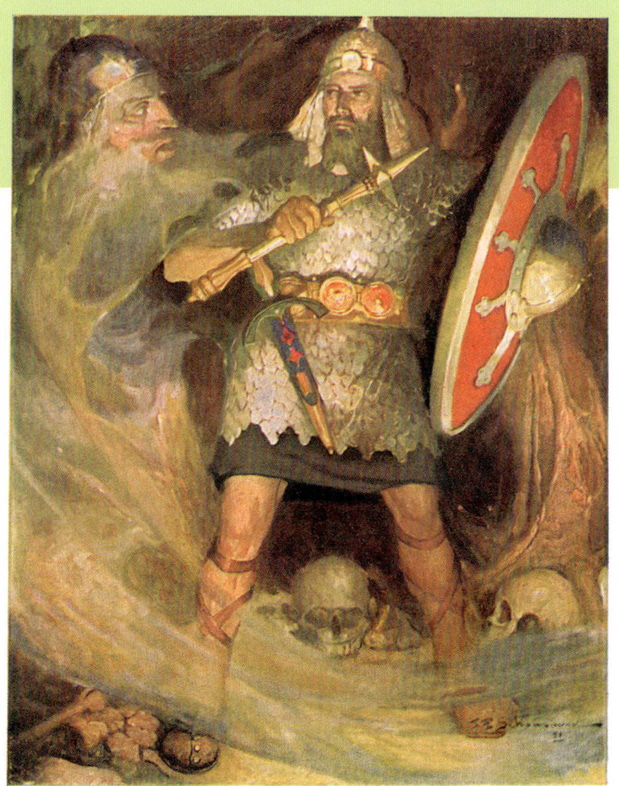

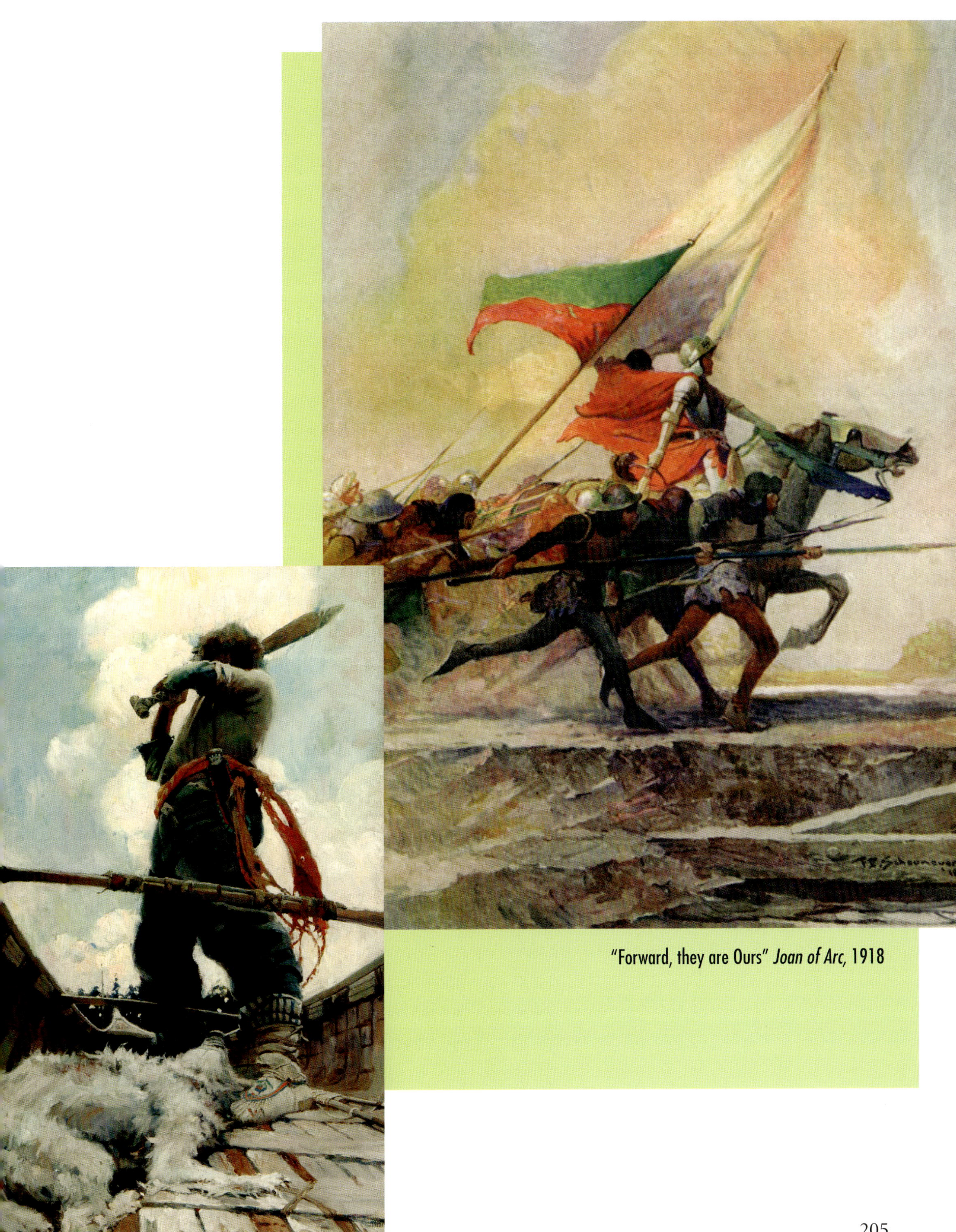

"Forward, they are Ours" *Joan of Arc,* 1918

BYAM SHAW

1872–1919, British

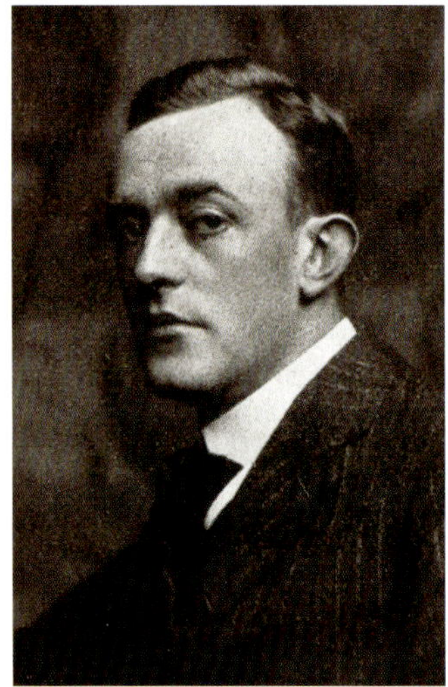

Originally born in India of English parents, John Byam Shaw came to England when he was six years of age, and began studies at the St. John's Wood Art School when he was 15. He went on to win several awards as a student, and was exhibiting at the Royal Academy at the age of 21. His ambition was formidable. Shaw's creative interests were broad—he was an accomplished gallery painter, mostly in the school of the Pre-Raphaelites. In the 20 years between 1896 and 1916, he had no less than five solo gallery shows.

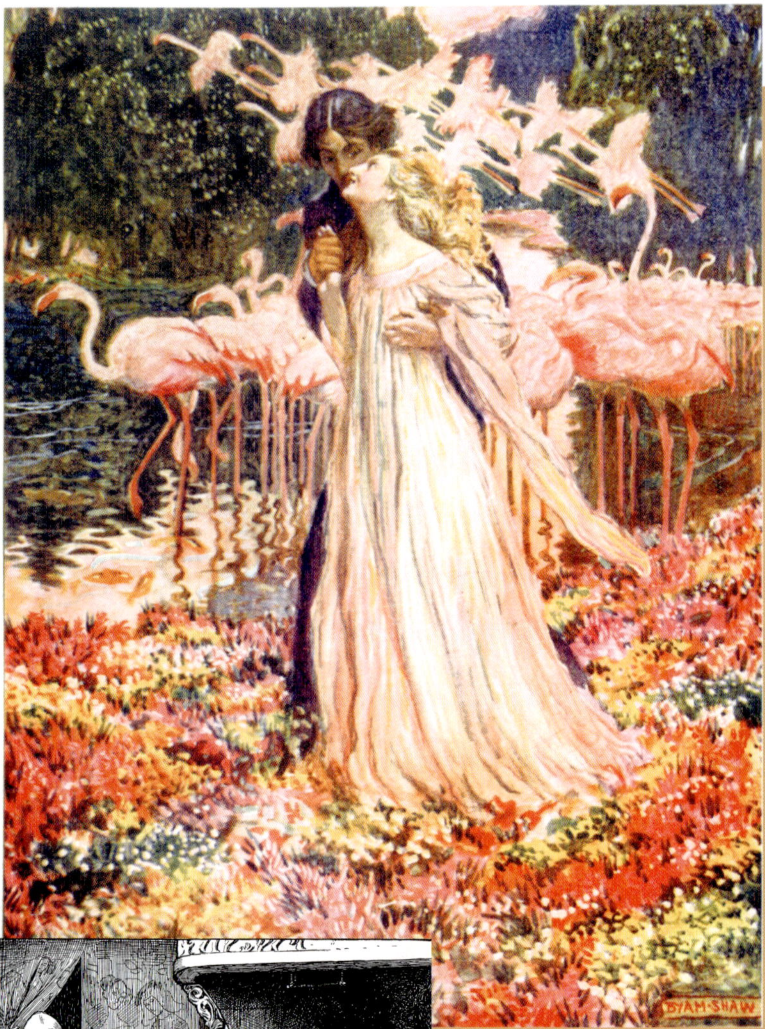

Shaw was greatly inspired by the words of others to create his large works, and he was frequently stirred by Rossetti's poetry. Before long, Shaw was sought out to illustrate a wide range of materials—Browning, Shakespeare, Haggard, and Poe were just some of the writers Shaw represented.

Teaching was also a large part of Shaw's later life—first at King's College, London, where he taught alongside other notable illustrators of the day, including Eleanor Fortescue Brickdale and Stephen Reid. In 1910, with long-time friend Rex Vicat Cole, Shaw taught at his own school; it was known as the Byam Shaw School of Art, and it operated under that name for nearly a century.

Mural and theater work were part of his repertoire as well. He worked with E. A. Abbey on a mural at the Palace of Westminster, and also painted depictions of actors, designed sets, and created backdrops. Wanting to contribute to the war effort during World War I, he and Cole joined the United Arts Rifles, though Shaw would transfer later to the Special Constabulary. He contributed to the effort with memorial works, poster designs, and portraits as well. Shortly after the war, the years of constant pressure caught up with Shaw; he collapsed and died at the age of forty-six.

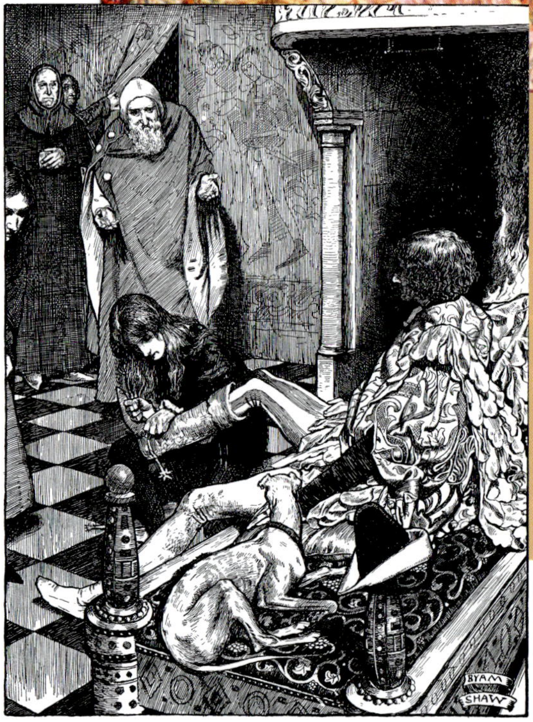

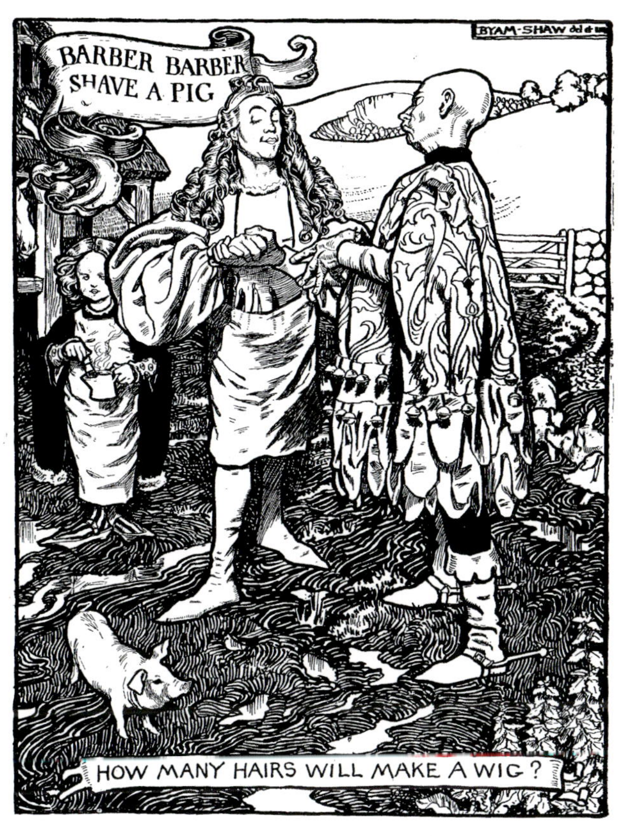
BARBER BARBER
SHAVE A PIG
BYAM·SHAW
HOW MANY HAIRS WILL MAKE A WIG?

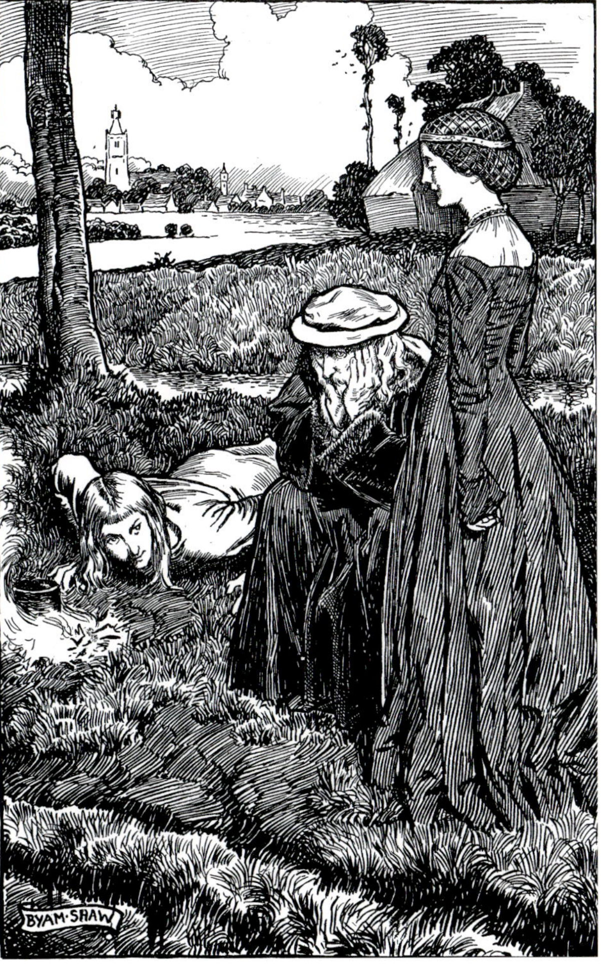
BYAM·SHAW

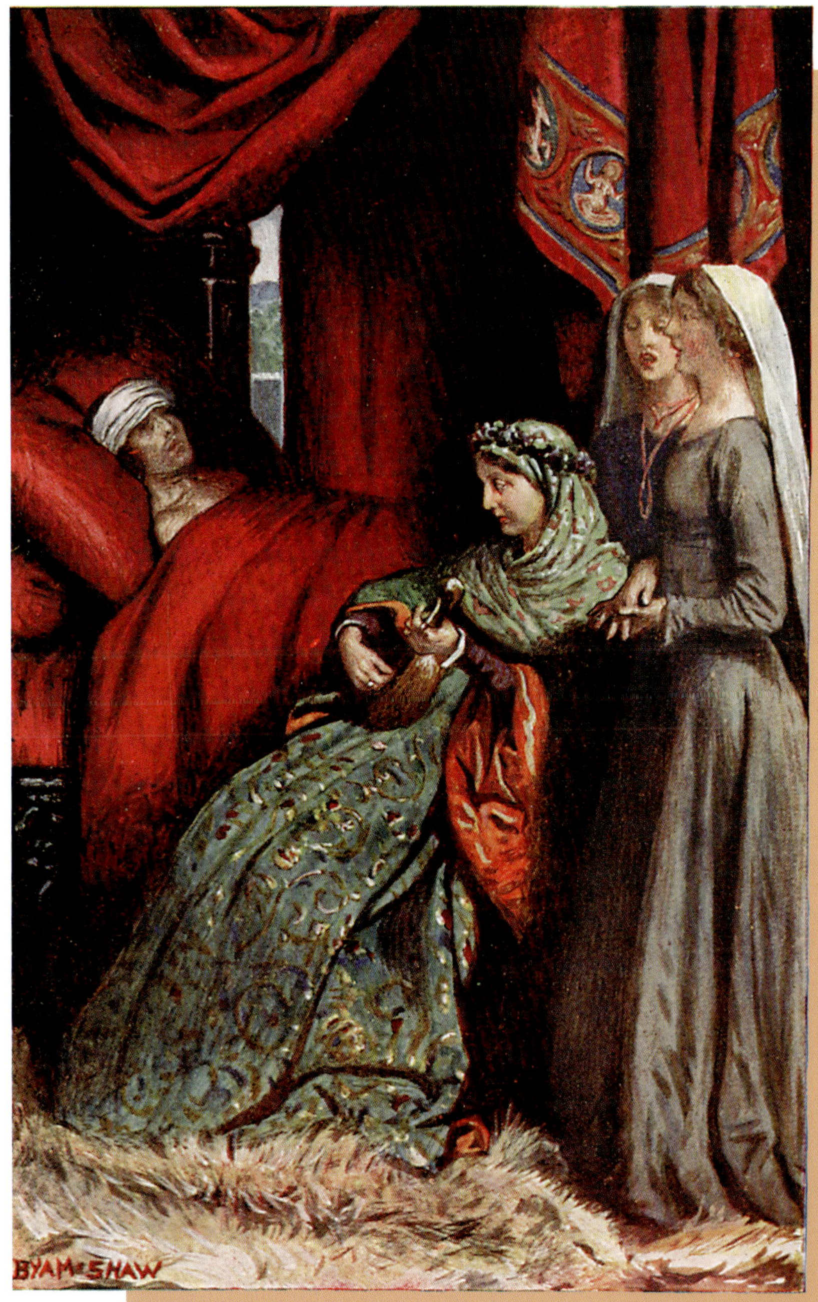
BYAM SHAW

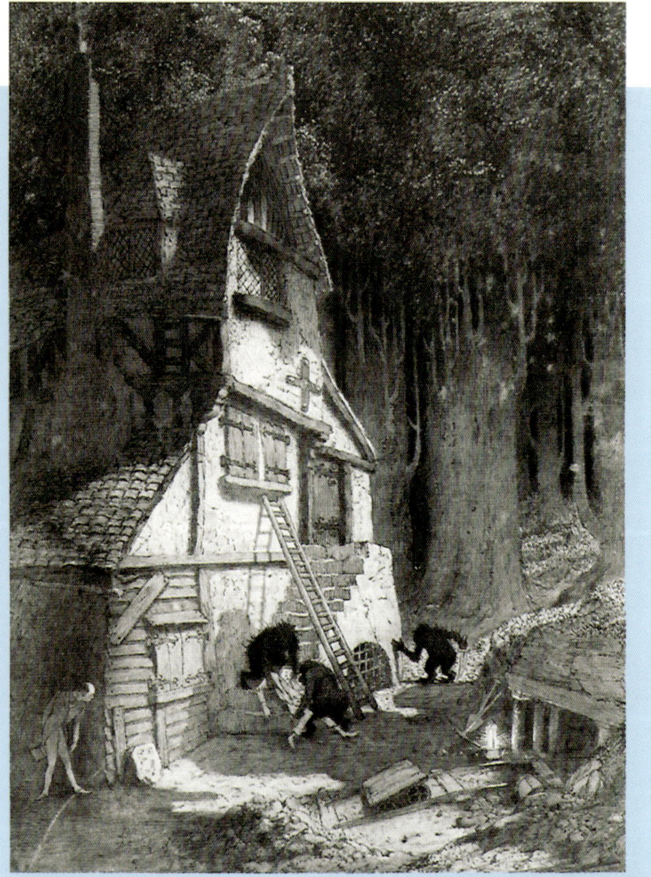

Sidney Sime

1867–1941, British

Prior to attending classes at the Liverpool School of Art, a young Sidney H. Sime spent time working as a coal miner, a baker, and a shoemaker, all before finding a job with a sign maker. Though he had always shown promise of artistic talent, it took a while before he could afford to take art classes while he worked. He was eventually noticed for his ability, and began to receive assignments as a freelance artist, mostly doing humorous cartoons. Sime's break came when he began working with the *London Illustrated News* in 1892. Over the next decade, he worked on a number of London-based magazines, including *The Strand, The Idler, The Sketch,* and *Eureka.* While illustrating some fanciful characters in these magazines, his work was noticed by an Irish author with some fantastic ideas of his own: Lord Dunsany.

In 1905 Dunsany approached Sime about illustrating a book of his short stories, *The Gods of Pegana.* With that book, a collaboration began between the two that existed for over fifteen years, and produced over 75 book illustrations painted by Sime. Most of these involved areas of fantasy and dream-like landscapes that had never been put on paper before. Sime was seen as an innovator, his work continuing to draw attention in even wider circles. Later that same year, he was offered a job by William Randolph Hearst in America. Sime accepted and moved to New York, but after half a year, he resigned the position, wanting to return to his friends and the familiar surroundings in England. On his return to England, he settled in Worplesdon, where he lived for the rest of his days.

The vision that Sime and Dunsany shared extended far beyond the work Sime did for the novels and short stories. Dunsany went on to become a markedly successful playwright, and Sime contributed to some of his stage designs, as well as the occasional frontispiece for a new collection of plays. Sime garnered high praise from critics, many of whom saw his work as visionary, comparing it to the likes of Blake and Doré.

When Europe became involved in World War I, Sime felt he must contribute to the effort, and, at 47, he joined the Army Service Corps. His contribution was cut short due to ill health, and on his return—aside from some sporadic magazine work—illustration assignments waned, and Sime's focus turned more toward painting. Two successful exhibitions of his work were held in London at the St. George Gallery in 1924 and 1927. A large collection of Sime's works can be viewed today at the Worplesdon Memorial Hall.

Sime, Sidney

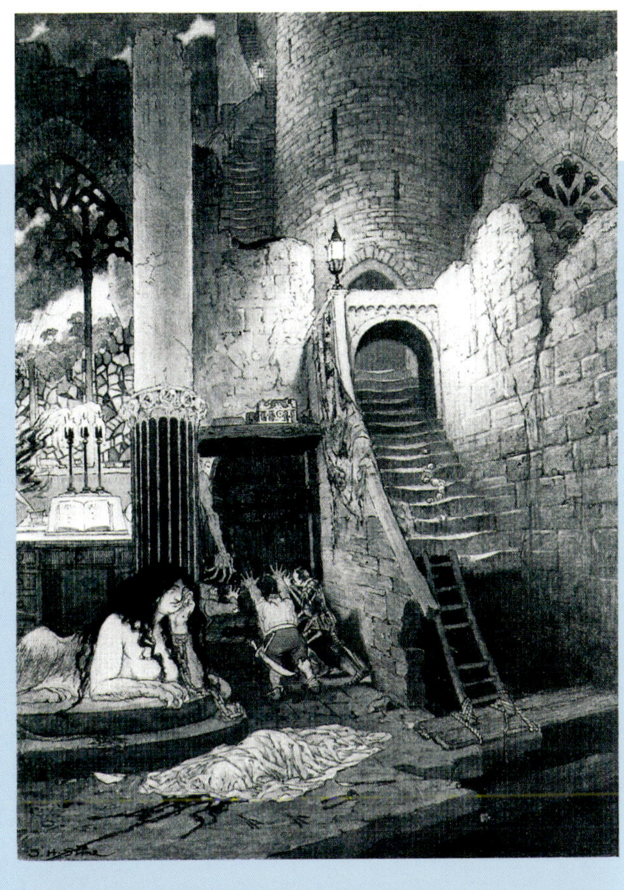

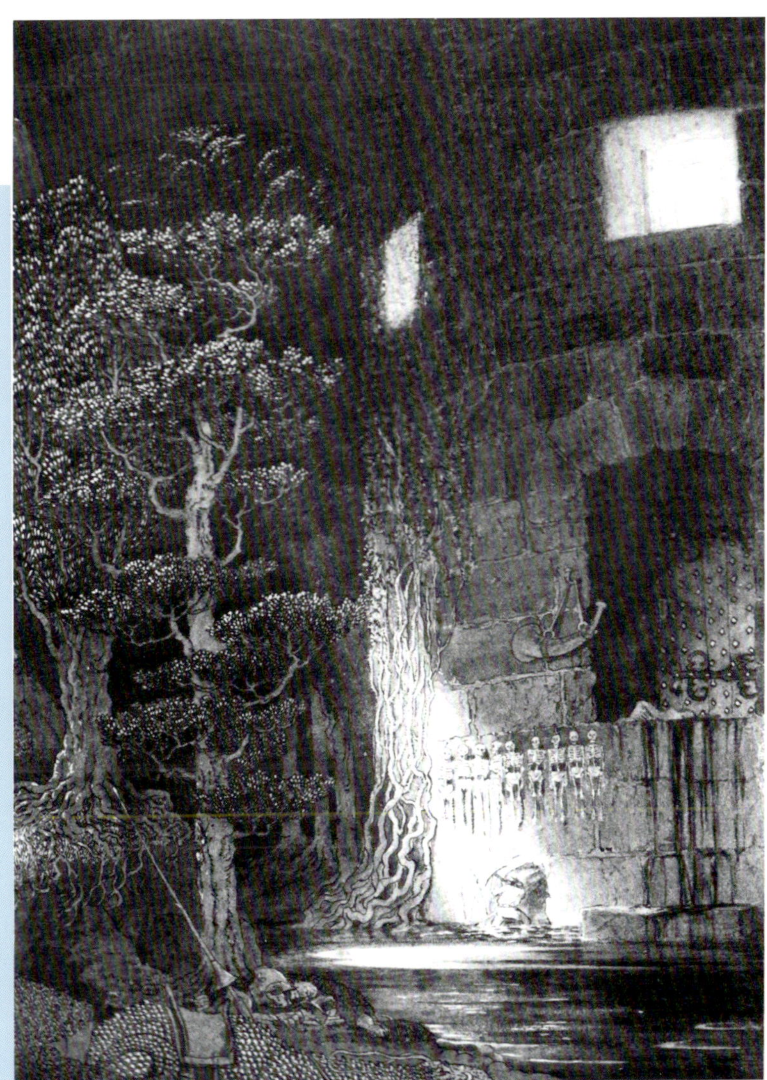

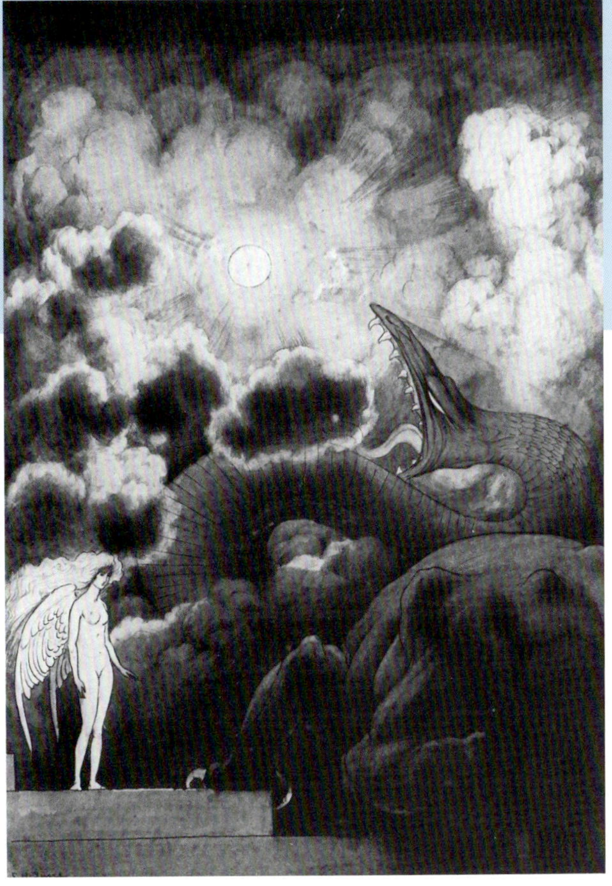

"...it was unlike anything that has ever been done before, anywhere else in the world..."

—Lord Dunsany, describing Sime's work

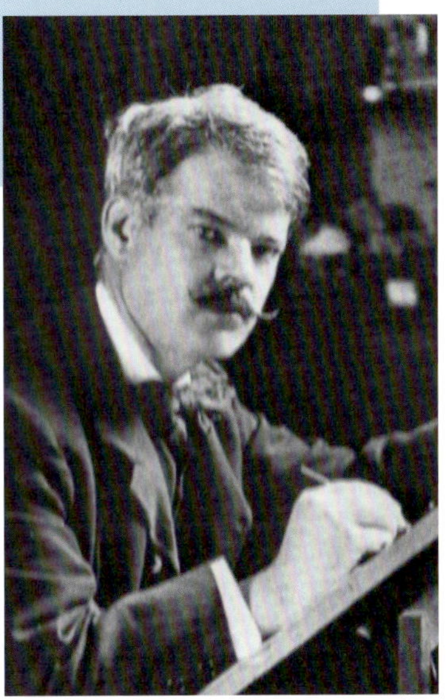

"Caricature is never a portrait; it's a comment."

—Sidney Sime

Jessie Willcox Smith

1863–1935, American

One of the pioneering women of illustration, Jessie Willcox Smith was already a teacher when Howard Pyle convinced her that she could make a professional career out of illustration. As Pyle's student at Drexel, Smith encountered Violet Oakley and Elizabeth Shippen Green, who would become close friends and later, studio mates, while all were studying with Pyle. Some of Smith's earliest works were collaborative efforts with the other two women artists.

With her charming illustrations of children, Smith was a well-sought artist for many assignments from both book publishers and magazines, especially where children and mothers were depicted. For many years she was a mainstay of *Good Housekeeping*, completing nearly 200 covers for the magazine in her career.

Her best-remembered illustrated work is her 1916 edition of Kingsley's *The Water Babies,* considered an ideal match for Smith's strengths. Some of the other books Smith illustrated were destined to become classics—*Little Women, At the Back of the North Wind,* and *Heidi,* all of which are fine examples of Smith's beautiful depictions of children. She concentrated on portraits and magazine covers in the latter years of her career, working with *Good Housekeeping* until 1933.

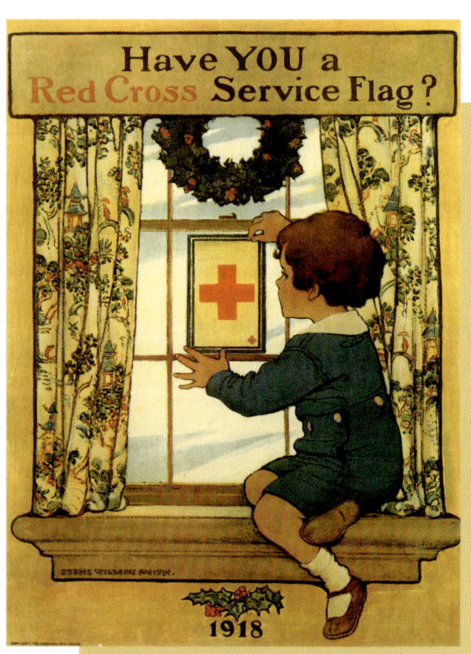

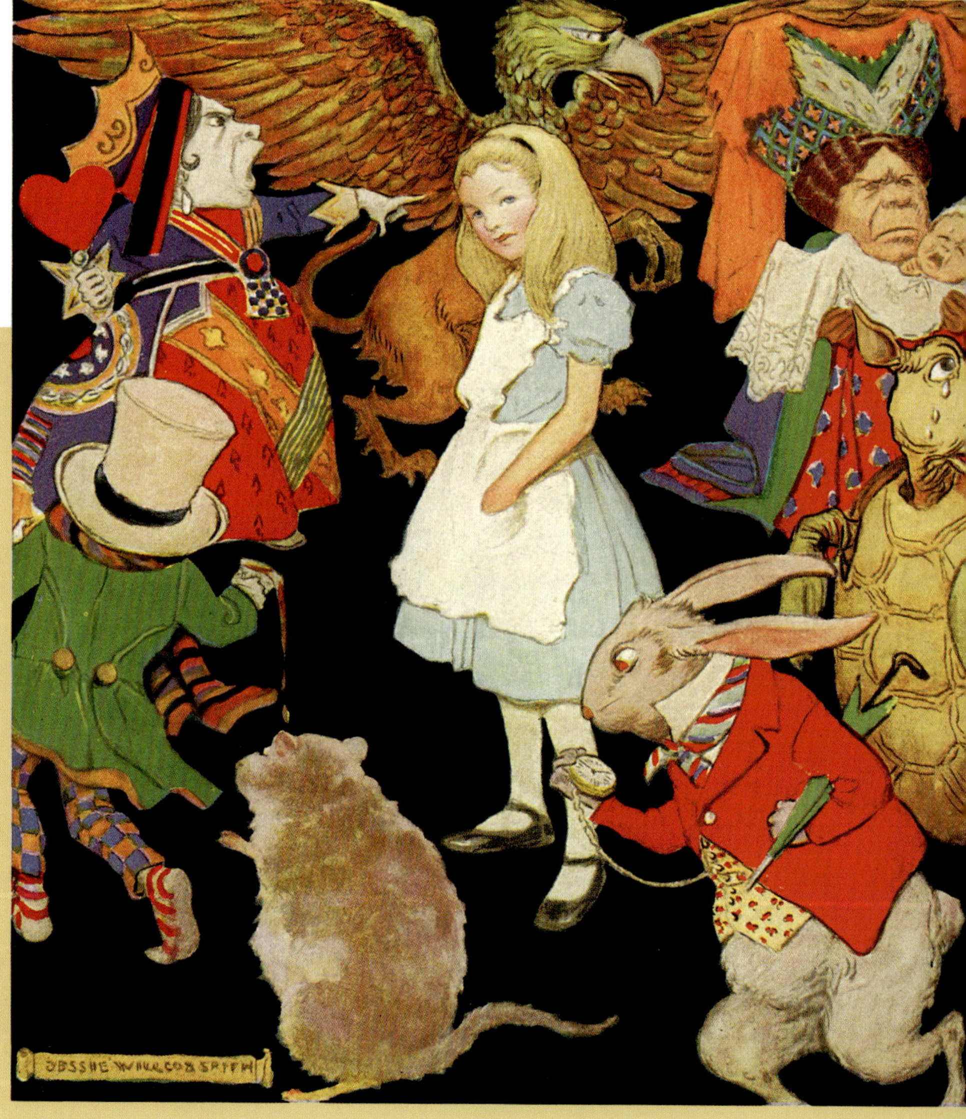

From the serious nature of wartime to the depths of Wonderland, Smith's work kept pace with the best artists.

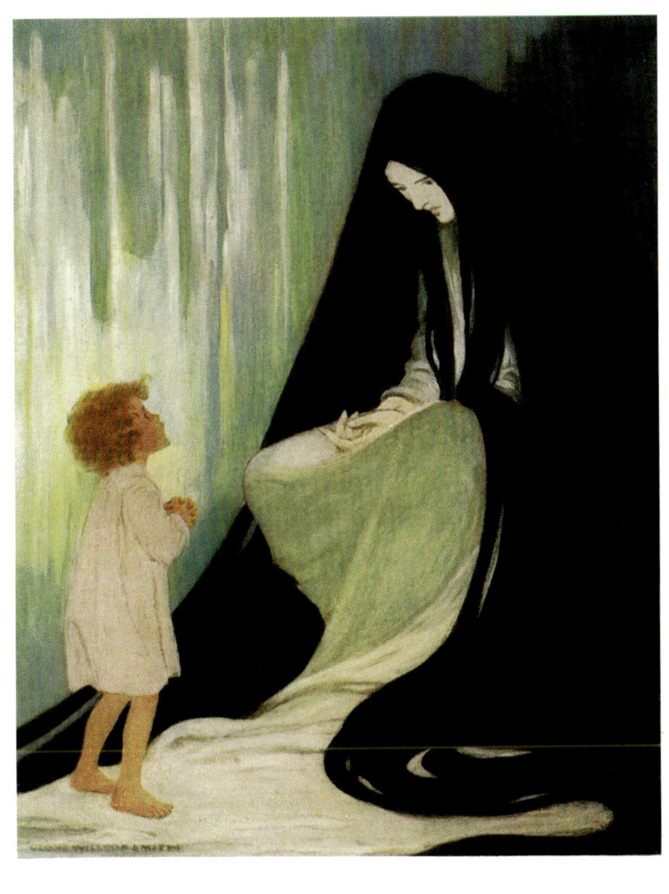

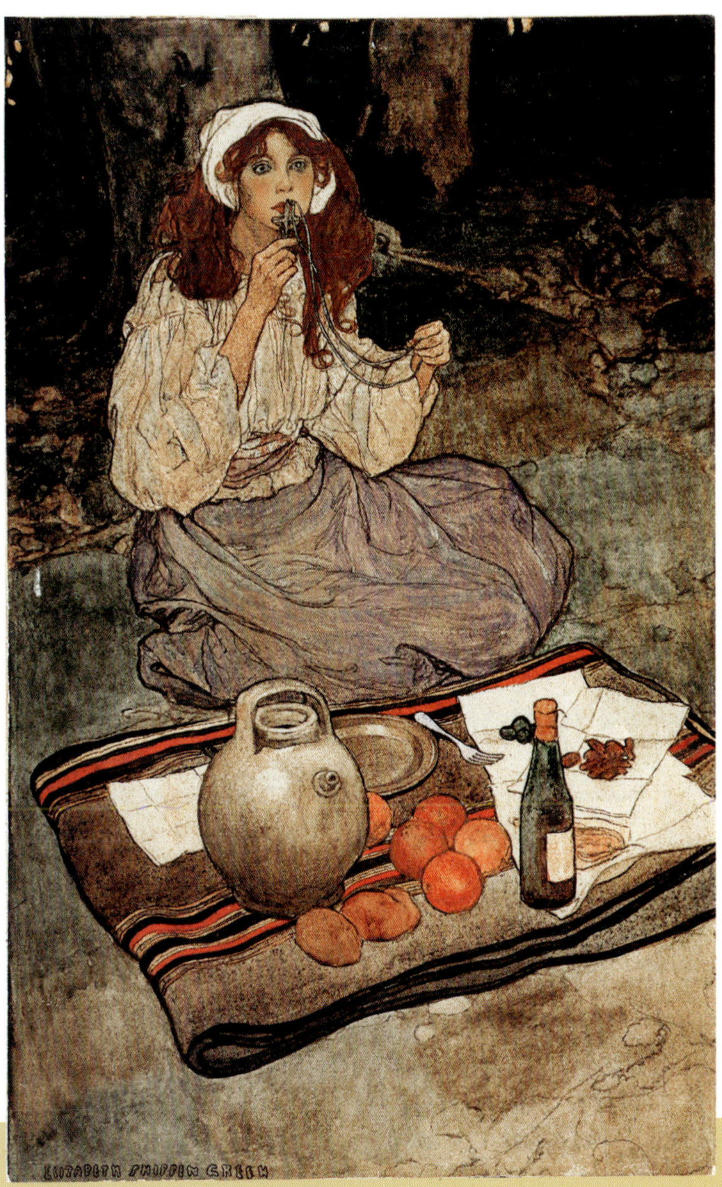

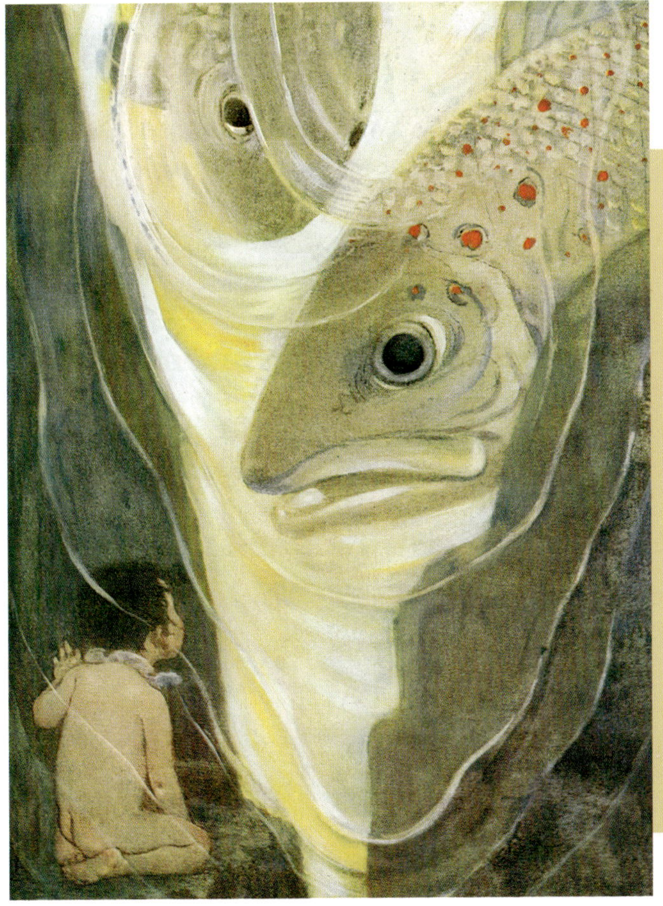

"That charm in children that appeals to all pervades her work, and, although it is essentially illustrative in its rendering, a high order of craftsmanship is displayed."

— A critic on Smith's work, *A Child's Garden of Verses,* 1905

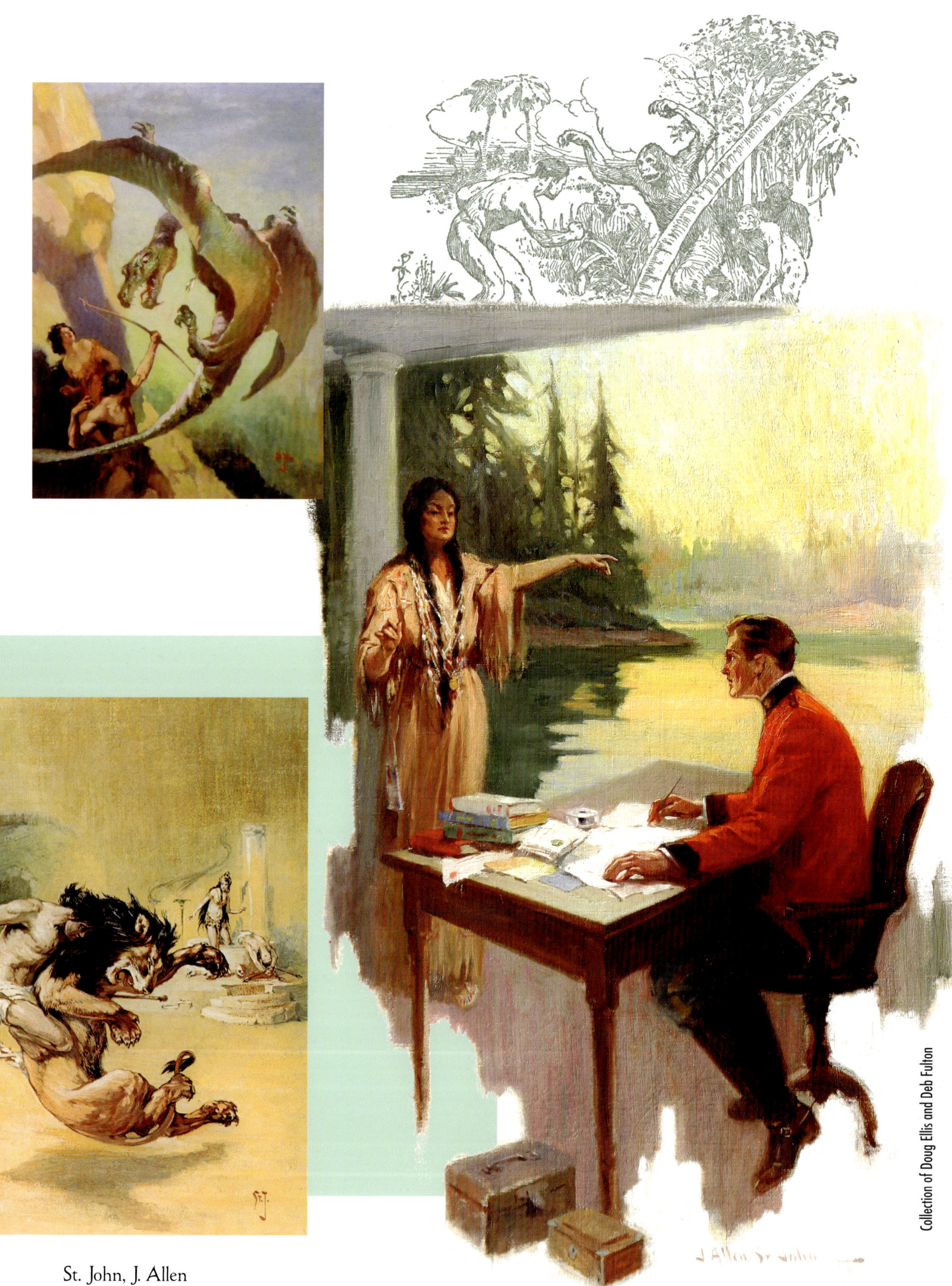

St. John, J. Allen

Collection of Doug Ellis and Deb Fulton

J. Allen St. John

1872–1957, American

At a very early age, James Allen St. John was exposed to the idea of an artistic lifestyle. Though his father was a practical man with a medical practice in Chicago, his mother was a free-spirited artist whose father was also a portrait painter. Though she studied for some time at the Art Institute of Chicago, she had greater aspirations, and in 1880 she left Chicago with her then-eight-year-old son, to study at the École des Beaux-Arts in Paris.

St. John spent the next three years in Paris, fascinated by his mother's circle of artistic friends, and visits to the Louvre and other Paris museums were some of his happiest memories. The family reunited in New York, where his mother opened a portrait studio after more studies at the National Academy of Design. As St. John finished his public school studies in 8th grade, his father sought to give him a solid start by buying a partnership in a trade company. St. John's career aspirations could hardly have been further away from his father's wishes. His father was determined to give his son some sense of a hard-working lifestyle, and the teenaged St. John was sent to work with an uncle and some cousins on a California ranch. Soon after, St. John found a teacher named Eugene Torrey. A landscape painter in the area, Torrey was an acquaintance of St. John's mother from her days at the École des Beaux-Arts, and he provided St. John with some formative art instruction for the next three years. Finally, St. John had found his path.

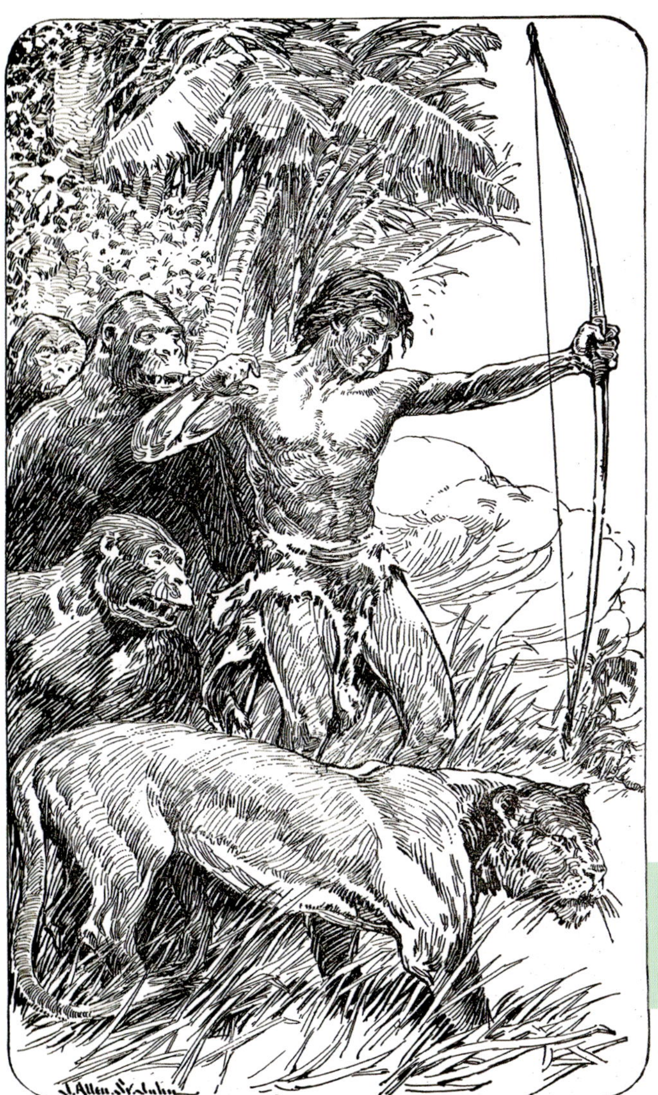

In the next decade, St. John moved back to New York, studying with William Merritt Chase at the Art Students League, and found his footing as a painter-illustrator in New York. In 1903, his father—who had moved back to Chicago a few years earlier—took ill, and St. John went West to help his mother care for him. Chicago remained an important base for St. John throughout his career, and he began to acquire work from Midwest publishers, including a book of his own. St. John wrote and illustrated *The Face in the Pool* for the A. C. McClurg Company in 1904.

Like his mother before him, St. John sought the influence and history of Paris. In 1908 he and his wife journeyed to France so he could study at the Académie Julian for two years. Returning to Chicago in 1910, St. John remained there for the rest of his life, including time spent living in the Tree Studio artists complex. Chicago's McClurg, which had published his book over a decade earlier, approached St. John to do interior illustrations for *The Return of Tarzan* in 1915. Edgar Rice Burroughs's writings, paired with St. John's art, formed a solid partnership, and the illustrator would continue to work on Burroughs's stories for the remainder of his career.

With a strong interest in the field of fantasy and adventure stories, St. John first regarded Burroughs's stories as just another project in his career, but it would become his legacy. Decades of working on those stories led to illustrating the pulp magazines of the 1920s and '30s, and the science-fiction and adventure magazines of the '40s and '50s. St. John also taught for most of his years in Chicago, at the Art Institute of Chicago, and later at the American Academy of Art.

Partner to Tarzan

St. John became Burroughs's most regular illustrator, working not only on *Tarzan*, but on the entire Burroughs library.

Frederic Dorr Steele

1873–1944, American

Born in a lumber camp deep in the Michigan wilderness, Frederic Dorr Steele found his way to New York, where he pursued the idea of becoming an illustrator, studying at the National Academy of Design. Steele worked for most of his career in a style that accentuated his drawing technique, using a dark stroke over a rough surface to achieve a halftone-like effect. He found clients in many magazines during the early part of the century, among them, *Scribner's Monthly, Collier's Weekly, The Century,* and *McClure's.*

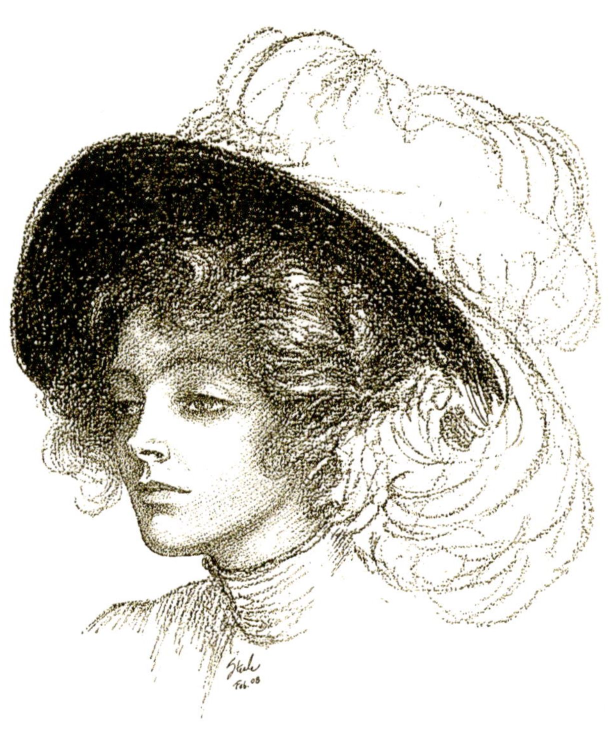

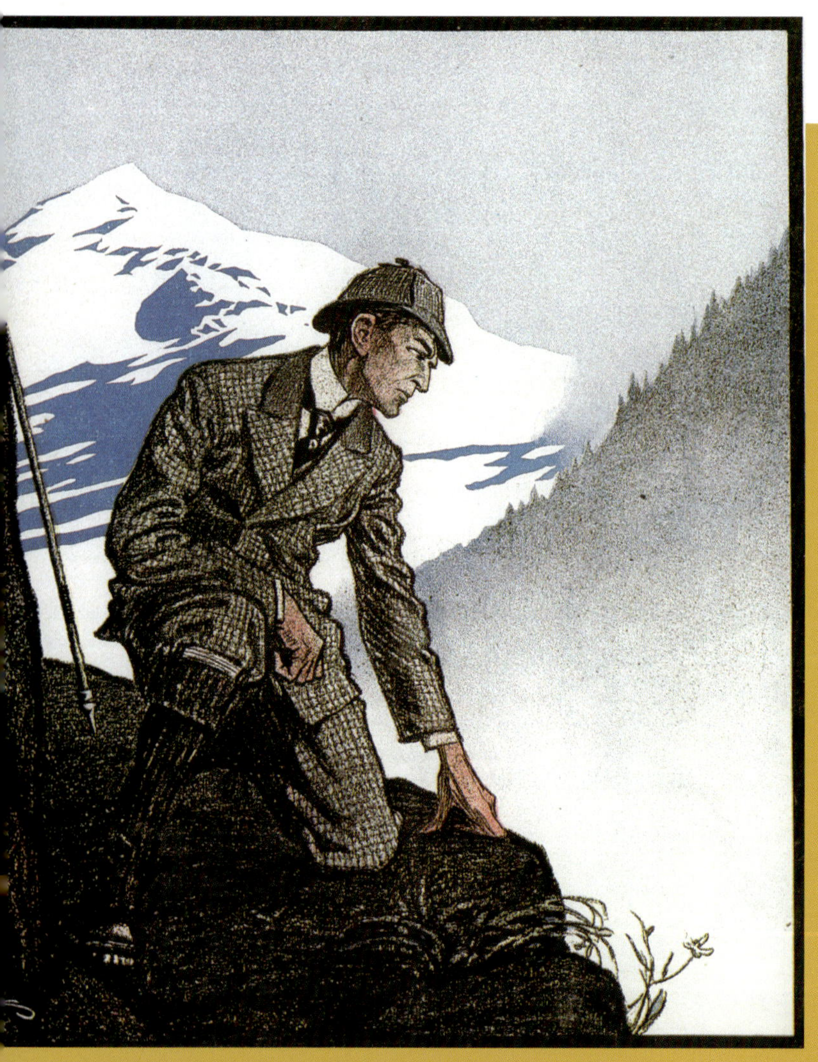

America's Holmes
Landing the Sherlock Holmes assignments for *Collier's* magazine gave a large part of Steele's work a lasting legacy.

In 1903 Steele was given an opportunity that would give his images lasting fame, and preserve interest in his work for posterity. *Collier's Weekly* hired him to illustrate the American edition of Sir Arthur Conan Doyle's *The Return of Sherlock Holmes.* It resulted in a long and productive partnership, and Steele illustrated Doyle's stories for most of his career. Actor William Gillette served as Steele's model for Holmes, and he has been cited as largely responsible for providing us with two of the character's most iconic symbols: the deerstalker hat and the calabash pipe.

Steele took the position of art editor at *Everybody's Magazine* for a period during World War I, and late in his career he found steady work doing theatrical sketches for the *New York Herald Tribune.* He also taught at the Art Students League in New York, where he had studied years before. In his twilight years he was still very much linked to the fictional character of Sherlock Holmes, and was working on a new collection when he passed away in 1944.

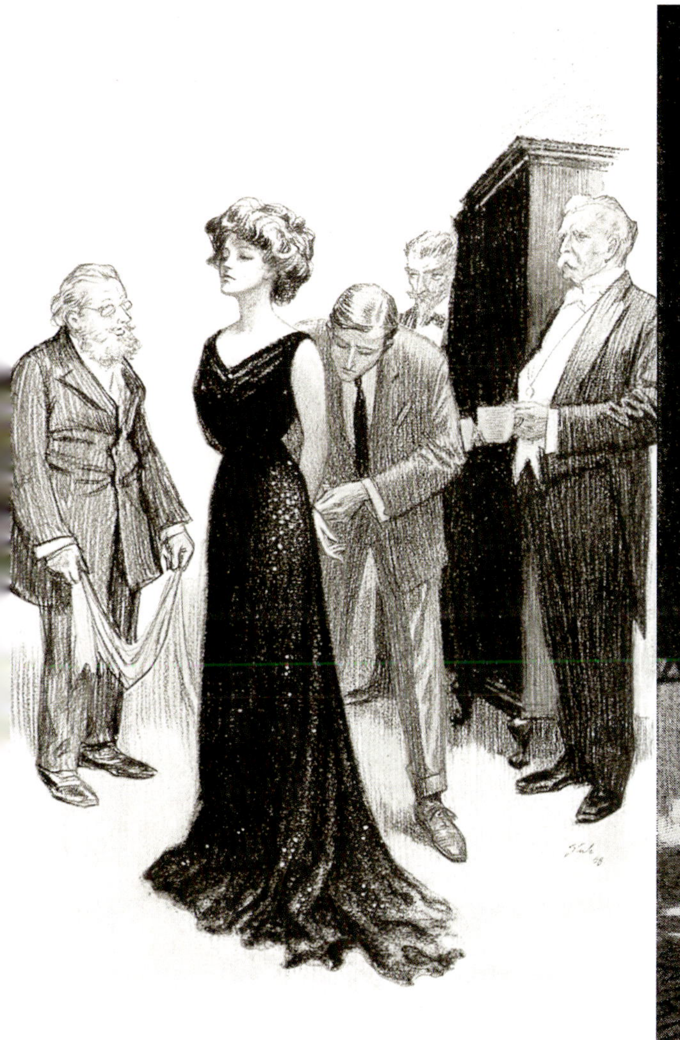

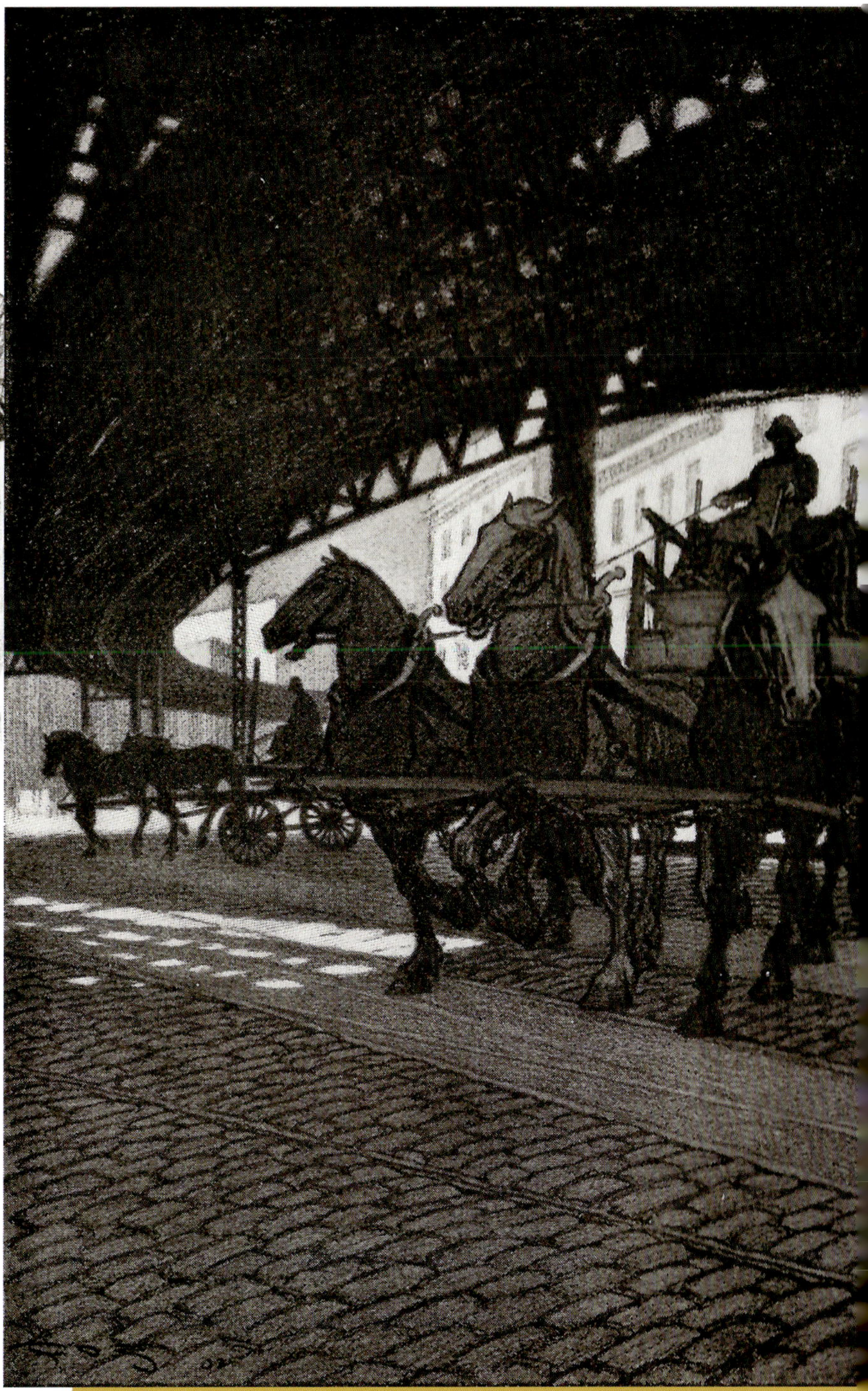

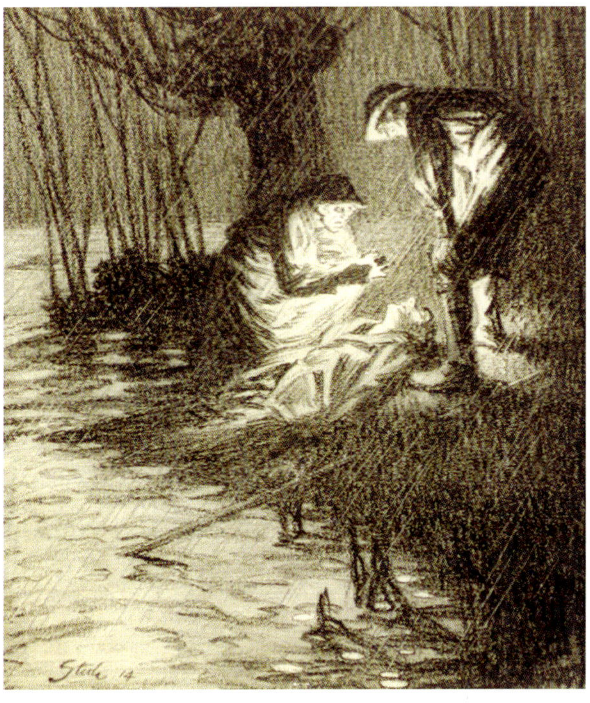

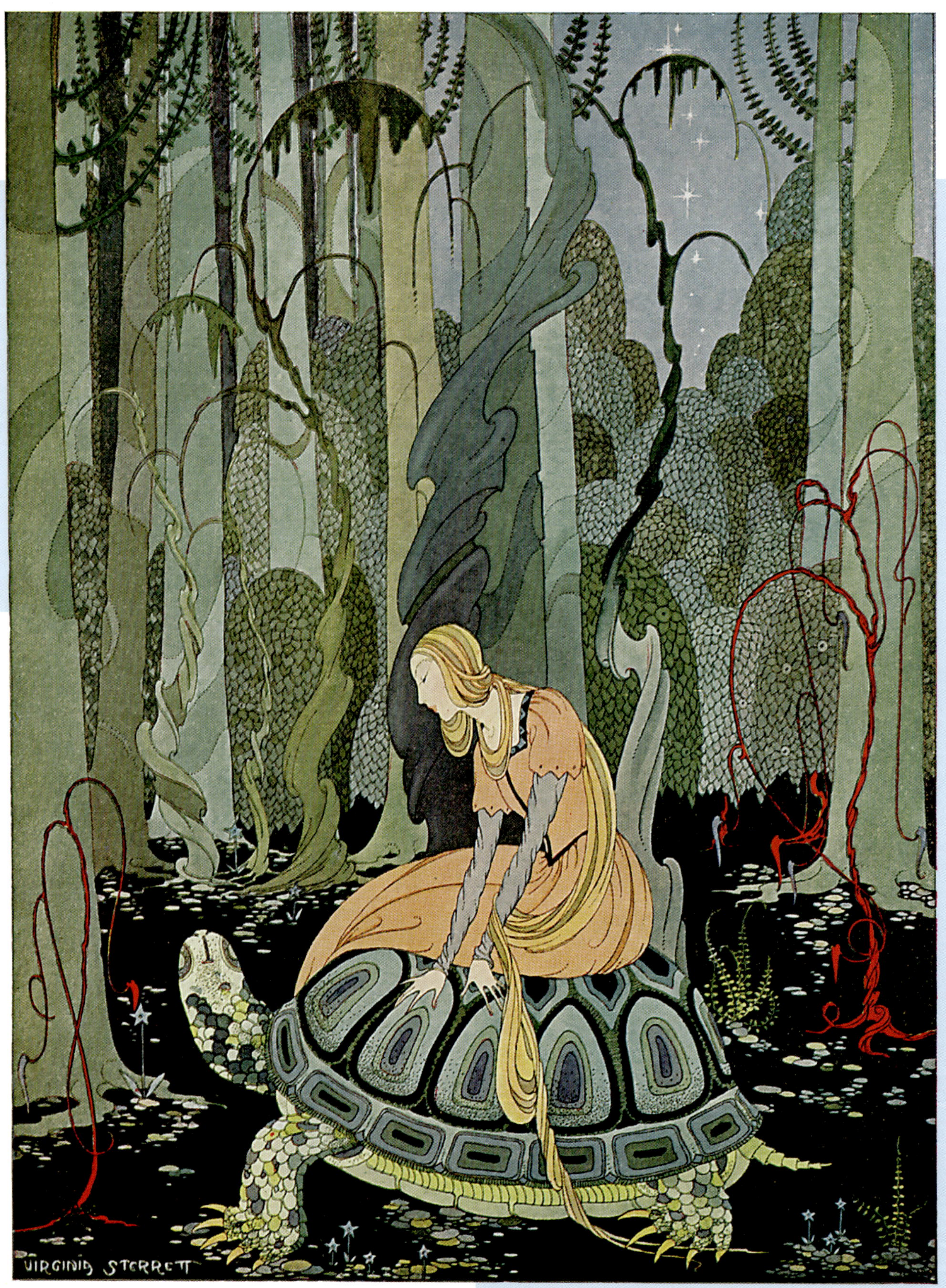

Sterrett, Virginia F.

Virginia F. Sterrett

1900~1931, American

We can only wonder what Virginia Francis Sterrett, a rising star in her teens, might have shared had she led a longer life. In fragile health from an early age, she experienced adventure through her artwork. Born in Chicago and spending her childhood in the Midwest, Sterrett was drawn to the imaginative, and her art became her outlet. Childhood was a tough time for Sterrett, as her father died early in her life, and her mother's health took a serious downturn when Virginia was still a teenager. Sterrett had exhibited promise in her drawing, and secured a full scholarship from the Art Institute of Chicago. However, she needed to leave after only a year of study in order to support her mother. Sterrett found work in Chicago's advertising agencies, and before she was 20, she received her first book commission: *Old French Fairy Tales* by the Comtesse de Ségur.

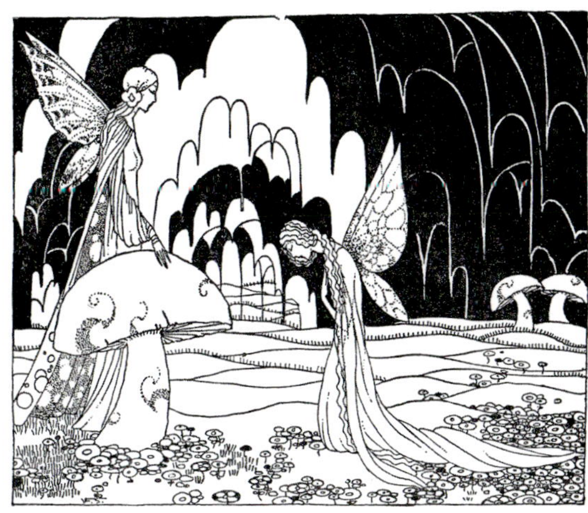

The Penn Publishing Company of Philadelphia would be the only publisher to hire her. They employed Sterrett to illustrate a fairy tale collection, followed by Hawthorne's *Tanglewood Tales* in 1921. Years later, in 1928, *Arabian Nights* would be Sterrett's last title, due to her poor health. Tuberculosis curtailed her career, and eventually would take her life. In 1930, after some improvement, Sterrett attempted a fourth commission—*Myths and Legends*—but it was not completed when her life ended on June 8, 1931. The three books she produced have become highly sought-after by collectors, though the *Arabian Nights* is considered by far to be her best work.

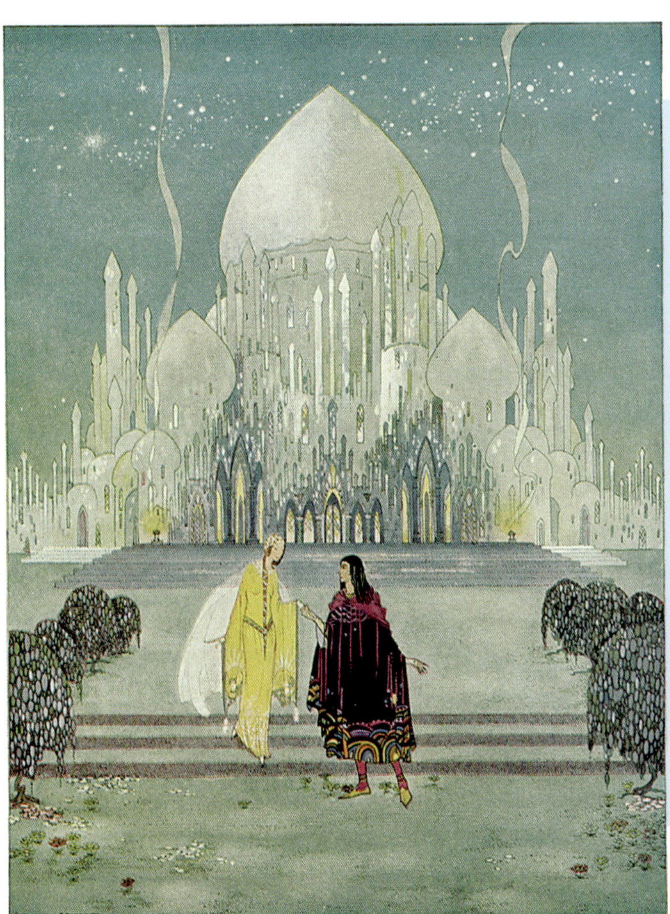

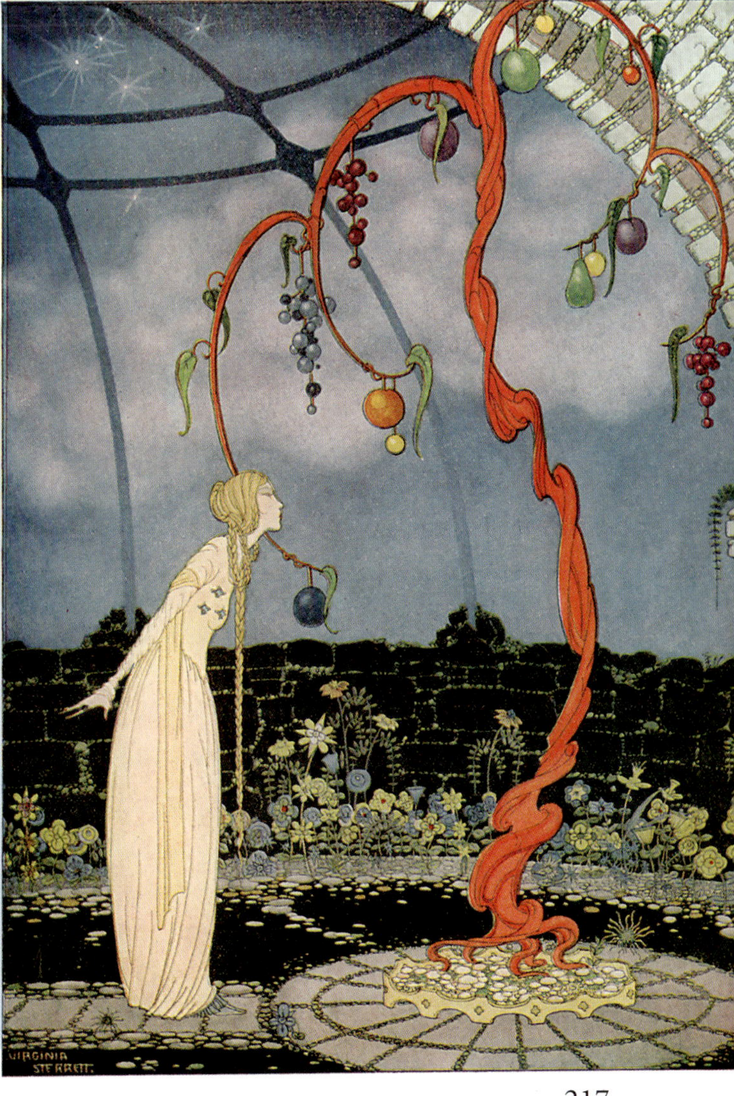

Helen Stratton

1867–1961, British

Helen Stratton was born in India, where her father was a prominent doctor and administrator. Stratton was still an infant when he retired and the family settled in England.

In 1891 Helen was studying art in Kensington, and within five years, illustrated books bearing her name were finding their way into families' homes. Fairy tales were often her subject matter of choice, and her comprehensive treatment of *Andersen's Tales*—initially released as magazine-like signatures, and later assembled as a book—held over 300 ink drawings by Stratton. In its compiled form, it is one of the most thoroughly illustrated collections of Andersen's tales available to this day. She concentrated her work almost exclusively in the fairy tale market, with little deviation in subject matter, until the 1920s.

Much of her later life was spent in and around Bath, England. Though she remained active in painting and portraiture, she is largely remembered for the artwork she created during illustration's Golden Age.

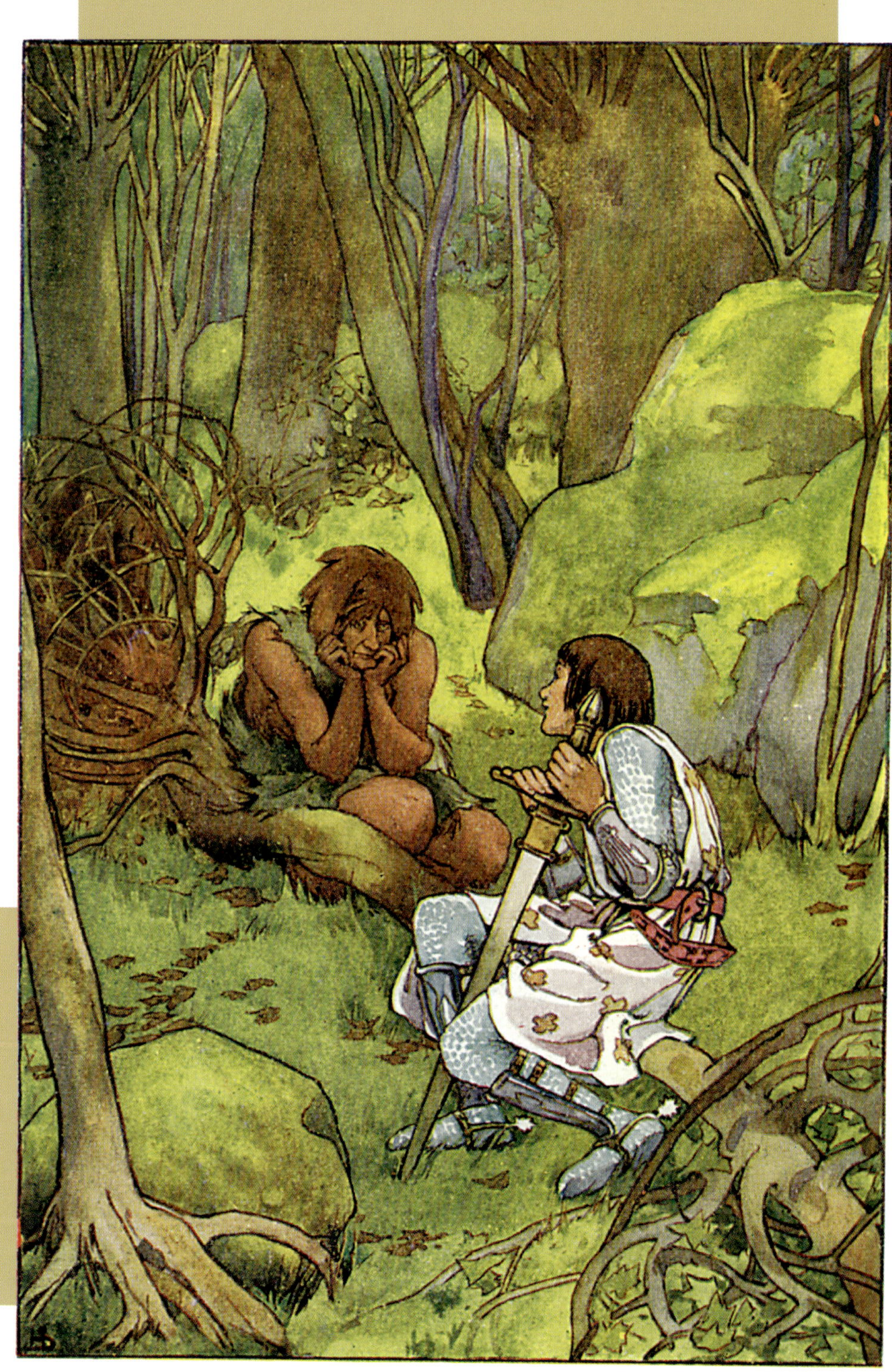

From *Heroic Legends*, 1908

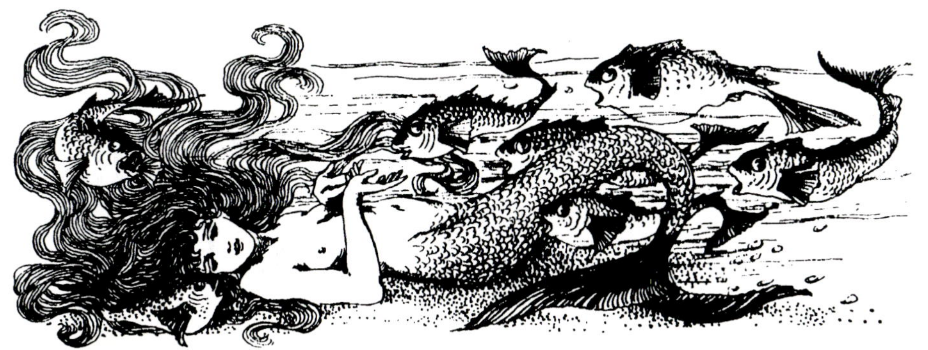

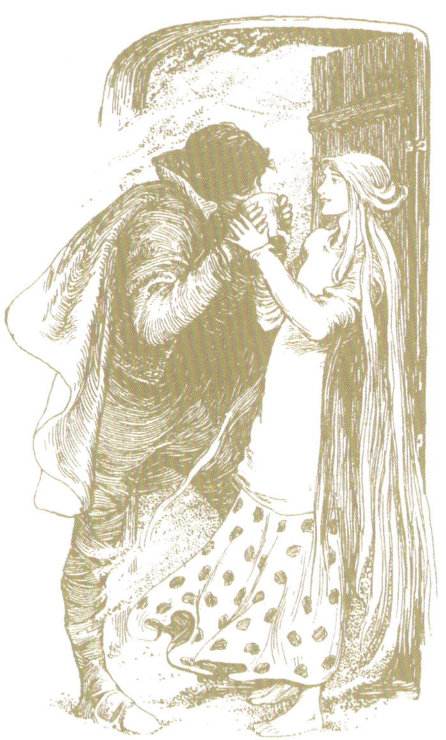

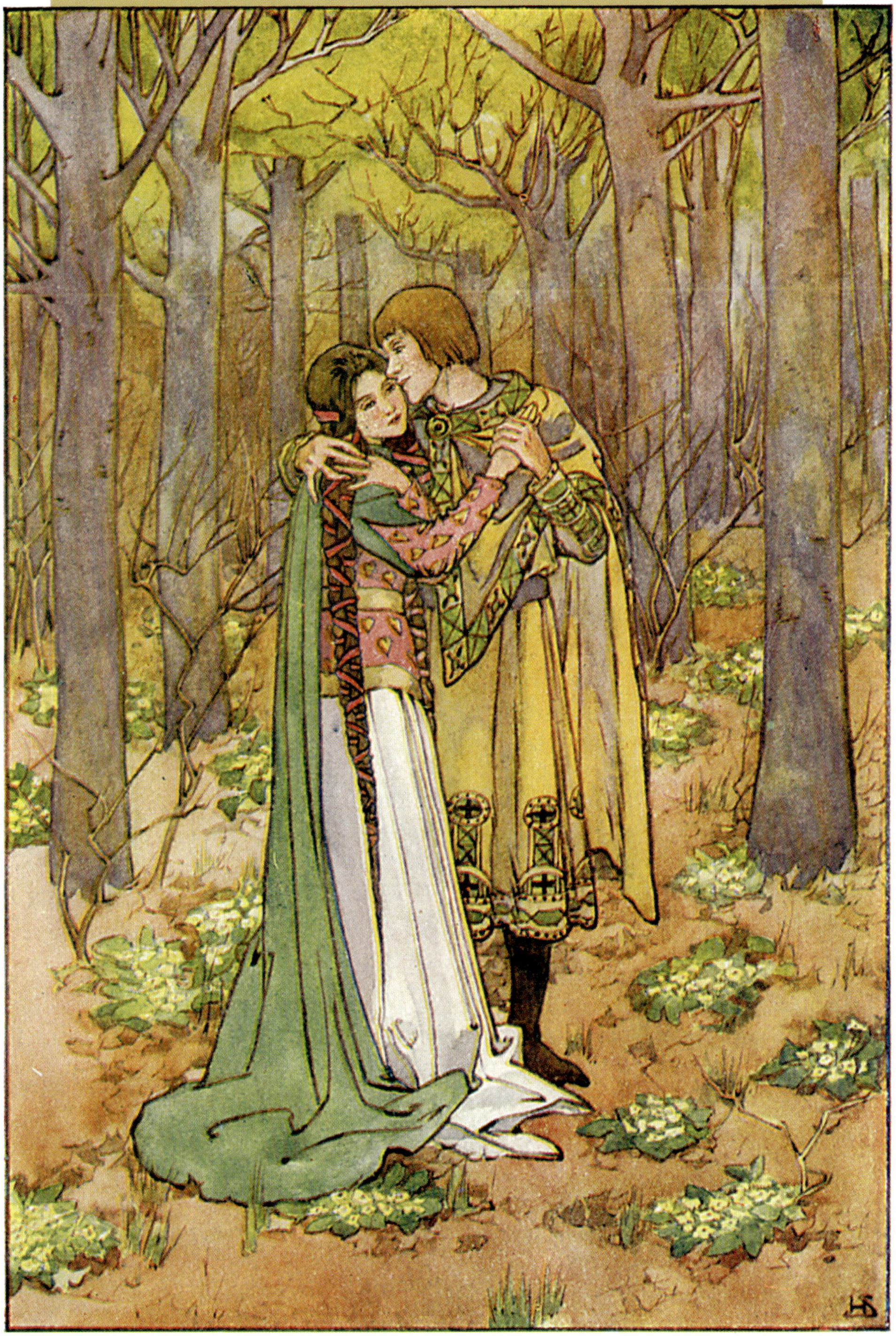

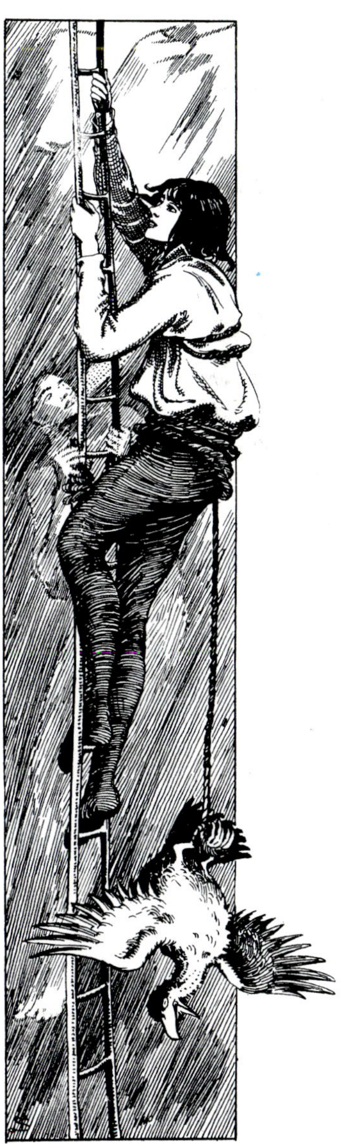

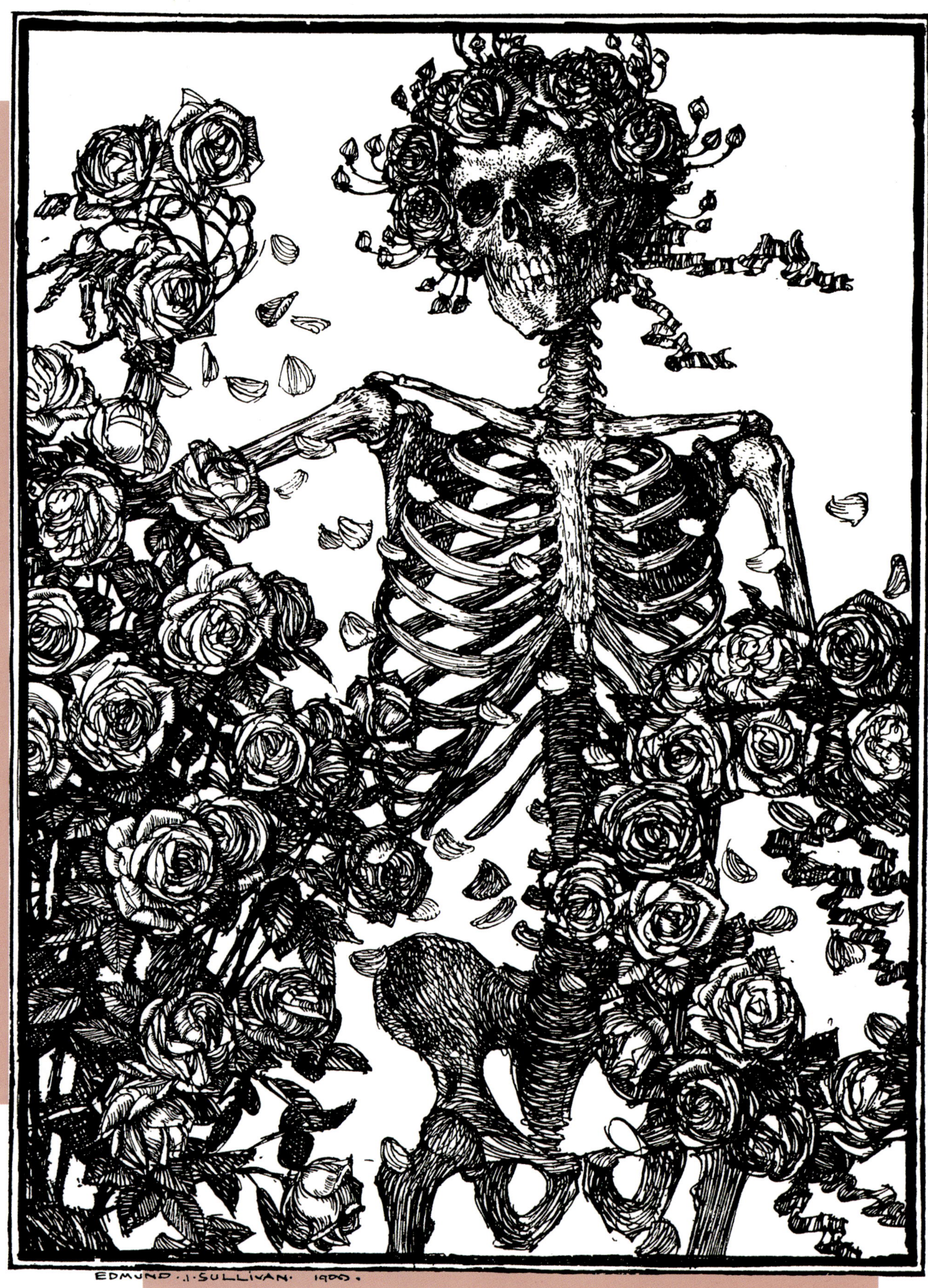

"A very bad picture or drawing may be a very good illustration—and a very beautiful one may contain very little demonstrative value." —Edmund Sullivan

Sullivan, Edmund

EDMUND SULLIVAN
1869–1933, British

Taught how to draw by his father, Edmund Joseph Sullivan was enticed by the graphic design that was a strong part of the growing print industry in Britain at the close of the nineteenth century. His work incorporates the approach of traditional illustration, but also embraces the strong design sense of the period.

With a start at *The Daily Graphic,* and work at *Pall Mall Magazine* in the early stages of his career, Sullivan received a solid foundation in the basic skills of composition, likeness, and inking technique. Illustrating fiction for the magazine soon led to book illustration, where his artistic voice was allowed to find its true expression. Sullivan's output was truly impressive, if not staggering. By 1896 he had illustrated four books—with a combined total of 262 drawings—and maintained his magazine work. Sullivan's styles often shifted in respect to his subjects, and as his career progressed, he refined his application of line to aid in better reproduction. Published in 1898, *Sartor Resartus,* with 79 line illustrations, is considered to be one of his best books. A philosophical tale by Thomas Carlyle, it contains a wild assortment of characters and symbolic ideas that suited Sullivan's tastes to a tee.

Like many who straddled the period between line work in magazines and the early days of four-color printing, his ink work remained his strongest method of creating images. Sullivan did venture into some areas of color work in the early twentieth century, most commonly using watercolor. Actively supporting his profession, Sullivan became president of the Art Worker's Guild, taught illustration and lithography, and wrote several books on the subject in the early '20s, including *The Art of Illustration* in 1921 and *Line* in 1922.

In the 1960s, an image of a skeleton with roses, originally done by Sullivan as an illustration for *The Rubáiyát of Omar Khayyám,* was repurposed for use in the iconography of the San Francisco-based rock group, The Grateful Dead. It went on to become one of the band's most widely used graphics, and a fan favorite—though few are aware of its origin.

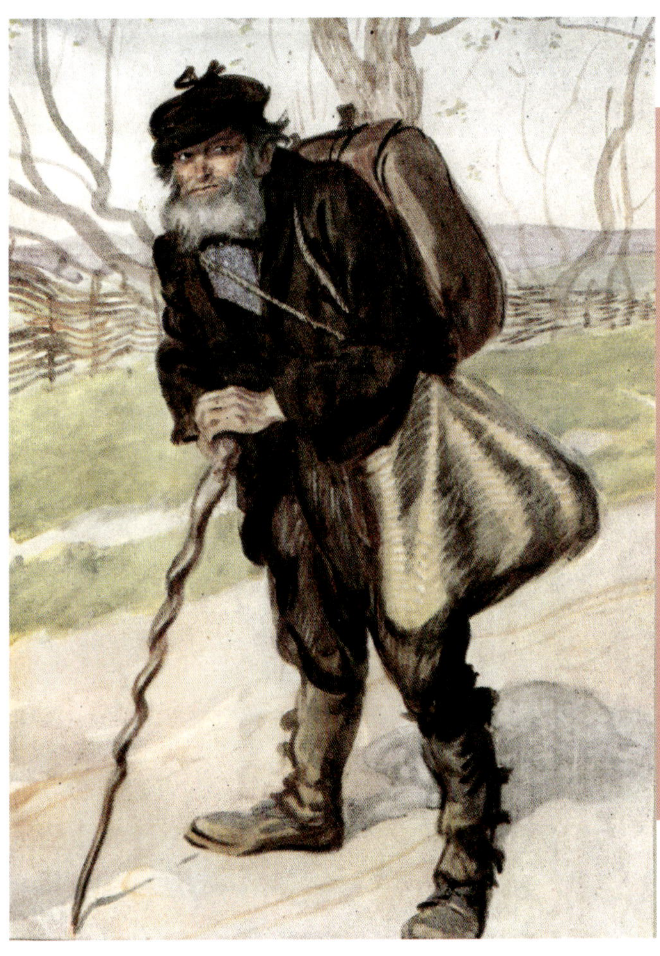

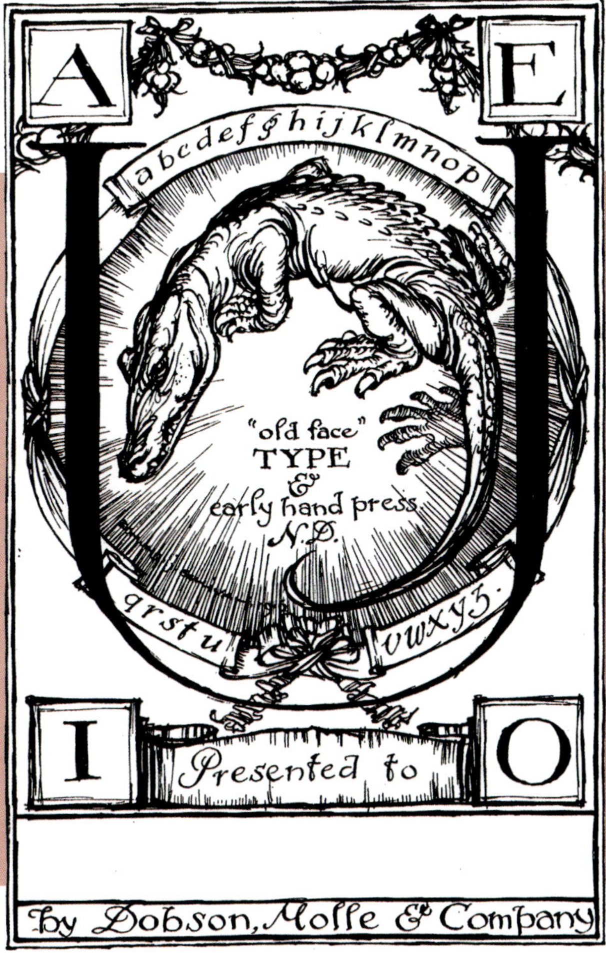

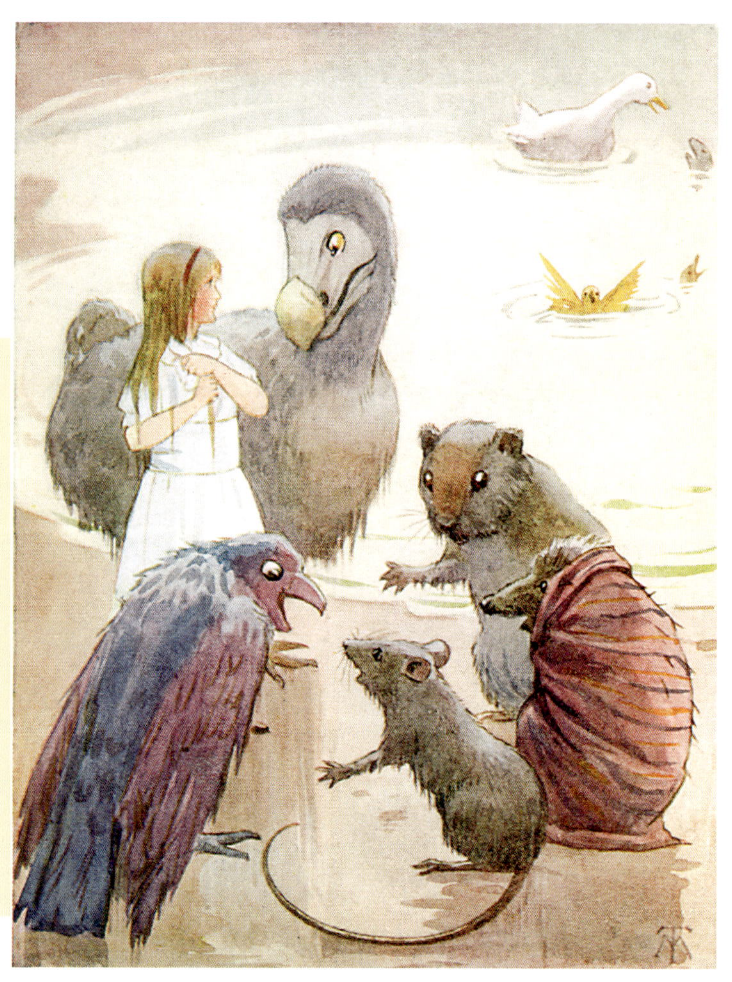

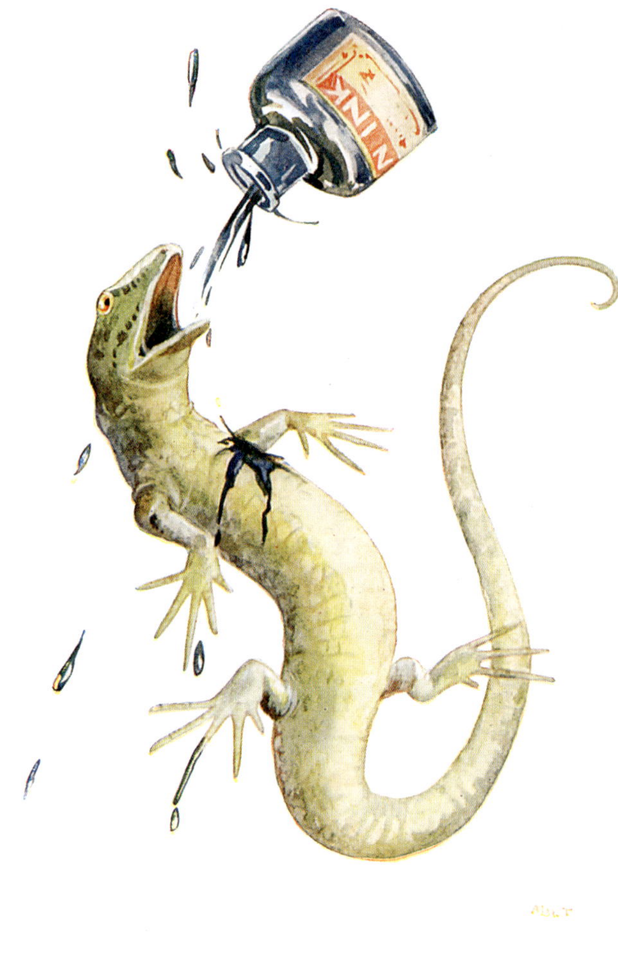

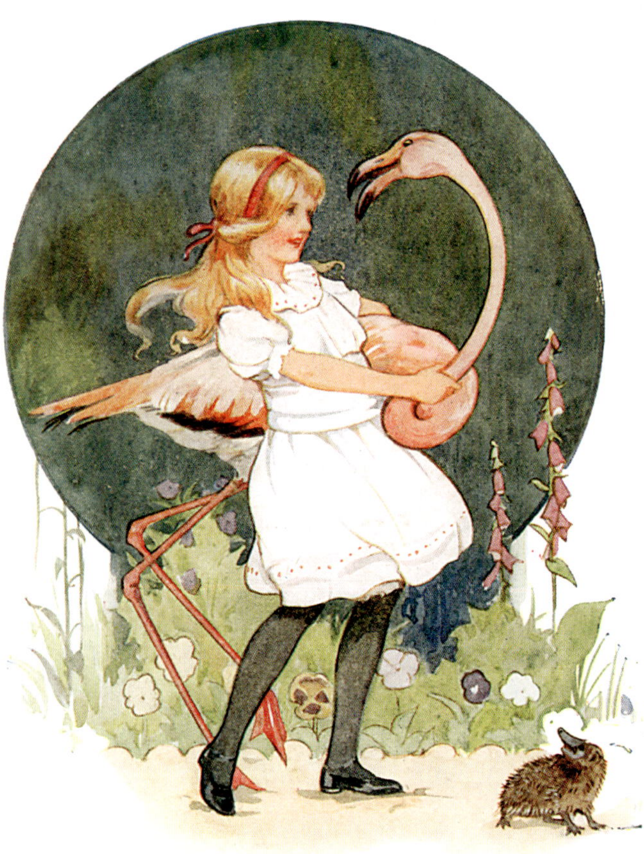

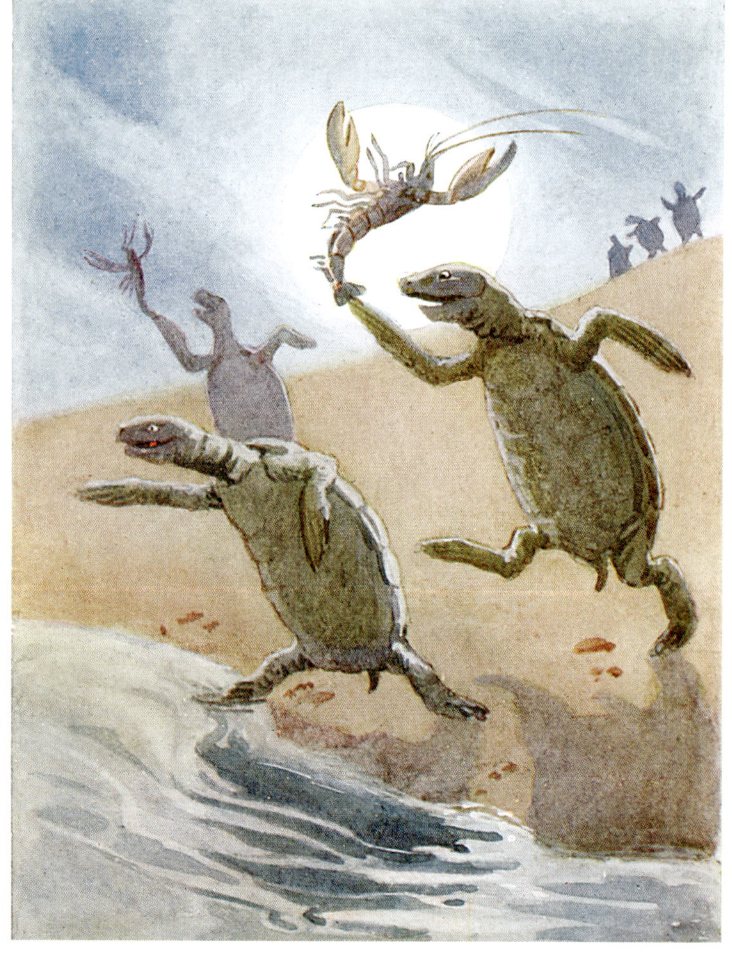

Tarrant, Margaret

Margaret Tarrant

1888–1959, British

An artist from childhood, Margaret Tarrant grew up outside of London, the daughter of landscape painter Percy Tarrant. Originally hoping to become a teacher, Tarrant found that art was her calling, and by the time she was 20, she had landed a book commission for an illustrated version of Charles Kingsley's *The Water Babies*. Book projects that followed were often in the domain of fairy tales; titles such as *Fairy Stories from Hans Christian Andersen* (1910), or *Nursery Rhymes* (1914), were typical of the type of children's tales where Tarrant's imagery found a home. She worked in a variety of mediums: pen-and-ink, watercolor, pencil work, and silhouettes, all of which were part of her portfolio.

Tarrant's gentle and youthful style was a huge hit with the public, and drew fans early on. Her work, used on postcards and prints at the time and made into calendars, grew in popularity alongside her book illustration. Card work was an integral part of her output from the very beginning of her career, when she started working at age 18 for a publisher of Christmas cards.

Christian themes were also represented in Tarrant's work during the 1920s and 1930s. One client that she worked with frequently during that time was the Medici Society, which used a great deal of Tarrant's imagery during the middle years of her career. She would continue to work until she was in her seventies, when her health began to fail.

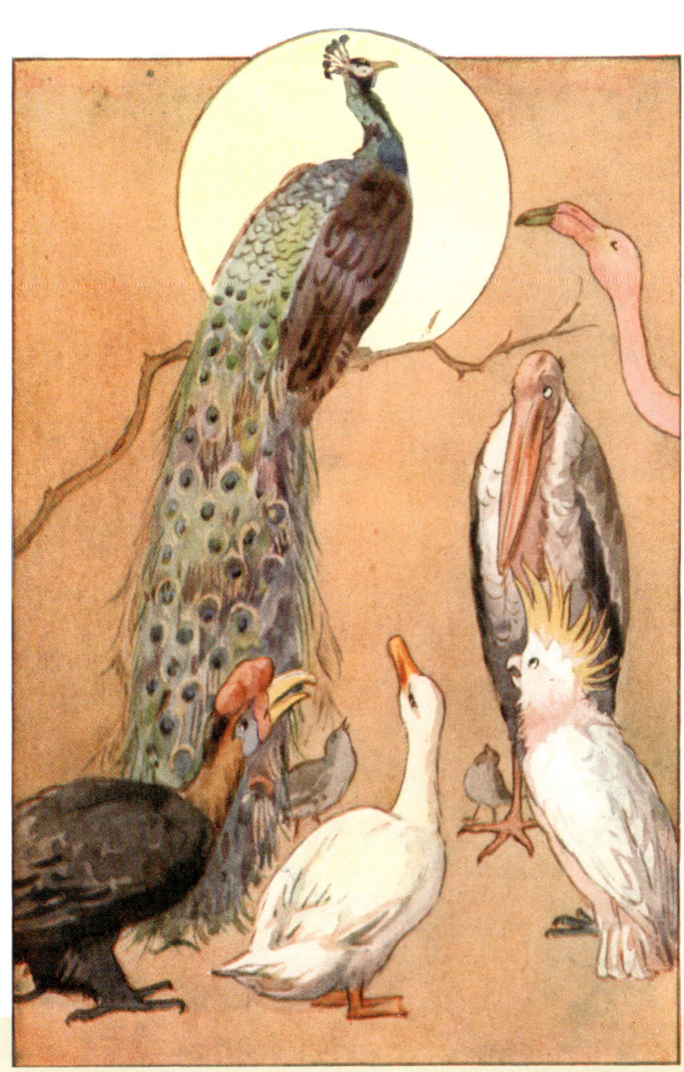

"I began drawing at a very early age and have never lost my love of it nor my great interest in all artistic work." —Margaret Tarrant

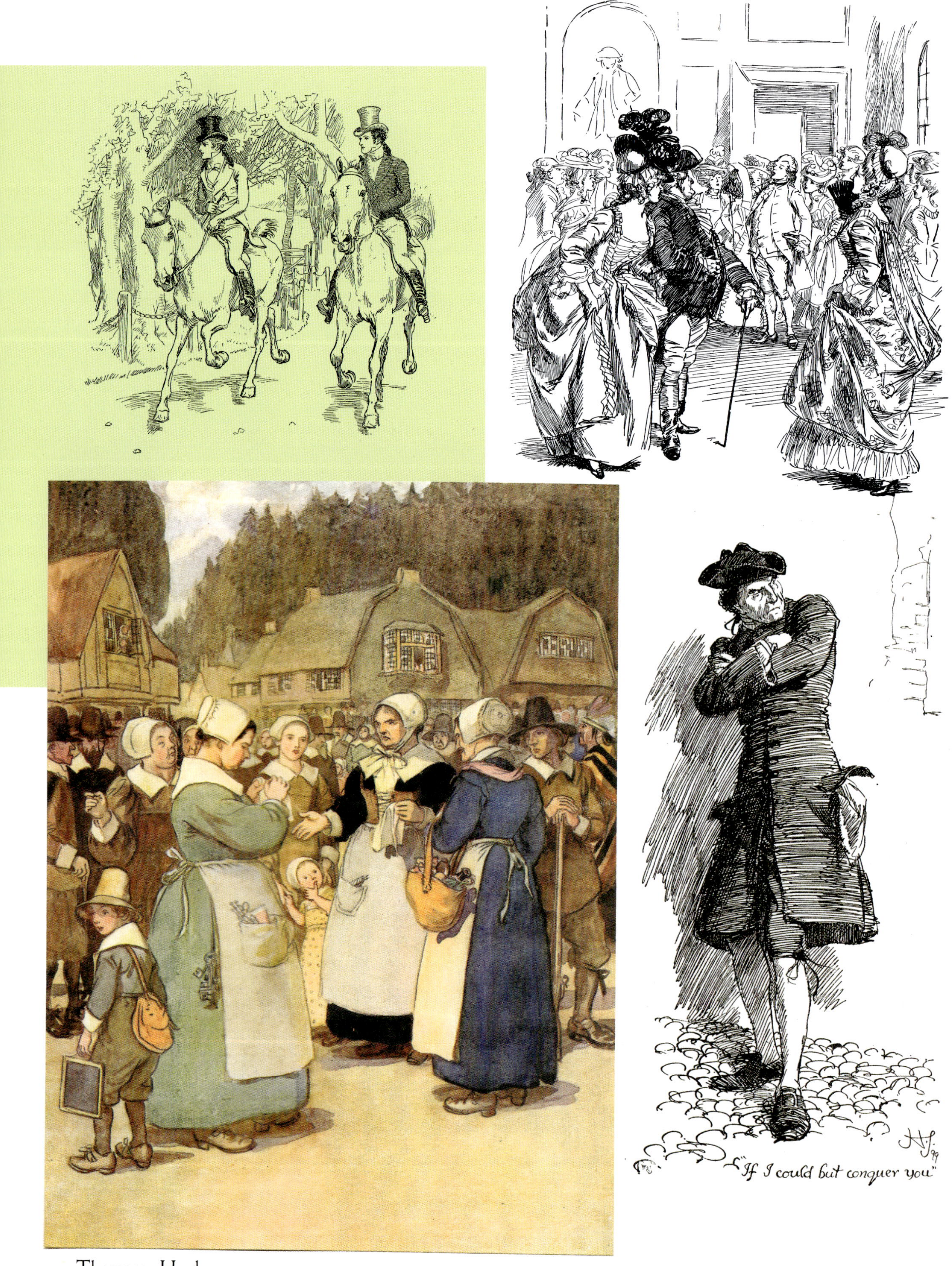

Thomson, Hugh

HUGH THOMSON

1860–1920, Irish

With no formal art school in his background, Thomson nevertheless became one of the most prominent illustrators of his time. Largely self-taught, young Thomson filled many schoolbooks with drawings, but spent his early working years as a clerk in the linen industry. In his late teens, his talent in drawing began to attract attention, and he was soon hired by a printing and publishing company. It was a supportive environment for a developing illustrator.

In 1883 Thomson accepted an offer to work with *The English Illustrated Magazine,* and went to London. He became a leading contributor there, learning from fellow illustrators Randolph Caldecott and Herbert Railton. He also became a recognized contributor to book illustration, and he depicted images for the works of Shakespeare, Austen, and Dickens. The subjects that Thomson excelled at fell into the category of classic literature, and for the last decade of the nineteenth century, Thomson was one of the best visual storytellers for that market. His work was praised for its attention to detail in historical works. Thomson was known to visit London's best art museums to find the right costumes, architecture, and settings that would be appropriate for what he was working on.

Although Thomson was primarily a pen-and-ink artist, later in his career, the technology of printing combined with publishing's demand for color led Thomson to add more color to his work. First he added a tone to a finished line work, and later illustrations were prepared in full color. His work is well-remembered as he contributed definitive imagery to many well-loved pieces of literature, most notably for the *Cranford* series by Elizabeth Gaskell, and the works of Jane Austen.

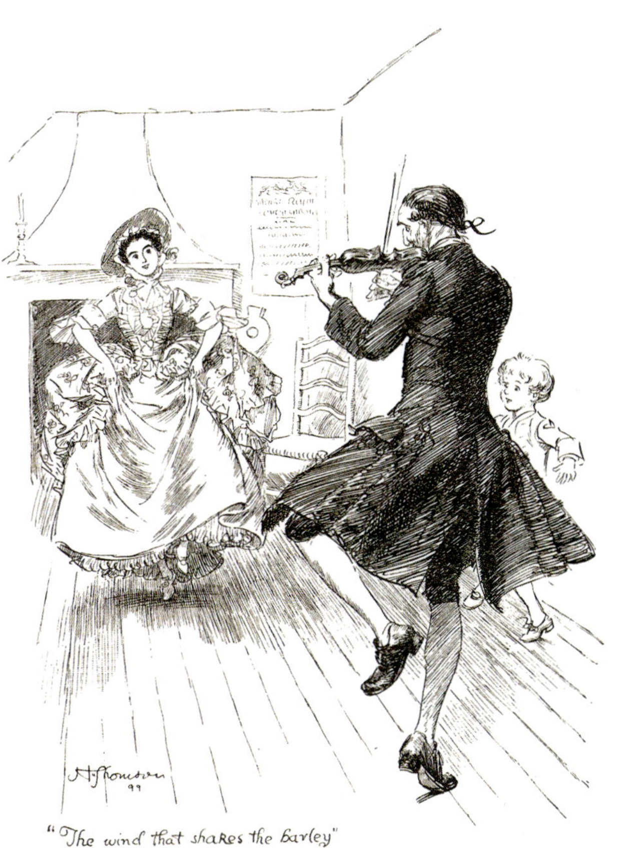

"The wind that shakes the barley"

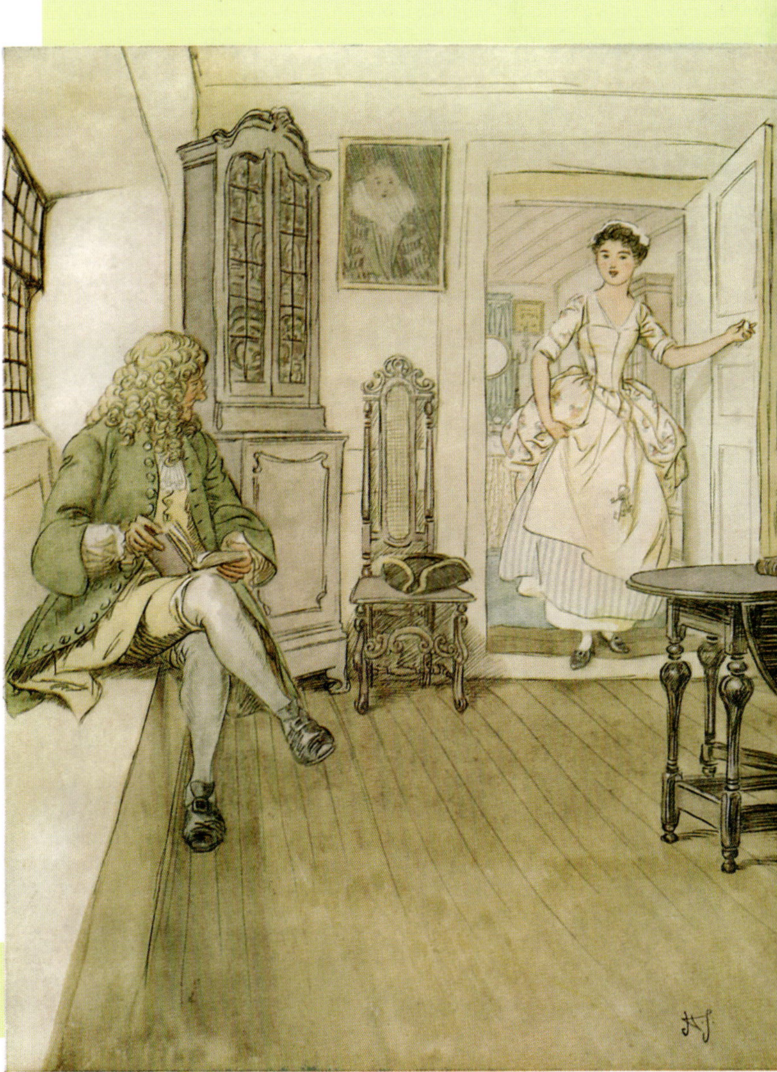

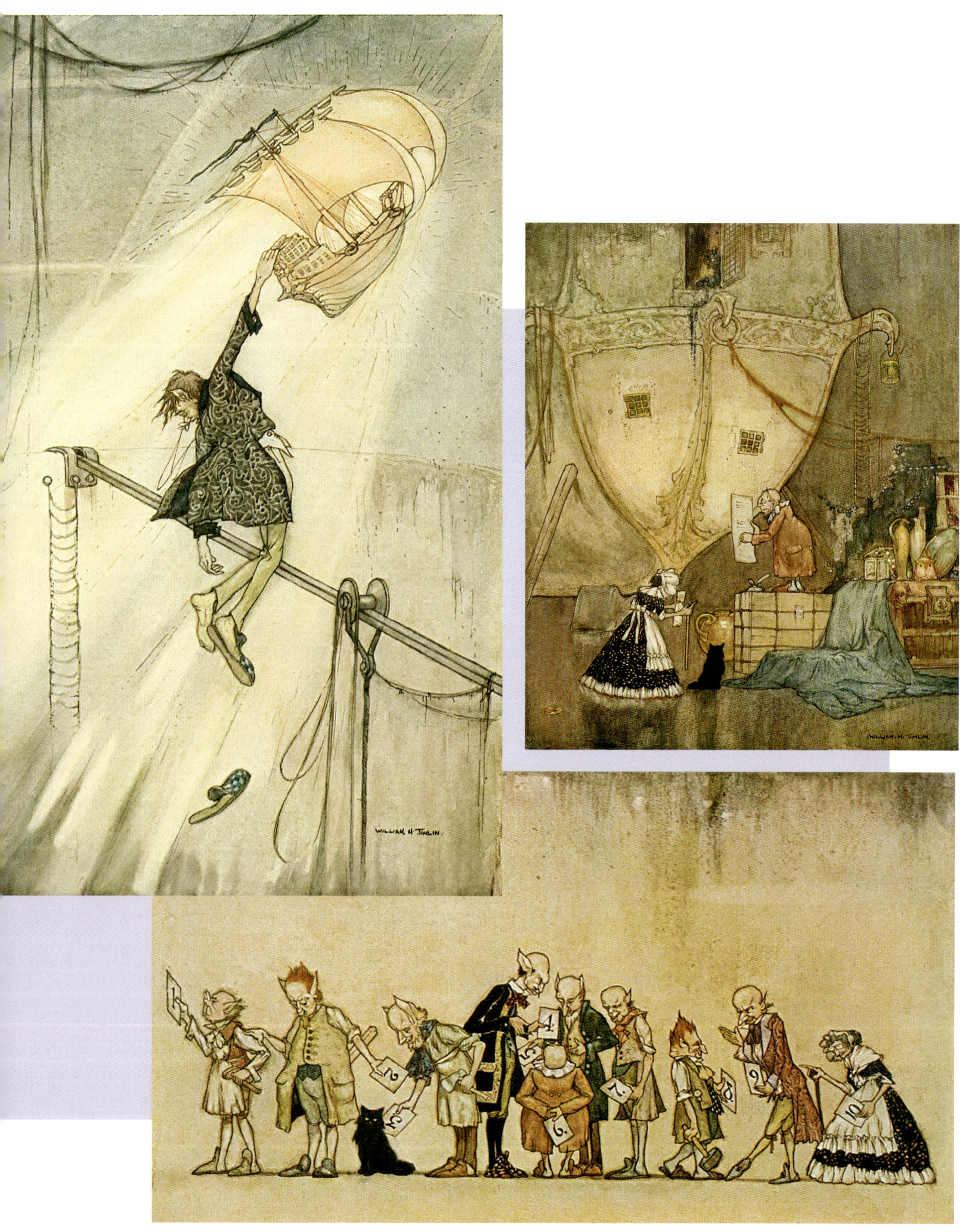

Timlin, William

William Timlin

1892–1943, British/South African

Though born in Northumberland, this architect and illustrator grew up and gained his reputation for the work he did while living in South Africa, having moved there with his family as a child. Timlin's route to becoming an illustrator was far from typical. Hardly prolific in his output, he produced one book—which he also wrote. Timlin illustrated the book with 48 color plates that compared favorably with the best work of the period, and he provided the calligraphic text as well. In November of 1923, British publisher Harrap released *The Ship that Sailed to Mars: A Fantasy.* At a time when book production values had begun to decline due largely to wartime conservation, this volume spared no expense, harkening back to the pre-war heyday of gift books.

With the detailed production also came a higher price, and fewer copies were printed. Though critically acclaimed, the book never led to further development. A movie based on the book was originally conceived, but it was never completed. A follow-up title from Timlin had been planned, but that, too, never came to fruition. He left us with his most brilliant effort, and faded from public view afterwards. Though he still painted on occasion, his subsequent creative output was largely focused on architecture, which became his primary career in South Africa.

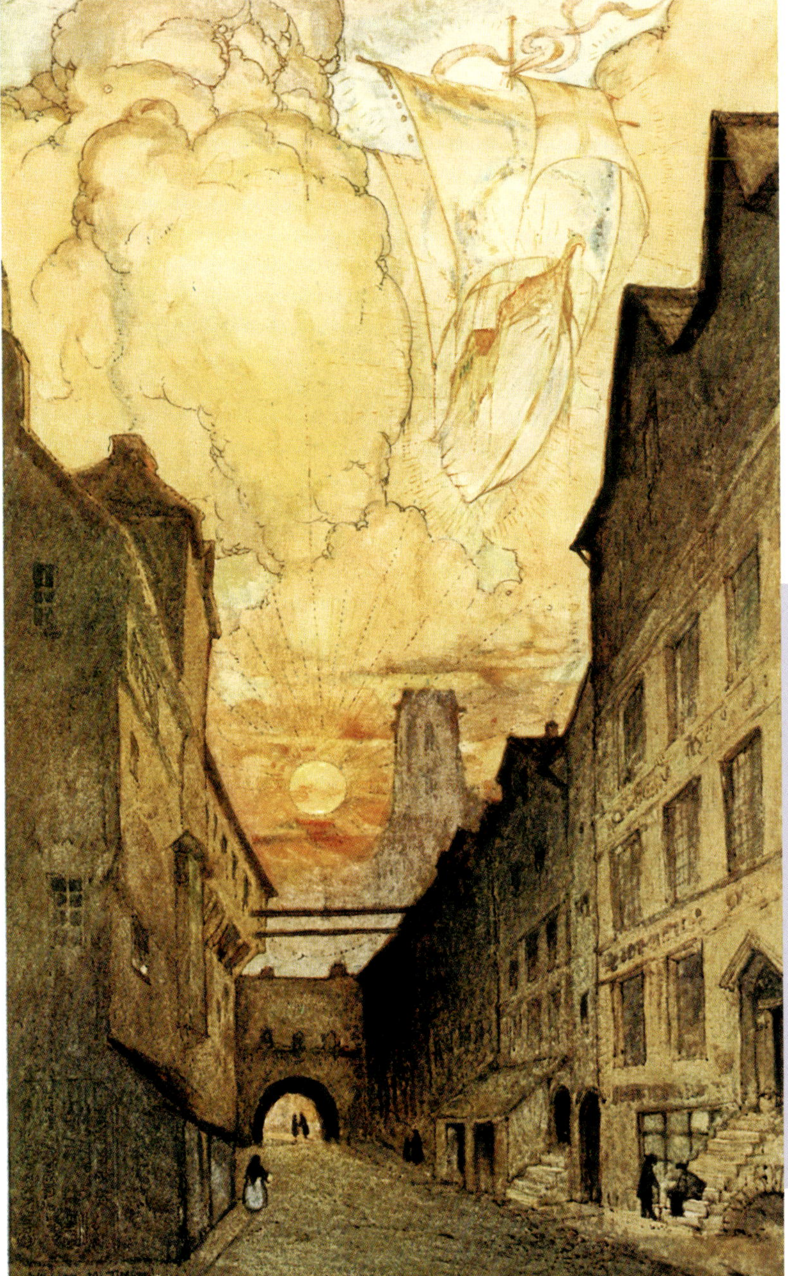

Timlin had achieved the goal to which most book illustrators would aspire in his earliest effort. Though he did not produce a lifetime of work to review, he bestowed us with one of the standout books of the period, still highly regarded nearly a century later.

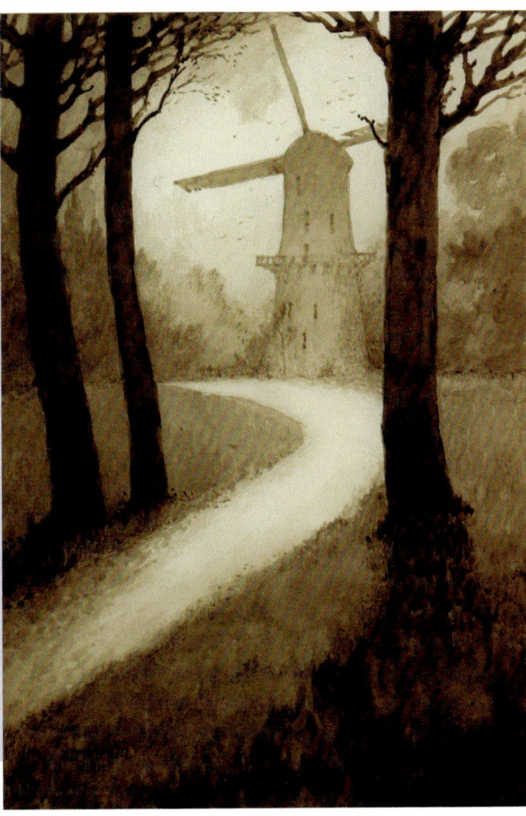

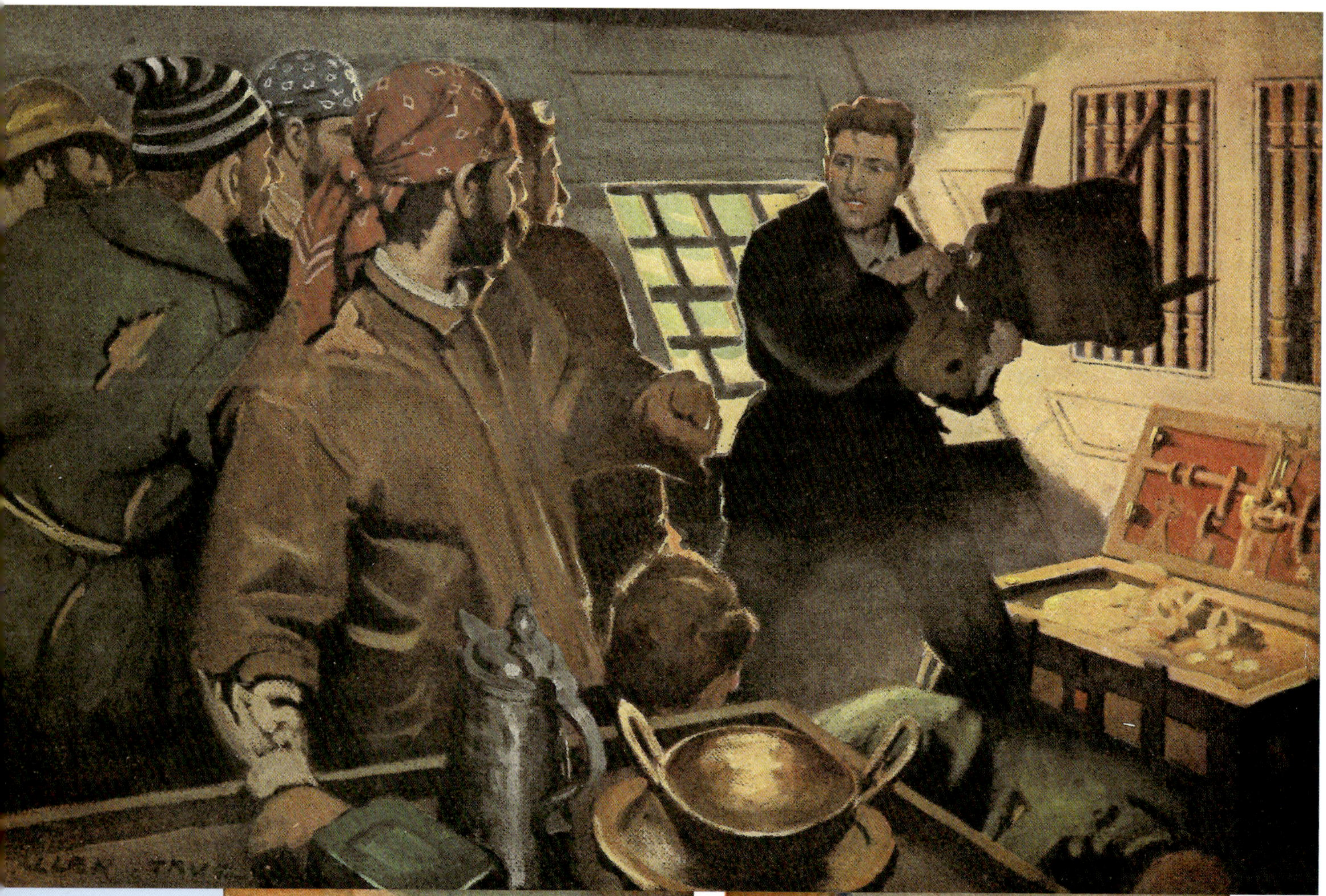

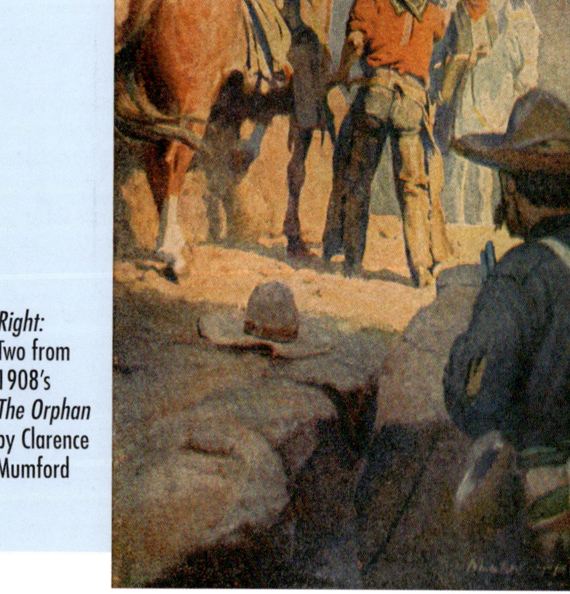

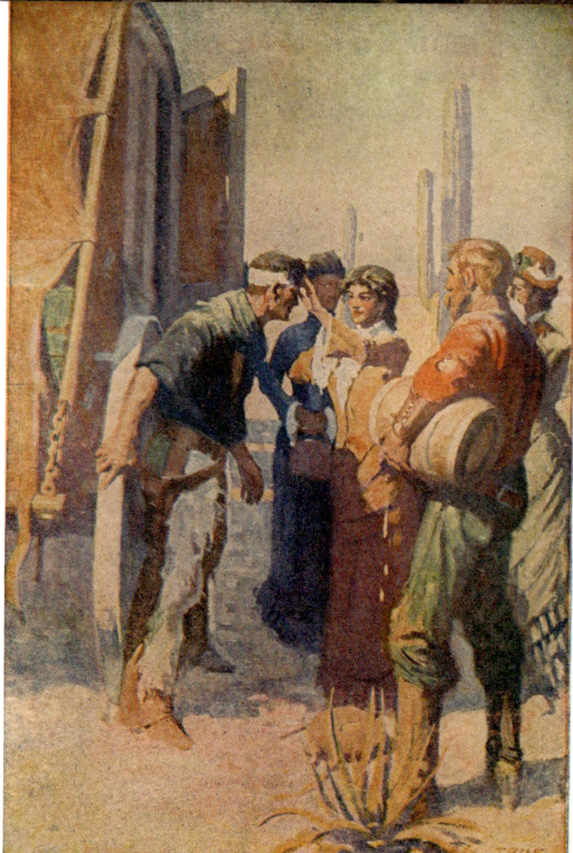

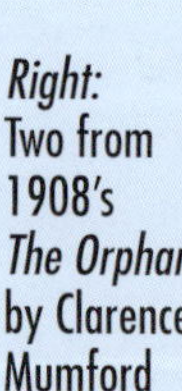

Right:
Two from 1908's *The Orphan* by Clarence Mumford

Allen Tupper True

1881–1955, American

In some cases, an illustrator's life is so strongly influenced by events in his childhood that they shape his expertise in the subjects he explores as a professional. This can certainly be said for Allen Tupper True. Born in Colorado and reared there and in Texas and Mexico, he was a bona fide child of the Old West. His father fought in the war of Texas secession, and his mother was a noted educator in the West. True had been exposed to all types of real-life frontier characters in the final years of the nineteenth century, and it became the theme he would most often explore in his work.

True obtained an exceptional artistic education. After two years at a Denver-based school, he came East to the Corcoran School of Art in Washington, D.C. He soon became aware that Howard Pyle was teaching a small group of hand-picked students in the Brandywine Valley, and in 1902, True joined them. He studied with Pyle until 1907, and in 1908, he journeyed to England, where he studied with and assisted Frank Brangwyn on numerous mural projects. Returning to the United States sometime in 1909, he had one of the most solid foundations a beginning artist could ever hope for.

Building on Brangwyn's impressions, True found his calling in (and passion for) mural work. He went on to produce murals for most of his active career; he was eventually considered an expert in the theme of the Old West. True produced murals for the state capitols of Wyoming, Missouri, and Colorado, where his work became a defining part of each state's identity. He covered many walls with his artwork, both public and private, civic and industrial. Banks, hospitals, schools, and hotels—all of these institutions found True's larger-than-life works on their facades.

One lasting reminder of True's contribution to the imagery of the West can be found in the state seal of Wyoming, which he designed. This emblem, of a bucking horse and rider, are so much a part of the state's identity that it can still be seen on the state license plates and the state quarter coin. A recognized authority on the designs of the Native Americans, True contributed designs for the major dam-building projects in the West during the '30s and '40s.

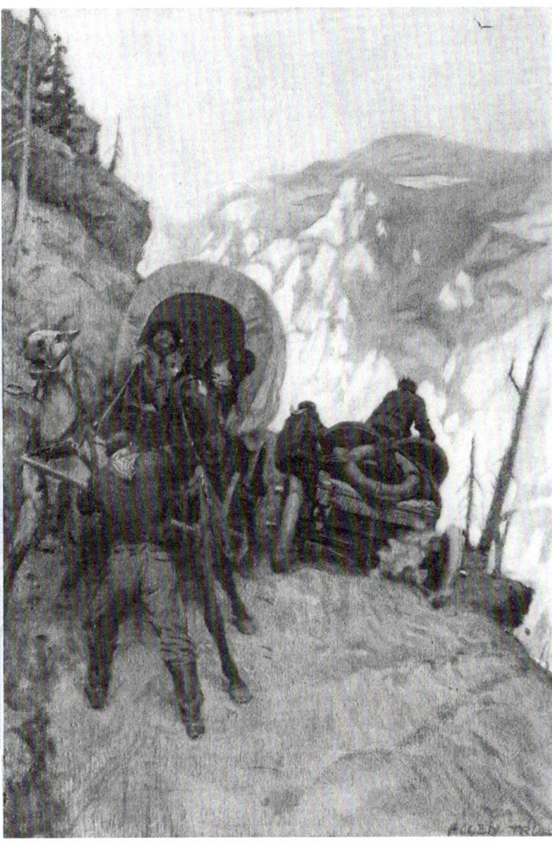

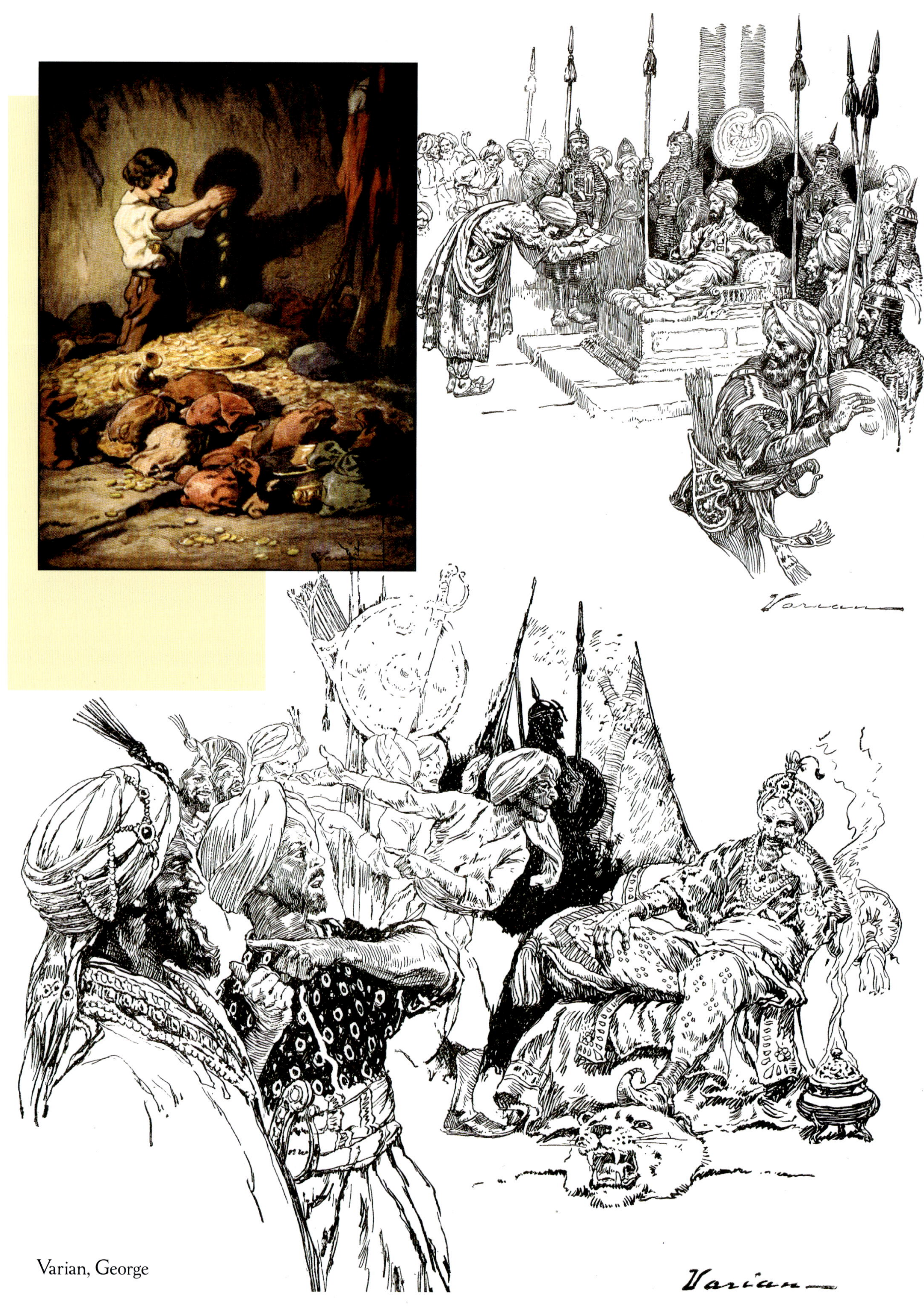

Varian, George

George Varian
1865–1923, American

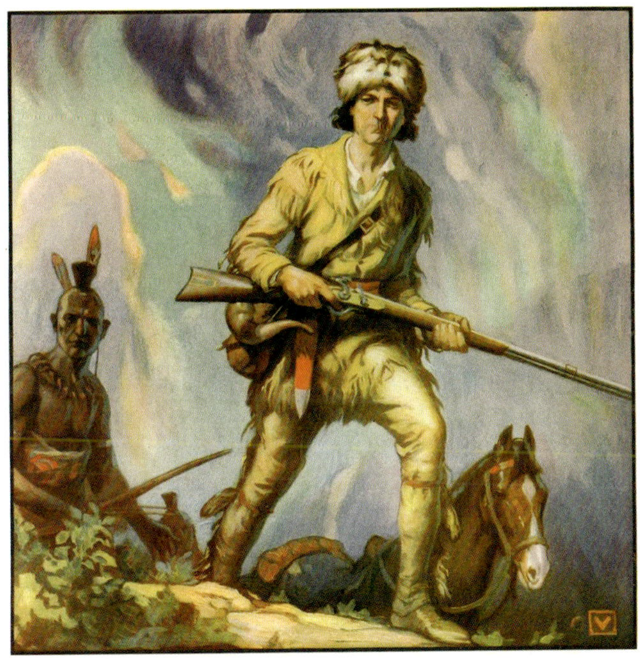

Born in England, George Varian traveled to America as a child, later studying at both the Brooklyn Artists Guild and the Art Students League.

One unique experience affected Varian in 1902, when he was an eyewitness to the eruption of Mt. Pele in Martinique; he documented the event for *McClure's Magazine* later that year. Varian's work often fell into the category of adventure for boys—he was equally at home with pirate stories, westerns, and historical works. Varian worked with a variety of established publications, and landed book work from many leading authors of the period. His illustrated edition of *Treasure Island* (1918) is one of the earliest available with color plates.

Unlike many of his contemporaries, Varian's transition from an early career of line-work, to painting in gray for halftone reproduction, to full-color work like his covers for *Youth's Companion,* was treated with equal levels of skill. He managed to succeed within all of these shifts in technology, adding to the longevity of his career. Today the archive that houses issues of *Youth's Companion* is named after him.

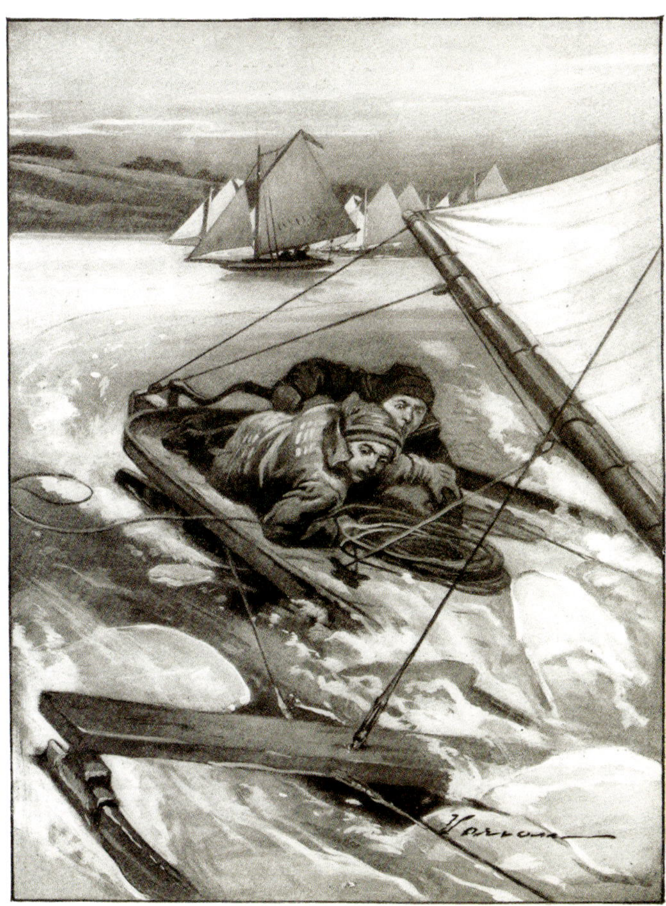

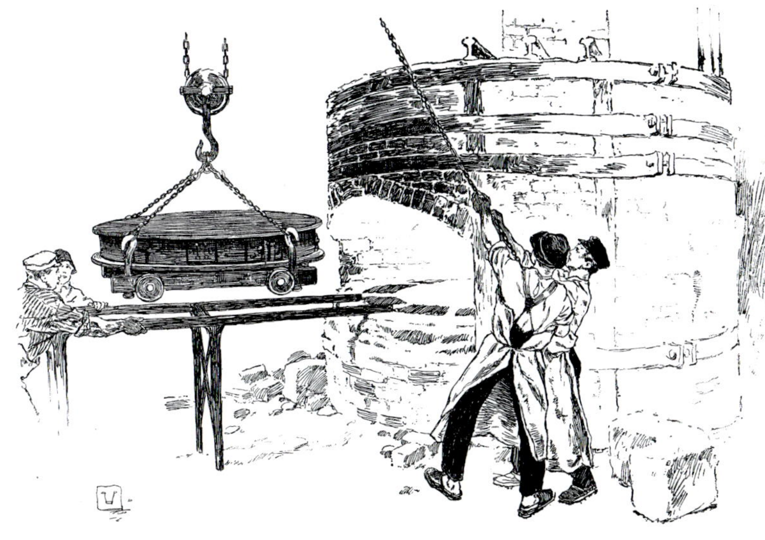

Daniel Vierge
1851~1904, Spanish

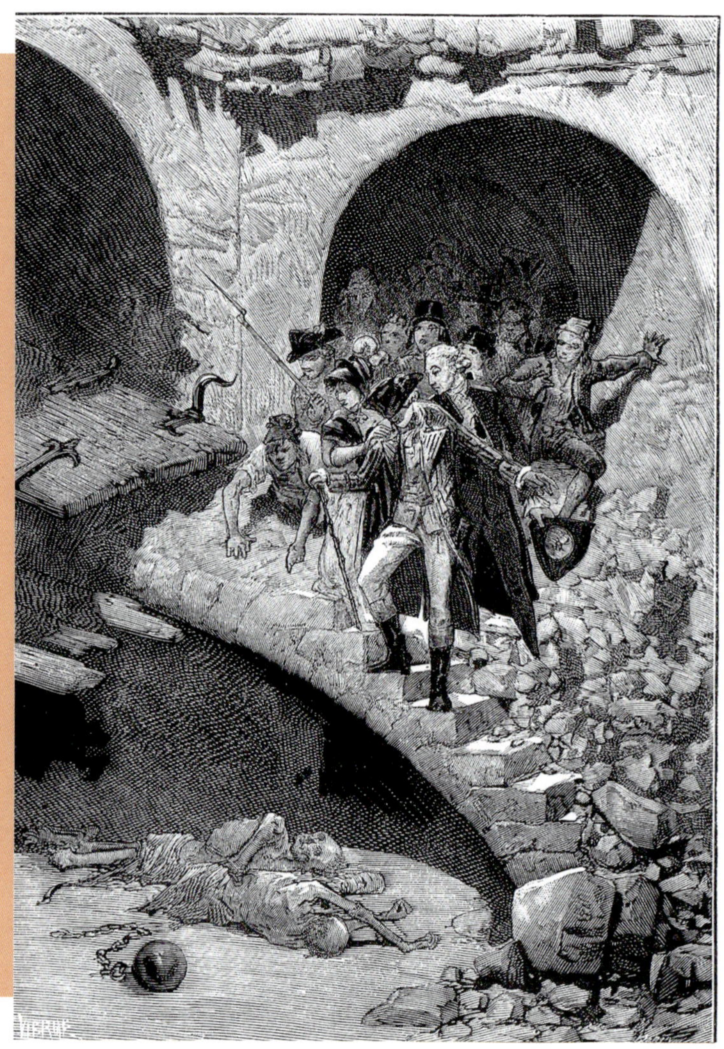

Known for his incredible mastery of line, Daniel Vierge also helped change the printing process that enabled his works to be presented so beautifully.

Born to a father who was also an artist, Vierge grew up in an environment where drawing was an ever-present part of his life. By the age of 13 he had entered the Academy in his native Madrid, and at 16 he was illustrating a leading paper there, *Madrid la nuit.* With higher artistic ambitions, Vierge moved to Paris to study painting while still a teen, and also found work there with a paper devoted to the use of art in reporting—*Le Monde illustré.*

Shortly after his arrival in Paris, the Franco-Prussian War began. Rather than leave France, Vierge saw the opportunity to produce meaningful illustrations for the paper, and became one of its leading artist-journalists. Growing more and more passionate about the images he was producing, he ventured into book illustration, which led him to new volumes of work, and some frustration at how they were reproduced.

In the early part of his career, all of the drawings that Vierge produced for reproduction needed to be redrawn on wood, and then engraved on wood to be put through a press. This meant the final result was the product of a craftsman's interpretation of the artist's work. Vierge conceived of a more direct method of producing plates for printing, while capturing all the nuances of the original drawings. With the help of a photo-engraver by the name of Gillot, Vierge developed the means to use photo emulsion on metal plates. When the image was exposed, every line remained true to the original drawing. It changed the process of printing images dramatically, and freed artists to be much more expressive with their line, knowing it would not need to be reinterpreted by an engraver.

Vierge produced some brilliant books to take advantage of the new reproduction method. During his work on *Pablo de Segovia,* the unthinkable occurred. With the project more than 80% complete, the artist suffered from a paralyzing stroke, at the early age of thirty. This left him unable to use his drawing hand. By sheer will, Vierge retrained himself to draw with his left hand, and months later, he was able to return to complete the project, with virtually no perceptible difference in style. He later created *The Tavern of Three Virtues,* and his masterpiece, *Don Quixote,* in 1906. He never regained use of his right hand, and lived until the age of fifty-one, when he died in Boulogne-sur-Seine, France.

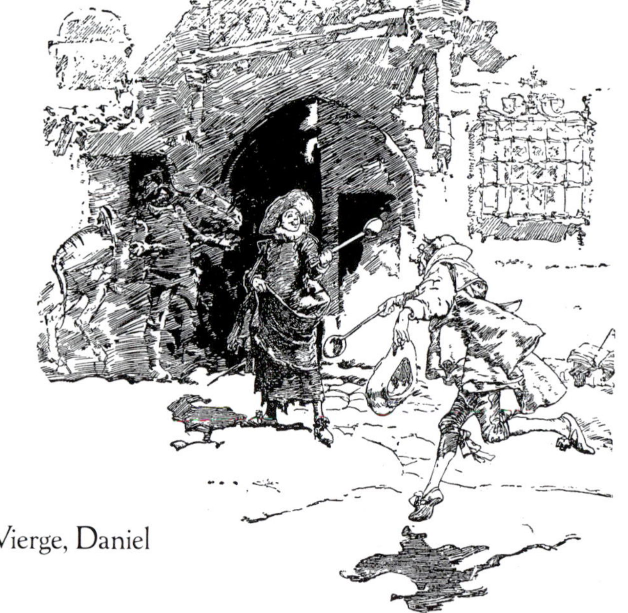

Vierge, Daniel

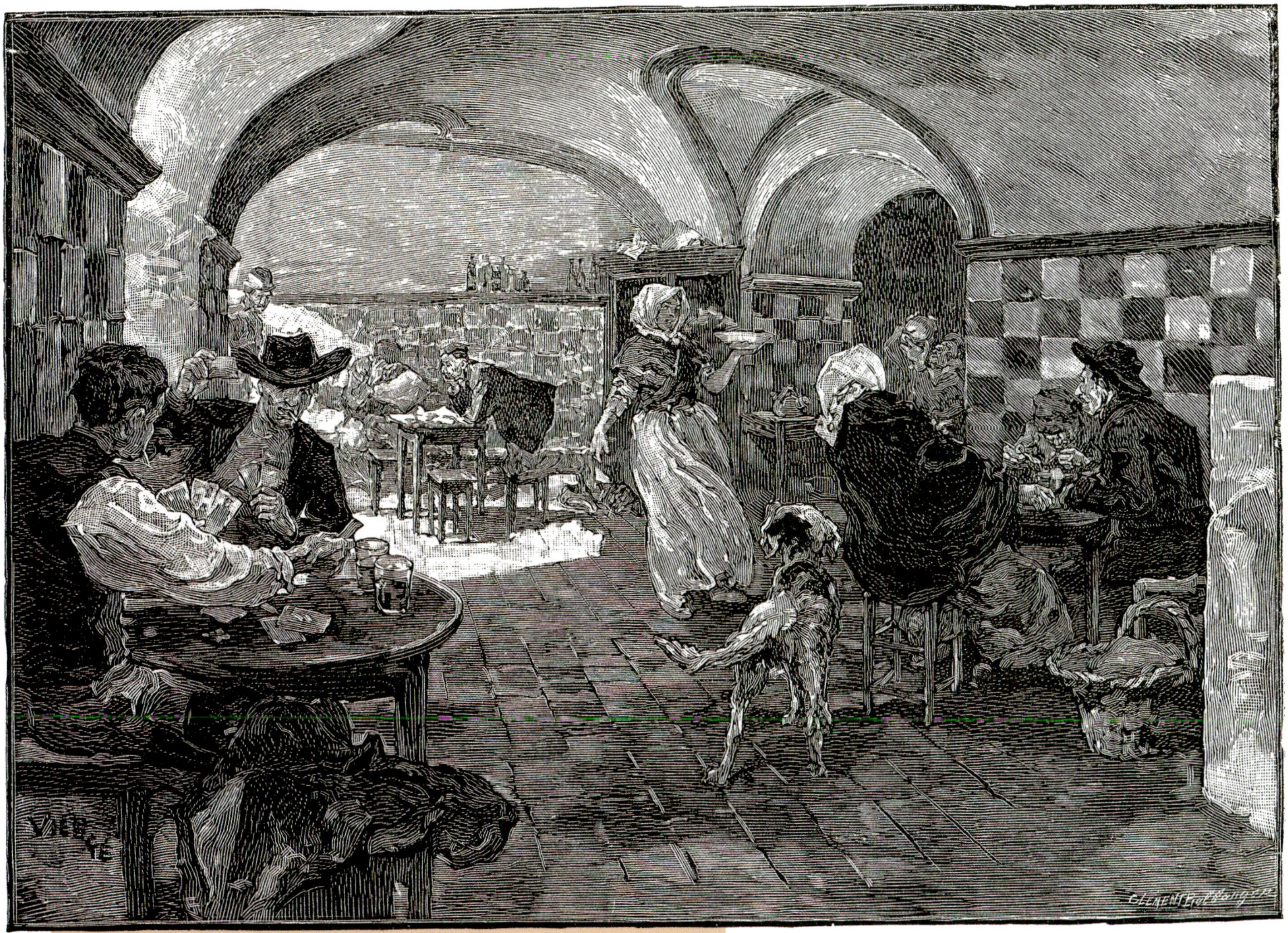

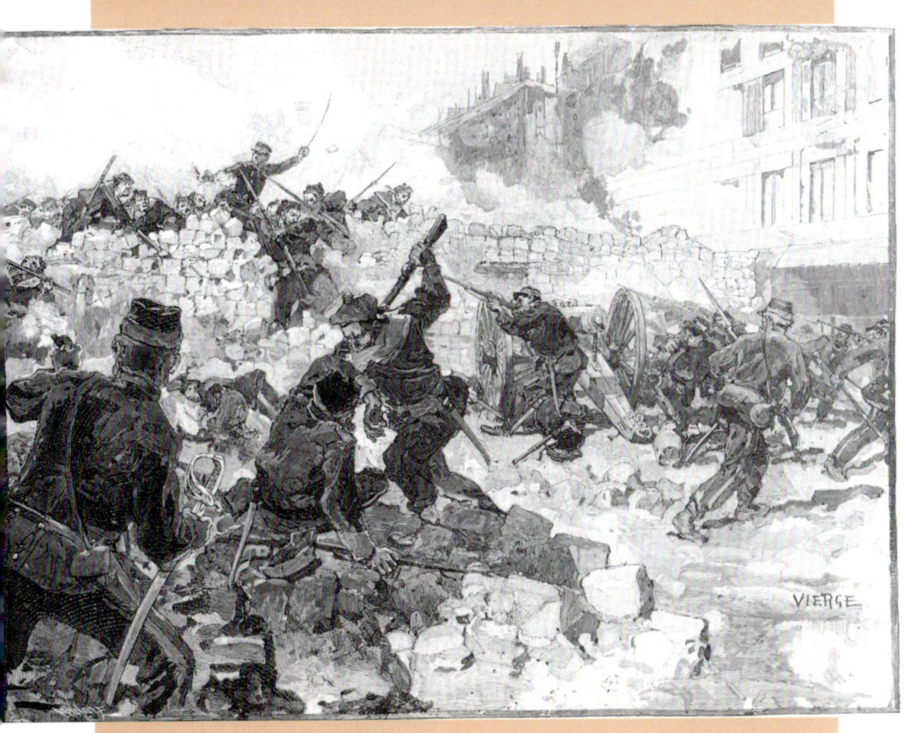
VIERGE

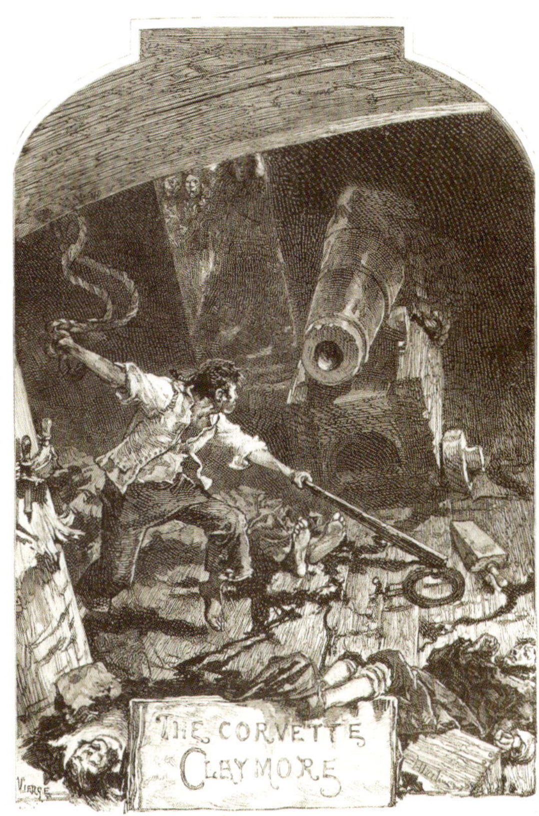
THE CORVETTE
CLAYMORE

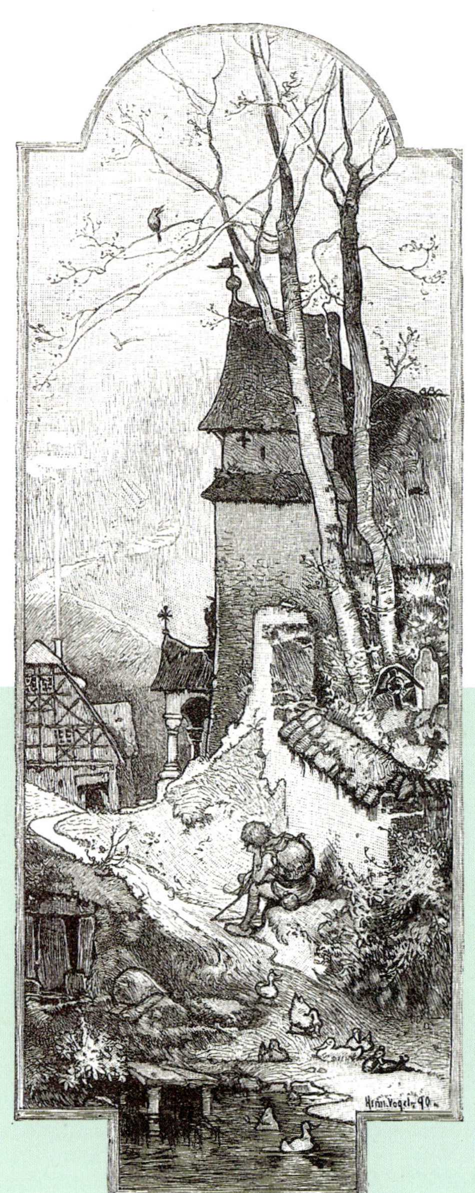

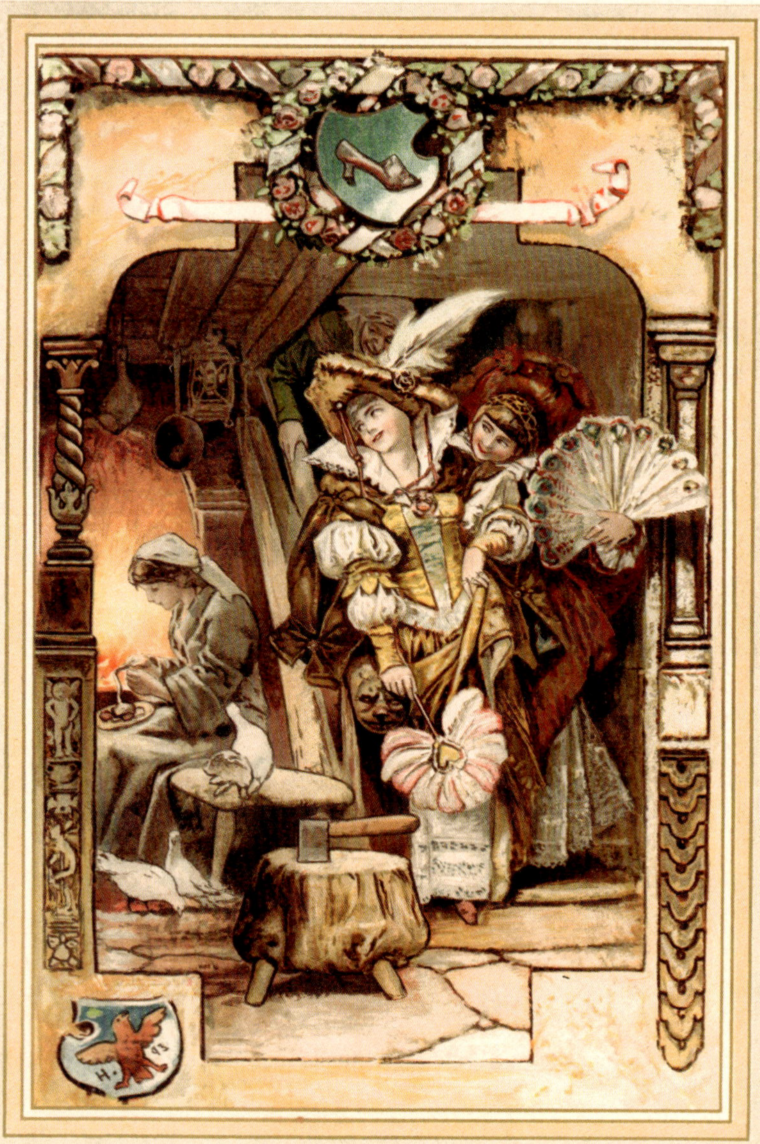

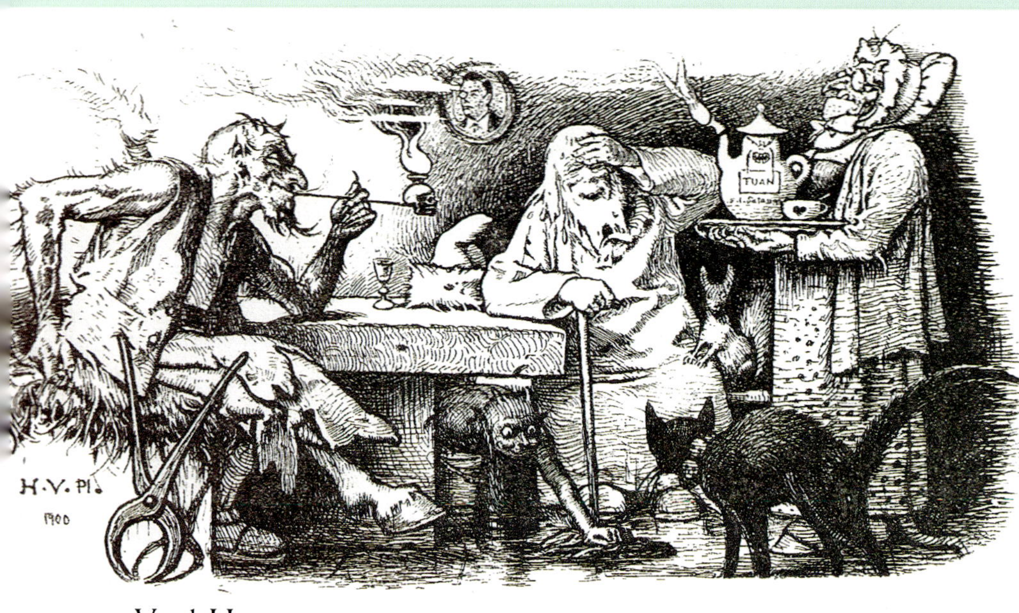

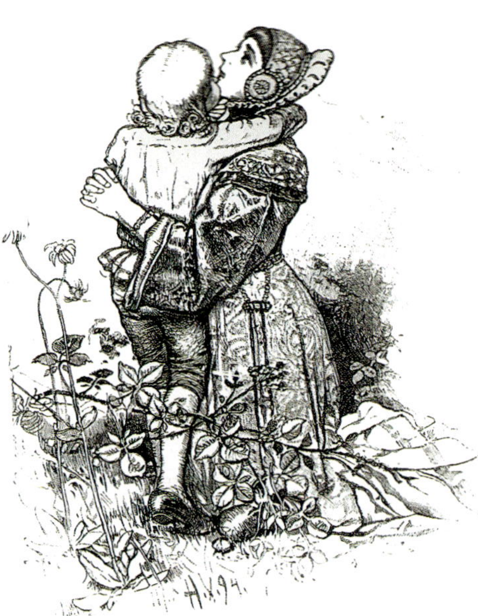

Vogel, Hermann

Hermann Vogel

1854–1921, German

Born in Saxony (now part of Germany), Hermann Vogel was the son of an architect and master builder. His earliest studies were in law, but he later moved to the Art Academy in Dresden, where he studied from 1874–75 before leaving the school to pursue professional work. After a short period in Italy, he returned to Germany, where he took up work with the publishing house of Braun & Schneider.

Beginning with his work in periodicals such as *Fliegende Blätter* and *Die deutsche Jugend,* Hermann Vogel became the definitive fairy tale artist of Germany. At a time when the stories of the Brothers Grimm were experiencing new life throughout the world, Vogel shaped how tales like these were viewed in their original language. Braun & Schneider assembled a four-volume collection of his magazine works from 1899–1908. Vogel also designed plates and covers for storybooks, including the fairy tales of the Brothers Grimm, Hans Christian Andersen's *Fairy Tales,* and *German Folk Tales.*

Vogel's work shows unbridled imagination combined with a great observational skill, and he rendered it all with great precision and passion.

During the last two decades of the nineteenth century, his output was impressive and significant. Vogel's real strength lies in his work in folk and fairy tales, and he imbued his illustrations of woodland creatures and imaginary fairies and dwarves with lively animation. His drawing talent would later become an acknowledged influence to the Disney Studios, influencing the look of *Snow White,* and other fairy tale-based films.

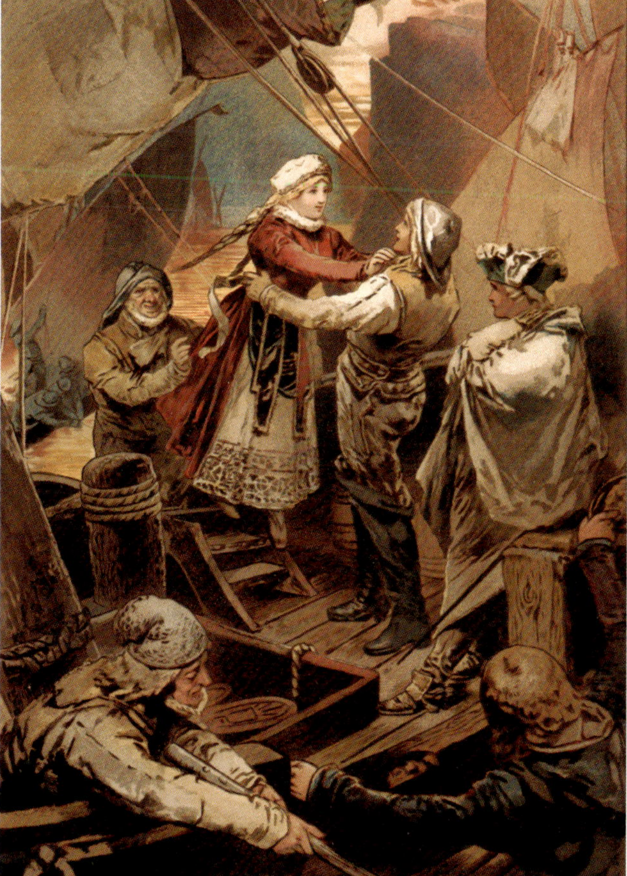

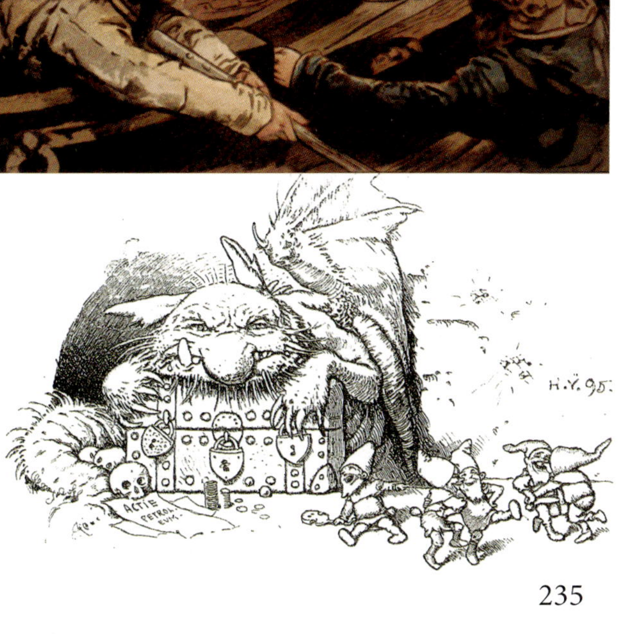

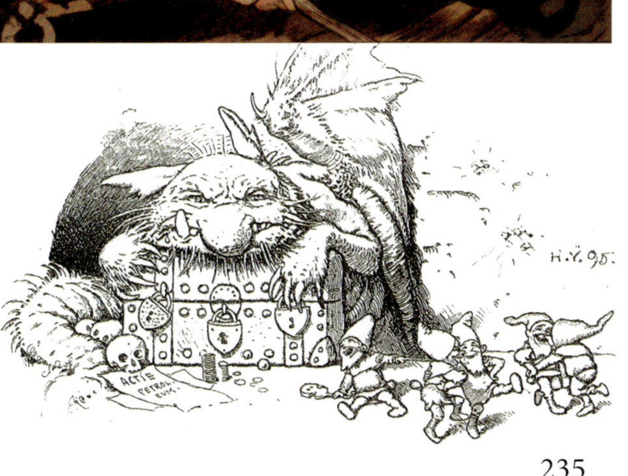

DUGALD STEWART WALKER
1883–1937, American

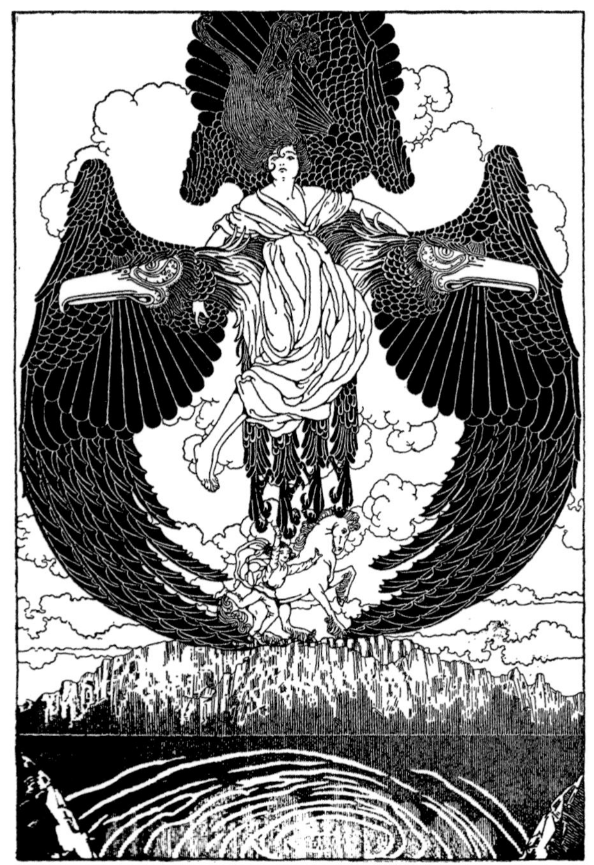

Raised in the area around Richmond, Virginia, Walker once credited both his style and imagination to an upbringing that allowed him little chance to travel and see "real things." The strong stylistic approach he took with his imagery was more akin to the style of Aubrey Beardsley than it was to the contemporary American artists of the Brandywine school. Walker studied drawing at the University of Virginia, and later at the New York School of Art. More influenced by the previous artistic generation than by his peers, the work he brought to the local Richmond galleries was not looked upon with great favor. His style was received much better in Europe, where his elongated figures and areas of flat design work drew comparison to French fashion of the period.

Walker's work did eventually find fans, and he became known primarily for his book illustration, beginning in 1912 with *Stories for Pictures* and

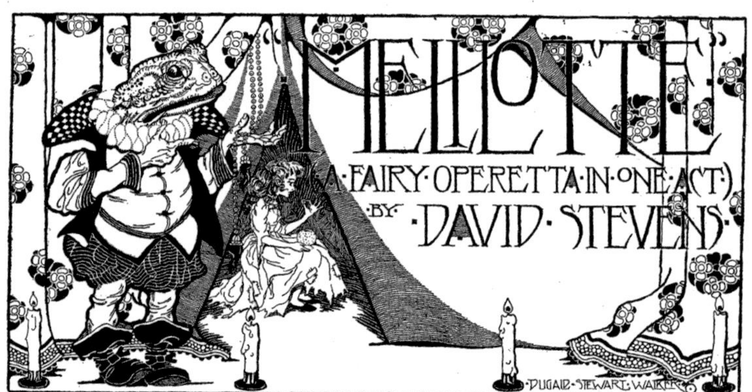

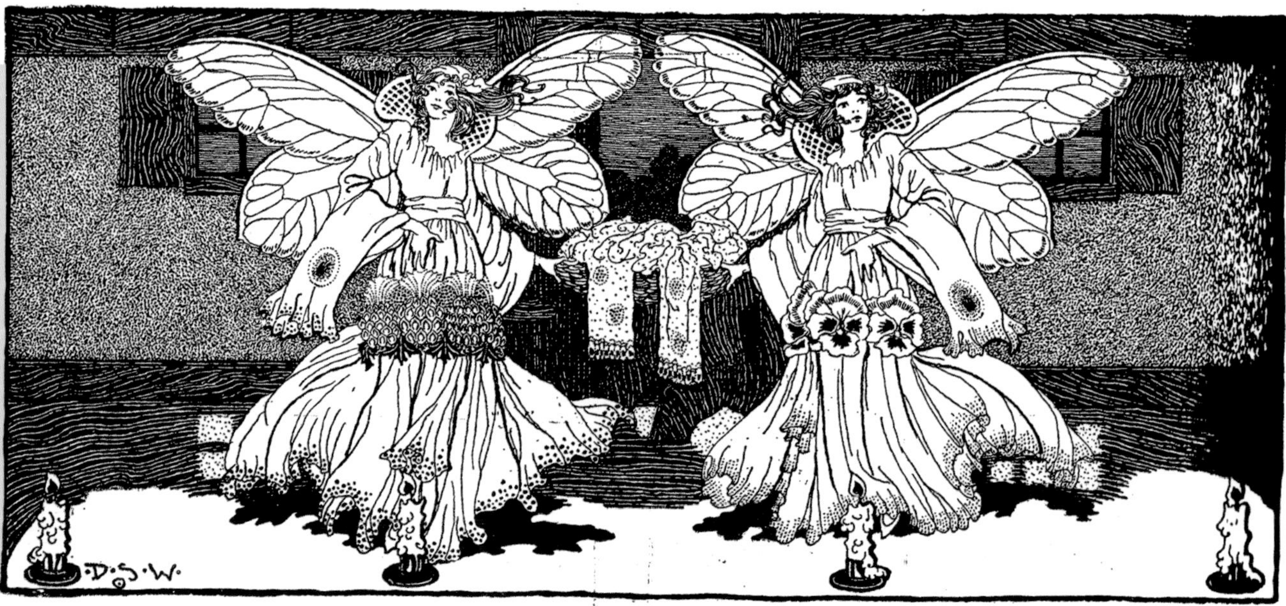

THISTLE BLOOM AND PANSY BUD BRINGING THE FAIRY ROBE.

ending with *Sally's ABC* in 1929. He also authored three books of his own, and was highly regarded as a book plate artist, creating personal works for those who wanted an identifying label for their libraries. Walker's bookplates were renowned for their extensive linear detail and complexity. They still reside today in a number of notable collections.

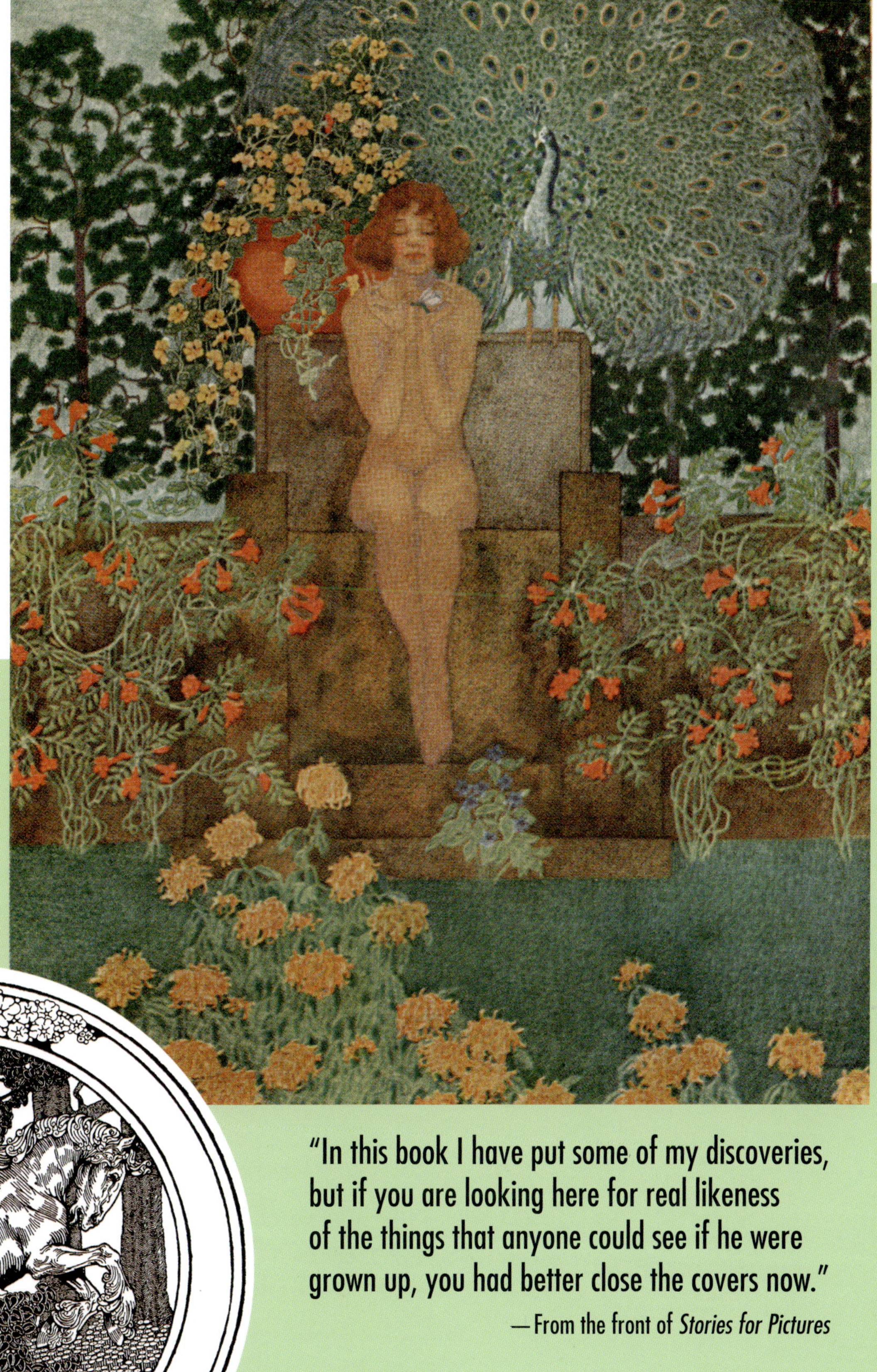

"In this book I have put some of my discoveries, but if you are looking here for real likeness of the things that anyone could see if he were grown up, you had better close the covers now."

—From the front of *Stories for Pictures*

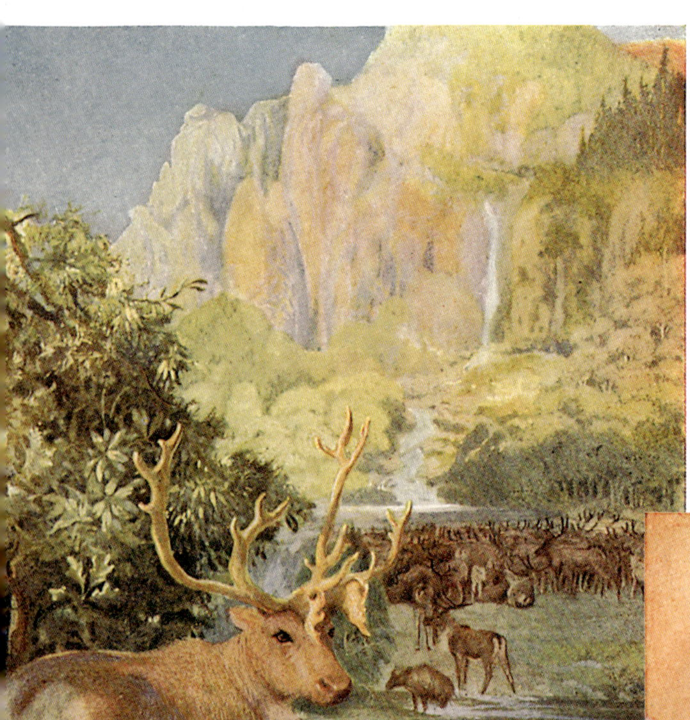

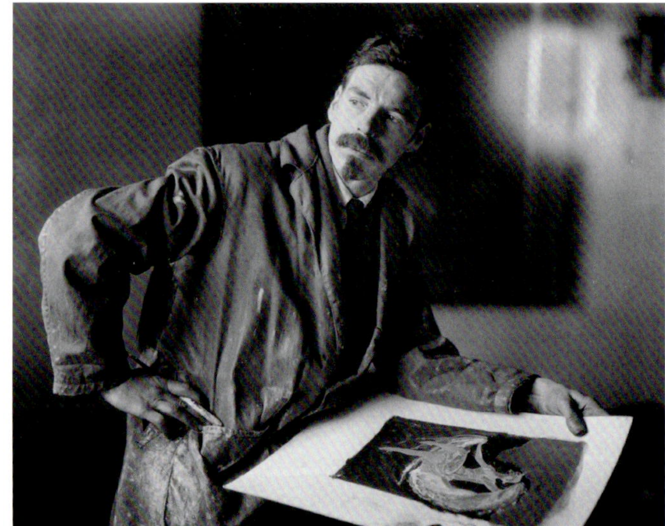

National Portrait Gallery, London

Wallcousins in 1926

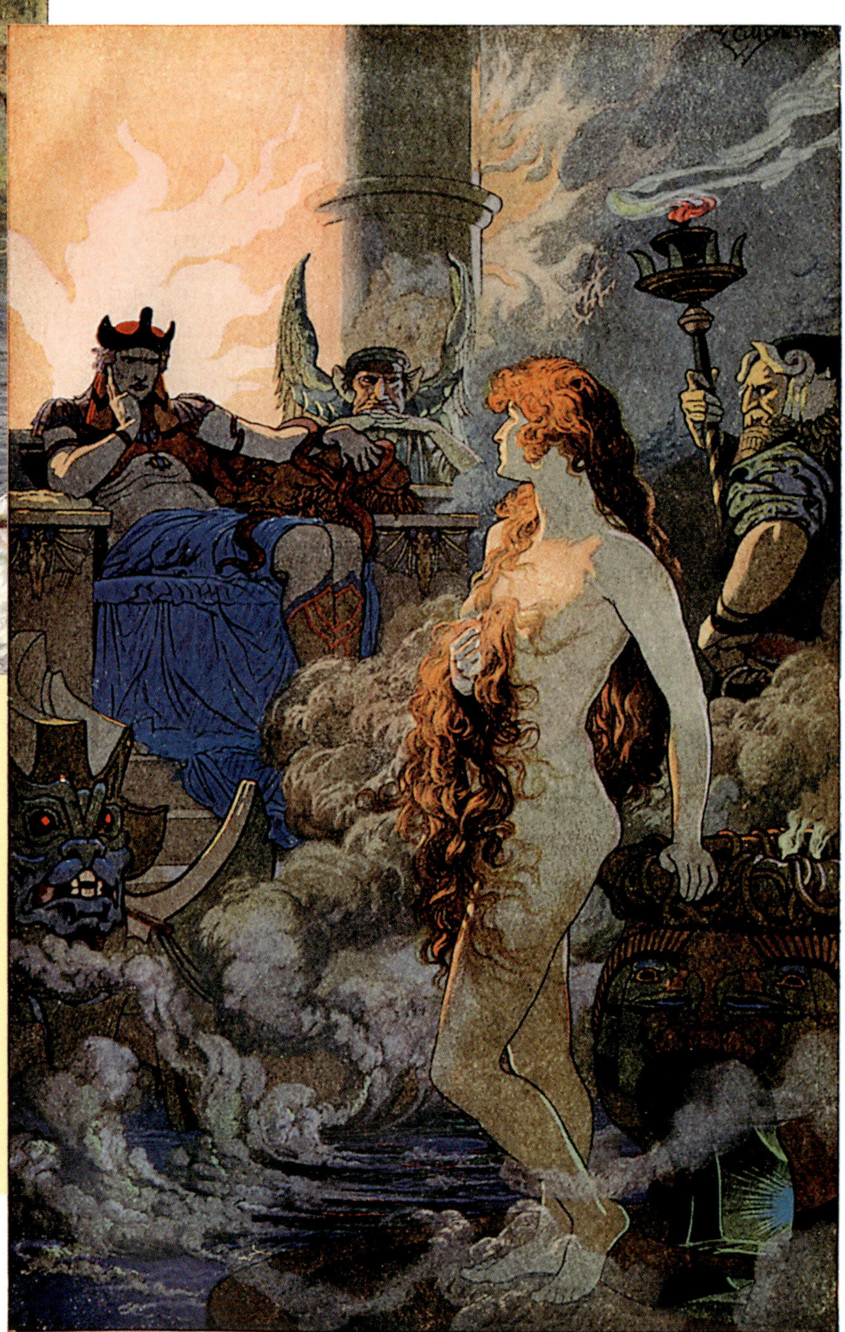

"In Mr. Ernest Wallcousins a strong play of original fancy and a sound technical skill in handling seem to go hand in hand."
—C. Matlack Price, *The International Studio*

Ernest Wallcousins

1883–1976, British

A member of the Carlton Illustration group, a London-based organization of working commercial illustrators, Wallcousins enjoyed a long career, which ran the gamut from illustration in books and magazines, to public works, and to fine portraiture at the highest levels.

As an illustrator, Wallcousins found work early in his career in a cycle of mythological stories published by the Gresham Publishing Company from 1910–1916. He contributed numerous works to titles for the series, including plates for *Celtic Myth and Legend, Poetry and Romance, Teutonic Myth and Legend,* and *Myths of Babylonia and Assyria.* He also had a long working relationship with a periodical called *Bibby's Annual,* for which he designed numerous covers.

In 1925 he designed a poster for the London Underground in conjunction with others from the Carlton group. He is perhaps best remembered today for a portrait he painted in 1945 of Winston Churchill for Oldham Press's *Victory Book,* published after the war in 1946. It was painted from life, and expresses much of Churchill's personality and accomplishments in a single still image. Another unique creation of Wallcousins' was a series of souvenir pamphlets he had designed for a number of royal occasions such as weddings and coronations, including one that went unused for the coronation of Edward VIII, who abdicated the throne in 1936.

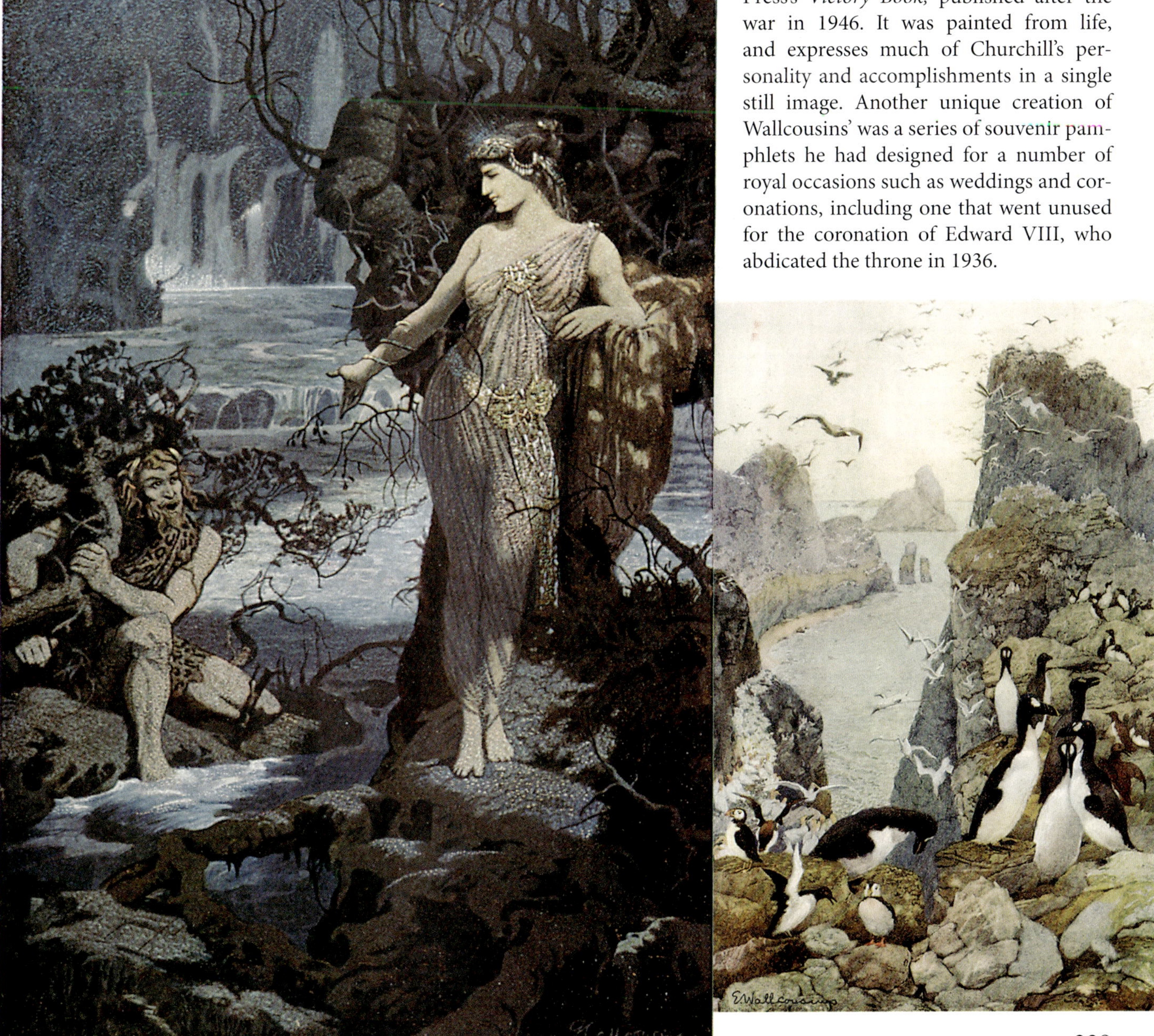

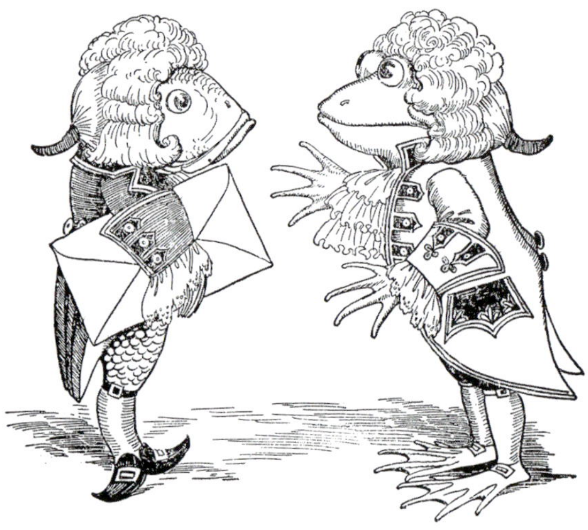

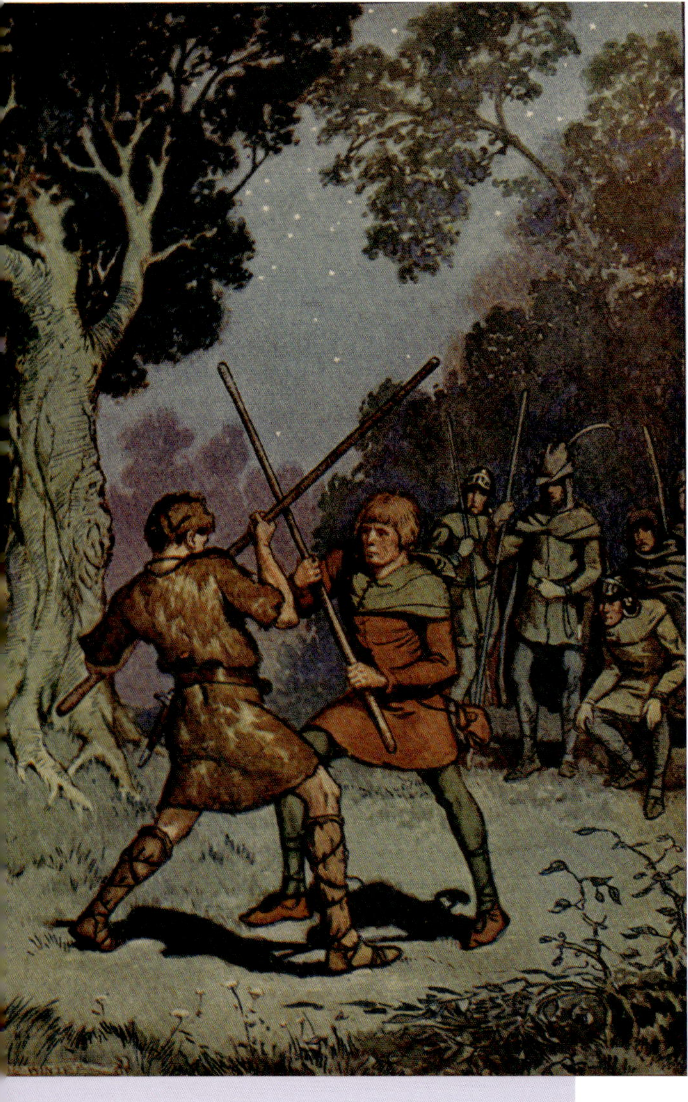

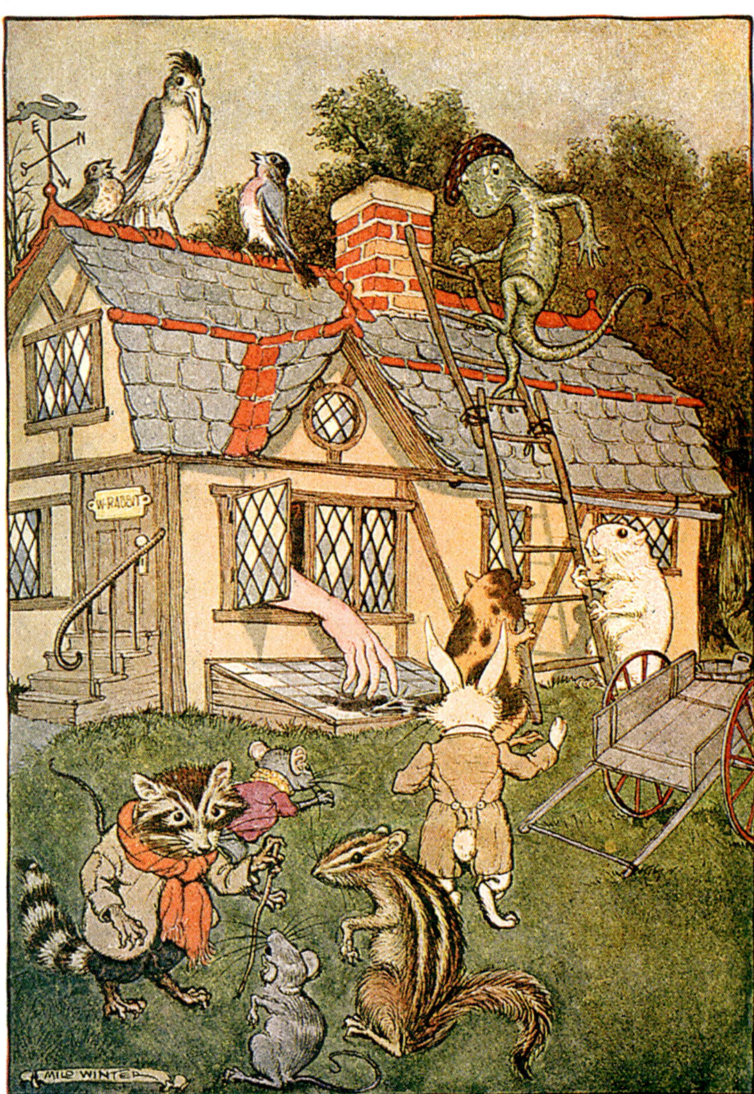

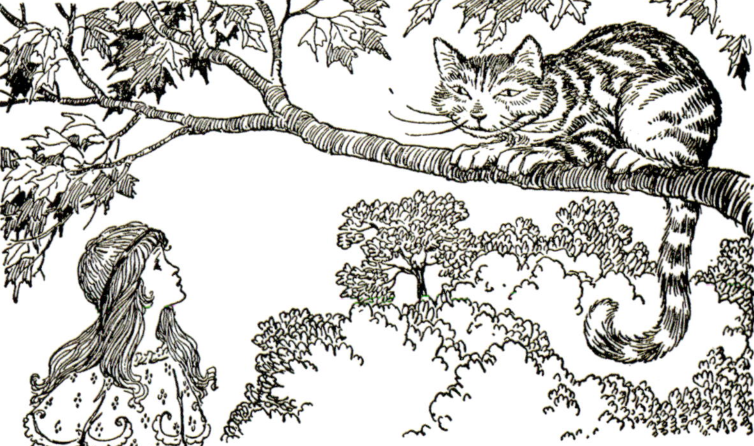

Winter, Milo

MILO WINTER
1888–1956, American

Born in Princeton, Illinois, Milo Winter grew up in Michigan and stayed in the Midwest for most of his working career. He attended the School of the Art Institute in Chicago, studying there until 1912. Earlier that year he began to obtain work in book illustration, which would become the majority of his creative endeavors in the years to follow. Winter both wrote and illustrated his first book, *Billy Popgun*. Winter's illustrations were playful, with a hint of humor, and often intricately detailed. Animals were a particularly strong theme in the imagery he chose to depict. Some of the titles he is best remembered for include *The Aesop for Children* (1919), *The Arabian Nights* (1914), and Nathaniel Hawthorne's *Tanglewood Tales* (1913), all of which were part of Rand McNally's Windermere series.

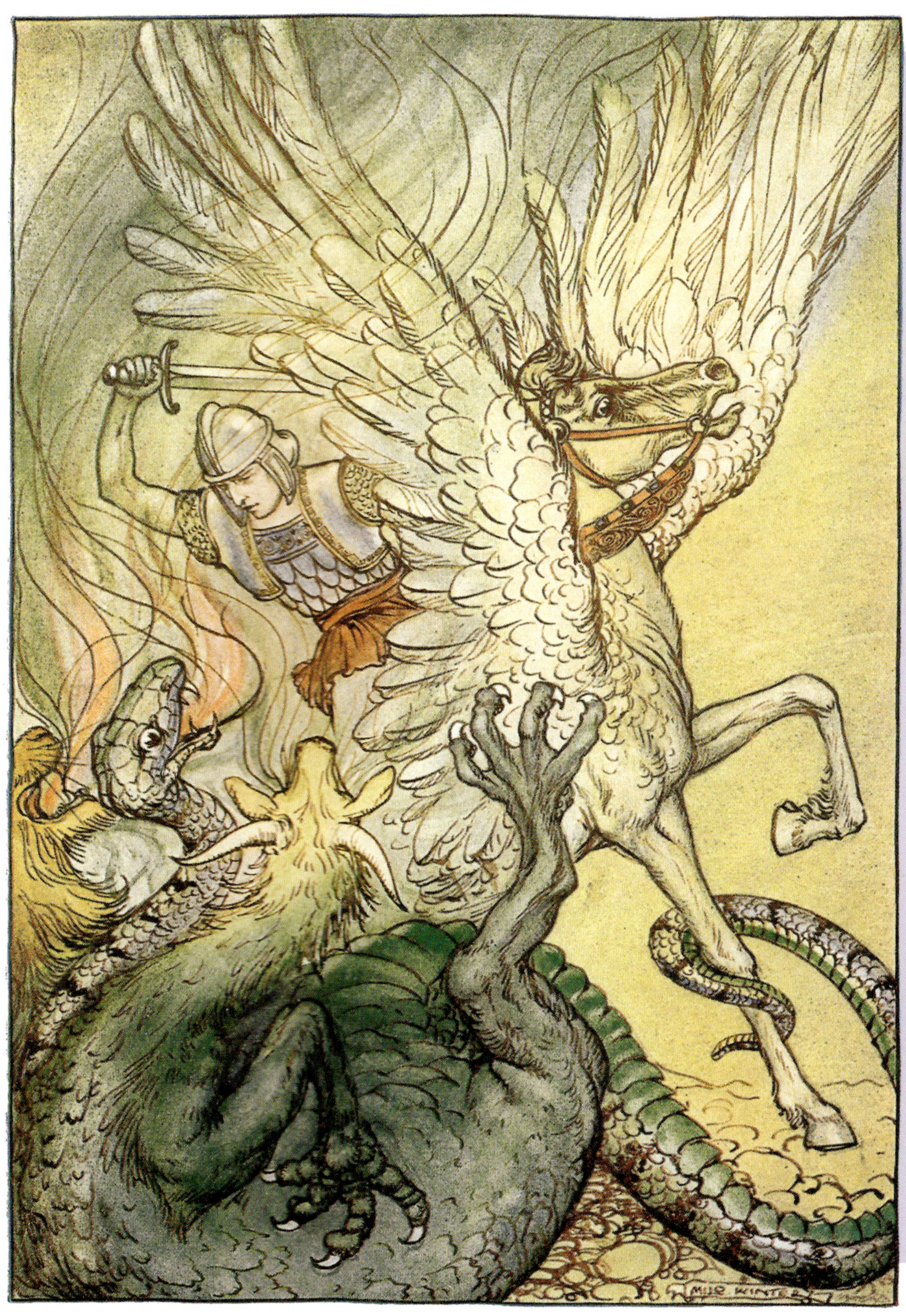

Winter had long periods of success working with Houghton Mifflin and Rand McNally—both located in Chicago—while maintaining work with the larger East Coast publishers as well, including numerous magazines.

In response to the popularity of murals in the 1930s—they were appearing in public buildings and larger institutions across the country, due to public works projects—Winter started his own company and developed *Muragraphs* in 1935. These were oversized posters, largely meant for classroom and library usage, to encourage reading and welcome a younger audience to a greater knowledge of literary figures. The prints featured characters such as Robin Hood, Joan of Arc, and Leif Ericson. At least twelve were produced, and they are highly sought after by collectors today.

In 1947 Winter took a full-time position with Field Enterprises, becoming the art director for their Childcraft books. The position did not suit him for long, and in 1949 he left to work with the Silver Burdett Company, as art editor of their film strip division. The following year, he left Illinois for New York City, where he lived until his passing in 1956.

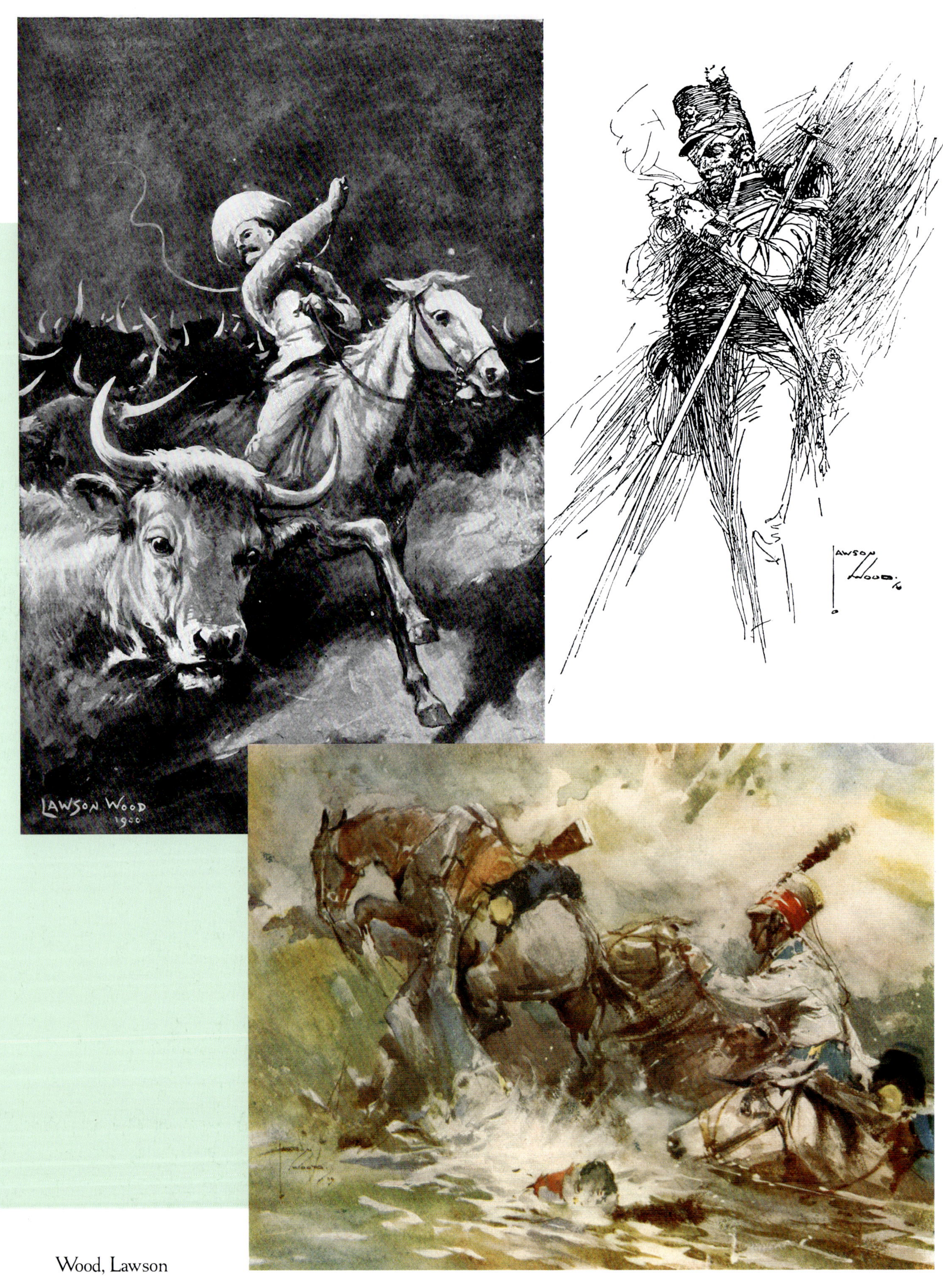

Wood, Lawson

Lawson Wood
1878–1957, British

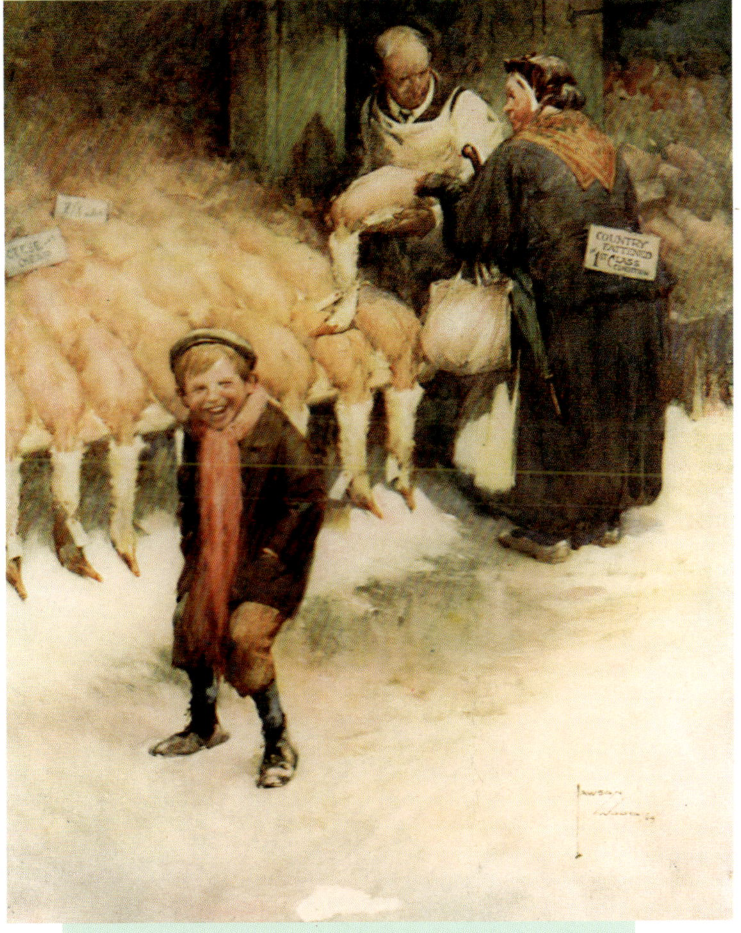

The son of a landscape artist and grandson of an architect, Lawson Wood developed his own specialty in illustration. Encouraged and supported by his creative family, Wood took on studies at both the Slade School and at Frank Calderon's School of Animal Painting. After schooling in London, Wood joined the staff of publisher Arthur Pearson *(Pearson's Magazine),* where he worked for six years exploring many aspects of the commercial art industry, before venturing into a freelance career. He soon grew into one of the premier animal illustrators of his day. Lawson's art also incorporated his humor, and the result was a unique combination of cartoon-like storytelling along with beautiful animal renderings.

Comic scenes involving Stone Age characters or policemen regularly found their way into his work, but Wood became best known for his animal characters. Lawson's affinity for animals permeated his entire life, to the point that his contributions to the improvement of animal welfare earned him a membership in the Royal Zoological Society. After a three-year interruption for service in World War I, where he served in the balloon wing of the Royal Flying Corps as a plane spotter, Wood returned to publishing.

His most famous recurring character was a red-haired chimpanzee known as Gran'pop, who was depicted on many *Collier's* magazine covers in the early decades of the century. The characters he portrayed gained even more popularity when they were transformed into wooden toys. Known as "Lawson Woodies," they established Wood as a commercial success outside of publishing. His characters would have gained more publicity in the late 1930s, when Ub Iwerks (previously Disney's lead animator) planned to use them in animated cartoons. Several cartoons were in production at the outbreak of World War II, but with studio energies needed elsewhere, the works never saw completion.

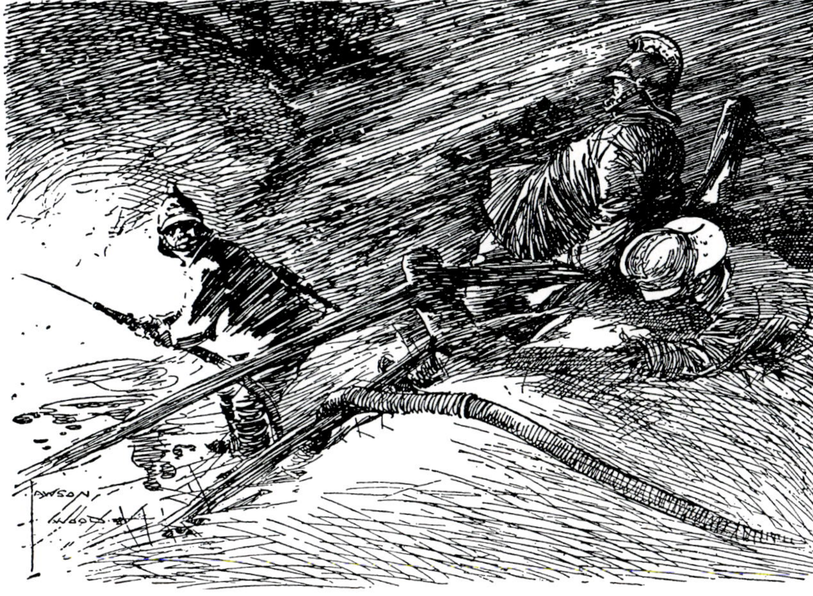

Wood's home was almost as interesting as his career. In his later years Wood lived in a fifteenth-century English manor house which he moved—brick by brick—from Sussex to a more attractive location on the Kent border. He became reclusive in his later years, but wealthy from the diverse work created during his career.

N. C. Wyeth

1882–1945, American

Many leading illustrators of the twentieth century passed through Howard Pyle's school of art. Perhaps his most successful pupil was N. C. (Newell Convers) Wyeth. Wyeth worked on classic adventures, historical pieces, and especially early in his career, was known for his depictions of Western life.

Wyeth grew up in a tight-knit family on the outskirts of Boston. After a short stint at the Eric Pape School, he became convinced that he needed to seek out the best instructor. Wyeth joined several of his classmates, who made the trip south to present their work to Howard Pyle in Wilmington, Delaware. When Pyle saw the promise in young N. C.'s work, he granted him a spot in his school immediately.

Wyeth rose through the ranks at the school, and before long, was part of the master's inner circle. When the time came, Pyle arranged for Wyeth to get an assignment through *Harper's* magazine out West, where he would craft his experiences into stories and pictures—and that proved to be the foundation of a significant career. Wyeth painted book and magazine illustrations, as well as advertising commissions, though he later detested the commercial applications of his work. He longed to be recognized as a painter rather than an illustrator—although museums and the public held varying opinions on his best role.

His ability to capture tension and a sense of adventure helped Wyeth land the work with which he is most identified—a

Wyeth, N. C.

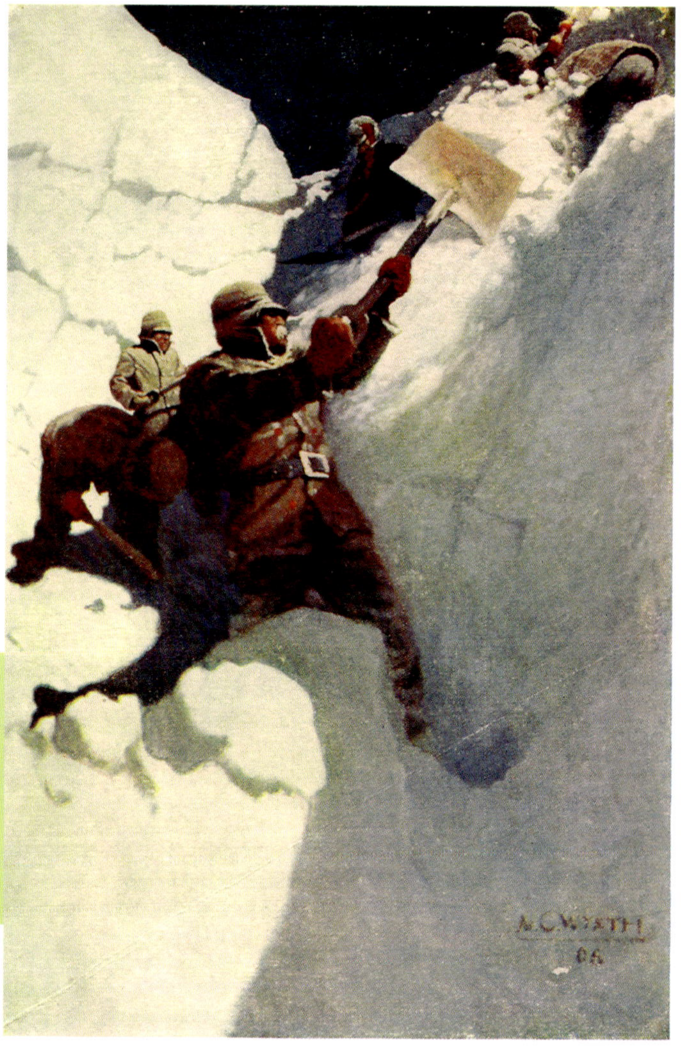

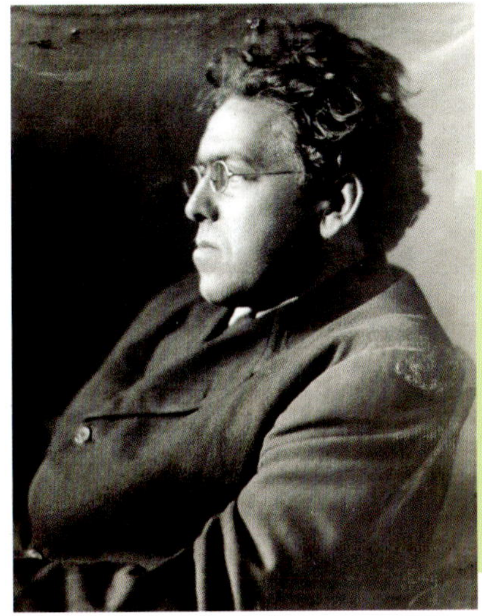

N. C. Wyeth, c. 1916

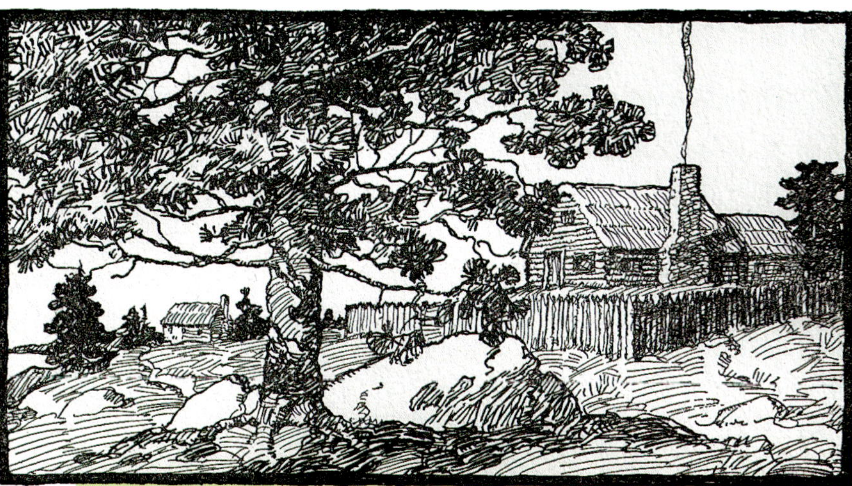

America's First Family of art, son Andrew and grandson Jamie Wyeth are just two of the many creatives that are part of the Wyeth legacy.

28-year stint working with *Scribner's Classics,* providing multiple large canvases for each story, and the occasional line work. It was for *Scribner's* that Wyeth painted the iconic images that define these stories in our memories. *Robin Hood, Rip Van Winkle, The Story of King Arthur, Treasure Island,* and *Kidnapped* are a small sampling of the 25 classics that Wyeth went on to produce.

A tragedy ended N. C. Wyeth's life. He was struck by a train while crossing the tracks near his Chadds Ford, Pennsylvania, home in 1945.

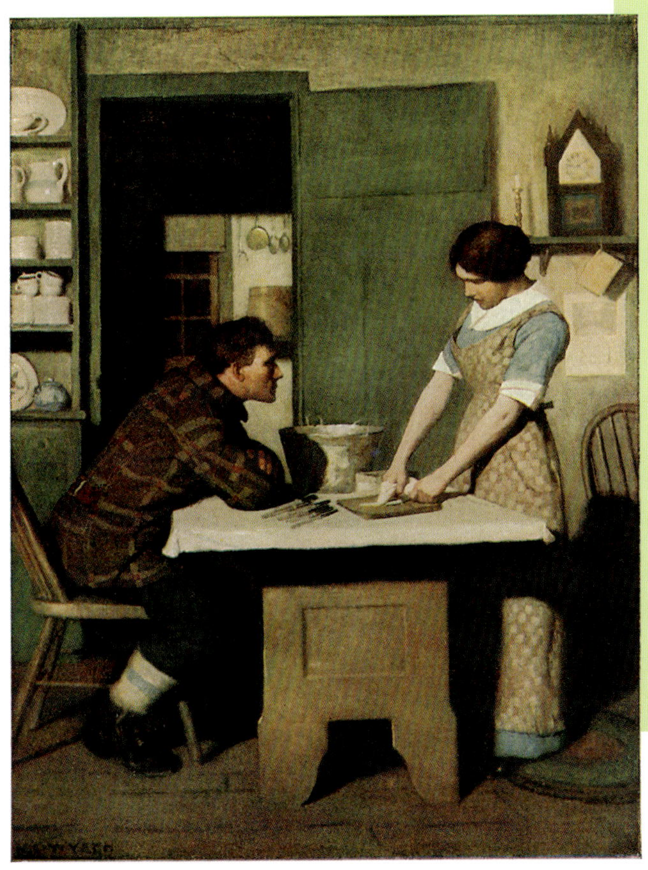

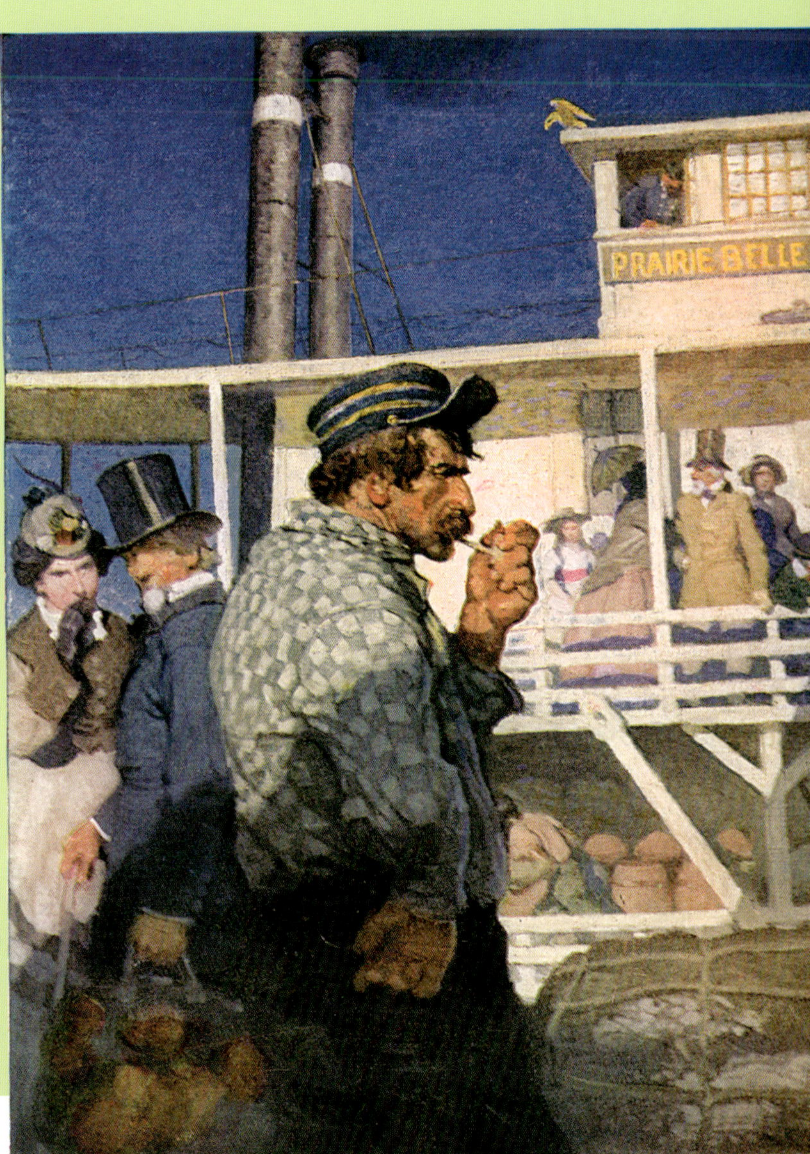

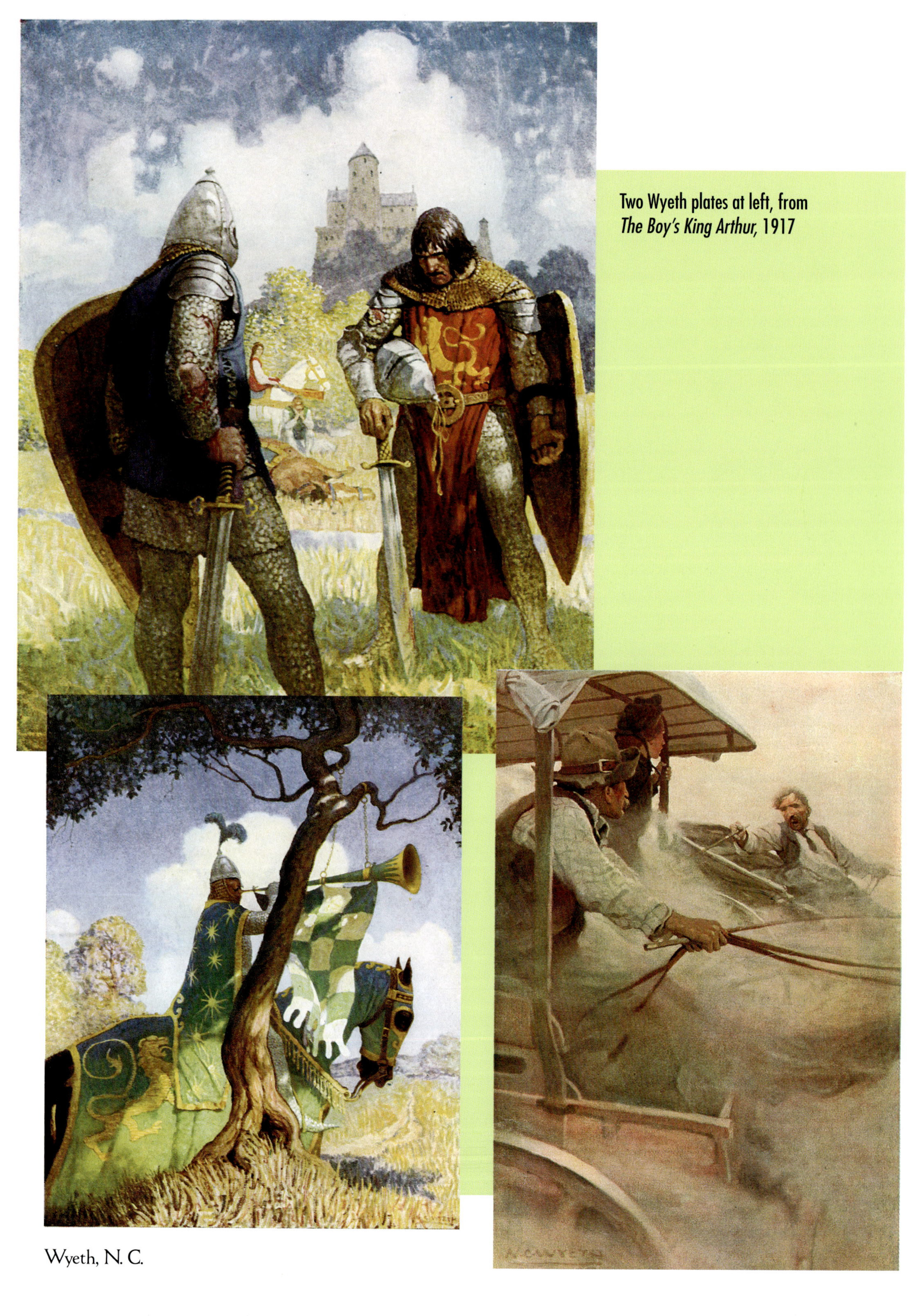

Two Wyeth plates at left, from *The Boy's King Arthur,* 1917

Wyeth, N. C.

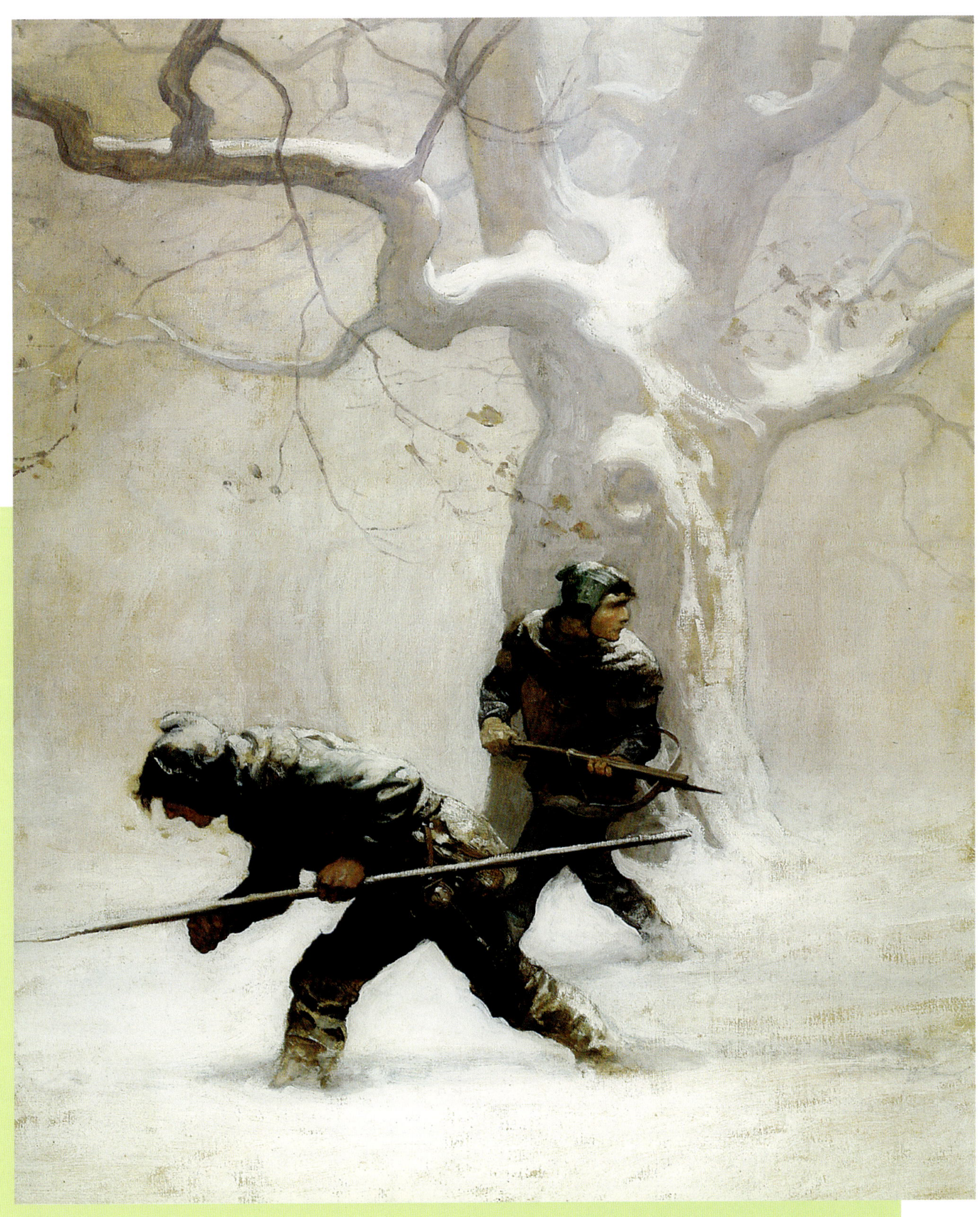

The Black Arrow, 1916

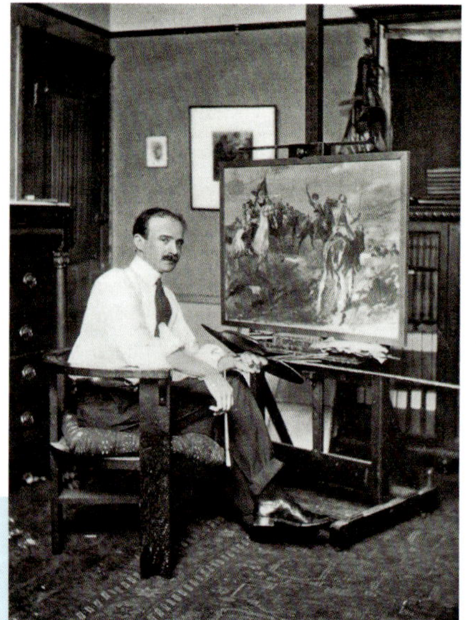

Frederick Yohn
1875~1933, American

In 1902 at the age of twenty-seven, during the prime of his career, Frederick Coffay Yohn was the subject of a very complimentary article in Scribner's *The Book Buyer.* As print was the primary source of news and entertainment for the public, such an article was about the best publicity an illustrator could receive. It went on to describe Yohn as "—a workmanlike, intelligent, sympathetic, 'all-around' Illustrator." The article ended with a discussion of his ability to clarify the minor details of a picture, whether in the nuances of individual characters or the historical details that defined a period.

While Yohn is not well-remembered for a fictional character he repeatedly portrayed—E. W. Hornung's *Raffles*—and he was not the best historical genre painter, he was a steady producer in illustration for the length of his career. Yohn did strive for historical accuracy. There were few publications of the period that did not include an F. C. Yohn illustration—he was a regular contributor to *Scribner's Magazine, Harper's,* and *Collier's Weekly.*

Yohn's earliest schooling in illustration was in his home state of Indiana, at the Indianapolis Art School. After a year he moved to New York, and attended classes at the Art Students League. His start in New York, publishing at *Harper's Round Table* in 1898, led to quick success. He became intrigued by historical works, a subject he had great interest in and for which he became well known. Yohn's work covering the Spanish-American War was widely seen in *Scribner's Magazine,* and following the war, the republications of Yohn's imagery (without recompense) was one of the driving points behind the formation of the Society of Illustrators. Yohn was one of the nine founding illustrators of that organization.

In 1929, Yohn received a national commission for the U.S. Postal Service, commemorating George Rogers Clark's victory over the British at Fort Sackville. His painting, *Washington at Valley Forge,* depicting a stoic Washington saluting the struggling remnants of his fighting force, remains one of his best-remembered images.

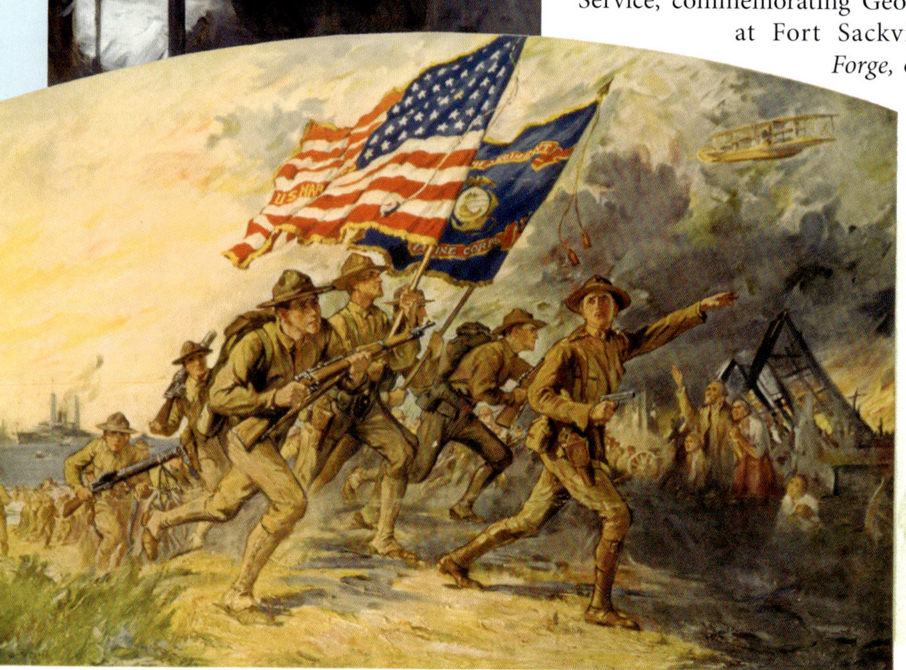

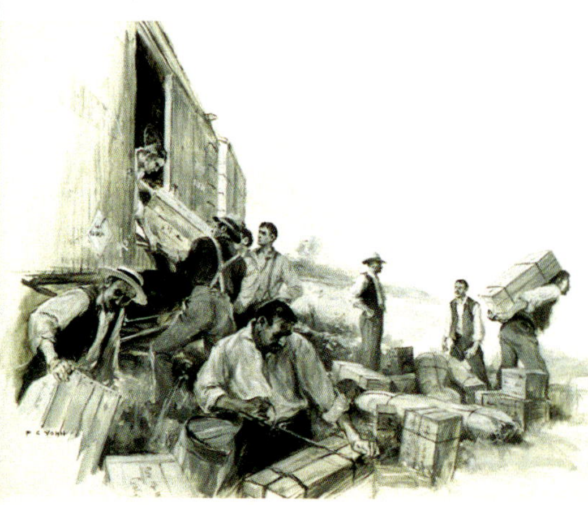

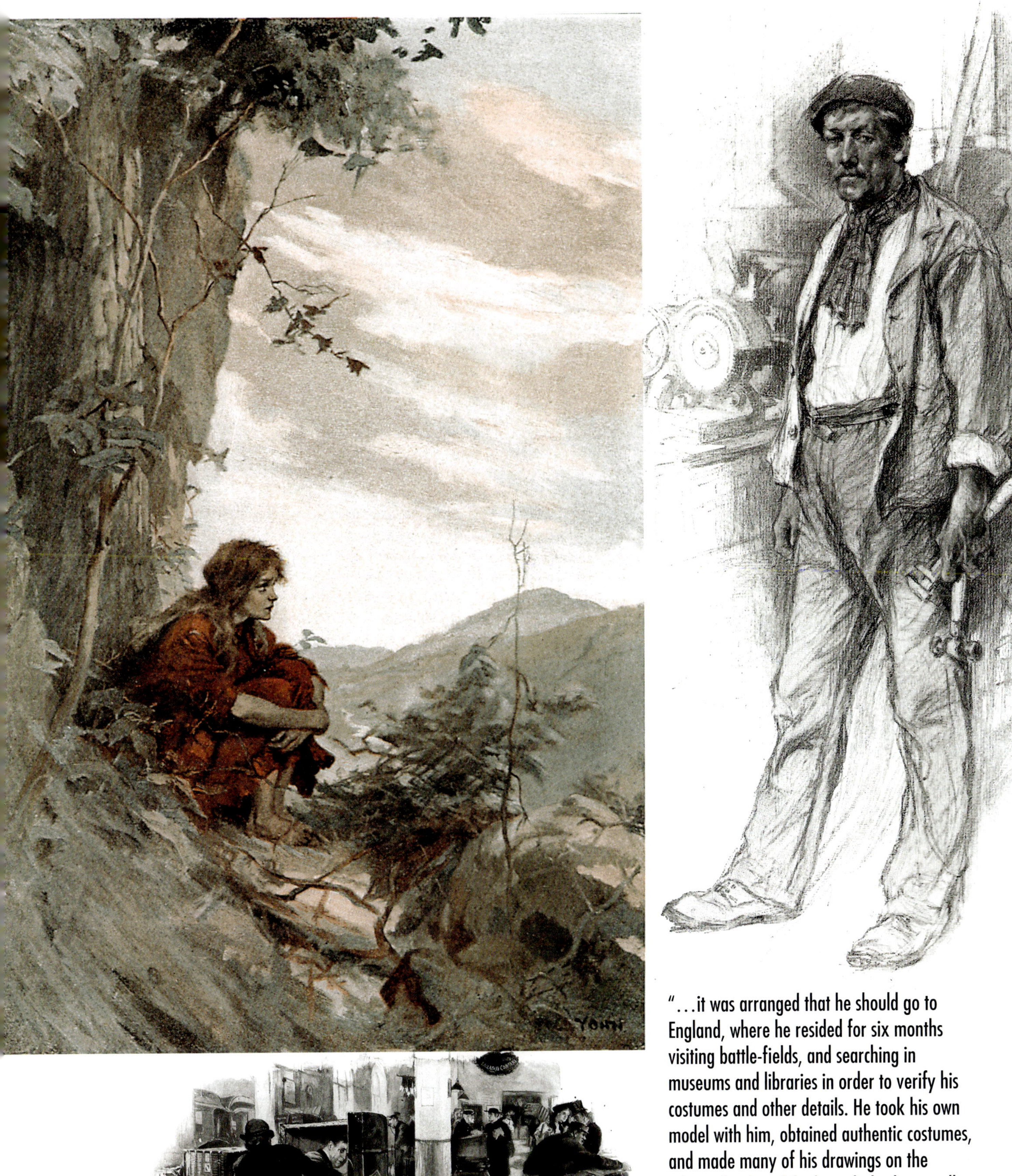

"...it was arranged that he should go to England, where he resided for six months visiting battle-fields, and searching in museums and libraries in order to verify his costumes and other details. He took his own model with him, obtained authentic costumes, and made many of his drawings on the other side, though he brought back a goodly collection of arms and armor, which served him well in his subsequent work."

—from *Scribner's The Book Buyer,* 1902

Selected Bibliography

Chilvers, Ian, ed. "Edwin Austin Abbey," *The Oxford Dictionary of Art and Artists.* Oxford University Press, 2009. Oxford Reference Online.

Dalby, Richard. *The Golden Age of Children's Book Illustration.* Michael O'Mara Books, Limited, 1991.

Elzea, Rowland and Elizabeth H. Hawkes. *A Small School of Art: The Students of Howard Pyle.* Wilmington, DE: Delaware Art Museum, 1980.

Elzea, Rowland and Iris Snyder. *American Illustration: The Collection of the Delaware Art Museum.* Wilmington, DE: Delaware Art Museum, 1991.

Furst, Herbert. *The Decorative Art of Frank Brangwyn.* London: John Lane, The Bodley Head, Ltd., 1924.

Holme, Geoffrey, ed. *British Book Illustration: Yesterday and Today.* The Studio, 1923.

Hornung, Clarence P. *Will Bradley: His Graphic Art.* Mineola, New York: Dover Publications, Inc., 1974.

Kelly, Richard. *Illustrating Modern Life: The Golden Age of American Illustration from the Kelly Collection.* Malibu, CA: Frederick R. Weisman Museum of Art, Pepperdine University, 2013.

Knight, Charles R. *Animal Anatomy and Psychology for the Artist and Layman.* New York: Whittlesey House, 1947.

Mahony, Bertha E., Louise Payson Latimer and Beulah Folmsbee. *Illustrators of Children's Books, 1744–1945.* Boston: The Horn Book, Inc., 1947.

Mather, Jr., Frank Jewett. *The American Spirit in Art; Graphic Arts; Illustration.* New Haven, Yale University Press, 1927.

Meyer, Susan E. *America's Great Illustrators.* The Netherlands and New York: Harry N. Abrams B.V., 1978.

Peppin, Brigid. *Fantasy: Book Illustration, 1860–1920.* Studio Vista, 1975.

Petrov, Vsevolod. *Russian Art Nouveau: The World of Art and Diaghilev's Painters.* New York: Parkstone Press, 1997.

Pitz, Henry C. *The Brandywine Tradition.* Weathervane Books, 1968.

——. *Howard Pyle: Writer, Illustrator, Founder of the Brandywine School.* Devon, UK: Bramhall House, 1965.

Ray, Gordon N. *The Illustrator and the Book in England from 1790 to 1914.* New York: The Pierpont Morgan Library, 1976.

Reed, Walt. *The Illustrator in America: 1860–2000.* Society of Illustrators.

Simon, Howard. *500 Years of Art & Illustration.* Cleveland and New York: The World Publishing Company, 1942.

Waldrep, M. C., ed. *Women Illustrators of the Golden Age.* Mineola, New York: Dover Publications, Inc., 2010.

Other Sources

The Jim Vadeboncouer Collection. http://www.bpib.com/illustra.htm

Appleton's Booklovers Magazine

Century

Collier's

Harper's magazine

The International Studio

Life

Scribner's

St. Nicholas Magazine

Acknowledgments

Libraries:
Reference Librarians of Northport Public Library, Northport, New York
Brown County Library in Green Bay, Wisconsin, and Mary J. Herber
The National Library of Scotland
The British Library

The Green Bay & DePere Antiquarian Society, and Debbie Ashmann
The Neville Public Museum of Brown County, and Louise C. Pfotenhauer

Vin Difate, Fred Taraba, the late Murray Tinkelman, and Walt Reed. Four guys who had direct impact on my interest in and appreciation for illustration history.

The staff of Dover Publications—most notably my editor, Susan Rattiner.

Melanie Reim and the MFA Illustration program at FIT.

Scott Gordley, and the Montclair State University Animation/Illustration Program.

Bud Plant, Jim Vadeboncouer, fellow collectors, and informants.

Tony DiTerlizzi, Charles Vess, Paul Alexander, John Howe, Ian Scheonherr, and Kev Ferrera, Jim Gurney, Leif Peng (and his *Today's Inspiration* Facebook group), and other creatives-turned-historians, always in search of paper treasures, and all willing to share.

The countless book and ephemera dealers who aided me in tracking down materials used in preparing this volume.

Pat and Jeannie Wilshire, for their outstanding energy and vision.

Doug Ellis, for use of images from his collection.

William O'Connor, for years of friendship, encouragement, and honest criticism.

Matt and Julia for dealing with a dad who is often buried deep in century-old paper.

Greatest thanks to my wife, partner, and sounding-board, Lynne. I'll paint the rest of the house now.

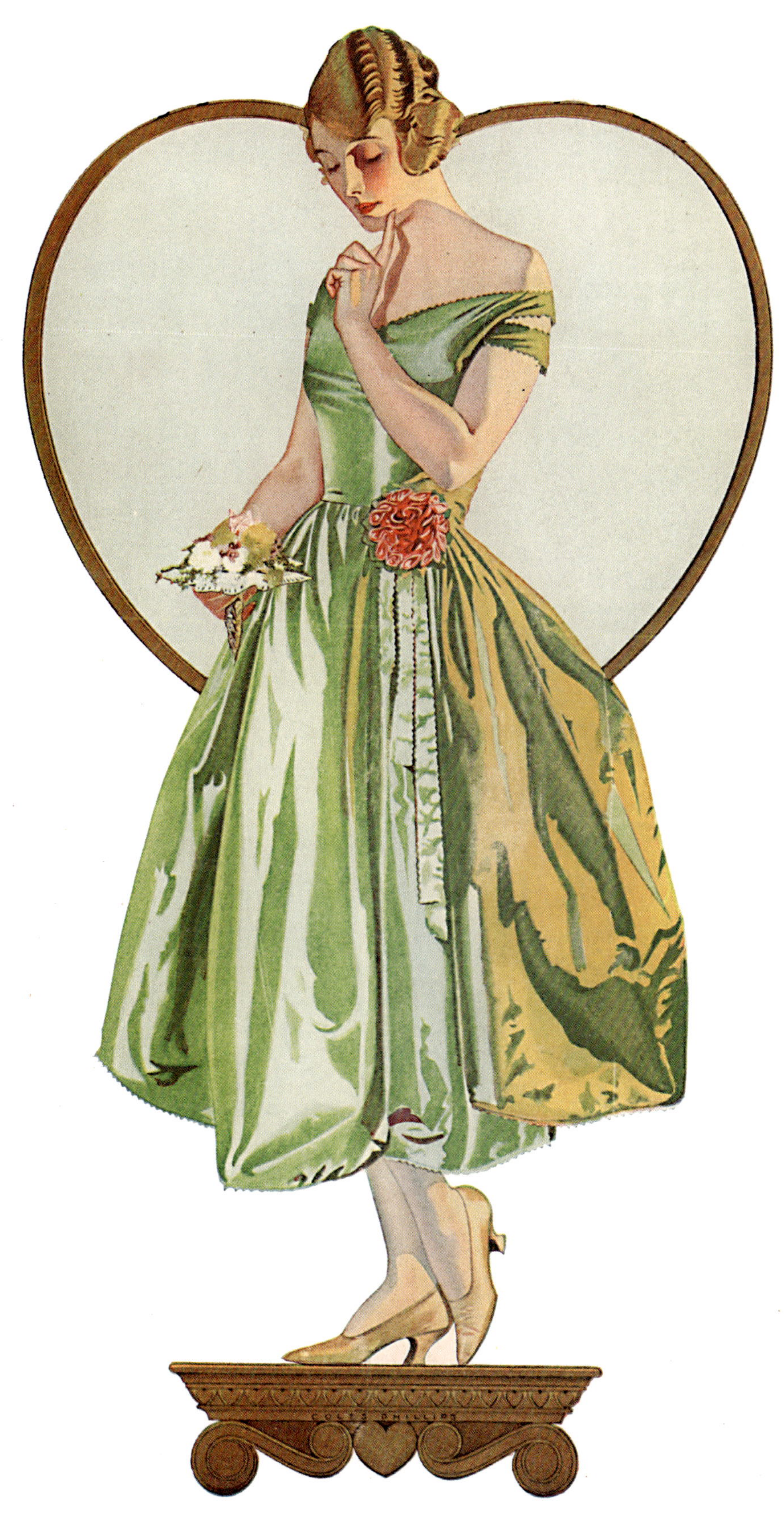

C. Coles Phillips